SEX

AND THE

GENDER

REVOLUTION

The Chicago Series on Sexuality, History, and Society
A series edited by John C. Fout

Also in the series:

Improper Advances
Rape and Heterosexual Conflict in Ontario, 1880–1929
by Karen Dubinsky

A Prescription for Murder
The Victorian Serial Killings of Thomas Neill Cream
by Angus McLaren

The Language of Sex
Five Voices from Northern France around 1200
by John W. Baldwin

Crossing over the Line
Legislating Morality and the Mann Act
by David J. Langum

Sexual Nature/Sexual Culture
edited by Paul R. Abramson and Steven D. Pinkerton

Love Between Women
Early Christian Responses to Female Homoeroticism
by Bernadette J. Brooten

Trials of Masculinity
Studies in the Policing of Sexual Boundaries, 1870–1930
by Angus McLaren

The Invention of Sodomy in Christian Theology
by Mark D. Jordan

Sites of Desire/Economies of Pleasure
Sexualities in Asia and the Pacific
edited by Lenore Manderson and Margaret Jolly

Sex and the Gender Revolution

Volume One
HETEROSEXUALITY AND THE THIRD GENDER IN ENLIGHTENMENT LONDON

Randolph Trumbach

THE UNIVERSITY OF CHICAGO PRESS

CHICAGO AND LONDON

Randolph Trumbach teaches at Baruch College, CUNY. He is the author of *The Rise of the Egalitarian Family.*

The University of Chicago Press, Chicago 60637
The University of Chicago Press, Ltd., London
© 1998 by The University of Chicago
All rights reserved. Published 1998
Printed in the United States of America
07 06 05 04 03 02 01 00 99 98   5 4 3 2 1

ISBN (cloth): 0-226-81290-1

Library of Congress Cataloging-in-Publication Data

Trumbach, Randolph.
    Sex and the gender revolution / Randolph Trumbach.
        p.   cm. — (The Chicago series on sexuality, history, and society)
    Includes bibliographical references (p.   ) and index.
    ISBN 0-226-81290-1 (alk. paper)
    1. Sex customs—England—London—History—18th century.
    2. Heterosexuality—England—London—History—18th century.
    3. Homosexuality—England—London—History—18th century.
    4. Adultery—England—London—History—18th century. 5. London
(England)—History—18th century. 6. London (England)—Social life
and customs. I. Title. II. Series.
HQ18.G7T785 1998
306.76′4′09421—dc21   97-52615
                                                        CIP

FOR BILL BURGET

WHO FIRST LISTENED TO ME ON THIS TOPIC

CONTENTS

ILLUSTRATIONS

MAPS

FIGURE

TABLES

Illustrations on the part titles are by William Hogarth. Part 1: *Sir Francis Dashwood at His Devotions* (painting in a private collection); Part 2: *A Harlot's Progress,* pl. 1 (engraving); Part 3: *The Denunciation, or a Woman Swearing a Child to a Grave Citizen* (painting in the National Gallery of Ireland, Dublin); Part 4: *Marriage-a-la-Mode,* pl. 5, *The Death of the Earl* (engraving).

ACKNOWLEDGMENTS

I began work on this book in the summer of 1976 when, to distract myself from the first of the City University's financial crises, I recast some material on the history of homosexuality that I had gathered for my dissertation on the aristocratic family but had not used. In the next year I made the first of a series of trips that allowed me in the summers and sometimes in January between 1977 and 1982, and again in 1986, to spend a total of fifteen months in the London archives. The Professional Staff Congress/City University research fund financed four of these trips and provided a research assistant for six months: I am very grateful that my University has in the hardest of times always managed to support the scholarship of its faculty. My own college, Baruch, granted me a leave of absence in 1988 that allowed me to write a first version of the chapters on prostitution. It regularly reduced my teaching schedule to give me more time for writing; it supported a number of trips to conferences to give papers on my material; it paid for the microfilming of some materials; and it gave me a prize that helped to finance a summer's research. The National Endowment for the Humanities made a grant for another summer's journey. And the Schoff Trust Fund of the Columbia University Seminars made a generous grant toward the cost of preparing the manuscript. Finally, the hospitality of two friends, Barry Davis and Phillip Winder, allowed me to work in London on a number of occasions.

Most of the manuscripts for this book are deposited in the London Metropolitan Archive. But I read them in the old days when the Archive was the Greater London Record Office. I am very grateful for the kind support and instruction of a number of the archivists there. Harriet Jones led me through the consistory court, as Richard Samways did through the Quarter Sessions and Alison Hotchkiss through the Foundling Hospital manuscripts. Pauline Suporova also gave me good advice at an early stage.

Harriet and Melvyn Jones became friends and made lunch pleasant on what were often otherwise lonely days. The staffs at the British Library, the Corporation of London Record Office, the Guildhall Library, the Westminster Public Library, the Royal College of Surgeons, the Public Record Office, and the Hertfordshire Record Office must also be thanked for their kindnesses and help.

Louisa Moy and Eric Neubacher, the interlibrary loan librarians at my college, have provided an endless stream of books and articles. Margaret Baar and Kent Gerard read newspapers for me. Carol Deacon has put endless different versions of these chapters through the word processor. My editors John Fout and Doug Mitchell have helped a very slow writer to finish, and I am very grateful to them. Over the years many friends and colleagues have made useful comments on my work and I thank them all, especially those I met at the Society for Eighteenth-Century Studies, the Social Science History Association, the Columbia University Seminars on Eighteenth-Century European Culture and on Legal and Political Thought and Institutions, the Maison des Sciences de l'Homme, the Berkshire Conferences, McMaster University, McGill University, the Seventeenth International Historical Congress, the Bay Area Eighteenth-Century Studies Group, the University of Pennsylvania, the Carleton University Conferences on the Family, the University of Limburg, and the City University Graduate School. A number of friends have read the manuscript in whole or in part: old friends like Polly Morris, who has been over it a number of times, always to its benefit; Trygve Tholfsen, who has been reading my writing since I was an undergraduate; James Jacob, who has also provided unflagging support over a weekly breakfast table; as well as newer friends like Beth Baron, Bryant Ragan, George Robb, Nicholas Rogers, and Karl Westhauser. My colleague Murray Rubinstein has provided steady conversation. And some friends have made it possible for me to get through life: Bill Burget, Rick Mathews, Thom Taylor, Scott Skipworth.

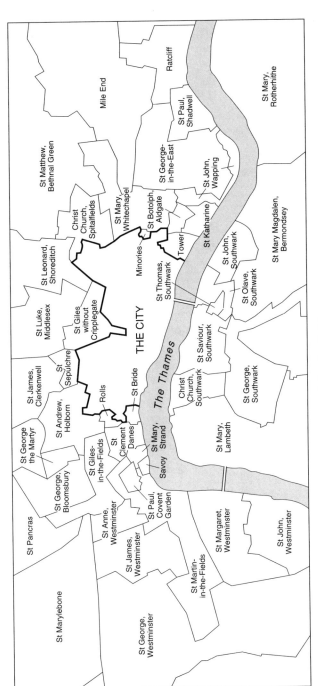

1. London Parishes

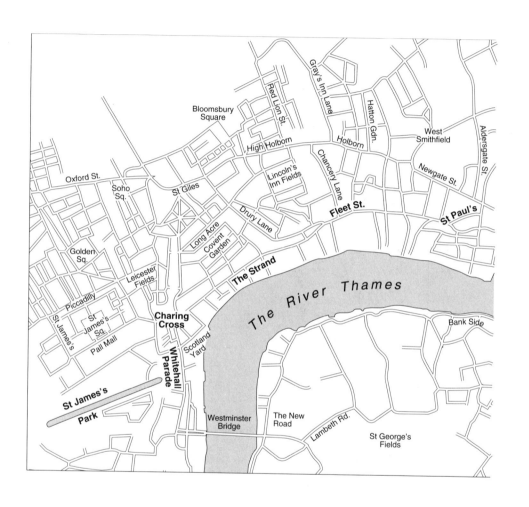

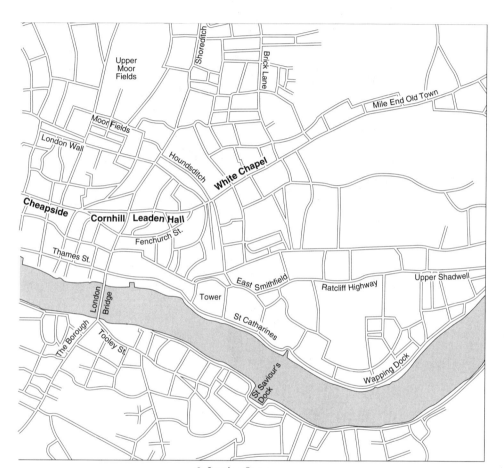

2. London Streets

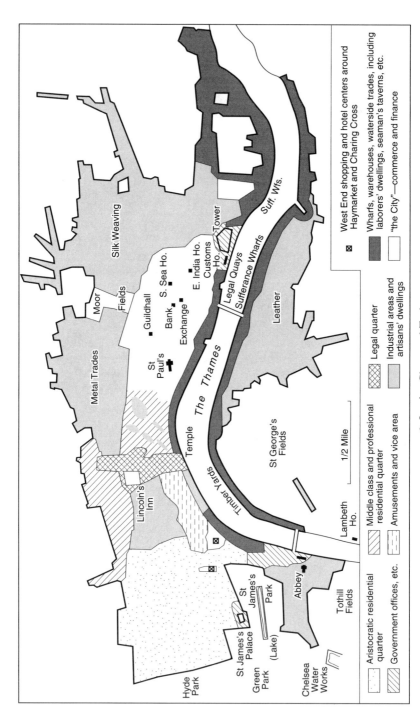

3. London Classes and Trades

Metal Trades

Silk Weaving

Moor
Fields

St
Paul's

■ Guildhall

Bank
Exchange
■ S. Sea Ho.

■ E. India Ho.

Customs
Ho.

Tower

Legal Quays

Sufferance Wharfs

Suff. Wfs.

Leather

Temple

The Thames

Lincoln's
Inn

Timber Yards

St George's
Fields

Lambeth
Ho.

1/2 Mile

Hyde
Park

St James's
Palace

Green
Park

(Lake)

St
James's
Park

Chelsea
Water
Works

Abbey

Tothill
Fields

Aristocratic residential
quarter

Government offices, etc.

Middle class and professional
residential quarter

Legal quarter

Amusements and vice area

Industrial areas and
artisans' dwellings

West End shopping and hotel centers around
Haymarket and Charing Cross

Wharfs, warehouses, waterside trades, including
laborers' dwellings, seaman's taverns, etc.

⊠ "the City"—commerce and finance

PART ONE

Introduction

CHAPTER ONE

Extramarital Relations and Gender History

A revolution in the gender relations of Western societies occurred in the first generation of the eighteenth century, and it is the purpose of this book to describe its consequences for the sexual behavior of most men and women. Around 1700 in northwestern Europe, in England, France, and the Dutch Republic, there appeared a minority of adult men whose sexual desires were directed exclusively toward adult and adolescent males. These men could be identified by what seemed to their contemporaries to be effeminate behavior in speech, movement, and dress. They had not, however, entirely transformed themselves into women but instead combined into a third gender selected aspects of the behavior of the majority of men and women. Since a comparable minority of masculinized women who exclusively desired other women did not appear until the 1770s, it is therefore the case that for most of the eighteenth century there existed in northern Europe what might be described as a system of three genders composed of men, women, and sodomites. The lives of these sodomites (and of the sapphists after 1770) have been described recently by myself and by other historians, and I mean in the second volume of this study to present a full analysis of London's sodomites and sapphists. But the consequences for the sexual lives of the majority of men and women of the appearance of the exclusive sodomite has not so far been undertaken. This book therefore aims to do just that, by writing the history of extramarital sexual relations between men and women in eighteenth-century London. It concentrates on extramarital relations because from legal sources such behavior can be more systematically documented for all social classes than can the sexual lives of husbands and wives with each other. The prostitution, illegitimacy, sexual violence, and adultery that can be described from such sources were all behaviors that had occurred before 1700, but they were reorganized and given new meanings after 1700 by the appearance of the modern system of three genders.

In the eighteenth century these new meanings and the reorganization of long-standing forms of sexual behavior produced among men (but not among women) what the late nineteenth century described as a heterosexual majority and a homosexual minority. The terms *heterosexual* and *homosexual* were nineteenth-century inventions. But the behavioral patterns they described came into existence among men in the first generation of the eighteenth century. It is difficult to understand that homosexuality and heterosexuality are conditions that were socially constructed first for men at a specific moment in time and then for women because the development of the late-nineteenth-century descriptions over the last hundred years has tended to leave most westerners with the conviction that a heterosexual majority and a homosexual minority are biological constants that must have been present in all times and places. The heterosexuality of the majority is usually taken for granted—how can the human race otherwise have continued to exist? The homosexuality of the minority has been more difficult to understand or to accept. For this very reason, a brief analysis of the differences in Western homosexual behavior before and after 1700 will clarify what it means to say that an exclusive male heterosexual majority first appeared in Western societies in the early eighteenth century.

To understand the nature of homosexual acts in European society before 1700, one begins from the presumption increasingly made by historians, sociologists, and anthropologists that homosexual behavior in all human societies has been organized by differences either in age or in gender. From this it is apparent that the postmodernist presumption that sexual forms are unlimited cannot be true. In some societies like ancient Greece or Renaissance Italy sexual behavior was structured by differences in age, and adult men had sexual relations both with women and with adolescent males who were sexually passive. In other societies like those of traditional South Asia the majority of both adult and adolescent males had relations both with women and with a minority of passive adult men who had been socialized into a lifelong third-gender role that combined elements of male and female behavior. This fundamental distinction is sometimes difficult for modern Western scholars to see since in their society any experience of homosexual desire assigns an individual to a decided minority without reference to the age or gender of the person desired. From this practice of their own societies Western scholars presume the presence in all times and places of an effeminate minority of males exclusively interested in other males and use this presumption to misinterpret the evidence for homosexual behavior in the ancient Mediterranean world and in European societies before 1700.[1]

This distinction between homosexual behavior organized by differences in either age or gender therefore reorients the historical quest into a more fruitful path and makes it possible to understand the nature of the change that occurred in Europe around 1700. In European society before 1700 probably most males felt desire for both males and females. Adult men expressed this by having sexual relations with adolescent males and with women. This pattern of behavior was of very long standing in Western societies. It had appeared in ancient Greece and Rome, in early Christian Europe, and in Europe of the later Middle Ages. This is sometimes doubted by modern readers because the sources are fragmentary and literary, and a historian like John Boswell was always determined to find an exclusive homosexual minority and to deny the plain presumption of his sources that homosexual activity occurred between most men and boys. But the brilliant work of Michael Rocke on the exceptional sources from Renaissance Florence allows the pattern to be displayed with statistical certainty. By the age of thirty, one of every two Florentine youths had been implicated in sodomy, and by the age of forty, two of every three men had been incriminated. Sodomy was therefore so widespread as to be universal. But it was always structured by age. Between fifteen and nineteen, boys were always passive. Individuals between nineteen and twenty-three were in a transitional phase in which they were either active or passive but with the older partner always active. After twenty-three men were always active. During this third period young men sometimes also went to female prostitutes. At thirty they married. Sodomy was illegal, and the church taught that it was immoral. But male opinion largely approved of it as long as adult men were always active. There were, in other words, two competing systems of morality in Christian societies, but the actual sexual behavior of men had changed very little from what it had been in the ancient pagan Mediterranean world.[2]

This pattern was also found in Venice and probably in the rest of Italy and in Spain and Portugal, as the Inquisition's records show. It probably also existed in northwestern Europe, but the records there are not so good as those for southern Europe. Statistics like those for Florence cannot be produced for seventeenth-century England, where there were very few prosecutions for sodomy. But the paucity of prosecutions does not demonstrate that there was very little sodomy. Instead it is likely that the severity of the law's punishment—death—made for few denunciations in a society that was not wholeheartedly committed to the Christian standard of sexual *but is the law really a deterrent?*

behavior. This had been the case in Florence in the late fourteenth century, when there were also few prosecutions because the penalties were
severe. But as these were lightened in the fifteenth century, the number
of prosecutions rose and revealed (to our twentieth-century eyes) that sodomy, while not completely approved of, was nonetheless so widespread
as to be the norm. In England during the Restoration, wild rakes like
Lord Rochester had wives, mistresses, and boys. King William's taste for
both women and boys was not criticized as was his friend William Bentinck's supposed sexual passivity; Bentinck was the king's contemporary
and therefore too old to be a catamite, which was a role for boys. In *Sodom;
or the Quintessence of Debauchery*, Rochester (if he was the author) wrote
of sodomy with women and boys as indifferently wicked and exciting.[3]

But in the 1690s opinion changed after a new way of organizing homosexual desire appeared throughout the modernizing societies of northwestern Europe, in England, France, and the Netherlands. No longer did differences in age justify sexual relations with males in the libertine's mind.
Instead adult men with homosexual desires were presumed to be members
of an effeminate minority. They were given a status similar to that of the
hijra in Indian society or the berdache among the North American tribal
peoples, who had passive sexual relations with the majority of males in
their societies. European society had begun to move from one to the other
of the two worldwide systems for organizing homosexual behavior: from
a system in which subordination was achieved by differences in age to one
whose focus was a third-gender role for a minority of men. In the old
system all males had passed through a period of sexual passivity in adolescence. In the new system, the majority of males could not conceive of
themselves as passive at any moment; passivity was instead for the minority, the homosexuals (as they have been called since the late nineteenth
century), who from childhood were socialized into their deviant role. European societies in the early eighteenth century gave such sodomites a
status equivalent to that of the most abandoned women. The majority of
men were supposed to avoid any sexual contact with them. But such contact nonetheless occurred, and when it did, it caused profound anxiety to
adolescents and adult men—but also perhaps profound excitement.[4]

The new effeminate adult sodomites can be documented among the
London poor because of the attacks against them made by the Societies
for the Reformation of Manners. These sodomites constructed around
themselves a protective subculture of meeting places and ritual behavior.
A few who seem to have been involved in prostitution played out a largely
feminine identity. They took women's names, spent nearly all their time

in women's clothes, and were referred to as "she" and "her" by their male and female acquaintances. Their male customers in some cases must have known that these prostitutes were genital males, but in other cases perhaps they did not, since some sodomites worked the streets as members of a group of female prostitutes. The gender identity of these transvestite males was not entirely feminine because they sometimes wore men's clothes and were prepared to take the active or inserter's role in sexual intercourse. They were neither male nor female but a third gender that combined some characteristics from each of what society regarded as the two legitimate genders. A few such men may have existed before 1700, when they were likely to have been confused with biological hermaphrodites who sometimes changed (though illegally) from the male or female gender to which they had been assigned at birth. After 1700, however, transvestite adult men who clearly possessed male genitalia and whose bodies showed no ambiguity were classified as part of a larger group of effeminate men who were supposed to desire sexual relations only with other males, who might be either adult or adolescent.

These men, for whom the formal term was *sodomite,* were in the slang of the streets known as *mollies,* a term that had first been applied to female prostitutes. Many of them could not be identified as sodomites outside the context of the molly-house, or tavern. Some of them were married with children, and others provided themselves with female companions so that they could pass with their neighbors. Once inside the molly-house, they displayed many of the feminine characteristics of the male transvestite prostitute: they took women's names and adopted the speech and bodily movements of women. On some occasions, especially at dances, some of them dressed entirely as women. Some sodomites in the molly-houses played men to match the role of female prostitute that others took. But all of these men were obliged to play two roles, one in the public world in which they worked and spent most of their time and another in the molly-house. Some men, of course, could not disguise their effeminacy in public and as a consequence were abused or blackmailed. This suggests that they had internalized their gender role to such a degree that they could not hide it, even though that would have been very much to their advantage in the public world. But in the public mind, all the men in the molly-houses—as well as those who used the public latrines, the parks, the cruising streets, or the arcades to find sexual partners—belonged to the same category no matter what their behavior in the public sphere. All were members of a third gender who deserved to be treated with contempt. Some were hanged in the few cases where anal penetration and seminal emission could be proven. And others were fined, imprisoned, and sentenced to stand in the public pillory, where a few were stoned to death.

Sexual relations between women, on the other hand, were not prosecuted. When they occurred, the women were not described as masculinized until the last generation of the century, when some women were categorized as sapphists or tommies, as the effeminate male minority had been called sodomites or mollies since the beginning of the century. Throughout the century there were some women who cross-dressed, and they were sometimes prosecuted for it; but their cross-dressing was undertaken so that they could pass safely in a male occupation rather than to sexually attract women. It was essential that their disguise be fully convincing; any ambiguity that might arise from the mixing of gender traits (as male sodomites mixed them) would have led to their discovery and the failure of their purpose. Among some of these cross-dressing women, there were a few who eventually married women and perhaps even engaged in intercourse with an artificial penis. These women had crossed the gender boundary and were condemned for it, but other women who lived as husbands to women for many years—but against whom no sexual charges were leveled—seem to have passed unscathed. After 1770 there were occasional examples of aristocratic women (sometimes singly, sometimes as part of a female couple) who were either romantically or sexually attracted to women and who cross-dressed in the ambiguous way that effeminate sodomites did. They were accepted when the romance was stressed and the sex vigorously denied, and condemned and ostracized when it was otherwise. It was, however, always much more possible to be unaware that sexual relations between women existed in any form than it was to be ignorant of the existence of effeminate male sodomites.[5]

For most of the eighteenth century, therefore, sexual relations between women still occurred in the context that had applied to sexual relations between males in the seventeenth century, when persons who engaged in sexual relations with their own gender were presumed to be attracted to the other gender as well, and when sexual acts with one's own gender did not compromise an individual's standing as masculine or feminine. Only sexual passivity in an adult male or sexual activity by a woman who used an artificial penis or a supposedly enlarged clitoris had endangered an individual's gender standing. Such individuals, along with biological hermaphrodites, were likely to be viewed as dangerous, since they passed back and forth from active to passive rather than remaining in the passive female or active male conditions to which they had been assigned at birth.

Only the temporary passivity of adolescent males whose bodies had not yet acquired secondary male characteristics did not threaten this system. Seventeenth-century society had therefore presumed that although there were three kinds of bodies (men, women, and hermaphrodites), there were only two kinds of gender (male and female).

After 1700 this system was replaced by another for men but not for women. For males, there were now two kinds of bodies (male and female) but three genders (man, woman, and sodomite)—since the sodomite was supposed to experience his desires and play his role as a result of a corrupted education and not because of his bodily condition. For women, the old system of three bodies and two genders could still be presumed. But men had entered a new gender system by changing the nature of their sexual relations with each other: men no longer had sex with boys and women—they now had sex either with females or with males. They were now supposed to be either exclusively homosexual or heterosexual. The majority of men now desired only women. This necessarily brought them into more intimate relations with women, and their intimacy could threaten the continuing male desire to establish domination. This dilemma was in part resolved by assigning those men who desired males to a third gender role that was held in great contempt. This role played its necessary part in the new relations between men and women produced by the emergence of individualism and equality in eighteenth-century society since it guaranteed that, however far equality between men and women might go, men would never become like women since they would never desire men. Only women and sodomites desired men, and this was true for males from adolescence to old age.[6]

The new heterosexual role for the majority of men that was produced by the system of three genders that came into existence after 1700 affected men of all social classes. It resulted in a pattern of extramarital sexual behavior that endured until the middle of the twentieth century and that is documented in this book by three sets of chapters, on prostitution, illegitimacy, and adultery and violence in marriage. The women who engaged in these extramarital relations did not, however, have their behavior structured by a standard of exclusive female heterosexuality. Their sexual lives were organized instead by the forms of family life that during the eighteenth century came to vary considerably by social class. Poor women, whether as wives, widows, or maids, were bound by the forms of the traditional patriarchal household and family in which servants, children, and wives were subordinated to the authority of older, dominant, and supposedly provident men. Women from the middle and landed classes, on the

other hand, lived in families constructed by increasingly egalitarian relations that found expression in romantic courtship, the close friendship of
husbands and wives, and the tender care of children. Male heterosexuality,
traditional patriarchy, and modern domesticity are therefore the principal
themes that run through the chapters that follow on prostitution, illegitimacy, and adultery. They will sometimes be found reinforcing each other
and sometimes be in opposition.[7]

These three standards of heterosexuality, patriarchy, and romance always operated in the persistent presence of men's violence. The violence
might appear as an expression of men's contempt for the prostitute or in
their attempts to cure themselves of the prostitute's venereal disease by
forcing themselves on prepubescent girls; or in courtship when marriage
could be offered as a compensation for rape; or after marriage by the husband who to establish his sexual domination of his wife or the absolute
possession of her property could treat her in ways that would certify him
as mad if used against anyone else. Heterosexuality and the family were
also in constant dialogue with Christian religion in its different forms.
The last gasps of traditional reforming urban piety appeared early in the
century in the Societies for the Reformation of Manners, which attempted
to control prostitution and other forms of extramarital relations by turning
to the secular magistrates after the church courts had failed. For them
sexual sin was equally reprehensible in men and in women. But the Evangelicals at the end of the century were more concerned about the prostitute
than about her male customer, for without realizing it, they had become
affected by the presumptions of the new male heterosexuality. Women
throughout the century were more likely than men to make Christianity
their bulwark against the libertine's justification of his practices. But since
male heterosexuality made it increasingly difficult for men to enter into
intimate relations with a male God, it is likely that the tie between sex and
religion was weakened even for those men who were not self-consciously
libertine.

The male heterosexuality, domesticity, and traditional patriarchal domination that run through the chapters that follow are displayed in the
physical environment of eighteenth-century London. In 1700 with a population of slightly more than half a million, London had become the
largest city in western Europe. A century later its population had doubled
to nearly a million. It dominated the rest of English society, and it remained throughout the century the political, economic, and cultural center
of its world, even though its total share of England's urban population
lessened as urbanization increased. London grew, however, largely as the

result of migration from the rest of England, since its death rate was staggering, especially in the first half of the century. This meant that only a quarter of those who lived in London had been born there. This pattern of migration was of great cultural importance. It meant that probably one in every six people in the entire country had spent part of their lives in London. The patterns of sexual behavior in London therefore had to some extent an influence throughout the country and cannot be attributed simply to the results of the urban environment. If one therefore finds modern male heterosexuality and domesticity in London, it is very likely that they also had made their way throughout the rest of English culture. But certain aspects of London's sexual life were certainly unique to it. It probably had more sodomites than anywhere else in England as a result of migration from rural areas. It certainly had the greatest number of prostitutes. And its level of illegitimacy was also different, but it is disputed whether it was higher or lower than the rest of England.[8]

The structure of London's economy and its role as the country's political center meant that there was present in it the full range of social groups, from the aristocracy and the gentry who spent a part of each year there (and who represented 2 or 3 percent of the city's population), through the professional men and the merchants who organized the national economy (and were 17 to 22 percent), to the poor who were divided between the largest group of skilled laborers in England and a still larger group of unskilled ones (75 percent). The London economy was organized around a service sector in the West End, a manufacturing district north of the City walls, and a third district in the East End tied to the port. These divisions were apparent in its sexual economy as well, since male servants and soldiers fathered the bastards in the West End, as weavers did in the parishes north of the City, and sailors in the parishes of the East End. By 1700 the development of East and West Ends brought a new focus as the parishes that still belonged to the four separate jurisdictions of Middlesex, the City, Westminster, and Southwark merged in daily life and became a single place. Through this newly unified town there ran a great thoroughfare made up of a series of interlocking streets from the Royal Exchange in Cornhill, through Cheapside and St. Paul's Churchyard and down Ludgate Hill to Fleet Street and the end of the City's jurisdiction. From there it continued into Westminster as Fleet Street joined the Strand, moving through Charing Cross and down Whitehall into St. James's Park. It is still London's principal ceremonious route. But in the eighteenth century it also became the beat of the army of streetwalking prostitutes around whom so much of the conflict between male heterosexuality and female domesticity was centered. In this huge sprawling city, however, each parish could still be its own separate world. And it was therefore possible to move from one part of town to another and to leave an old sexual life for a new.

The sources of information on the sexual life of eighteenth-century London come in eight different kinds. The consistory court (which was the bishop of London's court) heard suits for defamation and divorce. These records document the history of sexual reputation among poorer Londoners and adultery and sexual violence in marriage among the middle classes and the gentry. Three decades of cases were analyzed from the beginning, middle, and end of the century, and the rest were counted. The notebooks of the secular magistrates for the City, and the recognizances and house of correction calendars in the quarter sessions rolls for the City, Westminster, and Middlesex, are the foundation for the history of prostitution. But they also describe a variety of other sexual behaviors ranging from adultery to wife beating to sexual exposure. Two decades of the rolls from the first and second halves of the century have been read in detail (the 1720s and 1770s) and at least one year consulted in each of the remaining decades. The evidence from the trials at the Old Bailey that was printed in the Sessions Paper gives the histories of sodomy, rape, and infanticide, and all of the series has been included. Illegitimacy can be documented from the poor law examinations and the declarations made to the Foundling Hospital by women who surrendered their children, and four parishes spread across the geographical and economic variety of London provide the foundation for the discussion. The manuscripts of the Lock Hospital for venereal disease show the intimate connection between prostitution, venereal disease, and the life of London's poor families.

The newspapers are an endless source of information. They describe situations that would be difficult to visualize from the manuscript sources, but their record is always highly selective in reporting something like the arrests of prostitutes or the raids on bawdy houses. Sexual libertinism was recommended and opposed in an extensive printed literature. This has been widely sampled (it would be impossible to read it all) and as part of this project many of the more important items on masturbation, sodomy, prostitution, and venereal disease were reprinted in a forty-four volume series.[9] Sometimes a detail has been taken from a novel, a play, or a poem. But it has been an important part of the method of this book to base itself as far as possible on the reports in the legal sources of the behavior of actual human beings, however much those sources may be open to interpretation. Finally, there are the letters and diaries of individuals. These together with the libertine and the imaginative literatures have provided the sources for most of the previous general interpretations of eighteenth-century English sexuality. But these biographical sources are heavily weighted toward the lives of only 2 or 3 percent of the population. Only in the legal sources (however fragmentary or episodic they may be) is the behavior of the various social classes reported in something like their distribution in the general population. But it is necessary nonetheless to have as full an understanding of the sexual behavior and presumptions of the elite as possible, since it was they who policed society and produced the legal sources that document the behavior of the rest of society.

A study based primarily on legal sources documents behavior that for the most part was illegal. It cannot encompass (by and large) the history of legitimate sexuality in marriage. That can be found, however, in many of the recent histories of the family, to which I have already contributed a study of the aristocratic family in eighteenth-century England. This present book is therefore a study of extramarital sexual relations, and for this there need be no apology, since the history of modern male heterosexuality is substantially a history of extramarital relations. The sexual lives of women, on the other hand, were much more likely to have been confined to marriage, and it is probably a decided minority of London's women who appear in these stories of prostitution, illegitimacy, and adultery. This reinforces the point that women in the eighteenth century had not yet to any significant degree entered the world of modern Western exclusive heterosexuality with its concern for individual sexual identity and self-fulfillment.

The chapters that follow are grouped into three parts, on prostitution, illegitimacy, and adultery and violence in marriage. They are preceded by a chapter on sexual reputation and identity that seeks to establish the sexual roles into which the majority of women and men were socialized. A married woman was supposed to have sexual relations only with her husband, and her neighbors were very likely to gossip if they believed that she had sex with anyone else. They also gossiped if they believed that a couple were living together without really being married (which in some parts of the East End was frequently the case), or if a woman had borne a child before her marriage or been a prostitute. Widows and unmarried women were not supposed to have sex at all, and any misbehavior on their part also became the subject of gossip. This could have grave consequences for an unmarried woman since (as a subsequent chapter shows) she was very likely to be discharged from her job if she became pregnant. For poor women these distinctions remained vital throughout the century. But the old tripartite division of wives, widows, and maids was part of a world in which potentially every woman was a whore. Subsequent chapters will show, however, that men and women from the middle and the landed classes tended increasingly to divide women into a majority who were presumed to be motherly by nature and not especially sexual and a minority who from the circumstances of their poverty became prostitutes. A woman might still occasionally fall in love with someone other than her husband, as the last chapter shows. But she did not intend to make him a cuckold. It was instead that they had proven incompatible and the hope was that by divorce both partners might more happily remarry and reestablish their domesticity.

A man's sexual reputation, on the other hand, as chapter 2 shows, was no longer injured if he went to prostitutes. This now instead helped to establish his heterosexual standing. He was still not very likely to seduce the maids in his own household, since this violated the standards of both traditional patriarchy and modern domesticity. But the extensive population of young women who walked the streets between the ages of eighteen and twenty-three were fair game. This population of streetwalking prostitutes became the most distinctive aspect of the sexual lives of modern cities down to World War II. These women and the men who went to them are described in the five chapters that make up the second part of the book. Chapters 4 and 5 take up the number of prostitutes, the shifting geography of prostitution, and the management of the brothels, and how and why women entered and left the life of prostitution and their sexual behavior as prostitutes. Three chapters look at the men who went to prostitutes. In chapter 3 the libertinism of gentlemen is distinguished from that of poorer men. Romance and domesticity did modify the behavior of some gentlemen; but, as chapter 6 demonstrates, instead of giving up the prostitute, they domesticated the brothel and tried to reform the prostitute in magdalen houses. But male heterosexual desire could not be challenged directly since it was the bulwark men had built against the sodomite. The fear engendered in an adolescent by a man who made a pass at him and the terror of the adult man who allowed himself to be blackmailed because he was not certain that he could disprove a charge of sodomy once made are established in chapter 2. Appearing along with this new taboo on all forms of sodomy was another against masturbation that maintained that "self-abuse," whether it was solitary or with a group of other males, led to the gravest physical and mental degeneration. Male reputation and identity therefore grew out of a struggle to achieve an exclusive heterosexuality that avoided sodomy on the one hand and masturbation on the other, and that proved itself most easily by going to prostitutes.

For women neither masturbation nor female homosexuality were of much consequence. Before marriage it is likely that most women would not have thought much about sex, since sex for them was always subordinated to courtship and marriage. Their heterosociality (or their social relations with men) preceded their heterosexuality. But for men, masturbatory activity on their own or with other males and their social or sexual interaction with sodomites either preceded or accompanied their sexual interaction with the population of streetwalking prostitutes. This sexual development usually occurred before men attempted to court women in marriage or tried to seduce them for their pleasure. Male heterosexuality therefore came before male heterosociality. But the prostitutes with whom most men were likely to have relations before marriage were usually venereally diseased, as chapter 7 argues. They infected their customers, and these men took the disease home to their wives and children. The development of the male heterosexual role in the early eighteenth century therefore guaranteed that most sexual encounters were shadowed by the specter of disease. This remained the case until the late twentieth century, when widespread premarital intercourse, the decline in prostitution, and the development (before AIDS) of an easy and effective cure for venereal disease together instituted a new sexual regime.

The new male heterosexuality was not expressed, however, only in relations with the small minority of women who became prostitutes. It also affected men's relations with the majority of unmarried women, and this is described in the chapters on illegitimacy that comprise the third part of this book. The nature of the sources that survive does not make it possible to establish definitively the level of illegitimacy in London. But it is at least possible that London's illegitimacy surged ahead of the rest of England, as it did in the late twentieth century, when once again a new sexual system first made itself felt there. The sources do however, make quite clear that London's poor women were left to deal on their own with the harsh consequences of the seductions inspired by the new male heterosexuality and that they did not have the consolations of romantic love that were available to women from the middle and landed classes. The patterns of seduction varied throughout the city according to the economy of the parish in which they occurred. In fashionable West End parishes women were seduced either by the male servants with whom they worked or by the soldiers they met walking the streets. In those streets women also met gentlemen, but their own masters did not seduce them to any significant degree. In the East End the still tightly knit weaving communities north of the City walls produced a quite different pattern from the parishes east of the walls, where the sailors were found. But whether in the East or the West End, a servant lost her employment once she became pregnant, and after she had used up her savings and sold her clothes, she was obliged to turn to the parish for relief or to give up her child to the Foundling Hospital. Through all this she also had to deal with the disapproval of strangers as well as the ambivalence of the families in which she had worked and of her own family. For some women their pregnancies represented failed courtships. But never more than a fifth of them ever claimed to have been promised marriage, which makes it likely that a high level of sexual activity occurred without much thought for the future. Women because of their diffidence, however, always had great difficulty in resisting forceful advances from men. This becomes clear in the rape cases recounted in chapter 9 that conclude the third part of the book. These cases also show that men who violently assaulted women could afterward propose "to make the matter up" by offering marriage, and the acceptance they sometimes received demonstrates that self-conscious romance had not yet affected the sexual lives of the poor to any significant degree.

The role of romance among the middle and landed classes, and its inter-action with the new male heterosexuality and with traditional patriarchy, are the themes of the three chapters on marital violence and adultery that make up the fourth and final part of this book. Most of the evidence for these chapters is drawn from the divorce cases in the London Consistory Court. The nature of these divorces changed sharply around 1750. In the first half of the century women brought twice as many cases as men. They complained most often of their husbands' violence and less frequently of desertion. In these early cases men also complained of desertion and adul-tery by their wives, but they usually did so many years after the marriage had broken down and when they feared that they might become liable for the debts that their wives had contracted. After 1750 a great deal of this changed. Women still complained of violence, as chapter 10 makes clear. And it is likely that the new heterosexuality reinforced the old patri-archy for those men who beat their wives from the beginning of their marriages as a way of establishing their sexual and financial domination as well as for those who began their violence some years later after they had fallen in love with another woman. But some forms of violence disap-peared from the cases: it became harder to lock a woman away in a madhouse, and the number of widows whose second husbands beat them to gain control of their property markedly declined.

It was, however, the cases in which men sued their wives for adultery that changed most significantly, as chapter 12 shows. They increased in number, and men now brought twice as many cases as women. They made their complaints as soon as they discovered the adultery, and usually their wives had fallen in love with their best friend or a close associate. It is likely that the new heterosexuality had opened a space for intense friendships between men, and that one friend became more likely to ask another home to share the warmth of his new domesticity. But romantic love raised higher expectations of marital fulfillment in women who, usually after they had been married for a number of years, expressed their needs by falling in love with men who had recently entered their domestic world. This must have stung their husbands with all the force that the taboo against sodomy now carried and the fear that it created of any sexual subordination to another man. But it is also likely that the old belief that incompatibility ended a marriage was strengthened by the new romance. Chapter 11 argues that the poor and the middle class had often ended incompatible marriages by private agreements that were illegal in both common and canon law. But the landed classes in the early eighteenth century created a new form of divorce by which an act of Parliament allowed both spouses to remarry if the wife was adulterous. This device was used by a considerable number of the men who brought cases in the consistory. In this way divorces for the wife's adultery were transformed into divorces for mutual incompatibility. It was a clumsier device than the more straightforward divorces for incompatibility that appeared in revolutionary France and elsewhere in Europe in the second half of the eighteenth century. But the connection between sexual compatibility and modern marriage had been established, even though it was not until the generation after 1960 that divorce for mutual incompatibility became the legal standard throughout the Western world.

If it is the case that women appear in this book largely as the victims of modern male heterosexuality, it is also true that the behavior of the adulterous women in the divorces after 1750 establishes quite firmly that the new romance and domesticity did not destroy sexual passion in women. Before 1750 married women were frequently suspected of being unfaithful to their husbands, as the defamation cases from the consistory show. Similarly, in the divorces before 1750 (that are discussed in chapter 11) two kinds of passionate married women appeared. There were those who became prostitutes, some from economic necessity in the absence of their husbands; but there were other young women who seemed to have been released by their first intercourse in marriage into an overwhelming desire for many men. In a second category were the widows who used their financial independence to acquire younger, sexually desirable husbands. But in the divorce cases these attempts at sexual domination were usually literally beaten back by their husbands. This was a world, however, in which every woman was potentially a whore. After 1750 romance and domesticity divided women instead into a deviant minority who walked the streets as prostitutes and a majority who were faithful wives and devoted mothers and for whom sexual desire was supposed to be secondary. It is certainly true that women who intended to leave their husbands for a more satisfactory lover sometimes tried (but without much success) to ask for a reconciliation once they realized that a divorce meant that they would lose their children from their first marriage. But it is apparent that in the throes of their illicit love, they were overwhelmed by sexual desire, however much they might justify it to themselves in the name of romance and a higher standard of love. This passionate adultery coexisted after the 1770s with the newly emerged role of the masculinized sapphist who was exclusively interested in other women, and it may be that the presence of the sapphist role began to reorganize the desires of the majority of women into a female heterosexual identity. The appearance of the effeminate sodomite had certainly had that effect on the sexual identity of the majority of men at the beginning of the century. But the sapphist's presence was never as pronounced as the sodomite's. And what men did with each other was always of greater consequence than anything that might occur between women. It is therefore likely that women's sexual identity continued to be defined primarily in terms of their relationship to men and to the family and that there was still at the end of the century no exclusive heterosexual identity for women.

*   *   *

A number of the previous attempts to interpret the history of eighteenth-century sexuality have dealt with many of the forms of behavior described in this book. They have not, however, organized themselves around the presumption that heterosexuality and homosexuality are not biological givens but are instead socially constructed aspects of male and female gender roles that did not appear until the early eighteenth century, when the modern Western culture system in which we still live first arose. Michel Foucault originally intended that his history of sexuality should start in the early eighteenth century, and it is with that period that his introductory volume is mainly concerned. Foucault seems to have been struck by the literature against masturbation that first appeared in that period and used it to document the origins of what were for him the repressive structures of modern society. But he did not see in that volume any connection between masturbation and homosexuality. Instead he argued in a paragraph that has had an influence out of all proportion to its importance that the modern sense of the homosexual as a distinct kind of person did not appear until the late nineteenth century. In an interview two years before his death, however, he apparently changed his mind and declared that homosexuality first became a problem in the eighteenth century. But his followers (many of whom have tied their work to his first declaration) have not so far taken up their master's later position. Foucault's account of the eighteenth century (in what admittedly was to have been merely an introduction) is also unsatisfactory because it fails to deal with the histories of adultery and prostitution.[10]

Foucault's argument that modern homosexuality was a product of the late nineteenth century—which was simultaneously made by Jeffrey Weeks on the basis of a much more serious documentation—has been used by Jonathan Ned Katz and Kevin White to argue that modern heterosexuality must therefore similarly have been a product of the late nineteenth and the early twentieth centuries. But all four of these historians make the same mistake and fail to see that the late-nineteenth-century discussions of homosexuality and heterosexuality (in which the words were first coined) did not invent the roles that they considered. By 1880 modern Western homosexuality and heterosexuality had existed for nearly two hundred years. The new names therefore only represent a new stage in the public discussion of these roles, however much the discussion may have changed the political environment in which the roles were enacted.[11]

Five historians have discussed the sexual history of eighteenth-century England. Lawrence Stone in his general history of the family, sex, and marriage relied mainly on the letters and diaries of gentlemen. He asserted that in the eighteenth century sexual pleasure became a part of romantic marriage. He noticed an increase in prostitution as well as the new taboo against masturbation and a greater discussion of homosexuality. But he misinterpreted as a growing toleration for homosexual behavior what was in fact an unprecedented level of anxiety over its new form. And he did not consider that if masturbation, sodomy, and prostitution were put together with the traditional level of sexual violence (which he did not discuss), a sexual identity was produced in most men that could exist only in the most uneasy way with sexual romance in marriage. Roy Porter in three discussions of gentlemanly libertinism has produced a genial picture of sexual liberation tempered by hostility toward the sexual lives of women, the poor, the young, and the homosexual. In some ways it is similar to the history of aristocratic libertinism presented in this book and in two earlier essays of mine. But it presumes that heterosexuality is a biological given, and it accounts for a very small part of eighteenth-century society. G. J. Barker-Benfield has tried to show the way in which libertinism was modified by another component of Enlightenment thought, namely sensibility. But of the five accounts under discussion, his is the least satisfactory. Its evidence is drawn principally from novels; it discusses neither homosexuality nor domesticity; and it repeatedly asserts that sensibility was the product of a consumer society without ever showing how this could have been so. A. D. Harvey certainly gives homosexuality its due, in what he says is a discussion of attitudes and not actual behavior, and devotes a quarter of his book to the subject. But the discussion is out of focus because he presumes that the prosecutions for sodomy in European societies before 1700 show that modern homosexuality cannot have emerged in the early eighteenth century. He does not see that in the cases before 1700 adult men who were not effeminate and who were also attracted to women were prosecuted for sexual relations with boys. Not seeing this, he cannot make the most of his own observation (for which he seems to take exclusive credit) that homosexual effeminacy did first appear in the eighteenth century. Harvey's principal concern, however, is to suggest that sexuality after 1750 became identified as an exclusively male interest for the class of people who wrote books and that women were confined to another sphere. But since domesticity and adultery are missing from his book, this part of his discussion is also unfocused; and the heterosexual and homosexual roles in his world never engage each other. Tim Hitchcock in his historiographical essay is the most satisfactory of these historians. He claims that the majority of men moved from a culture of heavy sexual petting to one in which penetration frequently occurred and that this can be tied to the rise in population and to earlier and more widespread marriage and higher rates of illegitimacy. But he strangely does not believe that this resulted in higher levels of prostitution and venereal disease. He does not explain why the female partners of these penetrative males did not have a similar identity. He simply says that women came to be seen as more passive, without considering whether this reflected actual behavior or simply the views of the elite; and because he does not analyze the history of adultery and its connection to romantic love, he overestimates the extent of female passivity. Finally, the relationship between these identities in the majority of men and women and the male and female homosexual minorities is not adequately considered.[12]

The connection between the new male heterosexuality among men of all social classes and the appearance of domesticity and romantic love, which affected women more than men and which until the early nineteenth century was to be found only among the elites and the middle classes, is raised in two recent histories of gender by Anthony Fletcher and by Anna Clark. Fletcher maintains that the discussion of women's nature that occurred among the aristocracy and the middle class between 1670 and 1800 did not represent an improvement in women's place in the world. Instead women were subordinated to romantic love and separated from the outside world. Traditional patriarchy in this way reconstructed its basis: this was not the start of modern feminism, even though an older negative image of women was conquered. But Fletcher fails to discuss sexual behavior in the early eighteenth century, whether marital or extramarital, and as a consequence he does not see that the reconstruction of women's domestic role was accompanied by an even more startling change in men's role, represented by the new ideal and practice of an exclusive male heterosexuality. If domesticity was merely a reconstructed patriarchy, the level of male anxiety represented by the new heterosexuality becomes difficult to understand. This male heterosexuality preceded the ideology and practice of romance among the majority of men. Clark shows that it was not until the early nineteenth century that they came together in the lives of the poor. When in the 1820s, for instance, Richard Carlile tried to persuade working-class women that contraception would allow them to have more frequent sex with their husbands and provide the men with an alternative to the prostitution that (as I argue) was a necessary part of modern male heterosexuality, he received a shocked response from the women, who asserted that contraception insulted them as wives and mothers. Poor women had come to domesticity but not to heterosexuality, which remained a male defense against domesticity. Female heterosexuality would have been too much like the old presumption that women were sexual monsters. Motherhood and domesticity (while not to the liking of some kinds of late-twentieth-century feminism) did more for the respectability of women. Those women who in the eighteenth century used romance to reconstruct their sexual lives often had to endure ostracism and divorce, as chapter 12 in this book shows. But the new domesticity (if it was merely a reconstructed patriarchy, as Fletcher holds) had such a powerful effect on men's traditional roles that they constructed for themselves a separate world from women that this book calls modern male exclusive heterosexuality.[13]

There remain a series of large speculative questions that establish the need for a new kind of history, which this book begins to write. Why did a new sexual system come into existence in all of northwestern Europe (in England, France, and the Netherlands) in the early eighteenth century? Why did the division into heterosexual and homosexual roles occur first in men, and at what point did the distinction (or some variant of it) become crucial for the gender identity of women? What connection was there between the distinction into heterosexual and homosexual roles and the development of the ideals of romantic marriage and domesticity? When did a system that first appeared in northern Europe and North America spread to the rest of the Western world, to southern, central, and eastern Europe, and to Latin America; and how did the system change during this process of diffusion? And finally, why did a system of almost three hundred years' standing begin to change considerably after 1960, and did it change sufficiently to warrant the description of being postmodern? No-fault divorce, widespread premarital sexual relations between men and women who were not engaged to marry, widespread birth control, the expectation that women should have equal pay and equal access to work and that men should share in the duties of childrearing, the decline in prostitution, the control of venereal disease, and the appearance for the first time in most Western societies of a gay and lesbian movement—all these occurred together in a single generation, and in the very same countries that first experienced around 1700 the modern sexual system that these new forms of behavior have to some extent displaced. To these many questions, this book does not attempt to supply answers. It is apparent that we do not have much of an idea why or how cultural systems change rapidly in the course of a single generation, whether the change occurs around 1700 or around 1960. It is as baffling as trying to explain the rise and fall of diseases—the plague, syphilis, smallpox, or AIDS. It will be enough therefore in this book to begin the analysis of the division of the sexual world into a homosexual minority and a heterosexual majority that has been one of the most salient features of the modern Western culture that first appeared in the generation after 1700.

CHAPTER TWO

Reputation and Identity

The sexual reputation of women and men among their neighbors is one of the best guides to the varieties of sexual identity in eighteenth-century society. The present chapter contrasts the standards for women with those for men. A woman's sexual reputation was defined by her relationship to men, and by her status as a wife, a widow, or a maid. A wife could legitimately have relations only with her husband. The other married women in her neighborhood enforced this rule by making any violations the subject of gossip that discredited the woman and her husband. Defamation suits in the consistory court indicate that neighbors made four different kinds of accusations. They charged a woman with adultery. Or they said that she was not really married to her husband. They maintained that she had borne an illegitimate child before or after her marriage. And occasionally they suggested that she had been a prostitute before her marriage. Sometimes the charges were made as a result of a financial dispute or simply because of anger with a woman; it becomes clear that abusive language against women was more likely to be sexual than in the case of men. But sexual gossip was also a means to elaborate and enjoy one's sexual fantasies in a public forum. These points are established in the first half of the chapter through the defamation suits that married women brought against each other in the consistory court. A much smaller number of widows also sued those who said that they were presently having sex with a man, or that they were prostitutes or procuresses or had borne bastards. Single women brought the fewest cases, probably because they could least afford to do so and because they did not have husbands who were determined not to be thought cuckolds. But chapter 9 will show that a single woman who offended against chastity was more likely than a wife or a widow to suffer severe financial loss since she would probably be discharged from her place as a servant.

In these verbal exchanges the possibility of sexual behavior between two women was never raised, even though the modern masculinized sapphist role could be found enacted by some women after 1770. This is in marked contrast to the history of sexual reputation among men. The gender revolution of the first generation of the eighteenth century had produced the role of the adult effeminate sodomite and made it very difficult to discredit a man for any kind of sexual behavior with women. Instead, all males from adolescence onward had to display an exclusive dominant sexual interest in women. Sexual interaction between an adolescent and an adult male was therefore no longer acceptable, as it had been earlier, and boys who had passes made at them were thrown into a panic. Sexual interaction among adolescent males was also tabooed by the new doctrine that any form of masturbation produced grave physical and mental deterioration. The male body—whether one's own or another's—was closed off as object of male desire. Adult men socialized in this way feared the stigma of being labeled a sodomite so much that they sometimes allowed themselves to be blackmailed by men who threatened to swear sodomy against them, for the charge once made was difficult to disprove and therefore very destructive. In such a world an accusation of sexual behavior with women outside of marriage was no longer to a man's discredit; it was instead a welcome demonstration of his exclusive heterosexual interest in women. As a consequence the few cases brought by men in the consistory court in the early eighteenth century in which men complained of being called whoremongers disappeared by midcentury and were replaced by actions at quarter sessions in which men and boys brought charges of sodomitical assault and blackmail.

Men had entered the world of modern heterosexual relations. But women still lived in an earlier world (for which there is no convenient modern label) where it was of less concern what the gender of one's sexual partner was than whether the act had occurred outside of marriage. It is true that the number of defamation cases declined throughout the century. But it is likely that this was the result of changes in the values of the men who ran the court. The sexual language displayed in these actions had become too shocking for men of the elite, who had begun to have sentimental and romantic ideas about women that were not yet shared by those of lower social standing. The identities and the behavior displayed in this chapter can therefore be accounted for by the interplay among the three standards of traditional Christian procreative marriage, modern male heterosexuality, and elite concepts of romantic relations between men and women.

FEMALE HONOR: A WIFE, A WIDOW, OR A MAID

The material on the sexual defamation of women is drawn from the London Consistory Court, which was the bishop of London's court. Until the late seventeenth century such an ecclesiastical court oversaw the sexual lives of most communities and was known popularly as the "bawdy court." After the Restoration, however, the consistory in London more or less ceased to be the forum in which neighbors and parish officials complained about sexual misbehavior. This trend was reinforced throughout England after 1689 when the declaration of religious toleration led churchwardens to stop making presentments to the ecclesiastical courts. Instead in London after 1690 the members of the voluntary Societies for the Reformation of Manners took their concerns to the justices of the peace. By the first decade of the eighteenth century only 15 of 461 cases in consistory could be classified as being brought by the office of the judge, which was the traditional term for the court's general oversight of sexual behavior (table 2.1). Two of these cases were simply attempts to harass an enemy. Five of them were women who had borne bastards. The rest were against individuals who lived with a partner as though they were married when they were not. All of these kinds of cases were now far more likely to appear in the secular courts, and by the middle of the eighteenth century, they had disappeared entirely from the consistory court.

The consistory instead concentrated on cases for defamation and divorce or separation, and to a lesser degree on cases that questioned whether a legally binding marriage had been made.[1] At the beginning of the century nearly 70 percent (69.8 percent) of all cases were for defamation. They provide most of the evidence for the first half of this chapter. They were typically cases (64 percent) in which a married woman charged that another married woman had called her a whore, implying that she had committed adultery (tables 2.2 and 2.4). A lesser number of cases were brought by widowed or unmarried women (30 percent) and a very few by

Table 2.1 Actions in the London Consistory Court

Decade	Defamations	Divorces	Disputed Marriage Contracts	Office of the Judge	Total
1700–1709	322 (69.8%)	65 (14.1%)	59 (12.8%)	15 (3.3%)	461
1750–1759	134 (62.9%)	35 (16.4%)	44 (20.7%)	—	213
1790–1799	91 (43.1%)	86 (40.8%)	34 (16.1%)	—	211

Source: GLRO: DL/C/149–53, 171–74, 182–85.

Table 2.2 Number, Gender, and Marital Status of the Defamed

Decade	Wives	Spinsters	Widows	Males	Total
1700–1709	205	58	40	19	322
1750–1759	81	32	19	2	134
1790–1799	73	11	7	0	91

Source: GLRO: DL/C/149–53, 171–74, 182–85.

men (6 percent). These defamation cases declined in number during the course of the century, but even in the last decade they were still nearly half (43 percent) of the court's business.

The defamation cases show that it was far more important for a woman than for a man to be known among her neighbors as faithful to her marriage vows, since she was the plaintiff in most instances (table 2.2). Men were not careless of their sexual reputations, especially early in the century, when a few continued to bring defamation suits. But they were more concerned that it should be known that their wives were faithful to them. They cared less about being seen as faithful to their wives. But they were determined not to be taken for cuckolds. A number of defamation cases both in the bishop's court and before the justices of the peace, therefore, were brought by wives because gossip in the neighborhood had led to difficulties with a husband who had become suspicious that he was being mocked. It may indeed have been that for a woman the protection of her husband's reputation was a significant factor in all defamation cases. It did a woman no good for others to think her husband a cuckold.[2]

Most defamation cases in London were brought by women and usually by married women (table 2.2). In this regard London followed a pattern that had been established throughout England in the later seventeenth century. In the first half of that century and at the end of the sixteenth, men and women had in some areas (York, Norfolk) brought defamation suits in equal numbers. But in other areas (Wiltshire, Cheshire, Durham), women may always have been in the majority, though these figures have been reported somewhat vaguely. By 1700, however, women everywhere were bringing the majority of defamation suits and in fairly large numbers. After the middle of the eighteenth century in London, only women brought defamation suits. But as women took over defamation, the total number of suits began to decline markedly, and in early-nineteenth-century London, they eventually ceased to be brought. What is one to make of this history? To what extent did it reflect the changing relations of married men and women to sex, and to each other? Had the poorer

parts of society that brought these suits changed their behavior in regard
to the issues with which the suits dealt? Were they discouraged from
bringing these suits by their social superiors who ran the courts? Or did
the ecclesiastical courts no longer seem to the poor an appropriate forum
for their concerns, and did they find another?[3] There are no ready answers
to any of these questions. It is likely that magistrates and judges in the
first half of the eighteenth century did begin to feel that it was not their
place to punish adultery. Nonetheless, in the first thirty years of the century in London, a wife or a husband could have an adulterous spouse
arrested by the officials of the secular courts who might then send the
offenders to the house of correction, and 110 such cases can be recovered
for the 1720s. But this practice, in which the secular courts seemed to
take over some of the old disciplinary role of the ecclesiastical courts, may
well have been inspired by the fervor connected with the Societies for the
Reformation of Manners.

In the final decade of the influence of the societies, the cases for adultery
brought before the magistrates in the common-law courts show that men
were certainly reluctant to admit that their wives had misbehaved with
another man. In only two of the eighty-six cases from the 1720s in which
women were charged with adultery before the justices of the peace were
husbands plaintiffs against their wives. In one of them William Williams
said that his wife Elizabeth had threatened to stab him, had defrauded
him of his goods, and was living with Daniel Green as man and wife. In
the other case Francis Annesley charged his wife with adulterous conversation with Don Roderigo, the first step in what eventually became a divorce case. All the rest were complaints by wives against their husbands'
other women. A husband, on the other hand, was much more likely to
complain that another man had taken his wife—there were sixteen cases
of that in the 1720s. The adultery was often aggravated by other circumstances in these cases. John Justice assaulted Thomas Leach, married his
wife, and told Leach that he would lie with her whenever he pleased.
William Lewis was beaten by his wife's lover, who also received some of
the goods that Lewis's wife had stolen. Finally, some of these complaints
were evidently made by men whose wives were being seduced into prostitution. Robert Vero was found with Robert Whinwich's wife in a notorious house of ill fame. And Matthew Hartley sent out for James Buckley's
wife to come and join him in a similar place.[4]

Women complained that their husbands had left them or were seeing
other women. In half of these cases it was mentioned that the husband
had beaten his wife, and in three cases he had failed to support his wife

and children. One of the adulterous women in these cases was married herself, but more usually the women were prostitutes. Ann Rowse said that her husband John, who was a fisherman from Hungerford Market, had been found in bed with two such women at once.[5]

Women were more likely to charge that other women were having sex with their husbands or actually living with them as man and wife. It is likely that most of the women in the first group were prostitutes. It is harder to tell about the women who were charged with living with a married man. Grace Benjamin lived with her sister's husband. In some cases the adulterous woman was pregnant or had borne the offending husband's bastards. Mary Audrey was joined by John Leech in complaining that her husband Thomas and Leech's wife Mary had left their respective marriages, and that Mary Leech was pregnant by her lover. Mary Veal used her lover's name and passed as his wife and the legitimate mother of their two children for some years before Ann Talbot brought her to the magistrate. In both kinds of cases, of course, a woman and her children were likely to be suffering economically. This was sometimes specifically mentioned in a complaint, but it was probably always a factor. In some of these cases it is clear that the offending woman was a prostitute and that the cost of keeping a prostitute could be ruinous to a man's family. In this way Mary Lloyd had ruined a man's family and his business as well. When Mary Marks told the magistrate a similar tale about Elizabeth Unwin, she added that Unwin had also violently assaulted her.

Some women claimed that the other woman had either abused her physically or verbally or had caused a woman's husband to beat her. When Mary Garrett had an affair with Thomas Sarson, she raised a mob around his wife's house and threatened to set it on fire and kill her. Mary Wagstaffe tried to pull the nose off Mary Wiggins's face and to stamp her guts out because she wanted Thomas Wiggins to herself. These two women were poor and probably prostitutes. But a prosperous married woman like Elizabeth Pollard in the throes of passion could act similarly. Margaret Lee said that Pollard had subjected her to gross abuse with her threats to take her husband from her and would not let her live in peace. Finally, there were the adulterous husbands who beat their wives at the instigation of their mistresses, as Elizabeth Robinson said was the case with Susanna Ward. Ward first lived with Elizabeth's husband Thomas Robinson and then threatened her and helped Robinson and his servant to drag, assault, and abuse her. Robinson and his brother stood bail for Ward.[6]

In all of this it is apparent that a wife was far more likely to blame the other woman than to blame her husband. It may have been that this allowed her to feel that she had not lost her husband's regard and made it possible to reclaim him. It may also have been that wives felt that a husband's reputation suffered less if he could be regarded as seduced by the wiles of another woman. It was better than having a whoremonger for a spouse. Her husband's sexual reputation mattered to her perhaps as much as hers mattered to him. But in public it was always a woman's sexual reputation that was most likely to be discussed. In the case of sexual relations between women and men, it was women who were hardest pressed to maintain a flawless public reputation. This was a burden they bore so that no one could question the proprietary rights of their husbands in their bodies. A wife's reputation guarded her husband's sexual property.

When the Societies for the Reformation of Manners declined after 1730, adultery cases very rapidly disappeared from the sessions rolls. A quick survey of a few years of the Middlesex and Westminster rolls shows what happened. When the societies were flourishing, in years like 1704 or 1714, there could be thirteen to eighteen cases of adultery. In the last decade of the societies' power (1720–29), there were about nine a year. But twice in 1730, when such cases came before Humphrey Parsons, the lord mayor, in his role as a magistrate, he dismissed them as "being not properly before his Lordship." It was not that Parsons was soft on vice. He sent 60 percent of the prostitutes who came before him to the house of correction.[7] It was instead that on some ground he thought adultery did not come within his compass as a magistrate. There still could be as many as six adultery cases a year in the rolls in the 1730s (as there were in 1734). But by the 1740s, there were years with none. The last case in the rolls that I have seen appeared in 1755. In the entire decade 1770–79, there was not a single case of adultery brought before the magistrates in Middlesex or Westminster, or none at any rate that they punished as a crime. Instead adultery in the law became a private injury. Beginning probably in the 1690s and especially after 1750, husbands sued their wives' lovers for criminal conversation and recovered money damages that ranged from less than a hundred pounds to several thousand. Wives, of course, had no recourse against a husband's adultery. There was clearly an inequality between the genders. Nonetheless, adultery, despite the blazing publicity of the criminal-conversation trial, had ceased to be an offense against public order and had become a private tragedy that like other offenses against sexual honor (whether a rape or a sodomitical assault) could be "made up" or compensated with a money payment.[8]

These developments in the practice of the common law make it likely that the decline in defamation suits in the ecclesiastical courts was a reflection of changing attitudes among the classes of men from whom the judges and lawyers of the consistory came. It was not necessarily the result of changing standards of sexual or gender behavior among the poor, especially among women. This is confirmed by a simultaneous decline in the number of divorces brought by women in the ecclesiastical court (table 10.1; fig. 10.1). In the first two decades of the century, women had initiated two-thirds of all divorces. London's women in this regard followed the then-existing and subsequent pattern of all Western divorce courts, where women always have been the majority of the plaintiffs. But in the London court after 1720 the number of female plaintiffs fell to half of what they had been. This was partly due to an overall decline in the number of all actions in the court, from which it never recovered in the eighteenth century. But the number of female plaintiffs declined more than the male. After 1750 the number of male divorce plaintiffs began to increase, and by the last decade of the century they were two-thirds of the total, replacing women as the majority in this action. Between 1720 and 1750 the number of women who appeared as plaintiffs in all kinds of actions declined. This must have accounted in large part for the overall decline in the court's business. In 1700 the consistory had dealt mainly with women plaintiffs. By 1800, women were still in the majority because of the remaining defamation suits. But the number of male plaintiffs had become more significant, since they were the majority in divorce cases, and these cases had grown from 14 to 41 percent of the total business of the court (table 2.1).

After 1750 the law and the men who made it became less responsive to the public needs of women than they had been in the first half of the century. Susan Staves has suggested that something similar happened in the law on married women's property. It was perhaps (though Staves might not agree) a conservative reaction against the growing equality of women that romantic marriage and the domesticated family promoted. After 1750 gentlemen were likely to think of women as the loving mothers of children who ought to make their world in the family and not in the public sphere. Women were by their natures delicate, and this required that they should be shielded from the harsher aspects of sexual life. The explicit sexual language that was likely to be complained of in a defamation suit was something that a modest women should never have heard, and if she had, should never have taken notice of. Women should not have to deal with a man's adultery or his cruelty or his foul language. Adultery itself was no longer a crime, but a domestic tragedy. So divorce suits for women were to be discouraged in favor of private separations. Poorer women who could trade in foul language were discouraged from bringing their defamation suits to court. This is an explanation difficult to prove, but it very probably accounts for the decline in the number of women plaintiffs in the ecclesiastical courts.[9]

It is therefore unwise to find evidence for any significant change in the behavior of the poor in the decline in defamation suits. It is more likely that it was part of a general process by which a consistory that had previously dealt mainly with the behavior and concerns of women and the poor was transformed into an institution that monitored the domestic concerns of men from the middle classes and the gentry. The defamation suits, however, can still be the means of letting us into the sexual lives of the poorer, but respectable, women who lived in the alleys and courts of London. They show us how individuals and their communities created and maintained through conversation the boundaries of what they thought was proper sexual behavior. But they also demonstrate that individuals expressed in conversation the private sexual fantasies that they enjoyed and created out of the lives of those around them and that these fantasies often varied considerably from the prescribed norms.

Married women brought most defamation suits throughout the century—60 percent at the beginning and in the middle of the century, and even more (80 percent) at the end. It would seem that married women were more likely to be gossiped about than were spinsters or widows. It may be that society presumed that wives were the women who would probably be most sexually active, widows the least. But it may also have been the case that husbands were likely to be affected by gossip about their wives and would urge them to go to court. Spinsters and widows would not so often have had male defenders, so they brought fewer cases (table 2.2). These women without husbands were, on the other hand, more likely to be gossiped about by men than married women were, and this became increasingly true after the middle of the century. Men, many with wives of their own, were evidently willing to attack a woman without a husband. But the percentage of men who were charged as defamers was higher in the second half of the century in all kinds of cases even as the absolute number of cases declined throughout the century. It may have been that women grew less fond of gossip. However, it is equally possible that some kinds of cases brought in anger by one wife against another early in the century were likely to be compromised later in the century. But it may not have been so easy to ignore wounding words that came from a man (table 2.3).

Throughout the century it was always married women who did most

Table 2.3 Gender and Marital Status of the Defamed and Gender of Their Defamers

| Decade | Gender of Defamer | Status of the Defamed | | | | |
		Wife	Spinster	Widow	Male	Total
1700–1709	F	139	38	22	12	211
	M	66	20	18	7	111
1750–1759	F	45	13	6	0	64
	M	36	19	9	2	66
1790–1799	F	42	5	2	0	49
	M	31	6	5	0	42

Source: GLRO: D/LC/149–53, 171–74, 182–85.

of the gossiping. They were 46 percent of all those accused, and 69 percent of the women. Whether the victim was a wife, a widow, a spinster or a man, it was always overwhelmingly a married woman who had made the offending comment (tables 2.2 and 2.4). In three out of four cases it was a neighbor whom she attacked, or at least someone who lived in the same parish (table 2.5). It is apparent that the poor married women of London had constituted themselves the guardians of sexual morality in their neighborhoods. They played this role throughout the town, with a third of the cases coming from the West End (Holborn, St. Martin in the Fields, St. Giles, and St. James) and a quarter from the East (Whitechapel, Stepney, Wapping, and Shadwell). These married women maintained their vigil even after the men of the elite had ceased to do so and had turned their concern from adultery in families to the young unmarried girls who walked the streets as prostitutes. The boundary between a poor respectable married woman and a whore (which was sometimes lost on gentlemen) remained of the greatest importance to families at the poorer levels of society.

The standard of sexual behavior for a woman varied according to whether she was married, widowed, or single. But the sexual charges made against all women in conversation were remarkably similar. Wives who were defamed for sexual misconduct had four different kinds of charges leveled against them. Some were said to be presently engaged in adulterous affairs, and their husbands were often mocked for this. Some women were suspected of never having legally married the men with whom they lived as wives. And other women were charged with their misdeeds before their present marriage—either that they had borne bastards, or that they had been prostitutes. It is not possible to say in exactly what proportions these

Table 2.4 Marital Status of Female Defamers

Decade	Person Defamed	Defamed by		
		Wife	Spinster	Widow
1700–1709	Wife	114	10	15
	Spinster	22	7	9
	Widow	19	2	1
	Male	9	1	2
	Total	164	20	27
1750–1759	Wife	36	3	6
	Spinster	6	5	2
	Widow	4	0	2
	Male	0	0	0
	Total	46	8	10
1790–1799	Wife	36	3	3
	Spinster	4	1	0
	Widow	2	0	0
	Male	0	0	0
	Total	42	4	3
Total of 3 Decades		252	32	40

Source: GLRO: DL/C/149–53, 171–74, 182–85.

Table 2.5 Parish of Defamers

Decade	Parish of Defamer[a]	Status of the Defamed				
		Wife	Spinster	Widow	Male	Total
1700–1709	S	164	47	33	11	255
	D	41	11	7	8	67
1750–1759	S	51	21	12	0	84
	D	30	11	3	2	46
1790–1799	S	58	7	3	0	68
	D	15	4	4	0	23

Source: GLRO: DL/C/149–53, 171–74, 182–85.
[a] S = same parish as defamed; D = different parish from defamed.

charges were made since in many cases no information survives beyond the bare charge that a woman had been called a whore. The information for the cases in the last decade of the century is especially limited. It seems likely enough that one kind of charge—that of not having contracted a legal marriage—may have declined after the Marriage Act of 1753 eliminated the ambiguities about the form of marriage on which some of those charges had been based. On the other hand, the cases from the 1750s show a range of charges very similar to those made in the first decade of the century even though the number of cases had declined by 60 percent in the middle of the century.

In all three decades most of the disputes occurred between people of relatively the same social class, master artisans or poorer. Only one woman above this social level seems to have brought a case in the sample of three decades. In 1707, Mary, Lady Mordington, tried to punish Elizabeth Peere for saying that she should stand in the pillory for having two husbands. Lady Mordington had replied that she had one husband, Lord Mordington, not two. Peere then asked if she was not married to Mr. Laycock. Lady Mordington answered that she was but though she had been married to him, she was not now his wife. To which Peere retorted, "why what are you then, if you are not his wife, you are his whore." Lady Mordington's marital status must have been confused. She is not listed as Mordington's wife in the peerages. She certainly lost her case in court.[10]

It was not that gentlewomen were not gossiped about. The letters of Horace Walpole and almost any volume of aristocratic correspondence show otherwise. It must therefore have been that it was undignified for such women to use the courts to vindicate themselves. If this was so, it would explain why their husbands as the judges in the courts discouraged such suits by poorer women. A gentlewoman, however, could take steps to protect her reputation. In 1729 Sir Robert Walpole told the king and queen a scandalous story about the duke of Kent and Lady Kaye, who was a wealthy widow. The couple had had thoughts of marrying that in the end came to nothing, possibly because of the scandal. The story told at court was said to have come from Lady Powlett, who supposedly when visiting Lady Kaye had seen the duke reflected in a mirror as he stood before the fire in another room warming his sexual parts. Lady Kaye got Lady Powlett to deny that she had said this: she claimed that she had merely remarked that she "fancied his Grace was putting up to the rich widow" after she met Kent at Lady Kaye's. Lady Kaye therefore wrote to Walpole, who asked her to come to court, where the queen was very civil to her and assured her that no one credited the story. Lady Kaye then carefully filed away the packet of letters that vindicated her honor.[11]

Gentlemen had great difficulty taking seriously the honor of women beneath them in rank. A case at the end of the century that was fought across the great divide of gentility illustrates the anger that this obtuseness could generate. On a Saturday evening in March 1796, Thomas Clarke Jervoise arranged to meet some friends for dinner in an eating house in Panton Square kept by Sarah Dantan, a married woman. Clarke Jervoise was a young man in his early thirties, the eldest son of a very wealthy father worth about twenty thousand pounds a year. Jervoise arrived first and reserved five or six places at the table d'hôte for his friends. But only two of them showed up. In the meanwhile a number of other diners had been turned away, and their business was lost to the eating house. Dantan therefore charged Jervoise for all the places he had reserved, but he balked at the bill. Dantan complained that it was not fair that Jervoise with his thousands of pounds a year should refuse to pay. Taking a guinea out of her own pocket, she offered it to him, saying that if he needed a guinea, she would give him one. As a final thrust, she added that since lords would not pay their bills, she would put up "Lady Dantan" over her door; she had, she said, as much right to a title as they, for she always paid her way.

Jervoise's angry reply to this was disputed. Lord Strathmore's valet of thirty-five years said that Jervoise called Dantan a "damned old whore, a damned bitch." But Jervoise's two friends disagreed. The count de Bois-gelin (a French émigré fighting with the British army) remembered Jervoise as saying that Dantan was "an impertinent bitch." To this Dantan supposedly replied that that was very well, she would have him in the Crown Court for calling her a whore. (Other women also thought of the Crown Court or King's Bench before coming to the probably cheaper consistory court: in 1705 Mary Austin told Thomas Clements that "she would crown him, or put him in the Crown office.") Jervoise then told her that he had not called her a whore but an impertinent bitch. Lord Scarborough, Jervoise's other companion, agreed with this version—the phrase, he said, had been damned sniveling bitch. (In a case from 1701 a woman was similarly careful to deny saying "whore" and would admit only to using "strumpet," in which she did not believe there was any harm.) Scarborough then abetted matters by pushing Dantan around the room while Jervoise made rude and indecent gestures. Dantan claimed that Scarborough later returned to apologize. Scarborough denied this but agreed that he had said that Jervoise had used improper language in calling her a bitch. The punishment that the consistory could order against Jervoise—to do penance standing in a white sheet in church—which was so important to Dantan as the guarantee of her honor—was to a man like Scarborough quite comical and made him laugh heartily. But he carefully denied that he had mocked the court.[12]

Class divisions in the age of the French Revolution and the secularization of society had destroyed the spiritual community that had made public penance in the parish church a serious matter. That kind of community by the end of the century existed only among religious sectarians; among them religious discipline against adultery still had meaning, as a defamation case from 1794 shows. Katherine Rose, a married woman, complained that another married woman, Jean Graham, had defamed her. Graham had said that Rose lived in adultery with John Simpson. She had seen Rose come out of Simpson's bedroom in her bedgown and underpetticoat. Rose had sat on Simpson's knee as they kissed. Graham had also seen them on a bed together, or at least she had seen Rose's shoes and ankles and was sure they were "in the position of man and wife." She also had found them "in the very act on a great chair" and called out "for shame, for shame." Both women were Seceders, Presbyterians who had seceded from the Church of Scotland in 1733 and who had subsequently split into two groups. Graham said that she had told Rose that she went "to the meeting," or the worship of the group, only "to cloak your adultery." But Rose now complained in a consistory court of the Church of England that Graham had defamed her by saying these things in public to all their acquaintances. Graham insisted that she had spoken out only because all Seceders "on proper application or summons" were "obliged to give evidence of any transaction relating to any person of the said Sect, if called upon by those persons who compose the Session of the said Meeting on pain of being held contumacious by such Session and being forever dismissed from the Society or Meeting." But Rose had evidently decided to leave her religious sect and its discipline—her adultery was her private affair. In the consistory court, however, she had chosen a weak reed on which to rely for her vindication. Presbyterian discipline had always been stricter than that of the Church of England: the radical English Puritans before 1660 had struggled for a more thorough reformation in that regard. But for Rose the consistory must have represented the standards not of a sect but of general polite society. Through its agency she hoped evidently to maintain the modern principle that the sexual life of individuals was their own private business to conduct without any communal oversight.[13]

The wrangles over adultery in the consistory had far more meaning earlier in the century when they occurred between the men and women who lived in London's courts and alleys, where the good opinion of one's neighbors mattered, and where the court's sentence of public penance was a vindication worth having. The accusation of adultery in the first decade of the century was likely to be accompanied by the full panoply of ritual gestures and slurs that the husband wore horns and was a cuckold. Mary Sermon first told Jane Burston's manservant that she was not "as your mistress is." When Burston asked her what she meant, Sermon angrily held up her hand "and stretching out two fingers" (in the cuckold's sign) said, "do not speak to me, Impudence, but go to the cuckold your husband who found you drunk at two o'clock in the morning with your coats about or over your head or ears, go to Bridewell, Impudence, for that is the fit place for you." (Bridewell was the house of correction.) Similarly, when the neighbors became suspicious of Elizabeth Duncomb's way of life, someone put a pair of sheep's horns over her door when she was in bed, and a crowd gathered outside to ridicule her and her husband.[14]

Husbands were often taunted that others knew more about their wives than they did themselves, which was what Lucy Heartley added when she told Roger Phillips to "go you home you cuckold dog to the whore your wife." For this Sarah Phillips sued her. (Husbands themselves could not sue since being a cuckold was a misfortune, not a crime of which one might be illegally accused.) Jane Morris, a widow, said that Thomas Miller was a pitiful fellow because he had married a common whore of the town. His wife Sara sued her. Wives were perhaps most likely to sue for something said to their husbands when the speaker was another man. Men, at any rate, seemed to have had the most outrageous things to say. Thomas Fry told Edward Sedley that Mary, his wife, was a whore and that her brother Joseph Somner "stood pimp to your wife whilst a man fuckt her." Joseph Harrison went further when he told William Godley that his wife Grace had been incestuous with Godley's father to the couple's benefit: "You Godley, I might have as much money as you if my wife lay with her husband's father." Sometimes one man told another that he had slept with his wife, as John Farrington said to Michael Bliss: "your wife is a whore and my whore, and I have lain with her at the Goat Tavern in Hatton Garden and at the Red Lyon in Vane Street near Clare Market." William Parker was not so forthright, but his persistent mockery was perhaps harder to take. Oswald Dyke became suspicious of him when Parker said in Dyke's house that "he had and would have the private conversation and familiarity when he pleased" with Dyke's wife Barbara. When Dyke asked what he meant, Parker replied, "You by doing so will only prove

yourself a cuckold." After Parker left the house, he called out "cuckoo" at
the door several times in a loud voice. He returned many more times,
both when Dyke was at home and when he was away, and would stand
at the door and call out "cuckoo." He had gotten into another man's nest,
or so he was willing to claim in public.[15]

Wives also sued when their husbands were said to have profited from
their adultery. Elizabeth Swift claimed that Richard Anderson had said
that "it was not John Swift that procured the Queen's waterman's coat
for Thomas Groves but the gentleman that comes to John Swift's house
and knocks his wife that procured the Queen's coat for the said Groves,
and that he (John Swift) is a cuckold." Anderson denied he had said this
about Swift. There was clearly some confusion as to whom Anderson had
meant when he had said, "*his* wife." Anderson said that it was not a story
about Swift and his wife but one about Groves and his wife and a man
who visited her, and that the story was common knowledge. Anderson
also claimed that the entire suit was economically motivated: he kept a
public house that competed with the one kept by Elizabeth Swift's
mother. The Swifts had tried to get Groves to bring the suit. But the
court believed the Swifts and found Anderson guilty.[16]

The charge of simple adultery was made often enough against a married
woman. It could sometimes be an accusation of having had sexual relations
with a young servant or journeyman in the household. Arthur Nunnely
said to Rebecca Pitt that she kept her husband's servant John Anderson
for her stallion and that her husband was a poor cuckold dog. To which
Pitt replied, "damn you, if I was to keep a stallion I would choose a hand-
somer than him." The charge was in any case probably not seriously
meant. Nunnely and the Pitts were at odds because they thought he had
caused their servant to be impressed into the army. A woman could be
accused of keeping a young man in her house as though he were her husband. This was what Mary Hayes told Elizabeth Ridger that all their
neighbors said about Margaret and John Pinchon. There was "now evident
proof enough that they lived as whore and rogue together," which made
Margaret "a greater whore than Madam Blackburn, for that a Lord kept
her but that she Margaret kept Mr. Pinchon and if she kept a spark, she
ought to pay for him." Rowland Freid, on the other hand, boasted of
being kept by a married woman. When his friends in an alehouse asked
how he could spend so much (he was extravagant and drank a lot), he
replied that "his Prick was his Plough. . . . he had fuckt or use to fuck
Mrs. Ross," and she maintained him in his expenses.[17]

In a number of other cases, the offending words were spoken either to the woman or to others with the confidence that they would shock, or give pain, or simply make for titillating conversation. John Hart told Hannah Holden that she was an impudent, sorry, nasty whore and was "under the Presbyterian pulpit when Roger Henley fucked you." Margaret Coker said that Mrs. Ferrero was a whore and lay with a man against her own door in a "moon-shining" night. Judith Cross gossiped in a public house in Ratcliffe's Highway that Margaret Milward was Coffin's whore, who gave her the pox, and that she had given the pox in turn to her husband, which was why he drank so much water gruel. Thomas Williams triumphed that his brother-in-law John White "hath knockt Anice Watts as often as I have knockt my wife."[18]

After adultery, the second major charge of sexual irregularity made against a married woman was that she was a whore because she had not in fact legally married the man with whom she lived. The timing of a first pregnancy could raise doubts as to whether a sexual relation had begun before the marriage. Elizabeth Fisher said that Susanna Bagley came two months sooner than honest women used to come and that she had not been married long enough to have a child. Fisher even went further and by her questioning tried to make the neighborhood believe that a marriage had not occurred at all. It was therefore important that a woman's marriage be known to her neighborhood since this was likely to allay suspicion of her. Sometimes an adulterous or bigamous couple simply moved to another part of town and gave out that they were married. There are many instances of this in the adultery charges made either in the divorce cases or before the justices of the peace. This made it likely that a suspicious or hostile neighbor would try to smoke out an unmarried couple. A woman in such an irregular union might unwisely confide in what she thought was a sympathetic neighbor. But Mary Bell, when she quarreled with Martha Baldock, used her confidences against her and kept shouting in the street, "go in, get in, you whore, you whore, you whore, you told me you was not married, I had it from your own mouth. . . . you owned yourself to be a whore." This so upset Baldock's husband (if that was what he was) that he threatened to leave her. He agreed not to part only after a man in the neighborhood whom he respected said he would go to court on the couple's behalf.[19]

The offending words could involve a charge of bigamy, as the quarrel between the two sisters Dorothy and Elizabeth Bundyn with Elizabeth Elliott and her friend Elizabeth Hutchins did. Elliott and her daughter were known as very honest people in their neighborhood; the older woman was well liked and went to church regularly. Her daughter married Henry

Waldron. But Elizabeth Burdyn, who lived with her unmarried sister Dorothy, also claimed to be married to Waldron and seems to have had children by him. Elliott, however, told her friend Elizabeth Hutchins that Burdyn was merely her son-in-law's mistress. The quarrel came to a head when Burdyn, acting as Waldron's wife, intercepted a letter sent to him by his mother, who lived in Barbados. Burdyn and Elliott now quarreled, and after the older woman left, Hutchins heard Burdyn call her an old bawd and a bawd to her own daughter (Jane Waldron). Hutchins rebuked Burdyn for saying this behind the two women's backs. Burdyn then asserted that it was she who was married to Mr. Waldron. Hutchins replied that since Henry Waldron had been lawfully married before, and since his wife was still alive, Burdyn must therefore be little less than a whore, meaning thereby (as she told the court) that Burdyn had done an unlawful act and an ill thing.[20]

The third major sexual charge that was frequently leveled against married women was that they had borne an illegitimate child before or after their present marriage. A neighbor often claimed to know the actual father of the child, as Elizabeth Blanchard did when she told Mary Swaddell that she was a whore "and George Hutton's whore, and George Hutton is the father of your twins." More aggressively, Ann Gray pointed at Elizabeth Birchall and shouted, "come out you bitch and I will stone you"; and to Birchall herself she said, "I never was a whore, and never had a bastard by a baker." A husband like John Harris could, however, passionately defend his wife and his own honor against such a charge. John Parsons, who was a pork dealer, came into Harris's watchmaker's shop at ten in the morning when Susanna Harris was also in the shop with her child in her arms. Parsons pointed at the child and said, "You know very well that's not Harris's child, it's Meadow's child." Harris replied, "I'm sure it's no such thing, and I'll make you prove it." Parsons insisted that Susanna "has said so herself, and I'll bring two or three to prove it." The argument grew noisier, a mob collected around Harris's door, and the matter ended in court.[21]

When a child had clearly been conceived in a husband's absence, there was no doubt that it was spurious. Hester Byrne told Margaret Godman (as each woman stood at her own door) that she was a bastard-bearing whore because Godman had been married to four husbands and had been delivered of a child three or four months after Joshua Godman returned home. Supposedly Godman had said that the child was not his, and Margaret had confessed that it was Walter Scott's child whose whore she was, and that her husband was a cuckold. In another case James Quilter pointed out that his tenant Mary Buck had borne a child even though her husband had been away at sea for two years. Buck sued for defamation. But Quilter replied that she had sued to force him to abate the rent that her husband owed him; if Jonathan Buck were at home, Quilter said, he would not have approved of his wife's behavior.[22]

The bastards a woman bore before her marriage could be as damaging to her reputation as those she had in her marriage. It is clear that marriage did not wipe away previous offenses against chastity. Edward Collins wondered how Elizabeth Butcher could have the impudence to stand at her door. When she asked what he meant, he replied, "because you had a child before you was married." Neighbors were likely to tie their memories of premarital misbehavior to a woman's present life. William Phipps said that Elleanore Clancey had had a bastard before her marriage and now kept a bawdy house for which she had been indicted and found guilty. The two bastards Elizabeth Gregory had supposedly had before her marriage were similarly connected to the men she kept company with after marriage. After her marriage she befriended a young married woman, Eleanor de Colonia, who was warned against her. The de Colonia family was convinced that Gregory corrupted their relation. The two friends used a garret to meet two men and avoid discovery by de Colonia's husband. Eventually they rented a room together for these assignations. At this point Adrian de Colonia and Thomas Gregory became suspicious of their wives and went together to make inquiries. Two years later when Adrian was dead, Cornelia de Colonia had not forgotten Elizabeth Gregory's role in the disruption of her brother's marriage. She called Gregory a whore and made it clear that she thought that her bastards before marriage were a natural preliminary to her adulteries.[23]

Most defamation cases were actually concerned with a woman's sexual behavior, even though what the neighbors thought they knew was not necessarily accurate. But one has to end by noting (what has been apparent already in some cases) that sometimes words of sexual insult were employed when nothing sexual was known or suspected. Sexual abuse was simply the form of verbal abuse most likely to be used against a woman. A dispute often could have more to do with money or having a debtor arrested than with sexual reputation. Maria Grant charged that her former mistress, Lucy Russell, had told Ann Morgan that Grant did not scruple to say that Morgan had cheated her of money even though Morgan supported Grant, whom Russell thought a whore. Russell replied that Grant's witness Ann Morgan was a turbulent woman whose former neighbors had made a bonfire in celebration when she left their neighborhood, and that

Morgan owed Grant money and would swear whatever she asked. Morgan had also tried to make trouble between Lucy Russell and her husband by spreading false and scandalous stories. Russell explained that Grant and her husband were the Russells' former servant maid and apprentice. They had been married from the Russells' house. The Russells also gave the wedding dinner, paid the minister's fees, and lent the couple money. But the friendship soured when the Grants failed to repay thirty pounds, and the Russells had James Grant arrested. This, Russell said, was the motivation for the present suit as well as another in the Court of Common Pleas.[24]

The women who sued the least were widows. As in some of the cases brought by married women, the disputes were occasionally economic and not about actual sexual behavior. When the charges were really sexual, they maintained either that a widow was sexually active with one or more men, or that she was involved in actual prostitution either as a whore or as a bawd. A few widows were also charged with having bastard children. Daniel Mackay told Elizabeth Price that she had never married and that all her children were bastards. It must have been part of a larger quarrel since Mackay was also sued at the same time for having told a married woman that she was a common coffeehouse whore (coffeehouses were sometimes places of prostitution). But widows could hope to marry again, and a man could be concerned for his future wife's honor, as Alexander Cutting was. He courted Elizabeth Moody, and Mary Batchelour said it was he who inspired the suit against her. Moody had come to her house to complain about Batchelour's maidservant, in the course of which she called Batchelour a beast. Batchelour had replied: "I do not know how you can make a beast of me, I never did a beastly action; I never had a child but by my own husband," implying, of course, that Moody had.[25]

Sexual misbehavior was beastly, like that of the dogs in the street; so men were called cuckoldy dogs, and women bitches, since a bitch would go with any dog. John Colston accordingly told Fordice Skipworth that she was a common bitch and would turn up her tail to every dog. Elizabeth Dodge complained of similar epithets—Jane Adams had said that Mr. Dent used to turn up Dodge's tail as often as he pleased and that Dodge was "a hot ars't bitch" and as common as the highway. There was no implication of sodomy: it was instead that bitches were mounted from behind, and therefore a woman's vagina could be called her arse. But these two women had been trading insults with Dodge, saying that Adams had two daughters in prison who were eaten up with venereal disease and that Adams herself had been ducked at Portsmouth (a haunt for prostitutes because of the sailors) for playing the whore. Neighbors like Adams clearly kept a watch for a widow's lovers and were likely to call her a whore for each one she had, so that John Foukes could tell Anna Wright that she was Mr. Burlate's whore as well as Mr. Higgins's.[26]

A widow who was careless in what she said of a neighbor's children could meet with a harsh reprimand. Elizabeth Sais did not like the two sons of Eliza Holt. She said they were thieving bastards, had the gallows in their faces, and would come to be hanged. Holt replied that Sais was the old man's whore and her child a bastard. A widow also had to cope with vague general charges. As Elizabeth Jones waited for her friend Elizabeth Dun in Nicholas Douglas's alehouse, he asked her if she stayed for anybody. When she said it was for Dun, he sarcastically replied, "you stay for a very creditable person." Jones defended her friend, but Douglas insisted that Dun was a whore and he could prove her one. A vague charge that began more genteelly could still end the same: "Colonel Dornell," said Martha Junes, "is an honest gentleman but his daughter Mrs. Catherine Dennis . . . was a drab and a whore," and, determined not to be intimidated by her social superiors, Junes added that she would prove this before her betters.[27]

All these widows may have been indiscreet, but they were relatively respectable. Some widows went beyond this and actually became prostitutes or something very close to that. Katherine Newburgh had a bad reputation in her neighborhood in Whitechapel. For two years she had kept company with several men in a way that seemed suspicious. One of them, Captain Stow, was a married man with wife and children, but he spent all night in her lodging room. Newburgh had openly declared that she had lain with him and that she would do so again in anybody's sight. Then she quarreled with the children of Edmund Mathews as they played in the alley where they all lived, and she insulted their mother as well. When Mathews came home from work in the evening and was told what had occurred, he went to Newburgh's lodgings and asked why she had done this. In the course of a heated discussion he told her what all the neighbors said and maintained that he could prove that she was a whore and had had two bastards.[28]

Insults between neighbors reflect the widow's traditional role as a bawd in prostitution. Israel Hopper described Jane Freind as a poor woman addicted to swearing, cursing, blasphemy, and drink who quarreled frequently and was fond of provoking others. The constables had arrested her several times for cursing and swearing, and within the last four months she had been found guilty before Justice Ellis of swearing forty oaths in a row—clearly a shocking woman. But Freind added sex to her repertoire. She kept company with common soldiers; she made trouble between married couples in her attempts to recruit customers; and she was arrested as a bawd. She quarreled with Hopper as with many others, called him the son of a whore, and cursed him. Provoked, he called her old bawd, old bitch, old whore, and said that she had laid clean sheets on the bed so that her maid Kate could be debauched. Freind was clearly a bawd who had no claim to respectability. But Ann Theed still had pretensions in that direction. She said that her servant and companion Anne Nary, who was a loose woman, was married to John Clarke, the brother of Bruce Annam Lered. Lered denied this. So Theed called her an insolent slut, insulted her mother, threatened to slap her face, and told her to get out of her house. Lered responded that Theed was a bawd and a procurer.[29]

While sexual in their explicit content, many of the insults against widows, as with those against married women, arose out of disputes over debt or other kinds of economic conflict. James Dell had served Elizabeth Bridges as her journeyman in the draper's trade. But when he set up his own shop near her house, and probably drew away the customers he had found in hers, Bridges became enraged and threatened to make him fly Holborn, where both shops were. She said she would ruin him and had him arrested for debt. Dell was bailed by his friend Edward Mager. Both men denounced Bridges to her servant, Peter. Dell told Peter that Bridges was a whore and a bitch for doing this. Mager added that if she gave him half a crown, he would prove her a whore. Similarly, Rebecca Cooper and Eleanor Danger, who kept chandler's shops or general stores next to each other in Stepney and had a long history of mutual abuse, brought their quarrel, at some expense, both to the consistory and to quarter sessions.[30]

Some of the same kinds of charges that were made against married women and widows were also leveled against single women. Some of these spinsters were women of legal age who were able to bring suit themselves. But some were minors. In these cases, there occasionally was an out-of-the-ordinary level of concern in a girl's family or friends that she not be compromised by a situation that could do permanent damage to the rest of her life. But the usual charges of misbehavior with a man or of having had a bastard were made against both younger and older women. In some cases a woman became identified with a particular man. Sarah Clark said that Maria Hutchins was Thomas Marshall's whore, and Elizabeth Edwards was told that William Walker had lain with her on the steps of the vault (or toilet). In other cases a married woman became concerned for her husband's safety. Jane Burges complained that her husband had thrown

Rebecca Lawrence on the chairs in her father's house and kissed and hugged her, and that this had become known in their neighborhood.[31]

An unmarried woman had to defend herself against the charge of having had a bastard or trying to hide that fact. Two different women told Jane Gladman that they believed she had gone down into the country to give birth privately to a bastard. A girl from Stepney was said to have gone to London for six weeks so that she could lie in. More elaborately, Joseph Leeds described "Miss Lucy Spencer" as not being "that modest woman she appeared to be, that she was a lady or girl of bad reputation or character, and that she had been kept by Mr. Gore of the Temple and had had a child by him." Spencer was still young enough that her mother had to act for her. Anna Walter, on the other hand, was clearly an older single woman whose body had been carefully observed by her curious landlady. The landlady told another woman that Walter "has had as many children as you or I; I have had six. . . . I can see it by her breasts, nay by her very nipples." Very occasionally the charge went further and a woman was accused of being a prostitute. But the charge occurred less frequently than with wives or widows, even though the majority of streetwalking prostitutes were probably single women. Such women, of course, would not have been able to afford the costs of a consistory case. They might also not have cared if they were called what in fact they were. But it is interesting that the neighbors' fantasies about unmarried women did not much run to imagining that they might be prostitutes. It was perhaps the case (as Frances Place said) that the difference between those young women who might have offended once against premarital chastity and those who were regular whores was apparent to the neighborhood.[32]

Many unmarried women were employed as domestic servants, and the oversight of their sexual behavior that good masters or mistresses believed to be their duty could be the basis of a dispute like the one between Mary Mann, a minor, and Hannah Gould. Gould was herself unmarried and for seven years had been an upper servant to Mr. German and his daughter. German was a mental invalid cared for by a manservant, Joseph Barrow. Mary Mann was the new maidservant of two months' standing. Miss German observed familiarities between Mann and Barrow and told Gould to tell Mann not to let it happen again. But Miss German found it continued: Barrow spent New Year's Eve and the next night as well in Mann's bedchamber. Miss German now reproved Barrow and asked if he intended to marry Mann. He said he had not married her and did not intend to. Miss German now told Mann that she must tell her uncle and guardian, William Gardener, that she could no longer stay in the household. Mann

begged pardon and asked to be allowed to stay because she would otherwise be ruined. The girl was frightened and on Sunday (her day off) went
to her uncle and said Miss German had falsely vilified her character. Her
sister, Lucretia Mann, came the next morning and spoke to Hannah
Gould. Gould told her that because of what had happened between her
sister and Barrow, and that since Barrow did not intend to marry her, she
could only conclude "that he designed her for his mistress or his whore."
Lucretia Mann replied that she saw that her sister was guilty. She came
the next day again and spoke to Miss German and thanked her for taking
care of her sister. German promised to try the girl as a servant for a few
days longer. But the girl's uncle Gardener had decided on a different
course. He came to the house, raised a riot, and called German and Gould
whores. Early in February he arranged to sue Gould for defamation. He
was evidently not confident enough to sue Miss German.[33]

A dispute could arise because there was no single agreed standard of
sexual speech or conduct among London women. This becomes apparent
in the case of two families, the Battersbys and the Thurmans, when they
fought each other over the sexual behavior of their dependent children.
Jane and John Thurman had a son, Thomas, who was apprenticed to his
father, a tailor. Christopher and Mary Battersby had a daughter, Margaret
Davis, by Mary's previous marriage. Battersby was a butcher with a house
in Brewer's Street and a shop in John Street. Mary Battersby was a market
woman, and proud of it. She said "that she being a market woman had
a liberty to abuse"—that is, to use billingsgate, the language that took its
name from the market. Two years before she had been committed to
prison for a riot, and she was presently indicted to be tried at quarter
sessions for being a scold and a disturber of the peace. Jane Thurman's
mother hired Battersby's daughter, Margaret, as a servant, while the girl
apparently continued to live at home. The Thurmans' son, Thomas,
started to court Margaret and neglected his father's business to do so.
Thomas, according to Margaret, put his hands up her coats and tore her
shift, at which she declared that she had never been served so before but
once by someone who courted her. She clearly thought of herself as a
popular girl. Thomas's mother, on the other hand, said that Margaret had
allowed her son to do this. The Thurmans felt that since the two young
people were both only eighteen, it would ruin them to start courting. They
asked the Battersbys to forbid Thomas to visit their daughter and told
him the same, but to no avail. At first Christopher Battersby seemed to
agree with the Thurmans. But the next day the two families fought all
day with each other.

In the morning Margaret met two of the younger Thurman children at the water cock and threatened to beat them. She told them that their mother visited a Jew's shop and went down on her knees to beg for old clothes. At this point Mrs. Thurman called to her children from her door. Margaret spat at her and kept scornfully repeating: "Pogh a tailor, a tailor, good Lord, who would be troubled with a tailor," implying that she had no interest in Thomas Thurman. In the afternoon Thomas went to drink with Margaret and her parents at Jacob's Well, the alehouse next to his parents' house, but his father brought him home. Margaret's mother now knocked at the Thurman door and, when the couple answered, called him a white-livered dog and her a pocky pitch. Jane Battersby's neighbors at this point caught hold of her and took her home. Mary Battersby in the alehouse had also called Jane Thurman a Brumingham bitch, a brimstone bitch, and a Holborn bitch, and had told her to go to the Jews. Jane Thurman in her turn, according to one neighbor, later went to Margaret's door and called her a saucy, impudent jade, a draggle-tailed slut, and an impudent whore. But Jane Thurman denied that she had said these things. She was determined nonetheless to protect her son's future by preventing an imprudent marriage. Mary Battersby also wished to protect her daughter's honor, but she could only do so with a market woman's verbal skills. But those skills, to a woman like Jane Thurman, only made her a scold and a disturber of the peace. The poor women of London did not agree about what was acceptable, respectable speech in a woman.[34]

Some other cases arose when a master or a mistress felt that a former or present maidservant had been provocative; they retaliated by calling her a whore; and she sued them. Or a girl could get into an argument with an older woman, as Rebecca Hutchins did when she told Martha Long that the widowed woman had cuckolded her husband, only to receive the reply that Rebecca herself was a whore. A girl could tease a man, as Ann Cowling jeered at Henry Hall, "My Lord, how does your Hinny do?" and be told that she was an impudent whore. But what is missing from the cases brought by unmarried women are disputes over debt. They clearly did not borrow money and had none to lend. The closest thing to an economic dispute arose between Ann Serjeant and a Jewish couple, Ann and Christian Levi, who kept a shop. Serjeant pursued the couple over two years and several suits. She charged that Ann Levi had called her a whore. It was not far from the truth, since Serjeant had actually borne two bastards during the two years that the suits took. The Levis protested that Serjeant had begun the abuse by calling Christian Levi a Jewish rogue or dog. She had tried to pull Ann Levi out of her shop while saying to her, you impudent jade, you whore, come out. She then continued by telling her that "you are worse than all the jades and whores in the town, you gave nine shillings to a bailiff to lie with you, you whore." Serjeant eventually signed a certificate with the Levis quitting them of all quarrels. But that did not stop her from trying to bring still one last suit.[35]

The wife, the widow, and the spinster each had her separate place in the sexual economy according to her relationship to marriage. But it was recognized that any of the three could have a lover or bear a bastard. Each woman's misbehavior would of course have different consequences. The wife's was taken most seriously probably because her behavior was the most likely to affect the honor of males and possibly because she was in fact the woman with the greatest opportunities for irregular sexual relations—she could hide her bastards in her marriage. The widow did not have that protection, but, on the other hand, she was likely to have some degree of financial independence, and consequently a bastard was for her not so great a woe as it was to a single woman. She was also likely to be older and perhaps less concerned with sex. A single woman who became pregnant had to go away to have her child and had to find a way to hide its existence. But even if she did not become pregnant, a sexual indiscretion could ruin her for life and lose her any chance of marrying. The sexual fantasy of neighbors who gossiped about each other whether they had firm evidence or not seems to have operated within these bounds, with the wife the first object of sexual fascination and next the widow, and only then the unmarried girl. The woman who threw the entire system into confusion was the one who could not be classified by her marital status. Elizabeth Hampson, passing as a widow, sued Oliver St. John for calling her whore. But St. John pointed out that Elizabeth's maiden name was Plint and that she had married a man named Prigmore who was still alive: she could not be a widow: her suit was irregular. Susanna Conyers had a similar reaction to Jane Richardson, whom she had accused of keeping company with John Curry and having three of his bastards. Curry had called Conyers a brimstone whore and brimstone bitch, and it was he who promoted the suit against her. But Conyers had a question for Richardson. Was she a maid, a wife, or a widow, and hadn't she sometimes gone as one and then the other, and hadn't she used several different names? It was clear that Richardson was a woman without standing; although she had had a sexual life—which her bastards proved—she was without a clear relationship to marriage. She was neither a maid, a wife, nor a widow.[36] And a woman who was not one of these three was a whore, though she might not literally walk the streets in search of men.

Against this standard of marital sexual propriety, the chapters that follow consider three kinds of sexual deviance. First there are the small minority of women—mostly young and unmarried, but with some widows and wives—who were prostitutes. Then there are the women who became pregnant outside of marriage either as a result of a failed courtship or of sexual libertinage but sometimes as a prelude to an irregular long-term union. The prostitutes and the bastard-bearers were all poor women. But the adulteress (with whom the book ends) was found at all levels of society. From the discussion of these three deviant roles it will become apparent that the prostitute and the good wife and mother in the second half of the century began to replace for the middle and landed classes the older categories of wife, widow, and maid that were so apparent in the defamation cases from the early eighteenth century. Whoredom ceased to be a category into which any woman might fall who had sex outside of marriage. The prostitute instead was a woman who from the peculiarities of her life entered a state that was impossible for most women. And the woman who left her husband for another man very often did so to satisfy the highest standards of romantic attachment. Adultery ceased to be tied to cuckoldry and became a domestic tragedy. This was true at any rate for women from the prosperous classes. The sexual lives of poor women were less affected by ideas of romance and more subject to the traditional effects of shame and violence. But women of all classes were obliged to deal with men who imposed on them the less happy aspects of modern male heterosexuality. Most women continued to define their sexual identities in terms of their relationship to men, since for most of the century there was no female sapphist role from which to distance themselves, and when one did appear after 1770, it had less effect on women than the male sodomite role had on all men from the beginning of the century. Women, therefore, did not in the eighteenth century have heterosexual identities.

MALE HONOR: ADULTERY, SODOMY, AND MASTURBATION

In the early eighteenth century a man's sexual reputation could still be damaged by the charge that he was a whoremonger. Some men therefore brought defamation suits in the consistory court to protect their reputations against charges that they had been caught in adultery, or seduced the maids, or gone to whores. First there was the charge of adultery. In some cases a man defended himself against the woman who claimed that he had debauched her. Elizabeth Tenant told Richard Wastell that he had lain with her before she married her husband, but he denied it. When Jane Dowse declared to Mary Hieron, "I am Charles Hieron's whore and will be Charles Hieron's whore, and by God, I will see him by night or by day," Charles came to court and successfully defended himself. In other cases an individual claimed to know of a man's adultery. James Neale told William Bawcock, "you lay one night between your wife and one Hester Ruell in bed, and you did fuck the said Hester Ruell, and I will prove it." (Ruell also sued Neale.) Judith Rudge said that three different people had caught John Negus in his adultery: his wife and another woman who then told Negus's mother who went upstairs and saw the couple together in bed. Thomas Eardiwick was anxious that his reputation not be destroyed in a conflict between two women. He was a thirty-year-old bachelor who had lodged for ten years in the garret of a house occupied by Mary Summers, who was married with children. When another married woman, Jane Bentley, beat Summers's child, Summers asked her why she had done so and told her to come out and fight with her and not with the child. Blows were exchanged and charges of being a whore flung back and forth. The young man became handy ammunition. Bentley declared that Summers "was Thomas's whore and she could prove her to be Thomas's whore in the garret." Thomas brought Bentley to court, where she was found guilty. But he had probably sued her at his landlady's instigation, as much to save her honor as his own. If the gossip had gone unchecked, it could have become impossible for him to continue to live in the garret that had been his home for ten years.[37]

Some men defended themselves against the charge that they had seduced the household servants. The charge was sometimes untrue. Elisa Lewis called Abraham Barbour a rogue and told him to "go to that whore your maid . . . and play the rogue with her as you used to do," which Barbour protested was as good as calling him a whoremonger. He replied that Lewis was herself a common whore. When she brought a countersuit for his insult, he asked if he had not been provoked by what she had said. Barbour was clearly a man of probity. But Thomas Langley was guilty of seducing his maid. Isaac Wells, who was a mild, industrious man and a ringmaker, told Langley that "you knocked . . . your maid Hannah, and that the wench was heavy asleep and knew not of it till the next morning." Langley was an alehouse keeper who was known to be loose. His swearing and profaneness had shocked his neighbors, who rebuked him for his language and threatened him with the law. Wells, in his capacity as a parish official, had tried to admonish Langley and, when this proved fruitless, had applied to a justice of the peace, who had fined Langley twenty pounds for swearing. Langley then threatened to put Wells to greater legal charges than these and brought the defamation suit. But Wells said that the story about Langley's maid was the public talk of the neighborhood and that the maid herself had started it five or six years before. Langley had usually taken the story in good part. He subsequently formed a regular relationship with this woman, Hannah Zoan, but apparently the first time he had her she had been asleep after a hard day's scouring.[38]

In a third case, the gossip about a young man and the maid in his master's house seems to have been circulated by his master and mistress. But they then encouraged the young man, John Sheeres (whose father acted for him, since he was a minor), to bring suit against John Smallwood, whose original comment they themselves had spread. Smallwood was supposed to have said that he had seen Sheeres "fuck his master's maid in the garden adjoining to his master's powder house, then saw her walk round with her hands in his breeches." Smallwood admitted that he had called Sheeres into his shop and advised him to beware of the maid, who was an "ill woman." He had asked him why he allowed her to put her hands in his breeches. But he claimed that he had said all this to Sheeres privately. It was the young man's employers who then made it all public in the neighborhood because the boy's mistress disliked a reflection on her conduct that Smallwood's mother had made.[39]

From these two last cases of Langley and Sheeres, it is apparent that gossip about a man's actual sexual misbehavior could circulate in a neighborhood for some time until some conflict made the gossip a convenient weapon against a neighbor. It was also very common in the defamation suits for quarrels about other matters to lead to sexually charged language. The language of sexual accusation was one of the most disapprobrious that could be used. This can be seen in the quarrel between John Hughes and Jane Hyland. Hughes was a sober man who had been married for twenty years, a housekeeper who had held all the offices in his parish of Clerkenwell, and a man with a good trade. Jane Hyland was a married woman with children. Her husband was a sailor and away at sea. She lived with her mother, who took pregnant women into her own house and cared for them at their lyings-in. Hyland had a reputation for being very quarrelsome. In the midafternoon on an early September day, a quarrel broke out in the street between Hyland and Joseph and Judith Field. Judith threw a drink in Hyland's face, and Joseph took hold of her and struck her breast. The three together made such a noise that a woman in the neighborhood asked John Hughes if he could not make them be quiet or hold their tongues. Hughes replied that the Devil could not do that.

At this Hyland called him an informing pimp and told him "to kiss my britch, you shall not make me hold my tongue."

Hughes now told her to "get you home and mind your house and look after your children." Hyland retorted that he was a rogue (an equivalent to whoremaster); Hughes replied that then she must be a whore. So Hyland, probably alluding to Hughes's role as a parish officer who reported the misbehavior of his neighbors to the justices, told him that he was "an informing rogue and pimp" and added that he "lay with Frances Browne and had a bastard by her." Hughes replied that she was a saucy whore for saying so. For this last exchange they sued each other. Hyland added that when her mother asked Judith Field why she had abused her daughter, Hughes had come up and told her mother that she should not speak so much on her daughter's behalf since she was a whore, a common whore, and he would prove her one. It was no more probable, however, that Hyland was a whore than that the respectable Hughes had fathered a bastard. It is equally unlikely that when Hughes called Hyland a whore, he meant to say that she was a streetwalking prostitute. A whore in this context would have been a married woman who was adulterous—as a woman whose husband was at sea and whose mother delivered babies would have had ample opportunity to be. Similarly, Hyland slandered Hughes not as a man who went to prostitutes but as one who had fathered a child out of wedlock. Whoredom and roguery were therefore the opposites of faithful marriage.[40]

It was to protect himself against the consequences of a similar charge that John Purslow of Bishopsgate sued his mother-in-law for saying to him that he had had two bastards. Purslow was a buttonmaker whose wife Dorothea sued him for divorce. She said that Purslow had beaten her badly when she was pregnant. He had thrown her to the ground, beaten her in the belly, and threatened to murder her and rip her open as a butcher does a sheep. When she fled to her mother, who kept a shop, he followed and continued to beat her. Their child was born bruised and vomited blood shortly after birth. Purslow said that his wife had provoked him by calling him a dog and a rogue (the male equivalent of bitch and whore). She had said that she wished he were dead or bankrupt. She had also said that she had never loved him and that she loved another. To marry such a fellow as her husband was to cast pearls before swine. She taunted him with being a cuckold and called him a bandy-legged, tallow-faced fellow. She spat in his face and pulled off his periwig, scratched and kicked him, and threatened to cry murder when he tried to have sex. Because she wanted to abort their child, she ate coffee berries, and when she was told that they might abort the child, she said that she would hang herself if she were pregnant by him. She told her maid that "if she lay with any man, she could put her in a way to hinder conception," and declared that she would destroy her husband's child in her womb with savin or with tamarisk. She then sent her maid to the Stocks Market for threepenny worth of savin and had it boiled and drank it three mornings in a row, but to no avail since the child was born.

Purslow said that his mother-in-law, Dorothy Wallis, whom he was suing for defamation, had encouraged his wife to leave him and that Wallis had told his wife that she would never receive her again if she saw Purslow anymore. Wallis did in fact undertake to organize her daughter's divorce. She tried to get evidence of Purslow's adultery and urged a surgeon to swear that he had cured Purslow of venereal disease. And she told Purslow himself that he had had two bastards. To top it all off, mother and daughter tried to use the scandal to turn Purslow's creditors against him. The reputation of sexual misbehavior might give a man some swagger, but it was bad for his business with the respectable, and so Purslow sued for defamation.[41]

Some men who were defamed had in fact gone to whores. Francis Gotabed was seen by two different men as he lay in a field on top of a woman whose skirts were up. They made the story so widespread in the neighborhood that one wonders why he sued them. One of Gotabed's women was a married woman whom he paid three times a week and tried to persuade to leave the neighborhood. The two men whom Gotabed sued (one wonders if his name was a standing temptation to mockery) show that some men loved to gossip as much as women did. Jacob Chidwick was such a male gossip who had to explain why he had been obliged to mention that William Collins had picked up a whore in the Poultry and lain with her in an alley next to St. Christopher's Church. It had come up in the course of explaining to Sir Edward Clark the slanderous remarks that Mr. Buttler had complained Chidwick had made of him also. A final case from the first decade of the century shows, however, that whoremaster was an elastic term for sexual misbehavior, since Ann Baxter could say of Thomas Penne that he was a "whoremaster and a buggerer and that if he had not found favor, he would have been hanged for committing with some male child the crime commonly called buggery." It was a comment that also shows that the avoidance of an exclusive homosexuality was in the early eighteenth century not yet the test of male reputation that the sodomy blackmail cases show it becoming after 1730.[42]

All of the defamation suits that men brought in the consistory were

for sexual slander. By the middle of the century they ceased to bring
such suits. Had they stopped caring about their sexual reputations? Probably not, but the lone case of Thomas Penne, who was defamed as a
buggerer in 1708 had by midcentury become the many men who
charged in the secular courts that they had been blackmailed for sodomy
or had been compromised by a sodomite's mistaken advances. In such a
world, the reputation of being a whoremonger had become perhaps a
guarantee of sexual honor. Nonetheless, later in the century the occasional
man sued when the charges of his sexual misconduct with a woman were
spectacular enough that they were likely to injure his business. But a man
like Richard Shepley in 1776 did not use the consistory; instead he sued
in King's Bench. Shepley was a miller who traded at the Corn Market
in Mark Lane. In April of that year a man appeared in front of the Corn
Market and sold a sixpenny ballad that mocked Shepley for having had
an affair with a laundress. Thomas Sabine, the printer, admitted his role
in printing the ballad but would not say who the author was. Sabine had
arranged for handbills announcing the ballad to be circulated in advance of publication. These had perhaps been intended to warn Shepley
and to persuade him to buy off the actual publication. Certainly, Sabine
said that Shepley once he had seen the handbills should have asked him
to stop publication of the ballad. When Shepley asked Sabine why he
chose to sell the ballad on the Corn Market where he got his bread, Sabine
forthrightly replied that "he did it because he thought it would sell best
there."

The song, with five illustrations, came in ten stanzas.

The Miller and the Laundress
A New Song Founded on Facts.

I
Near Wandsworth town, this famed Miller does dwell
If his name is left out, it may do as well;
His wife brought him a fortune—and he's a tall man,
But what his wife longed for—he often gave Nan.
  Derry down &c.

II
It's Nancy the widow that humors his mind,
And to her a hundred times he has been kind;
There's six stones he works with, his business to do,
But Nan instead of his wife gets t'other two.

III

His wife's has had plenty of servants; but maids
   they're not long
For the miller plays well at the game of ding dong;
No miller's more amorous, no laundress more sly,
And they often in grinding their faculties try.

Shepley pointed out that he was the only miller near Wandsworth who answered the description, since he was a tall man and had married a woman of fortune. The next three verses mentioned that the miller had gone on business to France, as Shepley had. The ballad added that in his absence his wife had treated the laundress severely, and that on his return, Shipley took his wife's part and dismissed Nan. But he set her up in lodgings at Marylebone, and three times a week he visited her after work:

She goes for a laundress, and stands at the tub,
Till Jack comes to play the tune of rub a dub dub.

X

After this he comes home to prevent having strife;
And talks and looks pleasant and sups with his wife.
And loving together they both go to bed,
Then his wife gets the spoon, with which Nan has been fed.[43]

Richard Shepley's case is amusing but exceptional. When one turns, however, to the cases in which adult men were blackmailed or libeled as sodomites, or to those in which adolescent boys complained of a man's sexual advances, it becomes apparent that male reputation after 1730 came to depend on the ability to prove at any stage of life that one was exclusively attracted to women. In such a world it did no harm at all to be known as a whoremonger. The fear of being exposed as a sodomite left men paralyzed. Three cases make the point. In the first case from 1778 George Hadley was approached by Robert Harold in the vicinity of St. James's Park. Hadley, who must have stared at Harold, said that he thought at first sight that he had recognized an old soldier with whom he had served in India. After this exchange of glances, Harold told Hadley that he "must have something" from him. The peremptory tone apparently made Hadley hostile, and he replied that he would give him nothing. But when Hadley tried to resume his walk, Harold went around behind him, took him by the collar, and said, "God d[am]n your blood, you shall not escape in this manner." He then let go of Hadley's collar and with his right hand seized Hadley's left hand and forced it down under his greatcoat. Under the coat Harold's penis was exposed, and he touched Hadley's hand to it. At that moment, with his hand on a strange man's penis, Hadley said "the idea of resistance entirely forsook me." A mere robbery he would have resisted, he added; but this left him without any ability to act. Harold now said to him, "god damn your blood, you shall not escape so. There; There, you want to make an attempt on me. I will have justice." Hadley now understood Harold's entire scheme and was desperate that no one else should observe what was occurring. "Be quiet," he said to Harold, "I see what it is you want, it is not justice, it is my money." At this Harold looked carefully around and replied, "it is so; come, make me a present—I am a very needy man." So Hadley drew Harold aside and gave him what money he had, choosing a spot where they would not be observed, "for I was more afraid of anybody than he seemed to be at that time." Harold, however, demanded five guineas more. And Hadley agreed to meet him later and to pay the sum to him. He said he believed that if he had had a hundred guineas in his pocket at that moment, he would have given them to Harold.

Hadley thought of going to a lawyer at this point, but instead he met Harold a second time and gave him the five guineas. As he did so he told Harold, "Sir, this is a wretched way of getting money, and I am a wretched fool for giving it to you, but as I have been a fool in the first instance, I cannot help it, and must pay for my folly." Hadley saw Harold a third time seven days later. But by them he had gathered up the courage to talk to an attorney and some friends. They advised him to have Harold arrested, which he did with the help of two constables. This story raises the question whether Hadley was in fact a sodomite. A detail in his description of his initial encounter with Harold suggests that he might have been. He testified that when he saw Harold, he had stared at him. To the court he claimed this was because he recognized an old soldier. But it is possible that his stare had been one of sexual interest and that Harold had recognized this. Harold was evidently prepared for such an eventuality in the place where he encountered Hadley: it may have been a pickup spot for sodomites. He had come wearing a greatcoat, and he had his genitals exposed beneath it. Hadley's only recourse was to publicly insist that he was not a sodomite, and that he was instead a man terrified of the consequence of the charge. "My fear," he said, "was of my character."[44]

In a second case John Greene, along with another man who sometimes called himself Brown, sometimes Clark, extorted money from Samuel Tyas some twenty times over a twelve-month period in 1793–94, by threatening to swear sodomy against him. Tyas sometimes gave them five shillings, sometimes half a guinea. On the first occasion that Greene accosted Tyas he said to him, "You give money, I know you give money." On another occasion Greene met Tyas as he came down Ludgate Hill between eleven and twelve at night. He accosted Tyas by name, said he was himself poor, and that he wanted money. Greene did not actually threaten to charge sodomy on this occasion, but Tyas knew his meaning. Greene followed Tyas to his lodging at Mr. Bohn's in Salisbury Square, where to be rid of him, Tyas gave him four shillings and shut the door. Greene on other occasions came to Tyas's lodgings and became insolent with the landlord when he would not let him in to see Tyas. Tyas eventually told his employer what was happening to him. As a result, when Greene next came to the shop where Tyas worked and asked for him by name, there was a plan in place to capture him. Tyas came forward, "in a tremor" he said, and told his employer Mr. Ansley, "this is the man." Greene then ran away, but they caught him and took him to the magistrate. Greene denied that he had threatened to denounce Tyas as a sodomite and said that he had just come to London, had no lodgings, and had slept the previous night in a night house in Holborn.[45]

This case raises a number of questions. How had Greene identified Tyas as a potential victim? Had he in fact heard from others that Tyas had paid them in the past? Or was his statement that he knew that Tyas gave money made on the basis of an effeminate manner that Greene could observe for himself? It would also be interesting to understand the reactions of Tyas's landlord and his employer. Bohn, the landlord, came to the magistrate's to give evidence for Tyas, and Ansley, Tyas's employer, arranged for Greene to be captured. Did either or both of these men know or believe that Tyas was a sodomite, and if they did, had they based their opinion on Tyas's apparent effeminacy or on something else? If these men believed Tyas to be a sodomite, why did they help him? Were they sodomites themselves? Or did they care more that a respectable man, who had the misfortune to be a sodomite but who was otherwise a quiet lodger and a good worker, should not be tormented in this way? Or was it that the sexual and gender conventions of the world of Bohn and Ansley were best maintained by ignoring the likely meaning of Tyas's effeminacy and treating him as though he were a man of their own sexual tastes? There is finally the issue to consider of Tyas's own reaction. For twelve months he had lived in terror of being denounced. Had this happened to him before, as Greene's statement, that he knew that Tyas paid, may have implied? And why did Tyas eventually decide to tell his landlord and his employer what was happening to him? Had he come to the end of his ability to pay Greene? Had Greene's behavior made the situation so apparent that Tyas had nothing more to lose by taking Bohn and Ansley into his confidence? None of these many questions are answerable on the basis of the source. And we cannot know either the effect of these public declarations on Tyas's subsequent life.

A playful or flirtatious comment made by an ostensibly heterosexual man to another man could be interpreted in the most offensive way. In our third case Sir John Buchanan Riddle and a male friend were on their way into the park to see the fireworks at quarter to ten in the evening on June 19. Riddle said that he was also following a woman (almost certainly a prostitute) whom he thought he knew. But just before entering the park, Riddle stopped to talk to some other prostitutes who were looking out a window. Riddle was clearly excited by the bustle and the women. At the entrance to the park, Thomas Davis, a twenty-two-year-old guardsman, stood on duty as the sentinel. In his expansive state of mind, Riddle turned to Davis and said (according to Riddle's friend), "soldier, I suppose you would have no objection to do something to these girls." But instead of joining in the banter, Davis interpreted Riddle's remark as a sexual advance and asked Riddle how dare he propose such a thing. Riddle was infuriated and boxed Davis down. Another man came to the soldier's aid. Davis now threatened Riddle with his musket and bayonet and demanded a present. Riddle said that Davis also claimed in front of what must have been a growing audience that he had asked the soldier if he "wished to know a girl, and if his p[rivate] p[arts] stood," and that he had opened the flap of his breeches and taken hold of his testicles.

Riddle now became very uneasy in case anyone he knew should pass by, see the altercation, and put the worst possible interpretation on it. He therefore gave Davis a few shillings. But when Davis demanded more, Riddle decided that they should all go to the guardhouse. There the version that the two gentlemen told was given credence over the soldier's. Davis was brought to trial, found guilty, and sentenced to death. Whatever Riddle said to the guardsman raises two possibilities. It may have been common for sodomites to make sexual approaches to soldiers in the park by opening with some speculation as to the young man's prowess with women. Riddle's question and his evident state of excitement may therefore have misled Davis as to what was occurring. Riddle's question does, however, open the possibility that it was not unusual for an older heterosexual male like Riddle to enjoy the sexual good looks of a younger man like Davis provided that he could hide this from himself by supposing that what he felt was the excitement of a mutual interest in women that he shared with the younger man. The blackmail cases therefore open to us not only the interactions of the sodomitical minority and the heterosexual majority but may also bring to light the covert sexual interactions between men in the majority who were supposed to be exclusively heterosexual.[46]

Adolescent boys had to be socialized into the fears that we have seen displayed in the three preceding cases. This socialization can be observed in two ways: in their reactions to adult men who tried to seduce them and in the attempts made to prevent them from masturbating. The majority of boys who were seduced by sodomites had just reached the age of puberty. In the eighteenth century, this would have been around fifteen years of age. At that age aristocratic boys were often taken away from school because puberty had begun. One mother referred to her fifteen-year-old son as being at "his dangerous time of life." Schoolmasters agreed; and William Gilpin, for instance, was inclined to refuse to educate such boys, after they had come to what he called "the age of right and wrong." Fifteen was also the age at which many boys started to run after whores. Because of these considerations, lawyers declared fourteen to be the age of sexual consent for boys; after this a boy's passive role in sodomy made him as guilty as his active partner.[47]

Boys came to sexual consciousness at various ages. And even a sixteen-year-old could still be remarkably innocent. When Richard Branson attempted to seduce James Fasset, he began with the usual offer of a drink and then tried to excite the boy with sexually charged conversation. He "asked me," Fasset said, "if I never got any girls, or if I never f——ed them." The boy replied no, that he "was not old enough and had no such thoughts." Branson then tried, without success, to put his hand into Fasset's breeches. So he kissed him—putting his tongue into his mouth and sucking his lips. This the boy allowed; but he kept a firm grip on the waistband of his breeches. Branson now turned from whores to masturbation, and asked Fasset if "I never frigged myself; to which I answered, No." But the boy did not really understand the question, since when Branson asked about frigging a second time, he said "I did not know what it meant." At this Branson offered "if I would go back, he would learn me." But Fasset would not. Excited, perhaps, by this innocence, by the boy's sober, quiet ways (his headmaster said he was the most orderly boy in his college), and by what Branson told the boy were his soft, warm hands, Branson then "asked me if I had my maidenhead"; and knowing by now the answer, he continued that "if I had, he should be very glad to take it from me, but supposed I saved it for a young woman." But the thought of violating innocence (and treating the boy like a girl) was too much to leave alone, and so Branson again asked "if he should ravish me? I answered no. He said, he would not against my will."[48]

Branson was found guilty of attempting sodomy, though matters never went further than this flirtation. The Methodist preacher Charles Bradbury, on the other hand, was acquitted of the charge of sodomizing fourteen-year-old James Hearne, even though he had probably used the boy's innocence and his own authority to seduce the boy and then to force him in court to recant his evidence. Hearne, a Roman Catholic who had only recently come from France in 1755, went with a fellow apprentice to hear the Methodist preacher at Glover's Hall in Beech Lane. After Bradbury got rid of the rest of his congregation about nine o'clock in the evening, he took the boy on his knee, kissed him, and put his hand into his torn breeches. He then got up, put out the candle, and "unbuttoned his breeches and bid me play with his y[ar]d." When the boy grew worried that his master would scold him for being late, the preacher reassured him that he would find him another place. With this encouragement, the boy eventually told his master that he did not like the trade. The preacher then found him a lodging, where he spent the night with the boy. He "first tried with his finger to enter my body, then he tried with his y[ar]d, and did enter as far as he could, and his s[ee]d came from him." This occurred four or five times. Bradbury began to pay the boy's expenses and eventually moved him into the house where he lodged himself. But after Bradbury tempted fate and preached a sermon against Sodom and Gomorrah, the boy began to have qualms of conscience. Mrs. Whittaker, a woman in the congregation, had already observed the minister kissing another boy a little too fondly. This boy, whose name was Billy Cook, together with Hearne became involved with the preacher. When Hearne collapsed after the sermon, he told everything to Mrs. Whittaker. She observed that the way Hearne had kissed a baby in her house was "the way Mr. Bradbury kisses Billy Cook." The minister made various attempts to get the boy to retract his statement: he accused him of theft, reminded him that his father had disowned him for changing his religion, got him to sign a recantation, and sent him for a month to France. But on his return, Hearne pressed charges, only to break down weeping at the trial, declaring that Bradbury was innocent, and that "he wished he had never been born, and was sorry he had charged a person who had been his best friend." (Best friend was what sons called fathers.) Bradbury was acquitted.

The court had some difficulty in believing in the boy's sexual innocence. He was asked whether he had done everything that Bradbury told him to do. He answered yes. He was asked whether he did not know that these things were wrong. He answered that as they came from a minister, he did not. So they asked him his age, and he replied that he had just turned fifteen. He also said that he would not have thought these matters a sin with anyone else. So the questioning turned to his religious background: his father was a papist, but he had not received much instruction in the principles of religion; he had heard prayers read and had been to confession and to Mass; but none of this had led him to realize that sodomy was a crime. Only Bradbury's sermon had brought him to that belief. He had never heard the papist priests talk of sodomy, nor had he read about it in any book. The tack of the questioning now changed. Why had he gone to bed with Bradbury? "Because I was afraid of him, and I had no other friend but him in the world to stand by me." Did they talk about the acts? They had. "He asked me whether I could bear it. . . . I did." Bradbury had also asked the boy whether he had done the same things with anyone else and had told him not to speak about it to anyone. But that a fifteen-year-old boy in England could be so innocent before hearing Bradbury's sermon was evidently difficult to believe. The boy, however, had lived in England only a year. He had, it is true, been good friends with his fellow apprentice. But when he was asked, "Did you never talk about mollies with each other?" he replied, "No." But it is a question that reveals a world in which adult men remembered how obsessively they had discussed that topic in their own youths.[49]

By the age of seventeen—when a boy, if he was going to masturbate, had begun to do so—a boy's sexual orientation was probably settled. He might still allow a man to treat him and to flirt with him, and perhaps even to have some degree of actual sexual contact; but if a man attempted to turn the situation into a relationship, the boy would turn eventually against him. On the other hand, it is likely that some boys were happy to be seduced since their desires basically lay in a sodomitical direction. There is some evidence that an effeminate adolescent who was identified as a future sodomite might be used by men who did not think themselves to be sodomites and that they were likely to brush aside any objections he made. These contacts between sodomites and late adolescents were usually made either in the streets at night or in a shared bed.

In the streets at night, Richard Spencer invited seventeen-year-old William Taylor to have a drink and to talk over some affairs of his master. After the first drink, Spencer asked Taylor how big his cock was. When Taylor did not reply, Spencer held out his little finger and asked if it was as big as that. He then pulled out his own cock, and told the boy to lie on his side. When Taylor would not, "he said he would f——k me that night." He then asked the boy what county he came from; and when he replied, Herefordshire, Spencer kissed him several times, and said that he would take the boy there "in a coach, and make you drunk as an owl and all the way you go." (Traveling by coach and, indeed, having sex in a carriage could be a highly charged sexual suggestion.) At this point in this aggressive courtship, when the second pint of drink was brought, the boy went out and fetched a constable. The constable called Spencer a "black-guard old rascal for making such an attempt on a boy" and turned him out of the tavern. But Taylor had clearly been deeply wounded. "I did not think," he said, "he had punishment enough, ran after him, and with assistance brought him back again, and gave the constable charge of him, and he was committed."[50]

In a second example, Henry Wolf met John Holloway when the boy was on an errand for his master and asked him directions. Wolf then took Holloway around the waist, tickled him, and offered him a drink. As they drank, Wolf put his hand under the table and into the boy's breeches, but he stopped when the maid noticed. He then took the boy into a by-alley, but they were interrupted by a man, and they ran away. He then offered the boy a pint of wine to keep silent, and bought him a nosegay and a penny custard. As they passed Bedlam, he pulled the boy in to see the mad folks; and then he took him into the necessary house (or toilet), pulled down both their breeches, and fellated the boy. He told the boy he hoped to see him often and came to his master's house several times. They arranged to meet on Sunday. But this time the boy brought three friends along. Wolf gave the other boys the slip in the Posthouse Fields and looked unsuccessfully for a place where no one else would disturb Halloway and himself. But the three boys returned. Wolf suddenly became suspicious and dashed away with the four boys in pursuit. A young man asked what was the matter, and the boys replied that "there was a sodomite." The young man caught Wolf; Holloway went for the constable; and Wolf was taken to the justice.[51]

The third boy, John Meeson, was altogether more willing than the boys in the other two examples. John Dicks met him as he stood in the church-yard watching them lay the first stone for St. Martin's Church. Dicks repeatedly invited Meeson to have a drink. The boy said that after he became fuddled in the first alehouse that they had gone to, Dicks kissed him, put his hand into his breeches, and put the boy's hand into his own breeches. Then they went to a cellar in the Strand. But the boy had some goods to deliver in Fleet Street and told Dicks that he would return if he waited for him. When he did return, they went to two other alehouses looking for a more private place. Dicks settled for an apartment at the Golden Ball near Fetter Lane. The boy by then had drunk so much that he vomited. He later said that he knew that at this point when he lay down to sleep, Dicks had unbuttoned his breeches, turned him on his face, and tried to enter his body. But (no doubt to save his honor) he declared that whether Dicks had entered him or not, "I was not sensible enough to know." The three people on the other side of the thin partition—a man, a woman, and the alehouse boy—had no doubt. They heard Dicks kiss the boy and call him his dear, his jewel, and his precious little rogue. And they saw him "withdraw his yard from the boy's fundament" after making the usual humping movements. But when Dicks was about to enter the boy a second time, the woman cried out that she could "look no longer—I am ready to swoon—He'll ruin the boy"; and so they rushed in and seized Dicks as he lay on the boy's backside. The boy in our first example had become offended at lewd talk and a few kisses. The second boy was willing to be shown a good time and to be fellated—once. But this third boy had liked the initial flirtation enough to return for more; and once he was drunk enough, he had been willing to be sodomized. It would be interesting to know whether he became an adult sodomite.[52]

If the straight path of eighteenth-century heterosexuality was bounded on one side by the avoidance of sodomy, the avoidance of masturbation lay on the other side. After James Boswell had relieved himself one night by "low lascivious" means, he cautioned himself: "Have a care. Swear with drawn sword never *pleasure* but with a woman's aid." This taboo against masturbation and its supposed debilitating physical and mental consequences became of major concern in the early eighteenth century with the anonymous publication of *Onania; or the Heinous Sin of Self Pollution.* By no accident this same generation saw the emergence of the role of the effeminate sodomite. The taboos against sodomy and masturbation were mutually reinforcing. Modern heterosexuality required that men receive sexual pleasure only from women and never from their male selves or from other males. In the letters supposedly written by patients that were printed in the 1723 edition of *Onania* (which was advertised as the eighth edition), men confessed that they had started masturbation some time between eleven and seventeen and most often at fourteen or fifteen, the usual age of puberty. A few men had learned to masturbate on their own. But most had started in a circle of friends, and it probably was the homosexual implications of this sociability that made the practice suspect. One young man wrote that "about five years ago when I went to school, I and three or four more, on a holiday went bird-catching; and when we sat down, one of our companions who was about twenty years of age, the rest of us not being above fifteen, asked us, whether we ever saw the seed of man? We replied we never did. He told us if we would reach a leaf of cabbage, he would show us, which he did by self-pollution; and which, though it stirred my inclination, yet I attempted it not till a year after." Another young man saw it done in a circle of his fellow apprentices who told him that it would give him "unspeakable pleasure" and make his "fleshy robust body" become "fine and shapely." An elder brother could teach it to a younger, or one bedfellow to another; a servant could instruct his young master; or a man "old enough to have been my father, he was at least fifty years of age" could show the way to a boy of seventeen. A similar supposed collection of letters from boys published at the end of the century yields similar results: boys of sixteen to twenty-three saying that they had begun to masturbate between eight and fifteen and that they had usually been shown the way by someone else.[53]

It was therefore exceptional for a physician like John Hunter to write that he doubted that impotence could be the result of masturbation since impotence was relatively rare and masturbation was widespread. Hunter added that many men had made themselves miserable with this idea and that it was clear to him that the books on masturbation had done more harm than good. He even thought that masturbation was less harmful physically than sex with a woman, because a man's emotions were less engaged; and by the same token sex with a prostitute was only "a constitutional act" and of less physical consequence than relations with a woman with whom a man was in love. But Hunter's observation that so widespread a practice as masturbation ought to have more widespread consequences if it were really so dangerous did not occur to many other physicians or schoolmasters. A practical, skeptical doctor like William Buchan had no doubt that sexual "debility" was the result of masturbation. And Vicesimus Knox warned schoolmasters that it was their duty to tell their pupils of its "consequences in colors as frightful as the imagination can conceive." For "vice will occasion pain, distempers, imbecility, and premature old age. . . . Irregular and intemperate passions, indulged at a boyish age, will blast all the blossoms of the vernal season of life, and cut off all hope of future eminence."[54]

Nonetheless there seems to have been a general agreement that many boys (and perhaps most of them) masturbated. This taboo therefore did not really operate like the other. No one any longer supposed that most boys had sodomitical desires. But in some implicit sense, it must have been realized that boys had to be trained not to have such desires. The danger of adolescent masturbation (since it was usually a social experience and not a solitary one) was that it might lead boys to find sexual relations with other males acceptable. But no one could say this. It was necessary instead to maintain the myth that most males did not ordinarily experience any kind of sodomitical desire. The taboo therefore had to be stated in terms that stressed the physical and psychological dangers from masturbation for a boy's adult life. In this way an exclusive adult heterosexuality would eventually be achieved in which neither his own penis, nor the penis of another boy, but only a woman's body became the source of all sexual excitement in an adult man.

Masturbation in women was also discussed, but far less. Bienville claimed that its result in women was nymphomania; or in other words, a practice that in men was supposed to cause impotence and the loss of the drive to achieve, in women led to the desire for many men in violation of their standard of gender behavior. The fact that Bienville's book was published in 1771 was probably significant since it was in the 1770s that the modern sapphist role first appeared. This role in women paralleled the role of the effeminate sodomite in men that had appeared two generations earlier in the century. The emergence of the sodomite role had been accompanied by the appearance of the *Onania* against male masturbation. So Bienville's *Nymphomania* against female masturbation accompanied the emergence of the sapphist role. But it is likely enough that these were real differences in the incidence of male and female masturbation. Studies of twentieth-century Americans from the 1940s onward have found that while over 90 percent of males masturbated in adolescence, most women did not, and that even after marriage, many women still did not ever masturbate. From this John Gagnon and William Simon have suggested that Western males come first to the consciousness of heterosexual desire in the realm of their private fantasies and the circle of their male acquaintances and only later achieve heterosocial interaction with women; whereas with women, heterosociality precedes heterosexuality. It is a pattern of male exclusive heterosexuality that in all probability first appeared in the early eighteenth century and that this chapter and the remainder of this book attempts to document.[55]

PART TWO

Prostitution

CHAPTER THREE

Male Libertinism

The need to prove that a man was exclusively interested in women became the foundation of adult male identity in the early eighteenth century. But finding a willing sexual partner could be difficult. Relations with an unmarried woman were either not supposed to occur at all or to be a prelude to marriage, and a man who was callous enough to make a woman pregnant and not to marry her might still be forced by the magistrate to support her child. An affair with a married woman might be less complicated since she was already sexually active with her husband and could hide her bastards in her marriage. But the neighbors had sharp eyes, and the price of discovery could be high: disgrace and abandonment or divorce for the woman, and criminal damages from her lover. The most practical way therefore for a man to prove his heterosexuality was to go to a prostitute. Prostitutes could be found easily enough either walking the streets or in the bawdy houses. There were probably never more than three thousand of them at any one time, composed of a core who had made their living exclusively in this way for three or more years, with a smaller group of younger women who occasionally picked up a man. These women had put themselves beyond the pale and probably had great difficulty marrying when they left this life in their later twenties, but they were often enough conventional in other ways, refusing to perform certain sexual acts and retaining traditional religious belief. It is likely that most men who lived in London at some point went to a prostitute. The high rate of venereal infection, especially among groups like sailors, suggests this. Men who went to prostitutes offended against all the new ideals of romantic love and domestic affection, and women who walked the street destroyed the sentimental idealization of women. But the fear that men would become sodomites

if the outlet of prostitution were taken away always limited any attempt
to control it.[1]

For contemporaries the most startling aspect of this new heterosexually
inspired prostitution was the public solicitation in the street. This was
facilitated by the growth of London's population and the integration of
its neighborhoods into a single entity that stretched from Westminster
to Whitechapel. By 1690 London had a population of five hundred thousand. It has been suggested that in the nineteenth century, cities of such
a size were very likely to produce populations of streetwalking prostitutes.
In London, this had occurred by the 1690s. Thomas Pilkington, the lord
mayor in 1689, described this nightwalking as a fairly recent development
among men and women. It was probably a result of the degree of anonymity that could be achieved in a population of that size, since the scale of
the city now made it possible for individuals to live conventional lives in
one part of town but to visit a sexual subculture that was likely to be more
centrally located than their own neighborhoods. But nightwalking must
also have been facilitated by the introduction in the 1680s and 1690s of
oil-burning streetlamps maintained at public expense.[2]

The physical integration of the city meant that bawdy houses spread
westward into the area around Covent Garden from their traditional locations in Southwark and the eastern and northern suburbs outside the City
walls, where the majority of the poor lived. The new suburbs to the west
were as likely to have the rich living in them as the poor. The development
of this West End meant that there was now one continuous city of a half
a million that stretched from Westminster to Whitechapel. Through the
middle of this new city ran a great thoroughfare composed of a series of
interlocking streets. From the Royal Exchange in Cornhill in the heart
of the old City, it moved to Cheapside, around through St. Paul's Churchyard, down Ludgate Hill to Fleet Street and the end of the City's jurisdiction. It continued into Westminster as Fleet Street joined the Strand,
moving through Charing Cross and down Whitehall into St. James's Park.
It is still London's principal ceremonious route. From the 1690s on,
throughout the eighteenth century, and down into the early twentieth
century, it became the principal thoroughfare for London's prostitutes,
who walked it night and day, soliciting passing men to accompany them
into one of the nearby bawdy houses for a drink, or to go with them to
their lodgings, or simply to make do with a dark place in the street, a
courtyard, or the park.

Throughout the eighteenth century the respectable tried to stop this
public plying in the streets, inspired at first by religion, and then by hu-

manitarian zeal, and at the end, by a combination of both. Between 1695
and 1725, and again in the early 1760s, the late 1770s, and in the 1790s,
there were concentrated arrests of prostitutes that for a while cleared some
part of the great thoroughfare. But the women soon came back. There
were also drives against the bawdy houses, which were usually taverns with
rooms upstairs to which women brought men by agreement with the
keeper of the house. In time, the houses north of the City wall seem to
have disappeared. But this may have happened simply because they could
not be reached so easily from the great thoroughfare as the houses around
Covent Garden and in Westminster west of the abbey. In addition, new
areas for houses appeared in the Strand itself and along Hedge Lane as
it moved from Charing Cross into Soho. Furthermore, the houses in
Whitechapel in the East End, in Stepney and Wapping along the river,
and in Southwark across the river continued to exist.

These drives, however, are very useful to the historian since they produced what survives in the way of a systematic documentation for London's prostitution. These sources are peculiarly laborious to use since London north of the Thames was under the jurisdiction of three separate local
governments: the City, Westminster, and Middlesex. (Southwark on the
south bank was a further complication, which I have ignored except for
what turns up in the City records.) The arrests of prostitutes in these
three areas produced, in turn, three kinds of documents. There are the
magistrates' books, which contain a record of all of those arrested. These
survive only for the City, and only for a few years at that. There are also
lists of women committed to the three separate houses of correction.
These lists tell us a little about 60 percent of the women arrested; the
remaining 40 percent were usually dismissed with a warning. The lists
survive fully for the City but only sporadically for the other two jurisdictions. Finally, there are the recognizances given by those women who were
probably tied to bawdy houses and could therefore find individuals who
would stand bail for them. These recognizances were strung together into
bundles that were often then wrapped in the house of correction lists.
Together they made a quarter sessions roll. All of them survive for the
City, as do the first eighty years' worth for the other two jurisdictions.
Among these recognizances, especially in the early century, one also finds
men arrested for being with whores or for keeping bawdy houses. And
there are separate lists of those indicted for bawdy houses.

There is only one other large manuscript source. The Lock Hospital
was founded in 1746 to treat the poor who were venereally infected. Half
the patients were women, and most of these were whores. In 1787 it added

a small asylum to help back to ordinary life those girls who seemed likely
to change. The other asylum, the Magdalen Hospital (1758), has to be
described from its printed reports, since its records were apparently destroyed by bombing in World War II. Finally, among the manuscript
collections, one can find bits and pieces in the divorce and defamation
suits in the consistory court, and in the Foundling Hospital admissions.
But there is also a large miscellaneous body of printed materials: trials of
whores for theft in the Sessions Paper; biographies of whores; lists of
whores arrested and whores available; tours of the town; tracts of the reformers; and the newspapers.

The chapters that follow begin with a consideration of the male libertinism from which all prostitution flowed. There are then two chapters
that consider the lives of prostitutes by trying to answer a number of questions. How many women were prostitutes, and where did they live or
work? How did a woman become a prostitute, and what was her life like?
This is followed by a consideration of the attempts to sentimentalize and
reform prostitution. A fifth chapter considers venereal disease. Most prostitutes were probably infected, and they passed the disease on to the men,
who took it home to their wives and children, bringing the two worlds,
and the two halves of this book, together.

The men who went to prostitutes came from all levels of society, from
the titled aristocrat to the poor apprentice and the unskilled laborer. This
pursuit of women in the street by men of all classes was inspired by the
need to establish from adolescence onward that they were exclusively heterosexual in their desires. For poorer men this desire was limited in two
ways. Traditional Christian doctrine taught that sex ought to have a procreative purpose and should occur only in marriage. And patriarchy required that husbands, fathers, and masters should not endanger their families by improvidently spending their substance on loose women, or risk
the health of their wives and children with venereal diseases contracted
from such women, or tolerate irregular sexual behavior in their young male
servants or apprentices. But many men, if not most, broke these rules, as
the high rate of venereal infection shows. Some of these men from their
sexual experience came to believe that since nature, and presumably nature's God, had implanted sexual desire in human beings, it could not be
that the pursuit of those desires was evil, and that the example of the
patriarchs in the Bible with their many wives seemed to support such a
position against the teaching of a more ascetic Christianity.

The gentlemen who were libertine constructed for themselves similar
justifications that drew on the even larger store of ancient examples to be

found in the literature, philosophy, and religion of the Greeks and Romans. This aristocratic libertine religion in the early eighteenth century was usually one of inversion in which the Devil was substituted for the God of Christianity, but after 1750 it was more likely to be ruled by a goddess conceived as the divine generative power that held all the world together. Such libertinage had appeared before 1700, but in the eighteenth century it was transformed by two forces. In the new century's first generation the emergence of the role of the adult effeminate sodomite discredited those libertines who had pursued both boys and women. This promoted a libertinage that was exclusively heterosexual and required its devotees to systematically edit the ancient sources whenever they displayed their bisexual presumptions. Then in the century's second generation the sometimes Epicurean, sometimes simply riotous, libertinage of the previous generation was modified by the sentimental movement and its devotion to the free flow of emotions and its desire to produce in men behavior that was gentler and more subject to the influences of women.

GENTLEMEN AND THE RELIGION OF LIBERTINISM

In the fifty years between 1660 and 1710 male aristocratic libertinism had already passed through two stages of development that bequeathed a mixed legacy to the next generation. The abandonment of some of these developments under the influence of sentimentalism and the new ideal of the domestic family produced by 1750 a more unified libertine position; it held the field until in turn it was modified by the growth of Evangelical religion and the reaction to the French Revolution. This history is in some ways a difficult one to write since (as Dale Underwood said thirty years ago) libertinism was more a way of life than a systematic body of thought. Yet it produced attitudes and behaviors that tended to reflect a persistent set of ideas. It was part of a European world that had probably first emerged in the cities of Renaissance Italy. But by 1700 it had produced in England a number of representative theorists who in their lives and their writing set the terms of debate for the first generation of the eighteenth century. Three of these stand out. Lord Rochester was the great exemplar of the libertinism of the 1670s, but he was by the early eighteenth century discredited to a degree. William Congreve represented the libertinism of the 1690s; and throughout the early eighteenth century he and the beaus of his school were the most widespread ideal; but by 1750 Congreve was discredited and his plays were no longer performed. Instead, it was the aesthetic and moral idealism of Lord Shaftesbury that to a large extent after 1750 inspired alike the religious enthusiast and the libertines of the Dilettanti Society.[3]

Rochester was the most brilliant rake of the 1670s, and Sir George Etherege enshrined some of his wit and sparkle in the character of Dorimant in the play *The Man of Mode* (1676). Rochester in 1680, during his final illness, described for Gilbert Burnet the maxims of morality by which he had led his sexual life. They were two: "that he should do nothing to the hurt of any other, or that might prejudice his own health: And he judged that all pleasure, when it did not interfere with these, was to be indulged as the gratification of our natural appetites. It seemed unreasonable to imagine these were put into a man only to be restrained, or curbed to such narrowness." It was a doctrine that had a long life. Some seventy years later, John Cleland in his novel (which rapidly became a holy book to the libertines) made Mrs. Cole say that "she considered pleasure of one sort or other as the universal port of destination, and every wind that blew thither a good one, provided it blew nobody any harm."[4]

Rochester's sexual life was for him part of a larger philosophical system. This system (as Reba Wilcoxon shows) can especially be found in the poems that he wrote in the 1670s after a serious illness had left him more reflective. He first rejected the Christian ideas of immortality and of rewards and punishment; he had partly come to such a position by reading Lucretius and Seneca; and he was contemptuous of those who accepted the restraints that Christian doctrine imposed. Secondly, Rochester concluded that it was only through our senses that we perceived reality: "reason an Ignis fatuus in the mind, which leaving light of nature, Sense, behind." This he had found to some degree in Hobbes and Epicurus. Finally, Rochester held that morality was based on pleasure, which was good, and on pain, which was evil, but that some pleasures were superior to others. Obscenity and sex incarnated these principles in his poems, standing for the intensity of sensory perception and the morality of hedonism while opposing Christian asceticism.[5]

Rochester's obscenity soon discredited him even among those who shared most of the remainder of his system. This was especially so after 1750. Hume declared in 1757 that "the ancient satyrists often used great liberty in their expressions; but their freedom no more resembles the license of Rochester than the nakedness of an Indian does that of a common prostitute." Similarly Horace Walpole said that "Rochester's poems have more obscenity than wit, more wit than poetry, more poetry than politeness." Rakes like Rochester were probably also discredited because there was for them no contradiction between falling in love with one woman and having sex with another at the same time. Dorimant in Etherege's play is in love with Harriet, but he leaves her for an assignation with Belinda, telling himself that he is "not so foppishly in love here" to forget his appointment. "I am flesh and blood yet." Richard Steele by 1711 was already denouncing Etherege's play and over the next ten years continued to do so as a means of promoting his own more romantic productions. Etherege disappeared sooner from the early-eighteenth-century stage than did any of the other libertine playwrights, perhaps because his most famous character was so closely tied to Rochester's reputation. But Rochester's greatest liability as a model for the libertine may well have been his association with sodomy. There were several references to sodomy with boys in his poems, and, more notoriously, he had supposedly written during the 1670s his play *Sodom,* in which sodomy was presented as no worse than any number of other sexual irregularities. Editions of the play were published in 1684, 1689, and 1707. The publishers of the last two were prosecuted, and no printed copy has survived. But most significantly, no one seems to have printed it after 1707. It is very likely that John Marshall published the 1707 edition as a means of capitalizing on the mass arrests of sodomites in that year. But the men arrested for sodomy in 1707 were presented as members of a third gender who were effeminate and exclusively interested in other males. Rochester's bisexual sodomy was therefore beginning to take on a new meaning; it could no longer be used as the supreme symbol of license; it had come instead to be seen as incompatible with a libertine's driving interest in women. The new gender role for effeminate sodomites from this point onward stood as the very opposite of the role that the exclusively heterosexual libertine wished to play.[6]

By 1700 the libertines of Rochester's generation were old or dying. Some were unable to be true to their skepticism as they faced their ends. Bishop Burnet had of course published twenty years before the story of Rochester's deathbed conversion. Lady Cowper, a friend of Burnet and the mother of the future lord chancellor, noted in her diary the deathbeds of the turn of the century. In 1702 the "profligate Lord Warwick" had "divines to pray with him and died penitent, devoutly wishing he had never been born a lord." His doctors had warned him for a year that he would die if he did not change his way of life, but this had only made him "more outrageous and desperate." It was only when he was "in the jaws of death" that something had "appeared which with some goes for repentance." Lord Sunderland in the next year confessed the truth of religion before he died and twice received the Sacrament. Lady Cowper wondered what it meant. These after all were men "celebrated for sublime

parts"; yet "when they come to die," "these infidels are then in a horrible
fright, and it is rare to hear of any who stick to their pretended assurance."
Their conversions were explained away by some (who probably included
her libertine husband Sir William) as "the effect of melancholy fears,
bodily weakness, the result of ignorance." But Lady Cowper thought that
they must instead have been "overcome by irresistible conviction," since
the need "to maintain the honour of their party" would otherwise have
been "a stronger motive to dissemble than any other at that sad time."
She was kinder to Sir Charles Sedley, by whose wit she had been charmed.
Sedley had been "infamous for atheism," but she had seen copies of a
"seemingly devout" prayer he had composed a well as a sermon written
to confute Father Elliott. The sermon was ingenious, "but with what sin-
cerity he did either," she could "make no conclusion." But Sedley according to another report in fact had died in his bed "like a philosopher,
without fear or superstition." Nonetheless, it is apparent that a consistent
libertinism was difficult to maintain for men who had been brought up
in a Christian society, especially when their more conventional relations
hovered over their deathbeds.[7]

By the 1690s this generation of rakes from the 1670s had ceased to
dominate the fashionable world, and a more self-restrained kind of libertine had taken their place: the beau had replaced the rake, and the plays
of Congreve those of Etherege. Congreve's heroes, however, were still
unacceptable to the religious. Valentine in *Love for Love* was described
by Jeremy Collier as a "prodigal debauchee, unnatural and profane, obscene, saucy and undutiful; and yet this libertine is crowned for the man
of merit, has his wishes thrown in his lap, and makes the happy exit."
Valentine in 1695 came on stage reading Epictetus. Twenty years before
that Shadwell had opened *The Virtuoso* with his romantic lead reading
Epicurus. The patron saints of libertinism had changed.[8]

Epicurean license (for the 1670s misused his name in this way) had
given way to stoic self-restraint. And Epicurus had come to be more accurately known. St. Evremonde taught that the ancient Romans had followed two Epicurean paths. Those in the first "lived a retired studious
life." The others, who "were the greatest part of the ingenious men of
that time," knew "how to distinguish the gentleman from the magistrate
and apply their cares to the Republic in such a manner that there was
time enough left both for their friends and for themselves." Epicurus had
held that "the love of pleasure and the avoiding of grief are the first and
most natural motions that are observed in men." He was therefore "indul-
gent to the motions of nature," and he disapproved of dealing with it

violently: chastity was not always a virtue. But Epicurus was clear that luxury was a vice: "He would have sobriety regulate the appetite," and he "disengaged pleasures from the disorders that precede and the distaste that follows them." His doctrine, therefore, had only come into disrepute in England (so one of St. Evremonde's disciples said) because of "the irregular life of some libertines" who had "abused the name of this philosopher."[9]

Petronius was this school's other model, for he had (said St. Evremonde) "an ingenious politeness, far enough removed from the gross extravagance of a vicious man." He was "not so possessed by his pleasures as to be made incapable of business," and his tranquility was compatible with public employment. He was, except perhaps for Horace, "the only person of antiquity that knew how to speak of gallantry." But Petronius was dangerous because of the sodomy: William Burnaby carefully left some parts in Latin when he published his translation in 1694. Petronius had died well—better than Cato or Socrates even—since his soul was "more touched with the sweet and easy charms of verse than all the empty notions of philosophers." Poor St. Evremonde's assurance did him no good, however, with a redoubtable religious woman like Lady Cowper when she met him in 1701. She recorded that he had "a froward uneasy, discontented aspect"; she allowed that he was "far advanced in years"; but still she thought that it was "plain to perceive his Epicurean principles and practice neither give him inward satisfaction nor help him to appear other than a miserable spectacle." She concluded (with the defensiveness of her own uneasy mind and advancing years) that "these infidels are not firmly settled in their own opinions" and that "things remain doubtful to them, without that assurance they sometimes brag of and labour to make us believe they do possess and enjoy."[10]

Congreve wrote all of his plays during the 1690s, when he was in his twenties, and under the influence of his Epicurean philosophy of self-restrained sensuality. Jeremy Collier's attack and Congreve's bad eyes seem to have pushed him into retirement thereafter. But he may also have chosen retirement because he thought of himself as belonging to that sect of his philosophy who devoted themselves to a "retired, studious life." Voltaire misunderstood this when he visited Congreve and thought him vain to pretend to be simply a gentleman rather than a public figure. Samuel Johnson was even less sympathetic and thought Congreve's behavior "despicable foppery." But Congreve's contemporaries (or at least those who were not overly pious) thought him ideal. Addison declared in the *Spectator* that *Love for Love* (which Collier had denounced) was "one of the finest comedies that had ever appeared upon the English stage." And

Steele especially, who had denounced Etherege's characters, praised him
for his poem *Doris,* which gave "the character of a libertine woman of
condition" and "by the finest piece of raillery" made her impudence "only
generosity." But the English Epicureans ceased to produce much original
work after 1700. By the 1720s their movement had run into the ground,
and by the middle of the eighteenth century Hume and Voltaire strongly
attacked the philosophy. Through the 1740s Congreve himself and his
works continued to be presented in plays and novels as the quintessential
libertine. There were no new plays written by others who took his philosophical position, but his own plays (sometimes in bowdlerized form) continued to be a significant part of the repertory until midcentury. But after
1750, their popularity markedly declined. By 1781, Johnson could remark
that it was "acknowledged with universal conviction that the perusal of
his works will make no man better; and that their ultimate effect is to
represent pleasure in alliance with vice, and to relax those obligations by
which life ought to be regulated."[11]

Congreve and his school had been slowly displaced during the generation before 1750 and then were decisively overthrown in the generation
after 1750 by the influence of Lord Shaftesbury and his followers. From
1710 onward there was a steady published response year by year to Shaftesbury's ideas. The interest intensified in the late 1720s, just at the moment
that the Epicurean movement more or less died; and there was a second
efflorescence of Shaftesburian discussion in the 1750s at the very moment
that someone like Congreve had ceased to be a viable symbol.[12] Congreve's
restraint was no longer interesting to a generation that had learned to
trust its feelings and to surrender to enthusiasm. There is some irony in
the fact that Shaftesbury had himself come out of the libertinism of the
1690s, when he like Congreve had been a young man in his twenties
trying to find his way through the uproarious world of fashionable young
rakes and beaus. But there is no doubt that Shaftesbury's doctrine that it
was from our senses and our affections, and not from an externally imposed rationalism, that a true morality arose must have come out of the
libertinism of the 1670s, as much as it descended from the latitudinarian
or Neoplatonic religion, or the Lockean psychology and the new physiol-
ogy of the brain, to which it has usually been connected.[13]

Rochester would have recognized a great deal of Shaftesbury as his own,
and Rochester would have claimed that his own philosophy had arisen as
much from his libertine experience as from his classical reading. Shaftesbury was, in a way that can be shown, part of that libertine world. But
he insisted that the pleasures of the body had to be regulated: "satiety,

perpetual disgust, and feverishness of desire attend those who passionately study pleasure. They best enjoy it who study to regulate their passions." This was very close to the sensualism of Congreve and St. Evremonde. But Shaftesbury added his own distinctive note when he insisted that "the very notion of a debauch (which is a sally into whatever can be imagined of pleasure and voluptuousness) carries with it a plain reference to society." This was apparent to "the courtesans, and even the commonest of women who live by prostitution": they knew how necessary it was to the pleasure of their customers that it should seem that their "satisfactions" were recip-rocal, that "pleasures are no less given than received." It would even seem that the shared affection of a circle of friends justified for Shaftesbury even the sodomitical affections in himself, about which he was otherwise uneasy. All this was the doctrine of the first edition of the *Inquiry concern-ing virtue,* which Shaftesbury published in 1699 when he was twenty-eight years old.[14]

It was all directed in good part to the "youth of humankind, especially those who are above the laboring sort" and who early in life were "familiar-ized to the licentiousness of this passion." Shaftesbury had himself a healthy sexual appetite. It is hard to show this in the 1690s. But in 1702 Shaftesbury circulated to his two cronies or brothers a libertine fantasy and two scatological poems that he had composed. The fantasy was called *The Adept Ladies.* Two of the author's spiritual brothers have visited a set of ladies who are the heads of an angelic sect. Their bodily excretions turn to gold; they receive spiritual visitors at night and perform miracles; and they are quite licentious as a sign of the generosity and the nobility of their natures. Two of the three men who read this piece never married, and Shaftesbury himself did so reluctantly. But this was not for any lack of attraction to women: it was simply part of the late-seventeenth-century libertine pattern. It was also part of that libertinism when the two brothers in the tale took the Sacrament because it was "now in a manner our duty, at least for example's sake on the account of our stations in Parliament." It is a comment of the kind that Lady Cowper (who was a great admirer of Shaftesbury's virtue) would have rebuked with her story of the deathbed confessions of a frightened infidel. This man had said that once when some companions and he took the Sacrament "only for an office or place," one of them had "whispered him in the ear, saying, when the cup comes to me, I'll soup it away; whereupon putting out his hands to receive it, fell back and was taken away for dead; but coming to life again, continued so but a very few hours, then died."[15]

Religious skepticism and sexual libertinism were already part of Shaftesbury's life in the 1690s. But what can be more easily documented for that period is his protracted struggle to turn himself into a stoic. It was a private struggle that he experienced as a conversion. In his philosophical diary he kept as stern a watch on his sociability as any monk ever did. He admonished himself: "as to action and gesture . . . be in the same manner chaste; and leave that open, loose, independent boisterous way. . . . be a new man . . . no graces of speech: no repartees or sharpness of wit: no railleries, ironies or mockeries: no narrations of a certain kind . . . no . . . embellishing. . . . what is this but lying?" He was torn between public service and private retirement but wondered whether he would "lie, flatter, be debauched and dissolute to serve" his country. There was a story passed down in Shaftesbury's family that Rochester had said that his debauches had been the only way to make his "court at White-hall." Shaftesbury, in noting this story, was probably thinking of what was necessary to make his own court with his fellow politicians in Parliament. Such men, according to Toland, came to dislike Shaftesbury and "gave out that he was too bookish because not given to play, nor assiduous at court; that he was no good companion, because not a rake nor a hard drinker, and that he was no man of the world, because not selfish or open to bribes."[16]

Shaftesbury for his part, especially after 1700, was concerned to show the men of the fashionable world how they might move from the physical beauty of the human body to the beauties of poetry, painting, and philosophy. He complained to Lord Somers that their fellow aristocrats were corrupted by the pursuit of women and the superstitions of Christianity. He scoffed that the beaus "go no farther than the dancing-master to seek for grace and beauty." But the true virtuoso knew that "even in the arts, which are mere imitations of that outward grace and beauty, we not only confess a taste, but make it part of refined breeding to discover amidst the many false manners and ill styles the true and natural one, which represents the real beauty and Venus of the kind." From human beauty, then, one proceeded to the beauty of art. But from art, one went on to virtue: "Thus are the arts and virtue mutually friends; and thus the science of virtuosi and that of virtue itself become, in a manner, one and the same." This required gentlemen to surrender "brutality, insolence and riot" and turn to good breeding. They would then discover that "to philosophize, in a just signification, is but to carry good breeding a step higher." The virtuoso or "real fine gentleman" would be able to do this because he loved art and ingenuity and had seen the world. They knew the manners of the various countries of Europe, had "searched into their antiquities and records" and knew "their architecture, sculpture, painting, music, and their

taste in poetry, learning, language, and conversation." It sounds like a
program for the wits and libertines of the Dilettanti Society. But the won-
derful thing about Shaftesbury was that no one seemed able to discredit
him as a libertine and a skeptic, though they tried. The greatest rake in
the English novel was Lovelace, and Richardson had Clarissa write that
Lovelace had duped her into believing that he, unlike his libertine companions, had never "in pursuance of Lord Shaftesbury's test (which is part
of the rake's creed, and what I may call *the whetstone of infidelity*), endeav-
ored to turn the sacred subject into ridicule." But there were others who
either defended Shaftesbury as a friend to genuine Christianity or remained unaware or impervious to his deism. Shaftesbury spoke the very
language of his age and thereby provided a refined libertinism and sensuality with its greatest respectability.[17]

In the first three decades of the century, however, the libertine mode
was more likely to be Epicurean rather than Shaftesburian. The most brilliant example was Henry St. John, the future Lord Bolingbroke, who
turned twenty in 1698. Bolingbroke and Shaftesbury were apparently acquaintances, and it is clear from Bolingbroke's later mature writings after
he had fallen from power that he had seriously taken up some of Shaftesbury's ideas. (Shaftesbury, for his part, regarded Bolingbroke as a genius
corrupted by his desire for power.) Bolingbroke would have agreed that
men "have a natural sociability; that is we are determined by self-love to
seek our pleasure and our utility in society." But it was self-love, not an
innate moral sense as in Shaftesbury, that drove man to sociability. It is
apparent from those who recorded Bolingbroke's conversation when he
was a brilliant and beautiful young man in his twenties that he must also
have read Epicurus, Petronius, and St. Evremonde and have taken them
to heart. He complained to his friends, after he had become secretary of
state, that he had "too great a load of business." But he only did so, according to Swift, to show that he could "mix the fine gentleman, and
man of pleasure, with the man of business." This was, according to St.
Evremonde, the character of the second sect of Epicureans. Bolingbroke
also had "a great respect for the characters of Alcibiades and Petronius,
especially the latter whom he would gladly be thought to resemble." But
Alcibiades was perhaps too compromising a model because of all those
men who desired him in his youth.[18]

Bolingbroke must always in part have been attracted to the other Epicurean sect who lived in philosophical retirement, however much it went
against his gregariousness and his desire to be in the center of affairs. In
1709 (at thirty-one) he wrote that "whether it is owing to constitution or

to philosophy I can't tell but certain it is that I can make myself happy
in any sort of life. . . . happiness, I imagine, depends much more on desir-
ing little than enjoying much; and perhaps the surest road to it is indiffer-
ence." When he grew older and was at first in enforced and then in voluntary exile from politics, he returned more strongly to the theme of
retirement. It was no pose (as Sheila Biddle suggests) but a genuine part
of the equipment of the Epicurean rake. Bolingbroke's fondness for
women, on the other hand, became part of the libertine's lore. He had a
reputation for deflowering girls, and it is said that when he was appointed
secretary of state, a gentleman had asked a courtesan he met in the Mall
whether she had heard the news. The woman inquired what the office
was worth and was told about ten thousand pounds a year. "By God," she
said, "I'm glad to hear it with all my soul, for the whores will get every
penny of it."[19]

Young men like Bolingbroke, however, had difficulty keeping their
rakery within the bounds of decorum. He drank to excess (as Swift complained), and he was likely to be carried away when drunk. An early biographer was told by an old man that he had seen Bolingbroke "and another
of his companions run naked through the Park, in a fit of intoxication."
(A similar story was told of Rochester.) Bolingbroke does seem to have
kept his religious skepticism within bounds. Swift once found him "gone
. . . to receive the sacrament; several rakes did the same; it was not for
piety, but employments."[20] But other young men knew no bounds. Early
on a Sunday morning in 1703, a "parcel of drunken rioters" went into St.
James's Church with their swords drawn. They swore at and abused the
women attending the early service. Lady Cowper was told that they then
"pissed in the pulpit, and defiled the Communion Table in a manner not
fit to be named, tore the bibles and prayerbooks, sung lewd songs as
psalms, [and] preached in the devil's name." Lord Shannon, a son of the
duke of Monmouth, and a member of Parliament were three of the men.
These impieties may simply have been part of the physical uproariousness
of the male rake. In 1712 there was, for instance, a notorious group of
young rakes who attacked passersby in the street and were called the Mohocks.[21] But the rakes in St. James's Church were involved in something
more. Their sexual libertinism and its rituals had bred a profound disillu-
sionment with the rituals of an ascetic Christian religion. The great Alcibiades also in his time had been accused of desecrating the herms and
mocking the mysteries of Eleusis. But the traditional religion of ancient
Greece had incorporated sexual imagery into its cult. Christianity did not.
The libertines were determined to change that, and they kept at their

program even when they abandoned their physical uproariousness under the influence of the aesthetic stoicism of Shaftesbury. The rakes in St. James's Church probably knew of Sir Charles Sedley's behavior in the 1660s and took him as their model, even as Bolingbroke's naked dash in the park was probably modeled on Rochester's. But there was also a continuity of ideological aspiration and ritual enactment that can be seen going through the devil clubs of the 1720s, the rituals of the Medmenham monks in the 1750s, and the *Discourse on the Worship of Priapus* that Richard Payne Knight published in 1786.

These libertines in their fertility rituals sought to defile the Christian symbols by defecation, but more importantly they sought alternative forces or gods who might be seen as animating both their sexual practices and the world at large. Like Don Juan, some of them found that God in the Devil of the Christian religion. The rakes in St. James's Church "preached in the devil's name." Lady Cowper was also told in 1707 by the bishop of Litchfield that there was a "society" among the duke of Marlborough's soldiers who called themselves "the Devil's Club." When they met "they drunk a health to the Devil and other horrid blasphemies" that Lady Cowper said her "tongue nor pen shall never repeat." Similarly in 1721 the duke of Wharton and his friends were accused of keeping a Hell-Fire Club where the mysteries of the Christian religion were mocked, the Devil was worshiped, and whoring was promoted. The bishops took the matter seriously enough to promote a bill against blasphemies. A royal proclamation was issued, and the magistrates were instructed to root out the clubs. But the bill failed to pass, and the magistrates had to report that they were unable to find the clubs of young persons who met together to insult God.[22]

A few years later, in 1727, Mary Davys, who ran a coffeehouse and modeled her characters on Congreve's plays, put the Hell-Fire Club into her novel *The Accomplished Rake*. The club met at one in the morning in St. Martin's churchyard, where, using a tombstone for a table, they drank healths to the Devil until the watchmen scattered them away. The duke of Wharton in real life continued to organize such clubs, one of which Lady Mary Wortley Montagu described in 1724. There were twenty young men who met in Lord Hillsborough's house. They brought women in masquerade who were their sexual companions for the evening and who were supposed to be women of quality. The club met for "the advancement of that branch of happiness which the vulgar call whoring." They first met on Ash Wednesday, and then on every Wednesday in Lent thereafter, beginning their carnival on the day it should have ended and extending it throughout the season of penitence. "The whole generation of fathers, mothers and husbands raise as great clamour against this new institution as the pagan priests did of old against the light of the Gospel," wrote Lady Mary; and they did so "for the same reasons, since it strikes at the very foundation of their authority, which authority is built upon gross impositions upon mankind." This ritualization of sexual libertinism gave it a legitimacy in the eyes of its participants even though its rituals were those of inversion. But for men like Wharton, there was also a need for a ritual that worshiped a benevolent deity in a cult that was not sexual. Like Wharton in 1722, such men joined the Masons, in whose lodges they were more likely to find domesticity glorified and fidelity promoted than the enactment of libertinism.[23]

These rituals served a purpose similar to those that effeminate sodomites enacted in their molly-houses, as Ned Ward described them. There were interesting differences, however, between the rituals of the sodomites and those of the libertines. There is no evidence that the sodomites were deistical or satanic in the way that the libertines were. The sodomites, it is true, inverted the rituals of marriage, spoke of intercourse as marriage and the room with the beds as the chapel, and gave birth to wooden dolls. But these rituals were only incidentally religious: they were primarily in protest against the exclusion of sodomites from marriage and from all legitimate sexuality. The libertines, however, seemed to have aimed at a more elaborate reconstruction of their culture. The conventional Christianity of their day identified virtue with sexual abstinence, especially in women. The Reformation's abolition of clerical celibacy had made little difference in this regard. Those who were the most religious were also likely to be those who had the least to do with sex. Lady Cowper, whom we have seen sneering at the deaths of the libertines, was a good example.

Lady Cowper had married in 1665, when she was twenty-one. In the first five years of marriage she bore four children. Then, for no "other reason than to avoid having many children," she and her husband stopped having sex. They continued to sleep in the same bed for the next sixteen years, until she was forty-two; thereafter they slept separately for twelve years till her husband died. She was proud that she had borne four children "without knowing what it is to have an unchaste thought or sensual pleasure." But Lady Cowper over the years came to view those sixteen sexless years in the same bed as heroic: "had the Lady been of the Romish Church perhaps she might have been canonized, no doubt but some have for less matters." Still there was some humility left: "it may be truly said I have outdone Anna the prophetess in chastity, though not in piety and devotion. For she lived with a husband seven years from her virginity; whereas I scarce five in that sense, though in a matrimonial state near 43." Lady Cowper's husband, however, did not share her view of herself: they were frequently at odds, especially because he was a libertine. Delariviere Manley in a novel in 1709 described Sir William (who had died the year before) as "an old debauchee given to irregular pleasures, not such as the laws of nature seem to dictate"; he had married one of his sons to his own former mistress and then "died suddenly in the midst of his excesses." Lady Cowper vigorously denied the charge of unnatural pleasures. But during his life, she had frequently quarreled with Sir William over the relationship of the church to virtue and sexuality. He ended one argument by saying that "he found nobody the better that went so much" to church, since they would find that they made "such a stir against whoring, which he thought the least of sins."[24]

Whoring, then, was the least of sins, but still some sort of sin for many libertines. Women like Lady Cowper reinforced their sense of virtue that arose from sexual abstinence by going to the rituals of the church. Libertine men, by contrast, broke in on those rituals and parodied and degraded them and then, in company with women of their own cast (most of whom were prostitutes), celebrated sexual license in rituals of their own invention. It is difficult to say how seriously they took those rituals. How far did devil worship go beyond toasts and bawdy jokes? Did any one of them ever really conceive that like Don Juan he had made a compact with the Devil? There is no evidence. The references to the Devil apparently disappear after 1730. From that point onward the English libertines, especially those associated with the Dilettanti Society, seem, under the influence of Shaftesbury's ideal of the virtuoso, to have worshiped in their rituals a more benevolent goddess of fertility. By the 1780s, the goddess was dissolved into a more general divine generative force, which in Payne Knight's theory even subsumed Christianity and its symbols.

The Dilettanti Society was founded in 1732. It aimed at promoting the knowledge of classical civilization as it could be seen in its surviving physical remains in ruins, sculpture, and medals. Some of its founding members like Sir Francis Dashwood had traveled extensively, especially in Italy, Greece, and Asia Minor. It subsidized expeditions that surveyed the surviving classical monuments, especially those of Greece, and published engravings and descriptions of them. The members when they met wore robes and had various convivial rituals. The society also had an ideological program in their virtuosoship. They were libertines and often deists, opposed to conventional Christianity and interested in the justification for their sexual lives that the physical remains of ancient classical civilization seemed to provide. Some of them, under the leadership of Sir Francis Dashwood, evidently used their friendships as the basis of an additional fraternity that met in the 1750s at Medmenham Abbey, six miles from Dashwood's principal residence at West Wycombe. In 1763 and 1764 John Wilkes and Charles Churchill, as part of their campaign against the government, published accounts of this society that were enlarged upon in 1765 by Charles Johnstone in his novel *Chrysal*. What they described was a new Hell-Fire Society, in which the Bona Dea (the ancient goddess of fertility) was worshiped with parodies of Christian ritual and acts of sexual intercourse. It has ever since been difficult to separate fact from fiction in the history of the monks of Medmenham Abbey.[25]

Dashwood was largely responsible for whatever occurred at Medmenham. He was widely traveled and at home built extensively and with good taste. He remodeled the west portico of his house at West Wycomb on a reconstruction of a temple to Dionysus or Bacchus that stood at what had been the principal seat of Dionysiac worship in Ionia. The temple had been investigated and engraved at the expense of the Dilettanti Society. Dashwood also had a considerable interest in religious ritual. He printed in 1773 an *Abridgement of the Book of Common Prayer,* which revised the prayers in a more deistical direction. Benjamin Franklin, who was as committed as Dashwood to the principles of a virtuoso's libertinism ("rarely use venery but for health or offspring, never to dullness, weakness, or the injury of your own or another's peace or reputation"), helped him in his prayer book revisions. Dashwood also had his earthier side, which his most recent biographer ignores. Horace Walpole described him as "notorious for singing profane and lewd catches." Dashwood was fascinated by and contemptuous of Roman Catholic ritual. There is a sensationalist story that as a young man he had flogged with a horsewhip and with shouts of "the devil, the devil" the surprised penitents on Good Friday as they knelt in the dark of the Sistine Chapel, baring their shoulders in the expectation of a lighter discipline. In England he and his Dilettanti friends had their pictures painted, with Dashwood as St. Francis, with a chalice in his hand, at prayer before the statue of the Venus des Medici.[26]

Dashwood rented Medmenham Abbey, a converted Cistercian abbey, around 1750. Dashwood renovated it to look more like an abbey, adding a ruined tower and a cloister and, inside the cloister, a room from which "the glare of light is judiciously excluded by the pleasing gloom of ancient stained glass," which must have been intended to serve as the chapel or the chapter room. Dashwood invited down a group of friends, for whom there was a costume "more like a waterman's than a monk's." A motto inscribed over the door—*Fay ce que voudras,* or Do as you wish—was taken from Rabelais's Abbey of Thélème. To this much even the most skeptical historian agrees. The controversy remains over what the monks did there. Betty Kemp says that they came "to admire the gardens and to fish or sail on the river." Walpole said otherwise: each had "their cell, a proper habit, a monastic name, and a refectory in common—besides a chapel. . . . whatever their doctrines were, their practice was vigorously pagan: Bacchus and Venus were the deities to whom they almost publicly sacrificed." John Wilkes, who had certainly been to Medmenham, described "the English Eleusinian mysteries, where the monks assembled on all solemn occasions, the more secret rites were performed, and libations poured forth in much pomp to the BONA DEA." The gardens were filled with statutes and with other mottoes, and "the younger monks" took their pleasures there. But Wilkes was careful to say that those pleasures were with women: they "seemed at least to have sinned naturally." There was no sodomy at Medmenham, whatever else might have occurred in the chapter room. In that room, Sir Francis presided over the initiates in their mysteries, as Churchill wrote:

> [Dashwood] shall pour, from a Communion Cup,
> Libations to the goddess without eyes.[27]

It was a curious blend of Christian symbol and ancient Greek pagan rite. This very blending, however, was probably part of the instinctive belief of Dashwood and his brothers in the Dilettanti Society that there was behind all ancient symbols—both Greek and Christian—a single religion in which the generative powers of the world were worshiped, and whose cult was appropriately Dionysiac and priapic. What was implicit at Medmenham was eventually made explicit by the discoveries of Sir William Harcourt, and the theories of Baron d'Hancarville and Richard Payne Knight. Hamilton, while he was the British representative at Naples, discovered in the countryside what he took to be a priapic cult flourishing under the guise of a devotion to Saints Cosmos and Damian. He took it to be "a fresh proof of the similitude of the Popish and the Pagan religion." He had seen that women and children at Naples wore an amulet against the evil eye that was priapic, and he had been told that the country people actually wore the phallus. But he became truly excited by the feast of the Cosmos at Isernia in 1780. Ex-votos of wax made in the shape of the male genitals, some as big as the palm of the hand, were offered publicly

for sale. Women, especially, bought them and presented them at the altar
when they made their vows, saying "Blessed be Cosmo, let it be like this,"
and kissed them as they gave them to the priests with gifts of money.
Those with genital illnesses presented themselves at the altar and had
their affected parts anointed with St. Cosmos's oil. Hamilton reported his
findings to the Dilettanti Society. He collected examples of the ex-votos
and deposited them in 1784 in the British Museum so that they could
be kept with the phalluses from the ancient world. The society voted to
print his report with illustrations. Word of Hamilton's findings rapidly
circulated, and a dedicated libertine like Lord Pembroke set the tone of
the response when he wrote to Hamilton asking to "have an early sight
of your letter . . . upon the cult of Priapus. . . . So superb a Deity ought
always to have been treated with every possible mark of religion and respect; but from the natural perverseness and exclusive monopoly of the
Christian faith, he has been neglected for too long a series of ages."[28]

When Hamilton's letter was printed in 1786, it was accompanied by
Payne Knight's *Discourse on the Worship of Priapus.* Payne Knight in that
work relied on Baron d'Hancarville's *Recherches sur l'origine, l'esprit et les
progrès des arts de la Grèce,* which had been published in 1785 and which
he had heard about from Charles Townley, who was one of d'Hancarville's
patrons. D'Hancarville had stayed in Townley's house and had had access
to his great collection of antiquities. Townley promoted d'Hancarville's
ideas among the libertines, sending a copy of the book (with all of which
he did not agree) to John Wilkes. D'Hancarville held that the mythology
of the ancient world, or the mystic theology, as Payne Knight called it,
had not been understood because previous scholars had relied exclusively
on the literary texts. D'Hancarville concentrated on engraved gems,
painted vases, coins, and sculpture. The ancient theology as seen in those
images he interpreted to be intensely sexual in the sense that it worshiped
the powers of generation and creation. He also argued that a similar system could be found in the other religious of the world. Payne Knight took
up one part of this subject—the phallic symbolism—and made it central
to his book. And he insisted that the symbols of the Christian religion
were also a part of this ancient phallic cult.[29]

Payne Knight wrote that Christianity had attacked the worship of Priapus more furiously than any other part of ancient polytheism. Christians
had not understood that it was "a very natural symbol of a very natural
and philosophical system of religion," and, with a sly dig at Christian
sacramentalism, he pointed out that "the forms and ceremonials of a religion are not always to be understood in their direct and obvious sense;

but are . . . symbolical representations of some hidden meaning." "The
female organs of generation were revered as symbols of the generative
powers of nature or matter, as the male were of the generative powers of
God." The male organs were sometimes represented by other forms. One
of these was a cross in the form of a T. Sometimes a head was added to the
cross, "which gives it the exact appearance of a crucifix." It was therefore an
"emblem of creation and generation before the church adopted it as the
sign of salvation." The stone crosses of ancient England were also part of
this phallic cult, and "from the ancient solar obelisks came the spires and
pinnacles with which our churches are still decorated."

In Egypt a goat was kept as the symbol of the generative power; the
women had "the honour of being publicly enjoyed by him"; "it was one
of the sacraments of that ancient church." Fawns and satyrs were similar
symbols in Greece. The figure of Pan was represented as "pouring water
upon the organ of generation": the baptisms of St. John and of Christ
had a similar purpose. There was therefore nothing new in Christianity,
as Grotius had proved. The creator was both male and female: the nymphs
represented the female principle. The figure of the ancient hermaphrodite
presented both principles in a single person. God in Genesis, "prior to
the creation of woman, created him *male and female,* as he himself consequently was." The satyrs were often thought to have been represented in
intercourse with the hermaphrodites in such ways as "are rather adapted
to the gratification of disorder and unnatural appetites, than to extend
procreation." But it had been shown to be simply the "most convenient
way to get at the female organs of generation in those mixed beings who
possessed both." When the people in Exodus rose up to play before the
golden calf, they were therefore engaging in ritual sexual intercourse in
honor of the symbol of the generative power. Even Jehovah's name was
also merely a title of Bacchus.

Sexual intercourse had in fact been a common form of ancient worship:
"the male and female saints of antiquity used to be promiscuously together
in the temples, and honour God by a liberal display and general communication of his bounties." There were sacred prostitutes at Corinth and Eryx,
and "the act of generation was a sort of sacrament in the island of Lesbos."
The early Christian Eucharist had had its holy kiss. The agape feasts and
nocturnal vigils had given "too flattering opportunities to the passions and
appetites of men," and they had had to be suppressed by the decrees of
several church councils. "Their suppression may be considered as the final
subversion" of the ancient phallic religion, which nonetheless survived in
customs like the ex-votos of St. Cosmos and the obscene figures on Gothic

cathedrals. This phallic religion could also be found in ancient India, since it was a product of "the human mind in different ages, climates, and circumstances, uniformly acting upon the same principles and to the same ends." But Payne Knight had shown his deepest intent at the beginning of his book when he had repeated the libertine doctrine that "there is naturally no impurity or licentiousness in the moderate and regular gratification of any natural appetite" and had declared that "neither are organs of one species of enjoyment naturally to be considered as subjects of shame and concealment more than those of another." To establish this he appealed to the theology of the ancients as he understood it and to the universal workings of the human mind against the intolerance and austerity of the Christian religion.[30]

Payne Knight's book was privately circulated by the Dilettanti Society. Libertines like Charles Greville were liberated by the book. More conventional deists like Horace Walpole were shocked by its open and (to their eye) socially irresponsible attack on Christianity. Once the Revolution in France had broken out, and the worship of the Supreme Being had been instituted and celebrated by supposedly orgiastic rites, Payne Knight must have seemed even more outrageous. His book became publicly known, and he was to some degree ostracized. The book was therefore both the intellectual climax of eighteenth-century English libertinism and its closure.[31] But if libertinism in the second half of the century may have founded itself on the Shaftesburian program of the virtuoso, it operated within the restraints of the new prohibition against sodomy between men, and had to ignore the pederasty of the ancient world. Only the female temple prostitutes were cited, not the male. Still the great appeal of the book to some libertines must have lain in their own orgiastic experience: They had engaged in sacred fertility worship before the theory justifying it had been composed. But the libertine attempt to reconstruct the Christian attitude toward sexuality by appealing to the fertility religion of the ancient pagan world was doomed to failure. The rites of the monks of Medmenham stood no chance of being established.

THE SIMPLE LIBERTINE

The sexual behavior of the husbands, sailors, and apprentices who went to whores shows that there was a practical male libertinism among the poor that was driven by the same new standard of an exclusive heterosexuality that had transformed the libertinism of gentlemen. But the libertinism of the poor was less likely to be accompanied by a self-conscious religious skepticism. There was, however, some sense that sexual desire was an ordinary part of human nature and therefore natural, and that such desires must have been given to men and women to be enjoyed. The libertinism of the poor was constrained by the necessities of providing for a man's family and avoiding venereal disease, but there is no evidence for the presence among them of the sentimental and romantic ideals of marriage and the family that began to change the behavior of gentlemen after 1750. There is instead evidence for the breakdown of patriarchal supervision by masters of the sexual behavior of their apprentices that must have been occasioned at least in part by the concern that young men should have opportunities for sexual experience with women so that they might establish their heterosexual identities.

The sexual behavior of poor men with prostitutes can be described statistically as a result of the arrests inspired in the first generation of the eighteenth century by the Societies for the Reformation of Manners. These societies were voluntary organizations that appeared early in the 1690s and dedicated themselves to policing a city that seemed to them to have gone out of control. Their membership was apparently drawn from among the respectable middle ranks of society, and their reforming activity was directed primarily at those lower on the social scale. They concentrated on three forms of deviant behavior: first on cursing, swearing, and drunkenness; then on breaking the Sabbath; and finally on sexual immorality, especially of those (like prostitutes and sodomites) whose behavior could be openly observed in the streets and in public taverns. The societies flourished between 1690 and 1710, began to decline after 1725, and were moribund by 1738. The cursing, swearing, and Sabbath breaking to which they objected were all offenses against the honor of God. Those who broke the Sabbath were also failing to submit to the discipline of churchgoing. This was a national phenomenon encouraged by the (mistaken) belief that the Toleration Act no longer allowed churchwardens to present to the church courts those individual who did not keep the Sabbath.[32] The London church courts had, in any case, by the 1690s ceased to hear any significant number of presentments for immoral behavior and confined themselves to questions of marriage and defamation. The reformation societies were therefore obliged to use the justices of the peace to enforce their program.[33]

The societies were often accused of hypocrisy for going after the sins of the poor and not of the rich. No one could have accused them, however, of not seeking to punish the sexual sins of men as well as those of women. Prostitutes certainly were arrested more often than were their customers.

But the men were indeed arrested, whereas in the second half of the century only the women were. Up to 1730 both men and women were arrested in the hope that punishment would bring about their reformation, and in this regard the societies showed their descent from the Protestant reformers of the sixteenth century who had attempted to treat equally the sins of the flesh in men and in women. Sexual misbehavior was viewed as a sin rather than as a crime; and before God, a man was as guilty as a woman when he had sexual relations outside of marriage.

The Societies for the Reformation of Manners in the 1720s in the three London jurisdictions inspired the arrests of at least six hundred men for being with prostitutes either in the street or in a bawdy house. Most men were bailed, but a handful who could not find sureties were sent to the houses of correction. The number of arrests varied considerably from year to year. In Westminster and Middlesex there were 107 arrests in 1725, but only from 25 to 50 in most other years of the 1720s. The same thing was true for the first two decades of the century: 24 arrests in 1704, but 117 in 1714. From 1729 onward, when there were only 9 arrests, the practice of arresting men more or less disappeared. There were no arrests in 1734, 2 in 1737, and 5 each in 1745 and 1755. At the end of the century in a seven-year period in the City (1784–90), 36 men were arrested because they had been found in the act of sex with a prostitute. But 34 of them had been doing it in the public street or in Moorfields. Only 2 were in a bawdy house. It is likely therefore that the arrests were made because of the publicity of the act. In any case, 35 men were simply discharged, and only 1 was sent to the house of correction. The women with whom they had been caught benefited, apparently, from this leniency. Only a third of them (12 of 36) were sent to Bridewell, whereas half of the women arrested on their own as prostitutes were sent there.[34]

Even in the 1720s, however, more women were arrested as prostitutes than were men as their customers. In the entire decade, in Westminster and Middlesex, only 402 men were arrested. But in 1720 alone, 427 women in those two jurisdictions were sent to Bridewell, and they were probably not much more than half of those arrested. The reason for arresting both men and women in this period was, however, quite the same. It was to punish them and bring about their reformation. When Mary Carter was arrested on a night in March 1721 as she wandered the streets trying to pick up men, she was sent to the house of correction because she was "one that will not be reformed of her wicked course of life, though often punished for the same." In April a group of five women who had probably been wandering in the Strand were also committed under the same rubric. In May, Mary Kirk was described as "appearing to be incorrigible, though she hath often been sent to Bridewell" for plying in the streets. Mary Tindall and Mary Johnson were women "who will not be reformed though often punished."[35]

Men were less likely to become known to the magistrates and the constables as old offenders since they were not as likely to be arrested again and again. Those who were frequently admonished in their neighborhoods were probably poorer men who were not able to find sureties and had therefore been committed to the house of correction. This was the case with Edward Warburton, who was committed along with John Warburton, probably his brother. They had both been found in a bawdy house. Edward had been frequently told not to go to such houses. John was described as a "common player of interludes" that were often obscene. Thomas Inslay was also sent to the house of correction because he was a "person of lewd life and a whoremonger." The recognizances from the poor neighborhoods in the East End were more likely to note that a man was an habitual offender—as the constables of Spittlefields, Whitechapel, Wapping, and Limehouse complained of Charles Booth, Richard Moore, William Ruff, and Thomas Bradshaw. But in a western parish, the Clerkenwell constable also knew that Thomas Large had frequently gone to the bawdy house where he had been found locked up in a private room with a whore. The reformation societies said that by these arrests husbands were saved from contracting venereal disease that they would otherwise have passed on to their wives, and younger men had "by this seasonable chance been discouraged and turned . . . from following such sinful courses."[36]

A man's whoremongering was less likely to become known because men were seldom arrested for being with prostitutes in the street. It is probable that once a man had been picked up by a woman, it was difficult to prove that they were not a respectable couple taking the night air. In Westminster and Middlesex in the 1720s, only 11 percent of men were arrested because they were either strolling with a woman or having sex with her in the streets. Four of the men were arrested for having sex in an open field. In 12 percent of the cases, it is unclear where the man had been when he was arrested. But in 76 percent of the cases, he was arrested with his whore inside a well-known bawdy house. By contrast, women who were arrested and bailed for being prostitutes in the City in the same decade had in slightly more than half the cases (55 percent) been taken up in the streets and not in a bawdy house (44 percent); this is striking since these were the women most likely to have had ties to a bawdy house, given that there was someone to arrange their bail. But the men who were arrested and bailed in the City for being with whores had overwhelmingly been found in a bawdy house (82 percent) and not in the street (14 percent; 4 percent unclear).

The reformers in the 1720s therefore had two quite different but complementary strategies for dealing with prostitution—stop the women from walking the streets and punish the men for going to the bawdy houses. But the reformers also thought that in both cases there was sinful behavior that had to be changed. Otherwise they could more simply have pursued the policy that prevailed in the second half of the century, when the keepers of bawdy houses were arrested but not their male customers. A traditional concern for reproving sin produced a result whereby men and women were nearly treated as equals for their sins of the flesh. In the second half of the century, prostitution was less likely to be categorized as sin. The prostitute became a woman who had fallen because of the peculiarities of her environment; she could be redeemed if that environment were changed. She was not a sinner to be reformed by correction. The persons who ran the bawdy houses and profited from her prostitution were also part of that evil environment and had to be eliminated. But after 1730, it is clear that no one thought that it was necessary to do anything about the men who were the prostitutes' customers.

There were in the 1720s, however, considerably more women arrested as whores than there were men taken in bawdy houses. This may simply have been because it was harder to storm a bawdy house than it was to round up even a large group of young women in the streets. It was certainly the case that men were more likely to resist their arrest whether in the streets or in a house. These men had usually been drinking heavily, and this must have made them more obstreperous. Of the thirty-six men arrested in Westminster and Middlesex in 1723 for whoring, nine attacked or abused the constable. Edward Browne struck the constable when he was first arrested in a bawdy house and refused to give his name. But after spending the night in the Gatehouse, he had cooled down enough to be bailed. Nicholas Vincent was also violent when he was found with two women in a private room up one pair of stairs in a well-known house in Colson's Court. Norris John Hainky struck the constable, but since he was arrested in the street, he was able to gather a mob to make even more of a riot. Timothy Walters was, however, the most inventive. When he was taken at two in the morning with a woman in the street, he insulted the assistant to the Holborn constable and pretended that he had robbed him of fifteen yards of muslin.[37]

The constables often had to call for help in making arrests from by-standers, who sometimes refused and were charged for it. John Hall would not help the constable for the Tower district when he raided a bawdy house in Wapping and found four men in the upstairs rooms, two of them together on a bed with a single woman between them. But helping the constable could be dangerous. Timothy Smart got attacked by Richard Bramhall for doing so. The constables and the watchmen were not themselves above suspicion. John Tyle allowed a man in Whitechapel to escape after he had been arrested for whoring. Richard Hardy ignored the fact that he was on duty and picked up a whore himself; and when Francis Claxton complained that he should have been keeping the peace instead, Hardy attacked him. There were even magistrates like Charles Winyates, who after he had berated the watchmen and the beadles, released an arrested prostitute and went to a bawdy house to sleep with her.[38]

The violence of men against the constable, and their guile, was also used to protect their whores from arrest. William Ansley told the watchman that his woman was his wife. Obadiah Calvert and Richard Nicholls tried to rescue women who had been taken up in the street, and Robert Tippings successfully did this for a woman. Edmund Hacket, at three o'clock in the morning, insulted the constable, raised a mob, and allowed a woman to escape from her arrest. The men who must have escaped from their arrest never, of course, appear in the record.[39]

Watchmen and constables sometimes used their power to arrest as a means of extorting money from prostitutes. One constable, William Payne, complained that another constable, John Bull, had extorted gin and beer from prostitutes in return for letting them go. Payne had earlier charged four other constables with doing the same sort of thing. Three constables entertained themselves on a Sunday evening by arresting the two respectable daughters of a tradesman as they were on their way home from church. Another man pretended to be the brother of the keeper of the Tothill Fields bridewell in order to fleece girls who were actually prostitutes. Even some of the officers of the lord mayor's household entered this profitable line. They summoned the keepers of bawdy houses and dismissed them without a hearing once they had paid up.[40]

The status or occupation of a considerable number of the men arrested was given: 57 percent in Middlesex and Westminster, 74 percent in the City (tables 3.1 and 3.2). There were some striking similarities between the two sets of jurisdictions. There were about the same number of gentlemen in both cases (8 and 6 percent). Not all of these were literally gentlefolk, since gentleman was already an elastic term. There were certainly

Table 3.1 Occupations of Men Arrested for Being with Whores in Westminster and Middlesex, 1720–29 ($N = 402$)

Occupation	Number	Occupation	Number	%
Gentleman	34	Weaver	4	
Tailor	19	Bricklayer	4	
Yeoman	14	Victualler	4	
Laborer	14	Haberdasher	4	
Perukemaker	9	Other	27	
Sailor	8	Total	231	57.5
Carpenter	7			
Soldier	6	Unknown	171	42.5
Waterman	5			

Source: GLRO: MJ/SR/2340–2525.

Table 3.2 Occupations of Men Arrested for Whoring in the City of London, 1720–29 ($N = 197$)

Occupation	Number	Occupation	Number	%
Gentleman	12	Yeoman	4	
Tailor	8	Broker	4	
Tenser	5	Victualler	4	
Shoemaker	5	Other	93	
Butcher	5	Total	145	73.6
Ticket porter or porter	5			
		Unknown	52	26.4

Source: CLRO: SR, 1720–29 (Recognizances).

no titled men among those arrested. The percentage does probably reflect the actual number of leisured men in society. But it probably underrepresents their share in the world of prostitution, especially in the West End. The bastardy book of St. Margaret's, Westminster, shows gentlemen as 17 percent of the fathers of illegitimate children in the years 1712–29. The Societies for the Reformation of Manners in those years made the reporting of all men's bastards much more efficient. In the next two decades (1730–49), when the societies were not active, the number of gentlemen reported as fathers of bastards in that parish fell by half and more, to 7 percent, or about the number of men arrested for being with a whore in the 1720s.[41] But that 17 percent of the fathers of bastards in St. Margaret's should have been gentlemen in the 1720s, and that so many fewer of them should have been arrested with whores, strongly suggests that the constables in the 1720s were not very likely to raid the bawdy houses frequented by gentlemen.

It was claimed that from the middle of the 1690s houses for gentlemen took special precautions to protect themselves. "We admit no strangers," one bawd was presented as saying, "unless they bring a letter from the person they are recommended by, and therein an account of the last time they were here." The more "public houses of assignation" for gentlemen like the Three Tuns in Russell Street were more likely to be raided. In 1718 William Byrd safely went there with Sir Wilfred Lawson, and after the fricasseed chicken, two of the other men had had sex with one of the whores. But two years later Thomas Pendergass was arrested there with a whore; a year later still, William Thacker and Nicholas Hartwell were also arrested in that house. Even the more private houses were sometimes raided, though none of the gentleman customers seem ever to have been arrested. Elizabeth Needham and Sarah Jolly, who kept such houses, were arrested several times in the 1720s along with the women in their houses. But they simply moved to another house in another street. Needham was in Albemarle Street in 1721, but in Porter Street in 1723; Jolly moved from Pulteney Street to Suffolk Street. Arresting women in the company of gentlemen was dangerous. Swords were drawn and the constables' lives threatened when they arrested Susannah Larkin and Elizabeth Glover in the Rose Tavern near the Drury Lane Theater. Elizabeth Smith, who ran a house in Stonecutters Court, Pall Mall, had an even more gallant defender. Since the court in which her house stood was the principal way into the royal gardens, it was an annoyance to those persons "of very great rank and quality" who wished to go into the gardens when quarrels frequently broke out in the house late at night. One of the customers of the house—an unknown gentleman—came out into the court with a drawn sword in his hand and beat the porter of the royal gardens when he heard complaints being made. He "threatened to do mischief to anyone who should give disturbance to the said bawdy house, by reason it was his . . . bawdy house . . . and that therefore he should protect" it. Smith who kept the house was arrested, but not the gentleman.[42]

The two lists of men arrested strikingly coincide at one other point: in both of them, tailors were the single group of men (other than gentlemen) who were most likely to be found with a whore. Tailors were men with a well-developed taste in clothes. Campbell thought they had to be imaginative and quick-witted to succeed in their trade: "his fancy must always be upon the wing not awool-gathering, but fashion-hunting. . . . he ought to have a quick eye to steal the cut of a sleeve, the pattern of a flap, or

the shape of a good trimming at a glance." Campbell also indicated that
some of them would have been well paid: they could afford to treat
women. These were, perhaps, the men most likely to be beaus: able to
make their own clothes and with an easy air with women. They may have
been the City beaus and the beau apprentices whom Ned Ward loved to
mock. Their wigs, he said, were so full of powder that they looked "party-
coloured," and their coats were cut full "to show they had more cloth in
the skirts of one tunica, than any of their ancestors wore in a whole suit,"
which they could afford "because they were woolen-drapers." They patronized the milliners in the Exchange and paid double so that they could
boast what "singular favors and great encouragements they had received
from the fair lady that sold 'em." They fought to get into the pit at the
theater "when the girl is to sing a new bawdy song." Ward also explains
why the perukemakers came so close after the tailors in the list of those
arrested with whores since the "first rate punks" were to be found "sitting
in a head-dressers shop," which was "as seldom to be found without a
whore, as a book-sellers shop in Paul's Churchyard without a parson." In
the second half of the century, the tailors and perukemakers maintained
their reputation when Richard King described the nighthouses as "haunts
for the idle and vicious" that were full of "officers, rakes, barbers, tailors,
apprentices, bullies, and whores."[43]

In the City, the men arrested followed eighty-seven different trades; in
Westminster and Middlesex, it was ninety-one. The fourteen laborers in
Middlesex and Westminster show that some poor men were arrested and
went to whores. But laborers, though they were men who had not been
apprenticed to a trade, sometimes did well enough—they occasionally
even ran a bawdy house. It could be a vague category, though not perhaps
so vague as yeoman and gentleman. The men arrested in different parts
of town reflected the differences in the local economies. The West End
and Wapping were more likely to have soldiers and sailors who had picked
up a woman. Men arrested in the City reflected its economy. A tenser
was not a freeman or citizen, but he had paid a rate for permission to
trade in the City. Ticket porters wore a silver badge, were free of the City,
and gave two sureties of one hundred pounds for their honesty. They
worked for large merchants and bankers and around the Inns of Court,
were trusted with large sums of money, and frequently bailed others. The
brokers in the City were probably not pawnbrokers, but Exchange brokers:
"the word of some of these brokers will pass upon Change for some hundreds of thousands." Some of them were libertines, like Henry Ford, who
was arrested in 1722 and again in 1724. The second time he must have

Table 3.3 Addresses of Men Arrested for Whoring by Constables for the City,
and for Westminster and Middlesex, 1720–29

Address	Westminster and Middlesex	City
West End	135	14
Cripplegate etc.	22	54
City	17	39
Whitechapel	24	14
Wapping	14	1
Southwark	2	7
Elsewhere	30	7
Unknown	152 (38.4%)	62 (31.3%)

Source: GLRO: MJ/SR/2340–2525; CLRO, SR, 1720–29.

been quite angry when the constable took him as he was going into a
bawdy house with his whore, so he abused him. On the previous occasion,
the bawdy house he used had been raided.[44]

Men, from the addresses they gave, seem to have gone to whores in
one of the bawdy house areas near to home (table 3.3). Most of the men
who lived in West End parishes were arrested by constables from Westminster. Most of the men with City addresses were arrested by City constables; but it is not likely that there were houses in their own parishes
to go to; they had used the bawdy houses in the City's northern and western suburbs. The men who lived in Whitechapel and Wapping seem to
have used the bawdy houses in their own areas since they were seldom
arrested by City constables. The men from Southwark used the houses
there, since they were usually arrested by City constables. But for the visitor from out of town, it is apparent that the houses around Cripplegate
or those in Whitechapel and Wapping had little appeal. Four out of five
of them were arrested in the West End.

Wapping's bawdy houses were for the sailors. In the 1720s, thirty-three
men gave recognizances after being arrested there with a woman. Fifteen
of these gave an occupation; ten of them were sailors or connected to
shipmaking: seven sailors, two mast makers, and a shipwright. The bawdy
houses disturbed their respectable neighbors since the women stood at
the doors of the houses, trying to pick up men as they went by. John
Tennant, who kept a house, beat his neighbor John Browne when he
complained. Mary Ganston went out and picked up men for the house
she ran. Shadwell, which was next door to Wapping, was full of similar

houses; and so was Stepney up above it. In these two areas, English sailors mixed with Portuguese, Greek, Spanish, and East Indian sailors, or lascars. There were frequent fights between the various groups of sailors, usually over women. They hacked away at each other with their knives and sometimes demolished the bawdy house where the fight had begun.[45]

These East End houses were particularly difficult to police since the sailors' loyalty to each other and to the women made them very likely to riot. Still the magistrates tried. There was the occasional rounding up, for example, sixty women in Shadwell in 1759. There was occasional resistance, especially in a year like 1763 when the town was full of sailors released at the end of a war. Four sailors were killed in that September when they tried to rescue four prostitutes on their way to the Clerkenwell bridewell. Earlier in the year, there had been another riot when a number of bawdy houses were raided and prostitutes and sailors were arrested. The magistrates were threatened, and the soldiers called out. The men's officers managed to persuade them to disperse, but they rescued the women as they were taken to prison.[46]

The violence of sailors was easily turned against the women themselves or the bawdy-house keepers when they felt that they had not been dealt with fairly. "Docking" was a punishment inflicted on a prostitute who venereally infected a sailor: "it consists of cutting off all their clothes, petticoat, shift and all, close to their stays and then turning them into the street." Sailors who left their own neighborhood and ventured into the West End seem to have been particularly offended when misused. They were likely to return with a mob of others to demolish the bawdy houses. In 1749 two sailors who had been robbed returned with others and invaded a bawdy house in the Strand. The soldiers were called out, and by three in the morning the sailors were dispersed. But four hundred sailors returned in a day or two, marched down the Strand, and threatened to pull down all the bawdy houses. The riots continued for one day more. Twelve years later, in 1761, a sailor who was beaten by three of the bullies who belonged to a bawdy house in Eagle Court, just off the Strand, returned with a group of sailors the next day. When they could not find the bullies, they demolished the house. The keepers of other nearby bawdy houses now shut them up for fear that they would also be attacked. But the sailors only broke their shutters, doors, and windows. The next day the keepers moved out all their effects, expecting that the sailors would return on yet one more night.[47]

Pulling down bawdy houses in the early seventeenth century had been notoriously the business of London's apprentices, not of the sailors.[48] In the eighteenth century, the apprentices had a different relationship to the whores, and it is important to try to understand why. This new relationship was probably the result of three factors. The increase in streetwalking made it easier to pick up a woman, and many youths walked the streets themselves for mere entertainment. Secondly their masters were less likely to try to control their sexual behavior: the decline of patriarchal feeling made the apprentice more of an employee and less a member of the family. Apprenticeship was less common in general, and those who were apprenticed were less likely to live with their masters. They left at eight in the evening and were then on their own.[49] All this is confirmed by the decline and eventual disappearance of complaints by masters that their apprentices had been seduced by a whore or the keeper of a bawdy house. In Westminster and Middlesex, there were about two complaints a year in the 1720s. These continued to be made in the 1730s, but thereafter they stopped. This decline may have been the result of a sense that private sexual behavior ought not to be punished, and certainly complaints of adultery and of men for whoring also stopped at the same time. But it may also have been that masters increasingly felt that the adolescent males under their care needed sexual experience with women to establish their heterosexual identities.

The anxieties that the heightened concern over sodomy between males aroused in men of all ages were probably most intense for the adolescents who were newly apprenticed. Apprenticeship and puberty both began at fifteen; and boys from that age, and until they reached their early twenties, were the ones most likely to be approached by an adult sodomite. It is probable therefore that picking up a woman in this period of life came to have a deeper significance than before, since it was the best proof that one was not a sodomite. In addition, adolescents from the early eighteenth century were warned that masturbation had very destructive moral and physical consequences. Sex with a whore might be improvident, but it was at least healthy. Caught between the fear of sodomy on one hand, and of masturbation on the other, the London adolescent was likely to want to prove himself by picking up a prostitute, who would probably be a girl of his own age. This was easier to do than ever before since his master would not check on his behavior and since the streets were full of women plying.

It is apparent, nonetheless, that in the very early eighteenth century something of the traditional patriarchal relationship still existed between master and apprentice, and this was reflected in the desire to control the apprentice's connection to the world of prostitution.[50] There were certain refrains that recurred in the complaints to the magistrates. Seduction was an offense against good neighborhood: Hannah Mansley deluded "her neighbors' sons and apprentices"; Mary Parker seduced "her neighbors' sons and apprentices to her bawdy house, entertaining them whole nights with lewd women." Whoring was also improvident. Roger and Mary Phillips said that Elizabeth Jones had made their son-in-law and apprentice spend "several sums of money on her." Rose Hall and her daughter Elizabeth encouraged servants and apprentices to come to their house and enticed them "to spend their time and money" in their company. Masters who disapproved of such behavior in apprentices did not necessarily disapprove of whoring. Colin Wicks had his apprentice James Newton arrested when he found that the young man had taken a woman to a bawdy house, even though six months before Wicks had picked up Elizabeth Eyres and taken her to the Dean's Head, a well-known bawdy house, where he was arrested with her in a private room by the constables who searched the house and found two other couples there. It was a case of do as I say and not as I do.[51]

The young men most likely to resist the lure of the women in the street were those who had strong religious ties. Sir John Fryer complained that during his apprenticeship from 1685 to 1692, when he was between fourteen and twenty-one, his master had not made him sit in church where he could see him. Instead he met the neighboring apprentices and learned to spend his time as they did. They talked in the gallery during the service and sometimes went walking about the streets, and a few times he "was prevailed with by a loose companion to go to a public house on the sabbath day." Samuel Wesley recalled that the conversation in such a public house in 1693 was "fulsomely lewd and profane." But Fryer had a religious mother who had taken great pains with her only surviving child; he met another boy who was also religious, and together they went to the services at the Dissenting meetinghouses. Fryer turned out a success: his friend did not.[52]

There were masters who were more than merely indifferent and who sought to directly undermine the religious beliefs of their apprentices. John Swain was apprenticed to George Gorget, a fanstickmaker in Russell Street. Swain said that his master had tried to persuade him that "there is neither God nor devil, heaven nor hell." Gorget said that "the Scriptures were written by printers and that they set their apprentice boys to print the same when they had nothing else to do." He thought that the ministers of the Gospel were "dark lanterns and deceivers of the people." He held that there was "no harm in an oath" and that divine retribution would not follow perjury, and therefore "he would swear anything to serve a friend if he was sure not to be found out." John Hays, who ran a chandler's shop, was an "avowed atheist." He told the two young men in his house that the soul was not immortal, and that "men and women died like the brutes." He would not allow his wife to go to church. In neither of these two cases, however, is it possible to show that this religious skepticism was tied to sexual libertinism. Hays, however, did not seem to accept that sex should lead to procreation: he murdered two of his newborn children and left a third child to be brought up by others.[53]

But even a religious and ambitious young man, with no time or money to lose, could eventually feel the lure of the women in the streets. Dudley Ryder in 1715 was twenty-three years old, or about eight years past puberty. He had earned a degree abroad and was diligently reading for the bar. He came from a family of pious and prosperous Dissenting tradesmen. He went frequently to various Dissenting chapels, though he did remark that he could not bear the way his cousin Bilbo led the prayers: "I am always in pain for him when I hear him pray." He took advantage of occasions for discreetly lubricious conversation. When a cousin gave birth to a child, two male cousins came to visit, and together all three men talked about "matrimony and the pleasures and delights of the flesh." He also went to plays, which the strictly religious would have disapproved of as sexually stimulating. But the stimulation was not simply in the text of the plays. The theater was located in the heart of the Covent Garden bawdy houses, and the whores always stood in the passage to the theater and touched Ryder as he walked along. It flurried him when they spoke to him, even after he had thought in advance that this would happen. From time to time he considered talking to one of them on his way home at night as a means of giving himself "assurance and confidence." Eventually, as he walked along Fleet Street, full of the assurance that drinking in a tavern had given him, he "had a mind to attack a whore and did so." He walked a way with her and talked "tolerably well" with her. He then left her and tried the same thing with another girl. But all the while he was uneasy that "somebody that knows me should have seen me."

The conversations at his weekly club were especially stimulating. The members came as close as possible to justifying prostitution as they could by talking of polygamy. One man thought that polygamy was lawful and that there was no need for marriage to be lifelong. Ryder disagreed. But nonetheless, when he left between eleven and twelve, he was "so raised with our discourse about women" that he looked for a whore, with "a resolution not to lie with her but to feel her if I could." But he was relieved that he found no one. His hesitations annoyed him. His brother William was quite different: he seemed "to have no manner of regard to anything of decency on this side of downright bawdy." But Ryder had to admit that he could not "help envying him" and was "vexed" that he could not be satisfied with his "own superior merit." Religion and ambition, it is clear, placed powerful restraints on a young man's sexuality, even when the ability to conquer a whore might seem the measure of manly assurance.[54]

Poorer boys, with less to lose, and a great deal less religion, behaved quite differently, especially as the century moved on. Francis Place was apprenticed in 1785 at the age of fourteen. His father, who kept a public house, was severe with his sons, beating them frequently, determined that they should be respectable. He sent them to church as children but evidently did not go himself. Place's schoolmaster taught his students the New Testament, but he always separated morals from faith in a way that made Place later conclude that his master had never fully accepted the dogmas of religion. His teaching did inspire his student to be industrious and humane and to think things out for himself. Place eventually read Hume, who settled him in his skepticism. But his eldest sister, and the one friend from his apprenticeship years who turned out well, both became Methodists.[55]

The man to whom Place was apprenticed was a breeches maker and must have moved in the world of libertine tailors. He was certainly improvident. All his children were disreputable: the girls were whores and the sons were thieves. It was a neighborhood around Charing Cross and Fleet Street where, as Place said again and again, it was not unusual for the girls to have sex before marriage. There was, nonetheless, a sharp distinction between the girls one eventually married and the young whores who walked the streets. His master exercised no supervision over his young apprentice outside of his work. Like the other boys, he roamed the streets at night and was simply required to be in at ten, and then at eleven, and then as he liked. Place belonged to a gang of fifteen to twenty other apprentices who, with money in their pockets, would go up Fleet Street, shouting and clearing the pavement of everyone else. They were "fine men" to the prostitutes who walked Fleet Street, spending money on them, and sometimes receiving money from them. He also went to the low bawdy houses where the prostitutes wore no stays, "their gowns were low, round and open in front to expose their breasts"; some women did not wear handkerchiefs over their breasts in the summer; and consequently "the breasts of many of them hung down in a most disgusting manner." The women were frequently drunk and fought among themselves and with the men. Something in all this must have repelled the young Place. But it was certainly not the restraints of Christian religion. It was perhaps ambition. But whatever the origins of that particular drive, it does not seem to have been found in many others of his circle. Place noted that most of his fellow apprentices did not come to a good end, nor did his brother or his sisters. He instead married early, at nineteen, gave up his loose ways, and entered upon a provident and successful life. Sex and success did not go together. And religious skepticism was as likely to breed restraint as it did libertinism, even in a tailor.[56]

The improvidence of the behavior and the damage done to men's families were always the principal complaints of respectable poor women against whoring. The first Society for the Reformation of Manners seems to have had its origins in a voluntary society against prostitution and its effects that was formed in the parishes of the East End in 1691. Its broadside proclaimed that sons and servants were being tempted to debauchery; a man's debts were left unpaid; there was no bread for his children; and he was likely to infect his wife with venereal disease. Throughout the century other such voluntary neighborhood associations appeared with similar purposes: there was one around Covent Garden in 1764. When a woman in the 1720s charged a whore with seducing her husband (as opposed to saying that another woman was living with her husband), it was usually the economic deprivation of his family that was emphasized. Mary Marks had three children who were about to become chargeable to the parish because their father was keeping company with Elizabeth Unwin, a street prostitute. Mary Ellis was a Drury Lane whore who was ruining the life of Thomas Brickett's wife and family. But wives also complained of venereal infection. Sarah Sherwood prosecuted Mary Carraway for infecting her husband. Mary Fletcher had given the disease to Thomas Taylor, and he had passed it on to his wife. In both these cases, the wife, or even the couple together, focused their anger on the other woman. But Bridget Wildgoose was angry with her husband. He had beaten and bruised her. He gave her nothing to live on. Instead, he spent what he earned on lewd women and gave her the foul disease.[57]

Mary Morris showed how forceful a woman could be in reclaiming her husband. By 1751 she had been married for more than twenty years to John Morris, who was a clockmaker in Whitechapel. After John stayed out all night—"a thing," Mary said, "he was seldom guilty of"—she went through Whitechapel looking for him in the public houses she knew he frequented; but he was not in any of them. She met a man called Cowell, an old friend who came from the same county. He saw how distressed

she was, and when she said she was looking for her husband, he told her
that he had seen John two hours before. John was going to John Mills's,
a sheriff's officer, who kept a house of women in Bridges Street, Covent
Garden. Cowell agreed to show Mary the way, but he would not go in,
since he did not want John to know who had told her where to find him.
Mary entered, brushed past a woman who asked her business, said she
was looking for her husband, and went down into the kitchen, from which
voices came. John was sitting there with a woman on his knee, her arm
around his neck. Mary claimed that she then said: "John, will you please
to come home, I think it would be much better for you to be there with
your family than in such a place as this." At this Hester Mills (the wife
of the man whose house it was) said to her: "Damn you, you bitch, you
have no husband here; I have known this man for above this half year";
she added that the woman on John's knee had more right to him than
Mary did. Hester Mills, however, remembered the exchange differently.
She, of course, denied that her house was a bawdy house, and she said
that the three other women were her lodgers. Mary, according to her, had
burst into the kitchen as she was ironing and had said to John: "So you
rogue, what, I have catched you with your whores and spending my
money." To this Hester Mills supposedly replied that there were no
whores in the house, and that if John were her husband, she should peace-
fully take him away.

But it is likely that Hester Mills had not been nearly as pacific as that.
Mary said that she came up to her, thrust her out of the kitchen, and
pushed her against a bedstead. Mary, who was five months pregnant, cried
out and fell heavily to the floor. Mills kicked her in the small of the back,
and she cried out murder. At this point Mary's husband got up and ran
out of the house. The candle was snuffed out, and someone, probably
Mills, kicked Mary repeatedly in the dark as she lay on the ground. Cowell, Mary's neighbor, now came down into the kitchen and said, "What,
have you murdered the woman!" But Mills replied, "Damn her for a bitch,
what does she come here for after a man with whom she has nothing to
do." Cowell now took Mary out to a neighboring house; her bruises were
bathed; and someone came to bleed her as a precaution. They took her
home in a coach. She spent three weeks in bed, and a month later was
delivered of a child two months before she was due.[58]

The straying husband and the debauched apprentice who went to
whores certainly offended against Christian monogamy and worldly pru-
dence. But what they did with the women in the bawdy houses shows
that their sexual imaginations usually operated within the constraints of

the traditional Christian ideal that taught that sexuality ought to be tied to procreation and monogamous marriage. One hundred and ninety-seven men were arrested by the City constables in the 1720s. From their recognizances we can say what they were found doing. One man had attempted "unheard of lewdness" with a woman that was probably anal intercourse. One man had just been whipped; the rods were there for evidence. One woman was "stark naked." One man was being shown lewd postures by two women, and on another occasion, two men were similarly entertained by two women. Six men were unambiguously stated to have been found in the sexual act in the public street. (This is probably an understatement: 14 percent of all men were arrested in the street.) Three men were found in bawdy houses having sex on a Sunday morning during the "time of divine service." In three instances two men were found with one woman, and in fourteen cases, a man was "lying in state" with two women. All together, these cases make a total of thirty-one unusual sexual situations. In 166 instances (84 percent), one man was with one woman; they were indoors at night; they were at least partially clothed; and the sexual act they engaged in was probably vaginal penetration with the man on top of the woman.

The English were certainly instructed in other coital positions. The posture girls demonstrated them in the bawdy houses. When Nicholas Venette's sex manual was revised in the 1770s for an English audience of men apparently low on the social scale, descriptions of sex with the man on top, the couple standing or sitting, the woman on top, the couple lying on their sides, and penetration from the back with the woman on all fours were all given. Sitting and standing were disapproved because of the physical strain and the likelihood that conception would be hindered. The woman astride was rejected as base in a man since he gave up his power. The couple on their sides, and the woman on all fours, were approved when the man was too heavy or fat, or the woman was pregnant. But face to face with the man on top was described as the "common posture . . . which is most allowable and most voluptuous." It was probably the case that many of the couples who had sex in the streets did so in some sort of standing position, but this was not necessarily so. William Murrock said that a woman took him to the end of Cucumber Alley, "where she laid herself down upon her back." It is also probable that men were not likely to have sex with prostitutes who were so far advanced in pregnancy that it was convenient to use the position on all fours. (It was used between husbands and wives, and lovers, but it was controversial.) John Cleland did have one scene in which a young man has a woman sit astride him.

But this was an exceptional couple: the woman was stark naked, and she fellated the man as well. The woman was English, but the man, a "lazy young rogue," was an Italian, who enjoyed "her in a taste peculiar to the heat, or perhaps the caprices of his own country." It is unclear whether the total nudity or the position astride were the more surprising. Cleland, on the other hand, never described sex between a man and two women. Even in his orgies, the couples have sex only with each other as others look on. It would therefore be very interesting to know what happened when a man lay in state with two women. When two or more men had sex with one woman, on the other hand, it is very likely that they simply took turns at vaginal intercourse (as described in a subsequent rape case), since the taboos against sodomy and fellatio would have made difficult the sorts of ensembles that appear in the vase painting of the ancient Greeks. But voyeurism must have been more acceptable, as the men must have watched each other. They would have had some experience of this since they had often started their sexual lives in a circle of adolescent masturbators, and the showing of lewd postures was shocking but certainly not in the way that sodomy was.[59]

But most men who went to whores clearly had an encounter that did not stray far from a sexual act that was at that moment monogamous: there is even the later statement of a man to a whore that he would make her a good husband; and the act itself was potentially procreative. It was a sexuality that contemporaries would have called "natural." Whether one wrote for a libertine or a (supposedly) religious audience, it was always within the context of this natural sexuality. This can be seen in *Aristotle's Masterpiece*, which in its various editions was the best-known introduction to sex for young men. Francis Place by the time he was thirteen understood most of what happened in sexual intercourse from what he had overheard in the relatively frank conversation of adults. But for what he did not understand (such as the account of the miraculous conception of Jesus in the Gospels), he sought enlightenment in *Aristotle's Masterpiece*. He borrowed a copy, probably because he could not afford to buy one of the ones openly sold on the bookstalls. But a boy he knew clearly owned the book, and on the flyleaf of one of the copies in the British Library, another boy has signed his name over and over again, looking, no doubt, for personal identity through sexual knowledge. Most of *Aristotle's Masterpiece* in its first edition (probably in the late 1680s) took the form of a midwifery book describing the way that children were conceived and born. The female sexual organs were not described until page 99, and the male organs came even later on pages 172–44 and in a much smaller print.

The second edition that first appeared about 1710 had a similar emphasis on childbearing but was reorganized to begin with a description of the female sexual organs; it thereby more clearly distinguished itself from a midwifery book. It probably was intended to compete with the first translations of Venette's sex manual (1703) and John Marten's English imitation (1709) of that book, for which Marten was unsuccessfully prosecuted. The third version of *Aristotle's Masterpiece* in 1725 was rearranged again. This one began with a description of the male sexual organs that presumably was meant to heighten its appeal to a male audience. It had become less of a book on female diseases. But it still placed sex in the context of marriage and went back to Adam and Eve in Paradise.[60]

The libertines who wrote and bought these books, and the reformers who opposed and prosecuted them, had more in common with regard to sex than they realized. Libertine sexuality was usually procreative and natural. But the reformers opposed even ordinary whoring on the ground that it was unnatural, just as they opposed all kinds of sex in marriage that was not procreative in either form or intention. These two points of view can be seen in John Dunton and Daniel Defoe. Dunton was one of the promoters of the Societies for the Reformation of Manners and published a series of dialogues with male and female libertines. He had two basic points. The growth of religious skepticism in the form of Socinianism, deism, and atheism had encouraged sexual libertinism. Libertinism was contrary to divine law as represented in God's institution of marriage in Paradise between one man and one woman; and it violated the natural law that had designed sexuality for the procreation of children in marriage. His opponents, as he presented them, took the opposing view. Like Dudley Ryder's friends, they justified prostitution by comparing it to polygamy. A libertine priest, who disapproved of the reformation societies as "Presbyterians in masquerade," pointed out that polygamy had been "practiced by the best of men in the Old Testament, and he could never understand that it was repealed in the New." Dunton's answer was that God had winked at such acts but that now he called men to repentance; and furthermore the example of Adam and Eve had priority over that of the patriarchs. An older man did not bother to argue from Scripture but said that the English were monogamous and the Turks polygamous, simply because of a difference in customs that could not be justified by the "impertinent cant" of the religious. He said that he believed in God, but that he looked more to the example of his neighbors than the teaching of the Bible.

Others told Dunton that they were honest in their dealings with their neighbors, and that beyond that, they saw no harm in "satisfying the appetites of nature." But there was clearly a dispute as to what a natural sexuality was. For Dunton it was unnatural not to marry and procreate. But two young milliners, who sometimes worked as prostitutes, said to him that "everybody knew that all men and women were inclinable to bear one another company by nature." The wife of a sailor who was at sea went out looking for men because she "knew no reason why she should abridge herself of natural pleasures, seeing her husband took so little care of her." A young lawyer (Dunton said the Inns of Court bred Socinians, deists, and libertines, who were "practical atheists") was slightly more circumspect about the right of men to have women: he held that as "for women, provided there was no encroachment upon another man's property, he knew no hurt in the use them."[61]

If nature were taken to mean the feeling of desire, then prostitution and most forms of sex outside of marriage were justified: this was the libertine view held by both the educated and the simple. For such people the question of the teaching of the Bible did not arise, and when it did, there was the polygamy of the patriarchs to justify their desires. But for the reformers, sexual behavior was to be justified not in terms of the desire that inspired it: Christian tradition had long held such desire evil. Sex, instead, could be justified as natural only because it led eventually to the procreation of children.

Daniel Defoe therefore was anxious to say that desire as such had no role in Christian marriage: a husband driven by desire alone would be guilty of "matrimonial whoredom." Defoe, like Dunton, was inspired by the reformation societies: he began his book in the 1690s and published it in 1727. For Defoe, the law of nature had designed sex for propagation; the law of God had added to that the requirement of monogamy. Sexual behavior in marriage always had to be tied to procreation. It was therefore unnatural to have sex during menstruation and pregnancy and immediately after childbirth since children could not be conceived at those times. It was also unlawful to marry if one did not intend to have children, and all means to that end, like abortion and contraception, were illicit. It also followed that persons who were too old to have children should not marry.

In Defoe's case, however, the four chapters in which this traditional doctrine was set out were balanced by seven chapters insisting that the procreative aim of marriage could not be achieved unless the two partners had freely married each other for love. In this idea—to which some of the reformers were quite opposed, and to which some libertines subscribed—lay the seeds that would produce the modern justification of sexual desire. The plays of the 1690s were full of the doctrine of romantic love. But the reformers thought the playhouses unnaturally inflamed desire: John Dunton's libertines always had lots of playbooks when he visited them. Jeremy Collier, who led the attack on the stage after 1698, was quite opposed to romantic courtship. But by 1750 romantic courtship had fully justified itself, and this had presumably made sexual desire easier to accept. Romantic marriage, however, was monogamous marriage. There was, as we shall see, little room in its world for prostitution, even when sex with many women might be justified by the example of the polygamy of the patriarchs. But romantic love in the eighteenth century seems to have had its impact mainly on the landed and the middle classes. The sailors, tailors, and apprentices described in this chapter were therefore unlikely to have felt the tension between romance and prostitution that is described in a subsequent chapter. Their exclusive heterosexuality could therefore pursue the women in the streets, constrained only by the necessity of providing for their families and the fear of disease.[62]

CHAPTER FOUR

Prostitution: Numbers and Topography

T he only steady occupants of the world of prostitution were the prostitutes and the bawdy-house keepers. Male libertines and the constables entered and left this world at will. This chapter therefore begins with three questions about the women: how many were there, when did they start their lives as prostitutes, and how long did they last? It then turns to the bawdy houses and inquires as to their numbers, their location, and the identity of their keepers.

THE NUMBER OF PROSTITUTES

Saunders Welch, one of the reforming magistrates, estimated in 1758 that if one computed the number of women "whose sole dependence is upon prostitution," then three thousand would be a number that "falls far short of the truth." Two years later Jonas Hanway, one of the two founders of the Magdalen Hospital, agreed that "it is generally computed that there are 3,000 common prostitutes in these cities." At the time, the population of the city had grown to 675,000.[1] These men must have based their estimates on the number of women they saw on the streets and the number who were arrested. We cannot see the women, but we can look at the arrests.

From the middle of the 1690s to the middle of the 1720s, the Societies for the Reformation of Manners were very active in promoting the arrests of prostitutes, both those in bawdy houses and those who plied the streets. The societies always tended to overstate their successes, but their published lists of those arrested are nonetheless useful. Five lists survive for the first decade of the century, and they show the following numbers of prostitutes arrested: 791 in 1700; 820 in 1701; 805 in 1702; 890 in 1704; 651 in 1707. The lists from 1709 onward are less useful, as they lump

Table 4.1 Commitments of Prostitutes to the Westminster and Middlesex Houses of Correction

Jurisdiction	1720	1721	Total
Westminster	275	152	427
Middlesex	91	114	205
Total	366	266	632

Source: GLRO: MJ/SR/2342, 2343, 2344, 2348, 2349, 2351, 2353, 2354, 2356, 2358, 2361, 2363, 2364, 2366, 2368, 2369, 2373, 2374, 2376, 2378.

Table 4.2 Disposition of Arrested Prostitutes in the City of London, 1729–32

Year	Discharged	Bridewell	Total
1729	12	3	15
1730	16	24	30
1731	5	3	8
1732	7	18	25
Total	40 (45.5%)	48 (54.5%)	88

Source: CLRO: Mansion House Justice Room Charge Book, 1728–33.
Note: There were no arrests listed for 1733.

prostitutes, their customers, and others into a general category of lewd and disorderly men and women. One must therefore turn to the manuscript records.[2]

I looked at sessions rolls for Middlesex and Westminster for the years 1720–29. The house of correction lists survive in full only for 1720 and 1721. These do not tell us the number arrested but only the number committed. It is likely that these 632 women represent about 55 percent of the women arrested (table 4.1). This percentage can be calculated from two sets of magistrate's books that survive for the City. (There are none for Middlesex and Westminster.)

Tables 4.2 and 4.3 show that at two quite different points in time the same policy prevailed of dismissing 40 to 45 percent of those arrested, although the temper of the two periods was quite different. In 1729–32, the Societies for the Reformation of Manners had begun their decline, especially those societies that concentrated on the arrests of prostitutes. In 1730 there were only 251 men and women arrested for lewd behavior. There had usually been from four to eight times that many in 1720–24. The City arrests of prostitutes reflect that decline and averaged 22 a year

Table **4.3** Disposition of Arrested Prostitutes in the City of London, 1785–90

Year	Discharged	Bridewell	Total[a]
1785	46	44	104
1786	40	70	113
1787	63	81	161
1788	65	53	130
1789	24	54	90
1790[b]	73	120	200
Total	331 (41.5%)	422 (52.9%)	798

Source: CLRO: Mansion House Justice Room Minute Books, 1785–90.
   [a] The first two columns do not add up to the total because in 31 cases the disposition is unclear, and because 112 women, some of whom had been sent first to Bridewell, were passed to their parishes.
   [b] Record for 1790 ends with November 8.

in 1729–32. In 1785–90, on the other hand, a new campaign inspired by reforming societies had begun, and arrests averaged 133 a year. Nonetheless in both periods, 40 to 45 percent of the prostitutes arrested were simply discharged by the magistrate. The newspaper accounts from the early 1760s show the magistrates doing the same, at a time when there was once again a drive against prostitution inspired in part by a revival of societies for reformation. In December 1761, thirty men and women were arrested, but only "five of the most abandoned of them were committed to Bridewell." In the next April twenty women were on one occasion arrested, of whom "the most abandoned" were sent to Bridewell and the rest "dismissed upon promise of amendment." Saunders Welch himself can be seen following this policy of committing only "the most abandoned and profligate."[3]

The first thing to notice, then, about those arrested is that only slightly more than half were sent to Bridewell. The second point is that some of those arrested were arrested again and again. In 1720, for instance, there were 366 commitments to Bridewell in Westminster and Middlesex, but only 320 different women committed. Twenty-nine women (or 9 percent) had been committed more than once. Six more of the women were committed again in another year; and more of them may have been committed, since the lists survive capriciously after 1721. Of the women committed in 1720, it can be shown (at a minimum) that between 1720 and 1724, sixteen were committed twice, ten three times, five four times, and four of them six times. Some women can by chance be traced over what looks like the course of their careers as prostitutes. Constant Hilton was arrested at least five times in 1720: in February, March, May, July, and August; twice in the street, and three times in a bawdy house, on one of which occasions she was with a man. In February, she spent three days to a week in the Tothill Fields Bridewell. In March she was arrested with Jane Hilton, who may have been her sister. In May she spent two weeks in Bridewell, in July three days, and in August four days. Jane Hilton was in Bridewell only once in 1721. Constant does not appear again after August 1720. But in 1714 a Constance Hilton (who is probably the same person) gave a recognizance because she had been arrested for nightwalking and raising a riot around the constables when they took her. Patrick Pyot, who was a horse grenadier (or soldier) stationed in Westminster, stood bail for her.[4] Hilton had had a career of at least seven years. Catherine Oar lasted at least ten years. She was sent to Bridewell in March 1720, twice in November, and again in February and March 1722. She shows up for the last time in the records I have seen in March 1729.[5]

In the City at the end of the century there was a similar pattern. Between November 1784 and November 1787, 385 arrests were made. Forty-one names appeared more than once, half of them twice, the others from three to six times. This suggests that 309 different women were arrested and that 41 of them (13 percent) were arrested more than once. Mary Flannagan was arrested in January 1786 and sent to Bridewell for a month. In July she was sentenced to two weeks for picking up men and making a riot. By August she was out again, arrested once more, and sentenced this time to a month. She turned up again the next year in October, when she was sent to Bridewell for two weeks on the second of the month and again on the twenty-fifth for the same length of time.

We can now say that when the constables rounded up these women, 10 to 15 percent would have been experienced prostitutes who had been arrested many times over the course of a career that may have lasted for as many as ten years. Another 40 percent seemed hardened enough to be sent to one of the bridewells. But the remaining 40 to 45 percent were discharged after a warning and sometimes after promising not to appear on the streets again. Who were these women? And how did the hardened and the inexperienced fit together in the world of prostitution? It is likely, first of all, that the principal difference between the 40 percent discharged and the 40 percent committed even though they did not have a record of many arrests was a difference in age. The ones discharged were probably

Table 4.4 Age, Career, and Parents of 25 Prostitutes Arrested May 1, 1758

Age	Time as Prostitute	Whereabouts of Parents	Age	Time as Prostitute	Whereabouts of Parents
15	3 years	Mother dead; father at sea	19	1 year	None
15	2 months	Mother poor; father at sea	19	2 years	None
15	18 months	None	19	5 years	None
16	4 years	Mother dead; father at sea	19	5 weeks	None
16	2 years	None	19	1 year	None
16	2 years	Deserted by parents	19	1½ years	None
16	2½ years	Both dead	20	2 years	None
17	2 months	None	20	6 months	In the country
18	6 months	In Scotland	20	1 year	Deserted by both
18	3 months	Mother dead; father at sea	21	6 years	None
18	2 years	Mother left her; father dead	21	3 years	Deserted by both
18	3 years	Mother dead; father at sea	22	1 year	None
18	3 weeks	Mother ran away; father dead			

Source: John Fielding, *A Plan of the Asylum or House of Refuge for Orphans and Other Deserted Girls of the Poor of the Metropolis* (London, 1758), p. 18, cited by Francis Place: British Library, Add. MSS, 27825, fol. 245.

the very young ones. Unfortunately, the ages of prostitutes were never given in the records of arrest and commitment. There are, however, two samplings of their ages, both problematical, but useful as far as they go.

In 1758 Sir John Fielding, the most famous of the reforming ministers, gave an account of the ages of twenty-five girls arrested on May 1, 1758 (table 4.4). Fielding did not say how these twenty-five women were chosen, and he was intent on using them to prove the necessity for an orphan asylum. One of Fielding's contemporary critics—a reformed rake—also said that he had confined his attention to the starving wretches to be found in Drury Lane, Hedge Lane, and St. Giles and had ignored the better-off women in the houses in Bow Street and Covent Garden.[6] But in fact the ages of the women in *Harris's List of Covent Garden Ladies* (1788) are quite comparable with Fielding's of a generation earlier. Ages were given for forty-one of ninety-two women (table 4.5).

The principal difference between the two lists seems to be that the women who served gentlemen were more likely to survive into their later twenties, and in a few cases, even beyond that. But in both lists most of the women clustered around the ages of eighteen to twenty: fourteen of twenty-five in one list, and twenty of forty-one in the other. In neither list, however, are there girls under fourteen, and this is probably a serious misrepresentation. Fielding himself in another work said that it was not unusual when forty prostitutes were arrested on a "search night" to find that "the major part of them have been . . . under the age of eighteen, many not more than twelve." It was enough to move even a rake: "What a deplorable sight is it to behold numbers of little creatures piled up in heaps upon one another, sleeping in the public streets, in the most rigorous seasons, and some whose heads will hardly reach above the waistband of a man's breeches, found to be quick with child." These very young girls could be found walking the streets in groups with their bully, or male protector: a soldier was taken in Fleet Market with five girls about thirteen or fourteen years of age. There were also specialized bawdy houses, like the one kept by Mary Kelly with its four minors. But the two lists probably both started with fifteen because throughout the century fourteen and fifteen were given as the usual ages of puberty in girls. One physician added that puberty could come as early as thirteen and as late as sixteen. At all levels of society, a woman was taken to be most sexually attractive between fifteen and twenty-five, with nineteen or so as something of a peak. Aristocratic girls entered society and the marriage market at fifteen. But it was all over by twenty-eight. Anne Elliot smiled at her lover's well-meaning "blunder" when he said she had not altered from the girl of nineteen whom he had first courted: "it is something for a woman to be assured in her eight-and-twentieth year," Jane Austen wrote, "that she has not lost one charm of earlier youth."[7]

There is an early-nineteenth-century source for the ages of prostitutes

Table 4.5 Ages of Prostitutes in Two Lists

	Number			Number	
Age	1758	1788	Age	1758	1788
15	3	1	23	0	1
16	4	4	24	0	1
17	1	4	25	0	3
18	5	6	26	0	2
19	6	6	27	0	0
20	3	8	28	0	2
21	2	1	. . .		
22	1	0	40	0	2

Source: John Fielding, *A Plan of the Asylum or House of Refuge for Orphans and Other Deserted Girls of the Poor of the Metropolis* (London, 1758), p. 18, British Library, Add. MSS, 27825; *Harris's List of Covent Garden Ladies* (London, 1788).

Table 4.6 Ages of 111 Prostitutes in the City of London Bridewell, 1818

Age	Number	Age	Number	Age	Number
14	1	23	6	32	5
15	0	24	1	33	2
16	1	25	3	34	0
17	1	26	10	35	5
18	11	27	9	36	3
19	12	28	4	...	
20	0	29	6	54	1
21	10	30	7		
22	13	31	0		

Source: Parliamentary Papers, *Third Report from the Committee on the State of the Police of the Metropolis* (London, June 5, 1818), p. 30.

that tends to confirm that Fielding's sweep had not gathered up the older women in their twenties, who were still on the street even though their bloom may have faded. In 1818 the Guardian Society visited the London Bridewell and interviewed 111 women. There were no girls younger than fourteen, probably because such girls were not committed. Table 4.6 tends to confirm what the contrast between Fielding's numbers and those from *Harris's List* suggests. In the 1818 list, the women of eighteen to twenty-two were 41 percent of the total. But the women of twenty-three to thirty were just as many. In this list it must have been the girls under eighteen who were considerably underrepresented.

The girls under eighteen probably made up most of those who were simply discharged by the magistrates with a warning. But the women of eighteen, nineteen, and twenty, who must have made up most of those sent to the house of correction, fell into two groups: the old offenders who were repeatedly arrested, and the remainder. This remainder were probably 40 percent of those arrested. They can be explained in two different ways. Some of them may have been women who were taking their first walks on the street. One-third of the young women, for instance, who became pregnant with bastards (137 of 373) in the parish of St. Margaret's, Westminster, between 1712 and 1721 went to a disreputable public house either in their own neighborhood or around Covent Garden on the first occasion that they had sex with the man who fathered their child. They usually claimed that they had not had sexual relations with any other man. But it is also possible that unlike the other two-thirds of the pregnant women in their parish, they had not known the man before that first encounter. They had very likely been picked up in the street.[8]

But there is a second explanation possible. The 40 percent sent to bridewell only once may have been the women who went back and forth between the worlds of prostitution and respectable labor. John Dunton claimed in 1697 to have met two young women who explained that "we sometimes work to the change, and at other times to seamstresses, and now and then for gallants." Defoe a generation later described what he called the "amphibious life" of servants who "rove from place to place, from bawdy-house to service, and from service to bawdy-house again, ever unsettled and never easy": "if the bawd uses them ill, away they trip to service, and if their mistress gives them a wry word, whip they're at a bawdy house again." Defoe's explanation was quoted (without acknowledgment) a generation later by an experienced rake as "one of the chief reasons why our streets swarm with strumpets." Ann Pullen (alias Rawlinson) was an actual example of such a servant. She was an industrious servant, but when her master and mistress were in bed, she would "turn out and walk the streets, dressed in her mistress's best clothes, till four in the morning."[9]

The humanitarian movement that tried to remove these great numbers of young women from the streets, and to cure them of venereal disease, produced in the middle years of the century two other sets of figures that help us to see the numbers involved. The Lock Hospital was founded in 1747 to cure the poor of venereal disease. It was limited to those who could not claim a London settlement and would not therefore be treated in one of the London workhouses. Admissions were equally divided between men and women. About 15 percent of the women were wives infected by their husbands, and there were also a number of children infected by individuals in the belief that sexual relations with a virgin would cure the disease. No one could be admitted more than once—otherwise the hospital might have lost support on the ground that it encouraged vice. In the twenty-four years between 1747 and 1774, the hospital treated 10,897 patients. If half of these were men, and some were wives and children, this leaves approximately four thousand young unmarried women, most of whom were prostitutes. In a similar and partly overlapping period of twenty-six years (1758–84), the Magdalen Hospital, which sought to rescue the younger prostitute who was not yet diseased, admitted 2,415 women. If these two institutions between them could in a quarter century have dealt with approximately sixty-five hundred prostitutes, and if some prostitutes had an average career of ten years (from fifteen to twenty-five), Saunders Welch's estimate of three thousand active prostitutes in 1758 seems very likely.[10]

BAWDS AND BAWDY HOUSES

At the end of the seventeenth century, the London bawdy houses had, for the most part, been located in the poor suburbs to the north and west of the old City wall. This conformed to the spatial organization of the traditional city. But the growth of the West End and the emergence of London as a single spatial unit changed this, even though the city was still divided into three separate jurisdictions. London now had two centers of power: the City to the east, and the West End. The poor continued to live primarily to the north and east of the City walls, but they could also be found in pockets throughout the West End. The two centers of power in the eighteenth-century city were connected by the great thoroughfare that ran from Cheapside in the east to St. James's Park in the west. This thoroughfare became the principal place for prostitutes to ply for customers.

By the second half of the century the location of the bawdy houses conformed to this new spatial organization. The bawdy houses in the suburbs north and west of the City wall more or less disappeared. This was partly due to the City's more efficient policing, but since the City never managed to eliminate the streetwalkers from Fleet Street and Cheapside, it is unlikely that policing alone explains the relocation of the bawdy houses. The bawdy houses probably relocated themselves to the opposite ends of the great streetwalking thoroughfare. The areas at the western end of the thoroughfare also expanded from two to three; but at the eastern end, the two traditional areas remained. By the 1770s the three areas in which the bawdy houses in the West End were to be found were St. Margaret's, Westminster, west and south of the abbey; St. Ann Soho and St. James's north of the park; and especially around Covent Garden and the Strand. In the East End, the houses clustered in Whitechapel and Wapping; but these houses were always a distinct minority of the total. This changing pattern can be documented from the arrests and indictments for keeping disorderly houses. But the material from the two periods before and after 1750 is never exactly comparable; there are lacunae within each period; and the West End was always better policed and therefore better documented than the East End. The pattern nonetheless emerges clearly enough.

Table 4.7 Locations of Disorderly Houses, 1720–29

Covent Garden		Clerkenwell and Cripplegate		Whitechapel and Wapping	
Parish	Number of Houses	Parish	Number of Houses	Parish	Number of Houses
St. Giles in the Fields	193	Cripplegate	24	Stepney	36
St. Martin in the Fields	69	Clerkenwell	15	Whitechapel	10
St. Clement Danes	16	Shoreditch	15	Wapping	6
Westminster	11	St. Sepulchre	6	Aldgate	5
St. Ann Soho	1			Shadwell	1
Total	290	Total	60	Total	58
	(71.1%)		(14.7%)		(14.2%)

Source: GLRO: MJ/SBP/11–13.

There is a list of indictments for Westminster and Middlesex in the 1720s, when the Societies for the Reformation of Manners were still quite active. From it one can extract all those indicted for keeping a disorderly house. Not all of these were bawdy houses, but most of them probably were. From the result one can see that there were three principal areas: one around Covent Garden, a second around Cripplegate and Clerkenwell, and a third in Whitechapel and Wapping (table 4.7). The figures certainly underestimate the number of houses that there must have been in Cripplegate and Clerkenwell at the end of the seventeenth century. By 1720 the City magistrates and the societies had been quite active for twenty years. As early as 1697 John Dunton said that their actions had driven the nightwalkers from the City to Long Acre in Covent Garden.[11] But it is also likely that some of the Holborn houses should be grouped with the Clerkenwell area in the 1720s. The list also did not include any indictments for houses in St. Margaret's, Westminster, which is difficult to explain. They certainly were there and show up in the recognizances. In addition, a third of the women who were pregnant with bastard children in St. Margaret's in the years 1712–21 had had sexual relations in a public house, and half of these houses were in or near St. Margaret's. (One-third were around Covent Garden and the Strand, and the remainder elsewhere.) Some houses, like the White Bear in St. Stephen's Alley, just off King Street, had been used by several women; and there were a number of different houses in places like Thieving Lane, Long Ditch, and Peter Street.[12] St. Margaret's was by 1720 already a second nest of bawdy houses in the West End. But St. James's and St. Ann Soho had just begun.

Table 4.8 Locations of Disorderly Houses, 1770–79

Parish	Number of Houses	%	Parish	Number of Houses	%
	Covent Garden			Soho, St. James	
St. Martin in the Fields	149		St. James	23	
St. Paul Covent Garden	51		St. Ann Soho	21	
St. Clement Danes	32		St. George Hanover Square	4	
St. Andrew Holborn	4		Marylebone	2	
Liberty of the Rolls	3		St. George Bloomsbury	1	
St. Mary le Strand	2				
Total	241	71.1	Total	51	15.0
	Westminster			Whitechapel	
St. Margarets	18		Whitechapel	23	
St. John	2		St. George Middlesex	4	
Total	20	5.9	Total	27	8.0

Source: GLRO: MJ/SR/3221–3381.

Fifty years later the recognizances given by those arrested for keeping bawdy houses in the 1770s (table 4.8) allow the first and the second halves of the century to be compared. This is the last point at which this can be done, as many of the Westminster and Middlesex rolls after 1780 have disappeared. The City rolls show that except for the bawdy houses around Fleet Street, there were few houses left in the City. Only five recognizances show up in a year like 1777. By contrast, the recognizances for Middlesex and Westminster document at least 351 houses; there may have been more since some of the rolls in the first half of the decade are in bad condition and cannot be used. These recognizances give a better picture than the indictment lists. In 1755, for instance, there were nine indictments listed, but there are thirty-four recognizances in the rolls.

The most striking change between the two periods was that the houses in the poor suburbs to the north and west of the City wall had disappeared. There were, instead, two areas for bawdy houses at the east and the west ends of the great streetwalking thoroughfare. In the West End, St. James's and Soho had fully developed into an area of their own that was pushing forward into Hanover Square and even into Marylebone. St. Margaret's was now fully documented as a second West End concentration of bawdy houses. But it was Covent Garden that reigned supreme with 71 percent of the houses. Whitechapel in the East End was probably underrepresented with a mere 7 percent of the houses, and Wapping was not even there. But no arrests for Whitechapel were recorded at all in the first half of the decade, whereas three-fourths of those for St. Martin's in the West End had occurred in that period. The attention of constables and magistrates plainly turned from one area to another, with the West End always coming first. In a previous year, 1765, at the end of another drive in the early 1760s, there had been 21 different houses dealt with in St. Martin's; but there were 11 in Whitechapel; and there were 4 in Wapping, which was entirely missing in the arrests for the 1770s. But still in 1765, the West End parishes, overall, accounted for 70 percent of the arrests, as opposed to 30 percent in Whitechapel and Wapping.[13]

The disappearance of the bawdy houses to the north and west of the City wall is confirmed by changes in the incidence of recognizances given by women arrested for prostitution. These recognizances allowed a woman to leave the house of correction. Saunders Welch claimed that after 1752 the bawds bailed their best girls in not less than twenty-four hours. The women who were diseased, or otherwise undesirable, were left to pine away in prison because they "had no friends." It was not, however, literally the female bawds who stood sureties. Sureties were almost always men. They were supposed to swear that they knew the women. Sometimes plainly they did not. In the 1720s Thomas Morris, a laborer from St. Clement Danes, swore that he knew Mary Jenkins, who had been arrested for picking up men in the streets. He did not know her but had been paid a half crown to swear so: it was a common practice with him. Waller Duran, when he stood bail for Bridget King, swore that he lived in Arundell Street, off the Strand, paid thirty-five pounds a year in rent, was worth one hundred pounds, had his debts paid, and was a tailor and victualler. But it was all a lie.[14]

Victuallers, who often ran public houses, were in fact the occupational group most often found among the men who bailed whores (table 4.9). In the City in the decade 1720–29, 433 of the persons who bailed these women can be identified by name, occupation, and address from the recognizances. (One must hope that few of them lied as Morris and Duran had done.) Only 8 of the sureties were women: seven widows and a spinster. There were 120 different occupations given, but most of these appear one to three times. A dozen occupations, on the other hand, accounted for 50 percent of all the men. These were the men in the neighborhood most likely to have sufficient capital from their trade to look substantial enough to the magistrate. The neighbor probably expected such men to stand bail. There is a description of a brandy shop that was "going to

Table 4.9 Most Frequent Occupations of Men Who Stood Bail for Prostitutes in the City, 1720–29

Occupation	Number	Occupation	Number
Victualler	36	Watchmaker	14
Weaver	33	Gentleman	14
Joiner/Carpenter	23	Chandler	11
Ticket Porter	22	Tensor	11
Cordwainer	22	Perukemaker	10
Butcher	14	Silversmith	9

Source: CLRO: SR, 1720–29.

be demolished because the master refuses to bail some whore that's just arrested."[15]

The addresses of these men is our concern. Eighty percent of them can be easily assigned to one of the four then-traditional areas of prostitution. The women they bailed (presumably but not necessarily) had been active in the men's neighborhoods. The largest number (30 percent) of men came from the poor suburbs north and west of the City wall. Almost as many came from around Fleet Street and the West End parishes (28 percent). There were slightly less (21 percent) from the poor parishes east of the City wall (that is, around Aldgate and Bishopsgate). And there were a few from Southwark (2.5 percent).

The women who were bailed were those connected to bawds (male or female), and they were therefore tied to a bawdy house. By contrast, the women arrested elsewhere in London in the 1720s almost never gave recognizances. There were 259 recognizances for prostitutes in the City in that decade, but only 35 for all of Middlesex and Westminster. These two jurisdictions covered a much larger area, and hundreds of women were arrested in them each year, but very few of them were bailed. This was presumably because fewer of the women outside the City's jurisdiction were tied to bawdy houses, since most of those houses were in the City. By the 1770s this had changed entirely. Two years of the City's rolls in that decade (1770 and 1777) had no recognizances at all for prostitutes. By contrast, in the rolls for Westminster and Middlesex in the entire decade, 1770–79, there were at least 694 recognizances given by prostitutes. The women who worked out of houses had moved with those houses and their bawds out of the City's jurisdiction and into the concentrations of bawdy houses at the two opposite ends of London's great streetwalking thoroughfare.

The houses in Whitechapel and Wapping did not appear, however, in the recognizances for prostitutes in the 1770s. These houses are documented only in the recognizances of those charged as bawdy-house keepers. This was, presumably, a result of differences in the policing of the East and West Ends of town. Eighty-eight percent of the women arrested in the West End can be assigned to various areas. The addresses of one-third of the women were actually given. They usually lived in the same area from which their sureties came (often from the same court or street); this justifies assigning women to an area according to the addresses of their sureties. Forty-three percent of the women were from the Covent Garden area, which included the Strand and St. Martin's Lane. Twenty percent were from St. Margaret's, Westminster, and 16 percent from St. James's, in which Hedge Lane and Soho have been included. There were only two other significant concentrations: 4 percent around Fleet Street and 3 percent in Holborn; these were the last vestiges of the old City concentration in the northern and western suburbs.

There were two further differences between those who stood bail for prostitutes in the 1770s and those who had done so in the 1720s. Fewer women were bailed by persons with the same last name. Twelve percent of the recognizances in the 1720s had included someone who was probably the woman's relative. In less than 2 percent (1.7 percent) of the cases was this so in the 1770s. This suggests that the world of prostitution was probably becoming more of an autonomous subculture with fewer ties to the families from which women came. And it may also be (though this seems less likely) that more young women who entered prostitution were either orphans or immigrants from the countryside. In four cases in the 1770s, mothers bailed their daughters, twice being identified as "the elder." In the other seven cases, men bailed women with the same name. Humphrey Green twice bailed Phebea Green, once in December 1774, and again in January 1775. Phebea said she lived "at Mr. Green's, 8 Castle Yard, Westminster." This was Humphrey's address. In January, on the same day he bailed Phebea, he bailed Mary Smith as well. Both women lived in his house.[16]

In 10 cases a woman was bailed by the person in whose house she lived. It is a small number out of a total of 692. But it is something new to have the bawds (male and female) bailing their women themselves. There are probably more cases even than it is easy to identify, since those who bailed

prostitutes and lived in the same street or court may well have been directly
tied to the same bawdy house. In four cases a woman bailed another
woman who lived in her house. These women represent a second change
in sureties.

In the 1720s only eight women had been sureties for prostitutes. In
the 1770s, fifty-four different women appeared in fifty-five recognizances
(8 percent of recognizances) either on their own, or with a man or with
another woman. The mothers who bailed their daughters and the bawds
who bailed their girls explain themselves. It is likely that some of the
women who stood surety were prostitutes themselves. In 1779 Ann Harris, who lived in Bennet's Court, Drury Lane, bailed Charlotte Davis. But
a month before, Harris had had to be bailed herself for being a prostitute.
She was bailed by Margaret Green, who lived in St. Martin's Street; nine
years before it had probably been the same Green who had bailed Mary
Lloyd, when they both lived in Shoe Lane, off Fleet Street. There is no
doubt that it was the same Catherine Madden who bailed two women
who lived in her street when they were arrested in July 1777. Ann Stewart
bailed both Mary Bird and Elizabeth Luck when they were arrested on
the same day in 1772. Three years later she bailed another Covent Garden
woman. In both years she lived in Petty France, Westminster, and although listed simply as a widow, was probably a bawd. Ann Farmer, who
was herself twice charged with keeping a bawdy house, bailed Ann Williams. Farmer stood bail with another woman who, like herself, lived in
Catherine Street. Williams, in another year, was bailed by yet a third
woman. There clearly were networks among women that are hard to trace.
But most women seem to have moved in a single neighborhood. Mary
Egan bailed two different women, but like herself they all worked in the
Drury Lane, Covent Garden, neighborhood, where Egan was a fruiterer.
One of the women was at Mr. Reid's house in Cumberland Court, which
was a nest of bawdy houses; the other was a Drury Lane streetwalker.
Four women were, like Mary Egan, in the food trades. But most of those
whose occupations were listed (twenty-two of fifty-nine) were mantua
makers and laundresses, confirming the connection between women who
made or washed clothes and the world of prostitution.[17]

The greater number of women acting as sureties suggests that over the
course of the century, the role of women in the management of prostitution was increasing. The bawd has often been represented then and now
as being a woman. But in the earlier eighteenth century, it is likely that
there were more male bawds than female. One-half of those indicted for
keeping disorderly houses in the 1720s were men (table 4.10). There were

Table 4.10 Gender and Marital Status of Managers of Bawdy Houses (in percentages)

Status	Indictments, 1720–29	Indictments, 1752–59	Recognizances, 1770–79
Widow	15.5	22.7	1.9[a]
Spinster	8.7	13.1	41.4[a]
Wife	6.5	16.6	4.1[a]
Women	30.7	52.4	47.4
Husband and Wife	17.5	14.9	20.7
Men	51.6	32.3	30.1
Married Couples and Men	69.1	47.2	50.8

Source: GLRO: MJ/SBP/11–13, 16; MJ/SR/3221–3381.
[a] These percentages are not as precise as in the indictments; women are listed as spinsters whenever no clear status is given. Two percent of the recognizances cannot be assigned to women or men because they are defective.

also a substantial number of houses run by married couples. If these two groups are combined, it then appears that 70 percent of all houses were run by men. Women (including wives indicted without their husbands) ran only 30 percent of houses. By the middle of the century, on the other hand, women were just over 50 percent of those indicted. Management had come to be more or less evenly divided between women and men. The recognizances in the 1770s surveyed an even wider field since they included probably all of those arrested and not just those indicted. But the results were the same: management of bawdy houses had come to be equally divided between men and women. It is likely, though, that in both periods, bawdy houses were more likely to seem to be under the management of women because of the role played by wives. In the 1720s, for instance, if one combines the houses run by women with those run by married couples, one finds 48 percent of the houses with a woman manager, as opposed to 52 percent with a man. In the 1770s making a similar rearrangement produces a more dramatic contrast: 68 percent of houses with a woman managing and only 30 percent with a man. Prostitution in the second half of the century had become a business overwhelmingly managed by women.

This was true at least of the prostitution in the West End. In Whitechapel, it may have been less so because of the greater riotousness of the houses and class differences in gender roles. At three points after midcentury, the gender distribution of managers of disorderly or bawdy houses can be counted from either recognizances or indictments. In the indictments register for 1753, there are actually no couples as such prose-

Table 4.11 Gender of Bawdy-House Managers in Whitechapel over Three Decades

	1753	%	1765	%	1776–78	%
Woman	10		6		10	
Husband and wife	20		6		8	
Man	5		2		10	
Couples and men	25	71	8	57	18	64

Source: GLRO: MJ/SBP/16; MJ/SR/3305–65.

cuted in Whitechapel. But there are nine women listed as wives, and ten more listed as either both spinster and wife, or wife and widow. The indictments for other parishes also have women in the 1750s indicted as both wife and spinster or widow, but they are usually being indicted along with their husbands. It must therefore have been a common practice for a married woman who ran a house along with her husband to pass for either a spinster or a widow. It is therefore reasonable to suppose that at least eleven women in Whitechapel ran houses with their husbands, and by adding the nine simply described as wives, one arrives at the figure of twenty couples in table 4.11. The principal point of the table is, however, that the prostitution of the East End, which was likely to cater more exclusively to poorer men, was less likely to be run by women than the houses at the opposite end of town.

The various areas of prostitution were, nonetheless, connected by persons who had houses in both the East and West Ends of town. John Johnson, who was a cordwainer (or shoemaker) by trade, lived in Marygold Court in the Strand. It was a place well known for bawdy houses. In 1765 Mary Bartlet was in Mrs. Harris's house there, Mary Lee was at Mr. White's, and Mary Bartley and Ann Kilbury were both at the house of Thomas West, who bailed them. Johnson was arrested for his house in Marygold Court at the end of September, but at the beginning of August he had also been arrested for a bawdy house in Whitechapel. Elizabeth and James Robinson, who apparently lived in Aldgate, similarly ran houses both in St. Martin's and Whitechapel.[18]

The pattern of multiple ownership can be found elsewhere. Sophia Gray lived in Cumberland Court, where there was another concentration of bawdy houses. She was accused of keeping two houses. She may possibly have been in partnership with Charles Creamer, who also lived in Cumberland Court and kept two houses: one at that address, and another in Soho. A man called O'Hara was convicted of keeping a disorderly house in London-house Yard and stood in the pillory for it. It was claimed that he controlled five houses in all. Richard Haddock, who ran the best known of the Covent Garden bagnios (which were fashionable bathhouse brothels), was notorious for the string of other houses that he owned. He set women up as mistresses of coffeehouses, charged them two or three guineas a week, and threw them into prison when they could not pay. It may be that this kind of management explains the increase in the number of women who ran bawdy houses after 1750, but it is impossible to tell. Running several bawdy houses may also have made it easier to get away with robbing customers. It was said that the keepers of bawdy houses in Fleet Lane had houses elsewhere, and that as soon as a robbery was committed in one house, they moved to another for a few weeks until the matter was forgotten. Some of the houses, probably for the same reason, were also connected to each other by a back door and presumably under a common management.[19]

What is easier to document is the continued presence of bawdy-house keepers despite persistent legal prosecution. In a single decade like the 1770s, one can trace their continuing careers, especially the married couples. Margaret and John Grimes had a house in Eagle Court, Catherine Street, in 1773 and five years later were still there. Ann Dyas and her husband William were also in Catherine Street, in 1769 and in 1772. And in the same neighborhood Margaret Cassady and her husband were from 1771 to 1776 in a house in Cumberland Court, Drury Lane. But a woman apparently on her own (sometimes a woman's husband did not turn up at first) like Ann Sarsfield could survive from 1770 to 1774. Sometimes a couple moved from one house to another. In 1770 Thomas Burne and his wife Mary were in Clement's Lane, but in the next year they moved to Phenix Alley in Long Acre, where they still were two years later. Phenix Alley was another nest of houses: at least three other houses besides the Burnes' were there in 1773. Catherine Buckley and her husband Jonathan moved from one nest of houses in Crown Court, Russell Street, in 1771 to another nest of houses in Nag's Head Court, Drury Lane. All of these examples so far came from the Drury Lane, Covent Garden, area. But the same pattern existed in St. Margaret's, Westminster, as the cases of Mary Ashley and Agnes Cowan would show. The pattern was also present in the third West End concentration of bawdy houses. Patrick and Margaret Foran ran a house in Princes Court, Hedge Lane, at least from 1769 to 1772. Princes Court in 1771 had six bawdy houses, as their neighbors in Hedge Lane complained. Five were run by married couples and one by a single woman. The Forans were still probably running their house in 1777 since in that year, Patrick stood bail for a fellow bawdy-house keeper and said he lived in Princes Court.[20]

Nesting together in a single court like Princes Court was a persistent feature of bawdy houses. There were in the West End in the 1770s a number of other nests, as the recognizances show. The largest number were in certain courts and alleys around Covent Garden and the Strand: Phenix, Chymister's, and Jackson's alleys; Crown Court, Nag's Head Court, and White Hart Yard; Marygold and Castle Courts in the Strand; and Johnson's Court in Charing Cross. In Soho, there were Wardour Street and Meard's Court, and in St. James's, Princes, King, and Jermyn Streets. Finally, there were King Street and the Almonry at Westminster. The houses also grouped themselves in Whitechapel, especially in Buckle, Colchester, Plough, and Ayliff Streets, which all ran into each other. They were part of the "halo of brothels" that Sir John Hawkins in 1787 described as surrounding the Goodman's Field theater that stood in Ayliff Street.[21]

Some of the courts in the West End that were taken over by prostitutes were full of decaying houses. Francis Place said that in Johnson's Court there were thirteen houses "all in a state of great dilapidation, in every room in every house excepting only one, lived one or more common prostitutes of the most wretched description." The same thing was true in the 1750s and 1760s of places like Exeter Street and Eagle Court off Catherine Street and the Strand. When the leases of such dilapidated houses were near to expiring, it was no longer worthwhile to repair the houses until new leases could be granted. In such a situation, all the houses in a street or a court were taken in threes and fours by individuals who furnished them and then rented them to bawds who filled them with prostitutes. Exeter Street as a result became the haunt of apprentices from all over London because they knew that cheap women were to be found there. The houses in such places that were not occupied by prostitutes were taken by chandlers (small shopkeepers), brandy merchants, and publicans who profited from the women and their customers and who would not prosecute them. It could be dangerous for constables to venture into such a place. Two of them with their assistants were driven out of an Eagle Court house when a mob of thirty bullies (or pimps) attacked them. The only hope for such a place was action by the ground landlord. But that was necessarily a slow process. Eagle Court and Exeter Street in 1759 were inherited by a gentleman; he opposed the prostitutes; but it was apparent that very little had changed five years later in 1764.[22]

The management of bawdy houses less riotous than the ones in Eagle Court thrived on the ambiguity of their status. John and Margaret Hall ran such a house called the Robin Hood in Butcher Row, near Temple Bar. Benjamin Remnant went to drink there from time to time. Early in 1753 Remnant came into the kitchen of the house and began to abuse Margaret Hall. He said that the evening before a friend of his had come to her house with a "girl of the town" who had robbed him of his watch. He called Hall an old bawd. She dared him to prove it. He shouted that she was an old whore and that he believed "she would ruin all the girls she could." Remnant said all of this in a kitchen full of people. To protect her reputation, Hall brought an action for defamation against him in the consistory court.

Remnant tried to discredit her principal witnesses; these were Mary Askew, who had been a barmaid, and John Dearing, who was apprenticed to Hall's husband. When the trial began, Askew had recently married George Askew at Mr. Keith's Chapel in Mayfair. Together they ran a house in Clare Market called the Rising Sun. Margaret Hall had posed as Askew's mother and had signed the marriage license. Mary Askew was clearly enterprising. She had first worked for Hall as a chambermaid before being promoted to barmaid. She had also sued John Harris for not marrying her after he had promised to do so and had gotten one hundred guineas and her expenses from his trustee. John Dearing, Hall's other witness, had been suspected (according to another servant at the Robin Hood) of stealing from the till. They had found two shillings hidden in a flower tub; he had asked and received Hall's forgiveness.

Hall's third witness was less easily discredited. This was Martha Thomas. She was Hall's niece and a barmaid in the Robin Hood. She said that the house had reputable gentlemen and tradesmen for customers. She also said that she had heard her aunt give orders to the servants "not to let any women sit down with gentlemen company." But Butcher Row in the 1770s certainly did have bawdy houses. William Lemon and his wife Sarah kept the King's Head there and were arrested in 1774 and 1777. Thomas Hant was arrested in 1778 for his house. Margaret Hall's principal witness, Mary Askew, had also said that "she would make Mother Hale [the traditional epithet for a bawd] know that she was none of her . . . mother." The consistory court decided that Hall had not been defamed—or at least that her evidence was poor. Her house was probably, if discreetly, used by men who had picked up women of the town.[23]

The subculture of prostitution also thrived because London, although now united into a single great city, was still composed of very separate neighborhoods. It was still possible to change one's identity by moving from one neighborhood to another. The keeper of a bawdy house driven out of one neighborhood simply set up again in another. This was what Thomas Hance believed Mary Reeve was about to do in his parish in 1754, and he was determined to stop her. Hance was one of the church-wardens for Aldgate, and proudly aware of his duty to prevent bawdy houses, riots, and disturbances. He was a distiller by trade. He was a little hot-tempered; but a man who had been his apprentice said that Hance had never struck him. When Mary Reeve took a house in St. Catherine's Lane, Hance went to tell her that the house she had hired had recently been a bawdy house and that if she had come to keep it again as one, he was determined to rout her out as her predecessors had been. The previous tenants had run a riotous house: when their neighbors had complained of the noise, they had simply replied "in a bold manner that their house was a public bawdy house and not a private one." There had been a robbery in the house. People had also come there to "show indecent postures," a kind of striptease performance. Reeve insisted on her respectability. She said she had taken the house to keep a chandler's shop. She had been married eight or nine years before and had a little girl. Her friends—a stocking maker and a basket maker—swore that she had started out as an apothecary's servant and had then lived with a smith who was the sexton of St. Bennet's Church, before she opened her shop in St. Cather-ine's Lane. Hance, however, was certain that she was a whore and that she perhaps had been part of the previous establishment. He offered to lay a wager on it and went to get his money. He also said that her child was a young whore.

Hance was confident of his position because he believed that Mary Reeve had had quite a different history from the one to which her friends swore. Reeve, he said, had begun by keeping a house called the Shoulder of Mutton on Portsmouth Common. She was punished for this—made to walk at the tail of a cart, whipped, and forced to leave. She then came to London and took a house in Whitechapel. It was in Buckle Street—part of the group of bawdy houses around Goodman's Fields. John Smith, one of Hance's neighbors, said that he had passed outside this house and had seen young women and men pulling and hauling each other around the door, "behaving in such a manner as loose, idle, debauched and disor-derly people usually do about a bawdy house." But he had never gone in. Hance said that the Whitechapel churchwardens had forced Reeve to leave this house. She then had moved to another house south of Good-man's Fields at Salt Petre Bank near Rag Fair, until the churchwardens again made her leave. It was at that point, according to Hance, that she moved further south again to St. Catherine's Lane, just behind the Tower of London, from which place he had decided that he would make her leave. But Hance was probably mistaken about Reeve's identity. It was, however, likely that the neighbors would have viewed suspiciously anyone who moved into that house, which had so recently disturbed their respectability and peace. Hance probably also knew of a woman who had moved through all the houses he mentioned. She must either have looked like Reeve or have borne a similar name. It was, in any case, a history that made sense to a man confident of his knowledge of the ways in which bawdy-house keepers managed.[24]

The women who ran bawdy houses, even when they were not married, usually had men on their premises to serve as pimps, panders, and bullies. Pimps and panders were defined in the *London-Bawd* as a sort of "he-bawd and procurers of whores for other men." The pimp was "employed abroad, both to bring in customers, and to procure such wenches as are willing to be made whores." John Wiseman was such a man; he was charged with "being a common bringer of lewd women to strange men"; he was arrested in a bawdy house with the two women he had brought along. Panders, on the other hand, were those who were in a strict sense always "within doors, and have the management of matters in the house. These are they that bring the rogues and whores together, and wait upon them whilst they are acting of their filthiness." Abraham Brickwood, for instance, put a prostitute to bed with Thomas Brown in his house in Broad Street. The bully, however, seems to have been the more complex role. He stood ready to beat off the constable or any other enemy; and he was likely to be supported by women who were tied to him by emotional and sexual bonds. John Dunton described a bully who knew several prostitutes and "lived upon the pensions they allowed" him. But the man claimed that the sexual demands of "those horrid women weakened me so much that I fell into a languishing distemper." Ned Ward gave a less flattering description of the pimp or bully. He said that the poor Irishman when he first came to London was likely to enlist himself in "a whore's service, and has so much a day out of her earnings to be her guard du corps, to protect her in her vices." Sir John Fielding in 1770 described the bullies walking the streets with prostitutes to protect them from the constable. Sometimes in the commitments to the houses of correction the names of one or two men are included in a group of prostitutes taken up together: these men presumably were bullies.[25]

The bully was one of the persistent features in the management of prostitution throughout the century. But it is likely from what has so far been said that the management of bawdy houses in some respects changed significantly between the first and the second halves of the century. After 1750 more women than ever were to be found managing houses. This was most likely the result of the emergence of a number of men who had strings of bawdy houses and who hired women to manage them. It is less likely that women were showing more entrepreneurial ability. It is possible that the bawdy house represented one of the traditional female occupations that was not being taken over by men, as it has been claimed that millinery and midwifery were. The management of the houses after 1750 also seems to show the development of prostitution as subculture more fully separated from conventional life than previously: the women were less likely to be bailed by members of their families. Prostitution was increasingly a self-sufficient world. And the prostitute was presumed to have less in common with ordinary respectable women. Modern male heterosexuality had produced such women. Male sentimentality eventually made an attempt to restore them to the conventional world of honest work, the family and religion. But the effort was always halfhearted because it was overbalanced by the fear that in a world without prostitution male sodomy would flourish.

CHAPTER FIVE

The Prostitute's Life

Fifteen percent of the women arrested for prostitution regularly walked the streets, and some of them did so for as many as ten years, from their late teens into their twenties. Another 40 percent appeared to the magistrates to be experienced enough to be sent to bridewell. The remaining 40 percent were usually dismissed with a warning, presumably because they seemed young and inexperienced. Slightly more than half of the streetwalkers therefore struck contemporaries as making their livings entirely from prostitution. Who were these women, and where had they come from? How had they entered this world, and what were their lives like once they were in it? What happened to them when they left it? Some of them will turn out to be the daughters of the London poor. But most of them had probably come from the country to work in London as servants or milliners. A few were immediately snapped up by bawds, but a greater number took to the streets after they could not find work or had lost their jobs. Some had seen that there was money to be made in prostitution either regularly or occasionally.

All of these women had to be initiated into sexual intercourse before they became regular prostitutes. Most had probably been seduced by the men with whom they worked, sometimes by promises of marriage. Some were first picked up by one of the mob of soldiers to be found walking the streets of the West End. Some women had been raped. Some were married women. And some were enticed into the work by another woman who knew that procuring virgins could be profitable. By whatever means it occurred, first intercourse made women out of girls. This adult status could be cheerfully achieved, or accepted as the sad fate to which all women must come. But this was a transition that was supposed to occur in a marriage through which the property in a woman's body was trans-

ferred from her father to her husband. These women, however, were
owned for a moment by many different men; they were therefore no one
man's property; and this made them outcasts. But most prostitutes who
regularly walked the streets were tied to a male or female bawd who ran
the house where they lived and to which they brought their customers.
It was a financial arrangement, but it could also create a psychological
dependence, especially in younger women. Some women, however, were
independent operators, especially those who went to the bagnios that catered to gentlemen.

Prostitutes were outcasts because they had sex with many men outside
of marriage. But in other ways they remained conventional. Their rowdy
speech and public drunkenness did not necessarily distinguish them from
other poor women. Those who were willing to display their sexual parts
in a public show had probably gone the furthest into unconventionality.
This and whipping men were the most frequent irregular sexual acts in
which prostitutes engaged. Far fewer were willing to be part of a threesome whether with a second woman or a man. Fellatio was even less common, and anal intercourse hardly ever occurred. Most women retained
conventional religious belief and could distinguish themselves as Roman
Catholics, Nonjurors, Dissenters, or Churchwomen. But it was hard for
the rest of the world to see this conventionality. Instead prostitutes were
subjected to public scorn, imprisonment, and whipping. Their contracts
were not upheld in the courts. And they had to endure random public
violence. Eventually they left the life. In some cases they may have died
from the effects of hard living, though probably not because of any venereal diseases they had contracted. But in most cases they had probably
become too old in their late twenties to be sexually appealing. They presumably found their way back into the world of conventional labor. But it
seems unlikely that very many of them ever found their way into marriage.

RECRUITMENT INTO PROSTITUTION

The small minority of London's young women who entered the life of
prostitution did so either voluntarily or by seduction. The seduction could
be more or less coercive, and it could be a seduction either first into premarital sexual relations, or more directly into prostitution. But seduction
can be a difficult thing to distinguish from willing consent. Jane Birt
charged Eleanor Cavell with seducing her, keeping her money and clothes,
and assaulting her. Birt had lived with a Mr. Vanhagen as a shopwoman,
and her employer gave her a good character. But by "a train of artifices,"

Cavell persuaded her to leave her master, introduced her to a visitor, and arranged a tête-à-tête supper, with the result that the girl was ruined. She felt that she was in Cavell's power. Other gentlemen were brought in, and Cavell thrived on the girl's prostitution. But Cavell insisted, and the magistrate agreed, that it could all be read quite differently: "the girl was willing to be good natured, and the woman good natured enough to assist her." The girl may in fact have enjoyed having supper with gentlemen, but it is also likely that she had felt that she was in the older woman's power once the shame of her deflowerment struck her.[1]

Younger girls may have been especially affected by the apparent glamour of the prostitute's life. Ann Sissons was twelve years old and lived with her parents in Southwark. Her father was a cooper, her mother a japanner. At ten o'clock on a Tuesday night in July her mother sent her to buy some butter in the street around the corner. She met another young girl, Ann Walsham, who was her friend. As they stood talking, William Stoddardt, who was walking by, came up and asked them if they would go home to live with him: he would keep them as his own wife and buy them some things. They replied that they could not because they were on an errand. He offered to meet them the next night at the same time. They promised instead to visit him on Thursday morning and asked his address. Stoddardt apparently claimed that Sisson told him that "she meant to go upon the Town." But this the girl denied.

On Wednesday night she played with the other girls in the street. But the next morning, the two girls made their way across London Bridge to Stoddardt's little house in Talbot Court, Grace Church Street. Stoddardt now asked their names and where they lived. Sisson told him she was "going of 13," and that a boy in Southwark had taken her "up in a court" and debauched her. When Stoddardt asked her, she said she had been with no one else. She then went upstairs with him a little unwillingly. He took her into his bedroom and kissed and fondled her. He asked her to undress and get into bed, which she said she willingly did. She stayed until Sunday, when the other girl left and brought back Ann's father, who took her home. Ann said that she had come to the magistrate because her parents wanted her to, and that she would not have done so if she had realized that her testimony could affect Stoddardt's life. The charge of rape was dismissed.[2]

Benjamin and Rebecca Mordecai had greater success when they charged Mary Solomans with seducing their daughter, Hannah, who was thirteen years old. It is possible that something in the girl's behavior had caught Solomans's eye. But she may simply have been pretty. Rebecca

Mordecai at any rate said that Solomans had for some time been trying to entice her daughter away. Solomans took the girl one night to a bawdy house when she was supposed to be on an errand and introduced Hannah to a man. Hannah said that he "hurt her [and] she cried out." When he left, he gave her half a guinea, which she changed, giving Solomans half. When her mother was told that she was in bad company, and her father found out as well, she gave the money to a friend so that it would not be found on her. She confessed when her father threatened her. Solomans was sent to bridewell as a disorderly person.[3]

Ann Sissons and Hannah Mordecai were both drawn out of their initial venture into the world of prostitution by the actions of their parents. A careful mistress like Mary Gerrard did the same for her two young apprentices, Susannah Smith and Mary MacDonald. Susannah, or Hannah, was fourteen years old, illiterate, and apprenticed to Gerrard and her husband James, who was a vintner and had a house in Fore Street, Cripplegate. Both his trade and his location were often associated with the world of prostitution, but this couple was respectable. At Easter 1729 her mistress gave Hannah permission to visit her unmarried sister Mary, who lived across town in St. Margaret's, Westminster, where there was a nest of bawdy houses. Hannah took a shortcut through St. James's Park (another locale for prostitution as well as for respectable strolling) and met Winnifred Lloyd there. She previously knew Lloyd, but how we do not know. Lloyd was forty and a bawd who procured young girls for a Squire Janssen who had debauched her many years before. Lloyd invited Hannah to visit her in her lodgings in St. John Street, which was just south of the park and at the edge of a concentration of bawdy houses. When Hannah came to Lloyd's, she found Squire Janssen there. He told Hannah that she was pretty, asked Mrs. Lloyd to be kind to her and to let her want for nothing, gave her half a crown, and said she should come and visit Mrs. Lloyd often.

At this point Hannah's story diverged widely in the two depositions she made. In the first, she said that she had made four more visits, during which she was courted by Janssen but never actually debauched. In the second deposition she admitted that she had left out some things from "bashfulness," and that she had in fact been debauched on the second visit. Three weeks after her first visit, Lloyd had come to see her at five in the evening when her master and mistress were out, and together they had gone to Lloyd's lodgings. At ten o'clock they took a coach to the Horse Guards, where Janssen got in. The coach drove to a tavern opposite the Royal Mews in Charing Cross and left Mrs. Lloyd there. But before she got out, she pulled Hannah from her seat and put her next to Janssen. The girl and the man drove down Pall Mall to St. James's Street to the bagnio there.

The bagnio was fashionable. It actually did have a hot bath and a cold one. But it also had rooms where for an additional fee one could spend the night with a woman one had brought in or sent out for.[4] Hannah and Janssen were shown a room up one flight of stairs with a bed in it. He gave her a few kisses, threw her on the bed, and had sex with her three times before they left at midnight. They picked up Mrs. Lloyd at the tavern, and shortly after that Janssen got out. The two women drove to Lloyd's and spent the night. Hannah gave her the ten shillings Janssen had given her and discussed what had happened. Lloyd had previously told the girl that Janssen "would make a woman of her forever." She now asked her if Janssen had not hurt her. Hannah replied that he had almost stifled and killed her. "'O' says Mrs. Lloyd, 'when he first lay with me, I cried out Murder, but if you was forty years old, it would not hurt you.'" It is clear that for Lloyd the experience of sexual intercourse made a woman out of a girl.

Before the night of Hannah's debauching, Lloyd had hedged her bets and taken the girl to a person who lived nearby in the Broadway and told fortunes by tossing coffee. The fortune-teller told the illiterate girl that she had been given a present of money from a gentleman. The gentleman would give her a great deal more—enough to make a woman of her. If Hannah refused the money, she would not thrive. The gentleman was an acquaintance of Mrs. Lloyd's. Hannah went to her debauching thinking that she would make her fortune and become an adult woman.

Hannah's fellow apprentice, Mary MacDonald, had a similar experience. She first met Lloyd when she came to visit Hannah, but she later went to see Lloyd on her own. Lloyd took her into the park, where they met Janssen. They went to a public house in Pimlico, where he treated the girl to wine and cakes, kissed and fondled her, gave her nineteen shillings, and asked her to come again next Sunday. Mary returned to visit Lloyd, and once again they went to the park to meet Janssen. Lloyd left them there, and they went to a house and spent the night together. He gave her five guineas in the morning, which she gave to Lloyd. When Hannah described the night, Lloyd told her that "she was now made a woman of." Financial gain and adult status were always for Lloyd the lures with which to draw young women into the life of prostitution. But there is also contained in this phrase the profound pessimism about women's lives that another bawd in another case (which is analyzed at length in the section on rape) expressed when she comforted a young woman after her first intercourse by asking her why she was crying, for "it was what I must come to, and she must come to, and all women must come to." All women must eventually by sexual submission become men's property.[5]

The five girls in these stories were rescued, presumably, from the life of prostitution. Such rescue attempts were a common enough part of life. In a decade (1720–29) in the three London jurisdictions, for instance, there were at least twenty-seven such rescues made. Most of them are not very fully documented. But it is possible to say that thirteen of them were made by parents (eight fathers, five mothers), nine by the girl or woman herself, five by employers (three mistresses, two masters), and one by a husband. But three rescues a year versus three thousand women on the town must mean that while many of the stories of these young women may have started as the five did that have been told in detail, most must have ended quite differently. It was quite easy to move from one part of London to another and to be lost from sight: it was probably the most common way among the poor of ending one marriage and starting another. It is also likely that many of the girls seduced, as Fielding's table (table 4.4) of twenty-five was intended to show, had parents who were poor, absconded, at sea, or dead. These were girls who were often orphans and usually too poor to have been apprenticed. There were neither parents nor employers to rescue them, and they were unlikely to be motivated to rescue themselves.

It is also true, however, that some of the girls came from families who do not seem to have disapproved of their prostitution. Fielding claimed that he knew of mothers "who have trepanned their children into bawdy-houses, and shared with the bawd the gain of their own infant's prostitution." One mother wrote to a gentleman offering her pretty fourteen-year-old daughter. When another woman brought the girl, he had her and the mother apprehended.[6] Sometimes groups of sisters entered prostitution together. The arrest records from time to time have two women with the same last name taken up together. Thomas Hutchinson complained that Elizabeth Allen had seduced both of his daughters. Some fathers accepted the situation. The man to whom Francis Place was apprenticed had three daughters, all of whom were whores: the eldest plied the streets, the next was kept by a sea captain, and the youngest was visited by gentlemen at her lodgings. The middle daughter regularly visited her father: she was perhaps the most respectable. A boy who lived with his sister in a bawdy house in Chick Lane saw her bring home a man and go to bed with him.

She robbed the man and then killed and buried him after he had struck her for robbing him.[7]

Families sometimes came to a woman's rescue and stood bail for her when she was arrested. In the City in the decade 1720–29, whores gave recognizances 258 times. Eighteen women accounted for 41 of these, so that there were a total of 229 women. Twenty-eight of these (12 percent) were bailed by someone with the same last name. These were certainly a woman's relatives in some cases and probably in all of them. When Mary Geary was arrested in August 1721 for picking up a man, Edward Geary was one of two weavers who bailed her. In September 1722, he bailed her again, as he did in December when she was taken in a bawdy house as a known nightwalker. Earlier in December, however, it had been James Geary, also a weaver, who bailed her, when she was taken strolling the streets soliciting men.[8] Between July 1721 and October 1723, Catherine Green was arrested on four occasions: three times for strolling and once for taking a man to a tavern. Richard Green was always one of the men who bailed her. Each time he gave a different address, but he was twice described as a broker, and once as a dealer in wine and brandy.[9] Elizabeth Wallboyse was on one occasion bailed by two different Robert Wall-boyses—presumably her father and her brother; or perhaps her husband and his father. Some women certainly were bailed by their husbands or lovers. Catherine Moore, who was taken with a man in the private room of a bawdy house, was unambiguously described as John Moore's wife. John Buckmaster accompanied his wife as she picked up men and tried to rescue her from the arresting constable. James Timms, a drover from Cow Lane, was arrested himself when he protected Rebecca Timms and encouraged her to pick up men: they were probably married. Finally, there was Mary Blewett, who was twice arrested by that name. But on a third occasion, under the name "Blewett alias Blake" she was bailed by Richard Blake, a periwig maker—which is perhaps a situation open to too many imponderables to interpret.[10]

There were married women, then, who were whores, and husbands who accepted it, but very few in either case. John Dunton said that he tried to show one husband that it was the worst form of cuckoldry to have a wife who was a whore, but it had no effect. There was even the occasional man who coerced his wife into prostitution, whether genteelly or brutally. John Shaw was a ship's captain who did well out of the West India trade. He introduced his wife to the libertine friends with whom he went to whores. He kept for himself the gifts of money that his friends gave her after they had slept with her. Robert Allen, a butcher from Wapping, treated his wife brutally during the short time that he lived with her. He forced her into prostitution to maintain him and then abandoned her. She married another man at the opposite end of town. But she was found out, tried for bigamy, and sentenced to be branded.[11]

It was far more likely that husbands from the middle ranks would divorce their wives once they became common whores, as the cases in chapter 11 show. Three of them can be summarized here. Sarah Vallance in 1704 began seeing strange men soon after her husband sailed to the West Indies. She was turned out of her lodgings for it. Within less than a year of her marriage, she was procuring young girls for men, putting them to bed in her room, and charging a fee of a guinea or a half. Frances Edwardes acted similarly in the 1750s when her husband went to Jamaica. She at first received men in her various lodgings and then lived with three of them. Eventually she became the keeper of Wildair's Coffeehouse in Castle Court, Covent Garden, and was known as Kitty Wildair. It was a discreet place where there were no indecencies to be seen, but everyone knew that Kitty and her seven girls were common women of the town. She used her status as a married woman to escape from her debtors. Both Vallance and Edwardes, like Catherine Carter at the end of the century, once they had ceased to be faithful wives moved into the upper reaches of the prostitute's world because of their relatively prosperous origins. Vallance and Edwardes even became bawds. Carter was less enterprising. She either lived with men or joined various types of fashionable West End houses. After being recommended to Maria Theresa Johnson, she was interviewed to see if Johnson would "take her in her family." She then moved to Johnson's house in Jermyn Street, but after six weeks she was turned out for being frequently drunk. At another point she used Tom's, a bagnio kept by Thomas Hooper in Soho Square. Her name and address were put into the book that listed the women who used the house: the servants sent for them when they were needed. She paid five shillings "poundage" to the house each time she came. She was frequently sent for.[12]

The life of the middle-class woman who fell into the life of prostitution might have its moments of glamour; but it was usually a story of steady decline; and it was unlikely that she would ever be taken back by her husband. The poor were likely to be less unrelenting, especially with younger unmarried girls. When Sarah Ranson in 1732 was taken plying in the street at Temple Bar with three other girls, her aged mother came and gave her a good character. She was discharged, but her companions were sent to Bridewell. Ranson was very probably the same girl who had complained eight months before that Mary Yeates had enticed her from her parents and encouraged her to be lewd with her son William Yeates. Other parents and relatives very occasionally appeared to take home their daughters after they were arrested in the street. Elizabeth Rose's father came for her, as did Rosetta Webber's mother. Mary Lambert was held until her aunt appeared. The constable was directed to take Mary Ivory back to her mother. Sarah Powell was kept until her father in Scotland could be written to. Catherine Kendrick was sent to her godfather (her parents were presumably dead), who promised to take care of her. John Brown promised to take his sister home to his house in Black Horse Court after she had made a disturbance in the street with another woman. Her companion went to Bridewell. But in one fragmentary series of 644 arrests in the Guildhall Justice Room notebooks, there were only nine instances of families claiming their daughters. Fifty-eight percent of the young women arrested in this series were nonetheless simply discharged. One wonders how many of them had families to go home to.[13]

In another complete series of 798 arrests over six years in the City, when 39 percent of the women arrested were discharged, there was only one specific reference to a girl's family. Sarah Jennings was released from bridewell after being committed as a common prostitute when her mother agreed to take care of her and to stop her from streetwalking in the future. On the other hand, the Magdalen Hospital claimed in 1784 that in the previous twenty-six years it had reconciled to their friends (that is their families), or placed in service as servants, 1,571 of the 2,415 girls it had accepted. The hospital, unfortunately, did not separate families from employers—they were a single category of successful rehabilitation. In one case we can see that the categories overlapped. A girl was hired as a servant by a milkman and his family after she had spent a considerable time in the Magdalen Hospital. Ten days later they came home to find the house shut and a good deal of their clothes and linen missing. They pursued the girl to her relation's house. But she escaped by the roof to an adjoining house. When they pulled her down from a chimney, she was dressed in her mistress's stolen clothes.[14]

We have so far seen girls tempted into prostitution by the lure of money and the idea of achieving adult status as a woman. In most of the detailed examples it has also been the case that the girls were not freshly out of the country, but rather the daughters of the London poor. John Fielding certainly thought that many of the girls were the daughters of chairmen, porters, laborers, and drunken mechanics. The fathers died from drink, and the mothers, left with many children, tried to support themselves by taking in washing or keeping a green-stall or a barrow. Saunders Welch, on the other hand, thought it mistaken to say that "the bawdy-houses and streets are furnished with prostitutes from the children of the laborious poor." He thought instead that the women in "the bagnios and bawdy houses" came from "the next sphere of life to labourers," from parents who had given their pretty daughters an education in the hope that they might be ladies' maids rather than maids of all work. These girls first worked in the bagnios and, when they became diseased, walked the streets. Welch also believed, however, that some girls were recruited by the bawds in the classic manner: their agents met the young girls looking for work as servants as they arrived in town by the carriages and wagons.[15]

There was probably some truth to both theories. Many girls were the daughters of the London poor; some were fresh from the countryside, but more had been in London for some time working as servants or milliners. The poorest London families probably did account for some of the street-walkers. On the other hand, the girls in the bagnios, since they had to deal with gentlemen, did probably often have a little more education—though both of the girls Mrs. Lloyd provided for Squire Janssen were illiterate. Many of the girls started life as servants, and probably most servant girls had left their families in the countryside and come to London to find a place. But it was also a common observation that at least as many began as milliners, who would have had some training in needlework. "Take a survey," Campbell wrote, "of all the common women of the town who take their walks between Charing Cross and Fleet-Ditch, and I am persuaded more than one half of them have been bred milliners." In the last quarter of the century Adam Smith added that in London "those unfortunate women who lived by prostitution" were "said to be the greater part of them from the lowest rank of people in Ireland," who presumably could be distinguished on the street from the native English by their accents. The Irish were probably the poorest part of London's population, who were unlikely to be hired in the West End as servants, as the Chelsea poor law declarations show, and who instead settled for worse jobs in places like Shoreditch. Dorothy George rightly said that many of the women in the arrest records (it would be risky to say how many) bore Irish names. It is therefore possible that the number of poor Irish prostitutes increased in the second half of the century. This may partly explain why there are fewer parents rescuing their daughters from prostitution in the 1770s than in the 1720s and fewer relatives standing bail for women who were arrested. But whether they were Irish or not, it is likely that women whose parents lived in London made up a smaller part of the population of prostitutes in the second than in the first half of the century.[16]

It is clear that some girls and women were coerced into prostitution by dire necessity. Ann Evans was discharged for picking up men because she "appeared a poor ignorant Welsh girl just come from the country." But four days later she was picked up again by the constable, and a year later she was still on the streets. In many cases such a girl was there because she was being required by someone else to be there. One girl in a group of twelve women arrested in Fleet Street explained that she was forced out by the woman with whom she lived. The woman kept a gin shop. On the very day when the girl had previously been whipped and discharged from bridewell, the husband of her landlady had had her arrested for debt because she had said that she meant to make an honest living. Before he would allow her out of the debtor's prison, he forced her to give a note for eight pounds, and to promise that she would lodge with them and "turn out in the streets" as before. When after this she did not bring in enough money, he beat her as well.[17]

Some women became prostitutes because they were servants far from home who became pregnant and could not manage the consequences in any other way. This was Mary David's story. She was born in Herefordshire. Her father died, her mother remarried a man too poor to support them, and David was sent to London at a very young age to go into service. She served for two years in a fashionable household in Berkeley Square. The footman made promises of marriage and debauched her, but he was already married. She lost her place. He helped at first, and she took a place as a wet nurse. She put her own child out to nurse with a woman in Tottenham Court Road. The child she nursed was weaned, her milk dried up, and she went to live in the house in Tottenham Court Road. The landlady was "very civil, however, and suffered her to go on getting in debt. Till, one night, between eleven and twelve, she went upstairs to her with manners totally changed, and swore with the grossest abuse, that she would turn her into the street, child and all, unless she brought her some pay." When David asked how that was possible, she replied that "girls with worse faces than she often picked up a great deal." David now found that one of her fellow lodgers was a kept mistress, and that the house, in a quiet way, was a house for whores. David went out and walked the streets. But she was clearly determined to save herself. She swore her child to its father and gave it over to the parish. She found some poor friends who took her in. Then she returned to her mother in the country. But she found that she was pregnant again from her prostitution. In shame she went again to London. The first child had been left by the parish with the landlady in Tottenham Court Road and had died with whooping cough, a black eye, and a broken collarbone. The Foundling Hospital agreed to take her second child. For her future, Mary planned to sell her milk again and then to return home once more, as her story was not known there.[18]

For a younger and more vulnerable girl, Mary David's escape was impossible without the chance intervention of some outside agency. When Ann Lamb (her true name was Ann Hook) was not yet fifteen she entered the Lock Hospital because she was venereally infected. When she was discharged, she was asked what she would do to get her bread. She told her story. Her friends lived at Bristol and were poor. She became a servant, and when she was unemployed, she was persuaded by a young woman who had been in London to go there with her. When she arrived in the city, she was quite a stranger, very poor, and destitute. Her friend drew her into bad company. She made her very drunk and put her in bed with a man who debauched her and gave her venereal disease. Since her friend then deserted her, she took to walking the streets. Some of the other girls who "were kept by and belonged to" Fanny Finley urged her to join them.

Finley kept a bawdy house in Fleet Market next to another public house. Lamb went there with the other girls one night. Finley made her drunk and then extorted from her a promise to live with her. Finley provided food, drink, clothes, washing, and lodging for fifteen shillings a week. The girls earned this by picking men up in the streets and bringing them to Finley's house, where she sold them drink and they went to bed with the girls. But poor Lamb's venereal infection grew worse. Finley got her into the Lock Hospital. But she made her promise to come back when she was cured and went with her to the hospital, posing as her mother. Finley came to see her several times while she underwent the cure and brought her tea and sugar. She reminded the girl of her promise to return and said that she would send for her on the day she was discharged. Lamb said she supposed she would go back to her, as she was friendless and penniless and had no place to go. But she also said that she had seen "such a scene of wickedness there," and the girls treated so badly, that she dreaded to return. She was willing to do anything "to get her bread in an honest way," or to go back to her friends at Bristol if she had the money to do so. It would mean that she "could get out of the hands of this old bawd."[19]

Young girls like Ann Lamb, having come to town to seek a place as a servant, were sometimes, then, snatched up by a bawd. They were even met at the wagons. When two bawdy houses in Eagle Court just off the Strand were raided, all the girls were under eighteen; one was eleven, and another "had been taken out of a waggon by one of the [bawdy] house-keepers but three days before and debauched." But it was probably more usual for a girl, whether from London or the country, to have been a servant for a while before her entrance into prostitution, as Ann Carr was. In 1759 she said that she was eighteen. She was also illiterate. She had known Haddock's Bagnio in Covent Garden for twenty months, going there two or three times a week when she was sent for, sometimes at six in the evening, sometimes at ten. Four years before, when she had been fourteen, she had been a servant in a tavern in the Strand. She had then moved to a tavern at Hampton Court, and then to one at Woolwich. Sometime during that period, like many servants in public houses, she must have been seduced. But she aimed high. She moved to Clerkenwell, and then to Charles Street and Bridges Street, so that she could go to Haddock's Bagnio, which was "frequented by very good company."[20]

Ann Carr operated independently, but most streetwalkers were attached to taverns or lodging houses. Here they lived by day and brought their customers, and they were obliged to give the master or mistress of the house a share of their earnings. Susanna Eliot was given her clothes by a man called Phillips. He kept a house in Silvin Street, off Fleet Street, and the women gave him their earnings. Another male bawd, John Brett, complained that two girls, Ann Thompson and Elizabeth Webb, broke his windows by throwing brickbats. They said they lodged with him, paid fourteen shillings a week for board and lodging, and two shillings for every gentleman who came back with them. John Cleland described these cockbawds, or male keepers of bawdy houses, as letting the girls who boarded with them fall into debt. In the daytime, Cleland said, "the girls are kept within doors and out of sight, some without shoes, some without stockings, or in tawdry bed gown, without a shift, whilst their only one is washing, till towards evening . . . are they sent to cruize the streets or posted in the doors." These girls could take their revenge, but even that had its costs. One reported to the magistrate that she lived in a lodging house for prostitutes in the Great Almonry, Westminster, which was kept by a soldier in the footguards. She was angry because he extorted three shillings a week for a poor room with hardly any furniture. He was fined ten pounds, but the woman was sent to bridewell.[21]

Some women, like Ann Lamb, were held in a bawd's power by a kind of psychological dependence. Other girls were raped into prostitution and left demoralized. A servant in Whitechapel (another center for bawdy houses) was fourteen when she was so brutally raped by a fellow servant that she was unable to urinate and unable to do her work. When her mistress turned her away, she took to lying in the streets, until a previous mistress took her in and got the story out of her. Another girl was debauched by a captain and then went on the town, wandering in Fleet Street, picking up men. The bawds, male and female, participated in this violence, often with a degree of erotic glee. Hester Mason beat Elizabeth Turner and pushed her into a bedchamber where there was a man. She locked them in together and bade the man pox her soundly. Jane Dykes also locked the door on Katherine Allen and a man; but she bade him not to put Allen in a fever. John Fullerton beat Ann Drevenstead as he tried to put her to bed with a man.[22]

The most famous, and controversial, of these cases was that of Elizabeth Canning. In 1753 Canning disappeared for four weeks after she had been to visit her aunt and was on her way home to her mother. She was eighteen, but small, barely five feet. Her father had died two years before, leaving her mother pregnant and with four other children, of whom Elizabeth was the eldest. Canning had gone to a charity school and had learned to read and write. She had been in service in several places, had a good character, and at the point of her disappearance had been employed for ten weeks as a servant to a carpenter. Her neighbors thought her simple and good. She was religious and read the Bible and Thomas à Kempis. She may have gone with her mother to the Methodists. When she did not return home, her mother at first thought that she had been murdered. But she then consulted a cunning man about her who spoke of an old woman. The mother supposed it was a bawd and began to think that her daughter had been seduced into prostitution.

Then the girl returned. She was emaciated and her skin was black. Her mother immediately asked whether she had gone walking bad ways. The girl said no. But she could not give a coherent account of what had happened to her. She could remember that she had been seized by men as she crossed Moorfields, the shortest way home, but with a bad reputation. They had put her in a coach and taken her to a house at Enfield kept by Mother Wells. Wells's house was said to harbor whores and thieves. Along with an old gypsy woman, Wells had tried to see if Canning was "willing to go their way." The girl had resisted and gone into hysteric fits. She was put in an attic and kept on bread and water. She eventually escaped.

The midwife who had delivered her when she was born now visited her mother. She examined the girl and told her thankful mother that her daughter had apparently not been debauched. But the midwife was surprised that her shift showed no signs of excrement after supposedly being worn for so long. The girl's case began to attract sympathy and attention. Wells and the gypsy, whose name was Squires, were arrested, tried, and found guilty of abduction and theft. At the trial, Canning's confused recollections were supported by the testimony of Virtue Hall, a servant at the inn. But then Hall recanted her evidence. Squires found witnesses to prove that she had been far away. Canning was now tried for perjury, found guilty, and sentenced to seven years transportation. The town divided into two parties, the Canningites and the Egyptians, with a pamphlet war and crowds in the street.[23]

Alternative explanations were offered for her absence, all of a sexually discreditable kind. "Eighteen," John Hill wrote, "is a critical age; and what would not a woman do, that had made an escape to recover her own credit, and screen her lover." It was also said that she had had a private lying-in, or that she had been salivated—that is, gone for a cure for venereal disease. But a new midwife examined her and said she had never borne a child. (Skeptics noticed that the midwife did not say that she was a virgin or that she had never been pregnant.) A physician looked into her mouth and found none of the usual scars left by mercury in a salivation. Her friends explained away her clean shift. An apothecary said she had had no evacuations during her confinement. He had had to give her several glysters (or enemas) before she found relief. Dr. Cox pointed out that East India traders said that sailors had no evacuations when their food was down to biscuit and water. Besides, Canning was naturally costive and had not menstruated in the previous five months.

The best modern interpretation of Canning's story starts with that last point. The stoppage of her menstruation had probably (as it sometimes does) interfered with the action of her sphincter. It was part of her hysterical personality. She had started having fits at fourteen when menarche had probably begun. The threat of debauchment had thrown her into a fainting fit. She had also suffered a degree of amnesia. Some details she remembered, others she invented. It is all quite probable. She may have been abducted for some particular man. She had been saved by her hysteria. But her case would never have aroused the degree of attention that it did if her age and familial situation had not made her in the public mind (and in her mother's) exactly one of the sort of girls who could be seduced into prostitution. Her personal pain (though she eventually married and lived happily in America) was a consequence of the ruthlessness of the world of prostitution. But it is likely that that very ruthlessness was also a source of great erotic excitement to the men and women of her day who heard her story.[24]

Canning probably was not raped, and she also escaped the life of prostitution. But violence and violent seduction were never far away in this world. Ann Ward was a milliner and like many women in that trade slept with men for money from time to time. But she was raped when she attempted to control the conditions of her prostitution. She came from Warwickshire, where her parents lived, and had evidently been in London for some time. She lived in North Audley Street off the Oxford Road. She had worked as a servant but was now a milliner taking in plain work and washing smallclothes (underclothes and shirts). One evening, after delivering some work, she returned home through the Horse Guards and St. James's Park. When she was nearly out of the park William Caswell asked her to drink a glass of wine. Caswell, the son of an Irish attorney, was an officer who had come to England to raise forty men. Ward refused the offer at first but consented when Caswell said he would treat her very well. She was also impressed by his officer's clothes. He told her that he lodged at Mrs. Allen's in Great Suffolk Street. She replied that it was a house that entertained girls but went along with him, having "no other apprehension than that he took me there to lie with me."

At the house, Caswell did not go in but told her to ask for John Sullivan. Sullivan took her upstairs. Caswell then brought in another young woman whom he had met in the park a week before. Eventually a third man, William Fitzgerald, joined them. They sat drinking rum till eleven o'clock. Then Ward said she wanted to leave. She had been willing to be with Caswell: "but when I saw there were two more, I was not willing that any of them should lie with me." The men would not let her go. They locked her in a back room. They put the other young woman in another room from which Ward could hear her crying out. The three men then came to her. Two of them held her down while Caswell raped her. When she tried to get up, Caswell knocked her down and beat her. Fitzgerald stopped him: "Do not murder the poor creature; remember you came of a woman yourself; do not use her ill." But Fitzgerald also had sex with her. Caswell then picked her pocket of her money. It was now Sullivan's turn. After this the men left. In the morning, when she revived, the landlady, who had disliked the commotion she had heard, lent her a shilling so that she could swear out a warrant against the men. They were found guilty and condemned to death.[25]

Military men in general, according to a common saying of rakes them-

selves, treated their whores much less well than did sailors.[26] The prostitution in Westminster was in fact given something of its distinctive tone
because the greater part of the soldiers stationed in London were to be
found living there in barracks, or in their own lodgings, or quartered in
public houses. One can find the military rake and his servant making their
way through the pages of the bastardy examinations. Captain Jermyn
Duce and his servant between them made at least six different women
pregnant in as many years between 1718 and 1723. Captain Duce began
in 1719 in his lodgings in Killigrew Court, Scotland Yard, with Jane Jones,
whom he had twice. Then in 1720 there was Ann Archer, whom he met
at the races and had once in a coffeehouse and then several times in his
lodgings. In the next year he frequently saw Margaret Evans in the first
half of the year. Finally, in 1723, Sir Jermyn, as he had become, made
Mary Row pregnant. His servant, Thomas Atkins, saw Martha Stuart
several times in the course of a year, usually having sex with her in a public
house, first at the White Bear in St. Stephen's Alley, and then at the
Robin Hood in Thieving Lane. He also took other young women to these
two houses: Martha Smart, four months after Martha Stuart had born
her bastard, said that Atkins had regularly had sex with her in those same
places in the previous fifteen months. In fact in the parish of St. Margaret's, Westminster, in the years 1712–29, officers, common soldiers, and
officers' servants were responsible for a fifth of all the bastards in the parish. It is also clear that some of these young women came to work steadily
as prostitutes. Elinor Snowden in 1721 was an unmarried woman of nineteen who had served an apprenticeship of four years to a mantua maker.
Mantua makers made women's dresses: like milliners, they were frequently
prostitutes. Three years later she was pregnant by Thomas Hayes, and
three years later still, she was pregnant again by Colonel Bing of the footguards, who had had her twice in the Guard Room of St. James's Palace.[27]

The most notorious military rake of the early eighteenth century was
Colonel Francis Charteris. He was said to have been of the opinion that
when he "caught a fine sempstress or mantua-maker in the public streets
after nine at night, whether banboxed or bundled, it might still be lawful
to charge her in custody of the first hackney coach, and convey her to the
next bagnio." Charteris also seduced married women. He was found guilty
in Scotland of raping such a woman and had to flee in 1722, until he
received the king's pardon. But he seems to have specialized in servant
girls. Isabella Cranston in 1724 applied for a servant's place in the house
of Mrs. Sarah Jolly in Suffolk Street. Jolly had been arrested the previous
year for keeping a notorious house in Pulteney Street and had evidently

moved. She now hired Cranston and delivered her over to Colonel Charteris. Cranston became pregnant. Her parish probably forced the colonel
to pay for her. And Mrs. Jolly was arrested again. Charteris seems to have
preferred to have these young servants delivered to his house. One girl
had refused to leave when her sister came to find her. But Anne Bond,
who had been hired when Charteris used another name, would not do as
the colonel wished. So he horsewhipped her and raped her. The jury found
him guilty, but he escaped the gallows once more when the king pardoned
him again.[28]

Servants and milliners appear so frequently in these stories because
those were the two principal occupations of young unmarried girls. Gentlemen, on the other hand, are probably overrepresented as seducers in
these stories. Even in parishes like St. Margaret's, gentlemen accounted
for only about a fifth of the men who had made girls pregnant. At the
other two ends of London, in Chelsea and in Shoreditch, they were even
less significant as seducers. The previous chapter has shown that men
arrested in the 1720s for being with whores were not gentlemen (who
admittedly probably knew how to stay out of harm's way) but artisans and
laborers.

Being a servant was, however, a large, diffuse occupation. The milliner
was more highly particularized and probably more of an erotically charged
role. Servants had traditionally been part of the household and had a similar standing with children. Milliners, on the other hand, sold their services
and their wares. John Cleland had his Fanny Hill decoyed into prostitution when she was hired as a servant. But in the second, more libertine
half of the novel, she became part of Mrs. Cole's establishment, where
three beautiful young women of eighteen or nineteen sat demurely at their
work in a millinery shop. This was one of the places described by Campbell: "those who pretend to deal only with select customers . . . these . . .
take the title of milliner, a more polite name for bawd." But even real
millinery shops were erotically charged. Ned Ward described walking in
the Royal Exchange, where there was a row of millinery shops. The
"women sat in their pinfolds begging of custom, with such amorous looks,
and after so affable a manner, that I could not but fancy they had as much
mind to dispose of themselves, as the commodities they dealt in"—when
commodity was a name for "the private parts of a modest woman, and
the public parts of a prostitute." This place was the "merchant's seraglio."
Steele complained that a "young fop cannot buy a pair of gloves, but he
is at the same time straining for some ingenious ribaldry to say to the
young woman who helps them on." One man stood in front of the milli-

nery shops in Cornhill "acting in a very immodest manner," and when the young women were alone in a shop, he would go in and "behave with great indecency."[29]

All young women who made clothes came under suspicion of sexual misbehavior. Two of them were arrested by the constable after they had delivered a grown and a coat, even though he had not seen them in any illicit act. Phoebe League (who was twenty-three), on the other hand, was a seamstress who had borne a bastard. Her sister asked the Foundling Hospital to take the child, but with "all possible secrecy," so that her sister would not "lose the public confidence necessary to her livelihood." Ruth Plynn redeemed herself in another way. She contracted venereal disease and had a child, whom she kept. She entered the Lock Asylum for reformed women and eventually became the assistant matron. She used "her skill in mantua making" to save the charity a considerable sum of money by sewing clothes for her fallen sisters. The men who in their excitement seduced these young women suffered few consequences. The women were likely to lose their health, their reputations, and their livelihood.[30]

THE PROSTITUTE'S TRADE

The prostitute walked the street, approaching men, inviting them to go with her to a tavern, or to her lodgings, or simply to a darker place in the street. Defoe gave the classic description of these women walking between Charing Cross and Ludgate. He complained that as he walked at full speed, women moved into his path and stopped him with an "impudent leer." At other times they twitched at his sleeve or greeted him with a lewd suggestion: others simply grabbed him by the elbow and demanded to be treated with wine before they would let him go.[31] A man who was interested would, of course, have gone along with them. All these practices were described again and again by the constables who arrested whores, and by the men who complained that a woman had robbed them after a bargain had been struck.

Simon Jeffrey described how as he was going with a parcel of money up Fleet Street, a girl called to him. She asked him to go and drink with her. They went to Mrs. Sweetman's at the George Tavern at the bottom of Water Lane. They had two pints of beer. Then they went to another tavern. When they came out, the woman picked up another woman, and the three of them went looking for a bed. They found one and spent the night together in it. They also called up for some more drink. The next morning the women were gone, and so was his money. Henry Sweet was walking along in the piazzas of Covent Garden when Mary Hughes stopped him. She asked him to treat her with a glass of wine. He said that he could not afford wine but that, as she "seemed to be a good-natured girl," he would give her a pint of purl, which was hot beer with gin. He gave her two pints. He was going to Tower Hill. She was going as far as the Fleet Market. He said he did not want company. She went with him as far as Somerset House in the Strand, where she asked him to go down with her into the Yard: she had "something particular to say to me." Excited, no doubt, by the thought of what would happen, he went with her to the area of the stables where the coaches were. What then occurred is unclear. But after she bade him good night, he discovered that she had stolen his watch that had cost three pounds.[32]

These stories go on and on with interesting variations in the sessions papers and in the magistrates' notebooks. Michael Goodier passed through Honey Lane at eleven at night, on his way to or from Cheapside. He stopped "to make water" in the street, as was the custom for men. As he did so, two women came up, and one of them fondled his penis. The other put her hand into his breeches. Then they went away and took with them 9s 6d. John Northey reported that something very similar happened to him.[33]

But men who picked up women did so in the same manner, and not all whores were thieves. James Collins, a journeyman tailor, met Rebecca Pearce as he passed through Parker's Lane into Drury Lane, the center of London's sexual life. He stopped her and asked if she had a husband. She said she did not want him. He said he would make a good husband and asked where she lived. She replied that her room was down Parker's Lane and up one flight, and that she paid two shillings a week. He said that he would like to "go and lie with you." She answered, "you make very free the first time." So he asked what she drank. She said gin; he replied, "you must [fuck] for it." But she wanted to be paid. He proposed giving her a shilling in the morning when he left—the standard fee. She explained that she did not want to spend the entire night there: "here is such banditti"; for evidently, like a number of other women in these cases, she shared the room with others. She told him that if he had "a mind to have a bit" and then left, that would be acceptable. She probably also thought that she could find another man that night. He swore by Jesus that he would stay all night or split her skull. Another woman now came in. He liked her better and turned Pearce out, or so she said. He claimed that after having sex, he fell asleep. When he awakened his thirteen guineas were gone. He went with a friend and found Pearce walking in the

Strand, "dressed from head to foot." He found that she was called Black Bird. (Another woman was called Hell-fire Moll.) She said that she had met a sailor who had given her clothes and money. The jury believed her after the constable swore that when his wife was sick, Pearce had helped out and stolen nothing.[34]

Women who walked the streets had specific areas where they plied. When Hannah Sutton wished to attack another married woman in her neighborhood, she said that Susannah Parks dressed "like a whore" and was a common nightwalker whose "walk is from Charing Cross to White-hall." A soldier said that a girl had taken from him more than the shilling he had agreed to. He knew where to find her: "I have seen her about that corner; it is her *beat*." Women protected their areas from other women. Ann Brown shoved Mary Hughes in Fleet Street and pulled her hair, saying that the other woman "should not walk upon her . . . territories." One girl could give an area a bad reputation. Elizabeth Gough stopped John Hall and asked him to go home with her. When he replied that she was too small, she said she was not, took hold of his collar, whipped off his handkerchief, and ran down an alley. When he told the other girls standing on that beat what she had done, they damned her and said she did that to everyone who passed that way. A girl who appeared for the first time was obliged to treat the others. A group of women who plied the Birdcage walk in St. James's Park wittily turned this to their advantage. A gentlewoman was attacked as she went through the park. The prosti-tutes pulled pieces of her clothing from her until a man came up and stopped them. They had insisted that the gentlewoman pay "her footing as it was the first time they had seen her there."[35]

These women were as rowdy in their speech as in their actions. Their lewd conversations in the public street were both a means of creating erotic excitement and of showing the degree to which they had left behind con-ventional female behavior. Ann Way and Sarah Wright were arrested to-gether for talking lewdly in the streets. Elizabeth Fowler kissed people as she talked bawdy; Sarah Macdonell abused them. Sarah Lane and Mary Gray used this kind of talk as they tried to pick men up. One woman sang obscene songs. Such behavior could seem quite alarming to ladies. Maria Harris and Mary Williams used such "filthy expressions" before two ladies who were walking at night in Cheapside that they felt obliged to take a coach. But this behavior may have been less unconventional for poor women than it might seem. The defamation cases show respectable wives using extremely frank sexual language. The same was true of men. William Crocker was arrested for singing scandalous ballads in the street.

Edward Welsh sang an obscene ballad and then encouraged his young son to do the same. But such songs, though they might get one into trouble in the street, were sung by respectable tradesmen indoors. Francis Place remembered the singing of "very gross" songs in his father's parlor by men "who were much excited." Everyone who heard them clapped at the end and rapped the tables in delight. His friend Richard Hayward had to remind the now-respectable Place of the words of "Morgan Rattler."

> First he niggled her, then he tiggled her
> Then with his two balls he began for to batter her
> At every thrust, I thought she'd have burst
> With the terrible size of his Morgan Rattler.[36]

Prostitutes were more likely to depart from conventionality when men asked them to engage in any of those sexual acts that transgressed against a Christian society's taboo against nonprocreative sex. Probably the least offensive transgression was having sex in groups of three, but even this does not seem to have been very widespread. It was shocking, though, because it bordered on Mohammedan polygamy. It was nonetheless a frequent sexual fantasy. Boswell laughed when Samuel Johnson told him that thoughts of keeping a seraglio had often been in his mind. He had even worked out its details: "the ladies should all wear linen gowns—or cotton . . . no silk; you cannot tell when it is clean." But a man like Saunders Welch was shocked by the actuality of many partners at once. He had seen flophouses where debauchery was carried further even than having two separate couples in the same room: "for sometimes two women have been in bed with one man, and two men with one woman."[37]

In the bawdy houses, however, the constables found neither of these last two situations very common. Out of at least six hundred men arrested for being with a prostitute in the three London jurisdictions in the ten years from 1720 to 1729, there were only twenty-seven men found with two women (4.5 percent) and only four cases of two men with one woman (0.7 percent). It is not clear that a man with two women always had sex with both. It is also true that sometimes two women had set up this situation so that one of them could better rob the man while the other excited him. But in some cases the three people had clearly spent the night together in one bed when the constable broke in upon them. The second kind of threesome—two men and one woman—was much less common. Some women (like the milliner in an earlier case) may have feared that such a situation could easily become violent. The men may possibly also have found the potential of sexual involvement with another man too threatening. It is likely therefore that they went to the woman one at a time. Edward Dodsworth and John Theobalds were found with one woman. They both had their hands up her clothes, but only Theobalds was "in the act of adultery with her." Theobalds was evidently a younger man: his father bailed him. Another father and son who were visiting from Sheffield picked up a woman together and took her to a bawdy house.[38]

Anal intercourse with women, according to one English libertine, was the mode preferred by Italians and by some of the Dutch and the English. But only five cases turned up in the twenty-eight years of sessions rolls. They were spread, however, throughout the century: 1704, 1737, 1746, 1765, 1772. Four of the women were prostitutes, and the fifth was the man's wife. John Williams, a cabinetmaker, threw Dorothy Banger on a bed, gagged her mouth, and tried to sodomize her. He offered her nine shillings a week to let him do it. The price shows that it was a very controversial act. John Murray complained that when John Spives wrongfully charged him in the open street with having sodomized his wife, it raised a mob around him. And when the keeper of a Drury Lane bagnio called Lucy Earle a sodomite and a shoplifter, this also raised a violent mob against her.[39]

Fellatio was less controversial but still not common. To the libertines, it was no great matter. It could be used as a preservative against venereal disease. Miss Noble, in *Harris's List,* was said to have a tongue with "a double charm, both when speaking and when silent; for the tip of it, *properly applied,* can talk eloquently to the heart." Nonetheless, some men found it shocking. William Bligh said of the Tahitians that "even the mouths of women are not exempt from the pollution, and many as uncommon ways have they of gratifying their beastly inclinations." No one seems to have been arrested for doing it. It was probably not very common.[40]

Far more common were flagellation and what the eighteenth century called "showing lewd postures." It is likely that both of these created fewer feelings of aversion in both the women and their customers. Lewd postures was a form of striptease and can be placed in a continuum of various forms of sexual display. It was most directly tied to viewing "wanton pictures." Such pictures were seen as one of the principal "venereal incitements" along with "lewd books, women's company, and libidinous discourse." The pictures were very often depictions of sexual intercourse in various positions: they were often called Aretino's postures, after a notorious series of illustrations. Betty Sands was said to have shown "more odious postures than were invented by that most debauched nobleman of

Venice named Peter Aretino": "which immodest cuts," Captain Smith piously concluded, "ought to be committed to the flames." This kind of print was available at all levels of society throughout the century. Lord Dorset in 1704 kept by his bedside a book of them that was bound to look like a songbook. A curious visiting lady took a peep and found that it contained "the most obscene lascivious pictures that ever can be imagined." Francis Place said that in his boyhood at the end of the century, these prints were openly sold along with schoolbooks and offered to any boy or girl. Mrs. Roach in her shop would ask the young if they wanted "some pretty pictures" and then encourage them to leaf through her portfolio. Men went directly from the inspiration of the print to their actions with a prostitute. Lord Grosvenor was moved by the picture of a naked woman that hung over the fireplace of a bawdy house to ask Elizabeth Roberts to strip naked.[41]

Live women acted out the various sexual positions that could be seen in the prints. When the constables arrested James Reyney and William Cane, they found the men with two veteran prostitutes who had "shown them lewd and indecent postures." Ann Bailey, on another occasion, had done the same thing. Susan Brockway said that John Richmond offered her a crown to strip, and ten shillings if she would get a pennyworth of rods to whip him "and make him a good boy." After the third pint, he wanted her and her friend who had come with them to "strip naked and show postures, and let him whip us to make us good girls." There are two literary descriptions of women showing postures in well-lit bagnios. In one of them, girls who are naked lie on a table while they are surrounded by a group of men who look closely at their sexual parts. A glass of wine is then placed on top of the mons veneris and each man drinks from it. The women writhe and imitate various sexual postures and finish by masturbating themselves. In the other description, a girl who has arrived half drunk strips and goes down on all fours, as the men gloat over her and ridicule her. Ned Ward has one whore in Bridewell describe another as "one of Posture Moll's scholars" who could show "how the watermen shoot London bridge, or how the lawyers go to Westminster"—names of two erotic postures. But in commonplace bawdy houses it could be difficult to see at night. Mary Johnson said that Sarah Morrice had made her several times strip in the presence of a man so that he could look "into her privities" with the help of a candle. John Northey took two girls to Elizabeth Crawford's house (or so she said); he "gave them money to flog him"; and he "put one on the bed [and] had a candle to look at her."[42]

Flagellation and postures may have been found together in the fantasies and the actions of some individuals. But flagellation could be more openly discussed. It was, after all, not acceptable to show one's private parts in public; but prostitutes were stripped and whipped on their backs as schoolboys were on their buttocks. Men who exposed themselves to women in public were arrested. Their display occurred either as they went about the streets or stood in front of houses where they knew women would look out of the windows. Thomas Williams frightened women and children in the streets. Henry Wright shocked his neighbors by exposing himself in their common courtyard. Simon Jones stood in front of ladies' windows. James Cheesebrook ran naked in a field behind Southampton house where some ladies were walking. Jacob Duboys stood in front of a dancing school for young women. John Goff exposed himself for two hours to the young women in Bethia Townsend's house. Some of these men were probably mentally unbalanced: the man who ran naked in the field was probably having a lark.[43] Exposure could also be used as a deliberate threat, or sometimes as a calculated gesture of contempt. William Hastings forced his way into Sarah Hastings's room, even though she was his relation, and pulled out his private parts. Peter Dufree first beat Judith Gregory's husband and then took his privates out and showed them to her. Men sometimes inadvertently displayed themselves when they stopped to urinate in the streets. By the end of the century, it was proposed that men should be fined for pissing against a wall in public, and that public houses should be built for this purpose. But in the meanwhile men told jokes about women who took sly peeps. The duke of York, it was said, saw Lady H——n looking intently at a poor soldier who peed against her window. He asked her whether her milliner cheated her in her measure; "because, says he, you look so earnestly at the length of that poor man's yard."[44]

Women also exposed themselves in public. Sometimes they did so because they were mad, like the poor woman who stood naked in front of the statue of King Charles I at Charing Cross. It could also be done in angry contempt. Ann Rosamund abused her mother and sister as whores, bawds, and bitches and then took up her petticoats in the street and called her neighbors to see and kiss her arse. Whores like Isabella Smith or Jane Shipman when they pulled up their coats in various places or exposed themselves in the street presumably acted more like the men who exposed themselves to women for sexual purposes. But such exposure in them was probably less a sign of sexual disorder than it was in men, since sexual display was an ordinary part of the world of the bawdy house. When she wanted to speed things along in her own bawdy house, Mrs. Roberts pulled up her coats and told Aniel Price to "feel what she had got." In

Sarah Newell's house, Jacob Tansey took down his breeches and showed his penis to Margaret Saunders and Ann Mason: Newell then took hold and fondled it. Showing postures in this world was not so extraordinary as it might elsewhere have been.[45]

There seems to have been no need to explain the desire to know what the sexual parts looked like or how they worked. But in fact there was some uneasiness about it. A description of the sexual organs was the standard beginning for sexual manuals like *Aristotle's Masterpiece* and John Marten's *Gonosologium Novum*. Marten, indeed, was fascinated in his treatise on venereal disease by the ritual and religious modifications to the penis made in other societies: in his own society even the scientific description of the sexual organs was suspect (he apologized for its necessity), and modifications to the penis were made only to cure disease. The libertines therefore delighted in Richard Payne Knight's demonstration that there had been found in Italy a phallic cult flourishing in the ex-votos offered to a Christian saint (see chap. 3).[46]

But there was a difference in standing between viewing the sexual parts in private and flagellation. Without offering any justification, John Cleland in his novel has Fanny allow her nineteen-year-old companion to satisfy his curiosity by viewing her private parts. But Mrs. Cole has to reassure her that it was acceptable to whip Mr. Barville and to be whipped in turn: "she considered pleasure of one sort or other as the universal part of destination, and every wind that blew thither, a good one, provided it blew nobody any harm." Mrs. Cole "compassionated" rather than blamed those who were subject to "arbitrary tastes that rule their appetites of pleasure with an unaccountable control." An enterprising publisher like Curl brought out a translation of Meibomius's old treatise, in which flogging was described as a physical stimulant to erotic desire. Two different origins were commonly proposed for the desire to be whipped. It was said that boys who were whipped at school learned to feel sexual desire from it. Meibomius mentioned groups of schoolboys who flogged each other for this purpose. Snarl in Thomas Shadwell's play said that he was so "used to it at Westminster-School, I could never leave it off since." But Snarl's character also showed some of the ambiguities of the flagellant: he was a religious hypocrite; he was old; and he preferred (in his old-fashioned way) boy actors to female actresses. A second theory held that older men found that flogging stirred their declining sexual powers. In Ned Ward, a "flogging-cully" is also an older man, a "grave fornicator." Thomas Edsan knew that Susanna Hutchins would make him ridiculous by painting him as an older man who had paid her to flog him. He denied the flogging, insisted that she had robbed him, and was believed by the jury. John Cleland's Mr. Barville, on the other hand, was a young man: "What increased the oddity of this strange fancy was the gentleman's being young." We do not know Joseph Farrant's age; he was a loom maker from Shoreditch; but when the constable took him with a whore, it was clear that "she had whipped him naked with rods in a most scandalous lewd manner." It was a taste in a man that a woman could be brought to indulge perhaps with reluctance. In it a man surrendered his dominance. It was certainly far more common for men to beat women as an accompaniment to sexual desire, as the divorce cases will show. But a man who was whipped on the buttocks—where "the seat of male honour" lay—probably had raised in him anxieties about being passive in sodomy in an age when that fear had become one of the major hinges on which male identity hung. This may explain the correspondence in the *Gentleman's Magazine* on the flogging of schoolboys: why one man wanted it stopped, and another was determined to defend schoolmasters from the charge that they took particular pleasure in this part of their work.[47]

Prostitutes were also called upon in their trade to satisfy other forms of desire. Elizabeth Mob said that John Foster paid her "to let him spit in her mouth." Another man paid so that he could play mother and child with his whore: a disobedient child, who under the threat of the rod (but not its actuality), was a good boy and went to bed. Cleland in his novel has an old man who first wished to comb Fanny's hair; he then helped her on with white kid gloves, the tips of which he would bite off. But a woman had her limits. John Fitchell was arrested with a woman he had picked up and to whom he had offered "unheard of lewdness." What he had done is unknown, but his bail was unusually high.[48]

The prostitute played any number of roles with men. She was seductress and boon companion. But she was also a trickster and a thief. She was the monogamous wife to her good husband, and she was also one among the many women of his harem. She was dominated and abused, spat at and anally penetrated. Her private parts were a delight to a man's eye— a great unknown darkness through which he moved with a candle; but he was also contemptuous of her for making them public. He beat her to make her good and then submitted to her as his stern but loving mother. It is very likely, though, that most women moved through these dramas (or at least the ones in which they were willing to participate) without surrendering their basic conventionality.

The continuing connection of these women to the Christian society in which they lived can be seen in the prostitute's religion. In the early part of the century, the religious reformers thought that these women walked the streets because they lacked religion. But they would probably have claimed what a male libertine like Sir William Cowper said to his wife: that "he found nobody the better that went so much" to church, where they made "such a stir against whoring, which he thought the least of sins."[49] In the second half of the century, the reformers did not seek to make the prostitute good by punishing her; instead they thought that a steady dose of piety and work in an asylum would do the trick. The magistrates throughout the century certainly thought that they could appeal to a girl's conscience: which is why, in part, they let so many of them go once they had promised amendment.

Some, and probably most, of these women continued to have a marked religious identity. There is, alas, not much evidence for the Roman Catholicism of the Irish women. One woman did tell John Dunton that his threats of death and judgment for her behavior were "bugbears" that "might well frighten us who were Protestants, but for her part she was a Roman Catholic, and could be absolved when she pleased; and have the Eucharist brought her on her deathbed, which was a never failing Viaticum." Another woman told him that all the reformers were Whigs (and loyal to King William); he replied that he had heard that "all the whores in town are Jacobites" (and loyal to King James). She blessed God that she was "a true Churchwoman and love my King." Mother Wisebourn was the daughter of a clergyman. She was well read in the Scriptures, and the "deists, and they who make jest of all religion, were ever the subject of her reproach." Captain Smith claimed that Sally Salisbury, the most famous of Mother Wisebourn's daughters, was a Nonjuror: one of those who would not accept the new political regime on religious grounds. Her mother told Sally that she would not receive the wages of sin from her. Sally cursed her as an old bitch but continued to visit her. A whore, even a Protestant one, could die in the hope of heaven. It was said as a joke, but a revealing one, that when Mother Cole, a famous bawd who ran a milliner's shop in Russell Street, Covent Garden, was dying and heard the bar bell ring frequently, she exclaimed, "Why Betty! . . . no body to fetch girls to the gentlemen; oh! my God, what will become of this house when I am in the bosom of my sweet savior."[50]

One Dissenting preacher, Daniel Burgess, who on different religious grounds shared the political disaffection of some of these women, seems to have drawn some of them to his preaching. He set up his chapel in Brydges Street, Covent Garden, in the heart of what he called London's Sodom. He preached simply but eccentrically. One old rake said that Burgess was the only preacher he had ever heard who said that the prostitute's sins, "like those of Mary Magdalen, are forgiven, because of her loving much." "You see," Burgess exclaimed, "from what hath been said, that common strumpets, and the lewdest harlots, shall enter into the Kingdom of Heaven" before the clergymen of the Church of England. "There's comfort for you," he continued, "ye ragged whores at the door." This reduced Christopher Johnson to laughter, but as he left, he found "three or four of the strangest tatterdemalions" were indeed at the door. Unlike Burgess, though, he "could not say they had not a rag to their posteriours."[51]

Most prostitutes, if they did not steal, remained poor. The most usual fee mentioned for a common street prostitute was one shilling, sometimes two or three. Sometimes it was less than a shilling. Robert Harrison paid nine pence, and Catherine Speed accepted six pence from Thomas Winkfield. Francis Baldrey and Elizabeth Mathews had a fight over her price. Baldrey was a bricklayer's laborer. On his way home from work, he picked her up and asked her to drink. He was a married man and unable to stay the night. She said he told her that he was afraid of "getting a bad distemper." He offered her six pence. She would not take less than a shilling. So he raised his offer to six pence half-penny. She felt he was trying to ill use her, and she would not agree to it. He called her an "impudent bitch" and said he would swear a robbery against her if she did not agree. They ended up charging each other. When Baldrey's wife arrived at the watchhouse, she attacked him: "You dog, you brought me but twopence farthing last week." He had intended to spend almost five times as much for the woman. This suggests that common laborers cannot often have afforded one-shilling whores. It may explain why most of the men arrested for being with prostitutes were artisans. On the other hand, Francis Place knew a set of "horribly ragged, dirty, and disgusting" women who would take any customer behind a wall for twopence. When men debauched a virgin, on the other hand, the prices rose higher, to a half-guinea—ten times a one-shilling whore—or more. The women who served the aristocracy expected even more. They commonly received, according to the prices in *Harris's List*, from a half-guinea to two pounds.[52]

Contracts with prostitutes did not have any standing at law. Lord Mansfield did uphold a bond from a gentleman to pay a Miss Jones three thousand pounds. But he did so because "she lived with the gentleman at the time, giving her company to no other." He said that if she had been a common prostitute he would have set the bond aside. When the servant of a common prostitute brought an action for her wages, she claimed that she had earned them by finding customers for her mistress. She had written thirty-six letters; she had gone to the Gun Tavern in Charing Cross twenty-eight times looking for fellows, and five times to St. Paul's Church; and her husband had similarly gone on ships fifteen times. The servant did not get her money and was sent to bridewell instead. But the magistrate was kinder to Martha Smith. He sent her mistress to bridewell but made her pay her servant £6.6.0 in wages, and £4.6.0 to the girl's mother for doing her washing. Martha promised to leave her mistress and went home to her mother. Poor Susanna Corbet was arrested for trying to pass two counterfeit half-guineas. She said she had gotten them as pay from a gentleman. The magistrate thought that the coins were "so miserably bad as to make the story credible." So he simply sent her to bridewell for a month as a disorderly person.[53]

Prison, contempt, and violence were all common parts of prostitute's life. Throughout the century women were sent to the houses of correction for varying periods: a day, two or three days, a week, two weeks, or a month, which was the maximum sentence. Sometimes she was ordered to be whipped as well. There probably was less whipping as the century moved on. But the religious reformers of the early century probably put women in bridewell for shorter periods than did the humanitarian ones in the second half of the century. Some women regularly went in and out of Bridewell. It could be a demoralizing experience. Mary Sommers hanged herself in St. Margaret's Watch-house.[54]

Contempt for the prostitute could take various forms. Katherine Wilcox charged William Laurence with assault: he had thrown some urine on her. But since she was a common nightwalker, the man was discharged.[55] This contempt resulted in violence at all the various levels of prostitution. After the body of a woman was found in Cut-Throat Lane, in Shadwell, it was discovered that she had been seen with three lascars, or East Indian sailors, the preceding night. There was a center of prostitution for them along the river, a world that was often violent, and presumably they had killed her. But a young prostitute was also killed by the blow a man gave her with a large oaken stick as she walked in the Strand. Her murderer continued to walk calmly on after he had struck her, secure in his knowledge that no one would take any further notice than "to laugh at the brutality exercised on the body of an unfortunate, foolish, and miserable streetwalker."[56]

Ann Bell died because of what was done to her in a fashionable Covent Garden bagnio. She came from a reputable family in Norfolk. She had been seduced by an army officer and had eloped with him. Her family recovered her, but it was impossible for her to stay in their rural neighborhood. They therefore apprenticed her to a respectable milliner in London. But she soon left her new mistress. To become legally free of her family, she married a man with whom she spent one night. She then took up a friendship with an actor whom she had met in Norwich, and she lived in many different places under different names, making her way as a prostitute. Eventually she went to a Covent Garden bagnio with a group of libertines she knew through the actor. Her principal companion, William Sutton, was the son of a City merchant. It was suggested that he may have tried to force her to have anal sex, and that he cut her buttocks with a penknife when she resisted. She was kept in the bagnio for three days, continuously drunk on strong drinks like ratafia (a cordial with almonds and cherry kernels). Sutton cut her after his other two companions had left. He had also bent her fingers back almost parallel with the back of her hand. Eventually the girl was taken out of the bagnio and died in a fever. The legal question was whether she had died from her mistreatment or from the fever; and who was to prosecute her case—her husband or her family. The newspapers and an army officer took up her cause. The officer published a pamphlet attacking Sutton, who sued for libel but failed. He was indicted for murder, but the medical evidence did not seem to show that the wound had directly caused her death, and he was found not guilty.[57]

Ann Bell had been kept in an alcoholic stupor by her three companions. One of her defenders said that "so far from being a drinker to extremes," she was "remarkably sober for one of her unhappy profession."[58] Catherine Carter, one of the divorced wives in an earlier example, was dismissed from Maria Theresa Johnson's fashionable house because she was frequently drunk. From other examples it is clear that the most common approach by a prostitute to a man was to ask him to treat her to a drink. Ann Lamb and her companions were expected to bring men back to Fanny Finley's house to buy drinks before they had sex. Any drunken woman in the street was likely to be mistaken for a prostitute. Ann Griffith was arrested at eleven o'clock at night as she made a great disturbance near Billingsgate Churchyard. She was dismissed the next morning when it turned out that she was not a prostitute but simply "a poor woman a little overcome with liquor." A married woman was arrested, obviously drunk, as she picked up men in Chancery Lane: she said she did not know what she was doing, as she was "insensible" through liquor. Elizabeth Williams was taken in Fleet Street at midnight, drunk and picking up men; Bethia Atkinson was with a man at ten o'clock in the morning, and drunk. The drunken whore in the streets and in the bawdy houses was a commonplace sight. It was undoubtedly bad for their health, though it may have made their lives easier. It probably also denied them any slight chance they may have had to profit from their way of life. Moll King, who was one of the few women to successfully run a noted pickup house (she expected her customers to consummate their business elsewhere), did not get drunk, unlike many town ladies.[59]

Women also became pregnant from prostitution, which gave the lie to the folk belief that prostitutes did not conceive because the seed of many men had been mixed in their wombs. But it is impossible to say how many women or how often. From time to time a woman arrested on the street or found guilty of stealing turned out to be pregnant. Two women were arrested for being a great nuisance to the Cheapside neighborhood because they picked up men and used indecent language. They were both sent to bridewell: one was sentenced to be whipped as well, but not the other because she was pregnant. When Elizabeth Mob was convicted of theft, she "pleaded her belly"; the matrons found her pregnant. Sarah Edwards was arrested because she kept a house for pregnant prostitutes. Pregnant prostitutes sometimes show up in the bastardy examinations, but it can be hard to spot them for certain. But there was no doubt about Elizabeth Bottomley. She first met the duke of Montague in the house of the famous Mother Wisebourne in Drury Lane and then saw him several times at the china shop that Mrs. Lilly kept in Pall Mall. She said he had made her pregnant. Mary Fox can be traced over eight years and three pregnancies. In 1712 she said that a tailor she had had sex with at the Horn Tavern in King Street was her child's father; five years later it was an upholsterer with whom she had gone to an alehouse in St. Martin's Lane; three and a half years later it was a soldier at an alehouse in New Tuttle Street. There is a record of the second child's birth. What happened to it, and to the two other pregnancies, is not known. Some women were forced by the putative fathers of their children to abort. Margaret Hardin said that Thomas Dobney, who kept a public house, had beaten her because she would not take "the medicine which he offered her to destroy the child which she is pregnant of by him." Joseph Gayoh, who was also in the drink trade, actually forced Elizabeth Carr to drink the medicines he gave her. In some cases it is likely that women took these medicines of their own accord. It is also likely that in many cases a girl or a woman who had been with many men cannot have known who was the father of her child.[60]

Finally, we must ask why the women disappeared from the world of prostitution in their later twenties. There is a dispute on this question for the nineteenth century, when it is possible to gather some statistics. One view holds that the women died from disease and exhaustion; the other that they rejoined the ordinary world of working-class life from which they had gone back and forth into prostitution.[61] In the eighteenth century it is certainly likely that most active prostitutes contracted venereal disease, but it is unlikely that they died very soon, if ever, from it. It took James Boswell thirty-five years to die from the complications of his many venereal infections. If the women died, it was from drunkenness and the difficulty of their lives. The problem is partly solved by going back to the distinction between the 15 percent of women who were constantly on the street, and the remainder who probably did go back and forth between service or millinery work and the life of the streets. Some from the first group probably did die. The remainder left prostitution once the peak of their sexual attractiveness had passed.[62]

Some women also probably did marry. Certainly married women in the defamation cases often accused each other of having had an irregular sexual past. It is hard to know how seriously to take such abuse, but the women against whom such slurs were made may well have been those women who had only occasionally walked the streets. Francis Place had a naive friend who married a woman of forty who claimed to be a dressmaker and a milliner. But to Place's eye it was clear that she had been a prostitute. Place, who had passed all his life in the heart of London's largest bawdy house district, said that in the late eighteenth century all young girls had gone out with boys in a way that in the early nineteenth century was thought to be disreputable. Some of them became prostitutes, and Place's gang of Fleet Street apprentices had been fond of treating these girls, who were their own age. But they did not marry them. They married their sweethearts, who grew up to be respectable wives. Even those women who went back to respectable work probably had difficulty finding husbands. The Magdalen Hospital in 1786 claimed that in twenty-six years, it had sent 65 percent of its women back to their families or found them jobs. But only 122 women of 2,415 admitted (or 5 percent) were known to have married. It is therefore likely that reintegration into the ordinary world was never complete for those women who had walked the streets as prostitutes for any extended period.[63]

The stories used in this chapter to describe the prostitute's life have mixed material from both halves of the century to make a unified picture, but this is in some ways a misleading thing to do. The modern prostitute did not really come into existence until she was set apart from the majority

of ordinary women, sentimentalized, and reformed, as chapter 6 will describe. Before the sentimental movement began to describe the ordinary
woman's nature as maternal, every woman was at heart a rake, as Pope
said, and the prostitute was simply an extreme instance of this. The defamation cases give evidence that traditionally whore was a universal term
that could be applied to any woman for a variety of sexual acts that stopped
far short of walking the streets. The magistrates in their policing before
1730 also presumed that the prostitute's behavior was a sin of which men
could be equally guilty, and so they arrested the men also. They did not
necessarily presume that prostitution was a deviation beyond the nature
of most women. It is also possible that the London poor were more accepting of a woman's prostitution before 1750, when they were more likely
to bail their daughters, sisters, and wives and to try to rescue them out
of the hands of bawds. After 1750 a great deal of this changed. It may
have become less likely that prostitutes would be recruited from women
with families in London, since such families almost disappear from the
recognizances bailing prostitutes. The defamation suits with their general-
ized use of the term whore also declined. And the magistrates stopped
prosecuting men for going to prostitutes. Male heterosexual desire was
now protected in an unprecedented manner, and women were divided
into a maternal majority and a prostituted minority. Male heterosexuality
and the sentimental movement had joined hands together to create a new
deviant group against which the majority of the lives of ordinary women
could be measured.

CHAPTER SIX

Prostitution Sentimentalized

T he growth of sentimentalism—or the trust in the goodness and naturalness of human emotions—began to powerfully change sexual attitudes and behavior among the landed elites and the middle classes after 1750. Chapter 3 has shown how it modified the libertinism of those gentlemen, who used their sexual experience to construct a moral alternative to Christianity's view of sexual pleasure. This chapter considers the ways in which sentimentalism transformed the organization of prostitution for gentlemen and conceptualized the prostitute as a woman who deviated from the newly made standards of a domesticated, maternal sexuality. Sentimentalism in elite families led wives to expect faithfulness from their husbands and encouraged mothers to socialize their sons in the values of romantic marriage. But the need in men to establish an exclusive heterosexual identity placed severe restrictions on these points of view. Prostitution, instead of being abandoned, was domesticated in a new kind of brothel in which romantic feelings refined men's gallantry. All attempts at removing the young prostitute from the street were limited by concern that it would be dangerous to eliminate prostitution entirely, since men without the sexual outlet that it provided would turn to each other. The male heterosexual desire that lay at the foundation of all prostitution could not in the end be transformed into a purely marital sexuality because of the fear of sodomy.

DOMESTICITY AND THE BROTHEL

The rise of domesticity after 1750 effectively changed the attitudes of men in the fashionable world toward prostitution and its organization. By 1750 many aristocrats were marrying for love, and after marriage husbands and wives became each other's constant companion. This made it very difficult for husbands to have relations with prostitutes as well, and those husbands who did so were likely to make their wives hostile. In 1760, the young Lady Sarah Lennox, when she was fifteen and new to the fashionable world, observed the marriages around her and described to her elder sister the kind that she would not like to make. She had been told by another one of her sisters that the duke of Marlborough was "so entirely given up to women that it's quite dreadful, for he has a terrible disorder that hindered him dancing." The duke in this respect was like his father. The father had gone to women "after he was married, though he loved his wife." But Lady Sarah said that "that sort of love would not content me, for I have no notion of a man's loving his wife and following all those sort of people." Six years later, when the second Lord and Lady Bolingbroke were parting, Lady Sarah took the same view. Bolingbroke claimed he was "more in love with [his wife] than ever." But Lady Sarah had heard that "he had got a woman in the house already," and therefore she concluded that he was not as unhappy as he claimed to be "at the thoughts of having used her so cruelly," for "a man that had any feeling would not recover his spirits so easily."

It could be difficult, however, for a younger man to keep to his good intentions to love his wife and avoid loose women. Although Lady Sarah's sister, Lady Louisa Conolly, was a happily married woman, Lord Eglinton had told her husband "that as he was so young, he supposed he should not be constant to his wife." He offered to make things easy, according to Lady Louisa, so that his wife "should not find it out and that nobody might hear anything of it." He told Conolly that he could come to his house "and pretend to sup with him and so meet anybody that he chose to appoint." Lady Louisa, who must have been told the story by her faithful husband, remarked: "what a pretty character here is for a man of his rank to be a p[im]p." But even Eglinton seems to have realized that the times had changed and that a philandering husband now needed to be discreet.[1]

The libertine's reputation as a likely future husband markedly declined after 1750. In his preface to *Clarissa*, Richardson had explained that one of his purposes in writing was "to warn children against preferring a man of pleasure to a man of probity, upon that dangerous but too commonly received notion that a reformed rake makes the best husband." The libertines had insisted that they made better husbands than chaste men because they came to marriage with fewer illusions about women. "Chaste men," one libertine wrote, "seldom marry for anything but love, so they have framed to themselves such high extravagant notions of the raptures they expect to possess that they are mighty shocked at the disappointment."

But the experienced man, who would have tried several women, would know that "they all agree in one particular, and that after a storm of love, there always succeeds a calm." Such a man was prepared to make allowances for the human imperfections of his wife. Women knew that since it was "difficult to monopolize a man's affections, that he will have his curiosity about those affairs satisfied one time or other"; it was therefore safer (because of the possibility of disease) that a man should experiment before rather than after marriage. After 1750, however, a man's association with prostitutes was more likely to seem to make him unfit for marriage, since the experience would have left him contemptuous of women: "where a man by prejudice, and his connexions with loose women, comes seriously to despise the whole sex, it is very prudent in him to decline a connexion where virtue and mutual esteem are essential to happiness." Romantic marriage and whoring at any stage of life could be yoked together only with difficulty.[2]

Before 1750 even an Epicurean libertine like Lord Chesterfield ended with contempt for women, partly as a result of his sexual experience. Such a libertine was very likely to pass his attitudes along to his sons. In his letters to his son in the 1740s, Chesterfield distinguished between the man of pleasure and the rake. A rake was a composition of "all the lowest, most ignoble, degrading and shameful of vices" who was likely to end with his reputation ruined and his health destroyed by drink and venereal disease. Chesterfield later advised Lord Huntingdon always to wear a condom—"solid proof and armour"—and not to be taken in by attestations of health or even of virginity in a prostitute: "their vestal fire is hereditary and inextinguishable." Chesterfield at his marriage in 1733 had claimed that he married because he "found both my constitution and my fortune so much the worse for wearing" and it was "high time to lay aside the fine gentleman and to think of repairing them." Some of his excesses from his life in the 1720s did, however, return to plague his reputation as late as the 1740s, when Mrs. Phillips seems to have tried to blackmail him by implying that he had seduced her when she was fourteen years old. He therefore had cause to tell his son that "a man of pleasure, though not always so scrupulous as he should be, and as one day he will wish he had been, refines his pleasures by taste, accompanies them with decency, and enjoys them with dignity." Such a man did not affect to have vices that he did not have, and those that he did, he gratified "with choice, delicacy, and secrecy." It is hardly surprising then to find that by 1760s Chesterfield, along with other aristocratic parents, urged that boys at puberty be sent away from England to Geneva, "where appetites and desires will not be gratified" and that they be kept from travel in Italy, which was "the sink of atheism and of the most degrading and scandalous vices." In England boys would have too easy an access to prostitutes, as Westminster schoolboys did in London. And in Italy the traditional bisexuality of southern Europe was no longer acceptable to a northern European like Chesterfield, who had been reared in the new world of contempt for the adult effeminate sodomite.[3]

Chesterfield as he grew older became more conservative about the indulgence of sexual pleasure. But his contempt for women remained unvarying. It was, of course, a contempt that was never to be expressed in an openly hostile manner. Civility was due to women; it was their "only protection against the superior strength" of men. Women as a whole were not to be denounced, for then one unnecessarily made "a great number of enemies by attacking a *corps* collectively." Nonetheless a wise man did not waste his evenings "frivolously in the tattle of women's company." The man of pleasure was, after all, not a mere fop. Some association with women was necessary, however, since it "polishes the manners." Only the English booby professed to hate the company of modest women and to prefer that of whores. What Chesterfield did recommend was that his son attach himself to some "veteran woman of condition," because such women "being past their bloom, are extremely flattered by the least attention from a young fellow." They would then point out to him what manners had pleased them most in their youth. It was invaluable to have a small collection of such women as one's friends, since one might confess to them one's doubts and difficulties as to how to behave in society. But in conversation even with such women, one would find that they were "only children of a larger growth." They had "an entertaining tattle and sometimes wit" but never solid good sense. A man therefore "only trifles with them, plays with them . . . as he does with a sprightly forward child"; he would find that "no flattery is either too high or too low for them." Though unlike some rakes Chesterfield knew and enjoyed the company of women other than whores, it is very likely that his life of pleasure had reinforced in him a traditional misogyny that made it impossible for him to enter into a romantic marriage in which he would have wished his wife to be his constant and preferred companion.[4]

After 1750 a libertine like Lord Pembroke found that his wife would oppose not only his own libertinism but also his attempts to indoctrinate his son in his way of life. Pembroke was born in 1734, the year after Chesterfield's son; Pembroke's father died when he was sixteen, and he married in 1756 when he was twenty-two, the year after he returned from his grand tour. In the first twelve years of his marriage, Pembroke had two illegitimate children by two different women, and he and his wife separated after he eloped with one of his mistresses. In 1762 he was reconciled to his wife and came back to town after a strategic withdrawal. The great Casanova met him when he visited London that year. Casanova seems to have presumed that a libertine like Pembroke must be a bachelor, but it is probable that he was led to this conclusion because Pembroke had not yet gone back to live with his wife. Casanova certainly listened to Pembroke's authoritative advice with regard to the rules for moving in London's demimonde of fashionable prostitutes, the sort one courted and fell in love with. But Lady Pembroke was never reconciled to her husband's behavior. She did allow Pembroke's illegitimate son to live with the family, and she was fond of the boy. But when Pembroke tried to have him take the family name of Herbert, as he had promised the boy's mother, Lady Pembroke would not allow it; and she had her own son, Lord Herbert, oppose the move as disrespectful to herself. Pembroke never told her that he had another illegitimate child, but his libertine associate Captain John Floyd made certain that Lord Herbert knew where to find his illegitimate half sister in Paris. As a grown man Herbert ordered that the portraits of Pembroke's mistress La Bacelli that had hung at Wilton be taken down and stored away to avoid offending his mother. Pembroke simply dismissed the pictures as trifling objects. But Lady Pembroke in the end could not endure her husband's libertinism and finally separated from him.[5]

Lady Pembroke successfully struggled to detach her son from his father's libertinism and won him for religion and the domestic affections. The struggle was at its most vivid when Herbert was sent on his grand tour in the late 1770s. He was accompanied by William Coxe, a clergyman and a scholar who was his mother's agent, and by Captain John Floyd, his father's libertine friend. Pembroke wanted Herbert to read Voltaire assiduously, which Lady Pembroke wanted to prevent. She did ask Coxe when they were in France to point out to Herbert the superstition of Catholicism, and she complained that the French bishops were mostly libertines. She wanted her son to be a good man, "good not only from religion"; but as an apparent devotee of Shaftesbury (a fine example of the way in which both the religious and the libertine found Shaftesbury appealing) she wanted Herbert to be good "from his own feelings." She desired, and this she said no doubt with her husband's behavior in mind, that Herbert "should be sensible of the infinite pleasure of making others happy, and be *almost* . . . an enthusiast for virtue, which will support him at moments when the plausible language of libertinism may in some respects raise his doubts." Lady Pembroke was even willing to quote one libertine to avoid the other and suggested that Coxe point out to Herbert that Lord Bolingbroke made it essential to read all the ancient historians, since that would delay reading Voltaire: "mention Lord Bolingbroke's being a free thinker," she urged Coxe. Coxe in fact found that Herbert agreed with him and Lady Pembroke as to Voltaire's bad principles, and they managed to miss Voltaire when they tried to visit the philosopher, as Pembroke wanted.[6]

Lady Pembroke worried about the conditions under which Herbert's sexual awakening would occur. Here, curiously enough, she found her guide in Chesterfield's letters to his son, which had just been published in 1774, the year after Chesterfield's death. Other religious parents like Lord Dartmouth also found a great deal to admire in these letters. Lady Pembroke was concerned about Herbert's time in Italy: "I would not for the world have his passions first awakened there," since the Italians ignored all decency and morality and would "give him much too little trouble." But she was free apparently of any anxiety about Italy's sodomy. Lady Pembroke feared Italy's women, not its men, which probably reflected a difference between male and female sexual identity: it was male identity that now structured itself around the avoidance of effeminate sodomy; for women sex outside of marriage remained the issue. She hoped, since it would be "certainly the very best thing that can happen to a very young man," that Herbert would "fall desperately in love with a woman of fashion, who is clever, and likes him enough to teach him to endeavour to please her, and yet keep him at his proper distance"—which was Chesterfield's doctrine. This she wrote in March 1776. Three years later she simply told Herbert himself that she was "now too sure of your good principles to be afraid of your being hurt in Italy, either by their bad morals, or want of religion." Lord Pembroke, for his part, began to urge his son to think of marrying when he came home. Pembroke wanted a wife who above all was rich. She could also be as beautiful as Herbert wished. He pleaded against anyone who was deformed or mad. But he never mentioned love. Instead, then and later he passed along news of the sexual world both old and new. A master had been discharged for making love to the boys at Harrow. A Scottish lord who was captured during the '45 had tried to bugger the captain of a ship: Lord Lothian knew the details and could give them to Herbert "if you wish to know them." A libertine, it was apparent, knew the ways of male sodomites and quite firmly distanced himself from them. Pembroke also could explain to his son a particular kind of "pale and sallow" woman: "women who are teazed always have that appearance. Those who are rammed up to the Maker's name, look ruddy." Herbert was apparently not very interested in any of this. He chose his mother's niece for his wife, and when his father tried to make a social occasion of his marriage, he replied in the new domesticated way "that no one likes to faire spectacle de son marriage, and I have absolutely refused to let any of my nearest connections and greatest friends to be at it." Pembroke had lost the war for his son, and libertinism had fallen to enthusiastic religion and the domestic affections.[7]

Nonetheless, aristocratic men continued to go to whores after 1750; the standard of sexual behavior in men did not very quickly come to approximate that of women, even under the influence of domesticity. Aristocratic men instead patronized a new kind of prostitution that was more domestically organized. There was in this an interesting parallel to the way they had changed the education of their sons. Domesticity maintained that boys should ideally not be sent away from home to public schools: their fathers were their best teachers, and a domestic education would maintain affection between fathers and sons. Instead of doing this, however, aristocratic fathers after 1750 sent their sons either to small private schools where the boys were more closely attended to, or to houses inside the larger public schools where something of the same atmosphere could be maintained. Aristocratic fathers did not become the teachers of their sons; instead, they domesticated the schools.[8] Similarly, aristocratic husbands did not give up whores; instead, they domesticated the brothel. This was the male aristocratic response to the demand from their women that there should be a single standard of sexual behavior for men and women. But the male commitment to prostitution was deeply embedded in the gender identity of most men—prostitution was the means by which one proved that one was not a sodomite. This will become especially apparent in the next section when the reformers of prostitution will be found saying that there were limits to reform imposed by the need to have available a sufficient number of sexual outlets to ensure that men did not turn to each other and become sodomites. This might mean that one was obliged to treat some women as prostitutes and thereby violate every romantic and sentimental notion about the refined nature of women in their maternal role. The solution to this conundrum was to sentimentalize the prostitute, not to give her up.

By 1779 the two volumes of *Nocturnal Revels* organized the history of fashionable brothels since the 1690s around the theme of Mrs. Goadby's introduction at midcentury of the domestically organized brothel. Mrs.

Goadby had traveled to Paris and had come back inspired by the politesse
of the houses that she had observed there. She opened her own house,
first in Berwick Street, Soho, and then nearby in Great Marlborough
Street. The women in the house were examined by a surgeon to guarantee
that they were free from disease, and most of them were required to live
in the house. They were not allowed to become drunk or to talk bawdy.
They revealed to the "abbess" who ran the "nunnery" any presents they
were given above the usual fees. The men who visited the house came for
supper and a night of pleasure. After supper, the women congregated in
a large saloon where they played the guitar, sang, and did tambour work,
but did not drink. This was the plan of the French houses that Goadby
took over.[9]

Earlier in the century there certainly had been houses that catered
mainly to fashionable men. But even when they were run with decorum
and involved some kind of a social assembly, the women do not seem to
have lived on the premises. This was apparently the case in the house that
Elizabeth Wisebourn ran between 1690 and 1720. The same was true of
the houses run by Mother Douglas and Mrs. Gould. The houses that
Mrs. Smith ran in Queen Street and then in Jermyn Street in 1719 are
the best documented because William Byrd in his diary noted the visits
he made in the course of that year. Byrd was taken there by Lord Orrery,
who also introduced him to a similar house run by Mrs. Burton. But a
house like Mrs. Burton's was really a place of assignation: "we found two
chambermaids that my Lord had ordered to be got for us." Byrd returned
to Mrs. Smith's house some twenty-odd times on his own. Sometimes
he seems to have gone simply to make a social visit. Sometimes he drank
tea, sometimes he had supper before or after sex. He had sex at Mrs.
Smith's on fifteen occasions, during three of which he was impotent. One
or two of the women he saw a number of times. But none of them seem
to have lived with Mrs. Smith. This is clear from his experience on February 15. He went to "my good friend Mrs. Smith" expecting a girl Mrs.
Smith had arranged for, but the girl did not come. So they sent for Mrs.
Courtney, whom Byrd had seen at the house four times before, on three
occasions for sex, and once when he had taken her to the masquerade.
But Mrs. Courtney was not at home. They then sent for the widow Johnson, who came, and Byrd subsequently visited Johnson at her lodging in
Young Street. But when he next "rogered" her it was at Mrs. Smith's,
probably because it was unsafe to do so in Johnson's lodging—the neighbors and the landlord might object. On May 12, however, Mrs. Smith
had to disappoint Byrd entirely because she "could not get me a mistress"

when he visited her after going to the play. Mrs. Smith's (or Mother Smith, as he called her only once) was not cheap: one assignation had cost Byrd ten guineas for the woman, and a guinea tip for Mrs. Smith.[10]

Byrd's visits to Smith's house were, however, only a small part of his sexual life during his two years in London. He had over ninety sexual encounters in those months. Only seventeen of them were in a fashionable house. On twice as many occasions he picked up a girl in the park or in the street and consummated the act there or in a coach or at a tavern. Some women he took to a bagnio, one of them repeatedly. On only nine occasions did he go home with a prostitute, and only once did he have sex with a woman in his own lodgings, though several times he did kiss the maid there until he ejaculated.[11]

A generation later, in 1762, James Boswell spent a year in London as a younger (he was in his twenties, Byrd in his forties), poorer, less well connected man than Byrd, but it is instructive to compare the two men's sexual experience in town, since it helps to demonstrate the effect that sentiment and domesticity had begun to have on the libertine when he was set loose in London. Both men suffered from religious scruples about using whores, but their momentary twinges of conscience had almost no effect on their actual sexual behavior. Boswell was too poor to go to fashionable brothels or even to make use of a bagnio. Instead he set out to court a twenty-four-year-old actress. When she finally consented to sleep with him, he found a place to take her by pretending that she was his wife, since neither of their own lodgings were private enough. He crowed to himself that "the whole expense was just eighteen shillings." But he did lend Louisa two guineas, which he demanded back when the affair ended. Boswell could not afford the "splendid Madam at fifty guineas a night." He could do much better with the girl in the Strand or the park who was content with a shilling and a pint of wine. But he thought that "the dignity of his sex is kept up" when "paradisal scenes of gallantry" exalted a man's ideas and refined his taste. He wished to fall in love with his actress and to have her at no cost but love. He made certain that her affections were not engaged and told her that he could "never think of having connection with women I don't love." But soon after their first sexual encounter, he felt his affection for her disappear and became disgusted by hers for him. A few days later he became aware that he had become infected venereally. He was chagrined not least because he had boasted to his friends that he was safe from disease in the arms of a fine woman whom they had taken to calling his "ideal lady." His doctor insisted that Louisa must have known that she was sick. She confessed that she had had an infection three years before, but she maintained that there had been no symptoms for over a year. Boswell would not believe her and concluded that she was "in all probability a most consummate dissembling whore"—whereas he had expected from the affair "at least a winter's safe copulation."[12]

Boswell still hankered after a fashionable affair, but he was constrained by his lack of money. He had hopes about a widow who seemed to flirt with him. And Lord Eglinton promised to introduce him to "some women of intrigue of the highest fashion." But instead Boswell made do with a series of streetwalkers. With the first four he carefully wore a condom. Then he rashly acceded to the request of a fifth girl to leave it off as the "sport was much pleasanter without it." The next two girls he took together to the Shakespeare's Head Tavern and treated and enjoyed them. On the king's birthnight he sallied out like a gentleman in disguise and had two girls in succession and was refused by a third because he would not pay. On another night another girl picked his pocket of his handkerchief. It is unclear whether he had stopped using a condom. In the midst of these adventures Boswell met Samuel Johnson. When the two men were approached by a girl as they walked in the Strand, Johnson sent her away, and the two friends then "talked of the unhappy situation of these wretches, and how much more misery than happiness . . . is produced by irregular love." But a week later when Boswell was on his own, and "a fine fresh lass" tapped him on the shoulder, he went home with her. "Surely," he wrote to himself afterward, "when the woman is already abandoned, the crime must be alleviated, though in strict morality, illicit love is always wrong."[13]

Boswell's concern about venereal disease alone places him in a different world than Byrd. Byrd simply accepted the disease as a matter of course, and during his two years in London, he seems to have had a discharge on a number of occasions. He matter-of-factly paid for the cure of a milliner with whom he had contracted for sex and the care of his linen. But libertines by midcentury took greater responsibility for their own health. Such a libertine, especially one who had Johnson as a friend, was also likely to worry about prostitution as a social evil. This was rather different from Byrd's repenting his sexual encounters when he said his prayers at night. But Boswell's generation of libertines differed most from Byrd's in their presumption that sex unaccompanied by romantic feeling was less than satisfactory—though even Byrd had sometimes visited Mrs. Smith more for conversation than for sex. It is true that a libertine's love might dissipate very quickly, as Boswell's felt his do. But libertines after 1750 needed an environment where such feelings stood at least a chance of blooming. In a house like Mrs. Goadby's, which poor Boswell could not afford, they were more likely to find than at Byrd's Mrs. Smith's, women who were free from disease and drunkenness, and who were likely in the conversation that followed supper to try to add romance to sex.

In the 1760s and 1770s the most famous of these new brothels or "nunneries" was run by Charlotte Hayes, first in Great Marlborough Street and then in King's Place off Pall Mall. Her women were carefully examined for their health and supplied condoms to their partners. She had special elastic beds constructed that gave "the finest movements in the most ecstatic moments without trouble or the least fatigue to either agent or passive." She staged sex shows in which young men and women copied the postures in Aretino's prints. She may have inspired James Graham, who also had a special bed and recommended a variety of sexual postures and the use of lascivious prints and paintings to stimulate the languid or the old: except that Graham claimed to be dealing with happily married couples, not libertines. Charlotte Hayes's house was only one of several in King's Place, and the street became noted for its collection of other houses, with at least five of them in 1779. The houses had carriages attached to them and servants in livery. Their prices were necessarily high. In the 1760s there had also been such fashionable brothels in Bolton Row, Hanover Square. These houses in their fantasy provided those "paradisal scenes of gallantry" to which Boswell aspired. This arcadian fantasy had first been set out in Cleland's *Fanny Hill*, before such houses actually existed in England. Cleland may have known the French houses that Mrs. Goadby took as her models. But the frequenters of the English houses (as the *Nocturnal Revels* said) took Cleland for one of their holy books. They knew that the young men who supported Mrs. Cole's house in the novel had styled themselves "the restorers of the liberty of the golden age, and its simplicity of pleasures, before their innocence became so unjustly branded with the names of guilt, and shame."[14]

Some of the women who moved in this new world managed to keep themselves independent of any of the individual houses, but at the price of personal security. This was the case of Mrs. Ann Sheldon, who published her memoirs in four volumes in 1787. According to her memoirs, Sheldon was seduced at fifteen by a Mrs. Wilson, who came for her in a coach, pretending to be a relation. At Wilson's house she met Mrs. Horsham and her two daughters. They were visited by the marquess of Granby, who the girls said was their father, though they were in fact poor girls who had been procured for him. Sheldon herself was deflowered at fifteen by a Mr. Walsingham, who wanted to set her up in her own house, but who asked her instead because of her youth to return to Mrs. Wilson's house. She acquired other lovers, among them Lord Melbourne and Lord George Sackville. At this point she did well enough to keep her own carriage. Lord Bateman asked her to desert all others and attach herself only to him. Bateman's wife, however, seems to have required that Sheldon marry before she became her husband's mistress, probably to stop claims by any children that Sheldon might bear to Bateman. Bateman duly arranged her marriage to the complaisant Archer, whom Sheldon left on their wedding night.[15]

Mrs. Archer (as she now was) later set up on her own, supported by a changing clientele of two or three men at a time. She sometimes used the new nunneries to meet her clients. She visited Charlotte Hayes in King's Place. Mrs. Goadby from Great Marlborough Street proposed that Archer come into her house, but she preferred her independence. She also met clients at Mr. Kildare's in King's Place, where the financial arrangements were more generous than at Goadby's. Archer acquired a little cottage at Chelsea. She refused to settle for any one keeper: "in short I got too much money by seeing a variety of friends, to attach myself to the uncertain protection of anyone. Indeed, if I had pursued the economical plans of some of my female acquaintance, I should soon have acquired the independence which they possessed." Mrs. Matthews with her mansion in King's Place was one of these successful entrepreneurs who knew how to save and invest her earnings. The house was filled with girls from thirteen to seventeen who were kept locked in: the duke of Ancaster and Lord Lincoln were among the visitors. Mrs. Matthews proposed to take Archer into partnership, but Archer declined because Matthews was too unprincipled.[16]

At this point, Mr. Walsingham, her first seducer, came into Archer's life again. He had always possessed her heart despite her other lovers. This sounds rather like Fanny Hill and Charles, and one wonders how much life copied art. As a sign of love Archer became pregnant, but when Walsingham left her once again, she miscarried. At this point, she briefly tried to withdraw from the life by running a millinery establishment, but that did not last. Instead Lord Grosvenor helped her to set up a house of her own—"my seraglio"—and she in turn procured Negro women for him. But her house failed. Lord Bateman refused to help her, and her other old friends abandoned her. She began to let out lodgings and scrubbed her own floors. But her health was ruined. Her only resource was to write her memoirs. Her charms had failed, and her entrepreneurial skill had been insufficient. The golden age and the paradisal scenes of the King's Place seraglios existed only for the men who used them and the few women who knew how to manage them successfully.[17]

Archer did not tie herself to either of the two modes of fashionable prostitution most favored after 1750—the life of the kept mistress or residence in a King's Place nunnery; but the course of her career demonstrated two of the mutually competing forces of that world—the desire to have sex accompanied by love so as to make the sex more pleasing; and the increasing opposition of men's wives and families to these left-handed marriages. Archer had been obliged to marry another man to satisfy the wife of one of her lovers, and the deepest love of her life was taken away from her by the pressure from his family. The competition from wives increased significantly after 1750 because more gentlemen were likely to marry than had done so in the first half of the century. The number of aristocrats who married had fallen steadily through the Restoration and the early eighteenth century, and the size of families also significantly decreased. The lowest level of marriage occurred among those born in the period from 1700 to 1724, only half of whom ever married. It is very likely that these men who did not marry acted from a conscious libertine distaste for marriage such as one finds in men like Lord Shaftesbury and his friends. It is unlikely that (as has been proposed) the decrease in marriage was the result of an increase in homosexual behavior, since the early eighteenth century also saw the brutal stigmatization of sodomites as male whores. It is also not likely that it was from financial need, since aristocratic families had fewer children to provide for during the period of decline in marriage.[18]

The sexual lives of these men who were contemptuous of marriage must therefore have revolved around the world of female prostitution. Those who felt the need of domesticity but were contemptuous of marriage were likely to settle for left-handed marriages. Sir Charles Sedley had had such an arrangement. Lady Cowper wrote that "the left-handed wife of Sir Charles Sedley lately told me that [Sedley] verily believed" Lord Falkland "to be his true father and valued himself therefore, placing his picture by his own." Lord Albemarle Bertie lived with Mary Collbatch and had a son and five daughters by her. By Margaret Baines General George Hamilton had five children who were sent away to boarding schools; but she was listed among the mothers of bastard children by the reformers of St. Margaret's parish. These arrangements certainly continued to exist after 1750. There is the case of Lord Pembroke, but Pembroke was obliged to deal with the opposition of both his wife and his legitimate son and heir.[19]

The sexual lives of libertines were not, however, confined to mistresses and nunneries after 1750. The tavern and the bagnio continued to play their roles. The tavern could be the setting for an individual's extended fantasy. When Casanova was in London in 1764 and in despair over a love affair, he met the young Sir Wellbore Ellis Agar on Westminster Bridge and was invited to dinner at the Cannon coffeehouse, where Agar arranged for girls to meet them. Agar suggested that one of the girls dance the hornpipe naked, and she agreed if a blind musician could be found and if all four of them undressed. The musician was found and Agar undressed and danced with the girls. Casanova was too depressed to join in, but he was struck that Agar maintained an erection as he danced and wondered why he had not tried this himself. Agar then had sex with the two women repeatedly until he was exhausted. John Damer's naked frolic with his four women and a blind fiddler ended less happily. He supped with them at the Bedford Arms in Covent Garden, then dismissed them and shot himself. He had passed his life (though married to a woman who preferred her own gender) "with troops of women and the blind fiddler." Horace Walpole thought the blind man "an odd companion in such scenes," but it is apparent that his blindness must have made the naked dancing possible for the women who were otherwise too conventional to strip themselves.[20]

The bagnio was a more discreet alternative to the public tavern. One could either bring a woman there from a tavern or from the theater or the street, or once there, one could send out for a woman from the bagnio book that listed the names of women available. In the bagnios one could also have a bath or a meal. Archenholz described them as places "where noise and riot are banished, the domestics speak in a whisper." The bagnio in John Cleland's "The Romance of a Night," to which Felicia is taken in the course of the attempt to seduce her, is similarly described. These houses were very expensive, but Archenholz said they were often full all night long. Like the bagnios, some taverns also kept a register of available women. Casanova went to the Star and had ten women sent for but dismissed them all because none of them pleased him. Lord Pembroke later told him that he had to send for the better women by name, but that they could not be compelled to come.[21]

Beginning in the late 1740s an authoritative list of the more fashionable prostitutes was circulated in manuscript and then eventually printed and sold as *Harris's List of Covent Garden Ladies.* Jack Harris had been a waiter at the Shakespeare's Head Tavern and had kept a list of women whom he guaranteed to be free of venereal disease. There is a story that when

he enrolled the famous Fanny Murray, she had to be examined by a surgeon and sign an agreement with a lawyer that she would forfeit twenty
pounds if the information about her health was not accurate. The women
on the list paid Harris five shillings for each customer. There were earlier
occasional lists of fashionable whores that went back to the 1660s. But
Harris seems to have used his as a means of guaranteeing the health of
his customers. Harris died in 1766, but the lists continued to appear for
another thirty years. Archenholz claimed that eight thousand copies were
sold a year. The individual entry described a girl's age, her height, her
eyes, the coloring of her hair, her complexion, her legs, and the size of
her breasts. It gave her social accomplishments, whether she sang, or
danced, or conversed well. It said how long she had been on the town,
and whether she was innocent, or elegant, or liked sex. It sometimes told
what she would do in bed, and it sometimes described the size, appearance, and sensation that her clitoris and her vagina gave those who entered
her. It gave each woman's price. And it noted whether she encouraged
her clients to have repeated orgasms, an important point to libertines like
Byrd and Boswell, who carefully noted whenever it occurred.[22]

Harris's List described all these points about the women of the town
in the periphrastic and arcadian language of an elegant and romantic sensuality that had been brought to the pitch of perfection in Cleland's *Fanny
Hill.* Miss Lister's imagination was "filled with every luscious idea [that]
refined sensibility and fierce desire can unite." Her vagina was an "Elysian
font in the centre of a black bewitching grove." Miss Burn was a nymph
and Miss Hallond "a first rate ship" in which "to sail to the island of love."
Miss Linsay was free of the vulgarity often found in the "sisterhood." Miss
Hurdney had "beauty without pride, elegance without affectation, and
innocence without dissimulation." Miss Jones had "eyes molded for the
tender union of souls," and followed James Graham's sexual method because it increased pleasure and was clean and safe. Miss Clinton had "the
languishing eye of an Eloise." But a woman who drank was unacceptable:
Miss Brown was "too fond of the brandy bottle to give that sincere delight,
that mutual interchange of souls, so necessary to stamp the extactic rapture"; but then she had been on the town for seven years and was no
novelty. Miss Dodd, on the other hand, was forty and kept a house of
girls off Fleet Street but could still be alluring. She had erotic pictures to
revive the impotent and would give a "comfortable cup of tea in the morning." A number of the women used names they had taken from the man
who had kept them previously—in a sense seeing themselves as left-
handed wives. They could be found either at their own lodgings, which

sometimes had been provided by a present or former keeper, or in a house run by a mother abbess, or at the theater, or at one of the public hops or dances.[23]

The libertine desire to have romance and elegance accompany sex was necessarily vitiated by two inherent aspects of the world of prostitution. It was difficult for a poor uneducated girl ever to achieve real elegance of mind, and secondly, a love that was bought by many men from the same woman was hardly very romantic. Miss Emma Elliott had "fine blue melting eyes, with an aquiline nose, and a very pretty mouth." But her mouth lost its charm when she spoke, for once she gave "a loose to that unruly" tongue, she poured forth "such a torrent of blackguardism that shall destroy every attractive feature." She thereby spoiled "one of the most desirable girls in the Cyprian market" (for Venus's island was a place of commerce); consequently she was "the most agreeable looking girl when asleep"; and while after one aria of love, she "cries, *da capo*," for another, she also expected five guineas for her obliging ways. It is likely therefore, that the libertine could only find what he sought from women of his own social class—Boswell's "women of intrigue of the highest fashion." Such women would almost invariably have been married: there was too much disapproval for a man to seduce an unmarried girl of his own class. Before 1750 women of intrigue were likely to be women like Lady Vane, who wrote her memoirs for Tobias Smollett's *Peregrine Pickle* (1751). But after 1750, adultery like everything else became romantic. Aristocratic women like the young Lady Sarah Lennox, who at fifteen had objected to men who claimed to love their wives and yet went to whores, themselves eloped from their husbands with their lovers, even though the consequences for their lives could be more dire than anything Lord Pembroke had experienced when he briefly eloped from his wife with one of his mistresses. Still (as the last chapter will show) romantic adultery when it was followed by a parliamentary divorce allowed lovers to rearrange their lives, and Lady Sarah Lennox's second marriage brought her the domestic happiness she had missed in the first.[24]

THE PROSTITUTE REDEEMED, 1750–90

It is clear that after 1750 the new ideals of romantic love and the domesticated family affected the behavior of some husbands and induced them to give up prostitutes. But the need in men to demonstrate their exclusive heterosexuality in a world in which the gender differences between men and women were maintained by the role of the effeminate male sodomite meant that other men expressed their allegiance to the new ideals by modifying the milieu in which they went to prostitutes. The attempts after 1750 to reform the prostitute herself were similarly inspired by romance and domesticity and limited by men's need to display an exclusive heterosexuality. Radical reformers knew that the only effective way to end prostitution was to eliminate its clients—to persuade men not to use prostitutes. But no one was really willing to do this because it was always feared that if one eliminated all prostitution, men would seek sexual relief in each other's arms.

The idea for a house in which prostitutes could be employed and reformed seems to have appeared first in a pamphlet of Thomas Bray's in 1698. Bray was one of the principal organizers of the Societies for the Reformation of Manners; his proposal was part of the reaction to the increase in streetwalking by prostitutes that was first remarked on in the 1690s. Even the libertines, however, were struck by the need for some sort of institution. Christopher Johnson in 1724 remembered that in his earlier days, many of the prostitutes would moan to him after sex that they had been deluded cruelly by their first seducers, and that they had taken to the streets because there was no other way to live after losing their reputation and their friends. "How often," therefore, he had "wished we had such a provision for these unhappy females (and their offspring) as they have in other countries." Twenty-five years later, in 1749, the anonymous author of *Satan's Harvest Home* republished Johnson's comment (without acknowledgment in his usual way). He removed the women's confessions from Johnson's setting of postcoital sadness. And he secularized Johnson's remark that the prostitute's sins, "like those of Mary Magdalen, are forgiven because of her loving much," adding instead that "tho' they are the scorn and contempt of the generality of the unthinking world," they "are notwithstanding real objects of our pity and compassion."[25]

In the 1750s a group of reformers who were less inspired by punitive religious zeal or the regrets of the superannuated rake than Bray or Johnson promoted the cause of an asylum for prostitutes. Robert Dingley, a successful London merchant in his early forties who was married and the father of three children, took the lead. He seems to have been moved by civic pride in London's tradition of public charities, by humanitarian zeal ("humanity in its utmost efforts pleads their cause more powerfully than anything I can offer on the subject)", and by religious concern to be a "means . . . of rescuing many bodies from disease and death, and many souls from eternal misery." Dingley was soon joined by Jonas Hanway, his former partner and an active religious philanthropist. Saunders Welch and Sir John Fielding, the two London magistrates most active in trying to control street prostitution, also became advocates of the cause.[26]

Welch's proposals for the hospital neatly brought into focus the new attitude toward prostitution. He did not expect that the hospital would end prostitution. He thought that such an aim would be dangerous in any case since it might result in the increase of sodomy—"a horrid vice too rife already, though the bare thought of it strikes the mind with horror." His aim was simply to make prostitution less publicly apparent on the streets by removing the young streetwalkers. Picking these girls up and sending them to the house of correction had no long-term consequences: "punishment only prevents for the time it operates, but hardly ever produced one reformation." A hospital, on the other hand, would educate the girls and send them out as apprentices or servants, thereby "striking at the root of the evil." If there were, in other words, no mass of poor girls to be seduced into prostitution, its more public manifestations in the public street would be eliminated. Prostitution from Welch's point of view was objectionable when it was public and disorderly. But he presumed that it was needed as means of affording men a sexual release that would otherwise seek its outlet in other men—though he found such an outlet almost impossible to think about. The behavior of men was therefore unlikely to change. It was the behavior of the prostitute that had to be modified. Punishing her in the way that had been done in the early eighteenth century had no long-term effect. She had to be reeducated into appropriate behavior. He clearly did not presume that a woman once fallen could never be redeemed. And it is likely that his hopefulness about her redemption was based on an acceptance of the new view of women's nature that was now becoming fashionable. But this he did not say in as many words. William Dodd, the chaplain to the new hospital, did: "every man who reflects on the true condition of humanity, must know that the life of a common prostitute is as contrary to the nature and condition of the female sex as darkness to light: and however some may be compelled to the slavery of it, yet we can never imagine every line of right and virtue obliterated in the minds of all of them."[27]

The Magdalen Hospital, once established, could not ever have made much of a dent on the population of street prostitutes. It never had more than 60 to 100 women in it between 1758 and 1790. In its first twenty-five years, it admitted 2,415 women, when there were perhaps three thousand active prostitutes in London at any one time. It claimed that 65 percent of its young women were either reconciled to their parents or placed as servants. Twenty-five percent of the women left either at their own request or at the insistence of the hospital's committee when they were unable to conform to the discipline of the house. (A few died or became lunatics, probably as a result of the mercury they had taken to cure venereal disease.) Some went back to prostitution, as did 20 (12 percent) of the 164 women discharged in the hospital's first three years. But only 122 women (6 percent) out of a total of 2,197 by 1786 had married and sometimes become mothers. This may overestimate the number of former prostitutes who married, since by 1786 the hospital had begun to take in girls who had been seduced by men and alienated from their families but who had not yet "been publicly on the town." This policy may reflect the hospital's despair at an overwhelming task. Of the 20 to 35 girls who applied each month, it could take in only a few. Those who were venereally infected were sent to be cured and allowed to apply again. Some were supported until there was a vacancy in the hospital. Some were reconciled through the committee to their families and were never admitted, for the committee took the point of view that a woman with relations or friends to care for her would never become a prostitute.[28]

Life inside the Magdalen Hospital has recently been compared to the regime of the modern penitentiary, but it might as fairly be looked upon as a special kind of convent where the nuns made promises to reform their lives and stay for a while until they were prepared to rejoin the world. When the girls entered, they were reminded that "it never was intended that you should pass your whole life here" or live in idleness. Instead, they were there to "be enabled to return into life with a reputation recovered," "with a habit of industry, and the means to procure honestly your own bread," and with a mind "resolved through God's grace to forfeit no more the blessed hope of everlasting life." They were to attend the chapel twice on Sunday when the chaplain preached and visitors were admitted by ticket to observe them. They were to wear a "downcast look" on such occasions and to remember that a "bold and dauntless stare will give but mean ideas of reformation." They were to pray in private and read the Bible. In their conversation, they were to be meek to their superiors; and among themselves they were not to swear and never to "glory in your shame" by telling stories of their previous lives, "which should cover your faces with confusion."

If a woman wished to remain anonymous, she was allowed to assume another name. Each woman was given her own bed and a box for her clothes to which she alone kept the key. Their own clothes were taken away and stored, and they were given identical plain, gray gowns. They rose at six or seven, according to the season, and went to bed at nine or ten. They spent the day in needlework, which they were taught along with reading. They had meals at nine and one o'clock and stopped working at six or seven. Their friends or relatives could visit with advance approval, but they had to speak to the women in the presence of the matron or her assistants. Women were never allowed to leave the house except for some extraordinary personal occasion, and then not for more than a day, and they had to be in the company of the matron or her assistant. The change of name and clothes, the regularity of work and prayer, the limited contact with the outside world were all rather like the life of a strictly enclosed nun. There was even a similar purpose—"to save the soul"—but to this the hospital added others—to "preserve the life" from disease, and to "render that life useful and happy" when the young women left her confinement after a year or two. When Horace Walpole visited the hospital, he remarked that he "fancied myself in a convent." It was certainly a common fantasy among the libertines that a brothel was a convent, the bawd its abbess, and the women her daughters in religion. But a repentant prostitute in the Magdalen Hospital certainly came to know that reformation of life for which St. Benedict had long before written his little rule for beginners.[29]

The Magdalen Hospital remained the only institution of its kind in London until 1789, when the Lock Asylum was founded. It received up to twenty penitent prostitutes at a time after they had been cured of venereal disease in the Lock Hospital. The Lock Hospital (which the next chapter describes in detail) had been founded in 1746 to cure the London poor of venereal disease. Half of its patients were women, and most of these were young prostitutes. The men after their discharge usually had their "places of abode or occupations" to return to: the women had only prostitution to subsist on. The Lock Hospital by the late 1760s began to give some girls either money with which to buy their passage back to their families in the countryside, or a double set of clothes (cap, handkerchief, shift, gown, apron, petticoat, stockings, and a pair of shoes) so that they could take a place as a servant in London. The money to do this came from theatrical benefits, from bequests, and from the funds collected in the chapel that the Reverend Martin Madan had raised a subscription to build and to which his preaching drew a fashionable congregation.[30]

Madan had begun life as a libertine and a lawyer, but after a religious conversion he had taken orders. In the 1750s he became the chaplain to the Lock Hospital (see chap. 7), which tended in its program to stress the cure of disease rather than the reformation of manners. After ten years as chaplain, Madan became overwhelmed by the sense that neither sending a few girls to the Magdalen Hospital, nor locking up a great many more from time to time in a house of correction where they helped to corrupt each other and came out more abandoned, would solve the problem of prostitution. Instead a way had to be found to discourage men from seducing girls in the first place. The answer he hit upon was mandatory polygamy—oblige every man to marry every girl he seduced. He began to talk about it to his friends. Sir Richard Hill remembered that he had often "heard you deliver your sentiments on the subject to particular friends, but never could have imagined that you would have sent them abroad into the world." But after fifteen years of studying the matter, Madan in 1780 published his *Thelypthora, or a Treatise on Female Ruin,* to the delight of London's libertines and the pained shock of his Evangelical friends.[31]

Thelypthora was an eccentric but very interesting work because Madan in seeking a cure for prostitution undertook to question the entire Christian tradition of hostility toward sexuality to which most of his contemporaries were committed. He challenged the tradition by appealing to the Old Testament against the authority of the Christian Fathers. He began by justifying sexual desire: "Those who imagine that this appetite is in itself sinful, either in desire or act, charge God foolishly, as if He could ordain the increase and multiplication of mankind by an act sinful in itself." Madan insisted that polygamy was blessed in Scripture and that the New Testament had not forbidden it. Jesus had not spoken in favor of monogamy; he had merely condemned the abuse of divorce. Polygamy had probably been common among the first Christians, since Paul would not otherwise have recommended that bishops and deacons be chosen from those with only one wife. But the early fathers mistook Jesus and Paul as favoring virginity over marriage, and with "this unnatural plan of celibacy" they fostered the growth of sodomy; for Madan, like Saunders Welch, was convinced that a society that limited heterosexual contact very likely made room for sodomy; but unlike Welch, Madan saw polygamy rather than a regulated prostitution as the means of discouraging homosexual behavior. Madan, on the other hand, condemned Mohammedan harems, since women were bought to serve in them as slaves and men were made into eunuchs to guard them. England, however, had its seraglios in the public brothels, where a woman became "the temporary property of every visitor," and its streets "after a certain time of night" were "a kind of itinerant seraglio." All this would end if men were obliged to marry and take responsibility for the women they seduced.[32]

Madan's book was widely discussed. There were letters, epigrams, and lampoons in the newspapers. There were public disputations burlesquing him in places of amusement. His face appeared in the windows of the print shops. But there was also serious discussion. One clergyman found that the book was widely read in his parish and talked about everywhere he went, and he was frequently asked his opinion about the book. A young man in his parish who had set out to seduce a girl but repented, gave up his penitence and defended his behavior after reading Madan. The clergymen argued that either polygamy was never sanctioned in the Old Testament but was tolerated by God and taken up by the Israelites from the corrupt practices of those around them, or that it was unknown under the New Testament and therefore forbidden. Thomas Haweis said that Madan would simply confirm the infidels in "their prejudices against divine revelation" and "embolden them in the practice of sensuality." Henry Moore wrote that Madan should have published in Henry VIII's day and made his fortune, since only the libertines would thank him for his book. Madan's questioning of the Christian tradition of sexual asceticism was lost in the outrage against polygamy. He had perhaps forgotten how much the English libertine was likely to justify prostitution under the cover of polygamy, as we have seen the young Dudley Ryder and his friends do. Madan consequently became "a reigning toast among the jovial sons of pleasure at their clubs and taverns."[33]

For Madan's Evangelical friends like Richard Hill, preaching the Gospel was the only way to end seduction and uncleanness, and by the Gospel they meant traditional Christian asceticism. With this purpose the Reverend Thomas Scott, one of Madan's successors as chaplain to the Lock Hospital, set up an asylum for prostitutes. In theory, the asceticism of the Gospel applied equally to men and women, but in practice it was easier to enforce on women. Madan's program of polygamy presumed that men needed to be made responsible for the women they seduced into prostitution. But the Lock Asylum and the Magdalen Hospital held the prostitute responsible for her own condition and did not try to reach the behavior of the male libertine. This may in part have been because Christian asceticism had not yet accepted the new, more positive evaluation of women's nature. The temptress Eve may still have had her power in the minds of the religious. Certainly Thomas Haweis opposed Madan's idea because of its tendency "in the feebler sex to lessen the influence of conscience, and silence the pleadings of virtue against the violence of natural passion or persuasive seduction."[34]

The girls admitted to the Lock Asylum were those whom Scott had identified as the most tractable during the course of their cure for venereal disease in the Lock Hospital. One girl was rejected because she appeared "to be of such an artful disposition." The girls who seemed most promising were those who had been seduced, infected, and then deserted by a single man but who had not yet gone on to "more general prostitution": "these are the most hopeful and proper objects of compassion" and "may probably be almost all restored to society." The asylum, in its first eight months of operation, and within its limit of 20 girls, chose about 1 girl in 4 (33 of 117) of those released by the hospital as cured.

The clothes the women wore on entering were washed and set aside and they were given plain, neat dresses instead. They attended family prayers twice a day, listened to the chaplain's instruction, and decently dressed went to church on Sunday at the Lock Hospital. The women were let out to walk early every morning accompanied by the matron. Longer absences were discouraged for fear of the possible consequences: Mary Nunn, who was allowed for just one afternoon to visit her sick mother, "behaved so as to become again venereally infected" and was expelled. Inside the house, the women did needlework and were allowed to keep a quarter of their earnings. But there was little recreation or interaction among the women. No games were allowed, there was no strong drink, and only books approved by the chaplain could be read. They could have conversation only in the presence of the matron, who encouraged religious conversation and prevented other kinds. The women, except during working hours and in the matron's presence, were to spend as little time together as possible. This desire to separate the women from each other is a new departure, since it does not appear in any of the printed eighteenth-century rules for the Magdalen Hospital. Finally, their letters and boxes were subject to inspection. Not surprisingly, 40 percent (48) of the 120 women who had gone through this regime in its first five years were expelled for misbehavior or ran away from the house or the employer with whom they were placed. But as many girls (47) stayed with their employers. Nine girls died in the house. Only 16 girls, however, were taken back by their families (though many of those admitted were probably orphans), and a few of these married and had children.[35]

The Magdalen Hospital and the Lock Asylum were the greatest innovations against prostitution after 1750, and they peculiarly reflected the new views of the elite on the role of women, the domestic affections, and sentiment. But these houses were clearly failures, if for no other reason than the very small number of women they could admit. Nonetheless, a magistrate like Saunders Welch supported the Magdalen because he had

seen the failure in its latest phase of the traditional response of arresting
the prostitute and the bawdy-house keeper. This policy had failed despite
the rearrangement at midcentury of the relationship between the magistrate and the voluntary society of neighbors or religious reformers. In the
early eighteenth century, the reformation societies had pushed the magistrates into action. At midcentury, it was the magistrates who encouraged
the reformers. This was true above all of Sir John Fielding, and it was
largely through Fielding's efforts that a new act made its way on to the
statute book in 1752. But by 1758 Welch had declared it ineffective. The
act had been aimed at the keepers of bawdy houses and was passed in
the aftermath of the sailors' riots in 1747 against the bawdy houses in the
Strand. It allowed two inhabitants of a parish to ask the constable to arrest
the keeper of a bawdy house. The constable's expenses were to be paid,
and the two inhabitants received a reward if the prosecution succeeded.
But the act failed because Londoners dreaded to incur "the odious name
of informer." The number of indictments dramatically increased for a year
after the passage of the act, but after that they fell back to their previous
level.[36]

What two individuals might be reluctant to do, however, could be accomplished more effectively by a group. Such groups of neighbors became
active in the early 1760s. They were encouraged by a proclamation against
vice issued by the new king, George III, in October 1760 and by the
charges to the grand jury of magistrates like Sir John Fielding. The gentlemen and tradesmen of the Old Bailey formed such a group in 1763, and
in cooperation with the parish of St. Sepulchre they moved against the
bawdy houses in Fleet Lane. In the next year the inhabitants of the streets
around Covent Garden acted similarly. Finally, the Societies for the Reformation of Manners, which had not acted against prostitutes since the
late 1720s, began to do so again.[37]

In the 1730s the societies had largely confined their activities to prosecuting those who broke the Sabbath. In the next two decades they became
again (as they had been in the early 1690s) groups for prayer and the study
of Scripture. They seem to have been preoccupied with distinguishing
themselves from the new Methodist and Moravian societies. But by April
1760, a revivified society (there was now only one) was meeting every
Monday evening at six in the Justice Hall of the Old Bailey. It had started
to prosecute Sabbath breakers again, and it was planning to "extend itself
to other branches of immorality." By the beginning of 1762 the society
was in full swing. Constables belonging to the society arrested almost forty
streetwalkers: eleven well-known prostitutes were publicly whipped, one

was sent to the Magdalen Hospital, and the remainder were sent home. Fifty years later this particular night was recalled by another reformer, who, doubtful of the effectiveness of such actions, remarked that "such has been the practice, at long intervals, ever since, perhaps with some variations in the punishments inflicted, and, I am afraid, an omission of enquiring for their friends." Punishing the prostitute alone would never remove prostitution. The streets were still crowded with prostitutes in 1811, he said, because men were never punished for seduction. The reformation society of the early 1760s certainly did not try to do so.[38]

The society's efforts, overall, met with great hostility. It was criticized for going after the streetwalker and ignoring the more prosperous bawdy houses. Its agents were mocked and attacked. Some of those whom it arrested brought suits against its constables. The constables were sometimes vindicated, but the society failed when it arrested Mrs. Leman, who ran the Rummer Tavern in Chancery Lane. She sued for five hundred pounds in damages, was awarded three hundred pounds and costs, and had her award upheld on appeal. She won apparently because one of her waiters, who was later tried and found guilty, had perjured himself. The award against the society probably destroyed its effectiveness. But it is even more likely that the religious revival had not yet proceeded for enough to give the society any sustained support. The society formed in 1787 after another proclamation by the king fared much better: the spread of the religious revival and the fear of the French Revolution made its program seem much more pressing. In 1760, the society's preacher could only appeal to his countrymen's gratitude for their great victories in the war of his day: that they would support "this laudable design . . . as the best evidence we can give of our gratitude to God."[39]

The drive against bawdy houses clearly foundered because there were not enough households willing to use the act of 1752, and the voluntary societies of the early 1760s did not help much. It is, however, possible to look at the treatment of all the prostitutes arrested in the City and brought to the Mansion House Justice Room in the years 1785–90. This is in fact the best such surviving source for the entire century. It will allow us to see how the ideas about the reform of prostitution that became current after 1750 were put into force by a group of sober and responsible justices. And it will neatly conclude the story of the prostitute's reform by the humanitarians and the religious.

In the six years 1785–90, 798 women, some of whom were girls, were arrested as prostitutes and brought to the magistrates sitting in the Mansion House Justice Room. In 1785 and 1786 about 100 women were arrested each year. In 1787 and the subsequent years about 50 more women a year were arrested, probably as a result of the new reform movement. (See table 4.3.) Forty percent of the arrests were made in May, July, and August, which probably reflected the increased level of streetwalking associated with the great London fairs. About 40 percent of the women were simply reprimanded and discharged, probably after promising not to offend again. About 50 percent were sent to Bridewell. Of these, 40 percent were sentenced to a fortnight, a third to a month, and 15 percent to a week or ten days. Thirteen percent of the women imprisoned were also whipped. Compared with the early eighteenth century, the sentences were longer, but fewer women were whipped. These varying dispositions probably reflected the magistrates' judgments as to whether they were dealing with a young, inexperienced girl or a habitual prostitute. But out of the 40 percent who were simply reprimanded, there were only three instances in which a girl was clearly sent back to her family and three cases in which she was sent to the hospital because her venereal infection was so evident. It is true that 14 percent of the women were passed to their parishes, but it is unlikely that in most cases the intention was to send them back to their families, since 70 percent of those passed had also been sentenced to a term in Bridewell. The relatively low number passed does confirm that few prostitutes were girls fresh from the countryside: most of them must have been Londoners, or women with either a London settlement or no settlement at all. Some of those passed, in any case, were back on the streets as soon as they could manage it. Prostitutes in most cases must therefore have been passed to their parishes of settlement as a means of disposing of some of the incorrigible (Saunders Welch had recommended this) and not as a way of saving the young. That last aim was beyond the resources of most magistrates. They simply discharged the clearly inexperienced girl and hoped for the best.[40]

Such were the halfhearted attempts that men made in the second half of the eighteenth century to remove prostitution from the streets. These attempts were founded on a view of women's nature that arose from the system of gender relations that the late Enlightenment (or the sentimental movement) fostered throughout Europe. It was a system that presumed that men and women were close enough in the nature of their minds and feelings to meet each other in an intimate friendship that began to transform marriage and produced a new ideal of the couple's mutual care for their children. But it is apparent that a married man who went to whores did so in part because he wished to limit the degree of intimacy with his wife. The man without a wife who went to whores did so for a different but related reason. He was determined to show that his sexual interest was exclusively in women and that he was not an effeminate passive sodomite. Though it may not seem so at first, it is likely that this fear of male passivity and the new sodomitical role that it had produced in the early Enlightenment were also consequences of the anxieties induced by the new ideal of closer, more nearly equal relations with women. Men needed to establish that they could never be made passive as a result of intimate sexual relations. Adolescent males could no longer go through a stage of sexual passivity, and adult men who were passive were stigmatized as male whores. The changing sexual relations between men and women had transformed sexual relations between males. And since men's relations with each other were of much greater consequence to them in regard to questions of power than were their relations with women, the fear of sodomy was a stronger drive than the desire for intimacy with women. Men therefore could not give up prostitution. It was true that the figure of the prostitute contradicted all ideas about the natural domesticity of women. But she allowed men to establish that they were not sodomites. She also provided an escape from the demands of marital intimacy. Her public presence on the street was, however, an embarrassment—it flaunted too obviously the contradictions within the new system of gender relations. As a consequence, there were attempts to remove the women from the street and to reconstruct their lives. But these efforts never reached out to the male sexual desires on which the entire system of prostitution was founded. Those desires had to be left intact, since they were the bulwark men had built against equality with women. The sodomite and the prostitute guaranteed that ordinary men would never be transformed into women as a result of the intimacy or the passivity that might be produced by more nearly equal relations between men and women.

CHAPTER SEVEN

The Foul Disease

F or the majority of poor Londoners the sentimental movement probably made little difference in their experience of the widespread street prostitution that the new standards of exclusive male heterosexuality produced after 1690. But all social classes were affected by the pattern of venereal disease that accompanied this prostitution. Venereal disease in the sixteenth and the seventeenth centuries had probably been contained in specific social groups like gentlemen and soldiers and sailors. In the course of the eighteenth century, however, the gentlemen's disease became the common disease of the London poor in a world where there were no effective preventatives other than abstinence, monogamy, or washing, and where the supposed cures were either ineffective or too expensive. Many poor men did believe that sex with a virgin would cure them, and so they forced themselves on prepubescent girls, disrupting in the process the households, the shops, and the neighborhoods in which they lived. Men of all social classes also took the disease home to their wives and their children and destroyed the bonds of trust between themselves and their closest intimates, no matter whether their families were ruled by the old patriarchal ideals or the new romantic, domesticated ones. This pattern of disease was perhaps the harshest component of the new male heterosexuality.

INCIDENCE AND PROPHYLAXIS

From the 1690s onward, the new prostitution produced a new pattern of venereal disease that lasted in Western societies until the World War II. Venereal disease had first appeared in Europe two hundred years before, in the 1490s. It had been brought back by Spanish soldiers returning from America, where the disease was probably endemic among the Indians.

During the Italian wars, the opposing Spanish and French armies took and retook the same towns. The two sets of soldiers therefore slept with the same set of prostitutes, and by the medium of these unfortunate women, the disease passed from the Spanish to the French and eventually to the rest of Europe. This at any rate was the credible theory in the 1730s of Jean Astruc, the foremost authority of his day on the subject. Astruc showed from a systematic historical study of the medical literature that at first the new disease was treated as though it were epidemic in the sense that the plague was thought to be. Gradually, it became clear that it was spread principally by sexual intercourse; but that mothers could also give it to their unborn children, and wet nurses and their charges to each other. No nation wished to be held responsible for the disease and named it accordingly as they thought they had caught it. To the French, it was the Neapolitan disease; to the Spaniards and the Italians, the French disease. In Portugal it was the Castillian disease, in Persia the Turkish disease. The disease was carried through Europe by the armies of the sixteenth century. It was also spread through the public brothels. Astruc argued that the regulations of the medieval brothels showed that the disease had not then existed in Europe, and that the public brothels were closed in the mid-sixteenth century when the nature of the disease was understood. By the end of the sixteenth century the disease lost something of its initial virulence. It did not spread to the general population and instead tended to be contained among soldiers and gentlemen, the two groups most likely to go to prostitutes.

By the 1730s Astruc was optimistic that the disease, after a history of 240 years, was "going off the stage, tho' perhaps by very slow degrees." The symptoms described in the medical literature had grown less severe. It was true that "through the propensity of the present age to lewdness, it may perhaps be more frequently contracted than formerly, yet its rage is less violent." This may perhaps be translated as saying that while syphilis was less prevalent, more men were likely to contract gonorrhea than ever before because of the growth of prostitution. This was difficult for Astruc to see, however, since for him there was a single unitary disease that appeared in different parts of the body with different symptoms and that came in two stages of simple and advanced. Astruc did not realize that his evidence for the disease's being "more frequently contracted than formerly" substantiates the argument of this chapter, that a new 240-year cycle in the history of the disease had begun. Instead he argued that there was "reason to hope that by the assistance of medicine it may one day be conquered." If those who were infected overcame their prudery and sought early treatment with mercury, and if those who were well were careful to wash their sexual organs frequently before and after intercourse, the disease, Astruc was convinced, would disappear.[1]

Far from disappearing, however, the disease had spread in England by the 1790s to the general population of the London poor through the agency of the new street prostitution. "What was formerly called the gentleman's disease," William Buchan wrote, "is now equally common among the lowest ranks of society."[2] The growth of urbanization in the second half of the nineteenth century further increased throughout Western society the incidence of both street prostitution and the disease. But the modern patterns of venereal disease and prostitution first appeared in the great cities of the early eighteenth century, and not (as it has recently been argued) after 1850. In the modern pattern of the disease it was likely that in most countries the majority of men who lived in cities would at some point contract at least gonorrhea. This would also have been true of soldiers and sailors. The prostitutes to whom these men went would all have been infected. When these men married, they frequently infected their wives and their unborn children as well. Outside of the urban population, however, where there was no access to street prostitution, the rate of infection in the general population was lower.[3]

Statistical evidence for this pattern is difficult to come by, even for the twentieth century, but what there is supports the argument. In the United States, for instance (as the most recent systematic study shows), it was claimed in 1901 that eighty of every one hundred men in New York City had had gonorrhea; more certainly, 36 percent of the men who entered Boston's largest hospital admitted to having had gonorrhea; and 20 percent of the men who fought in the American Civil War and in the Spanish American War were infected. In the early twentieth century, from 70 to 90 percent of New York's prostitutes were diseased. On the other hand, only 13 percent of the general population drafted into the army in 1918 had been infected, which confirms the prevalence of infection principally among men from large cities. A similar pattern can be found in nineteenth-century England. In London in the middle of the century, more than half of the outpatients of major hospitals had venereal diseases, and one sick case in three in the army was venereal. In York with its large soldier population, half of the prostitutes who were treated at the expense of the poor-law guardians were sick from venereal disease, and a third of these women were recorded as having come directly from the brothels where they had been at work.[4]

Figures of this kind cannot be produced for eighteenth-century London. But in the forty years between 1710 and 1749, at least 15 percent of the women who sought divorces in the London Consistory Court claimed that their husbands had been venereally infected (17 of 115 cases). This can be compared with the nineteenth century, when about 9 percent of divorce petitions after 1857 cited venereal disease, but these were drawn from all areas of the country and a wider social range.[5] It is likely that in the eighteenth century the actual number of husbands who were infected was higher, since the medical writers frequently claimed that men were able to deceive their wives on this issue even after they had infected them. In addition, the couples in the consistory came at least from the middle ranks of society. The poor, on the other hand, according to Buchan, were far less likely to seek a cure or to persist in one. It is therefore very probable that the number of husbands among the poor who were infected was much higher than 15 percent, and that they frequently infected their wives. As early as 1691 the poor of London's East End joined together in one of the first of those voluntary associations that came to be called Societies for the Reformation of Manners. Their purpose was the suppression of the bawdy houses in their neighborhoods. In those houses "many a housekeeper is infected with a venomous plague which he communicates to his honest and innocent wife, whereby proper and timely means, through shame or ignorance being neglected, she lives a while a most painful, miserable, and perishing life, and at length falls by piecemeal, a dead sacrifice to her husband's unnatural cruelty and inhumane bestiality." But men who infected their wives sometimes claimed (as they did to Martin Lister) that they had been infected before their marriages and had thought themselves cured.[6]

Soldiers and sailors were among the men most likely to go to whores, and from them it is possible to estimate the number of unmarried men in London who were infected. It was claimed, for instance, in 1779 that one-quarter of the soldiers stationed in a Kent town were infected. But the best evidence comes from the logs of the ships in the Royal Navy, which recorded the fines paid by sailors who were treated for venereal disease. The number of men treated in ships in the Atlantic and the Mediterranean in the years 1755–63 varied from 1 to 20 percent of the ship's company, and the percentage in a particular ship could vary almost as widely at different periods of time (table 7.1). It is not possible to say where these men had contracted the disease, but most of them had probably passed through London's world of prostitution. In ships serving in the central Pacific from 1764 to 1795 even higher rates of infection appeared, varying from 20 to nearly 60 percent of the men (table 7.2). These men

Table 7.1 British Naval Seamen and Venereal Disease in the Atlantic and the Mediterranean, 1755–63

Ship	Men Treated	Number of Months[a]	%[b]	Ship	Men Treated	Number of Months[a]	%[b]
Lichfield	12	45	0.9	Elizabeth	20	11	4.5
	54	12	18.0	Achilles	8	5	4.6
Deal Castle	1	6	1.2		56	15	10.6
	5	6	6.2		28	5	16.0
	5	5	7.5		88	12	20.9
	6	6	7.5	Hampton Court	93	44	5.1
Barfleur	30	31	1.7		33	6	13.7
Magnanime	25	13	3.2	Dorsetshire	19	6	7.3
	55	13	7.0	Burford	30	9	7.5
	41	6	11.4		21	6	7.9
Monmouth	13	10	3.2	Invincible	59	12	8.2
Lynn	5	6	3.6	Edgar	29	9	9.2
	24	28	4.1	Ambuscade	161	75	10.3
	10	7	6.1	Fame	48	8	11.1
	30	13	11.1	Jamaica	61	54	13.5
	18	5	17.3	Arundel	67	32	15.7

Source: N. A. M. Rodger, *The Wooden World* (Annapolis, Md.: Naval Institute Press, 1986), pp. 367–68.
[a] Period over which the specified number of men requiring treatment was recorded.
[b] Percentage of ship's company per annum requiring treatment.

Table 7.2 British Naval Seamen and Venereal Disease in the Central Pacific, 1764–95

Ship	Crew	VD	%	Ship	Crew	VD	%
Tamar	109	20	18.3	Resolution	125	71	56.8
Dolphin	148	22	14.9	Bounty	46	18	39.1
Swallow	112	8	7.1	Pandora	136	27	19.9
Dolphin	155	28	18.1	Assistant	31	9	29.0
Endeavour	116	39	33.6	Providence	120	44	36.7
Adventure	90	17	18.9	Chatham	54	32	59.3
Resolution	122	31	25.4	Discovery	124	41	33.1
Discovery	68	30	44.1	Total	1,556	437	28.1

Source: Greg Dening, *Mr Bligh's Bad Language* (Cambridge: Cambridge University Press, 1992), p. 384.

would have been away longer from London and have had more opportunities to contract the disease elsewhere, especially perhaps in Tahiti. There
is also the possibility that the men on some ships gave the disease to each
other by having sex with the boys on board. But it is apparent that in the
second half of the eighteenth century it was not unusual for 20 to 40
percent of British sailors to be venereally infected. Contemporaries were
aware of these high rates of infection, and one pamphleteer in 1813 sensa-
tionally estimated that twenty thousand young men a year became venereally infected through London's prostitutes (who with Patrick Colquhoun
he improbably estimated to be fifty thousand in number). While it is
therefore not possible to statistically demonstrate that the modern pattern
of venereal disease existed in London from the 1690s onward, it is very
probable that a body of street prostitutes, who were almost totally diseased,
infected a large percentage of both the single and married men who lived
in the metropolises and the garrison towns, and that these men in turn
infected their present or future wives and children.[7]
    Once the pattern was established, the only certain ways of avoiding
infection were abstinence and monogamy. For many men in London neither of these were acceptable. They therefore looked for an effective prophylaxis but were usually thwarted by incorrect etiologies of the disease.
It is true that some etiologies once current were no longer given credence
by Londoners in the early eighteenth century. But country people still
sometimes believed that "the infection . . . was catching, as they call it,"
like the plague. They therefore avoided persons with venereal disease and
would not enter a house where someone had died from it or touch anything coming out of such a house. But even in London, there were those
(as a doctor could mock) who "fancied ways of catching it by common
conversation, drinking after one, sitting on the same close-stool, drawing
on a glove, wiping on the napkin after the infected person."[8] For those
who were aware that except in the case of mothers, nurses, and infants,
it was mainly through sexual contact that the disease was spread, there was
still a risk of infection because of a widespread misconception. Founded
on the observation that it was primarily through contact with prostitutes
that the disease spread, it was supposed that it came into existence because
the seed of many men had been mixed together inside a single woman.
(This mixture of seeds was also presumed to prevent prostitutes from con-
ceiving.) If a man, therefore, did not enter a woman's vagina, or even if
he simply did not ejaculate inside her, he was presumed to be safe from
infection. On this supposition, a number of ineffective safeguards were
taken.[9]

There were first a variety of sexual techniques that could be used in the place of vaginal intercourse, such as masturbation, fellatio, and sodomy. But in fact not even masturbation was always safe. Men reported that they became infected by a prostitute whose hand had touched her infected parts. One man picked up a woman at a playhouse and got into a coach to have sex with her there. He wanted her to masturbate him, but they disagreed over her payment. After the encounter, he became sick, and then he remembered that her hand had been wet as she held him. He therefore presumed that she had deliberately smeared her hand "with the filthy matter from her own body" in revenge for their disagreement over her price. Other men used fellatio. One libertine who had often been infected "prevailed with some of the women of the town to let him (as he called it) huffle with them." He stood in front of the woman as she sat down and then placed his penis between her lips. With the finger of one hand she stimulated his anus, and with her other hand, she masturbated him. But alas, one of the women had venereal ulcers on the inside of her lips and on her tongue, and infected him. Other men tried sodomy, in some cases presumably with the intention of avoiding disease. Men certainly had oral and anal intercourse with males with that intention as late as the first decade of the eighteenth century. As the century wore on, however, the new role of the molly made anal intercourse with either a male or a female very controversial. But it still occurred. In the 1690s Charity Parrot complained that Thomas Davis had attempted intercourse "against the order of nature." Lord Macclesfield thought such behavior worse than sex between males or with beasts. He agreed with the majority of his fellow judges that the keeper of a whorehouse at Maidstone was guilty of plain buggery when he sodomized an eleven-year-old girl in his charge—almost certainly with the intention of avoiding disease: "the unnatural abuse of a woman," the lord chancellor said, "seems worse than that of a man or a beast; for it seems a more direct affront to the author of nature, and a more insolent expression of contempt of his wisdom, condemning the provision made by him, and defying both it and him." Some physicians, however, could not believe that anything but vaginal intercourse spread the disease. Daniel Turner rejected the idea that one could be infected as a result of being touched with venereal discharges on the basis that the poison was activated only by the infectious person's sexual excitement: "the frigid or cold courtesan, however infected herself, yet having only her appetite to the reward; neither can be heated or excited to action, but continues merely passive; as she is least likely to infect her companion, much less can any matter which is but the vehicle of the poison, never roused or stirred up by the heat of such action, taken forth the body and grown still colder, be capable of doing the man an injury."[10]

Despite the hopes of libertines, it is apparent that the avoidance of vaginal intercourse, or even the avoidance of intercourse with women, was not a safe preservative from disease, since in anal, oral, and manual intercourse, either with females or with males, one might still become infected. But for many these sexual techniques or male partners were controversial in themselves, since they broke the taboo against unnatural or nonprocreative intercourse. It was otherwise with the only two effective techniques that could be used in vaginal intercourse: the condom and washing before and after the act.

Condoms—made from the dried gut of a sheep—were on sale in London possibly as early as 1701. They were mentioned by name in 1706 and 1708 as preventatives against disease, but John Marten in his book published in the latter year still did not know of them. Ten years later (1717) Daniel Turner took them for granted: "the condum being the best if not the only preservative our libertines have found at present." Some men, however, preferred to risk disease rather than use one, "by reason of its blunting the sensation." William Byrd did not record using one himself when he was in England in 1718. But when he went to the Three Tuns with some friends for supper, there were two whores present, and two of the men in the company had sex with one of them "in condoms." For Astruc in the 1730s, condoms were still an English practice. He was skeptical of their value since they might have cracks in them or tear during intercourse. A generation later, James Boswell in 1763 began to use condoms, probably on the ground that it allowed him the excitement of picking up the first low prostitute he found in the park or the street without the danger of disease. He did not then have to make inquiries of the girl or confine himself to well-run houses with supposedly safe women. But he complained that the condom dulled his sensation, and one girl asked him not to put it on "as the sport was much pleasanter without it, and as she was quite safe."[11]

From the 1720s onward, the condom became controversial in a new way when it became apparent that it could prevent conception as well as guard against disease. The condom was therefore as unnatural a means of prophylaxis as were anal, oral, or manual intercourse. But the libertines like Dean Kennett rejoiced that it was not only themselves who were now protected: young women as well were freed from the fear of the "big belly and the squawling brat." To another way of thinking, this was the sort of thing that "ought not to be allowed in a Christian country." A doctor like Joseph Cam therefore would not advise men "to use machinery and to fight in armour." For this reason, perhaps, the condom was not mentioned in serious medical works after midcentury. William Buchan in his practical guide for men did not discuss it, even though in his day it was no longer necessary to say (as men like Marten and Astruc had) that it was morally legitimate to discuss other preservatives from the disease. Condoms nonetheless continued to be quite openly sold in London, somewhat to the surprise of foreign visitors.[12]

Washing was the only effective prophylaxis that could be recommended without controversy. At the beginning of the century Marten had described how Venetian prostitutes after coitus bathed their privy parts in their own urine. He mentioned specially prepared washes that were to be used before and after intercourse. And he recommended washing afterward in almost any liquid. This would help even a man who after ejaculating stayed a long time in a woman's body because of "excessive extasy, heat and satiety"—which was much riskier, he thought, than quick withdrawal. Astruc held that only abstinence from irregular intercourse was truly safe, but he did admit that warm water or urine might be of some effect. At the end of the century, Buchan was convinced that venereal disease could be contained by a three-part strategy. Young men should be taught self-restraint. Prostitutes should not be allowed on the streets without some control; but he carefully added that too much restraint would lead men either to sodomy or to keeping mistresses at the expense of their families. And finally, Buchan said, there was simple washing with water and soap or shaving powder. Most men became infected because they were too drunk to pay attention to washing properly. Prostitutes could protect themselves by washing: a gentleman had tried to infect his mistress to punish her but had failed because of "her extraordinary attention to cleanliness." Buchan thought that even wives should wash frequently to stop their husbands from erroneously thinking that their wives had infected them with venereal disease when the inflammation had arisen from some other kind of vaginal discharge. He was skeptical that any of the specially prepared washes were worthwhile. But he knew men "who for many years had lived freely with regard to the sex" and never had contracted a disease. They simply washed in whatever liquid was at hand—beer, wine, punch, negus, brandy, or rum and water. Some preferred brandy to anything else, which Buchan pointed out could be warmed before washing by simply "holding it for a short time in the mouth."[13]

Buchan's essay was a handbook for gentlemen: he depended on the parish clergy to spread medical knowledge among the poor. He knew that gentlemen were more likely to seek medical help once they were infected, even if the young among them might delay too long or go to a quack who promised a quick cure. Gentlemen, moreover, tended to avoid street prostitution on the ground that those were the women most likely to be diseased. It is also probable that the bagnios with their lists of approved whores who could be sent for, and the seraglios with their women on the premises, were both used in part as a means of avoiding disease. The preference for virgins and for girls newly on the town, as well as keeping a mistress, also had this purpose in part. Gentlemen in their sexual practices therefore tended to do on an informal basis what Buchan had proposed when he recommended a degree of public regulation of street prostitution.[14]

But neither gentlemen nor the women they went to were consistent in their practice. Fanny Hill in Cleland's novel thinks herself safe from infection as long as she sees only the customers of Mrs. Cole's house. But she, like Boswell, has to have her fling. She picks up a sailor in the street, goes with him to a common bawdy house, and worries afterward that she may have infected herself. Fifty years before Cleland, John Dunton claimed to have spoken to a whore who had explained that she only kept company with the best, for she knew they would not "debase themselves to meddle with common prostitutes." Only "carmen, porters and such like fellows" followed "cheap jilts" and ended "poxt for their pains": "gentlemen and those of better condition will be more careful of their health." But Dunton told her she was mistaken; he reminded her of the saying, "foul water will quench fire," and predicted that sooner or later she would become infected, since when inflamed a gentleman would go to whom was at hand. Lord Grosvenor, for instance, in the early summer of 1770 saw twenty-one-year-old Elizabeth Roberts walking through Cranbourn Alley near Leicester Fields. When she stopped him, he offered her a glass of wine. But since he did not wish to be seen walking with her, he sent her ahead to a house called the Hotel. They went to a room upstairs with a green bed and drank a bowl of punch together. Then Grosvenor made his inquiries: "My dear little girl, are you well? because if you are not, tell me, and I'll give you double the sum of money I shall give you if I r[oge]r you." She answered that she was very well. He replied again that he would not be injured for all the world. Then he "rogered" her. Grosvenor was anxious about his health, but the girl was too tempting to pass up. James Boswell was far less careful with his women and came down with nineteen attacks of urethritis (probably gonorrhea) between 1760 and 1790. If one subtracts Boswell's four years of abstinence from whores, this was an infection every sixteen months. He probably died from their complications.[15]

It was therefore an illusion to imagine that the women like Fanny Hill who confined themselves to gentlemen who patronized a well-kept house were safe from infection by their customers. Dunton told of a bawd who when her strumpets became infected would "trappan unwary young fellows to help it forward"—on the theory that intercourse with someone who was not infected would cure the disease. Edward Strode in the early 1750s slept with the most fashionable women of the town: Charlotte Hayes at her lodgings in Pall Mall, and Frances Murray at her house in New Palace Yard. But Hayes gave him the foul disease. At the end of the century, John Cheetham seemed to specialize in infecting the women in his life. Within a few months of his marriage he started going to brothels. He would return home early in the morning and tell his wife about it. He became infected; and while he was being cured with mercury, he forced his pregnant wife to sleep in the same bed and to have sex with him. She became infected, and probably also her unborn child. Among the women Cheetham saw was Harriet Brown, twenty years old and illiterate. She lived in a less fashionable sort of brothel in Cherry Tree Court, Aldersgate. When she became infected, he sent her to St. Bartholomew's Hospital. She stayed for a fortnight and left. When she found that she was sick again, she returned to the hospital for three more weeks. But Cheetham blamed her disease on the other men she had seen in the brothel. He therefore decided to keep her. He put her into lodgings in Marylebone at the other more fashionable end of town and gave her six guineas a week. But he continued to see other women, especially Maria Taylor, who worked in a brothel. He again became infected, and he wrote to Taylor accusing her of being responsible. Other men who kept a woman found it did not work unless she was faithful. Marten told of a mistress who was kept by two different men, unknown to each other; they were both full of remorse when each infected her on separate occasions after going to common women when drunk or at the playhouse. A mistress who granted another man a single favor could infect her keeper, as still another of Marten's cases showed. The world of prostitution at any level was not designed to encourage mutual fidelity. There was unfortunately no safe haven from disease outside of monogamy or abstinence.[16]

CURES: RAPE, THE LOCK HOSPITAL, AND WIFELY TOLERATION

Once the disease was contracted, there was a vast army of quacks and doctors offering various cures. In 1697 Dunton described a "multitude of pretenders to cure that disease" whose porters walked the streets and forced "their bills upon us whether we will or not." This "multitude of papers and advertisements" showed that the disease had become "an epidemical distemper among us." Even women undertook to cure the disease (which Marten thought immodest) and sent their partners out with advertisements. Bills were pasted to "pissing-places, posts and doors, corner-houses, thoroughfares," proclaiming their stories of infallible cures. There were mountebanks on their stages in Moorfields proclaiming their skill. At the end of the century the young were still being seduced by the puffs for quick cures that were put into their hands as they walked the streets. Buchan, while he was writing out a prescription for a cure that would have taken weeks if not months to complete, saw his patient read an advertisement in a newspaper that promised the same thing in a few days. The young man put the doctor's prescription in his pocket and went off to the quack. The respectable medical profession devoted a considerable amount of its time to curing venereal disease. Campbell at midcentury estimated that "three parts in four of all the surgeons in town" depended on venereal disease for their practice: "it is not only the most frequent but the most profitable branch" of their profession. Surgeons probably did dominate the field. They made up three-fourths of the medical writers on venereal disease.[17]

Pills, powders, and liquids, often with some degree of mercury in them, sometimes with other drugs, were prescribed. A doctor like Astruc believed only mercury to be effective. He preferred to apply it externally rather than to take it internally. But however used, the intention was to bring on a salivation or sweating. In the second half of the century doctors began to use sharply different treatments for gonorrhea and for syphilis. John Hunter explained that "we know however that most gonorrhoeas are curable without mercury; and what is still more without any medical assistance." Instead the urethra was to be syringed; he was uncertain what kind of liquid it was best to inject. He did remark (somewhat alarmingly to a modern reader) that infection in gonorrhea came only from the discharge: men who were diseased but had sex with their wives before the discharge appeared did not infect them. He therefore allowed infected men to have sex if they syringed the urethra until it was clear, urinated, and then washed the glans of the penis. It is perhaps consequently not surprising to find him saying that the symptoms returned after a seeming cure more frequently in women than in men. Indeed he knew a woman in the Magdalen Hospital who was able to infect a man after she had been sexually abstinent for two years. It was therefore not so silly as Buchan thought that many women should "believe that a person once thoroughly infected can never be radically cured." There was in fact an important change in tone between the early and the late eighteenth century in regard to women. Marten and Astruc discussed the disease more or less equally in men and women. Hunter and Buchan did so mainly from a man's point of view. It was no doubt a result of new feelings of delicacy about women and about all sexual matters. But it was a reticence that must have made the treatment of women more difficult. There was no reticence, however, in their agreement that a pox was to be treated with oral doses of mercury in a quantity strong enough to make the mouth sore, the teeth shake, and the breath stink.[18]

This could be embarrassing. Buchan had a patient who complained that he had "made his mouth stink like the devil so that he could not go into genteel company." It could in fact ruin a man in a number of situations for it to be known that he had had venereal disease. Individuals declared (presumably those who had not been infected) that they would rather die than have it known. Those with a public reputation for religiosity found themselves hard put to admit that they had gone to a whore. Such a patient of Daniel Turner's claimed that one of his testicles had become "tumefied" from "lying cross-legged in his sleep." He tried to hide his penis, but when Turner got hold of it, he found a discharge. The man blushed, started to cry, and begged Turner "to be careful of his reputation."[19]

Among the poor, insults about being venereally infected were quite common; and they were usually tied to charges of being a whore, or of going to them. Katherine Newburgh was a widow who was known in her neighborhood to sleep with a married man; when she grew angry she called the respectable mother of a family, whore, bawd, and *salivated* bitch. To Dorothea Witty, Mary Cope was "a whore, a pockey whore, and the brewer's whore." William Waye abused Elizabeth Roe as a whore and a one-eyed whore, implying that she had lost her eye from the disease. The women gave as good as they got. Mary Harding, it was claimed, had mocked Michael Bayley that he had "lost his privy member." He charged her with saying that he was "a rotten old rogue and lost what he had twenty years ago, and his guts are so rotten they are ready to drop from him . . . he is a pockey old rogue." There was even a phrase—*docked smack smooth*—to describe a man who had lost his penis because of the disease. The loss of an eye, a penis, and finally a nose: Margaret Horne told Sara White that she was "an old bawd and an old whore and lay-in in Kent Street of a bastard at an old bawd's house with never a nose upon her face." Not to be diseased was to be respectable. Ann Pod's acquaintants came to her support when a neighbor called her "that pocky whore." Pod, they replied, who kept a draper's shop and also a public house, was brought up a gentlewoman; she was "a gentlewoman bred and born and never was poxed though people say she was."[20]

This abuse, however imaginary, had its force in part because it was founded on real-enough material. When Ruth Cason said that another woman had had the pox and not paid her doctor, she touched on one of the very real difficulties of the poor. Venereal medicines cost a good deal more than other kinds. Some doctors cured the poor for free. Marten said he did so to the value of one hundred pounds a year. He told the story of one poor patient, a sober modest woman whose husband had gone with the army and left her with the pox. She had a large ulcer on her leg and "fiery botches" on her face. After she was twice salivated in Kingsland Hospital, she had to apply a third time, but her money was gone; they would not take her again and told her that she was incurable. A surgeon gave her the same diagnosis. Starving, she applied to the parish for help, but they threatened to pass her to her native parish. When she decided on her own to go there to die, the wagon driver would not take her after he saw her symptoms. Marten, assured that she was industrious and that she had gotten the disease from her husband, cured her for free in six weeks. Her nose, he said, was saved, and her sores were healed.[21]

The London parishes were obliged to care for those who became infected when an individual had a settlement in the parish. The overseers in Wapping resented the cost. They put Mary Allen, who was a street prostitute, into the house of correction because they had had to pay for her cure. And they did the same thing to Thomas Groves because he had infected his wife, who became a charge on the parish. The parish workhouses seem to have kept foul wards for those undergoing their cure. A twelve-year-old girl died in St. Luke's workhouse after she was infected by the old man to whom she had been apprenticed. Seven of the man's other apprentices were in the workhouse for the same reason. It is not clear how Susanna Goodaridge became infected. She was probably an orphan from St. Margaret's. She had been apprenticed from the Grey Coat hospital to two different married women in Hungerford Market to learn housewifery. The market, however, was in the heart of a bawdy house district. She became venereally infected and spent a considerable time in the workhouse of St. Martin's in the Fields so that she could be cured.[22]

Sometimes a foul ward must have been full of prostitutes. There is a vivid scene of murder in one of them to show this. Elizabeth Tanner was in the ward and had been salivated by the surgeon who attended the workhouse. She had recovered and was fit enough to be discharged but was being kept cautiously for a week more. Around ten on a Wednesday morning, Ann Holding started to make a scene outside the ward and tried to get in the window. She was mentally unstable and had three or four fits a day. She shouted that they were a parcel of pocky whores and she would kill them all. One woman took her from the window, but she said she would get in and beat them all, for she was determined to get to the fire in the room, which was probably there to warm the women in their salivation. An hour later she returned. There was a cry of murder. Holding had taken the poker from the fire and had struck Tanner on the right side of her face and killed her. Holding declared that she had done it, and would do the same to the woman who restrained her, because she was "a street-walking bitch."[23]

These street prostitutes and poor married women, therefore, had three options for treatment: the private cure by a surgeon, which they could receive only in charity; admission to Kingsland Hospital (the venereal ward for women of St. Bartholomew's), for which they still had to pay; and finally the foul ward in a workhouse. This was free, but it was available only to those with London settlements, and it posed for others the danger of being passed to their native parish in the country.

The poor men of London, however, believed that they had a means for their cure that was free, but that in fact merely infected a new category of women—namely, the prepubescent child. They believed that sex with a virgin would cure one of the venereal disease. It was a belief present and acted upon throughout the century. It always produced expressions of horror in educated observers, who usually described it as a strange unknown custom of the poor. It is perhaps one of the most striking instances of the manner in which elite and popular culture were drawing apart, with little power to influence each other. And it shows that disease was viewed by the poor in what to the educated seemed to be a largely magical way.

As late as the 1690s, the literate still probably believed that virgins had the power to cure. Certainly John Dunton in 1697 when he described the practice was shocked by its cruelty, but he did not seem to doubt its efficacy. He told of a soldier who had been infected by his wife, a camp follower. He threatened to stab her; so to put him off, she offered him her daughter (who was eleven) in the belief that the girl "being fresh would cure him." It was a process that was supposed to work for both genders: consequently their ten-year-old son was seduced by another whore seeking her own cure. Dunton also mentioned that it was the common practice of bawds to cure their women by enticing fresh young men. Some of the beaus may have seduced young men for a similar reason. An anonymous writer commenting on the increase in sodomy in the 1690s (it may actually have been Dunton) pointed to a simultaneous growth in the number of cases of rapes on young girls. He did not realize that both the sodomies and the rapes may have been committed by men who were seeking safety and cure from venereal disease. Marten described the belief in the power of virgins as a wrongheaded notion of the libertines that had probably arisen from what was to him the equally bad theory that the disease was caused by the mixture of the seed of many men in the prostitute's body. But in 1715 Walter Harris unambiguously described the theory as one held by the common people. At the end of the century, Buchan explained that in most countries it was believed that one could be cured of a disease by giving it to another, and that in England, this was believed in regard to venereal disease. The result was that men raped and infected young girls without curing themselves.[24]

The best evidence for this can be drawn from the prosecutions for the rape of prepubescent girls held at the Old Bailey. Since puberty for girls arrived approximately at fourteen, the relevant cases are those of girls of thirteen and under.[25] Men may also have forced virgins of fourteen and over for the same reason, but it is too hard to distinguish such a possibility given the general cultural attraction to pubescent girls. Indeed, it may be difficult even with girls of thirteen. "The time of enjoying immature beauty," wrote a libertine in 1760, "seems to be a year 'ere the tender fair find on her the symptoms of maturity . . . before the periodical lustration hath stained her virgin shift, whilst her bosom boasts only a general swell rather than distinct orbs." Some men went through a succession of young virgins looking not so much for a cure as for freedom from infection. But a girl once seduced would soon have other men and thereby "seldom escape a taint." It was not practical to stay with her. But it is likely that the girls chosen for such a purpose would be at least thirteen and probably fourteen.[26]

The rapes of prepubescent girls can begin to be counted easily around 1720. There are printed trials before that, four for instance in 1707; but year by year, the survival of the sessions papers is not so good until 1720. After 1720 the number of cases varied from five to none at all in a given year. Since the reporting of the cases seems to have improved in its detail after 1760, the eighty-year period (1720–1800) should be divided in half. There were about sixty cases in the first forty years, and about a third as many in the second. But in only 30 percent of the cases before 1760 was it mentioned specifically that the girl was venereally infected, whereas after 1760 it was mentioned in 60 percent, or in twice as many. It is probable that most of the cases throughout the period actually involved an attempt by a man to cure himself. One must always, though, allow for men attracted to children. There were a handful of fathers charged with raping their daughters. The number of cases after 1760 does seem to decline, and it is possible that the poor men of London had begun to change their behavior. But it is also possible that the magistrates after 1760 were simply making it more difficult for all rape cases to come to trial. The cases that did make it to court were, of course, always a minority of the actual ones. The Lock Hospital, which was founded in 1746 to treat the poor for venereal disease, reported in 1753 that in its first seven years it had admitted eighteen hundred patients. Of these "upwards of 60 children from two to ten years old," had "suffered by ways little suspected by the generality of mankind, vizt, by adults in hope to get rid of the disease." The minutes added that "great numbers of these miserable distressed objects were frequently refused admission into the hospital for want of room, and most likely many of them perished." In those seven years then, when the hospital admitted sixty children ten years or younger infected in this way and turned away many others, only eleven such cases were reported at the Old Bailey.[27]

The Old Bailey reports nonetheless tell the story in greatest detail. They offer, for example, two reasons why so few of the cases came to trial. The expense of prosecution had to be borne by the injured child's parents, and they were often too poor to do so. In addition, the parents had often agreed to "make it up" with the offending party for a sum of money. Such payments in compensation for an injury to an individual's sexual honor were a widespread feature of society—from the great aristocrat who sued his wife's lover for criminal conversation to the servant girl who was paid by her rapists. But for reasons that are not always clear, some offers of compensation were unacceptable.

A case could fail in court for lack of money. Margaret East was a servant with a nine-year-old daughter. The husband of the woman who took care of her child raped and infected the girl. But East was unable to prove her case. Mr. Kennedy, who had examined the child, refused to come to court unless she paid him, and this she was too poor to do. Indeed, Kennedy had gone to her with two other gentlemen to try to persuade her to make it up for a sum of money. But this she felt she could not do. So instead, Kennedy appeared for the defendant. The child was swollen; her hymen was intact; she simply had had a bladder disorder, he said. Two other medical witnesses supported him. The man was acquitted.[28]

Mary Matthews and her husband were also poor. They put their ten-year-old daughter to work in a public house where she was raped. At the trial the mother had to say that the surgeon to whom they had gone, a Mr. Gloster, would not come to testify unless she subpoenaed him, but she could not afford to do this. The accused man, for his part, produced another surgeon, James Purdue, who said that the girl's hymen was almost intact and that the discharge was only the "fluor albus." The court was skeptical and ordered the man detained so that he could be tried on a lesser charge than rape.[29]

Finally, there was Joseph Fyson, who was a good friend of Jacob Sweetman and lodged with him. Fyson, who was fond of Sweetman's seven-year-old daughter, took her for a walk on Sunday afternoon and then raped and infected her. He said he was sorry and offered the parents a guinea or two in compensation. This the father rejected and asked him instead "how come you to use the *baby* in that manner?" The rape could not be proven, but the court gave Sweetman, who was a poor man, five guineas so that he could prosecute again on a lesser charge.[30]

Other cases make quite clear that men and boys committed these rapes to cure themselves. James Booty was born in London near St. Andrew's Church, Holborn. His father died when he was a child. At fifteen his mother bound him to James Peters, a cabinetmaker in New Street, Shoe Lane, for forty shillings. He had found the place through a first cousin, a girl of his own age who was Mrs. Peters's servant. The girl had been seduced by a "loose young fellow" who had left her diseased. She now seduced Booty (possibly to cure herself) and infected him. He described his condition, anonymously, to a friend, who said he knew how to get rid of it. "Why," said the friend, "I have heard say that a man may clear himself of that distemper by lying with a girl that is sound." The friend must also have specified that it was to be a young child. Booty now set to work. He took the five-year-old girl from next door up to the roof and raped and infected her. And he did the same thing with his master's daughter. The children's infection was discovered, and Booty was accused. This occurred over ten weeks. Mrs. Peters took her child to a surgeon who cured her for two guineas. Peters refused to return the forty shillings paid for Booty's apprenticeship. The boy was brought to trial and executed. His friends claimed that Peters could have made it up but had refused to do so.[31]

In a second case, an elderly man attempted to cure himself. David Scott was fifty-two, with a wife and daughter, a dyer from Scotland who lived near Moorfields. Mary Homewood was eleven. Her father was a weaver who kept a public house, the Golden-harp, in Lamb Street, Spitalfields. He employed Mary as a pot girl. On Thursday evening she was sent to deliver a pot of ale to Scott. She went to him at the dyehouse, where he forced her, apparently with the intention of curing his venereal infection. He offered her money to keep quiet, but she kept repeating that she would tell her mother. She did not do so, however, because she was afraid of being beaten. Her mother admitted that she was "very passionate to be sure and sometimes gave her a very heavy blow." When the girl was told again on Sunday to take beer to Scott, she refused. The story came out, and the girl's infection (she could not walk) became known. Her mother went the next day to complain to Scott's wife, and on Wednesday she went to the justices of the peace. Thomas Homewood, the girl's father, confronted Scott and told him he had "ruined my child." He went to Patrick Colquhoun, the magistrate in Worship Street, and thought of having Scott arrested. But he and his wife were afraid "it would make an alarm in the neighborhood and disgrace the child's character." But Homewood also hoped that Scott would leave for Scotland. He did not, and the story leaked out. Scott's fellow dyers discharged him and said they would not let him into the dyehouse again. At this point Homewood prosecuted. But he insisted that if Scott "had gone out of the way, so that it was not to be known, I would have put up with the misfortune." Before his arrest Scott tried to get Homewood to back off by sending him an attorney's letter. Scott's sister visited Homewood's house and said to his wife that they would bear the expense of the girl's cure. The girl had first been taken to a man called Tibbins, who was "not a regular bred surgeon." Richard Mann was; and he testified that her hymen was broken and that she had "clap or gonorrhoea." The court questioned him whether the disease could be cured by having sex with a young child; when he answered no, that it would only cause irritation, the court reaffirmed that "it cannot be too generally known that it does harm, not good." Scott was condemned to death.[32]

From this story, it is apparent that to most parents the possible stain on a daughter's reputation, and on their own honor, were more important than the issue of disease. It helps to explain why parents seemed to have attacked a child initially when they discovered her infection. It accounts for the fearfulness of so many girls in telling their parents what had happened. Phillis Holmes, who was ten, probably aroused the suspicion of her father because she was his bastard. She had been taken from her mother in the country to live in London with her father and his wife, who was ill. He ran a public house, the New Goose and Gridiron in St. Paul's Churchyard. The child passed there as her father's niece. When the girl was bathed by the nurse who tended her sick stepmother, it was discovered that she had the foul disease. The nurse could see that "her womb was open wide as mine who have had nine children." Her father kicked her on the backside and shouted, "Oh, you b[itc]h, you are poxed. Hussey, who has meddled with you." The harsh treatment was not unusual: the child had for a month been living on bread and water because she had given away four shillings. She was now threatened with being cut to pieces. She confessed that it was Ned, or Edward Brophy, the headwaiter, who had taken her into the cellar three times. Afterward, he had said to the child that she would be hanged if she told anyone. He confessed that he had had the disease twelve months before and had not gone to an apothecary. The girl was sent to the hospital to be cured.[33]

Children who lived and worked in public houses were especially subject to attack from the lodgers and the soldiers who might be quartered there. William Stringer, after he had lodged in a public house at Billingsgate for three months, infected the eight-year-old daughter of the landlord. He did this without penetrating the child, which the surgeon testified was possible. Ten-year-old Mary Mathews was attacked by a soldier quartered in the Red Lyon in Orton Street, Clare Market. The child kept silent until her discharge appeared because he had threatened to kill her, and "for fear of losing my place, and my daddy and mammy beating me." Another soldier, Thomas Davenport, raped an eleven-year-old as she lay asleep at the Brown Bear in Bedfordbury, which her father kept. He admitted to the surgeon, James Gale, that he was "in the habit of being with bad women." Gale squeezed his penis and produced a considerable discharge. The court presumed that Davenport had attacked the girl to cure himself and therefore asked the surgeon "a question for the sake of the public"—"is it possible for a man having a venereal taint of this sort to receive any benefit from connexion with a child?" Gale answered that it was "an extremely false idea."[34]

But the out-of-doors could be as unsafe as a public house. Elizabeth Hall's eight-year-old was raped (again without actual penetration) by a laborer in the tanning yard that Hall's brother ran. Hepzibah Dover (who was thirteen) was attacked by one of the carpenters when her mother sent her to get wooden chips and shavings. And once again, a frightened child apologized: "Mama, don't be angry, for he was stronger than I; don't send me for any more, for I will never go again." And then the child cried "most bitterly." Catherine Black (aged ten) was raped in Newgate Prison, which was not quite out-of-doors, but certainly out of control. Her mother was in prison for debt, as were Gerard Brown and Jonas Penn. Several times the girl's mother had seen Brown "playing and toying" with her daughter. She "be-rogued him very handsomely" and threatened "to make the gaol ring of him, if ever I knew him to meddle with her again." But he forced the child three times, and his friend, Penn, forced her once. The girl grew ill. Her mother examined her, showed her to "some knowing women," and they declared the child poxed. The mother confronted the girl: "Hussy, says I, tell me who it is that has been meddling with you." The surgeon confirmed that the child was violently lacerated and badly poxed.[35]

Whether in a public house or a private one, these attacks seem to have caused the greatest pain when they came from within the heart of the family. Susan Faucet's daughter (who was nine) was infected by her journeyman. At first she thought her child "forward," that is, menstruating at an early age. But a neighbor told her there "could be no such natural thing." Faucet then spoke to her child and promised not to beat her, after which she told her story. James Sharpe's Elizabeth (who was under ten) was raped in her bed, as she played with her doll, by Craige who worked for her father in his public house. She refused to say by whom since he had threatened to beat her. But when a neighbor, who had come to buy beer, told her that "your mammy won't get you cured and you will die," the child blushed, burst out crying, and replied that she would say who it was if she did not "tell my dadda." Her father then took Craige to the justice of the peace. But as he did so, he asked him, "How can you look me in the face after you have used me so ill, though I have been a father to you?" To which Craige replied that "his heart was ready to break."[36]

Sarah Batty felt similarly betrayed when one of her two lodgers raped her nine-year-old daughter. "I thought," she said, "I could trust my life with either." She had clearly been a careful mother and was full of disbelief that the girl was infected, since "the child never went outside my house." The girl had sometimes shared a bed with her fifteen-year-old brother because the family was large. Batty had thought that there could be no harm in this, as they were brother and sister. But in any case, the boy was not infected, and the lodger was. The girl herself had undergone a painful and baffling experience. "I thought," she said, "he ran his double fist right up my body." She had not understood the sexual act—"I thought he made water in me"—and this probably had made it more degrading.[37]

These stories show children caught between the need of one set of males to be cured of their disease at whatever cost to ties of intimacy and trust, and the need of their fathers to maintain their authority in their families and their honor in the world's eyes. But even the mothers and female acquaintances showed a tendency to blame the girls for their mistreatment. In the final case, however, Sarah Poultney seems to have been a mother who was more responsive to her child and determined to protect her against male power. But it is also the case where the offending male seems most likely to have been sexually interested in little girls. It was an interest supported by two attitudes familiar from similar cases in the twentieth century: first, the unwillingness of adults, especially men, to believe that the fondling of a child is sexual and not just friendly interest; and secondly, the tendency in adults not to be able to hear or understand the repeated protest of a child against abusive behavior.

When Sarah Poultney had come home on Saturday, her four-year-old daughter asked to be washed. Poultney told her she was too tired to do so. The child then explained that she was sore and could not walk. The girl's privates were swollen. A neighbor said it was the foul disease. The child said it was Mr. Wright's coachman, Charles Ketteridge, who had hurt her. Her mother then remembered that when two or three weeks before the girl had been late for dinner and she had asked her where she had been, she had replied "Mammy I could not come for Mr. Wright's coachman locked me in the stable." Her mother had then asked what he had done there, and the child had replied that "he took up my clothes before and behind." Her mother had inspected the child and found her very red. So she had said to her husband, "what does the fellow mean by playing tricks with my child, I'll go and kick up a dust with him." But her husband had skeptically replied, "pho, pho, the coachman is always playing with the children." Therefore, when the girl once again told her mother of being locked in the stable, she had taken no notice. Only the venereal infection proved the seriousness of the child's complaints.[38]

This Charles Ketteridge was a man known in his neighborhood, as were all the men in the cases described so far. Some attacks must have been made by strangers, but these could not be brought to court. Elizabeth Negus was six or seven years old and lived in Tottenham Court Road. Her parents were poor, and while her mother was out at work, she was attacked by an unknown man and infected. Her mother brought her to the Lock Hospital, which would not receive her until two housekeepers stood surety that they would take the girl back again. But even a mother like Elizabeth Batty, whose daughter, as she said, never went outside the house, found that her trusted lodger, apprentice, or journeyman might rape her child. And finally, the children who lived in public houses seemed to have been at special risk. James Eyre kept a lodging house in Coventry Court in St. Martin's in the Fields, which was full of journeymen. His wife, "having no spare bed . . . unthinkingly laid" their eight-year-old daughter with one of the journeymen, who ravished and infected her. But it is also probable that publicans were among those most likely to have the money to prosecute.[39]

The lack of money for a proper cure was one of the principal reasons for the entire practice of using virgins. (The other was probably the popular theory of how disease and cure worked.) Marten at the beginning of the century and Buchan at the end were aware of the difficulties the poor had in finding treatment. William Bromfeild, a London surgeon, in 1746 put into effect a practical solution. He founded the Lock Hospital. It was financed by subscriptions from the gentry and the aristocracy who were solicited by Bromfeild. Each week it admitted free of charge men and women who applied, and who often came with a letter of recommendation from one of the subscribers. It was intended for those so poor that they had no settlement and could not claim a cure in the parish workhouse. It therefore rejected in 1768 a suggestion from the vestry of St. George, Hanover Square, that the hospital treat that parish's diseased poor. In the late 1750s Martin Madan, who became the chaplain, built a chapel at Hyde Park Corner and preached there to fashionable congregations as a further means of raising money.[40] Between 1747 and 1771 the hospital treated 10,897 patients, half men, half women, most as patients in the house, but some as outpatients. Of the women, about 15 percent were wives who had been infected by their husbands. That at least is their proportion in fifty-two weekly admittances in 1756–57, and in the figures for 1747–56. Some of the other females (possibly another 5 percent) were young girls who had been raped. But the remainder, or at least four thousand, were prostitutes, some of them quite young. Of the men we know less, except that they were poor and that some were married. Some of them in 1781–82 were probably soldiers returning from the American war. The minutes from that time described "the numerous objects . . . many of whom arrived from abroad after the close of the last war and applied for relief . . . and who must, but for this charity, have absolutely perished in the streets." War had played its usual role in fostering venereal disease.[41]

Before patients were admitted to the hospital, it first had to be deter-mined whether they actually had venereal disease and not one of the innu-merable other diseases of the poor. There were individuals who either had the itch (that is, the contagious eruption caused by the itch mite), or had the itch as well as venereal disease, and therefore had to be cured of the itch before admission. Those who were consumptive were probably ex-cluded because it was feared that they would infect their fellow patients. Other patients were scorbutic, or had sore legs, or fistulas, or only piles. (These last two are evidence that the individuals had had anal intercourse because of the area of infection: one was a woman, two were men.)[42] Men and women with discharges that seemed to be "only a gonorrhoea" or "only a gleat" (i.e., a gleet, or a gonorrheal discharge) were also not treated.[43] Some were not admitted at first because their symptoms did not appear clearly enough but were subsequently admitted when they became unambiguously venereal.[44] Some were admitted on the chance that their case might be venereal and then were later discharged when it appeared that they had a fever or the dropsy.[45] Girls who were pregnant were also not admitted until after delivery, since the rigors of the cure would have been too dangerous to them and their child.[46] Their children must almost certainly have been born infected.

Once inside the hospital, these were not very tractable patients. They refused to rise and go to bed at set times. Some women cursed and swore and misbehaved in the wards. James Caton misbehaved in the chapel dur-ing services. Three women were discharged for "*gross* indecent behavior" in the wards. Bawds got in among the women patients and "endeavoured to prevail upon several of the women patients who were nearly cured to return to their former evil courses." The surgeons complained that the street door was not watched, and that this allowed "spirituous liquors" to be brought in, which retarded the patients' cure. The male patients in the long ward stood at the windows and behaved "indecently in sight of people passing and repassing the road." The windows were altered. Sarah Pope was cured and then ran away with the clothes and money of other patients. Helen Turner was discharged because she was too "disordered in her senses" to undergo the cure.[47]

The staff, or at least its poorer members, participated in this libertine atmosphere. The women's nurse was dismissed for drinking too much. But it was the aged porter, John Oram, who stole the show. Four women patients complained that he questioned them about their complaints and their wounds, and whether they had a discharge. He lifted up the clothes of some of them to examine them and tried to do the same with others who resisted him. He said that he had to report their cases to the surgeon before they could be admitted. He confessed it all but was forgiven by the board when he said that he acted "under the temptation of the devil." But he was probably unbalanced to some degree, as well as contemptuous of persons with the foul disease: some patients were so disgusted that they would not eat their food for days after they saw him emptying his chamber pot into the tubs of gruel.[48]

Even Bromfeild was accused of misbehavior. He retired as the house surgeon in 1770 and was succeeded by his son. But a decade later he was accused of using drugs paid for by the hospital to treat his private patients and of putting those patients into the hospital. Bromfeild convinced the governors that the charges were frivolous. Instead, they allowed him to apply to the hospital for medicine to treat the many poor people who daily came to his surgery in Conduit Street.[49]

The medical treatment inside the hospital is hard to recover. It was essential that the patients kept themselves clean. James Hunter would not do this. As a result he was so foul that the surgeon could not bear to be in the same ward. The most painful part of the treatment involved the cutting of a patient's ulcers. Elizabeth Richmond ran away rather than go through it once again. She hoped she could find some other cure. But she grew worse and returned since "she must either be cut again or be in danger of losing her life." Those patients who were being salivated (or taking mercury) were supposed to keep warm and dry. But some of them were made to wash the rooms of the hospital. This was stopped, as it discredited the charity. The matron was ordered to provide tin pots, plates, knives, forks, and spoons for those too poor to provide their own, but they were to be left behind when the patients were discharged from the hospital. In 1785 an infectious fever broke out in the hospital. It killed one of the house surgeons, the male nurse, and three of the women. All the patients were discharged, and the wards were fumigated and white-washed. Six months later the matron was sent to the seaside to recover from her exertions in coping with the fever.[50]

Conditions in the hospital were clearly physically rigorous. In 1797, it was proposed to set up three smaller wards for those who were otherwise sick or convalescent, or who tended to pick up illnesses in a common ward. Before that, it was not unusual to allow individuals who were too weak from a previous salivation, or unable to get well in the wards, to be treated as outpatients, with the hospital paying for lodging when necessary. Those with buboes were treated as outpatients, until the buboes suppurated, and then they entered the hospital. In 1756–57, 572 patients were admitted, but 79 were treated as outpatients for various reasons. But whatever the techniques used, there was often little to be done. Patients were sometimes discharged as cured as far as the nature of their case would allow. Some complained that patients who were discharged but not fully cured then applied for further help to the overseers of the poor in the parish in which the hospital was located.[51]

The organizers of the charity were, however, always concerned not only with the cure of the disease, but also with the reformation of the manners of those who entered the hospital. Consequently there was always a chaplain; but his role grew in importance after 1780 when the Evangelicals came to dominate the institution. It had always been the case, though, that a patient once cured could not be admitted a second time if there was a new infection. The hospital could not appear to be promoting vice by making it easy to escape its punishments.[52] When the hospital was first founded, a curate was appointed to read prayers to the patients in their wards, but he did not preach. In the 1750s Martin Madan volunteered to read prayers and to preach to those who could attend in the boardroom, and he visited some of those in the wards who could not come. Madan then raised funds to build a chapel. The money from the subscriptions and collections in the chapel was used to help some of the patients start life anew after their cure. Once the chapel was opened, Madan did not visit in the wards so often. He had always found that "the cure of their disorder was of such a nature as rendered it often impossible for him to converse with them in private." He therefore had a book printed for the patients instead. In the early 1770s, the Reverend C. E. de Coetlogen was appointed as Madan's assistant. He was a very popular preacher. The young William Wilberforce began his religious conversion when he heard him preach in the chapel in 1783. But de Coetlogen did not visit the patients in their wards. In 1781 and 1782, however, it began to seem that visiting the patients was essential. De Coetlogen thought that this was more than he was paid to do. So an assistant was appointed to do the visiting in the wards. The congregation in the chapel, meanwhile, was falling, probably due to the increase in the number of similar fashionable chapels in the West End. But de Coetlogen was blamed, and he resigned in 1785. The Reverend Thomas Scott was appointed, and with him the Evangelical regime fully prevailed.[53]

Scott declared that he "would feel a peculiar satisfaction in visiting the unhappy patients in the House," and in the peculiar idiom of his sect, he said that he would "be ready at all times when at liberty from the duties of the chapel, to preach for other gospel ministers." Scott put into effect a new regime for visitors to the hospital, since "very improper persons, who come for the worst purposes," frequently got in. Visitors were now allowed only on Monday afternoon between two and four-thirty. No one could come up who did not inquire for a patient by name and explain their business. Only that patient was to be spoken to, and in the presence of the nurse, who might also inspect any parcels. Scott visited the patients, who became "more orderly and tractable." Several expressed their gratitude for his "solemn warnings and exhortations." The governors concluded that "whilst the disease of the patients only is cured, they remain insensible and hardened in their vices . . . but if . . . they acquire a sense of religion and a detestation of their former courses, greatly must the utility and advantage of the charity be increased." Scott also persuaded the governors to set up a parallel asylum for twenty girls at a time: it was for those among the young prostitutes who appeared "willing to quit that miserable course of life" and desired to be restored to their families or to the world of honest labor.[54]

There had always been in the hospital a minority of honest women infected by their husbands. There was on and off an attempt made to provide them with a ward separate from that which housed the prostitutes. The matron's room was used for this purpose in 1766. A married women's ward in 1772 was subsidized by one of the women benefactors, Carolina Williams. It was proposed in 1780 that there should be an annual sermon to raise funds for this purpose. Two years later, infected married couples were being received together and cured, so that they could "become the parents of a healthy progeny for the good of the state and the benefit of society in general."[55]

Fifteen percent of the poor women admitted to the Lock Hospital were married. Fifteen percent of the somewhat better off women who sued their husbands for divorce in the London consistory claimed that their husbands were venereally infected. Four thousand prostitutes were treated by the hospital in the twenty-four years after 1746; and at the midpoint of this period in 1758, Saunders Welch estimated there were over three thousand street prostitutes active in London.[56] The numbers, for what they are worth, suggest the existence of a pool of prostitutes who were almost universally infected, and who through their customers circulated venereal disease to a substantial number of married women of all social ranks. These women, in turn, must have infected their unborn children. These children infected their wet nurses among those ranks where mothers did not nurse. Poor women who had been infected by their husbands infected the children they were paid to nurse. And a number of young girls were both raped and infected by single and married men seeking to cure themselves of the venereal disease that they had usually contracted from prostitutes.

Venereal disease shadowed all acts of sexual intercourse inside and outside of marriage. It destroyed relations within households, and between husbands and wives. It is likely that as the century progressed, more husbands infected their wives. This is what the divorces in the London consistory suggest on the basis of a detailed consideration of three decades, 1700–1709, 1750–59, and 1790–99. There was one husband who infected his wife in the first decade; none in the second; and four in the last. In addition the number of cases in which the husband's venereal infection was mentioned (but not necessarily as passed on to his wife) increased: two each in the first and second decades, but eight in the 1790s. The increase in infected husbands is even more significant because the number of women bringing divorce cases after 1750 was cut in half. But the total number of cases is, admittedly, small.

The husbands who became infected usually had a history of going to whores. John Abercromby, a cabinetmaker, married his wife Frances in 1694. For the next five years he also steadily picked up whores and took them to public houses. He got gonorrhea several times and was treated by several doctors. This alienated his wife. He begged for a reconciliation, and she slept with him after she was taken to a doctor who assured her that her husband was cured. But he continued to go to whores. The child born to them in May 1697 was very sick from the disease. John was diagnosed again. While he was being treated, he tried to force her to have sex; and when she resisted, he said he was sorry that he had not infected her, for then he could blame his illness on her. But she was in fact infected, since she had been able to pass the disease to their child.[57]

A century later Ann Rea found that ten days after her marriage she was attacked by a disease whose symptoms she did not recognize. She told her husband, who understood but did not explain. He treated her himself. She told her mother, who insisted on a doctor. She was treated for three weeks but grew worse. The mercury (which apparently she did not recognize) loosened her teeth and swelled her throat as it should have. She asked for another physician. Her husband refused and abused her for asking. Her mother then invited her home to Birmingham, and there at last, the surgeons and a physician told her that she had venereal disease.[58]

Robert Beeby did not go to whores, but seduced the female servants instead. He twice contracted venereal disease and infected his wife, who was treated by a surgeon, Alexander Barr. They separated because of his adultery. William Holland did go to whores, became infected, and passed it to his wife. He had to ask her to see the surgeon to whom he had confessed. Finally, there is Thomas Knibbs, who seduced the servants in the lodging house that his wife ran. He infected her and had to ask her to see a surgeon. In the cases of the two husbands who seduced the servants, it is very likely that they also went to whores. But the court required as much specificity as possible. A wife was likely to be best informed about her husband's sexual misdeeds among their own servants. Such husbands, though, were likely to have spread their infection not only to their wives and their prostitutes, but also to the unmarried servants whom they seduced.[59]

The wives in these divorces seem for the most part not to have made their husband's infecting them the heart of their case. It was the repeated adulteries and the physical violence toward them that often accompanied the infidelity to which they most objected. Many wives, especially when not infected themselves, seem to have philosophically accepted their husband's disease. Boswell's wife certainly did so. Mrs. Thrale helped to nurse her husband through his two infections, with only minor complaint on her part. But she did write the second time that "he has I am pretty sure not given it to me, and I am now pregnant and may bring a healthy boy, who knows?" Jane Cherry washed out her husband's clothes so that the maids would not know he was infected, but she did try to make him promise to give up whores. And Lady Mary Fitzgerald acceded to her husband's request and nursed him through his salivation for a bad case of the disease, even though she had only recently been delivered of her son. But she did use the occasion to extract a promise of better behavior. Some husbands did show a degree of concern for their wives. Henry Thrale in his embarrassment tried to hide the truth from his wife the second time, or so she thought. Daniel Timmings simply told his wife that he was in a decline and could not have sex.[60]

There were of course adulterous wives, and in two divorce cases, wives infected their husbands. In both cases, the women had had sex with many men, and in one case she clearly had become a woman of the town.[61] This strongly suggests that sexual relations between individuals accustomed to many partners was very likely to lead to infection. Promiscuity and prostitution almost always led to disease. Only abstinence and monogamy were safe, and even these two were safe only if one had in the course of life strictly passed from one state to the other, and one's partner had done so as well. Only in the marriage of two virgins were there no wages of sin to pay—provided, of course, that their parents had all practiced a similar restraint. The presence of the modern pattern of venereal disease cannot be statistically proven in eighteenth-century London. There are a few suggestive numbers. But it is more certain that the history of the disease's prevention and cure as it can be assembled from the medical literature, from the rape cases, and from the story of the Lock Hospital, as well as from the marital dynamics of the divorce cases, leaves little doubt that the modern pattern of infection had come into existence as a result of the new prostitution. All sexual acts in eighteenth-century London were bound to each other by the possibility of venereal infection. It was the harsh legacy of modern Western heterosexuality.

PART THREE

Illegitimacy and Rape

CHAPTER EIGHT

Courtship or Libertinage

T he new male heterosexuality produced a pattern of prostitution that the last five chapters have described. From that material it is apparent that probably the majority of men in London had sexual relations with a population of prostitutes who could be found walking from one end to the other of the great thoroughfare of interconnecting streets. This thoroughfare organized into a single city the separate jurisdictions of Westminster, the City of London, and urban Middlesex. But the city was now divided into an East End and a West End, and the houses of prostitution could be found together at these two ends of the thoroughfare. There were some class differences between East End and West End prostitution; but there was a very real similarity of experience no matter where along the thoroughfare a man picked up a prostitute to prove his masculinity; and the effects on his income, his relation with his wife, and the health of his family were also the same. The women seduced into prostitution, however, must always have been a minority of the young unmarried women in the city. The effect of the new male heterosexuality on the majority of these young women must therefore be sought elsewhere in the history of illegitimacy.

The level of illegitimacy in eighteenth-century London is difficult to measure. The parish registers that can be used for the early seventeenth century are less reliable later on, and there is no equivalent to the nineteenth-century census. Peter Laslett, nonetheless, has argued that until the twentieth century, London was always more conservative in these matters than rural England. The national census in 1842 found that London had the lowest illegitimacy ratio of all the English countries. This was probably inaccurate to some degree, and it has been claimed that before the 1880s at least a third of the city's illegitimate children were not recorded. But even if one increased the ratio by a third to allow for this, London would still have the lowest illegitimacy ratio in England in the middle of the nineteenth century. For the beginning of the seventeenth century, Roger Finlay has found from the parish registers an illegitimacy ratio that was lower in London than in the rest of the country. If these relatively low ratios were also present in the eighteenth century, it would make it very likely that London never experienced the very high level of illegitimacy that appeared in England and all of Europe at the end of the century and the beginning of the next.[1]

These high illegitimacy ratios have been used by Edward Shorter to argue for a fundamental cultural shift in which Europeans abandoned a sexual economy closely tied to marriage and the family for one that valued sexual fulfillment and romance. But the majority of historians have tended to say (as Nicholas Rogers does about eighteenth-century Westminster) that the increase in illegitimacy was the result of the pressures that economic change put on men who courted women and then abandoned them once they became pregnant. But the two positions can be reconciled if a sexual revolution occurred for men but not for women. It could then be argued that the new male heterosexuality encouraged men to seduce young women whom they had no intention of marrying, and that the young women usually consented in the belief that sexual intimacy was a prelude to marriage. If, however, there was no marked increase in illegitimacy ratios for London, this would create a problem in the argument. This might be resolved by arguing that young women who had the enterprise to come to London were able to defend themselves against exploitative men, and that there was no need for men in London to seduce respectable women since the streets were full of prostitutes with whom they could easily prove their masculinity.[2]

The question of London's illegitimacy ratio in the eighteenth century has been given, however, new life by Adrian Wilson's analysis of the records of the Foundling Hospital from 1741 to 1760. This hospital had been founded in 1739 to care for infants who might otherwise have been abandoned by their parents. Like the Magdalen Hospital and the Lock Asylum for reformed prostitutes, and the Lock Hospital for venereal disease, the Foundling Hospital can be viewed as inspired by the sentimental and humanitarian impulses that sought to cope with some of the more brutal effects of the new male heterosexuality. Between 1739 and 1746 about four hundred children were brought to the hospital each year, but fewer than one in three of them were admitted. Wilson points out that contemporaries usually assumed that these children were illegitimate, and he finds that the children's place of origin when it was indicated (as it was in 12 out of 119 he sampled) was always London. The minimum figure of four hundred bastards is increased by Wilson to one thousand by arguing that for every three mothers who brought or sent a child, a further two were deterred because their child had passed the age limit or died since the previous admission, or because they feared the publicity or believed their chances for admission to be slim.[3]

These supposed one thousand illegitimate children would have represented 5 percent of all the births in London in those years and would produce a higher illegitimacy ratio than the 4 percent to be found in the rest of the country. Between 1756 and 1760 the figures escalated when the hospital, supported by a grant from Parliament, took all the children it was offered. Children eventually poured in from all of England, but half of them came from London. From these figures Wilson estimates a London illegitimacy ratio of 10 percent for these four years. He admits, however, that his sources in both periods do not indicate whether a child was illegitimate or not, and he notes that in France some parents surrendered their legitimate children to orphanages. But he argues that the children were illegitimate because a third were brought within ten days of their birth and 70 percent in the first thirty-nine days and presumes that the parents of legitimate children would not have brought them so soon. But he does not justify this presumption, and along with the process by which he makes four hundred children grow to one thousand, it is among the weaker points in his argument.

If Wilson is right that London by the middle of the eighteenth century had gone from having one of the lowest illegitimacy ratios in England to having the highest, the argument as to the effect of the new heterosexuality on the great mass of young unmarried women in the city would change considerably. It would then seem that the men of the second generation to live under the new regime of male heterosexuality were actively pursuing their sexual desires with respectable women as well as with prostitutes. And it would suggest that London led England and the rest of Europe by two generations in this regard. The mid-nineteenth-century census cannot, however, be ignored. By then London would seem to have settled back into its conservative sexual ways, and this may well have happened as a result of growing working-class respectability and acceptance of the ideals of romantic love and domesticity. There London stayed, presumably, until the late-twentieth-century sexual revolution gave it once again an illegitimacy ratio that surpassed the rest of England. This would make an intriguing history, and the effect of changing sexual mores on London in the late twentieth century would support the possibility that a new

sexual system had similarly first appeared in London in the early eighteenth century before it passed to the rest of the country. London would
then have led the fashion in sexual mores, as it did in everything else.[4]

The material in the two chapters that follow cannot definitively answer
these questions. Instead they show that in different parts of the city there
were very different paths by which young women became pregnant. Illegitimacy was therefore less of a common experience throughout the city
than prostitution, which shows that London neighborhoods remained
highly differentiated from each other despite the unification into a single
city of the three separate jurisdictions. This becomes clear from the declarations that women made when they sought poor relief for themselves
and their child. They were then required to describe themselves, their
lovers, and the circumstances under which they had become pregnant.
Since there was no standardized form, the kind of information solicited
varies considerably from one parish to another. These bastardy examinations survive for about seven London parishes, usually in fragmentary
form. Four of them have been chosen, two from the West End and two
from the East End. Going from west to east they are Chelsea, St. Margaret's Westminster, Shoreditch, and Aldgate. In Chelsea illegitimate sexual
relations were domesticated. They usually occurred between fellow servants and must frequently have had marriage as their eventual aim. In St.
Margaret's sexual relations usually occurred in public houses and often
across class lines. They must often have been tied to prostitution, but this
was probably not so in those cases where women went with servants or
common soldiers. In Shoreditch the women who got pregnant were much
less educated than the poor women who were married. This was still a
tightly organized weaving community committed to conventional marriage. Its illegitimacy was therefore probably tied to the exploitation of
poor servants by their more comfortable masters, but between these
women and their lovers there was less of a social gulf than between the
servants in St. Margaret's and the gentlemen who made them pregnant.
In the final parish, Aldgate, sexual relations in and out of marriage were
less distinguished from each other than in any of the other three. It is the
place where the practical libertinism of the London poor (which elsewhere
turns up in bits and pieces) is best documented.

These pregnancies were disastrous for young women, as the next chapter shows. Most of them had left their families in the countryside and
come to London to find work as servants.[5] In Chelsea two-thirds of the
women who became pregnant had come from outside London; the rest
were born in London. These young women hoped to work for a number

of years and save their wages so that eventually they could leave service and marry. In the ordinary course of their lives they flirted with the men they met in the households where they lived and worked and in the streets where they walked. They did so sometimes for the pleasure of the thing itself and sometimes in the hope of finding a husband. But they had to be fairly careful since in both their households and the streets London was full of men who were prepared to force the issue beyond acceptable limits. But some young women did find themselves pregnant and unmarried because some men broke their promises or denied that they had ever made them; and some found themselves overwhelmed by passion for a man or by his physical intimidation.

Most women were overwhelmed with shame that they had lost their honor, and they often did their best to hide their situation from their masters, their friends, and their families, and sometimes even from themselves (as the infanticide cases suggest). Their pregnancies also had very serious economic consequences. Masters, no matter how much some of them might help, would not let a pregnant woman continue to work in their house. A woman who managed to leave her place without revealing her pregnancy then had to rent lodgings until her child was born, which usually forced her to use up the savings she had accumulated toward marriage and to sell her clothes as well. Once her child was born, she had to put it out to nurse since no master would allow her to bring her child to work. But the cost of a nurse was often equivalent to her entire annual wage. Some masters were prepared to hire a woman again, but others would not, even though they might be willing to recommend her to someone else. For most women their only solution was to seek public relief from the parish, which would pay the cost of their lying-in and take their child into the workhouse, where it was very likely to die. But the price of going to the parish was the public loss of a woman's reputation. As an alternative there was the Foundling Hospital. By the 1770s (after trying other standards of admission) it took the children of women who, it was thought, had a chance of maintaining their reputations and returning to honest work. A few women could not bring themselves to follow any of these rational courses. They hid their pregnancies and had their children while still at work. They delivered themselves and in the process deliberately or accidentally killed the child.

Some women must have persuaded their lovers to marry them, but they do not turn up in any of the sources used in this chapter. Other women entered into long-term liaisons with their lovers, and they do appear in the bastardy examinations, especially in the poor East End parishes. In some of those parishes women preceded or followed a bastard by one man with marriage to another. In parts of the West End the presence of the population of streetwalking prostitutes drew some women into their way of life, especially those who had sexual relations with gentlemen. But throughout London most women were seduced by men of their own social class.

The occupations of these men varied according to the local economy of the individual parish. In the West End they were often servants themselves or soldiers quartered there. In the East End, they were weavers in Shoreditch, Spitalfields, and Bethnal Green, and sailors in Aldgate and Whitechapel. But no more than 20 percent of the women ever claimed that they had been explicitly promised marriage before they started sexual relations. As many as a quarter of the women in the West End had relations with gentlemen whom they cannot have hoped to marry. And no matter how one calculates the numbers, it seems likely that half of these women must have begun sexual relations with their lovers without much immediate thought of marriage. For a small minority of women (but a number larger than the very small population of prostitutes), therefore, the force of sexual passion could break through the restraints of conventional female honor.

It is difficult to know, however, what sort of force may have led them to consent. A few women did charge that they had been raped. But it was usually their masters whom they accused or a man of their own social class whom they did not know. Women did not usually charge a fellow servant with rape, even though such men were often their seducers. It is apparent that before coming to court in many of the rape cases either the woman or her attacker had attempted to settle the affront to her honor by negotiating the payment of damages in money or by making an offer of marriage. For some of the women the violence of the rape excluded any possibility of courtship, but it is apparent that for many of the men and some of the women, marriage was a possible conclusion to a relationship that had begun in rape. Rape was a part of the continuum of courtship.

St. Luke's, Chelsea

The first of the four parishes to consider is St. Luke's, Chelsea. In 1724 when Daniel Defoe published his *Tour through the Whole Island of Great Britain*, Chelsea was at the westernmost edge of the city and in Defoe's view not yet fully incorporated into the city, but about to be so. "Westminster," he wrote, "is in a fair way to shake hands with Chelsea," which he called "a town of palaces." Chelsea was "itself to be made one time or other a part of London . . . in its new extended capacity . . . extending from the farther end of Chelsea, west, to Deptford Bridge east, which . . . is at least eleven miles." By the end of the century Chelsea was very much part of the great urban sprawl. There were 300 houses in the parish in 1705, and 350 in 1717. By 1795 there were 1,350.[6] Bastardy in the parish reflected this growing urbanization. No declarations survive from the first three decades of the century. But there are batches from the middle and the end of the century. The declarations made between 1733 and 1766 differ significantly from those made between 1782 and 1799 (those for 1795 to 1797 are missing). In the four middle decades of the century there were less than thirty declarations a decade, with only ten in the 1750s, but there were forty-five in the 1780s and at least sixty-two in the 1790s. This pattern of relatively few declarations at midcentury and twice as many in the last three decades shows up in other parishes throughout the city (see table 8.7 below on p. 266). The increase was probably the result of a number of factors: the growth of the parish's population, better policing by the parish authorities, and an actual small increase in the percentage of women who became pregnant outside of marriage. The increase in the parish's population is apparent from the fourfold increase in the number of houses over the course of the century. The greater vigilance of the parish authorities is displayed in the nine instances from the 1780s and 1790s in which a couple were coerced into marrying each other, which does not seem to have been done in the middle decades of the century. The change in sexual behavior is harder to document. But in the 1780s and 1790s there are for the first time declarations of women who were living in irregular unions with a man by whom they had had several bastard children. There were no such unions declared in the middle of the century. These unions were a long-standing aspect of London life and can be found in St. Margaret's in Westminster in the second decade of the century. So that it may have been simply that the increasing urbanization of Chelsea had brought with it one of the standard patterns of London life. In one respect, however, the Chelsea declarations were the same at the middle and the end of the century. A larger percentage of the male seducers were servants than anywhere else in London. It was 30 percent from the 1730s to the 1760s, and 21 percent in the 1780s and 1790s. Chelsea remained throughout the century a place where the rich lived and employed a considerable number of male servants.[7]

The domestic context of most seductions in Chelsea becomes apparent

when the declarations from the middle decades of the century are analyzed. A servant woman was liable to be pursued by any of the men who
might live in her master's or her mistress's house. The man could be her
master himself or his son or his nephew. He could be a lodger in the
house, or an apprentice, or a fellow servant. A woman's fellow servants
were the ones from whom she had the most to fear. Some women seem
to have become pregnant almost immediately; for others it took longer.
In either case it is likely that both servants were fired once this was known.
But while a woman's lover could go looking for another place, she was
obliged to make arrangements to have her child, usually without much
help from him or anyone else. After Honour Harris began sex with her
fellow servant, John Thompson, in their master's house in Chelsea in May
1739, she quickly became pregnant. By February she had had a son in
the lodgings she had taken in a carpenter's house. She applied to the parish
five weeks after her son's birth, when her resources must have failed her.
Martha Cleason and Richard Little John started a sexual relationship in
1733 when they served Mr. Russell in Chelsea. They were apparently
lucky, and she did not become pregnant until October 1735. In July 1736
she had a son and baptized him Robert Little John. She survived for three
months before she applied to the parish in October, while Richard became
a servant to a farrier in Chelsea.[8]

These men and women were often servants in the same household at
all the different levels of society, and they usually began sex in the houses
where they served. Amy Nixon and John Cuthbert were lovers in a fashionable house in Southampton Street, Covent Garden. Eight and a half
months after they began to have sex, she declared to the parish that she
was pregnant. They had made love several times in their master's house.
They either left or were discharged, since Cuthbert became a footman to
Andrew Hopegood at Hadley in rural Middlesex. Elizabeth White and
William Brown served a baker in Chelsea; Priscilla Howard and Edward
Lyon served a victualler in St. George, Hanover Square. Both these couples had sex in their master's house.[9]

Servants sometimes took home to a master's or a mistress's house a
lover they had met elsewhere, but the lover was still often a servant. Catherine Price made her living as a cook in fashionable houses. While she
was cooking for Mrs. Evers in Hanover Square, she met Richard Williamson, a footman to Mrs. Ann Fielding, who lived at Odium near Farnham
in Hampshire. Early in 1732 Catherine and Williamson had sex once in
Mrs. Ever's house, where Catherine lived. By May she had lost her place
and taken a lodging at Mrs. Buckett's in Swallow Street, St. James, West-

minster. There she and Williamson had sex twice more. She became pregnant in May, and this probably frightened Williamson away. They stopped seeing each other, and nine months later Catherine had a daughter. In October 1933 Francis Potts took Mary Neal to his master's house at Fulham, where he was a footman. Two months later they had sex there once more. They never did it again, but unfortunately for Mary, one of those two encounters left her pregnant. Jane Tapsell's lover was not a servant but a bricklayer in Chelsea. They used the house in the King's Road where she was a servant, but they never got around to certain formalities, since she did not know his last name when she became pregnant and went to the parish in November. But the parish officers found him—his name was Brittain—and forced him to pay for the child's support. The child died soon after.[10]

The apprentices in the household of a woman's master or from someone else's household had almost the same standing as a servant, but they do not turn up as a woman's lover quite so often. Mary Handbrooke was a servant to Captain Turner in Chelsea when she met John Evans, who was an apprentice to a shoemaker in Chelsea. They had sex three times in her master's house in March and April 1734. By November Mary must was seven months pregnant and applied to the parish. Ann Hunt and her apprentice in 1751 served an ironmonger in Piccadilly. They had sex in their master's house several times and must have been discharged since on December 29, Ann had a daughter in lodgings. A journeyman in a household had higher status than an apprentice, and if he fell in love with a maid in the house, he could hope to set her up in lodgings as James Randall, a painter and glazier, did for Lucy Robinson. She was twenty when she met him. He was a journeyman to her master who kept a public house, the Five Bells, in Chelsea. She left her place and they lived together. Within three months she was pregnant. But their resources must have been very slender, and when she was seven months pregnant she applied to the parish.[11]

A woman's master was at the top of the household's hierarchy. When he seduced his maidservant, he violated all the norms of traditional patriarchal authority, and perhaps for that reason it did not occur very often. Or it may be that masters who seduced their servants usually supported them when they became pregnant and that such women do not therefore show up in the record. But other masters clearly failed to offer any support even though they may have used considerable force to get their way with a young woman. Sarah Powell was coerced by her master into having sex in June 1754 just after her mistress had gone to market at two o'clock in the morning. He came to her bed, awakened her, pushed his way in, and had sex with her. They had sex on two other occasions in the house. Four months later Sarah declared to the parish that she was pregnant. He clearly had offered her no support. Men higher in the social hierarchy than Sarah's master behaved as badly. Mary Drew's master was described as a gentleman. He had sex with her several times in his house after a first encounter in July. Six months later she had to go to the parish. Some masters may have offered help at first and then stopped. In the two months that Mary Morris worked for Thomas Howard, they had sex several times. She became pregnant and had a child in lodgings at Hammersmith the night before King George's birthday (as she remembered it) in 1753. But she did not apply to the parish until January 1755. The king's birthday was on October 30, so her child must have been fourteen and a half months old when she applied. That would have been a long time for a woman to survive on her own. One wonders whether Howard had supported her for a while and then stopped. The parish officers could track down a master, or his son, or his nephew, and make them pay. But even then the story sometimes ends sadly. At twenty Elizabeth Edwards became pregnant by her master's nephew who came to her bed several times during the fifteen months that she worked as a servant in their house in Chelsea. Elizabeth left when her condition became apparent and applied to the parish. Her lover was made to pay for the child's upkeep, but the child died soon, probably in the parish workhouse.[12]

Women who worked in public houses may have been especially at risk, since they were likely to deal with men who were drunk and inclined to see them as prostitutes. Ann Mackenny served the Old George, a public house in Chelsea run by John Guerney. There she became pregnant twice by two different men over a three-year period. The first man, John Sparks, was a tidewaiter at the customhouse and lodged at the George. In March 1733 he and Ann began to have sex, and eight months later she was pregnant. What happened to her child is unclear, but she continued to work at the George. Two years later Ann met another man at the George who was a servant to Mr. Large at Chelsea College. After a year of having sex at the George, Ann was pregnant again. Sarah Randall was similarly seduced by one of the lodgers in the Bell Alehouse at Sand End in Chelsea. He worked nearby as a brewer's servant and lodged at the alehouse where he and Sarah had sex. She became pregnant right away and had a daughter nine months later at Mr. Gardner's near the Horse Ferry, where she had taken lodgings. But women who served in public houses had to deal with their masters as well. Ann Crockford's master, who ran the Swan and

Scotch Grey in Jews Road, Chelsea, had sex several times with her. When she became pregnant, he must have declined to keep her since she had her child in the Chelsea workhouse. But Chelsea parish was not inclined to take in the problems from the rest of London that were generated in public houses. Sarah Baldwin's master ran a public house, the Flask, near Avery Farm in St. George, Hanover Square, and they frequently had sex while she was his servant for ten months. When she became pregnant, he must have refused to help. The parish of St. George passed her to Chelsea, who appealed to the justices at quarter sessions and sent her back to Hanover Square.[13]

It is apparent that most women usually had sex in the safe enclosure of the house where they lived and worked. But occasionally sex occurred elsewhere. Elizabeth Bucknall was seduced by the son of her master, an attorney in Chelsea. They first had sex several times in the house and then once on Kennington Common, where they had gone presumably to stroll. Elizabeth Inwood first had sex with Francis Newton in an open field in Battersea. They also met once in her room in a little cottage in Chelsea Park where she lodged with Thomas Pinn. But most often they had sex in the fields. Nine months after they began, a week before Christmas, she gave birth to her child in her lodgings at Thomas Puiss's. A month later she applied to the parish. Martha Howard and Augustine Cooper, who was a husbandman, or agricultural laborer, first had sex in Richmond Park, and they went there several times with the same purpose. They also had sex in other places. Ten months after the relationship began, Martha had a daughter in the lodgings of William Downing. Downing was a gardener who lived in the stableyard behind the house to which Sir Hans Sloan had retired in 1742 with his library and collections—so that Martha's world met the increasingly fashionable world of an expanding Chelsea. Seven weeks after her child's birth, Martha's resources ran out and she applied to the parish.[14]

Women who went with men to public houses were probably engaged in prostitution. This was true for five of the fifty-seven women. Mary Hughes was very unlucky and became pregnant as the result of a single sexual encounter. The man was James Clayton, a chairman who was a lodger at the Marlborough Head public house in Great Marlborough Street. They used the Bunch of Grapes in Hartshorn Lane, which was opposite the Star Inn in the Strand and near Hungerford Market. Because of the neighborhood, one wonders whether Mary had been walking the Strand in the hope of being picked up and making some money. At any rate, eight months later she was pregnant and applied to the parish. She must have had some resources, though, since she gave birth to her daughter, Frances, in her lodgings at Mr. Harris's in Jews Row, Chelsea. Mary Snaggs applied to the parish a month after she had a son at her lodgings. She was almost certainly a prostitute. She had gone on April 1 to the bagnio (to which men took prostitutes) in Spring Garden near Charing Cross with Joseph Collett. Collett took her there on other occasions, and they also met elsewhere. Jane Rumbell had probably engaged in prostitution in 1754 when she was eighteen years old. She and Lawrence Sheet had sex for the first time in a house near Charing Cross. They continued to do this over the next three years, meeting in various places. Jane eventually became pregnant and had a son. A year after the child's birth, she applied to the parish. Because of the length of time that had elapsed, it is possible that Sheet had supported her and the child at first and had then stopped. It is possible that Rebecca Clements was also engaged in prostitution because of the places to which her friend took her and the length of their relationship. He was John Coustos, a jeweler who lodged in Theobald Row. Rebecca was lucky in that, unlike some girls who became pregnant immediately, she and Coustos saw each other for two years before she became pregnant. On the first occasion Coustos took her to the Angel Inn behind St. Clement's Church, and they returned there several times. But Rebecca seemed to think that she became pregnant on an occasion eight months before she approached the parish in April 1748 when she and Coustos had gone to the Cheshire Cheese near the creek that was next to Chelsea. Coustos had clearly been discreet and had never taken Rebecca to his lodging, but in the absence of effective means of birth control, even such discretion could not prevent a woman from becoming pregnant. The least certain case was Jane Phillip's. She began sex with Samuel Price, a carpenter, twelve months before she had her child. Their first encounter had been at the Black Horse, a public house in Kensington; later they met elsewhere. She had her daughter in lodgings and applied to the parish three months later.[15]

When a woman approached term, she had to make plans for her lying-in. Twenty-three of the fifty-seven women who applied to the parish authorities in Chelsea between 1730 and 1770 were able to afford to take lodgings in which they had their children. But after they had used up their savings, they were obliged to go to the parish. The other thirty-four women must not have had sufficient savings to take lodgings until the birth and applied to the parish before their child was born. Some of them were even delivered in the parish workhouse. Hannah Bradby tried to avoid these difficulties by appealing to her lover for help. She was twenty-eight years old and had been born in St. Margaret's, Westminster, and apprenticed to a purse maker. That arrangement did not work out, however, since she subsequently worked as a servant for three years with Dr. John Wilmer in Millman's Road in Chelsea for £5.10.0. a year. This gave her the right to apply for relief in Chelsea. At the beginning of 1760 she became a servant to a Mrs. Billister. There she met her mistress's lodger, Thomas Leigh, an attorney's clerk in the Rolls Office, and they had sex several times between February and May. Hannah became pregnant and by November was close to her time. She had either quit her job or been fired and expected Leigh to help with the expenses of her lying-in. But when she went to see him at the Rolls Office, he told her that "if one single halfpenny would save her and the child, that he would not give it to her," and pushed her out of the office. She then applied to the parish. Barbara Frampton's love affair also ended sadly, though it began auspiciously enough with sex on Valentine's Day in 1742. Her lover was a servant to Lord Frederick Murray but lodged at an apothecary's in Mealman's Row in Chelsea, where Barbara was probably a servant. After making love several times, she became pregnant but, evidently without resources, had her child in the Chelsea workhouse on October 20. The child was probably premature and was born dead. She must have had a difficult recovery and applied to the parish a month later for herself.[16]

Once a woman was delivered, it was very difficult for her to go back to work unless she found a way to provide for her child. If she could not give the child to the Foundling Hospital, only the parish workhouse was left. Martha Elmes at twenty served the Swan Tavern at five pounds a year for eighteen months. There she met Matthew Murphy, a waiter in the tavern, had sex, and became pregnant. She took lodgings, had a son, and baptized him Matthew. But the child eventually had to be taken by the parish and kept in the workhouse. A child's chances of survival in the workhouse were not very good, as Elizabeth Davis and Dorcas Edmonds both knew. When Davis was twenty-seven she served a baker in Chiswick for four months, became pregnant, took lodgings, and had her child. Ten and a half months later she applied to the parish. Her lover, Moses Gibson, who had been her master's journeyman, was taken up by the parish authorities and paid for the child's support. But the child was sent to the Chelsea workhouse and died. Edmonds at thirty gave birth to a daughter in lodgings in Chelsea. The father was a gentleman's servant who had gone to the West Indies and probably died. The child was sent to the parish workhouse and died there.[17]

If the figures from the 1780s and 1790s hold true for the middle decades of the century, only a handful of women would have come from families in Chelsea or from anywhere else in London. But those who did have families in London could not hope for much help. When Catherine Watson started sex with the Chelsea surgeon Alexander Reid on the first Sunday of August, they used her father's lodgings, where her son was born nine months later. She named the boy Alexander in honor of his father. But still she had to go to the parish eventually, probably to coerce Reid into paying for the child. Susan Street's story began in her mother's house at Wandsworth, where she had sex with John Sprawsley, a local shoemaker. This was at the end of July 1744, and nine and a half months later, on May 14, 1745, she had a daughter in the Chelsea workhouse. Her mother, presumably, had turned her out. Susan called her daughter Mary and gave the child her lover's last name. Seven weeks later she applied for further assistance. Elizabeth Powell first had sex with her lover (a journeyman barber in Chelsea) in a garret in the house where she was a servant and later met him several times in her mistress's stable. When she became pregnant, she went to her parents, and her child was born in their lodgings in the stableyard behind Great Cheyne Row. But they must have been unable to continue their support, and she applied to the parish five weeks later.[18]

A few women managed somehow to support a child on their own, as both Margaret Lumbey and Elizabeth Carpenter did. Lumbey came to the parish for help when her daughter was nearly three years old. The child had been born in lodgings in St. Martin in the Fields and was baptized Ann Johnson alias Lumbey. The child's father was a lighterman who lived in Chelsea. He had presumably not helped to support her. Carpenter had an affair with Richard Dickinson, who was a servant with her in Pall Mall. When her delivery was close, she took lodgings in Turks Row in Chelsea and had a daughter. Two years later she married another man who lived at Brentford. It is not clear how she had supported herself and her child for the two years before this marriage. But after a year of marriage, she applied to Chelsea saying that she could no longer support her three-year-old child by the first man.[19]

From the Chelsea declarations in the 1780s and 1790s it is possible to calculate the ages at which women became pregnant (table 8.1) and where in England they were born (table 8.4). This is extremely valuable since this information does not appear in the declarations for the other three parishes studied in detail. There are, however, ages from the 1780s and the 1790s for St. Martin's in the Fields in the West End (table 8.2) and for St. Sepulchre's in the 1790s, a poor parish northwest of the City wall

Table 8.1 Ages of Spinsters in Chelsea Making Bastardy Declarations, 1782–99

Age	1780s	1790s
13–17	3	1
18–22	17	20
23–29	16	26
30–40	10	9
Unknown	0	6
Total	46	62

Source: GLRO: P74/LUK/124–26.

Table 8.2 Ages of Pregnant Spinsters and of Poor Women at Marriage, St. Martin in the Fields and St. Clement Danes (in percentages)

Period	N	15–19	20–24	25–29	30–34	35–39	40–44
			Pregnant Spinsters				
1716–17	13	7.7	38.5	30.8	15.4	7.7	0.0
1745–52[a]	115	8.6	54.7	22.7	9.4	4.7	0.0
1780–86[a]	364	12.1	43.4	32.1	8.2	3.3	0.5
1790–95	205	12.4	47.1	26.8	9.6	3.8	0.5
			Poor Women at Marriage				
1750–52	244	21.7	26.6	25.8	11.1	7.7	7.4
1785–91	221	19.9	6.2	24.4	11.3	5.9	2.3

Source: Nicholas Rogers, "Carnal Knowledge: Illegitimacy in Eighteenth-Century Westminster," *Journal of Social History* 23 (1989): 355–75, tables 3 and 4.
Note: Figures are for the parish of St. Martin in the Fields except as noted.
[a] Parishes of St. Martin in the Fields and St. Clement Danes.

(table 8.3). In the 1790s (when there are fewer unknown cases than in the 1780s), about one-third of the Chelsea women were born in London West End parishes, with five of them in Chelsea itself. A fifth came from three counties near London. Most of the rest came from a dozen different English counties. But it is apparent that fashionable households did not employ the poor Irish women who were plentiful in some parts of London—only two came from Ireland. About half of all the women in Chelsea who made declarations were under twenty-four when the average age of marriage in England as a whole was 24.7 years. There was, however, in London a tradition of early marriage (see table 8.2) with about one-

Table 8.3 Ages of Spinsters in St. Sepulchre Making Bastardy Declarations, 1793–97 (*N* = 40)

Age	Number of Women	Age	Number of Women	Age	Number of Women
18	2	24	1	30	2
19	2	25	1	31	0
20	5	26	3	32	0
21	2	27	0	33	0
22	2	28	0	34	1
23	3	29	0	Unknown	16

Source: GL: MS9096.
Note: Sixteen of the women were pregnant. Nine had had children, four of them from one to three years before, which would lower their ages at the child's birth (from 22 to 19, 21 to 20, 26 to 25, 30 to 28).

Table 8.4 Birthplaces of Pregnant Spinsters in Chelsea, Declarations, 1782–99

Birthplace	1780s	1790s
London	5	18
Middlesex	3	1
Surrey	4	6
Hampshire	1	5
English counties with 2 women each	6	12
English counties with 1 woman each	8	9
Scotland, Ireland, America, East Indies	4	7
Unknown	15	4
Total	46	62

Source: GLRO: P74/LUK/124–26.

fifth of the poor women in St. Martin's marrying under the age of twenty. But only about a tenth of the women in St. Martin's became pregnant outside of marriage at such an early age. It is possible to argue that some of the Chelsea women who became pregnant under the age of twenty-four were intending to marry the men who had made them pregnant. With the women twenty-four and older the likelihood that they intended marriage (whatever the men may have thought) grows even stronger. But from the statements that some women made to the Foundling Hospital (which are cited in the next chapter), it is also likely that some were swept away by passion or coercion with no very specific plans as to marriage.

Unfortunately, the declarations do not say specifically whether promises of marriage had been made. About half of the women who were in their thirties were either pregnant or had recently had a child, but the rest were applying for relief for a child they had had up to ten years before. Seventy-one of the women as a whole made their declarations because of a recent pregnancy, fifty-seven of them before the child's birth, and fourteen within the child's first year. The other thirty-seven women had children older than a year. The fourteen women—a mere 13 percent—who waited until after their child was born may have hoped to marry or receive sufficient support from their lovers. Those with older children and those who made their declarations before their child's birth can have had little hope of marrying their lovers.

Six women in the 1780s and 1790s were living with men in long-term liaisons that show that some women did persuade their lovers to enter into a relationship. These women tended to begin childbearing at an early age and to come from London. But these liaisons can also be found among the Irish in the East End. The Irish did not marry because as Roman Catholics they did not care to use the Church of England, in which legal marriages had to be performed after 1753. Why the poor Protestant English failed to marry in church is harder to say—it was perhaps a sign of a religious disaffection that was a result of their social class. Two of these unions did begin at the conventional age of marriage. In 1786 Ann Lentler, who came from Bristol, was thirty-four and living in King Street in St. George, Westminster. She had two sons, George and William, both of whom had been baptized with her lover's last name of Bird. Beginning at twenty-four, Ann had served for five years as a servant in Chelsea. She then became pregnant, left her service, and had her first child when she was thirty. She apparently lived with her lover in King Street and probably passed as his wife. A year before she applied for relief, she had her second child in the same house. Another woman, Elizabeth Coleman, began to live with John Chart when she was twenty-four. She was born in Chelsea and began to work as a cook when she was nineteen. She kept that place for five years and left when she became pregnant. She and Chart then lived in different places in Kensington and Chelsea and had two daughters. He deserted when she was five months pregnant with their third child.[20]

The other four relationships began when the women were much younger. Esther Philpot started to live with Robert William Reeves after she quit service at seventeen. Over the next fifteen years, they had at least five children. Reeves was a gravedigger and so poor that their last two children were delivered at the parish's expense by the parish midwife. Elizabeth Hunt also stopped being a servant when she was seventeen to live with John Chuersey, a journeyman carpenter. They passed as married and had four children. But after fourteen years Chuersey left her to live with another woman who kept a shop in Streatham. The parish overseer tracked Chuersey down and made him promise to support his youngest child. Susannah Broom began her liaison when she was nineteen and had two daughters by George Perry. She like three of the others was a local London woman. Born in Edgeware, her mother had brought her as a child to Chelsea where she had grown up and been a servant for two years. It is striking that four of these six women were Londoners, and one wonders whether the presence of their families and the London tradition of early marriage had helped them to establish their relationships. But the sixth woman was born in Ireland. Elizabeth Foley became a servant in Chelsea when she was nineteen. She found a lover who was a private soldier in the footguards and within a year she was pregnant. She had her child in a house in Holborn and baptized her in the Roman Catholic chapel near Lincoln's Inn Fields. Two years later she had a son. For an Irish Roman Catholic in London, such a relationship was not unusual. But Elizabeth was only one of two Irishwomen who made declarations in Chelsea. Across town in the much poorer parish of Aldgate, there were lots of Irishwomen, and there it was the case that 12 percent of all women who made these declarations were in irregular unions.[21]

The parish overseers in the 1780s and 1790s occasionally urged or even compelled a couple to marry. When Ann Spond (to use her married name, since her maiden was not given) became pregnant in 1794 she was twenty-six years old. She said that Thomas Spond, a gardener, was the father. Spond was arrested and confined first in the cage at Fulham and then in the prison at Clerkenwell. When the overseer asked Ann if she would be willing to marry Spond, she said that she would rather not, as she did not like him. The overseer told her that she nonetheless "must have him" and compelled the couple to marry. They were allowed to spend the night in the workhouse and were then thrown out. After Ann went into labor in the public road, she was taken back to the workhouse and had a stillborn child after a painful labor. Catherine Wingate came to her marriage by a more circuitous route but ended happier with the arrangement. In 1783 she was eighteen years old and employed by a man and his wife who kept an academy for young gentlemen in Church Lane, Chelsea. Gordon Skelly, one of the students who boarded at the academy, seduced Catherine, and she left after she became pregnant. She said at the end of August that she was seven months pregnant, but her calculation must have been two months off, since it was four months before her child was born in the workhouse. Three years later in 1786 Catherine was pregnant again but by a different man, John Goldby. It is not clear how she had lived in the three years after the birth of her first child, since she gave her master at the academy as her last long-term employer. What happened to her two children is also unclear, but they had probably died. In 1787 Catherine got a job again as a servant and stayed for a year. Two years later she was pregnant for a third time by a third man, Henry Yates, a plasterer from Chelsea. This time, however, she married her lover in Chelsea church when she was three months pregnant.[22]

Did having three children by three different men in seven years make Catherine Wingate a prostitute? One presumes that the man who finally married her did not think so, and that her ability to identify him as her child's father meant that there had been a relationship between them for some time. Elizabeth Wheeler, on the other hand, could not accurately identify the man who had made her pregnant, and as a consequence, the parish overseers declared the friendship "to have been a bawdy house acquaintance." Elizabeth was nineteen, the daughter of a paper stainer, and lived at home with her father. A year and a half before she became pregnant, she went with two female friends to drink tea in a court in Bond Street. There she met James Creadon, who said that he lived in Wimpole Street and worked at the Treasury. Elizabeth and Creadon now began to see each other over a period of seven or eight months. They ate and drank at a public house where they had sex on a sofa. It is not clear whether Thomas Wheeler forced his pregnant daughter to go to the parish authorities, but when they tried to locate James Creadon at the Treasury, they could not find such a man. They concluded that Elizabeth was lying and that she had become part of the world of prostitution while living at home with her father. Five other women at midcentury who like Elizabeth had gone with men to public houses and probably engaged in prostitution have already been described. But most of the women from Chelsea who became pregnant were servants who had begun to have sex with a fellow servant probably (in her mind at least) with the intention of marrying. Male servants, however, could probably afford in few cases to marry or even to set up a household, and certainly in St. Margaret's more common soldiers than servants did this. A woman may have hoped for marriage, but her lover knew it was improbable when he seduced her.[23]

St. Margaret's, Westminster

Moving east from Chelsea and into London proper one encountered the second of the four parishes to be analyzed—St. Margaret's, Westminster. The parish contained the houses of Parliament, Westminster Abbey, and the main government offices. But St. Margaret's was less exclusively fashionable than Chelsea. Many of the tradesmen and artisans who catered to the elite lived in the parish. Many military men, both officers and common soldiers, also lived in the parish, some of the soldiers in barracks and others quartered in public houses. They set the sexual tone of the parish, and a flourishing street prostitution catered to them. The chapter on the topography of prostitution has shown that in the 1720s some of the public houses in the parish were bawdy houses, especially those in Thieving Lane, Long Ditch, and Peter Street. Fifty years later, in the 1770s, at least eighteen bawdy houses can be documented in the parish. This was nothing like the number around Covent Garden, but there were as many in St. Margaret's as in Whitechapel in the East End. In the 1720s one-quarter of the women in the bastardy examinations had gone with their lovers to public houses, the majority of them in the triangle of streets north and west of the Abbey and south of St. James's Park, and women who went to such houses were likely to be engaged in prostitution, as the Chelsea declarations also suggested.

The bastardy examinations for St. Margaret's cover the first half of the century (1712–52). They are the only examinations among the four parishes that survive from that period and are quite valuable in that regard. These examinations are also the only ones that come in a series of their own. In all the other parishes the bastardy examinations are found intermixed with the general series of poor law examinations. St. Margaret's "Bastardy Book" was probably begun as part of the program of the Societies for the Reformation of Manners. The societies conducted an extraordinarily close policing of bastardy in the parish. This can be shown by contrasting the entries before 1730 with those in the following two decades, when the societies were in decline. Their policing caught in its net between 1712 and 1730 a greater number of gentlemen than show up in any of the other sets of examinations. This provides a focus to discuss the extent to which bastard children were a result of class exploitation. The examinations also make it possible to consider the role of prostitution in bastardy, since St. Margaret's was the only one of the four parishes to have a considerable number of bawdy houses. Finally, the military men in the parish give bastardy in St. Margaret's its distinctive history, as do the male servants in Chelsea, the weavers in Shoreditch, and the sailors in Aldgate.[24]

The presence and then the withdrawal of the Society for the Reformation of Manners can be seen by comparing the entries in the bastardy book before and after 1730. If one begins with the women making declarations, it is apparent that the total number declined significantly after 1730. There were 287 in the first eight years and 418 in the 1720s. But in the 1730s and 1740s the numbers were more than halved to 164 and 142 respectively. Either there was a dramatic fall in bastardy after 1730, or there was a dramatic fall in reporting. After 1730 two categories of women either decline or disappear from the declarations. Between 1712 and 1721, 17 percent of the women with bastards were either wives or widows. Compared with the percentage of such women in other parishes later in the century, this was quite high. In Shoreditch (1759–99) it was half as many (10 percent) and in Chelsea (1733–99) even less (7 percent). In St. Margaret's itself the percentage after 1730 was higher than in these two parishes (12 percent in the 1730s and 13 percent in the 1740s), but it had still declined noticeably from the 17 percent of the first decade of the society's activity in the parish. The high percentage of wives and widows makes it very likely that the society had attempted to discover every woman in the parish who had a child but was not living with a husband, no matter what her marital status might have been. It is not even certain that all these wives and widows actually had asked or received support from the parish. This is made likely by the presence of thirty-one married women in the declarations before 1730 who had to explain that they were married and that their children were the legitimate offspring of their husbands who for various reasons were absent. There are no such women making declarations after 1730. The practice had stopped.

There is a final characteristic of the women making declarations before 1730 that suggests that the pregnant women of the parish were very closely monitored for two decades. In the first ten years (1712–21), 105 single women made their declarations after the birth of their child. Twenty-eight percent did so within the first two weeks of the child's birth, most of them within the week (21 percent), some on the very day. This practice turns up in none of the other three parishes. In Shoreditch no women at all made their declarations in the first two weeks of a child's life. But even in St. Margaret's it was hard to maintain this level of zeal. In the first five years of the bastardy book, sixteen women made their declaration in the first week (28 percent), but in the next five years this fell to six (13 percent). After the influence of the society waned (1736–49), the percentage of women making declarations in the first two weeks was halved (14 percent). These differences before and after 1730 in the number of women making declarations, their marital status, and when they declared their children to the parish, all suggest the kind of close supervision that St. Margaret's exercised over bastardy in the days when the influence of the Societies for the Reformation of Manners was predominant.

This policing by the societies is also apparent in the social class of the men who were charged with being fathers of bastards. In the first eight years (1712–19), sixty-two men were gentlemen (23 percent). In the 1720s, there were sixty-three, but they represented a smaller percentage (16 percent). In the 1730s and 1740s, however, gentlemen were only 6 to 8 percent of the men. Once again there is a pattern of initial zeal in which gentlemen who had made women pregnant were carefully noted in the first eight years. This zeal slackened in the next decade, and after 1730, when the societies became moribund, gentlemen declined to a fourth of what they had been in the first two decades. It seems most unlikely that there was an abrupt change in the 1730s in the sexual behavior of gentlemen. Instead it must have been that between 1712 and 1729 the parish authorities had registered all women, whether their lovers had taken care of them or not. But after 1730 only those gentlemen appeared in the record who had not settled with the women they had made pregnant. The military rake was probably overrepresented among these gentlemen, since throughout all four decades military officers made up about one-half of the total. If one adds common soldiers (some of whom were officers' servants) to the officers, military men equaled gentlemen as seducers of servants. But while the number of reported gentlemen declined after 1730, there was as high a percentage of soldiers in the 1740s as in the 1720s. The prostitute accompanied by a soldier in the street remained a common sight in Westminster throughout the century, as J. P. Malcolm bore witness in 1807.[25] The percentage of men who were servants also remained more constant than the number of gentlemen, at 17 and 22 percent in the two decades before 1730 and 25 and 19 percent in the 1730s and 1740s. The number of men who were journeymen and apprentices rose after 1730 from 5 percent in the 1720s to nearly 15 percent in the 1730s. It is apparent that the number of poorer men reported after 1730 either remained constant or increased. Only the number of gentlemen declined.

These figures from St. Margaret's suggest that the campaign of the societies revealed for a brief period the extent to which gentlemen were responsible for bastardy in the West End. The figures that can be culled from the examination books after 1730 therefore must always be much lower than the actual incidence. It is of course possible that over the century there was a decline in the number of gentlemen who seduced poor women. But it is equally likely that in the West End throughout the century gentlemen continued to account for at least the one-quarter of all illicit pregnancies that the zeal of the reformation societies had revealed between 1712 and 1719. In the second half of the century the number of gentlemen claimed by women from poorer parishes was 6 percent in Shoreditch and 3 percent in Aldgate. Shoreditch's figure is very close to the 8 percent in St. Margaret's in the 1740s. But it seems most unlikely that the figures from the two could actually have been so close given that Shoreditch would have had few gentlemen living there. But even in Shoreditch, the gentlemen may have been underreported. Mary Pellett said in 1798 that a gentleman from Hoxton "hath until very lately supported [her] child but now doth refuse to support it any longer."[26] It is therefore very probable that throughout London gentlemen who supported their children were not usually recorded in the examination books except for a brief period in the 1710s and 1720s in the parish of St. Margaret's. It must be stressed, however, that the many gentlemen among the seducers in St. Margaret's are accounted for by a world of prostitution that catered to military men. In a richer parish like Chelsea, gentlemen were only 2 percent of seducers because Chelsea was a more domesticated parish than St. Margaret's. In other words, gentlemen in London did not very often seduce servants in their own houses. In Chelsea that was left to the male servants. Gentlemen usually took their illicit pleasures away from home in other people's neighborhoods—unless, of course, one was an officer and lived in lodgings in St. Margaret's. It may therefore be that the purpose of St. Margaret's bastardy book was as much to keep track of the effects of prostitution as anything else, and that it ends in 1752 because Parliament had passed a new act that tried to give Londoners greater control over the prostitution in their neighborhoods.

The women who are listed between 1712 and 1719 as having had sexual relations with gentlemen (in the years when gentlemen represented one-quarter of the men in the declarations) had either been their servants or been engaged almost certainly in prostitution. For many it may have been their first venture into prostitution, but for some it must have been a fairly regular occupation. First there were the servants and masters like Sarah Leek and Sir Solomon Medeng, who began to have sex in his house in Pall Mall in August 1711. Eleven months later Sarah was pregnant. In four other cases, the woman seems to have been her master's servant in the countryside and to have come to London or been sent there after she became pregnant. Lydia Page had been with Edward Savage at his house in Hadley in Hertfordshire. Martha Hurrell began to have sex at Christmas with her lover in his father's house in Essex and was pregnant and in London by the next September. Frances Mills got pregnant in Richard Farnborough's house in Hertfordshire and had her child in a house in Westminster in Love Lane near the Great Sanctuary. George Cecil, Esq., who lived in Salisbury, made Mary Fulford pregnant in his house there.

The other London cases probably involved prostitution and occurred more or less equally in one of three places: the man's house or lodgings, the woman's lodgings, or a public house. In some cases the woman was probably a servant in the house where the man lodged, but this was mentioned only in the case of Mary Banbridge, whose lover had a place in the Exchequer and lodged in College Court. In the other cases it is likely that the man took home a woman he had met somewhere else. Some men had lodgings, some had houses. Henry Meriton had Arabella Fowke in his bedchamber in Petty France. Richard Newdigate, a barrister with chambers in the Temple, took Jane Jones there several times. Ann Squire and Ann Wigham were taken to houses in Queen Square, Westminster, and in Holborn. In most cases a couple did not have sex where the man lived, presumably to protect his reputation. James Kegwin, for instance, who was a more discreet barrister than Richard Newdigate, did not take Ann Fairfax back to his chambers in the Temple but used instead either her lodgings at Mrs. Taylor's in Thieving Lane, where there were other bawdy houses, or the Horn Tavern in King Street. Charles Blackmore also used the Horn when he had sex with Margaret Stewart. The duke of Montagu met Rebecca Bottomley at more fashionable brothels in Drury Lane and Pall Mall, one of which passed as a china shop. Richard Oglethorpe and Mary King used the Dogg Tavern in New Palace Yard. Margaret Newport and George Valentine met at Duck's Coffeehouse in Denmark Court. When a couple used a woman's lodging, it is not always clear whether she was a servant in the house. Elizabeth Coots unambiguously said that she was.[27]

Most of these women (nineteen of thirty-two) claimed that they had not had sexual relations with any man other than the gentleman who had made them pregnant, or at least with no other since the relationship had begun. Thirteen women, however, did not make such a declaration, and this may have meant that they were regularly employed as prostitutes. Three of these had used houses that were ambiguously described. But if they were prostitutes, it is probable that Mrs. Wright's house at No. 2

John's Street, where Alice Greenwood went with Mr. Walker—he lodged in Prince's Court, but she did not know his first name—was a brothel, as were the houses in White Friars and Black Friars (at the widow Pullin's) that Elizabeth Ovelever and Mary Roberts used.

The declarations were probably deliberate in their inclusion or exclusion of a phrase indicating whether a woman had had sexual relations with another man. For the first one hundred examinations, there was no indication in twenty-seven cases that this was the only man with whom a woman had slept. For the rest, there were three formulas used. Seventeen women said that they had had sex with "no other ever," or used an even more emphatic phrase. Thirty-two women more simply said that they had had sex with "no other" man. But in twenty-four cases the phrase was that they had had sex with "no other since" the man who had made them pregnant. The deliberation of the phrase indicates that these women had been sexually active with other men before this one. It was not an alternative to the phrase "no other," because in Elinor Jones's declaration the "since" was deliberately struck out to allow her to say that she had been with "no other person." Similarly in Frances Buckley's declaration the phrase was "no other person hath had carnal knowledge of her body since nor for several months before." Nine of these twenty-four women were widows, but the rest were single. If these twenty-four cases are added to the twenty-seven where none of the three formulas were used, the declarations would seem to indicate that fifty-one of the hundred women (only thirteen of whom had ever married) had been sexually active with more than one man. This does not mean that they were all prostitutes. And some of the women who had had sex with only one man may have been engaging in prostitution for the first time. Sexual experimentation and occasional or frequent prostitution must have been fairly common among the women in St. Margaret's who became pregnant with bastards.[28]

The forty women who became pregnant by gentlemen between 1712 and 1719 can be supplemented by the nineteen women who were made pregnant by army officers in the same years. Nine of them went with an officer to a public house, and six of them had sex where he lodged. In seven cases the women knew the officer only by his military title and his last name—Captain Wilson or Captain Boyle—whereas this was true of only two of the women who went with ordinary gentlemen. It is a sign of the sexual impact that a man's military bearing had and how it swallowed up his more individual identity. Six of the women said they had never had sexual relations with anyone except the officer. Two others used a slightly more ambiguous phrase "no other but him," which is less cate-

gorical than "no other ever." Five women said that they had been with
"no other since" the officer, which probably indicates that they had been
with other men at other times. Five of the women said nothing at all,
which certainly indicates that they were sexually experienced with other
men. This was probably true therefore for ten of the nineteen women.

The three of the women were servants in the house where they were seduced. In one case the officer lodged in the house; in another he did not;
the third is unclear. These women were probably not engaged directly in
prostitution. One of them, Mary Young, said categorically that she had
never had sex with anyone except Captain John Prendergass, a half-pay
officer who lived in Leicester Fields. And Elizabeth Turner was without
sexual experience when she was hired by Captain Courtney's landlady a
fortnight before Christmas. But in her first week in the house, Courtney
seduced her. Their relations continued for the next few weeks until she
left, less than a month after she was hired. One wonders whether her
mistress had learned what was happening and discharged her, for Elizabeth was pregnant when she departed.[29]

The women who went with officers to public houses were more sexually
experienced. Only three out of nine had never had sex before when they
went, respectively, to a cook's in Peter Street, the Cross Keys Tavern in
the Strand, and a chandler's shop in St. Martin's Street near Leicester
Fields that was run by Mr. Cock and where the lieutenant also lodged.
One of the other six women seems to have specialized in picking up gentlemen. In 1715 Johanna Pereya became pregnant after going several times
to the Red Lyon in Kensington with Captain Robert Hume. But in the
previous year she had gotten pregnant by another gentleman whom she
had taken to her lodgings in St. Martin's Lane. The public houses to
which the other five officers took their women were spread out across the
various London bawdy house neighborhoods. Three of the officers actually lived in St. Margaret's, and two of them used local bawdy houses.
Captain Copsey first had sex with Barbara Katherine Clay in a house in
College Street that was probably a brothel. Four or five days later they
met at the Buffer's Head Tavern, where they returned several times. But
eventually he took her to his house in Marsham Street. James French also
lived in the parish in lodgings in Petty France. At first he used a local
house, the Pheasant Alehouse in Thieving Lane, but later he took Mary
Batchell to a porter's house on Ludgate Hill. Captain Comerly, who also
lived in St. Margaret's, from the beginning used a house outside the parish, a Mr. Jonyman's in One Tun Alley between the Strand and Hungerford Market. Only one officer used a house in a distinctly unfashionable

neighborhood. He was Captain Pratt, who had sex with Barbara Tudor at the Three Cups in Aldersgate Street, where she was a servant. Major Manwell of the dragoons, on the other hand, situated himself in the heart of London's vice. He lodged next to a milliner's in Southampton Street in Covent Garden, when both the trade of milliner and Covent Garden were synonymous with prostitution. He first took Susan Smith to the Fountain Tavern in Great Katherine Street. After that they went several times to the Cock Tavern in Charles Street, Covent Garden, and to the Crown and Cushion in Great Russell Street. Susan said that after she began to see the major, she had not gone with any other man.[30]

The encounters that remain to be described ranged from the very indiscreet to the very domestic. Elizabeth Woodyar had sex several times with Captain Ledgard in the Tiltyard Guard Room. Jane Jones had the misfortune to go with Captain Duce, who was a notorious seducer, to his lodgings. Ann Jarvis, on the other hand, was seduced in her brother's house by the officer who lodged there. She had probably fallen in love. It was certainly her only sexual encounter. But there was not much chance that a gentleman in Her Majesty's Life Guards would marry a tailor's sister. Margaret Baines was General George Hamilton's mistress and came from Holland. They had had several children, three of whom were at a boarding school. What had happened to the general is unclear, but it is likely that Margaret would never have appeared in a bastardy book except for the zeal of the Societies for the Reformation of Manners.[31]

Military officers and gentlemen together made up the single largest group of seducers. Among poor men, servants were the only group that approached the number of gentlemen, and many of them were servants to the aristocracy and the gentry. But in St. Margaret's common soldiers were also a distinct group. In fact if one adds together officers, soldiers, officers' servants, pensioners, and sailors, there were as many military men as there were gentlemen. Twenty-one common soldiers were listed between 1712 and 1719. Only six of their women seem to have been sexually experienced. Ten said they had never been with another man. Three women had been married. Three of the soldiers had been living as man and wife with the woman who became pregnant. If to these one adds all the military cases until 1729, it appears that in the eighteen years that the policing of the reformation societies was most thorough, ten of fifty-one common soldiers (20 percent) had set up some sort of menage with a woman. By contrast only three servants (2 percent) did the same thing in those eighteen years, which confirms the likelihood that the male servants in Chelsea cannot have had much thought of marrying the women they seduced. Only one of the ten soldiers, however, was in a long-term relationship that had produced more than one child. Still it seems that the women who went with soldiers were less likely to have been engaged in prostitution than those who went with gentlemen. Their partners were of their own class. They were less sexually experienced. And they were much more likely to try to set up a household. Some of them must have married their soldiers. But a soldier's wife and children were likely to face a difficult future. In the 1740s the streets in St. Margaret's were full of women wandering about begging, many of them with children, who when they were questioned turned out to be the wives of soldiers who had either deserted them or gone with the army to Germany or Flanders.[32]

ST. LEONARD'S, SHOREDITCH

Shoreditch is the third parish to consider. With it we move from the fashionable West End to the unfashionable eastern half of London. Shoreditch, Spitalfields, and Bethnal Green were the three parishes northeast of the old City walls in which most of London's weavers were to be found. The weavers were the poorest of London's skilled workers. Silk weaving was highly susceptible to fluctuations in the economy, and the trade tended to have too many workers. This was partly because the relatively unskilled labor of women and children could be easily employed, and because weavers from Ireland and the English countryside came to London in search of better wages. Of the weavers who were hanged at Tyburn, 60 percent had been born in London and a fifth came from Ireland. The English weavers resented the Irish, and in 1736 rioted against them on the ground that they worked for lower wages. But the weavers had in general a history of militancy over the conditions of their labor greater than any other group. Poverty and debt were endemic, and the parish workhouses in the three parishes were often full with destitute weavers. Some of the poor law declaration books survive for Shoreditch from the last four decades of the century, but it is clear that the series is not complete. Still it is possible to extract the names of 581 women who either declared that they were pregnant with a bastard or had given birth to such a child.[33]

The Shoreditch bastardy examinations are the most laconic of the four sets under analysis. But with patience it is possible to establish the probabilities of who the women were, where their sexual relations occurred, and the nature of their tie to the men with whom they were involved. Ninety percent of the women were single, 2 percent were married, and the rest were widows. Twenty-five women (4 percent) were listed as having settlements outside of London, with only three of them from Ireland. But 85 percent of them had settlements in Shoreditch, and the remainder (11 percent) somewhere in metropolitan London. Those women with settlements outside of Shoreditch must have become pregnant while living in the parish. The declarations unfortunately do not explain why a woman had a right to relief in Shoreditch, but she must either have been born in the parish or have worked there. If these women were the daughters of weavers, and if the London birthplace of the 60 percent of the weavers who were hanged at Tyburn was typical of weavers as a whole, then many of the women may have been native Londoners, certainly in greater numbers than the servants in the West End. If the women had once been employed in Shoreditch, they had probably been maids of all work, which was the weavers' practice.[34] They certainly had not worked in houses with male servants, who were a mere 3 percent of the men who made these women pregnant. This is in striking contrast to the many male servants in the Chelsea, St. Margaret's, and the Foundling Hospital declarations. Male servants were largely a phenomenon of the wealthy West End parishes.

Instead of being seduced by servants or soldiers as in the West End, the women from Shoreditch were very likely to have had a weaver for a lover.[35] Eleven percent of all the men in the declarations were weavers. Forty percent of these weavers came from Shoreditch. There were about 20 percent each from the two adjoining weaving parishes of Spitalfields and Bethnal Green, and the remaining weavers came from a wide spread of London locations. But putting the matter in this way underestimates the role of the Shoreditch weavers in making the women of the parish pregnant. Only 25 percent of the men in all the declarations were living in Shoreditch. Another 17 percent lived in the adjoining parishes of St. Luke, Bishopsgate, Spitalfields, and Bethnal Green. The remaining men were to be found in the rest of London, many in the City, some in the West End, fewer on the south bank of the Thames, and the remainder in Kent, Essex, and the rest of England. It is not certain just what this means. Had the men from elsewhere come to Shoreditch and made the local women pregnant? Or more probably had the women with a settlement in Shoreditch moved out into the rest of the city, become pregnant by men who lived there, and then returned, or been sent back, to their parish? In any case, 25 percent of the women were made pregnant by men who lived in Shoreditch. If to this figure is added the 15 percent of women with settlements elsewhere than in Shoreditch, it is likely that at least

40 percent of the women lived in Shoreditch and that the other 60 percent lived elsewhere in or out of London. Of the men who lived in Shoreditch, 18 percent were weavers. Only three other occupations appear with any frequency among the 136 men from the parish. Fifteen were laborers (11 percent), seven were carpenters (5 percent), and six were shoemakers (4 percent). The rest were distributed among fifty different occupations.

It was therefore the case that if a woman from Shoreditch stayed in her parish or moved to the adjoining parishes of Spitalfields or Bethnal Green and became pregnant, there was one chance in five that her lover would be a weaver. But if she moved out to the rest of London, her lover might come from a very wide range of occupations. Few of them would have been gentlemen (5 percent) or servants (3 percent). This probably reflects the very limited range of places for which these women, as a result of their notable illiteracy, were qualified (table 8.5). In the early nineteenth century, Shoreditch had the reputation of being badly educated, and this has been attributed to the early age at which children were put to work. But in the Shoreditch poor law examinations of the eighteenth century, 32 percent of the married women were able to sign their names. This was nearly equal to the national average in 1750 of 36 percent. It was not as good as the 56 percent for London women that David Cressy has found in the 1720s, but the women in that sample must have been the wives of prosperous tradesmen and craftsmen. Certainly poor married women in St. Margaret's in the 1740s had just about the same literacy rate (32 percent) as did the Shoreditch married women in the second half of the cen-

Table 8.5 Literacy of Poor Women in Three Parishes

Parish	Period	Signature	Mark	No Mark or Signature
		Poor Married Women		
St. Margaret's[a]	1741–44	36	71	5
Shoreditch[b]	1770s, 1780s	88	189	
		Mothers of Bastard Children		
Aldgate[c]	1745–99	75	215	20
St. Margaret's[d]	1712–21	96	255	54
Shoreditch[e]	1758–99	53	293	6

Sources: [a] WPL: E. 3234; [b] GLRO: P91/LEN/1205–7; [c] GL: MS 52676, vols. 1–22; [d] WPL: E. 2574–75; [e] GLRO: P91/LEN/1200–1210, 1213–17.

tury. The Shoreditch women who had bastards, however, had a literacy rate (15 percent) that was only half that of the married women in the parish. This low a rate was not true for the single women who made bastardy declarations in other London parishes. Such women in St. Margaret's in the second decade of the century (1712–21) were nearly as literate (24 percent) as the poor married women in their own parish or elsewhere in London, and the same was true for the mothers of illegitimate children in Aldgate in the second half of the century (26 percent). The difference in literacy between poor married women and the mothers of bastards in Shoreditch therefore looks like an economic difference. This suggests that it was the poorest of poor women—those who probably were maids of all work, rather than those who helped with the spinning or the weaving—who were likely to be seduced, and it is possible that they were poor Irish women.[36]

A few women clearly began sexual relations with their lovers in the expectation that it would lead to marriage. Fourteen of the eighty-six (16 percent) declarations from the first ten years (1758–67) indicate that a woman began sexual relations after she received a promise of marriage. Four of the men who promised were weavers, two were dyers, two laborers. There were a shoemaker, a chamberlain, an ostler, a coachman, a clockmaker, and a coachmaker. Shoreditch (three), Bethnal Green (two), and Bishopsgate (two) together accounted for half the men. The rest were spread through the town, and one was a silkweaver from Manchester. All the women had settlements in Shoreditch except for one from Gloucestershire. All of them except one were illiterate. Twelve of them were pregnant, but two had had the child when they made their declarations. Both the men and the women, in other words, were typical of the entire population of 581. Not much other detail is given. Ann Chapman said that not only had Henry Plummer promised to marry her, the banns had even been published in Shoreditch Church. Ann presumably lived in the parish, but Henry was a laborer from Tottenham High Cross. David Pritchard, a dyer, after frequently promising to marry Ann Page, took her out into the fields on the evening of November 9 and had sex with her. Six months later she declared that she was pregnant. Most of the women said they had had sex frequently. Why did these fourteen women say that they had been promised marriage? Had the other seventy-two women from these years agreed to sex without a promise of marriage? In the Foundling Hospital declarations from the 1770s, only 20 percent of the women said that they had been promised marriage. This together with the Shoreditch declarations makes it likely that of the women who agreed to sexual relations,

Table 8.6 Declarations Made by Spinsters before a Child's Birth or When a Child Was under 12 Months

	Period	Total	Declared before Birth or Born in Workhouse[a]	%	Declared after Birth outside Parish Workhouse	%
Chelsea	1782–99	71	57	80.3	14	19.7
St. Margaret's	1712–21	305	227	74.4	78	25.6
Shoreditch	1758–99	480	313	65.2	167	34.8
Aldgate	1745–99	201	110	54.7	91	45.3

Sources: GLRO: P/74/LUK/123–26; WPL: E. 2574–75; GLRO: P91/LEN/1200–1217; GL: MS 52676, vols. 1–22.

[a] If the child was born in a workhouse, some sort of declaration must have been made before birth. Included in this column are 9 such children in Chelsea, none in St. Margaret, 49 in Shoreditch, and 11 in Aldgate.

it was a distinct minority of 15 to 20 percent who would not do so without an explicit promise of marriage. It seems unlikely, however, that there were no such women after 1770 in Shoreditch. Their absence from the later declarations must mean that whoever took down their information ceased either to ask or to record whether promises had been made.[37]

There are some other possible pieces of evidence to show that some women hoped or managed to turn their love affair either into marriage or an unofficial but stable union. Thirty-five percent of the women who had never married or (as far as we know) had a child before waited until after the child was born to make their declaration (table 8.6). All of them waited at least two weeks. Half of them declared the child within the next three to eight weeks, and the other half at various points in the next ten months. Almost all of the women had had the child somewhere in Shoreditch, but only a quarter of their lovers lived in the parish. Had many of the women become pregnant elsewhere and then moved back to the parish to have their child and protect their right of support from the parish? Or were all these women living in Shoreditch when they became pregnant? There is no way to be certain, but the practice in Aldgate will suggest that it was the first possibility that was true. The parish authorities were certainly not diligently searching out these women, since none of them came forward in the first two weeks, as had nearly 30 percent of the women from St. Margaret's early in the century, when the Societies for the Reformation of Manners were active in that parish. In St. Margaret's only 25 percent of the women waited until after the child's birth, as opposed to 35 percent in Shoreditch. But in Aldgate still more women

(45 percent) waited until after the child was born. When this figure is put together with the high percentage of Aldgate women (12 percent) who were living in stable but illegal unions with men by whom they had had two or more children, and the high number of women (44 percent) in Aldgate who baptized their children with their lover's last name, it becomes very likely that women who delayed making a declaration until after a child's birth were hoping to persuade the child's father either to marry or to live together. In some cases it may have been that a woman married her lover after her children were born, as Alice Broderick said she had done, though her husband left her for another woman and forced her to turn to the parish. But in Shoreditch the number of women living in irregular unions was low (3 percent) compared to Aldgate's 12 percent. There was not yet present in eighteenth-century Shoreditch the practice attributed to the weavers in the 1830s of not "having lawful married wives" but keeping instead "women whom they call tacks." Nonetheless one may presume that the 35 percent of Shoreditch women who delayed their declarations probably had hoped to form households with their lovers and went to the parish after it became apparent that this would not happen and when their own resources ran out. If this 35 percent is combined with the 16 percent who had received promises of marriage and the 3 percent who did manage to form stable but irregular unions, one may conclude that at least half the Shoreditch women had thought of sex as a prelude to marriage. But it also must be that at least the other half either had been swept away by passion without much thought of the future or had been unable to withstand the guile of a determined man. Certainly these women were notably less educated than the women in Shoreditch who did get married, and it is therefore very likely that their seducers must frequently not have considered them potential wives.[38]

St. Botolph's, Aldgate

Further east than Shoreditch, but lower down and closer to the river, was the fourth and final parish, St. Botolph, Aldgate. Aldgate was dominated by sailors or mariners (men in the merchant navy), but not to the same extent Shoreditch was by weavers. Nine percent of all the men who fathered bastards in the Aldgate declarations were sailors, as were 13 percent of the men who actually lived in the parish. But as in Shoreditch, there were few servants (3 percent). Male servants were always a distinguishing mark of West End parishes. (In Chelsea servants accounted for 20 to 30 percent of seducers, depending on the decade. At St. Margaret's they were similarly a fifth to a fourth of the men.) As at Shoreditch, a quarter of the men in the Aldgate declarations lived in the parish. Another quarter were to be found in the City parishes. The other one half were more or less equally divided among the parishes east of Aldgate like Whitechapel and Wapping, the parishes south of the river, the West End parishes, and English counties like Essex and Kent. Locations for 25 percent of the men were not given, but if they were known, it would probably change the distribution by only one or two percentage points. It is also the case that the occupations of 23 percent of the men were not given. But if one calculates the number of sailors in the declarations from the 251 known occupations, the percentage goes up from nine to eleven.

The women with settlements in Aldgate lived in a world less tied to a single craft than did the Shoreditch women. They also had more ties to the prosperous West End and City parishes and to the poorer parishes on the south bank of the river. But women only worked in the fashionable western and City parishes; they did not live in them once they married or when they formed long-term sexual liaisons without marrying. On the other hand, it can be said more definitely than in the case of Shoreditch that the Aldgate women were usually living not in Aldgate but in the parish of their seducers. The location where sex occurred was given in the first twenty-two years of the declarations. In 20 percent of the cases, it was in Aldgate. This is close to the 25 percent of men who in the declarations as a whole lived in Aldgate.

In a fifth of the known cases (six of thirty-two), a woman had had sex in either her mother's (four) or her father's house (two). Rachel Peter's lover was a cooper who made barrels and lived in her mother's house in Nightingale Lane in Aldgate, where she had her child. Richard Broxton, who was a brewer's servant in Hoxton, came to the house of Elizabeth Ripshaw's mother in Whitechapel, but Elizabeth had her child in a house in Mouse Alley in Aldgate. She had probably moved back into Aldgate to make certain that the parish would be responsible for her child. She baptized him Richard after his father. Sarah Smithson had her child in the Aldgate workhouse. Her lover was a farmer in Hertfordshire who several times had sex with her in her mother's house, but it is not clear whether the house was in London or in Hertfordshire. Had Sarah chosen to lie in at the workhouse to protect her settlement rights because she could not afford to take lodgings in the parish? Mary Walker was seduced by a servant in her father's house in Castle Street near Leicester Fields. She could afford to go to a house in Aldgate to have her child. One of the Aldgate sailors seduced Mary Norman in her father's house, but since the house was in Aldgate, she stayed and had her child there. She later married another man. But the house of a lover's parent could do as well as one's own, so that Thomas Smith, an upholsterer, felt free to take Jane Garter home to Moorfields where his pawnbroking father lived.[39]

In a pattern more familiar in the West End than in Aldgate, a woman could be seduced in her master's house by a fellow servant or by her master. Elizabeth Haines and Mathew Vernoll, for instance, had sex several times in their master's house in the Victualling Office. And William Griffin was a drawer who poured drinks in the house that Nathaniel Edmonds kept in the George Yard, Cornhill, where Mary Huggins was a servant. Female servants in public houses like Sarah Leggatt, seduced by her master, who owned the Clock at the corner of Sherborne Lane, were probably always the ones at greatest risk, since drink and sex so often went together. Margaret Ludgate's master was also in the drink trade—a distiller who lived in Whitechapel. Margaret moved back to Aldgate for her daughter's birth and baptized her Margaret Younger after herself and the child's father.[40]

Lovers who had left home and did not live in the same household could use either his dwelling place or hers. Some men could only take women home to lodgings in other people's houses. John Kennington, a Whitechapel silk thrower, persuaded Elizabeth Lockwood to go home with him to his lodgings in Buckle Street. Elizabeth Barber went home with a soldier in the First Regiment of footguards who lodged in the house of Mrs. Hines in Goodman Fields in Whitechapel. Some men were well off enough to have a house of their own. John Bullwinkle, who was a victualler and probably connected to the Victualling Office on Tower Hill, must have taken Elizabeth Phillips several times from the Aldgate neighborhood across London Bridge to Southwark, where he had a house in Ditch Side near Guy's Hospital. Thomas Jones's house was in Aldgate itself in Cooper's Court. He was a customhouse officer who took Isabel Morgan home with him several times. A man who had women lodging in his house might find one of them desirable, like the carman who kept a house in Slater's Court in Whitechapel and seduced his lodger Elizabeth Dennis. Carmen carted goods about. There must have been a lot of them in Whitechapel, since four of them seduced women with settlements in Aldgate, the only Whitechapel occupation to appear more than once.[41]

Eleanor Miller was also seduced by her landlord. She was born in Edinburgh and at some point went to London. In 1751 she was hired as servant in Aldgate and served for a year and a half. In Aldgate she met a fellow Scot who was a sailor and married him at the Fleet in 1753, the very year

that Lord Hardwicke's Act made such marriages illegal. Over the next
eight years her husband must have come and gone on his voyages. She
saw him last at Portsmouth in September 1761 when he went on board
a man-of-war bound for the West Indies. He had probably been impressed into the navy during the Seven Years' War. Four months later,
in January 1762, Eleanor left Portsmouth and went to London, where
she found a lodging with John Gunn, a laborer who lived in Spitalfields.
In the middle of the month she allowed Gunn to have sex with her. She
probably became pregnant immediately, since she had a son in September
in Gunn's house. She baptized the child Richard Miller using her husband's last name. Her husband as far as she knew was still alive in the
West Indies. But eventually she heard that he had been killed at the siege
of Havana, two months before her child was born. Eleanor and Gunn
now entered into an informal union and passed as married. Certainly when
she had a second child in April 1765, she baptized her Elizabeth Gunn
in the parish church in Whitechapel. But Eleanor had taken the precaution of having the child in a house in Aldgate. She and Gunn were clearly
no longer in the house in Spitalfields. Had they moved to Whitechapel?
And were the times bad enough for them to take the precaution of having
the child not where they lived but in Eleanor's parish of settlement? What
became of Gunn is unclear. But eight months after the birth of this second
child, Eleanor applied to Aldgate for relief and signed her declaration.[42]

Several couples after they met went back to the house where a woman
lodged, but it is never clear from the declaration why she lived there or
what kind of work she did. In two cases where a woman lived at a public
house, she was probably a servant in the house. One was the Bull Head
in Shadwell, and the other the Falcon in Old Fish Street, London. In
both cases the women returned to Aldgate to have their children, Martha
Snell in Nightingale Lane and Mary Stevens in her mother's room in Red
Cross Street. Four other women took their men back to private houses
where they were almost certainly servants. In the case of two women who
went with sailors, it is clearer that they lodged on their own. One of these
sailors, James Wright, often went from his lodging in Nightingale Lane
in Aldgate to visit Catherine Taylor at her lodgings at Mrs. Grainger's
in Three Ton Court in Wapping. For her child's birth, Catherine moved
back to Aldgate. Her child was eighteen months old when she applied to
the parish, and it may be that she had entered into some sort of steady
relationship with her sailor until he went to sea, leaving her without the
means to support their child. This was more certainly the case with Ann
Bond. She began to see her sailor, William Binmoore, in July 1753. He

lived in Wapping, she at a baker's in Fetter Lane in London. Ann soon moved to live with Binmoore. They were together in Wapping for nine months, and in May 1754 she had a child for whose birth she moved back to Aldgate. But in October 1755 she must have been on her own when she came to the parish with her seventeen-month-old son. Binmoore had probably gone to sea. In the final case Frances Sparks unambiguously said that Thomas Glossup lay with her in her own house in Swan Alley in Aldgate.[43]

There was probably more acceptance in Aldgate than in the other three parishes for women who became pregnant outside of marriage. This was partly the result of a more libertine environment. Whitechapel and Wapping, two of the parishes most closely associated with Aldgate, were centers of prostitution for poor men, especially for sailors. But in addition Aldgate was relatively isolated from the gentry and bourgeois standards of the West End. There were lots of sailors in the parish, and lots of poor Irish. One of the best tests of this proposition would be to determine the number of women who were pregnant when they married by calculating how many gave birth within the first eight months of marriage. The amount of such prenuptial pregnancy increased throughout the eighteenth century in rural England, where it was not uncommon in a parish for a quarter to a third of all women to be pregnant when they married. No one has yet calculated such a rate for London in the eighteenth century. It has been done for the first half of the seventeenth century, when 16 percent of women were found to be pregnant at marriage, as opposed to 21 percent in rural England. It is not possible to say whether this low rate of prenuptial pregnancy persisted through the eighteenth century in London, but it would clearly have risen if it is true that the London illegitimacy ratio then surged ahead of the entire country. In any case there must have been some increase from the seventeenth century level, as there was in the country as a whole.[44]

The rate of prenuptial pregnancy in seventeenth-century London varied considerably, however, according to the wealth of a parish. In poorer parishes it was twice that of prosperous ones and equal to the rate in the countryside.[45] If this pattern persisted in the eighteenth century, then it may well have been that in the poor parishes like Shoreditch and Aldgate 25 to 30 percent of the women were pregnant at marriage, as they were in rural England. Poor women in eighteenth-century London parishes certainly had literacy rates no greater than those of women elsewhere in England. There were probably other similarities between their lives and those of women elsewhere in England, and the rate of prenuptial preg-

Table 8.7 Bastardy Declarations in Four London Parishes

Parish	1710s	1720s	1730s	1740s	1750s	1760s	1770s	1780s	1790s
St. Margaret's[a]									
(1712–52)	287	418	164	142	42	x	x	x	x
Chelsea[b]									
(1733–99)	x	x	21	28	10	15	x	54	62
Shoreditch[c]									
(1758–99)	x	x	x	x	6	87	97	176	215
Aldgate[d]									
(1744–98)	x	x	x	8	23	35	89	85	91

Sources: [a] WPL: E. 2574–2578; [b] GLRO: P74/LUK/121–26; [c] GLRO: P91/LEN/1200–1217; [d] GL: MS 52676, vols. 1–22.

nancy may have been one of them. In the seventeenth century this rate could vary between poor London parishes by four percentage points. In the eighteenth century there was probably a similar variation. Since there are, however, no figures for prenuptial pregnancy in London, which would have to be drawn from parish registers, the argument must turn on the number of women who waited until after the birth of their bastard children to make a declaration to the parish (table 8.7). Such women (we have argued) delayed their declarations in the hope of marrying their lovers or living with them and must therefore have shared the belief that sex before marriage was acceptable if it led to marriage.

The variation among our four parishes entirely fulfills the expectations of the argument. The two West End parishes had fewer women who delayed than did the two poorer East End parishes. The lowest percentage was found in Chelsea, which was the richest parish. St. Margaret's was less prosperous than Chelsea. But although it was a center for prostitution, which was true neither of Shoreditch nor of Aldgate, and although its figures were produced during the most vigorous policing of bastardy in the entire century, the parish's declaration rate was still lower than in the two poorer parishes to the east. These two parishes had the highest number of women who delayed: 35 percent in Shoreditch and 45 percent in Aldgate, which (for what it is worth) were the proportions found for prenuptial pregnancy in some eighteenth-century rural parishes. In Aldgate the practice of women in naming their bastards supports the meaning that has been attached to the delay in making a declaration. Seventy-five children were mentioned in the declarations between 1744 and 1785. For twenty-one of them only a first name or neither name was given. Three of the fifty-four last names that are given were neither the father's nor the mother's. Eighteen names were the mother's. But thirty-three were the father's (44 percent of 75). In 61 percent of the cases in which we know a bastard child's last name, the mother must have presented herself as married to the child's father. This was her hope, but unfortunately we know only the cases in which it was not realized.

Aldgate markedly differed from the other three parishes in a second regard. It had the most women who had lived for a number of years with a man by whom they had had two or more children. They were 12 percent of all the bastardy declarations (40 of 325). In St. Margaret's between 1712 and 1721, there were 7 out of 371 (2 percent). Chelsea did not have any between 1733 and 1766, but in the 1780s and 1790s it had 6 (or 5 percent of 116). In Shoreditch there were 17 (3 percent of 581) between 1758 and 1799. What explanation can be offered for these unions in general? And why specifically do so many of them appear in Aldgate? John Gillis has proposed one general solution. The Marriage Act of 1753 put a stop to the quick informal marriages that were made at the Fleet, where in the first half of the century the London poor had gotten married in great numbers. After 1753 the same kind of privacy could be achieved only by getting a license to marry without banns being publicly called in the parish church, or by marrying oneself in traditional or newly made ceremonies. The result was that between 1750 and 1850, one-seventh of all couples were not legally married in church. There is probably a great deal to this argument, but it is not clear exactly how well it works for London in the second half of the eighteenth century. There certainly was a long-standing tradition before 1750 that couples had the right to marry and divorce themselves. Traditional Catholic theology had taught that couples administered the sacrament of marriage to each other and that the priest was only a witness. It had not accepted the corollary that couples could divorce themselves. But this nonetheless was widely believed and to some degree practiced before 1750. A subsequent chapter suggests that these beliefs probably had facilitated the attempts to legally provide the divorces for incompatibility that were promoted by the rise of domesticity among the elites and the middle classes after 1750. Among the poor the evidence for domesticity is harder to find, but other parts of the modern gender system like the contempt for effeminate sodomites was certainly as present among them as among the rich. The apparently increasing use of wife sales in London after 1750 may imply that the poor were also reacting to new ideas about marriage, divorce, and incompatibility, and not only enacting a long-standing belief in the right to self-divorcement.[46]

It is certainly true that in the first half of the century the London poor were increasingly married at the Fleet. Poor law examinations show this clearly, although St. Margaret's is the only one of our four parishes with declarations from the relevant period. Between 1714 and 1721, one-third (sixteen of thirty-nine) of the poor men and women applying for relief at St. Margaret's said that they had been married at the Fleet in the first two decades of the century. By the 1740s this had doubled to almost two-thirds (63 percent) who said they had married there in the 1720s and 1730s. But it was still the case that nearly 30 percent had married in London churches. A few had married in rural churches before they came to London (9 percent), and one had been married by a Roman Catholic priest in his house in Great Wild Street near Drury Lane.[47]

Despite this ease of marriage there were couples in St. Margaret's living together without the benefit of legal marriage. Between 1712 and 1721 there were eight women (2 percent of 371) who lived with a man and had had two or more children by him. In 1714 Elizabeth Yarnel said that she had had two children, eight and three years old, by a man whose last name they bore. The man, however, was said to be in Worcestershire. But Esther Morris before she married Henry Morris in 1714 had lived for at least fifteen years with William Rice and had two children by him, one in St. Katherine's under the Tower and the other in St. Margaret's. She said that she had not had sexual relations with any other men than these two, both of whom she must have counted as husbands. The sequence of Elinor Typto's two relationships was reversed. After her first legal husband died, she entered into a relationship with a pensioner (or retired soldier) in Chelsea Hospital and had two children by him. Mary Wheetly married her husband in the Fleet. But he was a sailor and went to sea nine weeks later. Eight months after he left, Mary entered into a more satisfactory arrangement with a corporal in the footguards with whom she lived but did not marry. By 1717 the relationship had lasted eight years and they had two children. Ann Higgons was married twice. After her first husband died, she married again and had three children. Her second husband, however, had a first wife alive in Worcestershire. He probably thought of his first marriage as over, but the law did not. In a final case Margaret Baines had had five children by General George Hamilton. She was a Dutchwoman whom the general had brought to England. Because of the difference in social class, it is not certain that this couple regarded their relationship as a marriage, but they may well have done so.[48]

After 1723 no more of these relationships with several children turn up at St. Margaret's, but occasionally a woman with a single child did say that she had lived with her child's father as man and wife. This all demonstrates that the presence or absence of easy marriage in the Fleet is not enough in itself to account for the presence of informal unions. But it may well be that the disappearance after 1723 at St. Margaret's of these unions with many children was tied to the increasing numbers who married at the Fleet in the 1720s and 1730s. Nonetheless the low percentage of these unions at Shoreditch after the Marriage Act (1758–99)—a mere 3 percent, or only a point higher than St. Margaret's in the second decade of the century—confirms that not all sections of the London poor took to informal unions after 1753. It was clearly possible to marry very discreetly in Shoreditch parish church among the throngs whose names were called out as promised in marriage. This was known to the couple who (in a subsequent divorce case) went there to be married with banns called even though the woman had merely separated from her husband by articles of agreement and was not legally free to marry again. It may also have been that at Shoreditch the very poor subset of women (judging by their high rate of illiteracy) who became pregnant outside of marriage were not in a position to form the long-term liaisons of the kind that appear in Aldgate.[49]

Six of the forty long-term liaisons in Aldgate were the result of the law of marriage. Two women married men who had a previous wife alive. This seems to have happened often enough and would not raise any difficulties for the new marriage until hard times came and a woman who had passed all her life as legally married would have to explain that she was not. This was the case with Hannah Puffey, who in 1789 had six children alive, the eldest of whom was nineteen. She had married John Puffey in St. Giles Cripplegate in 1765, but previously in 1752 he had married a woman in Staffordshire. He must have brought his wedding certificate with him to London, since Hannah said that she had seen it. Jane Stoneham's ten children by Joseph Mott were also bastards, since someone had informed her that his first wife had died only two years before she made her declaration in 1790.[50] The other four cases are accounted for by the legal situation of the Roman Catholic Irish. Roman Catholics were obliged to marry in Anglican churches. This was followed by a marriage performed by one of their own priests. But some poor Roman Catholics either had themselves married only by a Catholic priest or by no one at all. Mary Playford explained in 1798 that sixteen years before she had been married in the Roman Catholic chapel at Gosport, across the harbor from Portsmouth. Her husband was from Gosport and was probably a sailor. They had several children born in Portsmouth and Gosport, two of whom were alive in 1798. Mary had worked for three years before her marriage as a servant in the Dundee Arms in Nightingale Lane in Aldgate, and there presumably she had met her husband. But according to the law, she was not a married woman, and when she needed relief (probably because he was in the navy during the current war), she had to use her settlement and not her husband's. In the same year an Irish grandmother applied for relief for her son's four children. Eleanor Connor said that fifty years before she had married her first husband in Ireland. Twenty-four years later her son from that marriage, who was born in Ireland, was married to Elizabeth Hyde by a Roman Catholic priest in Glasshouse Yard in Aldgate. But they never went through the Anglican ceremony. Her daughter-in-law was dead, and presumably in her son's absence she had taken responsibility for his children.[51]

Sometimes the Irish did not trouble themselves with a priest of any kind. Eleanor Hays, who was born in Ireland, went to England and worked as servant in Liverpool. In 1785 she started to live with Alexander Young, first in Manchester where she had a daughter in a house in the potato market and then in Birmingham where another child was born. But Young died, and Eleanor moved to London with her lover's sister and the sister's husband, who was a soldier. She settled with her two children in Brush Alley in Aldgate. Her sister-in-law, Jane Fairbrother, told her story, perhaps because Eleanor was ill. Some Irishmen married as often as they pleased. Peggy Smith thought that she had managed to marry John Smith in Rotherhithe parish church. But then she learned that Smith had married four other women, all of whom were alive. He had married the first in Ireland, the second in Barbados, the third at Plymouth, and the fourth at Dartmouth. He was the classic sailor with a wife in every port. A year after her marriage, Peggy was hired as a servant by John Mark Brown. This lasted for six years. But the nature of their relationship changed after he made her pregnant. She ceased to receive wages, and they lived together as man and wife and had two children. Brown then fell upon hard times and was twice imprisoned for debt, once in the Fleet, and once in the Clerkenwell Bridewell, where he died. When he went to prison he signed over his goods to Peggy. After his death, Peggy lived with a carpenter from Aldgate until he was impressed into the navy for the war against France.[52]

Sarah Wickham's marital and sexual career was perhaps the most complicated of these Irish cases. In 1754 (when she must have been about twenty), she married an Irishman in St. John's Church in Exeter. After he died Sarah came to London and worked for more than a year as servant to Daniel Roberts, a victualler in Red Cross Street in Aldgate. This gave her her settlement. In 1769 she married again. She was clear that the marriage was performed by a Roman Catholic priest in a house in Holloway Lane in Shoreditch. She said this both in 1769 and in 1775. She was not consistent, though, about her husband's name. In 1769 she called him Thomas Farrell and said that he had deserted her and left her pregnant. She seems to have been surprised that her marriage had no legal force. But in 1775 she remembered that her second husband's name was Thomas Comer. It is the same first name. Had Comer lied to her in 1769 and said that his name was Farrell, or more improbably had she married two different men in the same Shoreditch chapel? Sarah also changed her story in 1775 as to whom she had worked for between her two marriages. She now remembered not Daniel Roberts but William Bradley as the Aldgate victualler who had employed her for a year. The child with whom she was pregnant in 1769 probably died. In 1775 (when she was probably in her forties) she had a seventeen-month-old daughter who had been born at the Dark Entry in Aldgate. She had baptized the child as Sarah Wickham. And this time she said that her lover was an Aldgate shoemaker named Thomas Bencraft.[53]

The Irish, however, do not account for many of these long-term irregular unions. What of the sailors? There were certainly lots of them in Aldgate and its neighborhood. Nine percent of the fathers of bastards were sailors. But sailors do not appear with any frequency as the companions in the forty long-term irregular unions. In twenty-two cases there is no information as to the man's occupation. Of the remaining eighteen, only two were sailors. Hannah Gotschin lived with a sailor for eleven years as his wife and had three children, the eldest of whom the churchwardens from Wapping apprenticed as a sailor. Ann Howard's first child was actually born on a ship, HMS Vengeance, when it was docked at Sheerness. She applied for relief while her companion was away on HMS Orion.[54] But there were as many tailors and gun polishers among the men. And there were more shoemakers (three) and laborers (four). There were also a carman, a waterman, a painter, a smith, and a carpenter.

Two-thirds of the children from these long-term unions were born in Aldgate, and nearly as many in the poor adjoining parishes of Wapping (15 percent), Whitechapel (5 percent), St. George (6 percent) and St. Catherine's Precinct (5 percent). Some (9 percent) were born outside London. Almost none (except for two in Holborn) were born in the fashionable West End or in prosperous City parishes. Women from Aldgate may have gotten pregnant in those parishes, but they did not raise illegitimate families in them. The rest were born either on the south bank (5 percent) or in the poor parishes (8 percent) north of the City walls.

Women in these long-term unions when they applied for relief had to explain where they had their settlement. Fourteen of them had worked as servants, four in Aldgate, and one perhaps may invent for them the scenario of the seduced servant who decides to live with her lover. But seven women indicated that they had grown up in Aldgate, and some of them made the point that they had never worked as servants. Rachel Clark's father served an apprenticeship to a gunmaker in Wapping and then married her mother. After her mother's death Rachel lived with her father and his second wife in a house in Aldgate that rented for four pounds a year. Her stepmother taught her how to make slops, that is, clothes and bedding for sailors. But Rachel was not apprenticed and she never worked as a servant. She eventually lived with a shoemaker in Aldgate and had two children. But she did not marry him, and for that she did not give an explanation. Ann Rubee also eventually lived with a shoemaker without marrying him. Her grandmother told her that her farther had served his apprenticeship to a butcher in Aldgate, but Ann herself was not apprenticed and had not worked as servant. These two women came from respectable enough families, and neither was a former servant seduced into a sexual relationship. They look instead like those women (described at the beginning of this section) who started a sexual relationship with a man who visited them in their parents' houses. Renee Tring's story was similar except in one detail. Her mother had told her that she was illegitimate; although her parents had married, her father had a previous wife living at the time. Since Renee never worked as a servant, she had also probably gone directly from her parents' house to live with her lover, a gun polisher. But the reason these women began to live with their lovers but did not marry is still missing. One can only conclude that Aldgate custom justified it and that sex, children, and an enduring relationship in that world were not tied to formal marriage. Such women must therefore have started sexual relations with their lovers without any necessary thought of marriage. It is possible, however, that sometimes a woman's family did not know that a marriage had not occurred. In one such instance, Sarah Hollindrake, a respectable widow herself, said that she had heard her daughter say shortly before her death that she had never married the man with whom she had lived for many years and had several children. It sounds like the deathbed confession of a fault covered over for a long time.[55]

Some women entered into more than one of these irregular unions. Mary Hemming lived with Thomas Curttler for over four years and had three children by him. After his death, she seems to have started a new relationship with John Russell, whom she did not marry either. Carolina Bell had two children by Thomas Bell and one child by Peter James. At first she posed as Bell's widow but then admitted that she had not married him either. Her desire to pass as a widow does suggest that these relationships were to some degree embarrassing to those who lived in them. Elizabeth Profitt did marry her first husband John, but after his death she had two children by another man. It was marriage, however, that ruined poor Grace Dalton's relationship. After she had lived with Daniel Dalton for at least five years, they were married. But Dalton—apprenticed as a tailor and turned soldier (one of their sons was born in Chatham Barracks)— ran away within a week of the marriage. The formality and commitment of the legal bond had perhaps frightened him away.[56]

To enter alternately into legal or informal unions, to have a bastard and then marry one's lover, and to have a bastard by one man before or after a legal marriage to another are all patterns that turn up frequently enough in the declarations. They suggest that in the world of Aldgate there was an acceptable fluidity as to how a union might be formed. William Tatum and Catherine Lee lived together as man and wife and had a child whom they baptized in Aldgate parish church, but they did not marry until two years later. They must subsequently have separated, since Tatum later had to reclaim their child after he was passed from St. George's to Aldgate. Catherine Bleasdale's marriage ended with her husband's death; they had had one child before marriage and two afterward. Joseph Bull and his wife Ann had a son in Southwark and then married in Shoreditch Church, after which they had twins and then a fourth child. Elizabeth Tipton married her husband in Stepney seven months after she had their child in the Hackney workhouse. Two years after his death, she began a new relationship and became pregnant by a winecooper from Southwark whom she did not marry.[57]

Some women began with marriage and followed it with a bastard. Alice Thomas had two children by her husband and then, after his death, had a third by a soldier. Elizabeth Gready did much the same thing. Ann Hannah married her husband probably in 1771. Less than three years after his death in 1781, Ann started a new relationship with a man with whom she lived but did not marry. They had a daughter, but this second relationship also ended when her companion died. Helen Gibbs sandwiched her bastard between two marriages. Her first husband died in April

1782. Six months later she began to have sex with the master of ship, became pregnant, and had their child in July 1783. She then married another sailor from Aldgate. For a woman to have a bastard by one man was clearly not a bar to a subsequent marriage with another. Amelia Ross also had a son by the master of ship and then married another sailor who deserted her. But some women, like Frances Smith or Elizabeth Gloster, seemed to stress that they had had their bastard child long before their subsequent marriage—as if to say that it was an early mistake that had been redeemed. But the pattern of Jemima Joyce's life was inherited by her daughter. As a young woman Jemima had an affair with a carpenter from Essex while she was a servant to a wheelwright in Aldgate. She became pregnant and had a daughter in the Aldgate workhouse and baptized the child Elizabeth Worksett. After this Jemima married and was widowed and then married again. But when her daughter Elizabeth was twenty-three, she also became pregnant by an Essex man to whom she was not married. Like her mother, she had her daughter in the Aldgate workhouse and in honor of her mother, no doubt, called the child Jemima. The women of Aldgate would have shocked those for whom there was a single standard of female chastity and for whom there was only one acceptable form of long-term sexual union. But they themselves were always aware that there was a predominant standard by which a woman might be judged and that that standard was marriage in church. Jemima had followed her bastard daughter with two legitimate marriages.[58]

The material from these four parishes certainly gives strong support to the supposition that by the second generation of the eighteenth century the new heterosexuality had modified London's traditionally low illegitimacy ratio. But it also makes clear that the way in which this occurred differed markedly in the various parishes across the city. The male servants in Chelsea and elsewhere in the West End must have known that they were not financially in a position to marry their fellow servants after they had seduced them, no matter what the women may have hoped. But this may have been clear to the women themselves, since no more than 20 percent of the men in the West End in the 1770s promised marriage before sex began. The West End was also full of women who engaged in regular or occasional prostitution with gentlemen and soldiers whom they did not expect to marry. The women who became pregnant in a poor industrial parish like Shoreditch were not the women whom the men expected to marry. They were much less educated than poor married women; only 16 percent of them had received promises of marriage; and they may have been poor Irish women of the kind who eventually walked the streets as prostitutes. In the poor neighborhoods of the East End promises of marriage before sex may simply have been irrelevant since men and women knew that it was possible to sustain a committed relationship over many years and many children without the formal bond of marriage. In that world sex and marriage had become separated from each other, and the question of entering into a union arose only after a woman became pregnant. But wherever and however this libertinism was produced by the new male heterosexuality across the variegated pattern of London's local communities, the judgment passed against sex outside of marriage by the traditional standards of family life could never be entirely avoided, as the next chapter shows. Women judged themselves harshly and could not sometimes believe or accept what had happened to them. Their parents sometimes abandoned them and, when they did not, often could do nothing to help them. Their masters and mistresses, however much they might like them, could not keep an unmarried woman and her child in their families. The woman whose illegitimate child died was in many ways the most fortunate. The men who seduced these women may have reinforced in their own minds the power and standing of their exclusive heterosexuality. But for poor women who became pregnant, there was usually no comparable standard of female behavior by which they could justify what had happened to them. And in the absence of efficient means of contraception, they were left to care for an illegitimate child without the economic means to do so. The new heterosexuality applied to men of all social classes. Romantic marriage with its new pattern of adultery and divorce was confined to the men and women of the middle and landed classes. But for poor women sexual libertinism usually came without romance and brought instead shame and the possibility of rape.

CHAPTER NINE

Shame and Rape

I t is likely (as the previous chapter has suggested) that the new male heterosexuality by the second generation of the century had begun to significantly change the sexual relationships between poor men in London and the majority of the unmarried women of their class who made their livings as servants and milliners. Poor women were to a large extent, however, the victims of this new sexual system, as this chapter undertakes to show in two ways. It considers, first, the shame and economic distress that women endured when they became pregnant and their lovers failed either to marry them or to live with them in an informal union. This is documented from the declarations made in the second half of the century by women who gave their children to the Foundling Hospital. These declarations show that after a woman had used her savings and sold her clothes, she and her child could survive only if she sought relief from the parish, went back to work, or gave her child to the hospital. Going back to work was difficult since a woman had to put her child out to nurse, and this was likely to cost as much as her year's wages. But only through work could she reenter the ordinary world from which her illegitimate pregnancy had excluded her. The injury that her reputation had suffered made her, however, unacceptable to many employers, and sometimes it led as well to rejection by her own family. The declarations show this vividly. They make clear that the lives of poor women were regulated by their relationship to the families of their masters and their parents and that neither kind of family granted them the sexual freedom that increasingly was given to adolescent males as they constructed their heterosexual identities. For poor women there was no ideology of heterosexuality to justify a child outside of marriage, nor did they have the belief in romantic love that helped gentlewomen through adultery and divorce. Instead there was the pain of their disgrace that led some women to conceal their pregnancies until the last moment. Alone and confused, they sometimes managed to kill their child during delivery, and sometimes, with greater deliberation but in perhaps even greater confusion, they killed the child after birth.

Unmarried women were also subjected to the sexual violence that men used to express desire for them whether in the courtship of women they knew or in passing encounters with strangers in the street. The rape cases show (in the last section of this chapter) that women had great difficulty in convincing others that they had not consented to any sexual act that had actually occurred since many men and women believed that it was impossible for a man to enter the body of a woman without her consent. Only the violation of a young virgin in an open field by a man she had never met or the gang rape of an elderly woman safely observed by all her neighbors from their windows were credible. The women coerced into having a drink or staying the night were never believed when they said they had not consented. Masters who raped their servants were strongly disapproved of but never found guilty of rape since some degree of consent by the young woman was always presumed. But the interplay of violence and consent is made clearest by two points. Women did not make charges of rape against the men of their own class with whom they worked, even though these were the men most likely to make sexual advances. These were the men they hoped to marry, and from them a very high level of coercion was therefore acceptable. The likelihood of this is confirmed by the practice of making offers of marriage in compensation to women raped by men who had not previously courted them. Some women strongly rejected such offers, but others accepted them because the violence of rape could be fitted into the continuum of ordinary courtship. Violence must therefore frequently have been an aspect of traditional courtship. And the new heterosexuality among poor men can only have confirmed this, since it was not leavened by the ideas of romance to which gentlemen increasingly subscribed.

Maintaining a Woman's Reputation

The aim of the Foundling Hospital was to maintain the reputation of an unmarried woman by taking her child and allowing her to return to the world of respectable work. Twenty-four bound volumes of the petitions made by mothers whose children were accepted by the hospital survive for the last third of the century (1768–99). The amount of information given varies from petitioner to petitioner, and from year to year. Totals

Table 9.1 Marital Status of Women Offering Children to the Foundling Hospital, 1768–79

	N	%
Spinsters	780	84.9
Wives	72	7.8
Widows	21	2.3
Other[a]	46	5.0
Total	919	

Source: GLRO: FH, Petitioners Admitted, vols. 1–10 (1768–79).
[a] Individuals who had become responsible for children not their own.

Table 9.2 Ages of Spinsters Offering Children to the Foundling Hospital, 1768–79

Age	Number of Women	Age	Number of Women	Age	Number of Women
15	1	22	3	29	0
16	3	23	3	30	0
17	2	24	1	31	0
18	3	25	0	32	1
19	5	26	0	33	0
20	3	27	1	34	1
21	0	28	2	Total	29

Source: GLRO: FH, Petitioners Admitted, vols. 1–10 (1768–79).
Note: The ages of 751 women offering children to the hospital are unknown.

have been made for the first ten volumes (1768–79), and the results are displayed in the tables (tables 9.1–9.6). A little over nine hundred women offered children to the hospital in these dozen years. Most of them were unmarried women (86 percent). But there were also a few married women and a few widows, as well as a scattering of individuals who had become responsible for children who were not their own (table 9.1).

Who were these unmarried women? Very few of their ages were given (a mere 29 out of 780), but it is likely that the span of the ages was representative of all such women offering children to the hospital (table 9.2). The youngest was fifteen, the age usually given for menarche in the eighteenth century, and there were six women aged fifteen to seventeen. But most of the women (17 of 29) were between eighteen and twenty-three. This was a good deal younger than the usual age of marriage, but it was exactly the age of most of the women who walked the streets as prostitutes. A third set of six women had ages that spread over the next decade from twenty-four to thirty-four. One-fifth of the unmarried women (158 out of 780) are recorded as saying that the men who had seduced them had made promises of marriage (table 9.3). Some of these women were of marriageable age, and their pregnancies may therefore have been the result of failed courtships. But some of them were too young to have been on the marriage market realistically. This does not mean that their seducers did not promise marriage as a means of gaining their sexual favors. It is also possible that the young women who presented their children to the Foundling Hospital belonged to that subset of servant girls who were seduced into prostitution. The men who seduced them came from the usual wide range of London occupations (table 9.4). Two groups were especially prominent: servants and men in the army or the navy. This makes it likely that women who were servants from West End parishes were more likely to go to the Foundling Hospital than were women from the poorer par-

Table 9.3 Spinsters Promised Marriage Who Offered Children to the Foundling Hospital, 1768–79

Total number of spinsters	780	
Number noted as promised marriage	158	(20.3%)

Source: GLRO: FH, Petitioners Accepted, vols. 1–10 (1768–79).

Table 9.4 Occupations or Whereabouts of Men Who Seduced Spinsters Offering Children to the Foundling Hospital, 1768–79

	Number		Number		Number
Servant	74[a]	Apprentice	6	Bricklayer	2
Gone abroad	55	Gentleman	6	Hairdresser	2
Gone to sea	35	Tailor	6	Ostler	2
Journeyman	30	Coachman	5	Schoolmaster	2
Gone to America	22	Shoemaker	5	Waiter	2
Impressed	17	Lodger	4	Waterman	2
Soldier	15	Gardener	3	Weaver	2
Carpenter	13	Barber	2	Other[b]	29
Married man	8	Blacksmith	2	Total	351
				Not given	429

Source: GLRO: FH, Petitioners Admitted, vols. 1–10 (1768–79).
[a] Fifty-three servants lived in the same house as the woman seduced; 21 lived elsewhere.
[b] One each boarding-school student, boatman, boxmaker, brickmaker, butcher, cabinetmaker, callico printer, carter, carver/gilder, coal porter, customhouse officer, floating mills, haberdasher, hatter, horsedealer, laborer, lamplighter, linen draper, merchant's clerk, pastry cook, pawnbroker, plaisterer, rigger, sadler, silversmith, stationer, wagoner's servant, wharfinger, workman.

ishes. A woman's fellow servants were usually the greatest danger to her chastity, and almost three-fourths of these male servants were employed in the same household. The number of soldiers and sailors was swelled at the end of the decade by the American war. Of the men who were described as having been impressed into military service, there was only one from 1771, while all the others turn up between 1777 and 1779. It may be that if these men had been in England, they would have married the women they had made pregnant. But it seems more likely that these sexual encounters were not a part of real courtships but were the result of the excitement in a town filled with men who were about to go away to war. Certainly the men who seduced their fellow servants did not marry them once they became pregnant. It is likely that most of these seducers would have been actually free to marry these young women, since only eight of them were listed as married. Many of these pregnancies were therefore probably not the result of failed courtships. They were instead the result of the aggressive passion of young unmarried men and the incautious yielding of young women who had taken their first step on the way to the prostitute's life.

These women may have been sexually incautious, but they certainly cared for their babies and tried to keep them as long as they could. This can be seen from the ages of the children when they were surrendered, which was noted in 30 percent of the cases (table 9.5). A few women (7 percent) gave up their child within two weeks of the child's birth— two of them within three days, but most at the end of the first two weeks. But the majority of women (60 percent) kept their children from three to eight weeks, with about the same number of women applying in each successive week of this six-week period. This means that two-thirds of

Table 9.5 Age and Gender of Children Offered by Spinsters to the Foundling Hospital, 1768–79

Age	Number	% of Ages	Known Gender	Number	% of Known Genders
3–8 days	17	7.1	Boys	163	57.2
3–8 weeks	145	60.2	Girls	122	42.8
9 weeks–6 months	75	31.1	Total	285	100.0
7–18 months	4	1.7	Not given	495	
Total	241	100.0			
Not given	539				

Source: GLRO: FH, Petitioners Admitted, vols. 1–10 (1768–79).

Table 9.6 Spinsters and Their Circumstances When Offering a Child to the Foundling Hospital, 1768–79 ($N = 780$)

	Number	Percentage[a]
Clothes and other possessions sold or pawned; savings from years of service as servant used up	129	22.9
Master or mistress had supported them in their crisis, or was prepared to rehire them or give them a good character as a servant	271	48.2
Help from families or friends	34	6.0
Families too poor to help	49	8.7
Families have rejected them	29	5.2
No friends	128	22.8
Charity from a person who was not a relation, friend, or employer	27	4.8
Shamed by their condition or determined to keep their situation unknown to the world	48	8.5
No information available allowing placement in preceding categories	218	

Source: GLRO: FH, Petitioners Admitted, vols. 1–10 (1768–79).

[a] Percentage of total number of women (562) whose circumstances are known to fall in one of the categories included in the table. Percentages total more than 100.0 because individuals may be included in more than one category.

all women found that they could not afford to keep their child longer than the first two months after the child's birth. The remaining one-third were able to hang on for up to four months more. But by the sixth month most women had depleted their resources: only four children were surrendered later than this. How did these unmarried servants manage to support themselves and a child for two to six months during which most of them did not work? Some indication was given in 70 percent of all cases (table 9.6). Almost half the women said that a master or mistress had either supported them in their crisis, or was prepared to rehire them or to give them a good character as a servant so that they could find work in another household, provided the hospital took the child. This must mean, however, that the majority of women had lost their jobs once their child was born. About a quarter of the women said that they had lived by selling or pawning their clothes or other possessions, or by using the savings they had accumulated in service, presumably with a view to marriage. A handful of women (6 percent) were helped by their families but twice as many women (14 percent) said that their families had either rejected them when they became pregnant or were too poor to help them. But nearly one-quarter of the women specifically said that they had no friends to turn to, which must mean that they were orphans or had come to London from the countryside. Most women, therefore, depended either on themselves or their recent employers to get through the two to six months that they survived on their own with a child. A few (4.8 percent) were helped by strangers, but nearly twice as many (8.5 percent) said that they were so ashamed to have borne a child outside of marriage that they wished to keep their situation from anyone they might know.

The stories that women told in their declarations sometimes began with the promises of marriage that men made to get a woman's consent to sex. Some of these promises were made as part of a public, open courtship. Martha Freeman's master testified that he had allowed a journeyman weaver to visit and court her for marriage but that the man ran away once Martha became pregnant. Ann Stafford's suitor also came courting in marriage with the consent of her master and mistress but then ran away to sea when she became pregnant. This was the most traditional pattern, in which sexual relations began well into the courtship and shortly before marriage. But sometimes the sex began at once. In such a situation women were aware that they ran the risk of becoming pregnant. Their lovers were therefore likely to promise to marry them if pregnancy occurred. But this was not quite the same thing as a courtship in which sexual relations began as a prelude to marriage. Mary Jewitt explained that James Frederick Smith had "most solemnly declared that if she proved with child he would marry her." Adrian Wilson has argued that in London this second pattern of sexual relations replaced the first by midcentury. But it is apparent that they coexisted in the 1770s. Some men were clearly willing to say anything to get their way with a servant girl. As nursery maid, Elizabeth Hall was sent with her master's child every day to the garden in Gray's Inn, where men often picked up women. There she met Mr. Featherstone, a young lawyer in Gray's, who told her that he would marry her, so that she would consent to having sex. But it is most unlikely that Featherstone was serious in his promise. In any event, by the time Elizabeth's child was born, Featherstone was dead. Persistent promises of marriage by a man who lived in the same house must have been confusing, especially to someone like Mary Teat, who had only recently come to London to look for a place as a servant. After she found work as a common servant with a family in Wood Street, a man who lodged in the same house pretended he wanted to marry her, and "after long solicitation at length obtained his wicked purpose."[1]

Because of the danger that sex posed for her, a woman could even read a promise into a man's silence, as Sarah Duke did. She admitted that while John Smith had kept her company, he had made no proposals of marriage. But she had "understood it to be a kind of negative promise." A woman could confess that she had been a fool. Marry Mose, "seduced by a stratagem," gave in "to the too great credulity of her own heart." Isabel Anderson's "greatest agony of mind" came from "her own credulity" in trusting a man she had "kept a correspondence with . . . for several years," but who deserted her the moment he found that she was pregnant. Elizabeth Jennings had the misfortune to listen to a man who "the moment after I had given up my honor, informed me he was married."[2]

Some women, however, admitted that they had been swept away by passion and that there had been no promises—only "one unguarded moment," as Ann James put it, when "she was ruined" by a gentleman's servant who lived in the same household. Mary Moorson had "been overpowered by the impulse of nature . . . through the artifice of a wicked designing man." Winnifred Richard, who worked with her needle and lived in Lamb's Conduit Passage with her mother, did not even know the name of her child's father because she had met him in the streets and he had taken her to a house in Holborn. She did remember that it had rained hard that night.[3]

A few women who brought a child to the hospital had been raped. Sarah Harbour was caught on July 29, 1768 by two sailors as she went from Chelsea to her master's house in Pickering's Court, St. James's. They dragged her into some new buildings in the Five Fields and tied her handkerchief over her mouth while one of them held her down and the other raped her. They then stole her handkerchief and four or five shillings she had in her pocket. Ten months later she gave the hospital the child she had borne as a result. Women who were raped elsewhere in England came to London to have their child, like Elizabeth Jardine Reynolds, who was raped by a soldier at Plymouth. Mary Whitcomb was raped by a man in Norwich who seized her in a narrow street at night as she went to get her mistress's medicine. He threw her down and stuffed a handkerchief in her mouth. Mary said she was so frightened that she did not realize what had happened to her until she found that she was pregnant. Some women were raped by men who knew and courted them. Ann Fleming said (and Jonas Hanway testified to the truth of her story) that the father of her child "gave her an intoxicating draught by which means he obtained his ends, and she thinks him a villain and therefore will not marry him." Ann Tuckey's friend, a man named Jackson, first courted her and then raped her in the fields near Islington, after which he disappeared.[4]

Single women with a child to support had few resources. If they did not seek public relief from their parishes, there were only three other possibilities. They could become prostitutes, or sell their clothes, or use up their savings. But some women who used the hospital were reluctant to ask the parish authorities to provide for their children. Their reputations were likely to be permanently damaged once they applied to the parish, making it difficult for them to find a job. Maria Hershaw of St. Savior, Southwark, said that "applying to her parish would disclose the affair, which would inevitably be her ruin" and that she had "undergone many hardships to prevent her character from being exposed to her friends and the world as her future support depends upon it." Elizabeth Hall did not wish to "expose herself to the parish as that would hinder her from going to service and getting her bread." Elizabeth Baxter worried about her family and said she was unwilling to disgrace them by swearing the child; they knew nothing about her situation. Another woman, F[rances] Story, said that although neither she nor her lover could support their child, they were reluctant to send the child to the parish workhouse because that "would make her unhappy conduct public, ruin her reputation, and deprive her of the means of getting an honest" living. She and her friend were in love; they hoped to marry as soon as they could afford to, and then they intended to reclaim their child from the hospital.[5]

A woman's desire to avoid dependence on the parish and to support herself could be quite strong. Two weeks after her child's birth, Sarah Salt explained that the wife of Mr. Buckle in Dragon Court, Snow Hill, St. Sepulchre's, "out of Christian charity," had taken her into her house, delivered her, and cared for her and her child to that point. But Sarah wished to go back to work so that she could "take care of herself again without being chargeable to her parish which is St. Paul's, Covent Garden, where she lived three years." Some of the reluctance of going to the parish arose from the necessity of swearing who the father of the child was, as Susannah Samworth's mistress discovered when she tried to get her to swear the child to her fellow servant. Sarah Picke's lover very cleverly made different excuses to stop her from swearing her child to him until he had a chance to escape abroad. The parish could make demands that were unacceptable. Elizabeth Eaton's parish told her that they would not take her child into the workhouse unless she entered herself. A woman with a settlement outside of London was especially afraid to go to the parish for help because, like Ann Barnes, she might find that the alderman would only offer to send her to her parish of settlement in Gloucestershire. Ann therefore asked the hospital to take her child since she preferred to remain in London with her mother in Maidenhead Court in Little Moorfields.[6]

Women in these difficulties sometimes thought of prostitution. Mary Abbotts, who had been seduced by her master's journeyman, asked the hospital to take her child so that she could "get my living in an honest manner and I should not be laid under the temptation of ruin and inevitable destruction." Catherine Jones actually became a prostitute. Once she was venereally infected, she entered the Lock Hospital. As a result of the religious instruction she received during her cure, she changed her disposition and was chosen for the Lock Asylum, which prepared women to reenter the world of legitimate work. Catherine, however, was also pregnant. Afraid that this would keep her out of the asylum, she concealed her condition until a few hours before her delivery. The Foundling Hospital accepted her child. When they did not take Ann Robinson's child, the Reverend John Prince, the chaplain at the Magdalen Hospital, took her under his wing. Her former mistress, Mrs. Tullock, said that Ann was honest and sober but that she "suspected her to be very gay." (This is an early use of what became a common nineteenth-century term describing a prostitute.) Mrs. Tullock also suspected Ann's sister, who was also pregnant. Mr. Prince, however, was satisfied that Ann was truthful and arranged for her to have five shillings a week so "that she may have no temptation to do ill from want."[7]

A woman's clothes were one of her principal resources, and repeatedly the declarations say that the clothes had been sold or pawned before or after the child's birth. Mary West who had "no friend that I can go to," had been "obliged before I lay in . . . to part with the best part of my clothes." But she at least had some clothes left. Leticia Smith, after being deserted by a young man who had promised to marry her, had used up all "her clothes except what is on her back." Jane Slater pledged her clothes and got charity from strangers after a man who had promised marriage denied that he had. Women were likely to use any savings they had first to pay for their lying-in. When these were gone, they began to sell their clothes to pay for their lodgings, which is what Mary Hewitt did. Even a lady's maid like Hannah Frankling who had lodged at the court end of town could become hard pressed. Her landlady, Mrs. Thomas, said that she paid her bills but had pawned most of her clothes. But it was unwise to sell everything since that left a woman without anything to wear when she was hired again as a servant, as Mary Taylor discovered when she went back to work after her child was born. She had sold so much that her new master found her "so bare of clothes that he advanced her a guinea to buy some."[8]

Servants were supposed to save their wages so that they could eventually leave service and marry. But these small nest eggs were quickly eaten up by the expense of having a child and taking lodgings when they could no longer live in a master's house. Mary Griffis of St. Ann, Soho, "exhausted the little she has saved in service" to pay for her lying-in. Mary Smith took lodgings to conceal her child's birth. She had been a servant in a gentleman's family, where she was seduced by a fellow servant who left her. Mary was careful to leave her place before anyone in the family knew what had happened to her. She dreaded the shame that would come once the existence of her child was revealed. Like Mary, Elizabeth Hill expended her savings to take lodgings in Hollis Street, Clare Market, so that she could "conceal her misfortune from her friends."[9] Women feared that bearing a child out of marriage would make it difficult for them to find work as a servant. Christian Bear, who had "nothing to depend on but servitude," said that she was deprived of this line of work "by this unhappy blot on her character." But Elizabeth Lumley had "so managed as to maintain her character" and told the hospital that if they took her child, she could get a place as a servant at five pounds a year.[10]

Most of these women worked as servants. This made them members of the families of their masters and mistresses. But a pregnant servant, or an unmarried woman with a child, raised serious moral problems for the head of any household. Masters might not care what a male servant did on his own time provided that he did not seduce a woman in their own house. But such a standard did not apply to female servants. When trust, however, had been established between a woman and her master and her mistress, they were less likely to abandon her once her pregnancy was known. Phoebe Gibbes of Goldsmith Street, Gough Square, who employed Sarah Aviary for a year and a half, was willing to take her back after her child's birth. Sarah had worked up to the day she was delivered without her employers suspecting "her condition, so well satisfied were they with her honesty towards them." They were also impressed by the preparations she had made to care for her child by providing baby clothes and finding a lodging for herself. Sarah, in other words, had shown no signs of intending to murder her child. Ann Carter at first discharged Susannah Scofield, no doubt because she thought it was the respectable thing to do, but it made her conscience uneasy, and in the end she took her back. She wrote that "when I discharged her, she said she had a countrywoman in town and she would go to her, so I have heard nothing of her since till now, and have been very uneasy upon the action for fraid [sic] she had laid some violent hands of herself, knowing she has nothing to support her and her little one for any time . . . and I will take her under my care till she can get her a place, and I dare be bound for her not to do the like again as I believe her disposition is not so inclined." But there were limits to trust, and even though Jane Whitaker's mistress allowed her to deliver her child in her house in Queen Ann Street, Marylebone, she was never able to make Jane confess the name of her child's father. Some employers, however, would not continue their support forever. Ann Stephens worked until the moment she was in labor. Her master and mistress maintained her for a fortnight during her lying-in, but they "afterwards told me I must do the best I could for myself, as they had acted a Christian part." Ann then managed to support herself and the child for three and a half more months with her savings. It sounds as though her employers had been torn between Christian compassion for her need and Christian disapproval of her behavior.[11]

Employers were likely to take a woman back into service when they were convinced that she was morally worthwhile. Mary Brown's former mistress from Philip Lane, Aldermanbury, explained that although Mary loved her child, both her lover and her Mary's father were too poor to support the child. She wrote that "we have, at her earnest request, agreed to take her again into our service, and that request is a testimony of her principles being good, and we sincerely believe her seduction was more her misfortune than her fault, and that she heartily repents it. If you should choose to enquire further about her, we should be glad to have it done privately, lest she may be exposed." The master and mistress whom Ann Brown served for two years said they intended to take her again if the hospital would care for her child. The expenses of Ann's lying-in and living for two months without a place had used up all that she had saved during several years of service.[12]

But a mistress could be concerned for the reputation of her household if she took back a girl who had fallen. Frances Moore's former mistress was willing to employ her again (if the child went to the hospital) but only because the whole affair had been kept a profound secret in her family. But while Mrs. Richard Crawley admitted that Mary McGowen was the best servant she had ever had, she would not employ her again because Mary's situation had become known in her household. Instead she offered to give her a recommendation that would ensure that she would find another job. Miss Mitford, for whom Kitty Plume served as a lady's maid, discharged her immediately after she discovered that she was pregnant. Miss Mitford said that she would have hired Kitty again "but for the bad example it would have set in her house." Mrs. Routledge's fear was even greater. Hannah Millington had been seduced by one of the Scotsmen who boarded in the lodging house she kept. Mrs. Routledge was concerned that the same thing might happen again and damage the reputation of her business. She said that as she had "a number of young men lodgers . . . it would be very improper" to have Hannah again. She was willing, however, to recommend her to another mistress.[13]

A servant who had borne a child could not expect to bring the child into her master's house and was forced to board it. This was very expensive. Mary Jewitt explained that she made six pounds a year as a servant but that boarding her child at four shillings a week would come to £10.8.0 for the year, or almost twice her wages. Thomasine Whely made the same point. She had grown up as a child in the Foundling Hospital and married a soldier, or so she claimed. (In one entry he is her husband, in another, simply a man.) When her child's father went abroad, Thomasine worked as a servant. But her wages were only seven pounds a year, and she paid £6.10 a year to have her child nursed. This left ten shillings for herself, on which she could not manage unless her mistress was very kind to her. After Mary Harpur became pregnant by a fellow servant, they both quit their places without saying why. Once she was delivered they put the child to nurse and got other jobs. She paid threepence a week for the nurse and had to sell her clothes to make a deposit of 10s 6d. Her lover, a butcher, had promised to pay three shillings a week but disappeared and paid nothing. If a woman had to nurse her child herself, she was prevented from going to work, as Elizabeth Hunt knew. A tailor in her neighborhood in Westminster had made her pregnant while courting her in marriage. She swore the child to the parish, but since it was not her own parish of settlement, the parish sent the child to her to nurse, making it impossible for her to go "to service to get her bread."[14]

A woman who had recently borne a child did have one new resource. She could sell her milk—but only if she put her own child out to nurse. After Mary Hendrie was made pregnant by a lodger in the house in Edinburgh where she was a servant, she came to London. For four months she supported herself and her child by selling her clothes. Then she was recommended to Robert Miller as a wet nurse and lived in his house for six months. But when Miller's child was weaned, Mary was obliged to take charge again of her own child. Amy Girling also served as a wet nurse for Mr. and Mrs. Henry Witham in Great Queen Street for twenty guineas a year. But when the child she was nursing was about to be weaned, she applied to the hospital to take her own boy. Her lover, a married man, had promised to maintain their child, but he had only once given her five shillings. It is curious that more women did not serve as wet nurses. But perhaps the mother of an illegitimate child was thought morally unfit, and many women would have been compromised by so public an acknowledgment that they had borne a child.[15]

Working women belonged, however, not only to the families in which they served. They had parents and siblings and aunts and uncles and cousins, with all of whom they had to deal. The women expected rejection for their fault, and sometimes an entire family did "turn their backs" on a woman. But even when they did not, a servant's family was usually very poor and able to help her for only a short time if at all. Women sometimes did not ask for help from their families because they did not want them to know what had happened whether their families were far or near at hand. After Mary Edwards sold her clothes, she was ashamed to ask for help from her family who lived at some distance from London because it would break "my poor mother's heart if she knew of my unhappy situation." Mary Taylor tried to give her six-day-old daughter to the hospital because her family in Southwark would be very distressed if they learned of her situation.

These stories come from the first twelve years of these records, between 1768 and 1779. In the last decade of the century, there was no change in the sentiments. Women either feared rejection by their families or were filled with shame at the thought of facing them. Women from respectable families in the countryside who had come to London to work dreaded to go home again. Frances Layton, Ann Pedder, Elizabeth Pernick all said the same thing. Elizabeth Morris was certain her family would abandon her if they knew. Catherine Pearce lived and worked with her sister in London, probably as a milliner. She concealed her situation and managed to go away for a few weeks while her child was born. But she was certain that her family would reject her once they found out.[16]

Some poor families did help their daughters and sisters as much as they could. But their resources were so limited that they could not do very much for very long. This is apparent whether one looks at the 1770s or the 1790s. In the 1770s it was usually a woman's mother, sister, or brother who came to her aid. Sarah Page had a sixty-year-old mother who could barely manage to support herself by her own hard labor. Sarah therefore had to sell all her household goods to pay for her lying-in. Elizabeth Williamson's mother had to apply to the hospital on her daughter's behalf because Elizabeth was "with great grief and sorrow brought to insanity" over the birth of her child, and a month after her delivery showed no signs of recovery. Help most often came from a woman's sister. Grace Scott's sister helped through her lying-in, but she was a married woman with responsibilities of her own and could do no more. Sarah Brown's sister, Mrs. Nelson, took her and the child into her lodgings even though she had children of her own and a husband who grumbled about it. But Mrs. Nelson was very poor and made her living charring and "getting a little broken victuals at gentlemen's houses." Sarah Williams went to her sister's lodgings when she came to London looking for the gentleman's servant who had seduced her in the countryside. "Please God," she said, "I was taken in travail at my sister's house who is but a lodger and her husband is in the Second Troop of Horse Grenadier Guards." She claimed that her sister and her husband had helped her all they could, but the landlady said that the couple had pressured Sarah to offer her child to the hospital.[17]

Brothers also helped their sisters, but less often, as did Elizabeth Owen's, who was a journeyman shoemaker. Nineteen-year-old Mary Smith said that her brother had helped her but only with great difficulty and that she had applied to no one else for relief "choosing to suffer rather than be exposed." A more distant relative could be of assistance when all the others deserted. All of Elizabeth Beety's family turned against her except for her cousin Alex Mills and his wife. But they had eight children of their own, a ninth was on its way, and Mills was only a journeyman dyer. Elizabeth bitterly complained that her young man had enticed her to London and vowed to remarry her but instead had forsaken her. Sometimes all of a woman's family were servants like herself and were able therefore to help her only for a short time. This was the case with Elizabeth Jones, who had had the misfortune to become quite ill during her lying-in.[18]

The information on a woman's family from the 1790s seems more detailed, probably because the interviewer was more probing. One thing becomes clearer. In most cases (sixty-three) a woman turned to her parents for help, together if they were both alive, or to the one who had survived. After her parents, it was her sister who was mostly likely to help. Brothers were called on much less frequently, and the more distant relatives made an occasional appearance. But all these women's relatives were poor and were unable to help very much or for very long. Elizabeth Barrow's parents were old and accepted charity themselves. A woman's parents were sometimes not only poor but also a hundred miles or more from London—as Mary Livesy and Elizabeth Barrett explained. Those who lived in London might be a family of servants like Charlotte Sophia Roberts's, all of whom worked for the Hon. Caroline Howe, her father as the butler, her mother as the cook, and her brother as the footman. Or like Ann Peter's parents, whose father was a poor blacksmith in Spitalfields, they might already have a large family to support, as did Rebecca Lambert's father who was a sixty-year-old waterman at Woolwich with a wife and two other daughters to support.[19]

Poor widows usually had occupations that left them unable to help their pregnant daughters. Sarah Guerry's mother wound silk for a Spitalfields weaver. Sarah's lover left her when she told him she was pregnant. He said "he was inclined to serve is [sic] king and country." Susan Smith's mother was a washerwoman, Ann Hayward's mother a servant. Mary Allen's mother kept a green-stall opposite the pump in Bloomsbury Market, but she at least was able to allow her daughter to be delivered in the stall. Other mothers could offer a place to stay, as did Elizabeth White's and Sarah Mason's. Some widows had other children to support, like Ann Macarty's mother. Some mothers though they helped could not avoid showing their distress. Sophia Wilson's mother was an aged widow who by her own labor for twenty years had brought up two girls with decency. She was crushed by her eldest daughter's imprudence. Sophia had not worked for five months when she applied to the hospital. She usually made seven or eight guineas a year as a common servant, but it cost a guinea a month to put her child out to nurse. The poor women of a family could club together over the generations to care for a daughter's child, as Elizabeth Finck's mother and grandmother did when they decided not to give her child to the hospital because they would not be able to visit whenever they wished. They were poor women who made their living as chars in gentlemen's houses or as nurses, depending on what they could find. The child lived with Elizabeth's mother.[20]

The widowed fathers of these women often had jobs that paid as little as a widow's. The fathers of Sarah Moore and Elizabeth Vinall were both agricultural laborers far away from London. Hester Broad's father was closer, but he was an old gardener at Tooting whose earnings were very small. A man who lived in London could be a servant like Charlotte Williams's father, who worked in Chelsea, or a laborer in the East India House like Sarah Clark's. Sometimes a man had failed in business. Jan Totty's father was an old carpenter who had suffered losses and misfortunes. Ann Sugg's father was a stay maker who had just gotten out of Fleet Prison after a long confinement for debt, as a result of the last Insolvent Act. He could hardly support himself.[21]

The stories become really harsh when a woman's father had died and her mother had remarried. Stepfathers could be odious. Mary McGovern said that hers was neither willing nor able to give any support. Because of her stepfather Sarah Benton ran away and left her child with her mother. When Sarah became pregnant, her mother had hidden her in the basement of the chandler's shop where they lived because she was afraid that her husband, a journeyman carpenter, if he discovered the child, would run away himself and leave them both. Elizabeth Gibson's stepfather seduced her. He threatened to leave his wife and small children if Elizabeth went to the parish for relief. Elizabeth had worked at a papermill since she had been a child. She was her mother's greatest comfort because of her "affectionate attention." The hospital took her child.[22]

The occasional seducing father appears in other sources. Jane Brabham in 1719 was pregnant by her father, with whom she had sex twice. On the first occasion he used his lodging in Mr. Roswell's house in Spur Alley in St. Martin's in the Fields, but then he took lodgings for her in another house, where he had sexual relations with her a second time. In Mary Doe's case, her father was a carpenter and her mother went out washing. When she was sixteen, her father made her pregnant. He delivered the child himself, wrapped it in a curtain, and left it in the horse manure at Tom-Turd's-Hole, where the "nightmen" took their refuse. A midwife who was called in to look at the girl (probably by her mother) concluded from the man's behavior to his daughter that he "was father to the child, as well as grandfather" and told him so. The girl confessed that this was true, and her mother gave the midwife a note that revealed the location of the child's body. It looks as though the mother disapproved but was unable to stop the relationship. Adam White was prosecuted for coming home at two or three in the morning and raping his eleven-year-old daughter. He probably venereally infected her as well, but since neither the surgeon nor the nurse who examined her came to court, the case was dismissed. But a shoemaker named Paterson did not escape so easily after he raped his nine-year-old daughter. He was sentenced to a year in jail and made to stand twice in the pillory, where the crowd pelted him. Men who went after prepubescent girls were therefore probably treated with greater hostility than those who made their daughters pregnant.[23]

It was usually to a married sister that a woman went for help in the 1790s. But they had families of their own and could not do much. Ann Windell's sister, who was married to a laborer in a manufactory, let her live with her until the landlord would no longer allow it. Sarah Hamerton was taken in by her sister, who made waistcoats, and helped with the work. But her sister was married to a mustard maker in Southwark and had three children. She was not able to help Sarah for very long and advised her to apply to the hospital. Mary Harpur's sister was married to a poor shoemaker in Somers Town and could not help at all, and the rest of their family were two hundred miles away. With an unmarried sister there could be a special bond. Amelia Friend was nineteen. She and her sister were orphans who had been brought up in St. James's parish school of industry and then apprenticed. They lived together at a washerwoman's. Amelia did needlework and had been helped by a collection taken up by their neighbors.[24]

A woman's other relatives—her brother, an aunt or an uncle, a cousin— made an occasional appearance. Ann Mockett's brother was the superintendent of the Southwark Penny Post Office. He had searched for her child's father while he and his wife supported her in their house. Ann Grainger's brother kept a shop in Fleet Market, but he was just starting out in his trade and could not help her much, and all her other relatives were servants. Elizabeth Powell lived with her aunt, whose husband was the servant of the Reverend Mr. Pennick of the British Museum, but they could not afford to maintain Elizabeth and her child. Elizabeth Pearson gave birth to her child in her uncle's house. He was a shoemaker in Charles Court, the Strand, where she continued to live with him. Mary Barrett had come to London from the countryside to be a servant eighteen months before she became pregnant. Her young cousin and his wife, who had just started their business, helped her so that she could save her reputation. Amy Webb after her delivery stayed with her cousin in her lodgings. Her mistress of eight months had liked her except for her very saucy answers, including the lie that she was a married woman who had had two children.[25]

Families in London sometimes rejected their pregnant daughters. Mary Browne said simply that her family would give her no countenance. Girls higher in status than servants and who made their livings by needlework may have been especially fearful of their families' disapproval. Jonas Hanway vouched for the truth of Mary Smith's long story. She had been in business for her herself as a milliner. But she had had to give it up when she was left with a child by the man who had promised to marry her. Her family was described as being "people of credit and character," and she was convinced that if they knew her situation, they "would forever desert her to infamy and ruin." She asked the hospital to take her child to preserve her parents' peace of mind and to protect them from shame. Another milliner, Eleanor Richardson, said that her friends had "turned their backs on her and her infant," whom she could not nurse because of her poor health. The woman who had employed her for four years agreed that all this was true. But even very poor families could feel a daughter's disgrace. A woman who used only the initials A.B. said "that her parents were very poor but very reputable people, and their sensibility of her disgrace plunges them into so much distress." All of Elizabeth Atwood's relations and friends turned their backs on her except for one who helped to get her into the Lying-in Hospital. Elizabeth Archer used the same phrase—"all my friends as [sic] turned their backs on me and will not see me."[26]

Pregnant girls from elsewhere in England fled to the anonymity of London once they were rejected by their families. Norman Herbert, a farmer at Barking, turned his daughter Susannah out of his house after she was seduced by one of his servants. The man absconded and Susannah went to London where she bore her child. Her father said he was prepared to take her home and forgive her fault "as far as in my power," but he was concerned that she should return without the child, so that the neighbors would not know—"to keep her disgrace clear of the world." When Elizabeth Bloxam was turned out by her indigent parents in Banbury, she went to London to look for her lover, who had run away the moment he heard that she was pregnant. She did not find him. Instead she had her son in Marylebone and lived on the charity of the people in the neighborhood. Mary Nelson's mother was more compassionate. When her daughter became pregnant by a man who had promised to marry her but married someone else, she sent the girl to London to have her child without telling her husband. Mary then returned home without her father's knowing anything about it. He was a poor country clergyman with an income of seventy pounds and five children to support who could not take responsibility for his daughter's child as well. But it is unclear where Mary and her mother had hidden the child (who was older than usual—eighteen months) when they applied to the hospital.[27]

The entire experience of bearing a bastards put an enormous strain on a woman, her family, and her employers. Some women became so profoundly depressed that they were tempted to kill their child or themselves. Ann Bartleet's mistress became suspicious when she began to complain of pains in her bowels three months after she was hired as a nursery maid. She ordered another servant to sleep with Ann and to keep the door locked so that she could not go downstairs alone and use the privy where she could deliver the child and kill it. Once the child was born, her master and mistress brought it to the hospital. Other women turned against themselves their desire to escape. Mary Pamplin's parents were gardeners who lived at Latham in Middlesex. After her delivery she left her child with her mother and took in washing to make a living. But this was a great decline in her fortunes, for Mary had first been apprenticed to a mantua maker, and then worked for herself, and later become an upper servant. A young lawyer from Ireland who lodged in the house where she worked debauched her, gave her five pounds, and left. When she was in the hospital to be delivered, "she suffered a mental derangement for some time" which was brought on, the matron thought, by her misfortune. But Mary Pamplins at least had not been rejected by her parents as Mary Partridge had, who came to London after she became pregnant and her parents had "discarded her . . . forever." A friend of her father's in London took her in without telling him. He said that Mary had to be carefully watched: he was afraid that she would try to take her life.[28]

INFANTICIDE: DELAY AND DENIAL

The shame and denial experienced by unmarried women who became pregnant is best seen in the strategy of those who continued to work and tried to hide their pregnancy (often successfully) from everyone else. This usually meant that when labor came on, a woman had to deliver herself. In the process the child often died. But sometimes when the child lived, the distraught woman flung it out the window, or smothered the child and hid it in the box where she kept her things, or pushed it down the vault or public toilet. When the child's body was discovered, the woman was tried for infanticide. In the first half of the century, she was likely to be found guilty, and the court usually tried to discover who had made her pregnant. But after 1750, she was likely to be acquitted, and the prosecutor and the judge were likely to be sympathetic. In 1784 the prosecutor actually began his case against Elizabeth Curtis by saying to the jury that he was sure that it was neither his wish nor theirs "to strain the law against this young woman."[29] In the cases after 1750 there was often no evidence given about the sexual relationship that led to the pregnancy. Instead the court heard of a woman's fondness for children, and the medical experts either stressed the ambiguity or uselessness of the test that supposedly determined whether a child had been born alive (did its lungs float in water), or they explained that a child was very likely to die when a woman delivered herself. The changing nature of the evidence after 1750 and the legal system's growing tendency not to convict in cases of infanticide are accounted for by two things. Changing ideals about family life among the middle and landed classes now insisted on the natural maternal feelings of all women and disregarded the traditional suspicion of women's sexual

depravity. And medical men were likely to assert their scientific authority
over all aspects of childbearing and to have that authority accepted. But
there is no real evidence that poor women or men were affected by these
new ideals. It is likely, therefore, that over the course of the century, the
behavior of those poor women who tried to conceal their pregnancies from
others, and in some cases from themselves, did not actually change. They
may have become pregnant as a result of the libertinism of poor men who
were driven to seduce them by the force of the new male heterosexuality.
But when they were left on their own to cope with the result of this libertinism, they were constrained by the standards of traditional female
honor.[30]

Three-fourths of the women accused of infanticide worked as servants
in a household. The rest were married, or lived with their parents, or
lodged on their own. Those who were servants knew that it was very likely
that they would lose their places once it became apparent that they were
pregnant. Frances Polsen explained that she would have been turned away
and lost a quarter's wages if she had said anything before her child slipped
from her as she sat at stool in the necessary house.[31] But most women in
her situation did not manage to conceal their pregnancies until the last
moment. They either went to the parish for support once their pregnancies
became known, or they quietly gave notice and went into lodgings to have
their child.

A few of the women accused of infanticide had followed the second of
these two paths. Mary Lewis, who was accused of strangling her son with
a ribbon, was lodging with Mary Williams in New Court, Little Chapel
Street, in Westminster. She had stayed there a number of times before
when she was between jobs as a servant. Three months before the child's
birth she had come again, explained that she was married and pregnant,
and asked the landlady to nurse her during her delivery. The landlady—
who said she could not have had a higher opinion of her if she had been
her own sister—agreed. But on the day of the child's birth, Lewis locked
her landlady out of her room. When the landlady eventually got in, she
found the room bloody and a dead child in the closet. Lewis claimed she
had miscarried, but her landlady did not believe her and would not allow
her to bury the child quietly. Lewis later told a surgeon who testified for
her that she had tied a ribbon around the child's neck so that she could
draw the child out. But the child was very large and had stuck at his
shoulders. The pain had been excruciating, and Lewis had had to pull at
the child for ten minutes. A second expert witness—a man-midwife—
agreed that ninety-nine out of a hundred children who stuck in this way

died. Lewis was acquitted. It is unlikely that she had planned to kill the child—she had made clothes for the child. But it was never explained why she did not ask her landlady to help her as they had agreed. Perhaps at the last moment her shame at her pregnancy made the delivery something she had to do alone.[32]

For most of these servants this was a first pregnancy. But Ann Taylor had had a previous child and knew the difficulty a servant had in providing for one. Sarah Mills said that Ann had been a "very tender mother" to her first child but that the child had died at eight or nine months. Her master at that time testified that she had been obliged to put her child out to nurse while she continued to live with him as his servant. The man who had made her pregnant that first time "had been very vile and wicked to her" and presumably had abandoned her. But Ann, he said, had loved her child and indeed had always been "very fond of children, she was ready to eat them up." Ann became pregnant a second time just as she started to work for Captain Crockat. After she was there for three months, she was challenged by Christian Osborn, the nurse in charge of their mistress, who had just had a child. To this experienced accoucheur's eye Ann seemed to be three or four months pregnant, but she denied it. This occurred on a Wednesday. On the following Saturday, Osborn came into the kitchen and found Ann standing by the dresser with blood over her. The girl said "something had come from her." A trail of blood led to the necessary house, from which a child was fished up with its head nearly cut off. Ann insisted that she had fallen down the stairs a few days before and had felt "a bearing down" but had not realized that she was going into labor by the kitchen fireside. She had called out for help, but when no one came, she had had to pull the child out on her own. She thought that in this way she had probably severed the child's head, and a surgeon agreed that this was possible. She had, however, first told the surgeon that the child had come from her when she was suffering from diarrhea and using the necessary house. This must have seemed less incriminating than admitting to him as she did a day or two later that she had delivered the child in the kitchen and then taken it and thrown it into the vault. The experience had clearly left her stunned. What is not apparent is how far her pregnancy had gone and what plans she had made to deal with it. The court in any case acquitted her.[33]

Similarities with Ann Taylor's situation turn up in other women's stories. Sarah Church like Taylor had gone to work for a new mistress in Chelsea at a time when she must have known that she was well advanced in her pregnancy, since her child was born three months later. Sarah, however, struck her mistress at first as very respectable: "I did not believe she was with child," she said, "I had too good an opinion of her." But something must have made her change her mind, and she told Sarah that if she were brought to bed in her house, she would throw her and the child into the street. Sarah therefore decided to go to her aunt's to lie in, but the child was born the day before she intended to leave. Locked in her room by her mistress, she delivered on her own. When she "came to myself," she found that the child was dead. She called out for help at first and then gave up because she was so "spent." But she had the presence of mind to hide the child in her trunk. When her mistress entered the room and saw the blood, she remarked that she was afraid there was "something in the trunk that should not be." She called the constable. The trunk was opened and the child found. A surgeon took out its lungs, inflated them, and floated them in water, supposed evidence that the child had been born alive. But the jury did not believe that Sarah had killed her child and acquitted her. Still it is not clear that Sarah had thought through an adequate plan to deal with her pregnancy. Her apparent respectability may have made it difficult for her to face her situation, but it may also have disposed the jury to believe her, especially in 1766.[34]

Poor Elizabeth Tea was not so lucky earlier in 1735 when like Ann Taylor she said that she had given birth prematurely after falling down the stairs. At first she had told her suspicious mistress that she had miscarried and was dismissed for that. But after her child's body was found in the garret, she was tried, found guilty, and sentenced to death. One wonders what her demeanor was. Certainly in the 1730s and 1740s young women like Sarah Allen or Ann Terry who were described as "a silly giggling creature" or as "hardworking but silly" were likely to have their ignorance and frivolity held against them when they were condemned to death for throwing their children out of a garret window three stories high. More sober young women like Mary Wilton or Hannah Perfect were acquitted. Wilton, who as a cookmaid was trusted with her master's money, was believed when she said that her child by the underfootman had been born dead. Perfect, the kitchen girl at the Dog Tavern on Garlic Hill, was also acquitted of suffocating her child because she had "always behaved like a very sober honest girl." But one might argue that these women were believed and the others not because it was difficult to accept that a woman's child could be accidentally dropped out a window—except that a man like Charles Cullam had his story accepted when he said exactly this after he was accused of throwing his daughter out a third-story window; but admittedly he was tried in the kindlier atmosphere of 1760.[35]

In 1735, on the other hand, not even Elizabeth Ambrook's evident distress of mind could save her from the gallows when she was accused of flinging her son out a window two stories high immediately after the child's birth three days after Christmas. Elizabeth was thirty years old and had been born in a village near Cambridge. After working there as a servant for different families, she came to London where her brother lived. She found a place in a house in Lincoln's Inn Fields where a fellow servant forced himself on her and made her pregnant. She then seems to have left that place and been hired by a watchmaker who lived in an alley in Shoreditch near to her brother's house. She had perhaps moved closer to her family knowing that she would need their help once her child was born. She prepared baby linen, but she did not tell either her brother or his wife that she was pregnant. When her time was near, she left the watchmaker and moved into her brother's house. On the day her child was born, she told her sister-in-law that she wanted to stool and needed some paper. But instead she delivered her child and flung it out the window. When her sister-in-law asked why she had done this, she replied that "she did not know what she did, for through the extremity of the pain, she thought the room was on fire when she threw it out." The ordinary of Newgate's account of her last days before her execution described her as "a simple silly creature"—which no doubt had told against her at the trial. He said that "she behaved with a great deal of humility and submission but was not much affected with guilt" and that "she died very penitent, believed in Christ, and said she was in peace with all the world."[36]

It is apparent that Elizabeth Ambrook was never able to admit even to her closest relatives what had happened to her—that she had lost her reputation by becoming pregnant. She was able to take some practical measures but never those that would have guaranteed the presence of someone to help her in her delivery. The ability of other women to hide their pregnancies varied. Even the surgeon at St. Bartholomew's Hospital said that he had not suspected that Ann Haywood, who was a patient in the hospital, was pregnant. Mary Samuel's sympathetic mistress took her lethargy for signs of dropsy and, pitying her, hired others to do her work.[37]

Other women displayed enough symptoms to reveal themselves to some eyes but not to others. A female relative of the attorney for whom Marie Jenkins worked did not notice anything. She was blinded by Maria's reputation, since she had always appeared to her to "be a very clever decent person; I never suspected her." But another woman was able to say to Maria, "I fancy you have stole a wedding." It was probably the same difference, between trusting to a woman's reputation and seeing the evidence before one's eyes, that accounts for the varying reactions to Sarah Reynolds. Her sister's mistress saw nothing when she allowed Reynolds to stay for a fortnight in her coffeehouse, but one of the lodgers was able to tell her "you must part with one of your maids soon, for she looks very big." But poor Esther Rowden could hide nothing from her sharp mistress's eyes. Mary Evans noticed her grow "bigger" and accused her of being pregnant, which Esther denied. But when Evans "perceived her grown thinner," she suspected she had been delivered, and "I looked all over the house" and found the child in the copper-hole. Esther had tried to deny her situation even when she was in labor. When Susanna Woan, a midwife, had asked, "how do you do? she said very well. I said, you seem to be in labor. She said she was no more in labor than I was. I said, come, go in, you are not the first that has done a fault." But Esther would not accept the offer of help. She delivered herself and later confessed to a third woman that she had strangled the child. She was condemned to death. Esther was not able to face the world's dismissive contempt that made light of a woman's tragedy.[38]

Some women delayed preparing for their child's birth because they misjudged the stage of their pregnancy. A few women delayed because in their innocence they had not quite realized that they were pregnant. Elizabeth Warner thought that she had three more months to go when her child was born. The expert witness in this case was Michael Underwood, who eventually wrote an influential book on the new ideals in childrearing. He said that he had begged Elizabeth "not to tell me anything that would do her hurt." He refused to say that her child had been born alive. Another woman, Elizabeth Wood, thought that her child had died because she had not felt it move in two months. Then there were the innocent girls like Ann Arbor who loved children well enough. Her master, who had three, described her as "humane and tender, I never had a servant like her, neither before nor since, so affectionate and tender" was she to his children, especially after their mother had died. But when the surgeon "asked her if she had been with child? she did not know." She had "found herself indisposed and went to the vault and something had come from her when she was on the vault." Sarah Hunter's mistress had suspected that she was in labor but "being very cautious of the girl's reputation" would not ask her "directly if she were pregnant." Sarah said that she "awaked in the morning and found there was a child; that frightened me very much. I was not sensible what I did. I can give no account how I did it." A third girl in Chelsea, Amelia Powell, who was sixteen or seventeen, had her child as she sat on the vault. Her mistress said that she was "a very ignorant girl . . . very diligent in her business but very ignorant; I question whether she knows how long a woman should go with child." All three of these young women presumably had some cognitive difficulty in connecting the birth of a child to the sexual experiences that had made them pregnant. These cases, however, all come from the second half of the century, when elite men had become more disposed to believe in the maternal feelings of women and their sexual innocence. But it may well be that both of those states of mind were often found together in many women throughout the century and that the evidence for this was not usually solicited in trials in the first half of the century.[39]

A few of the women in these cases, then, were so young and sexually innocent that they did not understand that the men who had seduced them had also left them pregnant. But most of them seem to have concealed their pregnancies because they could not cope with the loss of public reputation than an open admission entailed. They then deliberately or accidentally killed their child in the process of delivery or shortly thereafter. In doing so they opened themselves to the charge of murder and possible execution. But their experience shows more vividly than anything else the terrifying isolation that must have overcome a woman once she realized that what had happened between her and her lover (however much or little she had consented) had left her pregnant and unmarried. Her life was changed forever. She might eventually like the women in the East End manage to marry respectably, or she might enter into a long-term liaison. But she must also have known that for many men and women, for those who knew her best and for the total stranger, she had fallen from grace and virtue and lost her honor as a woman.

CAN A WOMAN BE RAPED?

The courtships of poor men and women grew out of their sexual attraction to each other and their hope (especially for the women) of marrying and having children. But this does not mean that sexual relations among them were yet affected by the self-conscious ideology of romantic marriage and domesticity that by 1750 had begun to transform relations among the middle and landed classes. The casual presence of violence in the sexual courtships of the poor is good evidence of this, and the best evidence of this violence is to be found in cases of rape.

In these rape cases, unlike those for bastardy, a woman unambiguously asserted that a man, or a group of men, had forced her into sexual relations against her will. The men who were accused, on the other hand, needed to assert that their victims had consented. A woman's husband, employer, family, friends, and neighbors, as well as the judge and the jury, were also obliged to form an opinion as to whether a woman had consented. For London in the eighteenth century the most readily available body of such cases are those printed in the Sessions Paper from the Old Bailey. The series is not very satisfactory for the first two decades of the century, but from the 1720s onward there is a substantial body of cases. The reporting varies in its density and is best in the 1770s and 1780s. In the 1790s the details of most cases were not printed on the ground that they were too salacious. The cases overall come in three kinds. There are rapes of prepubescent girls under the age of fourteen that have already been analyzed. In 60 percent of these cases after 1760 and in 30 percent of them before that date, it was mentioned that the girls had been venereally infected by their attackers. These men raped in the belief that sexual relations with a virgin would cure them of disease. The venereal infection was convincing proof that penetration had occurred and there was no need to raise the question of consent because of the ages of the girls. The cases that involve adult women come in two kinds. Individual married women or unmarried servants were attacked when alone with a man whom they often knew. The men in these cases were almost always acquitted, probably for two reasons. It was widely believed by both women and men that a woman who wished to avoid penetration could always achieve this by moving her body in the appropriate way. There was little sympathy or understanding for a woman's attempts to explain her feelings of psychological collapse during an attack. It is also apparent that the actions that some single women tried to classify as rape were remarkably similar to those used in the seduction of others. This continuum must have made it difficult to sustain a rape charge in court. Conviction was therefore most likely in cases of gang rape in which it was taken for granted that a woman had not consented or in those cases in which a single unknown stranger raped a young girl of an unimpeachable virginity. But even in these cases there had to be credible witnesses. The court was also careful to ascertain that a woman's case had not been weakened by any attempt outside the court to compromise the dispute by negotiating or accepting a money payment in compensation. The court's concern about money payments appeared, however, in all three kinds of rape cases, especially in the last third of the century. It was motivated in part by the fear that a rape charge might be used to extort money from innocent men. But there also seems to have been the sense that once honor had been satisfied by a payment, the court's intervention was no longer necessary or appropriate.[40]

There are fourteen cases to consider of married women who charged that they were raped. The rape usually occurred in their own house or lodging by a man known to the woman. It was sometimes a woman's husband who insisted that charges be brought to protect his honor. In five cases the woman's husband was in debt to the man who attacked her. This indebtedness was often used in the attacker's defense in court when it was suggested that the rape charge was part of an attempt by a debtor to intimidate his creditor. But it seems equally likely that a creditor felt freer to attack a woman because her husband's debt made him dependent on the rapist. Many of these issues appeared in the case that Betteridge May brought against her husband's employer, E—— J——, in 1734. At five o'clock on a Saturday evening, J——, who was a master carpenter, came to the house. He asked Betteridge if her husband were at home and said he was surprised to find that he was not since he had given May permission to come home early on Saturdays. J—— then asked to see some pigs, and Betteridge took him out to the stable to show them to him. In the stable, J—— threw her down, stuffed a handkerchief in her mouth, and forced himself on her. When he was finished, he tried to calm her down. But he also told her that he hoped she would not "tell your husband; but if you do, I'll turn him out of his work, and lay him in jail for what he owes me." J—— then gave six pence to each of her three children, one of whom she was still nursing. When Betteridge's husband came home that night, she said nothing since he owed J—— seven and a half guineas. A week later J—— returned to pay Betteridge her husband's wages and asked if she had told her husband. The six pence in change he told her to keep for herself. A few days later J—— sent a message asking Betteridge to come and meet him at a public house. She later said that she thought it was a message from her husband, but the servants at the inn insisted that she had asked for J—— by name. J—— threatened her with two pistols and a knife, forced her to have a meal, and then had sex with her again. When it was over, J—— said to her, "You may tell your husband of this if you will, for now you come after me."

This second rape occurred on a Friday. On the following Wednesday, John May said that he was "very urgent to do what married men should do." When Betteridge refused him, he "insisted upon knowing the meaning of it." She then told him of the first incident but not of the second. By this point she was in great physical pain. The pain was probably in part psychosomatic—she said she "had such a dread upon my spirits"—but she may also have contracted a venereal infection from J——. At this point, Betteridge told him of the second attack and explained that she had not mentioned it sooner because she was afraid that he "should turn her quite out of doors." The second incident was clearly more compromising to her than the first since it could be made to appear that she had freely gone to an assignation with J——. May and his wife, however, had no success against J——. Objections were successfully made to a first indictment for rape. The charge was then changed to assault with intent to ravish, but J—— was acquitted. They therefore indicted him for rape again (the evidence comes from this case), but he was acquitted a second time.[41]

Betteridge's story was not convincing in court for two reasons. There was first the conviction that a woman could not have intercourse without her consent. And there was the suspicion of her motive in bringing the case that her husband's indebtedness raised. Betteridge testified that J—— had "made use of what he had," which she was made to specify as his "yard," and that he had "put it into my body" and ejaculated, or done "all that was necessary on his part towards getting a child." When she was asked "could he possibly do that if you would not comply," she answered, "yes, he did it against my will." But when she admitted that he had not used "any means to terrify" her, such as a pistol or a knife, she was asked, "would not the least motion of yours have prevented him from doing as you say." To this Betteridge could only reply, "it was not in my power." But this answer and its implication of psychological debility, she was not asked to amplify. Instead the judge barked out that "the jury will judge of that," as to her power to resist. Sarah Denman received a similar response from her neighbors when she charged that John Clark (an alehouse keeper to whom her husband owed money) had come to her at eleven at night when her husband was away, dragged her around the kitchen, forced her into a chair, and had sex with her. Her neighbors insisted that they had heard nothing through the very thin walls, and the woman next door, Martha Powell, added "that no man can force a woman without she be willing."[42] The presumption clearly was that unless a woman was threatened by a weapon or held by several men, she could in any encounter with a single man always move her body in such a way as to prevent penetration. If penetration did occur, it then became a sign of consent. Except for the women who were actually raped, no one seems to have been willing to accept that a woman could despair and give in against her will. Only constant heroic resistance was credible.

The debt that John and Betteridge May owed to J—— also argued against their credibility. When Betteridge was told that if J—— was convicted of rape, he would be hanged, and that her husband's debt to him would then be of no consequence, she could only answer, "I know nothing of the law." John Clark, an alehouse keeper, similarly was acquitted in his case after he said that Sarah and Charles Denman, who owed him money, had charged him with rape to extort money, and that three friends of his had tried to negotiate a settlement of the rape charge. It is possible in all these cases that a poor couple saw their debtor's assault as an occasion that could be turned to their good, but this does not mean that the assault had not occurred. The rapist, in turn, may have felt freer to try the woman's virtue because of her husband's dependence on him.[43]

In all these calculations, the honor of a woman's husband as well as her own had to be considered. Betteridge May had been afraid that her husband would turn her out of doors when he discovered the second forced act of intercourse with his employer. Their persistence through two indictments and two trials may well have been motivated by the need to justify his honor as well as hers. Penelope Askew said that her husband had told her when Thomas Normansel forced himself on her, that "after such a heinous crime, and such a disagreeable affair, it was impossible ever to think of living with her." But Penelope and Richard Askew may have been disreputable, since he had been in prison for assault and perjury. Normansel, who came to Askew to have his portrait painted in miniature, claimed that the couple had tried to get money out of him. The rape, however, may still have occurred. Penelope said that she had tried crossing her legs to stop it but that Normansel had pried them open with his knees. She first told her sister about the attack and then her husband. She had been concerned that her husband would not be willing to take the trouble of prosecuting, but he went with her and her sister to Justice Wright in Bow Street for a warrant against Normansel. Samuel Stone insisted that Elizabeth Stone prosecute the young man she claimed had raped her and that if she did not "clear up her character, he would not live with her, for he would not be made a cuckold of by a one-eyed boy."[44]

It is not clear, however, that Elizabeth Stone had been raped by Simon Frazier. She fed him and two friends and then had sex with Frazier, with whom she was accustomed to spend time each day. After Frazier's mother peeped through the window and saw what was happening, she had burst open the door, shouting, "G[o]d d[am]n you, you whore, are you not ashamed to lie with three such boys when you have got a clever fellow for a husband and three young children." She then raised a mob in the neighborhood. From such a public disgrace, Elizabeth could recover and keep her husband only by charging rape. A number of her neighbors testified that Elizabeth liked to drink and that while she was modest when she was sober, "she would talk very badly" when she was drunk. Another Elizabeth, this one the wife of John London, seems to have charged William West with rape for a similar reason. She claimed that she awoke and found that West had gotten into her bed between herself and her child and had entered her from behind. She was asked to clarify that he had entered her vagina and not her anus. But it turned out that Elizabeth had been drinking with West, whose sister lived in the same house and that Mary Green had seen her going up into the garret with him. When Green had asked "what she did there with the young man," Elizabeth had answered, "what if I have a mind he should do me over?"[45]

It is apparent that if a married woman had a reputation for being troublesome or bawdy, it made it impossible for her to sustain her charge of rape. When David Taylor came to serve an execution against Ann Wingate's husband over an argument about knocking down a fruit stall (Ann sold fruit, but her husband was a smith), he put Ann in a coach, supposedly to take her to jail. In the coach he became familiar. She objected and got out. He then took her into Marylebone Fields and forced himself on her. After this they went to his sponging house (where persons were kept until they found bail). When she got out, she asked Sir John Fielding for a warrant. But Fielding took Taylor's part. He advised him to print handbills looking for the coachman, who when he was found swore that he had not heard any complaints from inside the coach. Before the trial, Ann tried unsuccessfully to get Taylor to make it up for five guineas, but he refused. The argument over the fruit stall was probably typical of Ann's life, and the case against her was concluded when several witnesses testified that she was a very troublesome woman.[46]

When Sarah Bethell charged Robert Moody with rape, it was said against her by her landlady that she was "not so good as some may be; she is very vulgar in her speech." Sarah lived at Wandsworth and had four children. When she was returning home from visiting her parents in London, she found that the waterman who usually took her on the river had gone. She therefore agreed to go back in Moody's boat. They both lived at Wandsworth and had known each other for years. They set out at four in the morning. Moody stopped at Millbank and at Chelsea to drink in public houses. Sarah drank a little herself and thought no harm of it since he was a neighbor. Back in the boat, he asked her to sing. She declined, saying "I cannot sing; I am not so light-hearted," because her husband had gone out of his mind. He had been put in the madhouse and then turned out as incurable and was now confined in the workhouse. "It lay on my mind," she said. At this, Moody swore that if she would not sing, she "should do the other thing." He pulled her down in the boat and threatened to throw her overboard if she resisted. When it was over, she told him, "Moody, I will expose you to everybody I know." He swore that he did not care if she did. Later he changed his mind and told her father, "For God's sake have compassion on me! Consider my wife and children." His neighbors rallied to him, and other women swore that he had never done anything to them when they traveled in his boat. Moody was acquitted, and poor Sarah had another woe to make her heavyhearted. Her plain speaking, which other women saw as bawdy, had done her in.[47]

Married women who were raped by strangers were not likely to be believed if their behavior seemed indiscreet. Mary Bradley met Ralph Cutler when she went out with friends, and he introduced himself to their group. As they all walked home, he asked Mary to go for a glass of wine, but she refused. After her other friends had turned off, he continued to walk with her, saying that it was not prudent for a woman to walk alone at that time of night. When she arrived, he went in with her. At a quarter past one, when her servant went home, she asked him to leave also. But instead he attacked her. Her servant, Caroline Taylor, who had sat with her four children while Mary went out that night, did not think much of her and said that Mary could "not be very modest, when at all times she would go out and come home at all hours when I was there, and sometimes very much in liquor." Mary's charge of rape had no chance of being sustained.[48]

Unmarried women were much more likely to be raped by a stranger who met them in the street than were married women (twelve cases). This occurred as frequently as the cases (twelve) in which a servant was raped either by her master or by a lodger in the house where she worked. Some women were raped in the context of prostitution (seven) and a few under promise of marriage (three). It was probably the case that unmarried women were more frequently attacked by strangers in the street than were married women because they were more open to courtship and flirtation by strange men since they still had husbands to find. Married women in the street must have been less approachable. But it is apparent that unmarried women had to be very careful in their response to men in the street since there were those who were inclined to take any expression of interest as justifying a ruthless and violent pursuit of their immediate sexual desires. Single women like married women were also raped at home by men on whom they were financially dependent, but their rapists were their masters rather than their husbands' debtors. It is important to note, however, that in no case did a woman charge a fellow servant or apprentice with rape. Yet from the bastardy examinations it is apparent that it was overwhelmingly such men who forced sex on young servant women. This makes it very likely that women tolerated violence as an ordinary part of courtship when there was any real likelihood that the men who attacked them might eventually marry them.

Rape cases are therefore not a safe guide to the incidence of domestic sexual violence against unmarried women. Judges and juries must have been aware of this, and it may explain better than simple male callousness why they refused to convict any of these masters. They did not necessarily approve of what had been done. Sixteen-year-old Elizabeth Smith told the court that two weeks after she had been in his house, her master, a married man with three children, had broken open the door of the garret where she slept, forced himself on her, and stayed from eleven at night until seven in the morning while his wife was sick in bed. He then went to the public house and bragged of what he had done. A man who heard the tale told Elizabeth's aunt that she should go to her niece's aid because her master had ruined her. She did so, and with her husband on the same day took the girl to the magistrate to charge the man with rape. The judge's response was to say that "to be sure, taking any method to persuade a girl, his servant, of this age, in his house, under his protection, he having a wife and three children, one cannot presume any thing more brutal and beastly than his conduct, but as to a rape, there is no pretense."[49] Young women or their families probably therefore brought charges of rape against masters either to restore a woman's honor or as a means to force a financial settlement. Judges (as we shall see) were always careful to ask whether compensation had been sought or made on the ground, presumably, that a woman should not be compensated twice for the same injury—once by a money payment and then again with a man's life. Most masters were not in a position to offer the third possible compensation, marriage, since they usually already had wives. This did not stop an enterprising man from making the offer. After Mary Swan's father quarreled with John and Mary Sutton (Sutton was a black man), he forbade her to visit the couple. But the wife got the girl to visit her, and after her husband came home, they made her drunk, forced her to have sex, and would not let her go home until five in the morning. Sutton then offered the girl's father either to make it up with a payment or to marry her. Her father declined, saying that Sutton already had two or three wives, and instead brought the case to court, where Sutton was acquitted of rape.[50] But a fellow servant or an apprentice who was unmarried and who had forced himself on a young woman could offer her marriage in return. And presumably for this reason, such men were not charged with rape.

The first category to consider of men who were charged with the rape of unmarried women are those who forced themselves in public on women whom they did not know. It was only in some of these cases, when a woman's virginal status was demonstrated, that the men were ever found guilty. In the first case to consider, Thomas Meller and John Litchfield met Marry Warnet and Mary Curtain when the two friends were taken to see the Compter (a prison). The two young women, who were seventeen and eighteen years old, lived in lodgings and were servants out of place for the moment. Warnet, whose parents lived at Camberwell, had worked on and off for a customhouse broker and his wife, but she suffered from fits and had had to leave her place when she had attacks. Meller was the more forceful of the two men and took the lead. He had a reputation for violence and had once been tried for knocking out a man's eye. Litchfield's father was a cowkeeper and prosperous enough to rent land worth four hundred pounds a year for the animals whose milk he sold. He had been married for three years but had no children. He was a more peaceable man than Meller but tended to get drunk. When Meller and Litchfield met the two young women, they offered to treat them to drinks. Warnet said that although she wanted to go home, Meller insisted and took them to a public house in a neighborhood she did not know. When Warnet asked to go home, Meller forced her to pay the bill and kept the change himself. As they left the public house, Warnet became afraid that a dog the two men had would be set on them. The women therefore went with the men into a field. Meller had chosen Warnet and, ignoring her cries, threw her down and entered her body with "what he had." (The court forced her to specify that she meant his "private parts.") He must have found it difficult to enter her, so he ripped her open with his fingers. A midwife who later examined her reported that "all round the thick part of her thighs, to the size of four of my fingers, were as if she had been cut with a horsewhip"; Warnet had explained to her that Meller's fingers had torn her in that way. As Meller ripped her, he asked her "whether I ever f[uck]t. I told him I did not know what he meant by it. He said if I did not know what he meant, he would make me know before he left." Meller then entered her with his penis and she felt him ejaculate.

Litchfield was experiencing similar difficulties with Mary Curtain. When Meller called to him and asked him if he had "f[ucke]d" her, Litchfield shouted back that, "no, d[am]n her, she was never f[ucke]d before.

I cannot." But he persisted and eventually entered her. By this point, Meller must have started a second time with Warnet, and to encourage Litchfield, he shouted "have you done her once." Litchfield said that he had.
"Then blast your eyes," Meller replied, "why don't you f[uc]k her again?"
Meller himself, after his ejaculation, put his fingers into Warnet's body
a second time. Litchfield, however, was ready to go and called to him and
begged him to come away. But Meller refused to leave. Warnet tried to
persuade him to do so by telling him that "he knew I was an honest girl."
But Meller only replied that "d[am]n his blood, he knew I was: for I had
never known a man before, and he did not know what to do with me
hardly." Eventually Litchfield came over and dragged Meller off Warnet
and helped her up. Curtain's landlady and Litchfield's wife and family
tried to persuade her to make it up, presumably with a payment. But she
refused. The two cases came to court, where both men were found guilty
and condemned to death.[51]

The details of this case reappear in a number of others—the approach
by a man totally unknown or barely known, his offer of a drink that a
young woman had difficulty in making clear she did not welcome, his
taking her through unknown streets and ignoring her pleas to be allowed
to go home, the physical force necessary to enter an unwilling virgin, and
his offer afterward to make it up or to marry her. Mary Currell said that
Simon Clark, the man from whom she had bought milk for two or three
weeks, offered to show her the way from Brook Street, where she lived
with her father, to Norton Folgate workhouse, where she was going to
see her cousin. As he led her down a turning different from the one her
father had told her to take, he asked her to have a drink with him. She
said she would rather not. He persisted, and in the end they stopped and
drank at several public houses. But she had been up all night nursing her
father and had not eaten. She became sick and vomited. The keeper of
one of the public houses said that she was so drunk that she could not
walk. Others swore that they saw her sit in his lap and put her hand into
his bosom. When she recovered, he took her into a tumbledown house,
put one hand around her waist, flung off her hat with another, pushed
her down among the bricks and stones, and threw himself on top of her.
To her cries of "Lord have mercy on me! Christ have mercy on me! I am
ruined!," he replied, "Humph! G[o]d d[am]n me, is there no entering
your body." Afterward, Clark went to her father and offered to make
amends and marry her. But he was in fact already married with three or
four children. In court, she was asked whether if he had been single she
"would have accepted that satisfaction." "I should not," she replied, "be-

cause of his ill usage." She pointed out that before the attack he had not even tried to kiss her or even to brush against her clothes. His violence, in other words, had been unmitigated by any attempt at courtship. It is possible, however, that during her drunken stupor, she may have responded to his physical advances. This is what some witnesses swore to, and they were believed. Consent of such a kind was enough to secure Clark's acquittal despite the evidence of Mary's virginity.[52]

In two other cases the man did not escape. Ann Lowther was approached by James Barrett while she was caring for a group of children in Stepney churchyard and he was attending a funeral. He asked her to run an errand, but she replied that she had to take the children home first. She returned accompanied by her friend Mary Stone. But she became suspicious of Barrett and suggested to Mary that they should go home because Barrett was going to follow them. Barrett now came up to the two girls (both of whom were fourteen) and said that he would pay them if they helped him to retrieve some smuggled goods. Seeing Ann's reaction, he asked her "what I was afraid of; I said I was afraid he did not mean any good." But he spoke "so fair that we did not think he could do us any harm." They followed him into a field. Ann's alarm returned, and she said to her friend that they would not know how to find their way home. Under the cover of a hedge Barrett now made his intentions clear and said he would cut their throats if they did not submit. Ann offered to submit to anything if he would leave the other girl alone, whom she mistakenly believed to be younger than herself. Barrett then threw Ann down and raped her while holding Mary fast. He eventually threw Mary down as well, but he said that he did not like her as much, and so he forced himself a second time on Ann. When the girls asked Barrett "if he was not ashamed of himself; he said, no, that he had served younger than us so." But it was one of those other girls who led to Barrett's arrest. Dr. Hatton's maid gave Ann's father a description of a man who had similarly assaulted her and offered her three guineas afterward. With the description Ann's father, James Lowther, found Barrett, who was identified by the two girls in a room with twenty to thirty other people in it. Barrett was found guilty and condemned to death.[53]

In the final case in which a man was found guilty of raping a virgin and condemned to death for it, Jane Bell, a girl of fourteen or fifteen who did not know her exact age, was attacked in Green Park by John Briant, who was thirty-seven years old. Briant was caught in the act by Sarah Scott and John Smith. Bell was a servant to Mrs. Sarah Pollard, who kept cows and sold milk. On a night in July when it was still light, she saw

Briant for the first time when she put her mistress's cows into the park to graze. Briant came up to her and asked her to go with him. When she refused, he took hold of her and dragged her to the upper basin. She managed to escape once while he loosened his underclothes, but he recaptured her and raped her. Sarah Scott and John Smith were in the park to talk over some business and heard Bell's cries. (Smith was a servant out of place, Scott a married woman whose husband was out of the country.) Scott urged Smith to go and investigate, and when he hesitated, she strode forward herself. Together they pulled Briant off the girl. Scott collared the man and "asked him if he was not a rascal." "I told him," she said, "there were plenty of unfortunate women he might take his pleasure with, better than a child." (In other words, streetwalking prostitution made the violent seduction of young girls unnecessary.) When she "collared" Briant, he said that "the girl belonged to him not to" Scott. But the girl denied that she knew Briant. Briant now ran away, but Smith pursued him (it is clear that Scott would not have let him do otherwise), captured him, and found a constable. There were no marks on Briant's underclothes, but a surgeon testified that he had seen semen on the girl's private parts.

At her trial Bell testified that she had been ill ever since the rape. She limped, and Briant had venereally infected her. It is clear that before the rape she had been without any sexual experience. Her mistress Mrs. Pollard explained that the girl had never menstruated and had never had any "followers," or young men who kept her company. Before the rape, she had examined the girl to see what she knew "about the course of human nature," and it hard turned out that "she did not know what I meant." "She was perfectly clean," Mrs. Pollard repeated, "she was as clean and fair a girl as ever sun shone upon." Briant's friends and Elizabeth Burns, with whom he lived (she like Mrs. Pollard was in the milk business), tried to come to his aid. Burns stopped Mrs. Pollard and asked what she meant to do. When Pollard answered that "it should take the law," Burns became insolent and called her an old bawd. In court Burns swore that the girl had told her that she had drunk three times with Briant. Another man and woman swore that they had seen them drinking. Hannah Cusack, who had known Briant for seventeen years, also swore that the girl had said that she had drunk with Briant. But Cusack overplayed her hand. She went to the girl and offered her five guineas and a gown not to appear in court and then threatened her as well with prison and the pillory. Cusack denied this. But Mr. Pollard must have placed himself so that he could overhear the discussion, and he swore to its truth in court. Briant's friends could not save him, and he was condemned to death.[54]

Younger women who were coerced into going home with a man and spending the night were never believed when they said that they had been raped, and the same was true of older women who could not claim virginal status of the kind that could be demonstrated for the girls whose rapists were condemned to death. Ann Keats and Elizabeth Hawkins were each accosted at night in the street by a man who insisted on forcing them to drink with him and who then took them back to a room where he raped them. But because they spent the night in the man's company, neither was believed when she said that she had not consented to the sexual act. L——l H——y, Esq. (a gentleman whose full name was not printed in the published trial) met Ann Keats at eight o'clock in the evening as she went to buy a bottle of Daffey's Elixir. After trying unsuccessfully to lose him, she consented to drink with him. When they were finished, he put her in a chair to take her home, as she thought, but instead he directed the men to take her to his lodgings. He forced her up the stairs when they arrived. He showed her gold watches and silver salvers that he said he would give her if she consented, and he tried to get her to drink some more. Eventually he stripped himself and asked her to undress. When instead she begged to be allowed to go home, he tore off her gown and shoes and stockings, but he could not (as she modestly said in court) get her petticoats off. So in that condition he raped her. She returned to her lodgings at two on the following afternoon, clearly distraught. "Miss Nanny," asked her landlady, "What is the matter with you. What made you stay out all night child?" "Don't ask me," she replied, "and fell into a violent passion of crying and so went to bed." In court she was asked why she had not cried out and replied that "I did break a pane of glass but he told me that nobody would hear me if I did cry out." She had not wanted to go up the stairs to his lodgings. She had not wanted to stay once they were there. But she was clearly unable to assert her will against him, and at each stage of the encounter, submitted, presumably with the hope that a way out would eventually present itself. But instead she was drawn in more deeply each time, and this allowed him to secure his acquittal by arguing that she had consented. Her landlady pointed out that she was not a servant and had thirty pounds a year of her own to live on. Her seducer's pretended offer of marriage may therefore have confused her resolution to leave him.[55]

But in the other case, nineteen-year-old Elizabeth Hawkins's inability to leave the presence of a man of her own class demonstrates that young women found it very difficult to assert themselves against men, to all of whom they had been socialized to defer. Hawkins was a servant to a fruiterer in Soho. At nine o'clock on a Friday night Philip Cratey stopped her in the street when she was sent on an errand. He was a chairman and had a stand in her street. She had spoken to him but did not know him. He asked her if she wanted a chair, and she said no. He then began to push her around and slapped her in the face. When she hurried on, he followed her, slapped her again, and pushed her about some more. He insisted that she drink with him and picked her up (chairmen had to be strong to carry their customers) and carried her into a public house. He then took her through a series of streets in the bawdy house district of Covent Garden, where she soon lost her way: she had only come to London from Devonshire six months before. Eventually he found a bawdy house he knew. He went up first while the landlady pulled Hawkins up the stairs into a room. She then left them and bolted the door from the outside. He undressed her, pushed her on the bed, muffled her, and raped her twice in the course of the night. When he let her go, she was afraid to return to her master's house (presumably because she had been gone the whole night) and instead went to her brother who lived in the same court. Cratey was on his stand the next morning. From his point of view, Hawkins had consented to their encounter. When she was asked why she did not call out for someone to arrest him when she saw him the next morning, she could only reply that "she did not know it was proper to call out to strangers." The people in the bawdy house (who must have known Cratey from his previous visits) of course agreed with him that Hawkins had voluntarily gone up to the room with him. He was acquitted.[56]

Older women who lived in irregular unions with a man, like the young women coerced into spending the night, had no chance of being believed in court when they said that they had been raped. Ann Clarke called herself a widow in court because her husband was a sailor from whom she had not heard in two or three years. But she lived with a man called Jenkins and passed as his wife. Edward Hatfield forced her into a house where he put his knee on her stomach and tore her with his fingers, telling her that she "was not large enough for him but he would make me big enough." Hatfield's attorney later offered her a guinea in compensation and said that if she did not accept he would prove that she was a common prostitute. Eventually they settled for three guineas and signed a receipt that was produced in court. The money was paid to her supposed husband, Jenkins, whom Hatfield had taunted by putting his hands to his forehead and saying, "look at the horns." But Jenkins lost his nerve and admitted that he was not married to Clarke.[57]

The gang rape of an older woman done in public view could not, however, be dismissed so easily. Margaret Maccullough was a widow who lived in Castle Court off Mercer Street, between Seven Dials and the Covent Garden Market. Between three and four on a Sunday morning in July she left her house to round up her two friends, Elizabeth Russell and Margaret Crouch, with whom she was going to buy mackerel. As she did so, John Whitney, a snub-nosed blacksmith who was called Pug, came up to her and knocked her down. He was quickly joined by Edmund Togwell, Peter Matthews, and Richard Arn. Togwell and Matthews were waiters in taverns, Arn was an actor. When Maccullough tried to get up, Arn knocked her down. Together the men dragged her to a toilet that they broke open. Togwell then stuffed a handkerchief in her mouth and raped her while the gang (which had grown to fourteen) held her down. When Togwell was done, he shouted to his friends that they should "[fuck] her to death," which Arn, Pug, a man called Harding, and three others proceeded to try to do. When Pug was done, he told his friends to "take a cauliflower stalk and [fuck] the bitch to death." They took his advice and also pulled off her shoes and beat her with them. One of Maccullough's neighbors, Joseph Tucker, who observed the scene from his window, said that he was afraid to go down and help her because he thought the gang was either drunk or mad. He added that when they were through with her, some of them had shouted "Let us put the bitch down the vault [i.e. toilet]." One of the other women was also attacked but not raped. Elizabeth Russell had fallen to her knees and begged the "gentlemen" not to hurt her when Pug took hold of her. They let her go and only stuffed mud and excrement into her eyes and mouth, leaving her so blinded that she could not see what happened to her friend. When the gang was finished, they roared off into Drury Lane. Some of Maccullough's neighbors were now brave enough to follow and saw them accost another woman, pull up her skirts, and whip her in the street. Maccullough said that she had never seen any of the men before. But a neighbor told her Togwell's name, and she was able to recognize him by a mark on his face. Matthews was identified when he bragged about the rape in a public house in Drury Lane. A group of violent drunken friends, fresh from their Saturday night debauches, had raped and humiliated a respectable woman on her way to market. Some neighbors had observed it all but had been afraid to intervene. But the evidence could not be ignored. No one could say that Maccullough had consented or received compensation. Togwell, Matthews, and Pug were found guilty and condemned to death.[58]

A young unmarried woman was as likely to charge that her master had raped her in his house as to say that a stranger had forced her. A man who raped his servant was likely to treat his wife badly and to make a practice of forcing himself on his servants. John Coates raped Anna Dixon on a night after he had beaten his wife and turned her out-of-doors. George Carter forced himself on Sarah Bishop twice on her first night in his house. He did not quite succeed on the first try, but he said that "he would be d[amne]d to hell if would not before he had done." When he put his hands up her petticoats the next morning, she told him she would not stay. So he gave her sixpence and some clothes and told her to go about her business. When she informed his wife what had happened, she was given another sixpence and told that if she proved pregnant, they would support the child. She added that her husband "always served all his servants so the first night when they came into his house." When Bishop swore out a warrant against Carter, his friends forced her to tear it up and to accept four shillings and a half crown. But she got a second warrant and brought her case to court. There they trapped her into saying that for her injury she would expect to receive six or seven guineas, or about sixteen times what she had been offered. The judge then directed the jury to acquit Carter, presumably on the ground that Bishop had brought her case to force him to make a larger settlement.[59]

Some families refused to support a young woman who brought such a charge against her master. Anna Dixon did not tell her father that John Coates had raped her because she was "afraid that he would lick me." At the trial her father appeared as a witness for the man she accused. When Elizabeth Russ was raped by her master, she went to her aunt's expecting sympathy. (Her parents were dead.) Instead he found her master's brother-in-law there telling his version of the story. Her aunt said to her that she had heard that Russ had been rude to her master and that "if you have, I will not encourage you in my house, it cannot be a rape." She repeated that "she would not encourage me, she would not have the trouble of it," and then put Russ in a coach and sent her back to her master. From other women she received more sympathy. The washerwoman agreed that her master had called Russ a bitch and had said that he had only managed to put his hand up her body and that "his thing went in but three inches and that could not get the bitch with child." Russ had a strong emotional reaction to the rape. She fainted when her master forced her, and she continued to have some kind of shaking fit. She was first sent to the country to be nursed for a week, and when that did not work, she was put in the hospital. That same day she decided to go to a

justice of the peace to charge her master. In the court one surgeon who
had examined her said that her body did not appear to have been torn
and another said that he thought that country air would cure her fits.
Between them the various authorities closed the matter up without any
of the usual discussion of her consent or possible compensation.[60]

Sarah Tipple had a similar strong emotional reaction to her ordeal. She
fainted during the rape, was sick for three weeks thereafter, and did not
get up. Her master John Curtis was being treated for a venereal infection
at the time of the rape—"he was obliged to take the plaisters off before
he could meddle with her"—and he left her infected. When she asked
him to put her into a hospital, he sent for a constable and charged her
with trying to extort money from him. She filed her charge against him
when she was released three hours after her arrest. Her master tried to
claim that she had been discharged for being found in bed with one of
the lodgers and that she took money from gentlemen. She denied all of
this and said that she had lived by selling her clothes while she was out
of work. But her case in court was destroyed by the well-meaning neighbor
who had helped her by allowing her to stay with him. Robert Carroll
testified that Tipple's master "was rather fond of a woman," but he also
said that Curtis had had sex with Tipple more than once and that he had
"promised to take care of her." Those multiple encounters and that promise destroyed the charge of rape. It was probably the case that Curtis had
forced Tipple the first time but that this violent and unfree beginning had
been resolved into some kind of a relationship that must have soured. It
was exactly the situation that the court feared might exist in cases when
a master was charged with rape. And the absence of cases against women's
fellow servants, makes it likely that in some cases, the court was right.[61]

In a third category are cases in which a young woman was raped as a
means of recruiting her into prostitution. These were usually instances in
which a woman helped her male friends or customers to violently debauch
a young woman. Ann Cooley, for instance, charged that Lucy Roberts
had made her drunk on Christmas Day and forced her into a room with
a young gentleman who then locked the door and put a chair against it.
Roberts had called out to the man, "Here is your girl," and he had flung
Cooley a half-guinea when he was finished. A week later Roberts tried
to force her to dress to receive company, but she refused. It was pointed
out that Cooley (whose parents lived by London Wall) had known the
place to be a "bad house" before she went there. Roberts was therefore
acquitted of abetting a rape, but the house was indicted, and Cooley was
sent to the hospital to be cured of venereal disease. In two other cases the

seduction occurred outside of a brothel, and the girls (both were fifteen) were more innocent. In the first case Mary Cove seduced Sarah Sharpe for her lover Joseph Dowling and then helped him to rape the girl. She had gotten to know Sarah's mother, Margaret Molineux, two years before when she was sick and had hired Molineux to nurse her. Sarah worked as a servant for a tailor in Conduit Court, Long Acre. Cove came and borrowed her from mistress for a night or two. She told Sarah she would explain what she wanted when they arrived at her lodgings in Great Wild Street. Once there, Cove gave Sarah some rum and asked her to play cards. Then Dowling came in. He and Cove passed as a couple, but she was actually married to John Cove. Sarah did not know Dowling, who made his living as a herald painter (i.e., of coats-of-arms). He kissed Cove and gave her some money to go for beer. But even before she left, he pulled Sarah's stomacher out of her stays and began to feel her breasts. She cried out and said, "pray let me alone." But instead, once Cove was gone, he took Sarah by her hands, dragged her into a back room, and threw her across the bed. He was unable, however, to penetrate Sarah until Cove came back and held down her hands on either side. Cove and Dowling then went to bed together and asked Sarah to join them. But she refused and sat in her shift in the front room until they allowed her to leave the next day. Cove promised Sarah (whose wages were a shilling a week) that she would give her a silk gown and a fine handkerchief if she did not tell her mistress. But Sarah did. Her mother and stepfather were informed, and they began to negotiate compensation for the rape. An offer of two guineas was made, but her stepfather said that that would not cover his expenses and that twenty pounds "would make it up." But he left the final decision to Sarah because he was only her "father-in-law" (i.e., stepfather). It must therefore have been her decision to bring the case to court. But Dowling and Cove were acquitted because "the offer of satisfaction . . . stifle[d] the prosecution."[62]

It is not clear what Cove and Dowling had planned should happen to Sarah after this first encounter. But from comparable cases in the chapter on the lives of prostitutes, it is very likely that Cove was engaged in some sort of prostitution and intended to induct Sarah into that life. In a similar rape case it is clearer that Ann Lock (a twenty-six-year-old woman) was a soldier's whore and that she had decided to seduce Martha Linett (who was fifteen) for one of her soldier friends. Martha (whose father was dead) had come to London from Oxfordshire nine months before the rape to join her mother, who had preceded her there nine months earlier still. Ann Lock lodged in the same house as Martha's mother, had gotten to know the girl in that way, and had taken her to see the soldiers encamped in St. James's Park. On an evening in July, Lock met Martha as she was going to see her former mistress and asked her to go with her again to the soldiers' camp to collect money that a young man owed her. Together they walked about the camp until eight o'clock. As they went through the Horse Guards, Lock ran up to meet one of the soldiers, Christopher Morris. Morris must have been instantly attracted to Martha and plucked away her handkerchief, which revealed the tops of her breasts. When Lock said that she would go home by way of Pimlico, Martha went along as she did not know her way. Lock now picked up a second soldier, John Mills. As the four walked through a field at ten o'clock in the evening, Lock and Mills ran away and left Martha with Morris. He immediately pushed her down and began to try to have sex. He did take time to ask "was you ever laid with before," but Martha's "no" did not stop him. On his third try he entered her body. When Lock returned she found Martha crying. She asked her "what was I crying for. . . . it was what I must come, and she must come to, and all women must come to." With this advice, she left her, and once again Morris pushed her down and entered her. When Martha's cries of murder brought two men, the soldiers drew their bayonets and frightened them away. Mills and Lock then walked on so that Morris could have Martha a third time. When she cried out again, Mills returned and hit her with his bayonet and told her to be still. It was now too late for Lock to get into her lodgings, so the four of them stayed out all night. In the morning when Lock went to retrieve Martha's handkerchief from Morris, her mother came looking for her. Susannah Linett said nothing to her daughter when she heard the story but could only cry.

Mrs. Linett examined her daughter and found her private parts bruised and her eye blackened. A surgeon later said that she had been venereally infected as well. Mrs. Linett now confronted Morris, who asked her to go and drink with him. She replied that she did "not choose to drink with such wretches" and that she "had no notion of soldiers at all." She thought he was impudent when he called her "mother." "Mother," he had said, "don't be angry." But she was angry and pressed charges against him. He was discharged at the Bow Street office, however, when Martha failed to appear. Morris claimed that she had not come because he had offered her ten shillings that she had accepted. Mrs. Linett had a different story: "The sergeants and his acquaintance who were there persuaded the girl not to appear, and kept her back, and persuaded her that as soon as he was discharged, she would have a husband; and she, silly girl, minded them more than me." This made Mrs. Linett so angry that she beat her daughter in the street. When she discovered that the girl was venereally infected, she brought a fresh charge against Morris, and this one came to trial. But before the trial, Morris asked Mrs. Linett to come and see him in Bridewell, where he offered her ten shillings. She would not take them herself, but another woman with her did. They spent four shillings on drink, and the other six, Mrs. Linett said, "I received for my loss of time." But what she did not realize was that those ten shillings guaranteed that the case against Morris would be discharged and that her daughter's honor would have no vindication.[63]

The offer of marriage with which the soldiers deluded poor Martha Linett brings us to our final point. It is apparent that for some women and some men, marriage was a possible conclusion to what began as a violent sexual assault. But for other women the initial sexual violence precluded the possibility of marriage. In a way familiar from the bastardy examinations, a man who became violent might initially make promises of marriage when all he sought was sexual conquest. After Thomas Coventry had raped Catherine Southall, he boasted to some soldiers in an alehouse that he had "longed for a maidenhead, and by G[o]d, he had got one, and swore the girl was sixteen years of age," and that she was "as fit for the business" as the girl's mistress—who sat listening without knowing that Coventry was speaking of her servant. To Catherine, Coventry (who had lived in a cellar next door) had promised marriage and a wedding ring. But instead, she said, he had "hauled me into a dirty place at Ivy Bridge, and laid me down, and then laid upon me, and wanted to unlace me, then took up my coats and laid with me." When Catherine told her mistress that a man had "deluded" her away, she sent for her mother, and the decision was made to charge Coventry with rape. But in court Coventry insisted that the girl had been nice to him, and this evidently was enough to secure his acquittal. Premarital sexual relations between engaged couples were frequent enough that it was as difficult to accept that there was no consent between a courting couple as between a husband and wife. One wonders why, however, this couple did not proceed to marriage. It must have been either that the violence made him no longer acceptable to Catherine, or that Coventry had made clear, once he had gotten Catherine's maidenhead, that his proposals of marriage were not serious.[64]

Barton Dorrington made a practice of seducing young women by promising marriage and kept a notebook with their names. He met Eleanor Masters when she was on an errand. He told her that he had often seen her in the street, and that he was very much in love with her and wanted to make her his wife. He then began to visit and court her at her master's house—the height of respectable behavior. But choosing an occasion when the rest of the household was away, he tied her hands, stuffed her mouth, and raped her. When it was over, he told her again that he would marry her if she said nothing about the rape. He even at some point got her to sign a note stating that she would forfeit twenty pounds if she did not marry him. (He had a series of these notes from other women pinned together.) Although she had been tied, gagged, and raped, the offer of marriage was acceptable enough to Eleanor that on her own she visited him and they had sex again. When she admitted this in court, the judge stopped the proceedings since any sexual consent subsequent to the rape argued that the matter had been made up between them. Eleanor eventually left her service and went to live with Barrington in a house in Foul Lane in Southwark without telling her friends. When they searched for her and found her, Dorrington made it difficult for them to take her away.[65]

Mary Brickinshaw, on the other hand, totally rejected John Sheridan's offer of marriage after he raped her. She was twenty years old and a servant in an inn at Hammersmith. Sheridan, who was single, lived next door for the six months she worked at the inn, and they knew each other fairly well. When Mary was returning from delivering a pot of beer, she met Sheridan and asked directions from him. In answer, he put his hand around her waist, pulled her down a lane, and put his hand over her mouth when she tried to cry out. There were no houses in the lane. He said he wanted to lie with her. She said he should not. He put his legs between hers, threw her down, and raped her. After a while he got up and dragged her down another lane and raped her again. At that point she said she did not have the "strength left to struggle as before." When he was finished the second time, Sheridan tried to change the mood. He got up and then helped her up in his arms. He asked if she would forgive him, but she said no. He asked if she would kiss him, but she said no, she would neither kiss him nor forgive him. He then said that he could not help that, turned down the lane, and left her to get back to the inn on her own. His tenderness after the rape suggests that for him this was a rough and ready form of courtship that also satisfied his immediate desires. But it is clear that for her it was violation.

When Mary returned to the inn, she said nothing to anyone at first. But when the last customer of the evening was leaving, she would not let him kiss her. This must have been a common enough thing between a customer and a servant at the inn because her mistress asked her, "what

makes you look so scornful?" When the man was gone, she therefore explained what had happened to her earlier in the evening. She made clear
that she wished to prosecute Sheridan for rape. (Her master said that he
would not have encouraged her to do it.) The day before the trial Sheridan
offered her five guineas to withdraw the case. And he proposed marriage
to her: "he said he would have me if I would have him, and he would use
me well." But "as to having him" Mary replied, "I never will." He then
appealed to her not "to take his life away." To which she flintily replied,
that "I would not spare him an inch if I knew it." Sheridan was found
guilty and condemned to death. Eleanor Masters had consented to marry
her rapist; Mary Brickinshaw scorned a proposal of marriage from hers.
In this harsh world where sexual reputation and marriage were so important in a woman's life, there is the real possibility that there were more
Eleanors than Marys. But there is no way to prove that.[66]

Sex for poor men and women was a traditional part of courtship and
a responsible prelude to marriage. But it is likely that by the middle of
the eighteenth century in London, the new standard of male heterosexuality had disrupted this pattern. Sex came first and marriage was thought
of only once a woman became pregnant. This was fine for men but dangerous for women, since there was no standard of female heterosexuality by
which they could justify themselves, and since they suffered alone most
of the consequences of bearing a bastards. Courtship among the poor had
also traditionally made room for a degree of sexual violence by men. The
new male heterosexuality very likely reinforced this, especially since there
was no countervailing ideal of romantic love among poor men as there
was among gentlemen. Some poor women accepted this violence. But it
is also apparent that others expected tenderness and attention in a lover
and would not marry a man who had raped them. Poor women, however,
could not consciously draw on the resources of romance, and it is likely
that they suffered the most from the construction of the modern sexual
world.

PART FOUR

Adultery and Violence in Marriage

CHAPTER TEN

Violence in Marriage

V iolence against women was in the eighteenth century a major source of sexual excitement for men. For some poor men (as the last chapter has shown) rape could even be followed by a proposal of marriage. A degree of violence in courtship must have been acceptable to those poor women and their families who accepted such a proposal. But for the men and women from the middle classes and the elite who mainly figure in this chapter, it is unlikely that courtship could ever take such a form because of the increasing influence of romantic love. Once marriage had occurred, however, it is clear that men from these classes felt free to violently dominate their wives, inspired by a combination of traditional patriarchy and the new heterosexuality. Whipping a grown woman was not in itself that shocking. Prostitutes were whipped in the house of correction, and children, servants, and wives could all be beaten legally. But there were servants who objected to this and who sometimes successfully took a master to court. There were also parents who refused to whip their children because of the influence of the new domestic family—standing a child in a corner became more acceptable. And there were wives who objected to the level of a husband's violence against them and either swore the peace against him before a magistrate or, in extreme cases, brought him before the consistory court in the hope of receiving a divorce *a mensa et thoro* that would allow them to live separately with a maintenance for her.

The women who sued in the consistory court are the subject of this chapter. Divorce in the consistory court can be arranged in a two-stage history of adultery and domestic violence. In the first half of the century women brought 60 percent of all divorce cases for the violence, adultery, and desertion of their husbands. This changed dramatically in the four decades after 1760, when men instead of women brought 60 percent of

Table 10.1 Numbers and Genders of Those Seeking Divorces in the London Consistory
Court, 1700–1799

Decade	Total	Women	Men
1700–1709	65	40	25
1710–1719	65	46	19
1720–1729	40	22	18
1730–1739	36	19	17
1740–1749	39	24	15
1750–1759	35	15	20
1760–1769	36	13	23
1770–1779	82	21	61
1780–1789	66	27	39
1790–1799	86	29	57
Total	550	256	294

Source: GLRO: DL/C/149–85.

the cases. Between 1720 and 1760 the total number of all cases in the court
declined, but the number of divorce cases brought by women declined far
more than those brought by men (table 10.1 and fig. 10.1). The decline
in divorce suits by women is partly accounted for by an increase in the
number of women who brought cases for restitution of conjugal rights,
which makes it likely that the consistory had begun to encourage women
to restore their marriages instead of separating from their husbands. But
between 1700 and 1760 the number and relative proportion of women
and men who used the consistory remained constant when the divorce
and the restitution cases are added together. After 1760 this changed in
every way. Men brought the majority of cases for the adultery of their
wives, and the total number of cases in the last three decades of the century
exceeded the numbers from the previous highs between 1700 and 1720.
Both the increase in the total of all cases as well as the increase in male
cases were accounted for by men who after they had received their separations from the consistory went on to seek a divorce by act of Parliament,
which allowed them to remarry as a consistory divorce did not (table 10.2).
But despite the change after 1760, violent and abusive husbands are to
be found in the consistory in relatively the same numbers in every decade
of the century.

Some men beat their wives from the very beginning of their marriage.
In this way they asserted their sense that marriage gave them total possession of a woman's body and her property. This was a traditional patriarchal

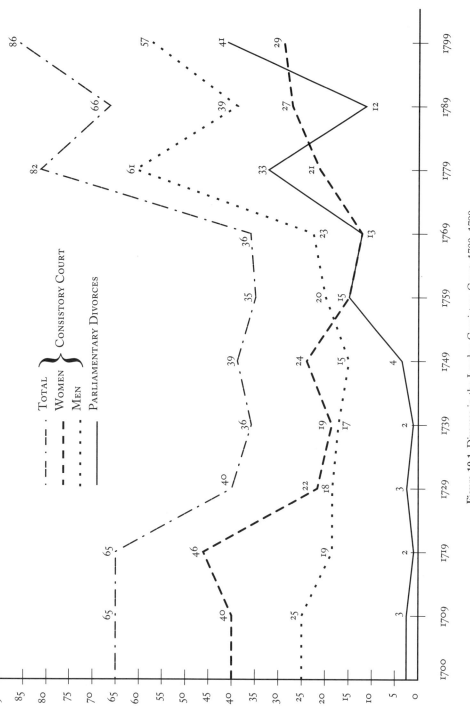

Figure 10.1 Divorces in the London Consistory Court, 1700–1799.

Table 10.2 London Consistory Divorces and Subsequent Parliamentary Divorces

Consistory Divorce	N	Parliamentary Divorce	%	No Parliamentary Divorce	%
		1770–79			
Brought by women	21				
Brought by men	62[a]	30	48.4	32	51.6
Total	83[a]				
		1780–89			
Brought by women	27				
Brought by men	39	8	20.5	31	79.5
Total	66				
		1790–99			
Brought by women	29				
Brought by men	66[a]	35	53.0	31	47.0
Total	95[a]				

Source: GLRO: DL/C/176–85.

[a] These figures differ from those in table 10.1 because one divorce in the 1770s and nine in the 1790s that resulted in parliamentary divorces could not be located in the London consistory manuscripts.

idea; but it must have been powerfully reinforced by the new heterosexual need to demonstrate an exclusive attraction to women; and it may be that the men who resorted to violence immediately after marriage were those who were especially intimidated by the weight of these two reinforcing norms. Some men began to beat their wives only after many years of marriage and usually after they had fallen in love with another woman. In their case, the impossibility for most men of easily receiving a divorce that allowed remarriage may have contributed to their violence. In both kinds of case the extreme violence that women often endured for years, and the encouragement that their families gave them to return to extremely abusive men, establish how necessary it was for a woman to be under a man's protection whether her idea of the family was the old patriarchal or the new romantic one. Two forms of violence did, however, slowly disappear from the consistory cases. It became unacceptable to lock a woman away in a madhouse. And the abuse of a wealthy widow by her second husband markedly declined for reasons that are complex and still speculative. One clear conclusion, however, is that the new gender roles and standards of sexual behavior that appeared in the early eighteenth century did not to any great extent lessen the role of violence in the sexual relations between men and women.[1]

SEXUAL DOMINATION AND THE NEW MARRIAGE

The number of cruelty cases in the consistory court in which both partners had married only once remained the same at the beginning and at the end of the century, with twenty cases in the first decade and nineteen in the 1790s. There was a decline in the middle of the century, with only seven cases in the 1750s. But this was probably the result of the legal strategy that encouraged some divorce cases to be brought as cases for the restitution of conjugal rights. All these cases fell into two kinds. There were husbands who from a variety of motives started to beat their wives almost immediately after the marriage began: these are the more difficult to explain. The second category is more straightforward: the men who anywhere from two to ten years after the marriage began to beat their wives when they became involved with other women. The number of both kinds of cruelty case may have remained constant. But there were differences between the two halves of the century in the situations that seem to trigger the violence of men who began to beat their wives immediately after the marriage, and it is likely that these differences were tied to the increasing influence of the ideals of romantic marriage and the tender care of children. But the social distribution of husbands who were cruel to their wives remained the same throughout the century—about a fifth were from the gentry and the remainder were in trade or in the professions—so that it would seem that the ideas of romance did not have a greater impact on the men of the elite than on the middle classes.

In the first half of the century a husband's desire for the total sexual domination of his wife and his inability to achieve it might or might not be combined with his seeing other women. Other men became violent when they perceived that their financial control of the household economy was threatened. Two men who kept public houses provide examples of the way in which a husband's need to establish his sexual domination could result in violence from the very beginning of a marriage. In the first case Robert Winch married Ann Goodwin in August 1699. He kept a well-known coffeehouse, Richard's, at the back of the Royal Exchange and made over twenty pounds a day from it. She brought a portion of at least two hundred pounds to the marriage. Within a month of the marriage he began to beat her, at first with his fists, then with a bag of farthings aimed at her head. He damned her and said he would knock her brains out; she cried, "Murder." He forced her out of bed. She ran down-stairs into the maid's room, and the maid bolted the door. He broke down the door, pulled his wife out with cries of bitch and whore, and struck her head and face and eyes. She had to use cosmetics to hide her bruises. Two months later she became pregnant, and the beatings apparently ended. But in September 1700, as she lay in bed after the delivery of her child, Winch tried to choke her. In January 1701 he bit her hand almost to the bone. She decided to go to the justice of the peace. A reconciliation began, and it was agreed that bonds would be signed. But in August, just before the signing, he knocked her down and continued to beat her until the gristle of her nose was loosened and her right eye became distorted and bloody. As he beat her he said, "Damn you, you whore, I will give you something to go before the Justice for." The maid meanwhile cried out murder. The watch entered the house and arrested Winch. He was imprisoned and the next day bound over by the lord mayor to appear in court. He was then sent back to jail. There, speaking to his friends, Winch said that he wished he had beaten his wife fifty times worse and that he would be content to be hanged for killing her. He declared that he would flatten her nose to her face, beat out the teeth in her head, and spoil her marrying with anybody else. That last phrase may perhaps provide the key to the story. Winch had married a beauty, but the sexual part of the marriage had possibly not worked in the first month, and he therefore began to beat his frustrations out on her. During her pregnancy, when the sexual relationship between spouses was usually suspended, the tension may have lessened. But immediately after the child's delivery, the physical abuse began again and grew worse when he felt further challenged by her complaint to the justice. She left him and filed for divorce with her friends' support. Winch said that as a result his business had declined because he lost his best customers, and that he could not pay his rent, for which he blamed his wife and her friends. The court granted her divorce.[2]

In a second case Thomas Briggs combined his domination of his wife with going to prostitutes. His wife Mary came from Chelsea, Briggs from Westminster. They had two children. He kept the Blue Ball alehouse in St. James's Street and made between two and three hundred pounds a year from that and from dealing in horses for noblemen and gentlemen. Briggs beat his wife so badly that on three occasions between 1751 and 1757 she had to be treated by a surgeon. He called her names, kicked her, punched her and threw things at her. He made threats against her life. He threw her out of the house and forced her to sleep in the stables and the hay crofts. He burned her face and throat with candles. He throt-

tled her as she lay in bed after childbirth. In 1751 when she was getting
into bed in her shift, he hit her with an iron candlestick that cut her eight
inches on her neck and down her back. He punched her and left one of
her eyes so swollen that she could not see out of it for days. She was
treated by a surgeon. In 1755 he threw her down in the public room of
the alehouse, kicked her in her head and sides, and beat her face until it
was "in a gore of blood." He then drove her out of the house. She was
treated by a surgeon for seventeen days. Initially her friends and relations
could recognize her only by her voice. During the last major beating in
1757, he threw her down the cellar stairs. When she landed on her face,
he called to her, "Damn you for a bitch, have I not killed you? If I have
not, I will." Then with all his force he threw an iron candlestick that hit
her in the face. She bled profusely and was under the care of a surgeon
for some time. She thought this beating would cause her death. The abuse
went on for ten years and grew worse over time. The facts are not clear,
but it probably started immediately after the marriage. During these ten
years, Briggs frequently had sex with whores: an alehouse keeper in Westminster had lots of opportunity. He contracted venereal disease and was
treated for it by a surgeon. Both Briggs and the husband from the previous
example kept public houses, and it may be that the heavy drinking and
prostitution that were often associated with such places help to explain
their sexual violence.[3]

An extravagant husband was likely to feel challenged by the economy
of his wife. Rebecca Bradford married John Austin in December 1695.
She was single and he was a widower. He later claimed that her father
had turned her out of his house for her loose character and that he had
picked her up in the streets, kept company with her, and been "drawn"
into marrying her. But he was probably lying to cover his own extravagant
behavior. She at any rate had a very different tale to tell. Austin had a
place in the Stamp Office that paid only thirty pounds a year, but he liked
to appear expansive, and to treat his friends beyond what his wife thought
prudent. Within six months of marriage she said that he dragged her out
of bed by her hair and beat her when she tried to dissuade him from giving
one of his treats. He had cursed and thrown things out the window and
awakened the house. She was persuaded to spend the rest of the night in
another woman's bed. There were other quarrels and threats to leave her.
He sent for her to come to a tavern where he was drinking with his friends
and ordered her to give him a silver spoon so that he could pawn it to
help a friend. But since she kept the money herself, he quarreled with her
and kicked her when he came home. Her father died in February 1702

and left her six thousand pounds. She asked a friend to get her husband to settle the money on her as a hedge against his extravagance, but Austin absolutely refused to make a settlement. He continued to get up at two or three or four in the morning so that he could ramble from alehouse to tavern. He would return home drunk and curse her to the pit of hell and call her bitch and whore. In April 1703 he threw a case knife at her, and in May when he tried to strangle her, she had to bite his hand until it bled and the neighbors broke in to help her. When she filed for divorce, he could only respond that she had sworn at him and bitten him (for which she had a different explanation). He added that she had run away from him. She had threatened him with being arrested—which again she probably had done as a way to stop the beatings. He had, he said, become weak from her behavior. No doubt she had challenged the expansive unreality in which he had tried to live beyond his means.[4]

In other cases a husband's violence was tied not to his wife's efforts at good housekeeping but to his desire to break up their household and free himself from any financial responsibility for her. William Bowden seems to have been helped by his own father in a war against his wife's family. Hannah Bryant married Bowden in November 1704. He was a barber and periwig maker earning £80 a year. For the first three months they lived with her parents; they then moved into a house of their own that cost £30 a year and that Bowden asked her father to furnish at a cost of £120. Once they were on their own, he began to call her names—bitch, whore, beast, monster, beggar brat, bog trotter. He cursed her father and mother and wished them damned in hell. He said he would work to make her life as uncomfortable as possible. For a month he would let her have only one meal a day while he was away; her mother and her friends fed her instead. He then beat her. He lured her out of their house, went back, locked it up, told her his goods had been seized for debt and that she would have to shift for herself. She was pregnant and frightened and nearly miscarried. At midnight he put her in a coach and sent her to her father. Bowden went to his father, and the two of them sold off the couple's household goods. When she went to his shop to get her clothes, he detained her and took her to lodgings, where she miscarried that night. He later beat her with an oak stick and with his fist and accompanied this with threats and insults. He kicked her out once more, and she returned to her father.[5]

The cases that have just been considered came from the first half of the century, when the ideals of romance and domesticity had not yet come to prevail among the landed elite and the gentlemanly part of the middle class. But in many of the cases after 1750 the power of these new ideals becomes apparent if in nothing more than the shape that women and their lawyers gave to their complaints. Even after 1750, however, a poor but pretty and amiable young woman like Mary Meredith, the sister of Sir William, could be unwisely persuaded to marry a rich nobleman like Lord Ferrers (his estates produced about eleven thousand pounds a year) even though he was a drunkard and probably quite mad. The Ferrers case is especially useful because it establishes that the behavior against wives that has been described so far would have proved a man to be mentally unbalanced if directed against anyone to whom he was not married. A rational man in eighteenth-century England could behave toward his wife in ways that only madmen behaved toward others. After two tries Lady Ferrers eventually managed to be separated from her husband by an act of Parliament (31 George II, c. 39). But Ferrers in one of his fits of anger killed his steward because he thought that he had taken his wife's part. He was tried for murder by the House of Lords, who disallowed his plea of insanity and found him guilty. He was duly executed. In his treatment of his wife, Ferrers's behavior was certainly no more extreme than that of most of the men whose wives accused them of cruelty in the consistory court. He differed from these men only because he treated other men and women in the way he treated his wife.

Within two months of the marriage Ferrers began to display irrational behavior that seems to arise from sexual jealousy and his need to establish a total domination of his wife. When Lady Ferrers was invited to a music meeting, he forbade her to go and she submitted. But at tea that day with his sister Elizabeth Shirley and her sister Ann Meredith, Ferrers became enraged and said that his wife had arranged for the invitation so that she could carry on some bad design. A male servant of nearly seventy then came in with the teakettle, a lamp, and a napkin. The napkin caught fire, and Lady Ferrers got up to put it out. Ferrers became enraged and pinched her because she had touched the servant's hand. In July of the next year when Ferrers and his wife and her sister were returning from a trip, he called the two women bitches and damned whores in front of others at an inn at Loughborough. He made his coachman get down from the coachbox, stripped him of his livery, and discharged him. He then forced the women into the coach and drove it himself along bad roads with young, untrained horses. When they were at a ball at Litchfield races, Ferrers suddenly ordered Lady Ferrers home. At their lodgings he called her a damned whore. Lady Ferrers could only burst into tears and ask him why he had accused her of impudence and indecency in a ballroom. When they played cards, Ferrers snatched his wife's cards and threw them into the fire. As he was about to strike her, Lady Ferrer's sister stopped him. He therefore pushed his wife down. When she protested that she had not deserved such treatment and could not bear it, he replied, "Damn you, you are my wife and I'll use you as I please, and since your sister has been so damned impertinent to interfere, she shall never come into my house again."

Ferrers kicked, beat, and pinched his wife when her brother did not do a piece of business for him as quickly as he expected. When they dined with his sisters, he began to pace and said to Lady Ferrers, "Damn you, why don't you go to bed? You shall not cabal with these damned bitches by God, you shall never see them again: I know you are all talking of me and laughing at me." When they denied that they were, he swore it was a damned lie. He said that if Lady Ferrers did not confess, he would murder her. He gripped her hand and, gritting his teeth, said, "I pray God of his infinite mercy to damn me to all eternity if I don't murder you tonight." On an occasion when they had company to dinner, Lady Ferrers came in from paying visits dressed in a "sack or negligee without hoops." Ferrers looked at her with scorn and indignation and said in front of her brother and the rest of the company: "A woman dressed like you looks like a whore that some fellow had picked up at the Shakespeare, lain with all night, and turned reeking out of bed at Haddock's Bagnio at eleven o'clock the next morning." Lady Ferrers could only reply that "his comparison for all she knew might be very just, but she had never seen such a creature, and hoped she never should."

During their marriage Ferrers behaved similarly to others. Constantly drunk, he carried loaded pistols in his pockets, as well as a large knife that he drew on anyone who got in his way. When he became enraged with his brother, Captain Washington Shirley, he forced one servant to bring pistols and another to load them. He then ordered the second servant to go downstairs and shoot his brother or he would blow the servant's brains out. Lady Ferrers tried to calm him. They tried to lock him in a room. He swore he would murder them, but before he could get downstairs, his brother and his wife escaped the house. When he became fond of one of his housemaids, he forced Lady Ferrers and her sister to go to the Leicester races so that he could debauch the girl. He made his attempt when she warmed his bed. The girl resisted but to escape him she had to throw herself out the window. On another night he ordered Lady Ferrers to get up and call her maid. When the woman came, Ferrers began to beat her. When Lady Ferrers got up to stop him, he said he would kill them both. He threatened to burn the room and tried to light the paper

hangings by the bed with a candle, but they would not catch fire. He
threatened his wife the rest of the night until he left to go hunting at
seven in the morning.

When Lady Ferrers eventually decided to leave Ferrers with the help
of her brother and sister, he pursued her with loaded pistols and a double-
barreled gun. He threatened to shoot his servants if they did not come
along. He forced Lady Ferrers's coach to turn around, pulled her sister
out, left her in the road, and got in himself. He then forced Lady Ferrers
to ride by horseback in the dark until they got back to his estate around
midnight. He would not allow her out of his sight. He forbade her to
have pen and paper. He threatened to kill her if she tried to escape. The
servants in fear watched constantly at the door. Her brother applied to
King's Bench for a writ of habeas corpus. Ferrers refused at first to obey
but eventually did so by surrendering Lady Ferrers to her younger brother.
In London she swore the peace against him and sued for divorce. Ferrers
continued to resist in various ways, but eventually she received her release
by an act of Parliament. Ferrers was executed in 1760, and in 1769 Lady
Ferrers made a happier second marriage.[6]

Lady Ferrers's family in the end had protected her, and other aristocratic women who in the middle decades of the century married a man
who turned out to be a rake and would not settle into marriage found
that their families would by and large protect them when they separated.
But some men did not allow marriage to change their sexual behavior
even briefly and either went to prostitutes or seduced the servants. They
might be more or less discreet in doing so, and they might accompany
their adulteries with either psychological or physical cruelty. In May 1793
John Cheetham courted and married seventeen-year-old Mary Fielding.
Soon after marriage Cheetham began to stay out at brothels until four or
five in the morning. When he returned home, he told his wife about his
sexual encounters. Eight months after the marriage he became venereally
infected. He went to a surgeon to be cured with mercury. But during the
entire cure, he forced Mary, who was pregnant, to have sex. She also
became infected. In the next year Cheetham seduced Sarah Eagling, who
was his wife's nursery maid and helped with the two children. When Eagling became pregnant Mary discharged her. Eagling bore her daughter
in the workhouse of St. Leonard Shoreditch in May 1796, and Cheetham
paid the parish officers thirty-five pounds for maintenance. In the summer
of 1796 Cheetham regularly saw different prostitutes. There was Ann
Jacobs or Wilson who worked in a brothel in Leathsellers Building, All-
hallows. And there was Harriet Brown, of whom Cheetham boasted at

home in front of the servants that he had picked up a very pretty girl and slept with her, taken her to Sadler's Wells, and had thoughts of bringing her home to be his mistress. Cheetham also took to verbally abusing his wife and striking her. In July 1796 Mary left him and went home to her parents at Tottenham.

Six months later, after Cheetham had said how sorry he was and had promised to change, Mary went back to live with him in Cheshurst, Hertford. But Cheetham had no intention of changing. He was still seeing Harriet Brown in early 1797, paying her three guineas a week, and staying with her all night. Harriet Brown became venereally infected and at Cheetham's suggestion entered St. Bartholomew's Hospital for a fortnight initially, and then for three more weeks when she discovered she had not been cured at first. Cheetham now decided that it was too dangerous for Brown to continue to see other men who might infect her again, so he "took her into keeping" at lodgings in Queen Ann Street East, Marylebone, where he gave her six guineas a week. In October Cheetham also began to see Maria Tyler who worked in the brothel kept by Isabella Anderson at 2 Berry Court, Love Lane. Mary Cheetham must now have realized that her husband would not change, and she left him again. Her agents discovered the record of Cheetham's subsequent visits to Maria Tyler: two hours on Wednesday November 15; two hours the next night; all night two days later on Saturday; and supper and all night again three days later on Tuesday. Cheetham also intended to call again on Tyler at the end of the month. But he found instead that once more he was venereally infected. So he wrote Tyler telling her that if she had not infected him, he had infected her, and that she should see a surgeon. Mary Cheetham sued her husband for divorce six months later and was granted it.[7]

It is not clear whether Mary Cheetham was in love with her husband when they married. But a woman unfortunately could fall in love with a rake and make her life a hell, as Mary Hunt did with Anthony Daffy Swinton. In this story there is a new element to the adultery. Swinton fell in love with his wife's close female friend, and his wife was never able to break the bond between the two lovers. It is the one case in which a husband's adultery parallels the adulteries of the many women who in the second half of the century were divorced for falling in love with their husbands' best male friend. Sex with the servants or with prostitutes was traditional. An affair with a good friend who visited the family was in the modern pattern of domesticated adultery. But it was something that a wife was far more likely to do than a husband. In 1786, as adolescents,

Anthony Daffy Swinton and Mary Hunt married each other twice, once at Gretna Green according to Church of Scotland rites, where underage couples could run away to be married, and once again to be sure according to the Church of England at Hornsey. Swinton was nineteen, Mary seventeen. Swinton's family were the owners of the well-known patent medicine Daffy's Elixir. From 1787 to 1790 the young couple lived in Norfolk. Swinton was from the beginning violent and adulterous. When he was bitten by one of his dogs, Mary rushed into the room to help, but at the sight of her husband's blood, she became faint. This enraged Swinton, and he tried to hit her. As Mary ran out of the room, he threw a knife that struck her in the back. Mary was in advanced pregnancy, and this brought on her labor. The child was born dead, and she was in danger herself for some time. On other occasions Swinton punched her so violently that she fell to the ground, where he kicked her in the stomach even though she was pregnant. Swinton also seduced the female servants. Mary Denny swore her child to him before a justice at Lynn, and Swinton had to give a bond to support the child. It turned out that she had twins. Swinton then had sex with the cook in the poultry room and the dairy. She also had a child whom Swinton acknowledged and supported. But Swinton did not neglect his wife. Mary became pregnant again. After one delivery, Swinton came into her room and damned her and the child in front of the nurse and the servants. He also beat Mary around the room in front of their guests—all of which left her ill.

In 1789 Mary invited Ann Moore, a young unmarried friend of hers, to visit. Swinton seduced Ann and ran away with her to London. After Mary went up to London to see him, she was persuaded by her affection for him and her concern for her children to forgive him. But she stipulated that they must move to London (her family was there) and that Swinton must send Ann Moore back to her father in Norfolk. Swinton agreed, but Mary was never to be free of Ann Moore. In London Swinton continued to beat her, and when they took a house in Kent, he seduced another young woman. But he also (without Mary's knowledge) brought Ann Moore from Norfolk to London and installed her in lodgings at a tobacconist's, where Ann bore his son. In April 1791 for reasons that are not clear, Swinton and his wife moved to Bruges and then to Brussels. He continued to beat Mary. He also sent for Ann Moore. In January 1793 Swinton was imprisoned in Brussels. When Mary visited him, he beat her and would not let her stay with him. Instead Ann Moore visited him until the magistrate noticed and forbade it. Mary secured her husband's release in February, but she had decided not to live with him again.

Mary and Swinton returned separately to England. From 1793 to 1796 Swinton was imprisoned for debt first at Maidstone and then in London. Ann Moore lived with him in both places, and when Swinton was released they continued the arrangement. During these years Mary supported herself. But in December 1797 when she was in distress, she appealed to Swinton. Swinton by then was doing very well as one of a growing number of druggists. He had a business in Fleet Street from which he sold his family's nostrum, Daffy's Elixir. He made over five hundred pounds a year from this in addition to his general business as a druggist, from which he earned at least another three hundred pounds a year. Swinton spurned his wife's appeal. Mary therefore filed a suit for restitution of conjugal rights. The same day Swinton came with two men and a cart and took away Mary's goods and bedding. Mary he put in a back garret of his lodgings and secured her with a chain and padlock. When Ann Moore tried to persuade him to let her give Mary some necessaries, he refused. He swore that Mary would never come out alive and that he would shave her head the next day. He said that she must be mad since she otherwise would never have allowed him to get his clutches on her again. When Ann Smith came to see Mary, Swinton told her that "he had caged the damned bitch . . . and that she should never get out of her cage again alive." But the next day Mary's father William Hunt came and insisted on seeing her. Hunt obtained a warrant for assault from an alderman, Swinton was taken into custody, and Mary was freed. Swinton was jailed and found guilty at the next quarter sessions, but Mary agreed not to punish him if he gave a bond to keep the suit for restitution. But the marriage was clearly over. Swinton went back to living with Ann Moore, and Mary sued for divorce.[8]

Marriage to a rake was clearly dangerous, but women whose marriages were founded on the new domesticity did not necessarily fare better. At the center of the new ideal stood the figure of the pregnant wife and the mother who did not use a wet nurse but suckled her child herself. It must have been the case, however, that women in either of those two situations aroused in some husbands intensely negative feelings since they were likely to be sexually unavailable during their pregnancies and preoccupied with their infants to the exclusion of their husbands. The husband who systematically beat his pregnant wife, tormented her as she nursed, and alienated the affections of her children became a fixture of the divorce cases. There are two cases to consider. In the first, the protagonist, Benjamin Brogden, was a man-midwife whose professional role was itself one of the more controversial parts of the new domestic system. Such a man claimed that he had a technical knowledge about childbirth superior to that of the traditional midwife. Many husbands and wives employed these men-midwives to guarantee the safety of the mother and child. But to others the man-midwife violated the chastity of women and was more likely to butcher babies with his instruments than to save them. A year before Brogden married Anna Maria Wade, as an example of these tensions, a brawl broke out at a meeting of the Royal College of Physicians between Dr. Frank Nicholls and Dr. Robert Nesbitt after Nicholls attacked the competence of men-midwives like Nesbitt and said they "were of no profession." Nesbitt took Nicholls by the collar and struck him with his fists. Nesbitt was then pulled down into a chair by others while Nicholls kicked and struck him until he was pulled back himself.[9] The man-midwife in this consistory divorce case was clearly something of an operator. Brogden's future wife Anna Maria lived with her mother in Queen Square in 1754. Her father was insane. Anna Maria had twelve hundred pounds in South Sea annuities as her fortune. Brogden "got himself introduced" and courted her. Mrs. Wade, however, refused her consent to her daughter's marriage when Brogden would not agree to a proposed marriage settlement. She forbade Brogden to visit, but he continued to see Anna Maria privately. They were married in December 1754 when she was twenty-one. Brogden had a considerable practice that brought in two to five hundred pounds a year. At the time of the divorce one servant described Brogden's patients as persons of rank and fortune; but his maid said that they were persons "in a middling station"; and a third servant added that she had never known Brogden to be "averse to his going to attend a labour when he was sent for." He rented two houses: one in Frith Street at £135 and another in the country at Lipson Green for £28.

Within four months of the marriage, in April 1755, Brogden began to beat his wife. When they were in bed he would kick and beat her. When she fled to the maid's room, he dragged her back to their own and beat her again. But this man-midwife began to beat his wife in earnest once she became pregnant in December. (He must have delivered babies by day and come home to beat his pregnant wife at night.) A man who lodged in the house was awakened by Anna Maria's screams at night. On a Sunday afternoon this lodger rushed into the parlor and found her weeping bitterly in a chair as Brogden stood over her with a raised fist. Six weeks before her delivery, Brogden blackened her eye, and she wore a patch to hide it. Three weeks before delivery, he pinched her in bed so violently that she had to wear gloves to hide the marks. (She spent that night running back and forth to the maid's room for protection.) Two weeks before delivery her maid ran into the parlor to find her stretched out across the chairs and Brogden beating her. Brogden took her to St. James Park and then forced her to find her way home in the dark. She arrived to find him smiling. When she asked how he could treat her that way, he punched her in the head.

Once their son was born, Brogden began to use the child's presence as part of his wife's torture. He questioned her as to the amount she had given away at her churching and began to beat her in her head as she nursed the child at her breast. She begged him for God's sake not to hurt the child, which only made him try to pull the boy from her by his head. She knocked on the floor for a servant, who came to take the child. Brogden then flung Anna Maria to the floor and beat her until he was quite tired. He finished by pouring a large bottle of water over her. There were other beatings in which he tore her ear until it bled, hit her in the breast with tongs, and banged her head against the wainscot. He beat her one day as she held the child in her arms. The child became so frightened that it screamed and nearly went into fits. To frighten her, Brogden would snatch the child from her arms, hold him up by his head as though to drop him, and then shake the boy who cried all the while. He was probably expert at holding children by their heads from his experience in delivering children. When the boy was eating cake or sugar, Brogden took it away and ate it himself to make the boy cry and to torment his wife. All this while Anna Maria was reluctant to complain to her mother and her family since she had married against their advice and because she was concerned for her son. She also must have continued to have sex with Brogden, since by December 1757, when her son was seventeen months old, she was pregnant again. Anna Maria, however, had had enough. She left her husband on December 17 and filed for divorce in April. By the end of the year it was granted with costs of forty pounds and alimony of twenty pounds a year. Who kept her son is unclear.[10]

The second case that can be tied to the new world of domesticity brings together all the themes of sexual jealousy and domination, contempt for women, and the determination to destroy a woman's hopes for domestic happiness. Abraham Adams married Sophia Downing in 1787 when they were both twenty-one. They lived at Bayswater, and he had an income of about five hundred pounds from a number of coach houses and stables that he owned. The marriage lasted ten years, during which they had five children, two boys and three girls. From the very beginning Adams abused his wife with foul language that terrified her and sent her into hysteric fits. The physical violence began during her first pregnancy in May 1788, when she was close to delivery. He tried to strangle her in their bedroom, but the nurse in attendance heard Sophia's screams and forced open the door to help her. Over the next four years (during which she bore a second child) he knocked her down with his fist several times and told her he would have to kick her out of the house. He also threatened her with a loaded gun and a large knife when she was in bed, saying that he would either blow her brains out or rip her up. This usually frightened her so much that she went into hysteric fits. The bedroom setting guaranteed that there would usually be no one else there to stop him, but it also probably fed Adams's sexual excitement. Throughout the ten years of abuse, the couple certainly continued to have sex, as the record of Sophia's pregnancies attests. Sophia was pregnant a third time in 1793, and once again Adams attacked her violently and tormented her during her meals.

In 1794 Adams's violence peaked. In April while they were at breakfast, he tried to pour boiling water from the kettle down her bosom. When the charwoman stopped him, he tore Sophia's cloak and bonnet to pieces instead. In July he threw himself on top of her in bed and tried to smother her with a pillow. He pinched and bruised her stomach and bit her arms and sides so hard that he left the imprint of his teeth: all of this was probably sexually charged for him. It occurred over two nights. On the third morning he tried to force her out of a second-story window. The entire summer of 1794 passed this way. He spat in her face. He threatened to throw her petticoats over her head and expose her to the first man who would come to the door. He ran up to her with clenched fists and said "how ardently he wished to rip her bowels out and that he would not care to be hanged for it and that he would never cease using every aggravation and cruelty until he had either broke her heart or driven her into a state of madness." By the end of the summer Adams had succeeded in his second aim. Sophia was delirious and out of her mind. When she was confined to bed, he ordered the house to be unroofed and repaired. When she complained of the noise, he called one of the carpenters into her bedroom and let him beat Sophia with a stick. Her doctor found her much worse the next day, inquired the cause, and wrote Adams a letter of protest. On August 13 Sophia fell down the stairs as she fled from Adams who then kicked her out into the street. At the advice of her friends, Sophia got a Middlesex justice of the peace to swear the peace against Adams. But after Adams promised to behave, she did not proceed with the legal action. Adams, of course, immediately began his abuse again. At first it was psychological. He told her that he "knew how to baffle all law since he could at any time procure a fellow for three guineas who would swear anything he should request" so that he could thereby accuse her of adultery. He then attacked what must have been the tattered shreds of her domestic security. He said he would introduce a mistress into the house. He threatened to give her for support only what the parish gave a pauper. He taught his two sons to call her a damned bitch and a gallows' whore. He sent one child to her with a cord to tell her that he had brought it so that she could hang herself.

Three months later, in November, when Sophia was pregnant for the fourth time, Adams began to beat her once more. The child was born in June 1795, and since Sophia was too sick to nurse it, she was soon pregnant again and was delivered of her fifth child, a girl, in July 1796. Three weeks later Adams attacked Sophia as she was rocking this last child. He came from behind and struck her and then threw a quarter-pound pot full of water that hit her in the head and knocked her out. The nursemaid told him to leave. He struck her, and she took him to court. On another occasion he destroyed all the tea "equipage" in front of a guest and punched Sophia several times when he came home and could not find his dog. But Adams seemed to concentrate his attacks on Sophia at those moments when she cared for her new infant. This suggests that Adams deeply resented his wife's attention to their children, which he must have seen as so much less for himself. He especially resented the presence of his daughters. He kicked Sophia down the stairs as she held the infant and locked them out in the street. Sophia said that she had to struggle not to go into a hysteric fit, which would have left her unable to care for the child. In July when the girl was eleven months old, Sophia took the child with her to bed to suckle her. Adams came in and called the child a devil. He then exposed the child and would not allow her back in bed. The next morning he told Sophia that "he would take care of his sons George and Samuel but as to the three other children who were girls, and his said wife, they might go to Hell and be damned, for he did not care about them." Sophia must now have been near the end of her endurance. The next day Adams (who was clearly out of control) jumped up at dinner and threatened to blow out her brains with two pistols he had. A friend who was dining stopped him. But Sophia, on the advice of her friends, had decided to leave Adams. On that very day she took her youngest child and went to her father at Enfield. A year later she filed for divorce. One hopes that Sophia managed to put together some kind of a new life for herself. But it is apparent from her case and the others in this section that for some men of her social class neither romantic marriage nor the domesticity that followed had modified the violence that reinforced the male domination out of which their sexual fantasies grew.[11]

Violence, Adultery, and the Established Marriage

In the second half of the cases brought by women who sought to end what was a first marriage, the men had begun to beat their wives anywhere from two to ten years after the marriage and usually because they had become involved with another woman. These wives usually had spent a number of years in childbearing and must often have lost their charms. But unfortunately for them, they were often still very much in love with their husbands, as was Jane Adams. As Jane Neville she was courted in 1728 and 1729 by William Adams, whose first wife had died the previous year. They were married in July 1729 and consummated the marriage, but they agreed to keep it secret a while from her father. She returned to her father's house in Newport, Shropshire, for the next five months. They then openly acknowledged their marriage, lived together, and in three years had three children. A year after the birth of the third child, Adams failed in business. They gave up their house and separated, and she went for a year with the children to live at her father's, where Adams visited them two or three times a week. After Adams settled his affairs, they took a house together again, and two more children were born. In 1736 they moved to London, where Adams had managed to secure a place in the customhouse as the examiner of duties on wines and currants. There was later a good deal of acrimony as to what the salary was. It was originally forty pounds a year, but by the 1740s it was augmented to eighty pounds. There were also perquisites of ten pounds and some other fees, so that in all it must have been worth one hundred pounds. Adams hired a clerk and paid him twenty pounds out of the total, so that he himself only went to the office occasionally (its regular hours were from 9:30 to 1:30) and on no schedule. In the afternoon when they were free, Adams and his clerk worked for merchants who paid them as well. Adams was therefore able to keep a single-horse carriage and to have a servant in livery. He also had various pieces of property in Shropshire and money in the funds and other securities. Once the marriage broke down, Jane began to make her living by running a business as a mantua maker with her sisters, from which her husband said she made at least one hundred pounds a year; but one of her customers said that her gowns were not well made and that she doubted that Jane could save from her business.

Two years after they moved to London, and ten years after they were married, Adams met Ann Johnson. She was a widow whose first husband had been a trussmaker in Little Britain, and she continued the business. Adams and Johnson became lovers, and soon after he began to beat his wife. The lovers were seen together by Adams's eldest son, who told his mother. When Jane spoke to Adams about the affair, he flew into a rage. He called her "a long chin picked-nose bitch." Her servant said that Jane meekly replied with tears in her eyes, "Well, well, I was once reckoned as handsome as Whore Johnson." In response Adams threw a book at her that cut her eye and made the blood gush. But he would not allow her to get help, and she lost the sight in the eye. He then went upstairs and came back with his penknife, which he sharpened on the stairs. He called her into the parlor to come and "kill or be killed." She replied, "Aye, with all my heart I would choose to die by your hand." But her servant stopped her from going to him. The next Sunday he told her that if she asked him for one penny, he would blind the other eye and beat out her brains. He then beat her with his horsewhip even though she was pregnant.

Adams now more or less began to live entirely with Ann Johnson in her lodgings in Little Britain. They also rented a house in the countryside at Finchley where Johnson passed as his wife. (Adams later tried to pretend that his marriage to Jane had never occurred, but he did not get far with that.) Johnson became pregnant. She and Adams had an intense sexual life. Rebecca Woodward, a married woman who served as Johnson's cookmaid for five months, said that she had seen the couple together in bed, and "that they were two of the most lewd and debauched persons she ever met with for filthy and obscene talking." She had heard Johnson "in a very immodest manner boast in a morning after she had come down how much Mr. Adams had pleased her, and that he had given her a good bout, and she wished she might prove with child by him." Adams's increasing pleasure with Johnson only seemed, however, to increase his fury against his wife. He went to her house and took away all the furniture, and forbade the baker, the brewer, and the butcher to give her any credit. Ten months later Jane Adams sued for divorce. It took six years for the case to be resolved, but in 1752 she was awarded her divorce with twenty pounds alimony a year.[12]

Adultery was probably the most disruptive when it had had time to develop in the midst of familial intimacy—when a man seduced his wife's younger sister. Incestuous fantasy in the eighteenth century centered around the sibling tie at least as much as around the parental. The wife's sister and the brother's wife were powerfully charged figures. This was in part because the nature of English kinship made the sibling tie the strongest of bonds. But domesticity also sentimentalized the wife's sister in a new kind of way. It was proposed throughout the eighteenth and the nineteenth centuries that if a wife died, her husband could hope to find no better new mother for their young children than her own sister. This was especially appealing to the middle classes, who viewed marriage as an alliance that could be maintained by remarriage. It was opposed by the aristocracy, who preferred to legitimate cousin marriage (which was often shocking to the middle classes) and to treat marriage as an act of incorporation. Bourgeois marriage in the course of the eighteenth century came to forbid a widow's remarriage but attempted to legitimate a widower's remarriage to his wife's sister. When such marriages occurred, they were, however, illegal. In the first decade of the century they were still occasionally brought to the consistory and declared null and void. But those that probably occurred later are almost impossible to trace since the consistory ceased to be a forum for seeking out the sinner.

In the first decade of the consistory records consulted, Henry Yeamans married his wife's sister in 1699 in St. Stephen's, Coleman Street, a year after his wife's death. Thomas Taylor married his wife's sister within a few months of his wife's death in 1702, and John Bull's marriage to his sister-in-law was declared null in 1709. John Quick wrote against such marriages in 1703 because he said he knew of four men of "quality" in the city who were involved in these sinful marriages. In this context it becomes apparent why the magistrate should have sent Grace Benjamin to Bridewell in 1719 for living with her sister's husband. The man, of course, went unpunished since the intention must have been to send him back to his wife.[13]

A case of incestuous adultery with a sister-in-law from the end of the century a illustrates how such behavior could lead to divorce. John Dance married and courted Catherine Anne Dawes in 1791, when they were both single and twenty-one. By the time of their divorce seven years later Dance was making about twelve hundred pounds a year as a fruiterer in Oxford Street and had about five thousand pounds in securities. In 1796 he bought the business from his father-in-law, agreeing to pay an annuity of eighty pounds for three years, then sixty pounds for three more, and after that forty pounds for life. As part of the arrangement he was to employ his wife's brother James Dawes and her younger sister Jane Dawes, who came to live with Dance and his wife. Shortly thereafter Dance began to fight with his wife. In front of the servants Dance hit Catherine on her head, face, neck and breasts. He knocked her down and kicked her. He humiliated her by ordering the servants not to obey her. He threatened her with candlesticks, shovels, and pokers. He turned her out of the shop. He refused to sleep in the same bed or the same room with her. Six months after this change of behavior, a servant revealed its cause to Catherine.

Dance had begun to have an affair with Jane Dawes. Jane was seen coming out of Dance's room in only her shift and without shoes by a servant to whom she said "don't tell." Jane had shared a bed with this servant and had frequently wanted them to rise early so that she could go into her brother-in-law's room. It was this servant who revealed the affair to her mistress; she was fired by her master for doing so. Before it all came out, Dance took a house at Sudbury Green so that he and Jane could sleep together more easily. Jane's brother John had seen her stand in the parlor and the kitchen without her handkerchief, lacing her stays in front of Dance, who instead of rebuking her, laughed and joked with her about it, to her stricter brother's surprise. Other servants saw the couple kiss and Dance put his hand into Jane's bosom. Jane was clearly more carefree than her brother or her married sister, who usually went out on Monday and Wednesday evenings to "attend divine service at chapel." For five months after Catherine was told of the affair, Jane Dawes stayed in the house. In October Jane was sent to her father's house in Sussex, where Dance secretly corresponded with her. In December Catherine left her husband because of his violence. His adultery she apparently had found more tolerable. In the following May she sued for divorce and was granted it a year later. Her brother John was set up by their father as a fruiterer in a shop directly opposite her husband's. Catherine helped her brother in the new shop and stole many of her husband's customers. Dance said that his wife and her brother had declared that they intended to ruin him. Catherine Dance ended the quarrel by bringing her case to the consistory. She clearly had the support of her family against her younger sister, and there is no evidence that she had been passionately in love with her husband, as poor Jane Adams had been with hers. But both these women (and all the others who brought similar cases) had had to swallow after many years of marriage the bitter pill of rejection for a younger, more attractive woman.[14]

THE INCARCERATED WIFE AND THE REMARRYING WIDOW

The men who sought to dominate their wives by violence from the beginning of their marriages, and the men who became violent as a result of their distaste for an old wife once they had acquired a new lover appear throughout the eighteenth century. There does not seem to have been any notable changes in either pattern of behavior except perhaps that after midcentury the dedication of some women to the new ideals of romance and domesticity gave their husbands a new weapon with which to torment them. But two kinds of violent behavior did lessen and more or less disappear from the consistory cases. At the beginning of the century there were husbands who, in a display of a patriarchal power more daunting than mere beating, declared their wives mentally unbalanced and imprisoned them in madhouses. Some of the women escaped through their own initiative and sometimes with the help of their families. By midcentury, probably as a result of the new ideals of romance and domesticity, there was revulsion against this practice; laws were passed that made it more difficult to do; and by the 1790s a wife who was threatened by her husband in this way could use the law to hold the madhouse-keepers at bay.

The widow who married a second and often younger husband who then abused her either to squeeze her money out of her or to assert his manhood in the face of her attempts to dominate him with her wealth is the second kind of case that gradually disappeared from the consistory. These cases had made up exactly a third of all the cruelty cases in the first decade of the eighteenth century (ten of thirty). By the 1750s they were only two out of nine cases, and by the 1790s only one case out of twenty could be classified in this way, and the violence in it was minor compared to the cases at the beginning of the century. The level of violence in other cruelty cases continued much the same throughout the century, although it may have been triggered by different causes in the first and second halves of the century. How is the disappearance of the rich widow to be explained? There are a number of possibilities. Widows may have stopped remarrying, either because they were faithful to a husband's memory or because they wished to protect the rights of their children from a stepfather. Women may also have entered second marriages after making legal settlements that could not be easily shaken. It may also be possible that there were not as many rich widows because husbands had ceased to make their wives their heirs. Finally it may have begun to seem dishonorable for a man to financially exploit a woman in this way, especially when the marriage was between an older woman and a younger man whom she had married for his charms.

At the beginning of the century men fantasized about locking away an erring or an inconvenient wife and sometimes actually did so. William Durant told his wife Margaret that she behaved as badly as the German princess, the wife of the future George I, who had been locked away for adultery; and it is quite likely that he was thinking of having her locked away for the dishonor that she had caused him by flirting with an army officer. Failing that, he beat her.[15] Two other husbands in the first decade of the century incarcerated their wives in the same notorious madhouse

at Wood Close, Islington, which James Newton ran. In the first case, Jane
Cherry had married Richard Cherry in Magdalen College chapel, Oxford,
in 1694. She brought a portion of over seven hundred pounds. He was a
confectioner, making over one hundred pounds a year at the time of the
divorce. They lived together happily for four years. But then Cherry seems
to have lost interest and to have begun to go to whores. He apparently
decided to get rid of his wife and locked her up in Newton's madhouse.
Jane was released through the intervention of her family and friends, but
she returned to her husband, who would come home early in the morning
and beat her. When she became ill, her husband employed an apothecary
whom she distrusted: she lost her sight and blamed a plot between her
husband and the apothecary. Her family intervened again and Cherry
signed a bond to treat his wife well. In the bond he agreed not to go to
whores any more. He had contracted venereal disease and had been treated
for it three times while his wife was locked away in the madhouse. The
disease had broken out on his genitals and his nose. Jane had herself
washed out his clothes so that the servants would not know of his infection. But Cherry disregarded the bond. He now locked his wife up in a
room at home. He chained her to the floor next to her bed, and made
her lie in bed chained by the leg. When she broke the chain with the help
of her nurse, he got a heavier chain. When the apothecary prescribed
medicine, he asked that Jane should be unchained while it purged her,
but her husband forced her to remain in bed. He told her friends that she
was raving mad when they tried to see her. But she got a letter out to
them. They complained to a justice of the peace, and she was able to leave
and go to a friend's house. After ten years of marriage, for five of which
she had been mistreated, her divorce was granted, with alimony of twenty-
five pounds a year, and eight pounds in costs.[16]

In the second case John Edwards and some associates "trepanned" his
wife Dorothy into Newton's madhouse. He at first agreed to give Newton
twenty shillings a week and later contracted for forty pounds a year if he
would keep her for life. Edwards seems to have visited Dorothy twice in
the madhouse. On the first occasion he took away her diamond ring, her
silver snuffbox, and her tortoiseshell case by force and kicked and beat
her. The episode seems to have ended when she had a convulsive fit. On
another occasion he told her that he would make settlements on their
children if she gave up her jointure. She refused once more. So he threatened her and beat her and ordered her to be locked up in a dark room
again. At some point she was given a medicine "to deprive her of her
senses." But after nineteen days in the madhouse, she managed to escape.

She sued and was granted her divorce with alimony of forty pounds a year—what it would have cost to keep her in Newton's madhouse.[17]

Public opinion turned against these practices in the middle four decades of the century. James Newton and his madhouse became the subject of a case in 1728 in which the court declared that a man might reasonably confine his wife in his own house but not in a madhouse. By 1754 proposals for legislation to control private madhouses were being made. A select committee of the House of Commons was appointed in 1763 and finally an act regulating the London madhouses was passed in 1774, extended in 1779, and made perpetual in 1786. The difference the act made can be seen in the 1790s, when Edward Eagleton tried to confine his wife in a madhouse so that he could better enjoy his mistress. Eagleton married Elizabeth D'Rippe in 1782 when he was twenty-one and she was twenty-eight. The marriage lasted eleven years, and they had eight children. By the time of the divorce in 1793 Eagleton was a very well off tea dealer making nearly twelve thousand pounds a year from a trade throughout Britain. He was well known for his innovative marketing and advertising. He had agents and warehouses at Norwich, Birmingham, Leicester, Derby, Bath, Evesham, Gloucester, Newberry, Liverpool, Manchester, Monmouth, Andover, Lymington, Gosport, Glasgow, Exeter, Hereford, Brecknock, Edinburgh, Portsea, Ross, and Southhampton. Four or five times a year Eagleton traveled to supervise his trade. In 1790 after eight years of marriage he met Elizabeth Coventry on his way home and started an affair with her. When his friends learned of it, he arranged for Elizabeth to be apprenticed as a milliner at Worcester, where he visited her. But Elizabeth's mistress insisted that she leave once she learned the nature of the arrangement. Eagleton therefore began to travel with Elizabeth as his wife, taking her with him to Birmingham, Leicester, Gloucester, and Newport. When his wife visited her relations in May 1792, he brought his mistress home. He then took lodgings for her in Kent and visited her daily. But he could not get the lease of the house because its owner had discovered that Elizabeth was his mistress. Eagleton therefore found a place for her in Vauxall. Elizabeth bore his children, of whom one daughter survived.

As the affair took over his life, Eagleton began to mistreat his wife. He beat her and tried to turn her out of the house. He threatened her with death and told her that a howling dog was the presage of her end. He said that if he could not get her out by fair means or ill usage, he would send her to a private madhouse where her friends would not be able to help her. In August 1793 he asked Thomas Warburton (a quack who kept a series of madhouses at Bethnal Green that were notorious for improperly detaining people and mistreating them) to come and bring someone with him to look after his wife, who was insane. When a couple arrived from the madhouse, Elizabeth Eagleton rang for a servant who threatened her husband into being quiet. She then explained the situation to the two visitors. They asked if they might stay to observe her for a day or two since they had come with orders to confine her and put her in a straitwaistcoat. The couple found her sane and apologized. They advised her to apply to a magistrate. She did so, and the lord mayor bound her husband for one thousand pounds to keep the peace with her. She then left him and three months later filed for a divorce, which was granted. She had been saved from the madhouse but was thrust out of her marriage. Without the madhouse Eagleton had achieved his goal. He was ever the daring entrepreneur.[18]

Men who were entrepreneurs of a different kind than Eagleton married widows. But these widows were often women of some initiative themselves. When they were very self-confident, they sometimes attempted to dominate a younger husband whom they viewed as a social inferior, and if as well they considered these men as sexual objects whom they had to some extent bought, then the mixture of emotions could become quite volatile. Sarah Bishop's marriage to a poor younger man failed because she emphasized his dependence and humiliated him. In 1691 she was a young widow with a daughter eight years old and a son of eighteen months. Her first husband had been a leather gilder, and she had inherited the trade with his apprentices and journeymen. One of the journeymen was John Mould, and she married him. But Sarah was contemptuous of Mould. She told him in front of their servants that "she had made her dishcloute her tablecloth." She struck him and pulled off his hat and his periwig. She flew in his face and tore at his hair when he advised her or disciplined the servants or the children. She said she knew of no duty a wife had to a husband. She encouraged her friends to call Mould a pitiful fellow and told them that Mould had not had sixpence in the world and would have remained a journeyman all his life had he not married Sarah. Mould responded in kind. He said that he could be as cruel as he pleased and do what he liked to his wife, except kill her, for there was no law to stop him, since if he crippled his wife, he simply had to keep her.[19]

When Ann Stewart and John Ryves married half a century later in 1745 there was a similar dynamic, though Ann was a richer woman than Sarah Bishop and even more independent and tempestuous. Ann was a rich widow; Ryves had been the tutor to her children. She had made the first overtures about marriage to him. But Ann was determined to keep control of her property. Four days before the marriage a settlement was made that gave her all her property except for fifty pounds a year. She had a jointure of 250 pounds a year from her late husband Alexander Stewart, the interest on fifteen thousand pounds, and a Jamaican estate left to her by her grandmother that brought in four thousand pounds a year. Ann was also unwilling to take any vow that limited her freedom. At the marriage ceremony she refused to pronounce the word obey, and in their subsequent disputes, she often told her husband that since she had not promised to obey him, she was not bound to do so and would not. When she left him, in a neat reversal of the usual situation, she took all the money and ordered the butcher, the baker, and the brewer not to give him any credit so that he was unable to provide for himself and the five servants in the household. Ryves was arrested for her debts of three thousand pounds and had to hide to avoid the creditors. He was able to go out only after the duke of St. Albans made him a servant in his family and thereby gave him immunity from arrest for debt. Ann had been obliged to borrow because her relations as well as those of her dead husband disapproved of her marriage to Ryves, and her father Dr. Alexander Stewart had held up the payments from the Jamaica estate. The dispute was taken to Chancery and not yet resolved when the marriage broke up. Ryves said that Ann's relatives had threatened him with hostile, anonymous messages. He was told that someone had been hired to kill him. As part of this intimidation, John McAllister came into their house five months after the marriage and broke his arm. Ryves began to carry a pistol for protection, and when he forgot to take it, Ann would bring it to him or send a servant with it. But when they started to quarrel, Ann used the episode against him. "You cowardly villain," she had told him, "I have got the pistol to shoot you; if you had not been a coward, your arm had not been broken. I wish John McAllister was here, I would give him thirty guineas to break the other arm."

The couple began to quarrel seriously in July 1748, three years after the marriage. It escalated for four years until she left him in March 1752 and sued for divorce in June. She charged him with cruelty. He admitted that he had occasionally beaten her, but he insisted that it was not severely and that it was within the bounds of due correction. It is also apparent that Ann was openly contemptuous of her husband, that she used her financial power against him, and that she refused to sleep with him when he wanted her to. Ann in fact had a violent temper. Once when she was angry with her five-year-old daughter, she ordered the nursery maid to bring a pan of red-hot coals. She then held the child's hand in the pan until all the skin was burned off. Eight years later there was still a scar to be seen.

The couple in their statements to the court disputed what had occurred in a dozen incidents from the four years of fighting. In July 1748 Ann said that when they were going to bed, Ryves had pinched her and driven her around the room for hours. He claimed that she flew into a rage when he insisted that they go to bed. She took off her dress and threw it in his face. A lead in the sleeve hit him in the forehead, so he took her by the wrists and seated her on a chair. In October 1749 Ann said he boxed her on the ear and beat her with a horsewhip on her neck, shoulders, and arms. She was so bruised that for a fortnight she could not lift her hands to her head. Ryves said the episode began when he employed a man to clear a vault and lay in coals. He sent a servant to ask for the man's pay of a half-crown. She became enraged and said that if he employed people without her leave, she would not pay them and that Ryves could rot in jail. After this he was out of sorts for a few days. But when he said he was going to play the violin, she answered that if he would not speak to her, he would have no music: she locked the music room and kept the key, which he then took from her. She dropped to her knees and called upon God to strike John Ryves dead with thunder. She called him a beggarly dog and said she had done him the honor to raise him out of the dunghill to her bed. But when she called his mother a vile whore, he struck her slightly three or four times with a horsewhip but not hard enough to make her bleed, as she had claimed. In fact two days later she accompanied him on the harpsichord in front of their guests, kissed him after they had left, and asked him whether she didn't play well.

Ann began to sleep apart from Ryves in 1750 as a further challenge, no doubt, to his sexual control. She used a room above his and put a padlock on the staircase door when they were in the country. In London he frequently asked her to come back into his bed and threatened to pull down the tester bed in which she slept. On the same night that he forbade her to visit Dorothy and Mary Murray, who he thought were his enemies, he insisted that she should sleep with him. During the night he saw a shadow and started up for a pistol. She said that he had pointed the pistol at her head when he thought she was asleep, but that she had shouted, "You villain, you are going to murder me," and had called for the servants. When Ann got up and cursed him, he slapped her. She fled to the housekeeper's room. He went for her and brought her back with the help of the housekeeper's persuasion. She said that after this he confined her to the house. He replied that she had had guests.

In March 1751 after a violent quarrel she applied to the lord chief justice for a warrant against him. The quarrel began after she returned from visiting Sally Clark, who Ryves thought caused quarrels between them. Ann banged on the harpsichord; he threatened to smash it with a poker. She brandished another poker at him; he took it away and told her to go up to her dressing room instead of provoking him. She came down with a walking stick and struck him, saying, "You villain, you shall see I can fight as well as you can." She ran back up and returned with a pistol. He took it away. As he sat reading at his desk, she rushed in and said that she wanted to provoke him to strike her and spat in his face. He wiped it away with his handkerchief and told her that it was the gravest insult a gentleman could receive, but that since she wished to vent her rage, she could spit on his hand, which he stretched out to her. She took it with both of hers and spat on it and on his face again and again. The maidservant knelt down and asked her to stop. Ryves took a small cane and struck her two or three times on her back and shoulders.

She left the house after this but later returned. She claimed that he now began to demand to see her marriage settlement and threatened to make her burn her settlement if she did not give him a thousand pounds a year. When she objected, she said that he told her that he had a right as her husband to treat her as he pleased and that he had an absolute power over her person. He denied asking for the money or saying that he had an absolute power over her. He had simply reminded her of her duty and had rebuked her for not promising to obey him when they were married. But he probably had asked for one thousand pounds to be settled on him and to have his debts paid. Helena Brett, who otherwise supported his version of events, said that she heard him ask for this, and that he had told his wife that she did not know the power of an English husband, and that her settlement ought to be burned.

These painful arguments ended on a note of farce. Ann said that Ryves accused her of flirting out of the window of her dressing room with a Life Guardsman (or soldier) in the street. He forced her to shut up the window and to dress herself by candlelight in the daytime. She said that he also told her that she had been a whore from the age of eleven and that he could count nineteen men she had whored with. Ryves denied calling her a whore. He said that he had learned that several horse grenadiers used to frequent an alehouse with a window that looked into the window of his wife's dressing room, and that the soldiers would stay at the alehouse for hours especially when his wife was dressing. He was told this by several neighbors. He therefore asked Ann to keep her curtains drawn. She became angry and shut the windows. The soldiers had begun to call his house "Fun-Corner."[20]

Ann Stewart was clearly able to take care of herself. But an older woman like Elizabeth Wywall fared less well when she surrendered to the charms of a beautiful man and married someone much younger than herself. Her first husband, a wholesale tobacconist, had died in 1745 and left her all his estate, which amounted to seventy-seven pounds a year in land in Kent and Sussex and five hundred pounds in money and goods. They had lived in a house at Dulwich. She had married him in 1741 after her parents' death (for whom she had probably cared) when she was about forty. After five years as a widow, she was courted by William Peirse and married him after settling her property on him. Peirse was a young man of twenty-six. Within a year of the marriage, he left her for a younger woman and told her in a letter that he had been "very base" to himself "ever to consent to think of a marriage with you, so different in years, and so monstrous in temper." But Elizabeth's "pride and vanity deserves much worse usage, to expect that a woman of your age, almost old enough for my mother's mother, should spend her days with a young fellow of about twenty-six."

Peirse had the backing of his own parents in what looks like a determined scheme to trick the old widow out of her money. After the marriage, the couple had lived briefly in her former husband's house and then went to Peirse's father in Cloth Fair. They later took a house in Hatton Gardens that was furnished with furniture from the house of Elizabeth's first husband. After a supper at an attorney's, Peirse sent his wife back to his father's but told her he would go to their new house to guard the plate. Instead he sent for Priscilla Edwards, a married woman with a husband in Shropshire and a whore in London living in Theobald Court. When the servant whom Peirse sent for Priscilla told Peirse's mother, Hannah, what had occurred, Hannah laughed and told him not to tell Peirse's wife. Priscilla went to the Hatton Gardens house and lived there with Peirse for over a month.

Peirse now decided to leave his wife. While Elizabeth was on a visit to her old neighborhood in Dulwich, he made off with her plate, linen, jewels, and clothes after forcing open her chest. He also wrote her a letter deriding her as an old woman and left it for her at his parents'. In the letter he told her "to think of another world and endeavor to make your peace with God." He advised her to take a lodging of two rooms (his parents refused to let her stay with them) and said that he would see that she had enough from the estate to maintain her. Elizabeth found lodgings. Six months later Peirse's mother brought her a second letter but refused to say where her son was. The letter was full of insults. "I methinks I hear you cry out in one of your accustomed whining deceitful tones, 'What, won't the villain allow me nothing to maintain me; how does he think I must live after stripping me of everything'; then sighing, or sobbing, or perhaps one of your stomach aching fainting fits, with your ugly withered face more frightful than the witches in Macbeth, 'Sure, never was any woman so miserable and so ill used as I am.'" Peirse especially resented that she had frequently complained about him to his parents, "telling them how often [two words scratched out: I beat?] your old dry bones." Elizabeth finally saw Peirse briefly when Mrs. Cartwright, from whom Peirse was trying to borrow money, sent for her. In front of Mrs. Cartwright, Peirse abused Elizabeth, threatened her with his stick, and told her never to come near him. He wrote to her repeating these sentiments and told her that he would give her thirty pounds a year, or less than half of what she had settled on him at marriage.

At the same time Peirse began to live with Priscilla as man and wife: she bore him one child and lost another. He rented a large house at the sign of Grasshopper near Spittal Square in Bishopsgate and began to trade as a grocer. The house cost forty pounds a year, and Peirse kept two journeymen, an apprentice, a porter, and two maidservants. He also rented another house in Hackney for twenty pounds a year and kept a saddlehorse. His trade was worth three to five hundred pounds a year. Four months after these arrangements were made, Peirse came to see Elizabeth. He told her with a sneer "that he had a good habitation of his own and that she might come and live there." "What," Elizabeth replied, "with your whore?" "No," he replied, "but I have a dark room there which will do for you." He also sent her a letter telling her to call off her friends and her lawyers—Elizabeth had clearly been busy—and saying what "millions would I give" that he had never seen her "unfortunate face" or called himself her husband. In May when Peirse came to pay her rent, he pinched her nose and struck her in the teeth with his fist. There the story ends until three years later when Elizabeth filed for a divorce. She received it a year later and was given fifty-five pounds a year in alimony.[21]

The three widows who have just been described were each women capable of taking initiative for themselves. But many others were much more dependent women whose fearfulness allowed them to be easily exploited by an aggressive and unscrupulous man. A widow who remarried without having her property settled opened herself to the easiest kind of exploitation. In May 1695 Ann Swaine married Edward Hart. He was a widower "in low and mean circumstances." She was a well-off widow who owned a house in Southwark. They had agreed that the house was to be settled on her, but after they were married he refused to do so. He also got fourteen gold pieces out of her for his business that he promised to repay. He failed to do so, and when she asked for them, he abused her. In the first two years of their marriage, there were periods when he refused to speak for days. In 1697 he left her house and rented lodgings for himself in Aldermanbury. He took her to Hampstead and announced to others that she had left him. When he would not give her money to pay for the Hampstead lodgings, she borrowed the cost from her friends and returned home. At home he told the servants to disregard her, and when one of them struck her, he told him to do it again. In 1701 Hart began to beat and kick her. He forbade her friends and relations to visit. For two days he refused to let her eat. When she became ill, he said that he had given her a pill (that is, poisoned her), and that if that pill would not do her business for her, he would give her another that would. Ann filed for divorce. She had not gotten from the marriage what she had hoped for. Hart had done well enough. He was making over one hundred pounds a year as a clothworker, had two apprentices, and was a yeoman in the queen's guards with a salary of forty pounds a year and twenty pounds and more a year in perquisites. But Hart was hoping, apparently, that the rich widow could be squeezed even more.[22]

The widow who remarried with jointure or annual income that was guaranteed by a deed was not necessarily protected from an unscrupulous husband who was prepared to use violence to force her to sign the deed over. This occurred at all the levels of society where jointures were made, except perhaps the highest. In April 1700 Jane Mary Anderson married Brownlow Sherrard. She was the daughter of Sir John Methuen, the ambassador to Portugal, and the widow of Sir Richard Anderson. She brought to the marriage over two thousand pounds and a small estate of a few hundred pounds a year. She also had a jointure from Sir Richard. Sherrard was single and worth two thousand pounds or more. After the marriage he began to beat Jane in an attempt to force her to sign over her jointure. He locked her in her dressing room, pinched and kicked her, and held a sword and a pistol to her breast. She eventually signed the deed as well as a statement that he was a good husband and she a devil. He once threatened to murder her if she would not deny that they were married because he said that he abhorred the thought of a wife. He beat her because, he said, he did not like her looks. He dragged her down two pairs of stairs and threw her out of the house because she said the neckcloth he wore that day was made of muslin. When she asked him not to let a prostitute into their house, he beat her for two hours. He mistreated her during her pregnancies and after childbirth. He pulled her out of bed after the first child was born, called it a bastard, and threatened to kill it. During her second pregnancy he struck her in her belly with a wooden window bar. While the child was being delivered, he pretended to go away to sea. He left her no money and took out an advertisement not to give her credit. Finally, after five years of marriage Sherrard and his brother Richard tried to force her into a madhouse, at which point she sued for divorce.[23]

Elizabeth Ridge and Thomas Bowen were lower in the social scale than Jane Anderson and Brownlow Sherrard, but the dynamics of their marriage were similar. Elizabeth married Bowen in 1707. She was a widow with sixty pounds a year in rents and a jointure. He was the sergeant at mace for the Poultry Compter prison, making (according to her) over five hundred pounds in perquisites and with an annual salary of over £260. It was also his second marriage. They were married at Hertford. But as soon as they were in London he began to beat her and threatened to kill her to force her to assign her jointure to him. In May he put her into a coach and took her to Mr. Gillets's madhouse at Horton. She was confined for three weeks until Gillet released her after he discovered that she was not disturbed and that it was a trick of her husband's. Five months later in October Bowen forced Elizabeth into another madhouse run by the more compliant Thomas Newton, where she was kept for two months. In January she capitulated and agreed to mortgage her jointure for three hundred pounds. But over the next year Bowen continued to beat her until in January 1708 he turned her out of the house, while he kept her rings, her watch, and her clothes. Bowen for his part said that Elizabeth was a drunken woman who abused his mother and his children by his previous wife and who threatened him with a hammer. Her first husband he said had described her in his will as base, barbarous, and lewd. He also claimed that she had seen other men during her first marriage, and that she did the same when she was married to him. It is unclear whether any of this was true. The court, at any rate, believed Elizabeth and granted her divorce.[24]

By the 1790s the widow with the abusive second husband disappeared from the consistory either because she was likely to solve her difficulties with a private separation rather than in the more public divorce court or because the trustees of her settlement were powerful enough to protect her. The single case from the 1790s in which a man sued his wife for restitution of his conjugal rights illustrates this. Thomas Oliver was a watchmaker who preached occasionally at various Dissenting chapels and meeting houses. The Kensington chapel of the Reverend Dr. Lake was one of these, and there Oliver met Frances Mackintosh. They had both been previously married, and Oliver had a daughter by his previous wife. Frances was a well-off widow with more than one thousand pounds a year, but Oliver was worth less than five hundred pounds in total. A settlement was made when they married in June 1798 that apparently left most of her wealth at Frances's disposal. Oliver was dissatisfied and soon after the marriage began to try to force his wife to change the terms of the settlement. Two months after the marriage as they rode in her carriage on a Sunday morning going to Mr. Martin's chapel, Oliver abused Frances in front of his daughter and proposed a separation with four hundred pounds a year for himself. During their August holiday at Brighton, Frances's health declined as a result of their quarrels and Oliver's threat to lock her in a room and horsewhip her every day.

In October Frances became so ill that she was confined to her bed. She called Oliver into her room and said that she wanted to die in peace with everyone. She asked him to send for his daughter so that all three of them could pray together. But Oliver flew into a rage, refused to pray with her, and told her that she was going to hell immediately. Frances then sent for Dr. Lake (at whose chapel they had met), asking him to come and pray with her. Oliver refused to be present and later abused her for sending for Lake. In December he threatened her with a stick as they rode in a carriage. She cried out murder, and passersby in the street came to inquire. Oliver told them she was mad, but her servant helped her out and took her to a house where she had a fainting fit. On other occasions he took up the theme of her madness and threatened to send her to Bedlam as a lunatic, but this was no longer a threat with much force. Frances finally left Oliver in July 1799 after thirteen months of marriage when he shook her and threatened to fling her down the stairs because she would not give him the key to the storeroom. Frances went to one of the London aldermen for advice. The alderman visited Oliver and negotiated a separation in which Oliver was to receive three hundred pounds a year. But after the deeds were drawn, Oliver refused to sign them. He wanted more. He had once tried to persuade Frances (after he had failed with her trustees) to sell some property so that he could buy an estate in the country and had even begun negotiations with some landowners. Presumably he still aimed at some such scheme to fulfill his mechanic preacher's dream of the life he was to have after marrying the rich widow. But Frances and her trustees were not to be intimidated. Oliver's only recourse was to bring his forlorn suit for the restitution of his conjugal rights. He could not make his way around the solid prenuptial agreement and his wife's responsible trustees: these kept Frances's wealth and her person secure. The increased use of such settlements may therefore explain as much as anything else the disappearance of the abused widow from the divorce court record. But in the end it must be said that while her disappearance is apparent, the causes for it remain speculative.[25]

MARITAL VIOLENCE AND THE POOR

The cases in the consistory court document the history of adultery, sexual violence, desertion, and marital separation among the middle classes, the gentry, and the aristocracy. It is harder to find information on these matters about the poor. It is certainly not that they were of no concern. The defamation cases in the second chapter show how frequently the actual or supposed adultery of wives rankled their husbands and their neighbors. The husband who deserted his wife and lived bigamously with another woman can be documented from the poor law declarations of their abandoned wives. Poor women were quite ready to complain to the justices of the peace about their adulterous husbands and their lovers. But by the middle of the century the justices were no longer willing to deal with such matters. Throughout the century they did continue to hear cases of wife beating among the poor as well as from the other classes of society, and they sometimes arranged for what were in effect separations with alimony for the poor, much as the consistory did for those who were better off. But since these separations do not appear in the sessions rolls, they can be documented only from the notebooks of justices, which survive only in a broken series for the City and not at all for urban Middlesex and Westminster. Finally, the quarter sessions records of wife beating in the rolls and separations in the justices' minute books never record the kind of detail that the consistory did. Still, the sketchy records that do exist make it plain that the experience of poor women and men was roughly similar to that of the well off, even if the subtleties and ideological contexts of their lives are more or less lost from our sight except in the defamation suits.

Early in the century the violent husband appeared in the quarter sessions records when he was occasionally sent to the house of correction or more frequently when he gave a recognizance. In July 1704, for instance, Henry Bannister, a framework knitter from Cock Lane in Bethnal Green, was charged with beating his wife Elizabeth and gave his bond along with two of his fellow framework knitters. In October Mary Blaker complained that her husband had assaulted and threatened her. He refused to maintain her and she had had to seek relief from the parish of St. Martin in the Fields for herself and her child. John Blaker was probably an older man with a young wife: one of his sureties was his grown son who bore the same name; but it may have been that it was the younger man's own mother who had been mistreated: these are the uncertainties that the brevity of these records create. Ten years later in 1714 John Bayne, who was a hosier in St. Martin's in the Fields, beat his wife Ann and turned her out of the house. John Lewin, like the wealthier men in the consistory cases, began to beat his wife once he started to see another woman. He was a turner in St. Ann, Westminster, who beat his wife Catherine after he became involved with Margaret Kennedy. He threatened her life and refused to support her. His father and his brother—Abraham senior and junior (or possibly his two cousins)—who were also turners came to Lewin's aid as his sureties. Robert Wildgoose also beat his wife Bridget once he became adulterous. He went to whores and caught a venereal infection that he gave to her, and he stopped supporting her as well. Wildgoose was a pipemaker in Fulham, and two of his fellow pipemakers in the neighborhood were his sureties. Johanna Broom, however, at first sought help from a power greater than the justices after her husband John deserted. She complained that Benjamin Parry had cheated her by pretending that he could "cast a figure" that would put such pain in her husband's heart that he would have no peace of mind until he returned to her. Johanna had paid Parry six shillings for his services. The number of such cases varied by year, but for instance in the rolls for 1737 for Westminster and Middlesex twenty-three men gave recognizances for beating their wives, and one was sent to New Prison.[26]

The notebooks of the justices for the City for the second half of the century document separations arranged by the magistrate. In 1761 Thomas Rottam, who had beaten his wife and run away, agreed to give her 3s 6d a week. Ann Hands in 1775 made it clear that she wished to live separately and to have an allowance. Her husband agreed to seven shillings a week. Edward Lewis and his wife Elizabeth agreed to separate in 1782 after he had beaten her, but a financial provision was not made. The justices sometimes effected a reconciliation. Seven days after the Lewis case, Henry and Martha Gray at first agreed that they would separate and that he would pay her five shillings a week, but they later changed their minds and decided to live together after all. In 1790 John Gromand was more dramatic after he became drunk on a Saturday evening in March. He told his wife that he had a letter from God Almighty to kill her at ten o'clock on Monday morning. He repeated this the next morning when he was sober. His wife Frances took him to the alderman, where Gromand said that he was very sorry. Frances forgave him, and they went home together. But in other cases from the 1790s a reconciliation was impossible. When Elizabeth and John Round decided to separate, she asked for an agreement to be drawn up in which she was given a half-guinea a week and allowed to keep the furniture in her possession. William Williams also agreed to let his wife keep the furniture and promised as well to pay six shillings a week which his wife Mary was to collect from his master, a method of payment that probably gave her greater security and guaranteed that the couple would not have to deal directly with each other.[27]

Most of these cases were initiated by an abused wife. But occasionally it was a husband who complained. Thomas Knight said that his wife Elizabeth had repeatedly left him over the years. But in 1793 when the man she was living with died, she returned to molest her husband. He by then had lived for some years with another woman by whom he had had two children. Thomas and Elizabeth had in effect privately divorced each other and made new marriages. This the magistrate could not support. Instead Knight agreed to pay Elizabeth two shillings a week without taking her home again. But Knight was not rebuked for his second family. In a second case the couple had never legally married but had lived together for years. John Dutton complained that his companion Amy Lee had assaulted him and taken away his property. He told the magistrate that he wanted a separation and the restoration of his property. Lee promised the magistrate that she would no longer molest Dutton and was discharged. There was, from the magistrate's point of view but not from Dutton's, no need to declare a separation. In these cases the official and unofficial systems of marriage and divorce met and made the most of each other that they could.[28]

Poor men, middle-class men, and rich men all beat their wives, and for relatively the same reasons. Traditional patriarchy taught men that the property of their wives and their bodies belonged to them and that they could dispose of the one and beat the other into submission. Modern heterosexuality may not have concerned itself with women's possessions, but it reinforced in men the desire to have exclusive sexual access to women, and the best way for some men to achieve this was violence. Modern ideas of romance and domesticity certainly moderated the violence of some men among the middle classes and the elite, but they fought an uphill struggle against the forces new and old that upheld male violence and domination.

CHAPTER ELEVEN

Desertion and Incompatibility

V iolence by men and adultery and desertion by either a husband or a wife were the only grounds on which the consistory court could grant a divorce or legal separation, which did not, however, allow the spouses to remarry. But there existed at all levels of society a strong feeling that a marriage ended once the spouses proved incompatible. The gentry and the aristocracy could express such feelings, but they could not act upon them since their visibility in society forced them to stay within the forms of the law. But middle-class and poor people through simple desertion and by invented rituals and private contracts divorced each other for incompatibility and married again. The middle-class men and women who used the consistory court before 1750 therefore seem to have used it as a court of last resort when a spouse's actions became financially inconvenient after they had been separated for many years and sometimes even married someone else. Women sued husbands who had deserted them after financial difficulties or for another woman and left them and their children dependent on her family or on public charity. Men sued wives who had left them for another man or who had become prostitutes when they feared that they might be responsible for her debts or her bastards. But the adulterous wives in this chapter, especially some of those who became prostitutes, like some of the remarrying widows in the last chapter, show that a woman's sexual desires once they were activated in marriage could be as powerfully felt as those of men. Yet their desires differed from the new male heterosexuality since for most of the century there was no sapphist role to divide women into a heterosexual majority and a homosexual minority. After 1750, as the next chapter shows, the divorces in the consistory became largely the history of the adulterous wife. It was an adultery, however, given its distinctive character by the ideals of romantic marriage and the domesticated family, and it was as likely to appear among aristocratic women as among the middle-class women who before 1750 had dominated the divorces in the consistory court. These aristocratic women were then able to legally marry their loves after their divorces, since their husbands had found that by act of Parliament they could give force to the traditional feeling that the incompatibility of a husband and wife brought their marriage to an end.

THE DESERTED SPOUSE

The number of men who in the consistory court cases deserted their wives remained stable throughout the century: eight in the first decade of the century, six in the 1750s, seven in the 1790s. Men deserted their wives for two different motives. Some ran away after they fell into financial difficulties and usually went to London where they made new lives for themselves and married a second wife. But eventually their first wives found them in London and sued for divorce when the men were unwilling to take up their first marriages again. The second group of men left their wives after they fell in love with another woman. In both kinds of desertion the original legal marriage had lasted from one to eighteen years at the point of desertion. Ten had lasted five years or less, five under ten, and seven under twenty years.

Charles Harding was a husband who deserted under financial difficulties. Catherine Felder had married Harding in 1736 when they were both twenty-one and single, and within a year they had a son. When Harding went bankrupt, Catherine began to live with her father in Dartford because she was pregnant with their second child, who was born in August 1738. Harding left Catherine at this point, hid from his wife, who was cared for by her father and her brother, and began to live at Wapping with Sophia Brand. For two years from 1739 to 1741 Harding and Brand pretended to be married, but when she became pregnant, Harding took out a license to marry her as a bachelor. Although they both knew Catherine to be alive, they married each other in July 1742 and lived together and had three children. Brand died in January 1755. When Catherine learned of Harding's whereabouts she filed for divorce seventeen years after he had left her, and the divorce was granted.[1]

A man like Henry Crimes appeared and disappeared throughout the course of a long marriage, leaving his wife and children to be supported by her family or by public charity. Crimes had married his wife Ann in 1681 and received with her land worth four thousand pounds. On his own he had a Treasury pension of seventy-eight pounds a year. In eighteen years of marriage Crimes fathered four children on Ann. In 1689 he left her with her mother in Plymouth during her pregnancy and lying-in. For three years in 1696–99 he put her into various lodgings in Westminster and the City while he took other lodgings for himself. He failed to pay her rent, and her clothes were seized by creditors. In 1699 their children were being kept by her family, but three of them had lived for two years in a Devon almshouse. He told their friends that she had tried to poison him, that she had given him venereal disease, and that she had become a Roman Catholic—none of which were true. What brought her, finally, after eighteen years to sue for divorce is unclear.[2]

The cases of men who left their wives to live with other women often give no more detail than the names of the other women, where the adulterous couple lived in London, and whether they had had children. Occasionally there is some information about the other woman. Thomas Walter Williams married his wife in 1782 when he was nineteen and she was a young widow. They lived together for eight years and had children. At twenty-seven Williams fell in love with their maidservant Jane Kenny and eventually left his wife to live with Kenny, who bore their child. Thomas Webster, on the other hand, fell in love with someone else's wife. In 1788 as a bachelor of forty-five he had married Mary Hunter who was single and twenty-four. Her portion was two thousand pounds in bank stock. He was a large merchant who provided supplies for vessels in the West India trade and made about three thousand pounds a year. The couple lived together for nine years and had two children. In 1797 Webster began an affair with Sarah Jones, a married woman. In September and November Webster and Sarah met in hired lodgings under assumed names two or three times a week. In June 1798 Webster persuaded Sarah to leave her husband and to move into a furnished house he had taken for her. When Mary Webster discovered this in November, she left her husband. Sarah's husband John Jones sued Webster and was awarded £550 by default. Mary Webster sued for divorce six months later and received it in a year's time. Her husband does not seem to have contested her suit. Webster and Sarah presumably continued to live together.[3]

A woman sometimes struggled unsuccessfully to win back her husband's affections. Ann Fawcett married Thomas Ward in 1781 when they were both single and twenty-one. They lived together until the end of 1785 when Ward met Elizabeth Smith and fell in love with her. Smith was a nursery maid in Wardour Street. Ward persuaded her to leave her post and to go into lodgings that he provided. He paid her daily visits, and they passed as a married couple with Ann using Ward's name. In September 1786 Smith had a child. Ann Ward now discovered the affair and spoke to her husband. He confessed and was contrite. As a means of ending the relationship Ann agreed to take care of the child Ward had had by Smith. (There is no indication that she had a child of her own.) But Ward continued to see Smith, and eventually he left his wife again to live with her. Smith passed as Mrs. Ward and had two more children. Then in August 1792, five years after he had left her, Ward came to Ann, who had moved from London to York. Once again he was contrite and promised to break with Smith, and Ann agreed to live with him again. But whatever the reason for Ward's reappearance in 1792, it was weaker than his bond with Smith. After four months he left Ann once more and went back to Smith. Five months later Ann sued for divorce.[4]

When one turns to consider the women who were sued in the consistory court for deserting their husbands, two patterns emerge. Most women were divorced because they had deserted their husbands for a single other man, but some women became prostitutes with many men. Among the women with only one lover, there were significant differences between those early in the century and those from the middle and end. Almost none of the early cases involved couples from the gentry or the aristocracy, and divorce proceedings were often started years after a woman had left her husband. After 1750 the gentry and the aristocracy appeared quite frequently; proceedings were started very soon after a woman had eloped from her husband; and in at least half the cases, the husband went on to seek a divorce from Parliament that allowed them both to remarry. None of the plaintiffs from the first decade of the century received a parliamentary divorce that allowed remarriage. In many of them a divorce was sought only after years of separation and when an alienated wife's behavior seemed likely to make financial difficulties for a husband. There is little evidence either that a husband had sued in revenge for his shattered domesticity or that a couple had agreed to part after rearranging their romantic commitments, as often happened after midcentury.

Before 1750 a wife's financial demands after a separation had been made could drive her husband to seek a more formal divorce. This was George Debbertin's case. He seems to have been a good enough man whose life was threatened by his wife and her lover. In 1683 he had courted Maria Christina Schulman and married her in the Lutheran church. She was an indigent widow with three small children and many debts; it was his first marriage. He took care of her children and paid her debts. In 1696, after they had been married for thirteen years, she began an affair with Bernard Chancellor, and together the lovers plotted to murder Debbertin. They agreed to marry each other afterward and broke a piece of gold between them to seal their contract to marry. Maria Christina now tried to poison her husband when she gave him his usual mess of milk in the evening. Debbertin did not like the taste and gave a spoon or two of the milk to a cat, which began to vomit. He became sick from the little he had taken himself. The lovers tried to get a maidservant to help them. But she refused and revealed the plot to Maria Christina's son-in-law, who told Debbertin. Maria Christina now left the house, and Debbertin agreed to support her with five pounds a week. In March 1699 she suggested that if he gave her a lump sum, she would go abroad to the West Indies to try her fortune. She then wrote out in German a confession of what she had done, which was duly witnessed. She took the money (thirty-five pounds) and started to live with another man as though they were married. They eventually moved first to Ireland and then to Barbados and Jamaica. But when the man left her to go to Africa, she returned to London in November 1703. She took a house in Wine Office Court, Fleet Street, where she practiced physic and fortune-telling, making, Debbertin claimed, from twenty to forty pounds a week. She continued to threaten Debbertin, saying that she would be his ruin and would have him arrested for the fifty-five pounds rent of the house in which she lived. At this point Debbertin filed for divorce and received his release.[5]

In most cases, however, the evidence is not full enough to say what induced a particular man to file for a divorce after his wife had left him and had lived with another man for some time. It may simply have been that a husband filed when he discovered where his wife had gone in London's great anonymous world. George Loriston, for instance, married Elizabeth Adams in 1677. After nine years she left him for Thomas Bayles. Elizabeth and Bayles lived together in Whitechapel and had a daughter whom they christened Martha Bayles. Three years after Elizabeth's elopement, Loriston filed for his divorce and received it. Joseph Carroll also sued for divorce three years after his wife Martha had left him for John King. During that time Martha bore more than one of King's children. In both these cases, it may have taken the aggrieved husband some time to find his wife. Her illegitimate children and his possible responsibility for them may have acted as an additional spur to action. George Stoney from Wapping seems to have found his wife Catherine after her conviction for a crime. They had married on Christmas Eve in 1700. Six years later she eloped with John Dexbrough and lived with him as man and wife. After she stole from one of her landlords, was indicted at the Old Bailey, found guilty, and burned on her left cheek, Stoney sued for his divorce and received it.[6]

A husband whose wife eloped, of course, had other options than either accepting her absence or suing for divorce. He could also forgive her or turn her and her lover over to the magistrate. William King tried both of the latter before he decided to divorce his wife Ann. King married Ann in 1683, and they had several children. In 1702 after nineteen years of marriage, Ann left King for five months between June and October. But when she asked forgiveness, he took her back. Ann, however, seems to have liked her taste of freedom, and a year later she ran away again taking some of her husband's goods with her. She lived with several men. Pretending that King was dead, she married Thomas Haines, and lived with him in another part of town. When someone heard that she was alive and told King, he got the constable and took his wife and Haines to the magistrate who sent the lovers to the workhouse. Haines then went to sea. Ann took to the streets and was sent to the Wood Street and the Poultry Compters (or prisons) several times for prostitution. This King evidently could not forgive and filed for divorce.[7]

There were cases, however, in which a man tolerated for years his wife's living with a succession of men in what in each case must have been intended to be a new stable union or marriage. This tolerance made it legally very difficult for him to receive a divorce, and in one of the cases a wife claimed that her husband had tried to bribe her to accept the divorce. In two cases that can be described, it is still not apparent why a man decided to seek a divorce after so many years. It is also not clear why his wife resisted. It may have been her lawyer's advice, or a strategy for making a favorable financial settlement. It may simply have been a woman's determination not to allow a former partner to have his way. In the first case John Sharrow courted his wife Sarah in June 1703 and married in August. Two years later she started to have sex with different men, especially Philip Bridgeman and Francis Rawlins, using their names to pass, presumably, as their wives when they took rooms together. This was the story Sharrow told, and it may have been true. But his wife was not ready to be divorced. She said that he had offered her ten guineas if she would come to court and swear that she was a whore. It was at least certain that their marriage was at an end and that they were not living together. Sarah Sharrow also claimed that her husband, who was the third mate on an East India ship, had kept company with many prostitutes before their marriage and was now living as man and wife with another woman. He had been found with a prostitute by the constable in an alehouse near Billingsgate and had been committed to Bridewell. He had had to find bail or lose his place on his ship. He had taken away his wife's goods to keep his whore Bess Yates when she was in the Gatehouse prison. This was perhaps a failed marriage between two libertines.[8]

In the second case James Amson courted and married Margaret Hicks early in 1693. She was a clergyman's daughter and brought him four hundred pounds. He was a journeyman to a Mr. Brittain who ran the Goat Tavern in Bloomsbury. Six months after the marriage, he took a tavern of his own in Red Lyon Square, probably using her money. This lasted two years, and then he took another tavern on Snow Hill for three years. But he failed in business, and she left him. She said that he had promised to pay her twenty pounds when they separated but had never done so. He became a purser on a merchant ship, sailing to Newfoundland, Leghorn, and elsewhere. In the eleven years after their separation he said that Margaret had relationships with three different men. The first, with Obadiah Wesnincott, had begun before they separated. She had entertained him in their house on Snow Hill and given him money, and they had met frequently at a midwife's house near Covent Garden. With her second lover, William Royston, she took a coffeehouse in Devereux Court near the Temple where they passed as man and wife, but Royston was already married. His wife came to the coffeehouse, broke the dishes, and made such a row that they had to quit the business. Finally in 1705 and 1706 Margaret Hicks kept another coffeehouse, first in Old Bedlam and then in King Street near Towerhill, where her companion was Thomas Haynes, by whom she had a child.

Margaret denied none of this. She only said that during their marriage her husband had given her the foul disease and that he had been charged with being the father of a bastard. His adultery, in other words, prevented him from using hers to get his divorce. This was a marriage, however, that had ended by mutual agreement years before. Amson presumably now had some unstated financial motive for trying to end it more formally. In this it was fairly typical of the early-eighteenth-century cases where a divorce was sought as a protection against the legal uncertainties that could arise after a couple had separated for some time and formed new relationships. Whatever pain there may have been in the dissolution of the original marriage had often long disappeared by the time the divorce was sought. It was only after midcentury, with the growth of romantic marriages, that the tragedy of failed conjugal love became central to the divorce case.[9]

Margaret Amson lived with three different men after she left her husband, but she always did so under the appearance of being married to her new lovers. There was, however, before 1750 a second pattern among adulterous wives in which a woman deserted her husband to become a prostitute, and a few women had even been prostitutes before they married. The number of these women declined over the course of the century, another piece of the evidence suggesting that London families and the world of prostitution drew further apart after 1750, with prostitutes drawn increasingly from women who had left their families in the country. The prostituted wife appeared in nine of twenty-seven cases of female adultery brought between 1700 and 1709, in four of the twenty cases from the 1750s, and in only two of fifty-four from the 1790s. In the most straightforward kind of case a young man or a careless libertine inadvertently married a prostitute. Although Peter Henley seems to have been an experienced man-about-town when he married Susannah Roberts, he said that in June 1748 he had been induced to marry her even though she had almost certainly been a prostitute. Elizabeth Porter, who on and off for many years was a waiter at Haddock's Bagnio, claimed to have known Susannah before her marriage when she went by the name of Sucky and brought her customers to the Bagnio. Susannah, on the other hand, said that James Simpson, with whom her husband accused her of committing adultery, was her husband's good friend, and that the two men had colluded against her. It is quite possible that she was right, but in that case the two friends had found a way to get a divorce from a woman whom neither of them would have wished to marry because she was a whore.

The two friends had apparently arranged for two occasions to be documented. In November 1752 Simpson and another man ordered supper for three in a room at the Cardigan Head Tavern and left instructions that a woman in a brown and red striped gown was to be shown in. Susannah arrived an hour later. According to Henry Waartz, the waiter, a lot of claret, burgundy, and champagne were called for. Susannah became drunk, behaved indecently, and was carried away in the arms of two chairmen to Haddock's Bagnio where a bed had been ordered. The two gentlemen followed. At Haddock's, Elizabeth Machoun served breakfast to Susannah and one of the men, and she was put to bed by Elizabeth Porter. In December a similar scene was played out at the other principal bagnio, the Royal in Long Acre, where Judith Willis waited on Simpson and Susannah after they had gone to bed. Willis was also familiar with Susannah's husband Peter Henley who had been a customer of the bagnio for four or five of the ten years that she had worked there. Another waiter at the Royal Bagnio had also been in the room when Susannah and Simpson were in bed together, but this man, Garret Cavanaugh, had not actually seen her: the curtains of the bed had been drawn and he had only heard a woman singing behind them. But he said that Susannah later confessed to him that it was she who was in the bed and that she had once asked him "to help her to some gentleman to lay with at his house that would give handsome and she would . . . make an acknowledgement" to Cavanaugh. She also told him that a Jew called Mr. Mendez (whose linen was cared for by her cousin Mrs. Clayton who lived with Cavanaugh and passed as his wife) had met her one evening at Cavanaugh's house and gone home with her to spend the night. Mendez had given her a guinea in the morning. The court granted Peter Henley his divorce, and Parliament passed an act that allowed him to remarry.[10]

The lives of the women who became prostitutes after their marriages fall into three patterns. Some women became prostitutes because of the extended absence of their husbands, as Frances Edwardes did after her husband was imprisoned for debt. In the summer of 1742 Frances Taylor was courted by John Edwardes when she was twenty-one and he was eighteen. They married in September and lived together for three-quarters of a year in his house in Castle Court off the Strand until he was arrested and confined in the Fleet for the debts she had contracted before and after their marriage. Edwardes stayed in prison for eleven years and went to live alone in Jamaica when he was released in 1753. During the years of his imprisonment, Frances became a prostitute; but it is possible that she may have been one before her marriage—the nature of her debts were never described. During her husband's imprisonment, she sometimes lived on her own and received company. At other times she lived with a man as husband and wife. At one point she ran a coffeehouse with seven girls who were prostitutes. For the first year after her husband's arrest, Frances lived in three different sets of lodgings and received company. At the end of 1744 she met Dr. Thomas Champanty and lived with him in his house near Covent Garden. Six months later she met another man and lived with him for four months around Clare Market. And then Edward Milborne came into her life, and from 1745 until 1751 they lived together as man and wife. Milborne was an officer of the Marshalsea Court who was already married. The couple fought frequently and at least once had to change their lodgings when their landlady discovered that they were not married. During this relationship, Frances also ran a coffeehouse known as Wildair's in Castle Court, Covent Garden, and was called Kitty Wildair. Her landlord at some point arrested her for the costs of her board, lodging,

and clothes, and she was imprisoned in the Marshalsea. But the landlord
did not pursue the case because he knew that she would plead that she
was a married woman and that her husband was liable for her debts. A
brandy merchant who had her arrested for debt came to the same conclusion. Milborne left her at some point before or after her imprisonment.
When Frances was released from the Marshalsea, she briefly stayed with
Dr. Champanty, whom she had continued to visit over the years. She then
lived on her own again until October 1753 when she met Robert Gray.
With him she lived very respectably in Carolina Court, Saffron Hill. Her
landlady said that she "never saw any loose, abandoned or profligate behavior" in her. But when a publican at the Stationers Arms discovered
Frances's past, she admitted that her husband was in Jamaica. Her landlady (who was married and thirty) said that this made her "blameable" for
living with Robert Gray. Why Edwardes sued for divorce in 1755 is unclear. He perhaps feared that he would once again be made liable for
Frances's debts.[11]

In a second pattern found at the beginning and the middle of the century, a woman became a prostitute with many men after she left her husband initially for a particular man. Mary and Charles Trefy married in
September 1725 after three months of courtship. Since he was still a journeyman to an apothecary, George Bowl of Grace Church Street, with two
years to serve, he continued to live with his master, and she lived with
her mother. He then set up his own shop, where they lived together for
five years. But she spent a great deal of money; he had to abscond for fear
of being arrested for debt; and all his stock was seized. In the last year
that they lived together, Mary started to see other men. In 1731 she went
to Portsmouth, supposedly on a visit, but instead she met a captain in the
army who followed her back to London, where she entertained him after
her husband fled to avoid arrest. Once Trefy had settled his affairs and
taken new lodgings, he sent for Mary to come and join him. But she swore
that she would never live with him again and would instead see men she
liked better. She refused to see him when he came to call on her and went
to live in the Strand where the army captain visited her. But like other
women, she eventually fell lower and became a common streetwalker. She
usually worked out of the Hoop and Bunch of Grapes in Battersea, where
the proprietor John Adam often sent for her for his customers. For seventeen years Mary Trefy left matters this way. Trefy in time did well enough.
His business brought in over one hundred pounds a year, and he had an
appointment at St. George's hospital for another one hundred pounds a
year. Mary, on the other hand, at forty or so and, with her looks presum-

ably gone after a hard life, was not doing so well. In 1749 she wrote a
letter to Trefy admitting all that she had done. But he evidently did not
respond as she had hoped and so, three years later, she filed in the consistory for restitution of her conjugal rights. In response he sued a year later
for his divorce.[12]

In a final category are the young women who shortly after their marriage
began to see many men and eventually became prostitutes. They are the
hardest cases to understand. It is almost as though their first experience
of sex in marriage with their husbands stirred in them a need for constant
sexual experience with other men. These are cases where there was clearly
no economic need that motivated the sexual experimentation as there
might have been with some of the wives who became prostitutes. Instead
these women display a sexual energy equal to that found in libertine men.
But whereas young men could begin their pursuit of women immediately
after masturbation began in puberty, it would seem that women had to
go through marriage before they could experience a similar release of their
sexual desires. For women social experience with men always preceded
sexual fulfillment, but such fulfillment for women usually came at the price
of social ostracism because heterosexuality had not yet become the norm
of sexual honor for them as it had for men. The cases of Mary Pettiver
from the beginning of the century and of Catherine Carter from the end
of the century illustrate these themes. William Pettiver courted Mary
Steward in August 1694, and they were married in September. But within
a year of her marriage Mary began to go out at night with other men.
Whether her husband knew this is unclear. In 1697 Pettiver went to work
for a month in Hertfordshire, leaving his wife behind in London. She
went to the playhouse every night, where she picked up men and brought
them home. Her neighbors became aware of this, and someone told her
father, who found her with a man. When he asked the man his business,
he was beaten for his pains while his daughter looked on. After Pettiver
returned to town, he asked his wife whether they were going on Sunday
to dine with her father, as they usually did. She began to cry and said
that her father had ruined her, but she would not explain what she meant.
Pettiver learned the story from his father-in-law. He questioned his wife,
and she went away to think for six days. Through her father's intervention
she promised that she would behave, and Pettiver received her home
again. But she continued to take away his goods and stayed out late at
night to see other men. In 1698 she left her husband and became a common whore, picking up men in the street. She swore in 1703 that she had
borne a child by George Flower, and in 1704 she was taken to Bridewell

for picking up men. Pettiver during all this time was arrested several times for her debts. He sued and was granted his divorce in 1705.[13]

Mary Pettiver's behavior at the beginning of the century cannot be taken as an example of a new female heterosexuality because there was yet no exclusive sapphist role to match the effeminate sodomite in reaction to whom the majority of men constructed their exclusive heterosexuality. By the last generation of the eighteenth century such a sapphist role had begun to exist, but for most women, their sexual relations with men remained of far greater importance than any possible sexual interaction with women. Catherine Carter's sexual career in the 1780s and 1790s did not therefore substantially differ from Mary Pettiver's at the beginning of the century. George Carter met Catherine in 1780 at the house of his friend Robert Welton at Chertsey in Surrey when Catherine was a student at a boarding school in the town. She came from Reading, where her parents kept the Black Bear Inn. Carter fell in love with Catherine and married her fresh out of school when she was still a minor. He received with her a small portion from her father of £280, as well as her clothes, linen, and china. Carter was an attorney who by the time of the divorce had a house in Clement's Lane, Lombard Street, and enough business to need several clerks. He made at least eight hundred pounds a year from the law, and he had inherited land from his mother and his uncle that probably brought him another five hundred pounds a year. In August 1784 after they had been married for four years, Catherine's mother in Reading became quite ill and seemed about to die. Carter and Catherine went together to Reading to see her. He could stay only a few days because of his business in London, but Catherine remained behind. Carter later said that since he had left his wife with her father and her brother, he had not doubted that she would "be secure from any insult of the guests using the house." But Catherine in fact fell victim to the widespread feeling of the male customers of public houses that all the women present were likely to be sexually available. Catherine's mother died, and she stayed for the burial. She wrote Carter love letters that he later said were intended to hide what she had begun to do. When Carter was told of his mother-in-law's death, he went down to Reading. Catherine seemed cold and languid and treated him with aversion. When he tried to reason with her, she said to him that the gentlemen who frequented her father's house had told her that they were surprised that in London she had not gone to masquerades, balls, operas, and plays. She said to Carter—a serious attorney who apparently did not spend his money on such delights—that as soon as she returned to London, she would go to all these places.

Carter became frightened and asked his friends in Reading what had been taking place. To his "poignant distress of mind," he heard that Catherine was now shunned by all her previous friends because of her conduct with the gentlemen who came to her parents' inn. Catherine had been seen sitting on various men's knees, and it was thought that she had slept a number of nights with one of them who was riddled with venereal disease. She was also involved with two other gentlemen, Arthur Annesley and Gilbert East, who had used the inn when they attended the Reading assemblies. Before one ball Catherine disappeared for two hours during which Annesley's room was firmly locked. She later told a waiter in the inn who had seen her with Annesley, "you know that I'm a whore for Mr. Annesley was doing me." James Wyatt, another young man of twenty who had stayed at the inn, became friends with Catherine. She told Wyatt that she disliked her husband and that as soon as she was back in London, she would leave with the first man who would take her away. When Wyatt asked if she would go with him, she said yes, and they made an appointment to meet in London. Catherine's husband in the meanwhile had decided that he had to get her back to London immediately so that he could have time to think.

Two days after they arrived in London, Catherine packed her clothes and went to meet Wyatt, who like her husband was an attorney but evidently livelier. She told Wyatt that she had seen Gilbert East (another of the men from Reading) that day and had arranged to meet him at a play that evening and to spend the night with him. She asked Wyatt to see her safely to the playhouse. While they were going there in a coach, Wyatt put his hands into her bosom and up her petticoats, and Catherine told him that she would have slept with him but for her engagement with East. Catherine then asked Wyatt to recommend a place where she could go with East. He suggested the Fountain in Catherine Street, a well-known bawdy house. Wyatt took her to the theater, where she met East. The play was the first night's performance of *The Marriage of Figaro*. Wyatt himself picked up another woman, and the two couples later followed each other into the Fountain. Both couples slept there that night, and Catherine told Wyatt the next morning about her sex with East. A few days later she wrote to Wyatt that she was living at Mrs. Elizabeth Roberts in Dartmouth Street in Westminster under the name of Clive. She invited him to call. When he did, she told him that since East slept with her every night, she could not see him also. Wyatt after that saw her many times in theater lobbies dressed and behaving like a prostitute. She frequently asked him to go home with her, but since she looked "so common" and he had heard that she might have become venereally infected, he always refused.

Gilbert East visited Catherine in Dartmouth Street as her husband under the name of Clive. The house was clearly a respectable one. Catherine's husband Carter knew a barrister, Michael Burton, who stayed there with his wife when they came to town. Carter went with another attorney to consult with Burton and found to his surprise that Catherine was in the house entertaining a man. When he saw them come downstairs, Carter rushed up to her room and searched it. He found East's monogrammed shirt, with his initials in colored thread and "East" in black ink. When Catherine returned to her room, she found Carter showing Burton the shirt. She passionately said to her husband: "Give me back Mr. East's shirt; keep it at your peril if you dare; if you don't return it to me, I shall set off to Oxford to him tomorrow morning and he will make you give it up. I once loved you but now I love another man better. I'll do you all the mischief I can." But if Catherine was in love with East, it did not stop her from seeing other men, like Charles Wilson who visited her in Dartmouth Street.

In February 1785 after her first three months as a woman of the town, Catherine, as a result no doubt of the scene with her husband, moved to the house of Theresa Maria Johnson in Jermyn Street, Piccadilly. Catherine had been recommended to Johnson by a lawyer named Lutwicke; Johnson went to interview Catherine and "engaged to take her into her family." Catherine stayed there six weeks, sometimes calling herself Carter, sometimes East. Gilbert East came to sleep with her nearly every night, but she also saw East's brother Augustus, as well as Lutwicke and some others. But Johnson did not keep Catherine on because she was frequently drunk. Such a house prided itself on the absence of drunkenness and disease. Catherine now began a series of frequent moves. In the spring she was at Sadler's, a well-known brothel in Newman Street in Marylebone. In the summer she moved to another house in Marylebone, kept by Martha Willis in Queen Ann Street East. Catherine was now part of the world of fashionable brothels that catered to gentlemen. Men of that class had begun to excite her in Reading and had opened to her a world larger than those of her husband or her parents. But evidently she could enter that fashionable world only by becoming part of its demimonde. She could not move there respectably as though she were among her social equals. Her state of mind was perhaps in part the product of those illusions that critics sometimes claimed were engendered in young women of her social station by a boarding-school education of the kind that she had

had. Her marriage to her husband had been a step up in the world. Her lovers (many of whom like her husband were lawyers but of higher social standing) had moved her higher still, but at the price of losing her respectability as a woman.

Catherine, however, was as excited by men beneath her social class as well as by those above. In the middle of 1785 she met Michael Underwood, a hackney coachmaster who lived in Marylebone. Catherine and Underwood used Tom's in Soho Square for their assignations. The house was kept by Thomas Hooper, and had a list of women who used the house so that the servants could easily send out for one of them when a customer wanted a woman. For every day or night the women were sent for, they had to pay the house five shillings as their "poundage." Catherine's name was put into the list, and she was sent for so frequently that she became known to the waiters. But her affections had become centered on Underwood, who was a married man. Underwood's wife began to notice Catherine walking around their house looking at her husband, and Underwood started to come home with his clothes full of powder and smelling of perfume. When Sarah Underwood (a laundress) confronted her husband, he beat her, and she left to live with her sister. Subsequently a friend told her that if she returned she would find Underwood and Catherine together in bed. Sarah put a ladder up against a window, climbed into their room, and found her husband sleeping in a pair of drawers that hung over his knees and Catherine without stays and in a petticoat so loose that her knees showed. Sarah went downstairs and got a man from the stables and together they awakened the couple. Sarah told Underwood that she had caught him, which was true enough; but she had lost him to Catherine.

Catherine and Underwood now went to live together in Charlotte Street, with Underwood's daughter Sarah as their servant. The girl slept with them in the same bedroom. This lasted ten days. They then moved to a bawdy house kept by William Robson in Portland Street, where Underwood's daughter remained as their servant. When Catherine and the girl went to the Pantheon to see Lundard's Balloon, Catherine was accosted by Richard Warren, an ensign in the Third Regiment of Foot, who called himself Captain Warren. Together they took a coach to her lodgings, and Warren made an appointment to dine with Catherine the next day when he came and spent the night. Warren decided to take Catherine "into keeping," that is, for his exclusive use. He lodged her at James Spring's in Portland Street with young Sarah Underwood as her servant. Catherine lived there several months and took her lover's mother, Elizabeth Underwood, as a second servant. Warren, of course, did not know of Catherine's relationship with Daniel Underwood. When he discovered it, he turned Catherine out and discharged the lodgings. So Catherine went to live with Underwood at his house in Tottenham Court Road.

Catherine was still living with Underwood in Tottenham Court Road three years later when her husband George Carter sued for divorce in the consistory. Carter also brought an action for criminal conversation against Gilbert East, but not against Underwood, who must have been too low in the social scale to sue. Carter was granted his divorce in 1791. But unlike Peter Henley in the first example of a man married to a whore, he did not seek a parliamentary divorce that would have allowed him to remarry. He was perhaps on the wrong side of the social divide of those injured husbands who did, higher in social standing than Daniel Underwood the hackney coachmaster but lower than Gilbert East, a baronet's son. Carter seems to have acted like the middle-class men and women who used the consistory court in the first half of the century to free themselves from the legal responsibilities of a marriage that had ended many years before. But because he was an attorney, it is likely that he did not use any of those usually illegal private contracts and ceremonies that throughout the century the poor and the middle classes used to free themselves from an incompatible spouse, as the second half of this chapter now shows.[14]

INCOMPATIBLE SPOUSES

Before 1750 divorce on the ground of incompatibility did not legally exist in England. But private ceremonies and contracts were used by individuals to divorce themselves when their marriages fell apart, even though these forms were not recognized by either the ecclesiastical or the secular courts. The force of these forms of self-divorcement becomes clearer when placed in the context of the tradition that held that individuals were able to marry themselves by making promises of marriage without the intervention of a priest. Such marriages by private promises were legal, if difficult to prove, until 1753, when the Marriage Act made marriages in church the only legal ones. Before 1753 the ecclesiastical courts—or at least the London consistory—were often unwilling to support the validity of private marriages when they were brought into court, but the cases do show that individuals felt that they could marry themselves without the intervention of the church or the state. A couple could seal their union by using the forms of the official church marriage or by taking communion together;

or they could exchange rings or a piece of gold. Five instances show the range of customs. In the first case Henry Owen started to court Mary Scurlocke in 1700. Owen was a man of considerable public standing: a barrister and justice of the peace for Carmarthen, with an estate of over five hundred pounds a year, and in his thirties. In January 1704 he and Mary read together the marriage liturgy from the Book of Common Prayer and exchanged a ring. This became the subject of gossip. When Mary's mother learned of it, she dismissed the marriage and threw the ring in the fire. In the second case John Ramsey's claims about his contract with Ann Raby were similar but not so formal. Although he was asked by her stepmother not to visit so often, Ramsey and Ann continued to meet. He gave her a ring, and they contracted themselves in the garden as man and wife. They acted out the change in their status by going into her bedchamber when her family was at church and "continued together for many hours saluting and embracing each other and behaving themselves as such who were to be speedily married together." In the third case Elizabeth Bayley claimed that the agreement between herself and Peter Durrand had been made with her parents' consent. A written contract was made, and Durand took the Sacrament with her family as a pledge of fidelity. In the fourth case Margaret Rigby said that she and her fellow servant Edward Turpin had similarly sealed their contract by taking communion together. They later drew up contracts, which he kept, and she gave him a piece of gold. And in the fifth case a piece of gold was broken between William Frances and Mary Hallows when they promised never to marry anyone else and declared each other man and wife.[15]

All these private marriage contracts come from the London consistory in the first decade of the eighteenth century. By the 1750s there were no such cases in the consistory. The passage of the Marriage Act in 1753 may have made it worthless for anyone who believed that they had made such a contract before 1753 to bring it to court. But it is also likely that the practice itself had died out at some point in the first half of the century. By the middle of the century disputed marriages in the consistory were over irregular marriages made before unlicensed priests in the environs of the Fleet Prison or in Mayfair that could be made quickly and without the supervision of family, friends, or employers that an open marriage with banns called in the parish church entailed. It is likely that such marriages replaced the private contract for the poor who wished to be married quickly and for the rich who wished to be married quietly. Certainly in a West End parish like St. Margaret's, Westminster, from one-third to two-thirds of poor couples were married at the Fleet between 1700 and

1750. Marriages before Roman Catholic priests were similarly valid but illicit since it was still illegal to act as Catholic priest in England. The Marriage Act made both of these kinds of irregular marriages impossible. Therefore, by the 1790s almost all the disputes in the consistory questioned whether one of the spouses had been under twenty-one at the time of marriage or had married without the consent of a guardian.[16]

Two cases of disputed marriage from the consistory court in the 1750s, one before a Roman Catholic priest and the other in the Fleet, show how these irregular marriages could be used by fortune hunters to trap young men and women. In the first case the fortune hunter was a woman, Sarah Holland, the daughter of a clothier and dyer from Leonminater, who married Thomas Meigham the younger in 1737. Meigham's family were Roman Catholics, and the marriage was performed by a Roman Catholic priest in Thomas Saunders's house in Milk Alley near Wapping Chapel. The young couple were obliged to keep the marriage a secret from his parents since Sarah had been a servant in his father's house in Drury Lane. The priest who married them was "old Middleton," and Thomas Meigham's mother Martha used to complain "how ill Mr. Middleton . . . who was their intimate friend, had used them in marrying her son" to Sarah Holland. For the first four years of the marriage Meigham continued to live with his parents while visiting his wife at her lodgings. After the birth of their daughter, a reconciliation of sorts occurred, and Thomas Meigham the elder, a bookseller by trade, brought his granddaughter to live with him. The child was named Martha after Meigham's wife, and he was determined to give his granddaughter the best education he could. On the recommendation of Elizabeth Robinson, a milliner, he sent Martha to the Ursuline nuns in Boulogne, where Robinson's own granddaughter was being educated. But Meigham refused to be reconciled to his son's wife and even forbade her to come into his house. For seven years Sarah Meigham therefore lived in a room at the back of the house. In a room opposite to hers was John Canhill, who by the time of the divorce in 1756 was eighty-five years old. Other witnesses said that Canhill was a Roman Catholic priest, but he himself refused to admit it and would only say that he lived upon his fortune, which tellingly reveals the illegal status of such priests in England. Canhill remembered that when he had asked the elder Meigham why he behaved so inhumanely to his son's wife but treated his granddaughter so well, Meigham had answered "that he had reason for it and was not obliged to tell everybody."

In 1749 after twelve years of marriage Thomas Meigham left his wife Sarah and began to live with Rose Meigham, his unmarried first cousin, the daughter of his father's brother. They had several children, two of whom were alive in 1755. At first Meigham and Rose lived abroad, but in 1755 he returned with her to his father's house in Drury Lane and claimed that they were married. Meigham said that the Roman Catholic friends of his family were angry that he had married his first cousin since such a marriage was contrary to the canons of the church of Rome. (The marriage was legal in England.) Doing his best to appeal to the English hatred of papists, he insisted that it was at the urging of Roman Catholic priests that Sarah Meigham brought her case to prove her marriage. But John Canhill said that no one was upset with Meigham except "for his being so wicked in marrying Rose Meigham when he had a lawful wife" who was still alive.[17]

In the case of the marriage in the Fleet a young woman with the help of her servant was trapped into marrying a fortune hunter who almost immediately deserted her. Lucy Naomi Gough had been raised by her uncle Ferdinando John Paris after her father died in 1733, when she was eight years old. In July 1745 Jane Jay, a servant in her uncle's house, introduced her to Edward Strode, who was a clerk to an attorney in Gray's Inn. Without the knowledge of her uncle Lucy married Strode in August in a house in Mayfair when she was twenty years old. This marriage (like the Meigham marriage) was valid but illicit since it was performed by a priest of the Church of England without a license or the calling of banns in a parish church. Four months later on December 6, Jane Hay let Strode into Paris's house, where he consummated his marriage to Lucy. When he left (the footman was bribed to let him out), he took with him a diamond ring that Lucy's uncle had bought. Six days later Strode returned at night. He swore at Lucy and flung her to the floor. He drew his sword, took away her keys by force, and wounded her in the arm. He ransacked her drawers and took all her valuables except her clothes. These he pawned since, as her husband, they were now his property. He even tore from her hair a diamond star that she wore. Lucy tried to enquire about Strode through a friend who had heard of him "at several gaming houses and bawdy houses in and about Covent Garden, but could never see him." Lucy never saw Strode again. Her uncle, Paris, learned the entire story on January 4. He discharged his servants and told Lucy that she must leave and go to her husband. But Lucy's mother found lodgings for her and gave her an allowance to live on. Nine months later her uncle relented and took her back home. Strode in the meanwhile lived the life of a man about town, sleeping with fashionable prostitutes like Charlotte Hayes and Frances Murray. By 1754 Strode was a gentleman with a considerable fortune. (How he had gone from being an attorney's clerk to his later affluence is not apparent.) In that year he sold his officer's commission in the footguards for nine hundred pounds. He lived in a fashionable house in Hanover Square and kept his chariot. He had a coachman, a valet, and other servants. He must have been spending (so Lucy's brief estimated) two thousand pounds a year. Ten years after Strode abandoned Lucy, she filed for a divorce, which was granted in four months.[18]

Private marriages made without the presence of a priest and valid but illicit marriages before unlicensed priests seem to have created a sense that the couple could undo their contract if they proved incompatible because they, not the priest, had made the marriage. George Farquhar's play of 1707, *The Beaux' Stratagem,* has Mrs. Sullen say that it was only compatibility of tempers that made a marriage possible and that when this was missing, divorce ought to be possible. Dorinda tells her that the courts never grant divorces except for "uncleanness." "Uncleanness!" Sullen answers, "O Sister, casual violation is a transient injury and may possibly be repaired, but can radical hatreds be ever reconciled?" Farquhar ended the play saying that "consent is law enough to set you free." He seems to have taken his ideas from Milton, but unlike Milton, Farquhar presumed that women as well as men had a right to expect a compatible spouse.[19]

George, Lord Warrington stayed closer to Milton's point of view that a man needed a wife whose mind was compatible with his own. Warrington's opinions arose out of his personal experience. In 1702 as a means of restoring his family fortunes he made an arranged marriage to one of the two daughters of a wealthy London merchant. Warrington paid a marriage brokerage fee of one thousand pounds and received a portion of twenty-four thousand pounds with his wife Mary Oldbury. But the marriage fell apart after the first two years, and Warrington and Mary agreed to live separately in the same house after the birth of their daughter. Warrington complained that Mary was extravagant and that after he spoke to her about it, her one good quality (that "she seemed good-natured and easy in being advised") turned into "a sour dogged temper." Nine years after his marriage, Warrington told his uncle that Mary had "no conversation," that her only good quality was "being virtuous in the narrow sense that comprehensive word is used," by which he presumably meant that she was chaste in her actions. Her tongue, however, shocked Warrington, whose family traditions were straitlaced and who was unable to accept the sexual freedom that the daughter of a London citizen could use in conversation: "sometimes she'll have such discourse, where she's free as don't become a virtuous woman: and a little matter would bring on strong liquors." But since Mary did not take a lover, Warrington could not escape his marriage because there was no divorce for incompatibility. Without mentioning his own case directly (though the description of an unsatisfactory wife on pages 21–22 was based on his view of Mary), he therefore wrote a tract in 1739 advocating divorce for incompatibility, saying that two of the three purposes of marriage, namely the procreation of children and the avoidance of fornication, did not apply to some marriages, and that only the need for mutual society, help, and comfort was present in all. Mutual comfort could not be achieved, however, unless a husband was able to talk to his wife. When he could not, he ought to be able to divorce her, since the marriage did not really exist.[20]

Individuals in a more private station in life than Warrington's sometimes solved their difficulties by making public declarations or giving bonds that a marriage had ended and that both the former spouses were now free to remarry. James Hall (b. 1704) and his wife used the public declaration, as Hall explained when he was executed for murdering his master in 1741. He had married as his first wife a woman with a dubious sexual past. They lived together for some years and had children. But since they quarreled constantly, they both agreed that it was best to part. They therefore declared themselves free from each other in front of several witnesses. Hall then married again. In a second case, William and Elizabeth Phelps ended their marriage more formally, with a bond. After William went to sea, Elizabeth began to live with Robert Wilkins. When Phelps came home, he asked Elizabeth to return to him. When she refused, they agreed to live separately and to disown their marriage. On October 1, 1700, they signed a document renouncing the marriage, and Phelps gave a bond to Wilkins for five hundred pounds agreeing not to trouble Elizabeth. She took Wilkins's name, and they lived together as man and wife until he died. As a widow she was courted by John Pickard and married him on September 30, 1706. But Pickard discovered that her first husband was still alive. Since he was not willing to accept their private divorce act, he sued in the consistory court and had his marriage declared bigamous and null. A third possibility appears in 1722 in *Moll Flanders*. There Daniel Defoe presented an ecclesiastical divorce as though it gave the right to remarry, which it did not. This is what Moll's bank clerk husband proposes, and it is possible that Defoe knew that it was done. In the novel the problem is solved by having the divorced wife die from remorse, leaving the man free to remarry. But Moll in the meanwhile has unfortunately married a husband and parted from him. The husband, however, tells her that he gives her liberty to marry again and will never expose her. Moll's female friend solves this problem by appealing to the doctrine that consent makes and breaks marriages: "that as we parted by mutual consent, the nature of the contract was destroyed, and the obligation was mutually discharged."[21]

In the second half of the century William Webb and Ann Rider ended their marriage with a formal bond. But in this case the agreement was somewhat against the wife's will. In 1779 Webb, a shoemaker and a widower, married Ann, who was twenty-one. They lived together for three years until Webb turned her out of the house because he had fallen in love with her fifteen-year-old niece, Mary Brewer. Mary Brewer as a minor applied for a marriage license, and her mother gave her consent as a widow, though in fact her husband was the beadle of the Merchant Taylors Company and very much alive. Webb and Brewer were duly married and were still living together in 1793 when Ann Webb sued for divorce. Ann said that Webb had offered her twenty pounds when he turned her out and advised her that if she did not accept this payment, he would leave England and she would starve. Webb made a bond to pay the twenty pounds with his partner, Samuel Wyatt Farmer, as trustee. He paid for four or five years. When Farmer mislaid the bond, Webb refused to pay any more. But Webb told the consistory that Farmer's word was not to be trusted. It was Farmer who paid the costs of Ann Webb's divorce case, which she brought ten years after Webb stopped paying. Webb said that Farmer had told his friends that he had been to Doctors' Commons and "given Billy a lift," and that he had arranged for seventeen witnesses to be examined because he was determined to ruin Webb. Webb added that Farmer had once been tried for perjury. But Webb did not dispute the story of his bigamous (but not incestuous) marriage to his niece-in-law.[22]

A formal deed of separation could be used by one spouse as justification to remarry without the consent of the other partner. This was especially easy to do in the anonymity of London. But even in London gossip eventually made its way to an offended partner's ear. In 1779 Edmund Nash married Mary Johnson. They lived together in lodgings until Nash left to enlist in the army of the East India service in 1783. In his absence Mary had a love affair with a surgeon, John Irvine. After Nash discovered this, he and Mary separated by articles of agreement in December 1786. Mary Nash went to live at Wormley in Hertfordshire, where she kept a school under the name of Newman. Irvine joined her and took a house of his own and practiced as surgeon. After Mary and Irvine decided to marry, they went back to London, had their banns announced in St. Leonard Shoreditch, and were married there on September 12, 1787, with

Mary using the name of Nash and claiming to be a widow. They then
went back to Horsley. Mary gave up her school and moved into Irvine's
apothecary shop. They lived together until Irvine went to sea and died.
Edmund Nash heard of their marriage soon after it occurred. He had
searches made of a number of parish registers, trying to find the record
of the marriage, and succeeded in December 1789. By then Irvine was
dead and Mary had moved to Westham in Essex to keep a school under
the name of Irvine. Four months after finding the record of Mary's bigamous marriage, Nash sued for divorce.[23]

The form of popular divorce used by the poor that has recently been
most discussed by historians is the wife sale.[24] In it a man sold his wife
to another in public and usually by prearrangement. The practice seems
to have been especially prevalent in the century from 1750 to 1850, but
there are examples earlier than this. These sales should be seen as reversals
of the processes by which private marriages were made by exchanging
promises or a valuable object like a ring or a piece of gold or by writing
a contract. The wife sale denounced an existing contract sometimes by
words alone, sometimes by a written contract, and sometimes by exchanging an object of value. In the marriage contracts a virgin gave herself to
a man and passed from her family's to her husband's keeping. In the wife
sale a husband gave his wife into another man's keeping. The poor law
declaration that Thomas Carter made to the officials of Blackfriars in
London in the summer of 1783 neatly illustrates the process of sale. Carter
(who also used the name Cooke) ended one marriage by desertion and
entered another by buying his wife from her husband. He married Rebeccah Riddle (also called Brighthemstone) in Sussex in 1777 because she
had sworn that he was the father of her bastard child. It is likely that
Carter was forced into the marriage by the overseers of the poor. He did
not care for this contract, and within three months he ended his first
marriage by leaving Rebeccah. He then bought Mary Collingham of Lew-
isham from her previous husband for a bottle of beer. This marriage he
settled into, and seven years later he had two children, one born in Sussex
and the other in Hertfordshire. Within a year of the birth of his second
child, Carter and his family came to London and applied for relief. He
said that he believed that his first wife was still living.[25]

Wife sales in London began to be reported in the newspapers in the
1730s. In 1735 the keeper of an alehouse near St. Clement's Church in
the Strand, after nine years of marriage, sold his wife to a tolling-press
printer for ten guineas. Half a guinea was paid down, and two notes were
given for the payment of the rest. The alehouse keeper then arranged for

the common crier to announce in Milford Lane and Clare Market that he was no longer responsible for the debts of his divorced wife. But the arrangement did not work. The wife and her new husband after a few days asked the alehouse keeper to take her back, and he did. Thirty years later a sailor returning from China found that his wife had married a sentinel in the guards during his absence. She had done what others did: declared one marriage to a missing spouse over and contracted another. The sailor demanded his wife back; the soldier agreed. But then they drank together and reconsidered, with the result that for a treat of two pounds of beef sausages and a crown's worth of gin punch, the sailor gave the soldier back his wife. In the same year another case ended less happily. A journeyman carpenter in Southwark sold his wife in an alehouse to a fellow worker. But then he was sorry for what he had done and entreated his wife to return. When she refused, he hanged himself. A bricklayer's laborer had a different sort of regret a year later after he sold his wife: she inherited two hundred pounds from an uncle in Devonshire. His wife and her new husband had sealed their new union with a conventional marriage ceremony in a church.[26]

The reports of the sales in the 1790s describe a more elaborate public ritual. When Thomas Parsons sold his wife (whom he had married five years before and by whom he had had two children), he took her with a halter around her neck to a public house in Whitechapel and sold her to a cooper for a gallon of beer. A publican who gave his wife to a dealer in flowers used the public ceremony to seal an affair that had already been arranged by written articles of agreement. He took his wife into Smithfield market with a rope around her waist and tied her to the railings opposite St. Bartholomew's coffeeshop. After she was exposed for a quarter of an hour to a crowd that gathered, she was sold to the other man for a guinea. An attorney had advised the two men that the sale would not be valid unless it was completed in the open market. The florist with his new wife received from her previous husband a portion of twenty pounds's worth of "Birmingham" (or bad) halfpence. When a butcher sold his wife in Smithfield market to a hog-driver for three guineas and a crown, he put one halter around her neck and another around her waist, which he tied to railings near the Ram Inn. On some occasions there seems to have been no arrangement made in advance, and the bidding was genuine. A man who put his wife on sale in Smithfield decided that she was too valuable to part with after the bidding reached four pounds: a wag said he had decided to take her to the West End of town to see what she would fetch there. In another sale, a tailor outbid eight competitors. But a man who bought a wife could already have another at home, as did the carman from Compton Street who for a guinea got a second wife from a militiaman in Covent Garden.[27]

The wife sales demonstrate that the poor were able to invent their own rituals by which to end marriages that had become incompatible. But the forces that opposed such an idea of marriage were stronger than those which promoted it, and they were usually able to have the law on their side. Nonetheless, among the middle classes and the gentry, lawyers and married couples were able to subvert the law to their own purposes by collusion and plain fraud. This is shown by the advice given by John Andrew and William Strahan, two reputable practitioners in the consistory of sixteen years standing, to Jocelyn Sydney and his estranged wife Elizabeth. Sydney, who became the seventh earl of Leicester, married Elizabeth Lewis in 1717 when she was fourteen years old and he was thirty. In a settlement before the marriage, he agreed that once his wife was twenty-one, he would in return for her portion settle land to provide a jointure and pin money for herself and portions for their younger children. He in turn was allowed to cut timber to raise money to pay off a mortgage. Sydney cut the timber but never made the settlement. When the marriage fell apart, they lived separately, and each of them took lovers. Sydney said that Elizabeth went to wakes and country dances with people entirely unsuitable for the wife of a man of his quality. She also took two different young men with her to a favorite sand bank a mile from her house. Sydney eventually employed men to trap Elizabeth who broke into a cottage and found her (she was now twenty) with James Jenkins. Jenkins, whose clothes were unbuttoned and his stockings loose, confronted the men with a drawn sword as Elizabeth sat on the bed. Three years later the proctors from Doctors' Commons advised the couple how to end their marriage. John Andrews said that Sydney should get an ecclesiastical divorce and then an act of Parliament and that Elizabeth should not recriminate, that is, plead Sydney's adultery against him. In other words, Andrews recommended collusion between the couple as the only way for them both to regain their freedom.

But Andrews also advised that to protect Elizabeth, Sydney should be obliged to enter into a penal covenant to do whatever her counsel required if it became necessary to obtain a reversal of the ecclesiastical divorce. William Strahan advised Elizabeth to enter an appeal against the ecclesiastical divorce and to keep it going until Sydney complied with an agreement to give her back her property. Sydney signed the agreement but then fulfilled none of it. Instead he and Elizabeth pursued a suit in Chancery for ten years that eventually compelled him to pay her pin money of one hundred pounds and its arrears and to settle land for her jointure. Elizabeth lived with Paul Beeson and had children by him, one of whom succeeded Sydney as the eighth earl of Leicester since he was presumed legitimate, as Elizabeth and Sydney had never been divorced. Sydney, however, left as much of his estate as he could to his illegitimate daughter Anne Sydney. At Sydney's death, Elizabeth, now countess of Leicester, thought of contesting his will but did not. She also declined to marry Paul Beeson after all those years. Sydney's two legitimate nieces did contest his will and eventually a division was made between them and Ann Sydney. The nieces tried to claim that in his last two years Sydney had gone mad. After Sarah Allen, his daughter's mother, died at Penshurst, where they had lived together, he had put her body in a lead coffin and kept it in an open vault in his chapel until he died. He had seen ghosts and apparitions. He had spent his time obsessively cutting out patterns for clothes: several sacks of them were found. He had up to thirty tailors at a time in his house but was always dressed poorly. He had grown nasty and dirty. He grafted crab apple trees with ones that were nonpareil. A sad end, if only a small part were true, to a difficult man's life. Both he and Elizabeth would have been happier if he had followed the advice of their lawyers and colluded with her to get an act of Parliament that would have allowed them both to remarry.[28]

Fraud rather than collusion was used when the desire of spouse to end a marriage was strong enough. In 1781 George Kemp married Jane Lumsden when they were both thirty years old. For sixteen years they had a happy marriage. But in June 1799 Kemp sued Jane for divorce on the ground that she had had an affair with her cousin, Charles Farquharson. Farquharson, an ensign in the army on half pay, had left his wife and family in Scotland in 1796 and come to London on business. Jane urged Kemp to let Farquharson stay with them to save him money, which he did until Farquharson was arrested for debt in 1797. Kemp later claimed that during his visit, Farquharson and Jane conducted an affair, especially when Kemp, a busy tailor, was away for most of the day. After Farquharson was released from prison Jane persuaded Kemp to take him in again. Jane now pretended to be ill. Kemp took a house for her at Mill Bank where Farquharson pursued his love affair with Jane. Kemp said that when the landlady told him of it in July 1798, he informed Jane and her relations that he could no longer live with her and filed for a divorce in June 1799.

Jane countered that Kemp's entire suit was a lie designed to end their marriage so that he could marry another of her relations, Margery Farquharson. When Margery visited them in 1797, she and Kemp began an affair. Kemp now started to mistreat his wife after many years of happy marriage. Margery became pregnant and left Kemp's house. After bearing a daughter in May, she returned and they continued their affair. Kemp promised Margery that he would try to get a divorce from Jane. He even made a contract on February 2, 1799, to marry Margery on the death of his wife or after he had divorced her. Margery read the contract out to various people. The idea of such a contract had occurred to Defoe in *Moll Flanders*. Moll's banker husband proposes before their marriage that she should "sign and seal a contract with him, conditioning to marry him as soon as the divorce could be obtained, and to be void if he could not obtain it." Jane Farquharson got hold of the contract her husband had made and was able to introduce it as evidence. She denied that there had ever been anything between her and Charles Farquharson, who was a man of sixty with a wife and six children. Farquharson had called on her at Mill Bank to ask about her health and at her husband's suggestion. But Kemp had urged his wife to live at Mill Bank so that he could pursue his affair with Margery. After Kemp filed for his divorce in June 1799 Margery took lodgings and Kemp visited her. She had a second child by Kemp in November. At her delivery Margery told the man-midwife that her name was Kemp. Jane Kemp's story stopped her husband's attempt to end their marriage, but it is apparent that emotionally the marriage had dissolved once Kemp fell in love with another woman.[29]

Neither collusion nor fraud were, however, very satisfactory ways of ending a marriage in which the partners no longer found themselves compatible. Middle-class couples therefore began to privately make separate maintenance contracts instead. These contracts allowed a woman to live on her own (and possibly with her lover), made her financially independent, and sometimes gave her custody of some of her children. It is possible that women were encouraged to use these private separations rather than the more public forum of the consistory court, and this may explain the decline in the number of consistory suits brought by women after 1750. But by the first decade of the nineteenth century the common law courts turned their face against these innovations as much as they could by limiting the terms of these contracts on the ground that marriages were not "fluctuating contracts" that "at their pleasure" couples could dissolve, if only partially. Nonetheless the contracts continued to be made—a sure sign that some couples thought of marriage in exactly the terms the court disapproved of. And for individuals beneath the level of the gentry, it is likely that these contracts were sometimes used to justify a second, but technically bigamous, marriage.[30]

This middle-class world of secret marriages, private separations, bigamous marriages, and consistory divorces is displayed in a consistory case from the 1790s. In February 1788 Timothy Goldsmith, a widower and the mate on an East India merchantman, married Ann Green, a spinster. The marriage occurred without the knowledge or consent of her father, who lived in Hull, or of her brother, who lived in London. Since Goldsmith was due to sail soon for India, the marriage was left secret and unconsummated. After the marriage ceremony Ann returned to her brother's London house and five days later left for her father's house in Hull. But Goldsmith almost immediately asked her to return to London. When she arrived, he told her that he wished to consummate the marriage, probably because consummation would have made it impossible to later declare the marriage invalid. Ann was afraid of becoming pregnant since he was going to be away for nearly two years and she was supposed to continue to pass as an unmarried woman and use her father's name. But Goldsmith insisted, and the marriage was consummated. A week later Ann returned to Hull. Goldsmith continued to demand secrecy, but he made no financial provision for Ann: she even had to borrow the cost of her journey back to Hull from her brother's father-in-law. At Hull Ann received an offer of marriage from a gentleman in the neighborhood that she declined. This made her father suspicious that she and Goldsmith (the family must have known of their friendship) had in fact married. He therefore forced Ann to leave his house but gave her a small allowance.

By April Goldsmith had reached Madeira, and from there he wrote to Ann disowning the marriage. He said "that he was obliged to give her up, that he should not have deserted her after his marriage with her, if a friend had not accused him of ingratitude which he declared he should be guilty of if he did not instantly resign his pretensions to her." It is not clear what had occurred. Was Goldsmith involved with another woman? Was he under some sort of obligation to Ann's brother or father that the secret marriage destroyed? Had he decided that there was no chance of profiting from the marriage? Was he simply a rake who had been intent on deflowering a young woman he did not especially wish to marry? Ann claimed that Goldsmith had kept various prostitutes in London, so there may have been something to the last possibility. Ann now destroyed all his letters after showing them to her friend, Ann Bateman. She must have been relieved to know that at least she had not become pregnant. Seventeen months later when Goldsmith's ship returned to London, Ann tried to see him, but he refused to meet her. Four months later she revealed the affair to her brother. He advised her to come to London and with his help for a month she tried unsuccessfully to find a husband: better bigamy than no marriage at all. She and her brother next attempted to get Goldsmith to sign a deed of separation so that any property she might inherit from her father would be protected. But Goldsmith refuse to do this unless he received five hundred pounds. He added that once he was paid and the separation signed, he would advise Ann, since she would still be without a husband, "to go to some obscure market town and marry again if she thought proper." This was clearly a well-known solution in a world where absolute divorces were possible only for adultery and by act of Parliament.

Goldsmith's letter does suggest that he had entered the marriage from the beginning for financial gain, but he must soon have decided that he did not wish to live as Ann's husband. Instead, he would wait until her father died and then as her husband claim her inheritance. But it is not possible to say for certain what his scheme was. Whatever his purpose, Ann had made a marriage from which she needed to escape as far as was possible. In this case a private separation would not have been adequate: she needed the stronger guarantee of a consistory divorce against an unscrupulous man.[31]

The aristocracy and the gentry after 1760 began to draw on this longstanding tradition that couples had the power to marry and divorce themselves if their tempers proved incompatible, or if one of them fell in love with someone else. But it was very difficult for them to institutionalize this in England where one had to first receive a divorce or separation in the consistory, then a judgment in the common law courts for criminal conversation against a wife's lover, and finally an act of Parliament that allowed both husband and wife to marry. Nonetheless, from the midcentury onward, one-third of the women accused of adultery in the consistory divorces were gentlewomen, and adulterous wives came to make up two-thirds of the business of the court. The sexual behavior of married women had always dominated the business of the court, but in the early eighteen century they had appeared in defamation suits trying to prove that they were not adulterous as a neighbor had claimed, and most of them had been women from the middle and lower ranks of society. After 1760 the aristocratic husbands in the consistory divorces were not trying to mend their marriages but to end them, and it is very likely that both the increase in the number of husbands petitioning and the change in the social class of adulterous wives were a consequence of the rising expectations of marriage with which individuals now came to it.

The rise in divorces for incompatibility occurred throughout Europe, but the law on the Continent was always more accommodating, as English men and women discovered if they married a foreigner. In France after the Revolution it even became possible for a time for a couple to divorce either for the fault of one of them or for mutual incompatibility, and it was relatively cheap and simple to do so. The difference between the two legal systems in the 1790s is neatly demonstrated in a consistory case. In 1772 James Woodmason married Mary Magdalen Gavelle, who was then nineteen years old. The marriage lasted eighteen years, and they had ten children, two of whom survived. In August 1789 Mary Magdalen went with her brother James to visit their parents, who lived in Paris. She stayed there until June 1790, when she met Woodmason in Flanders. He soon returned to London, but she remained to take their sickly child to the baths. Woodmason came back to Flanders in September and found that Mary Magdalen had neglected their child and had never gone to the baths. They quarreled and agreed to separate. She went back to her father. Woodmason agreed to pay her two hundred pounds a year and took the child back with him to London. In 1792 the French Assembly passed Europe's most liberal divorce legislation, which allowed a woman to sue with relative ease for a divorce and permitted her to remarry. In June 1796 Mary Magdalen obtained such a divorce without Woodmason's knowledge and married Joseph Antoine Guibert when she was forty-four. Woodmason then had to undertake the more tedious English procedure to achieve his own freedom. He filed in the consistory in January 1798, and that divorce was granted in March. There was hardly much point to suing for damages so that step was omitted. His divorce act passed in Parliament in May 1798. He and his wife were now under English law each free to remarry. It had all only taken five months—record time for England.[32]

The law of divorce in Sweden also allowed divorces on the ground of incompatibility, though the process was more elaborate than in revolutionary France. In the case of Elizabeth Lishman her Swedish lover persuaded her to enter into a sexual relationship by promising that he would take her to Sweden where she could divorce her husband and marry him. Lishman had married her husband in 1787 and had lived with him for four years. But he neglected and mistreated her and eventually left her. About two years later she met the Swede. But after he had made her pregnant, he also left her. Since Elizabeth worked as a servant, she had to leave her place when her baby was born. Unable to find another place as a servant as long as she had to provide for her child, she offered the child to the Foundling Hospital in 1794. As a poor woman in England, Elizabeth had no effective remedy against her husband when he deserted her. She could not afford a divorce in Parliament, and such divorces were granted only to men. Legally she was tied for life to her absent and abusive husband.[33]

The increase in divorces for incompatibility after the middle of the eighteenth century was part of the rise of romantic love and the domesticated family that occurred throughout much of Western culture. The new ideals and their practice brought with them higher expectations of marital compatibility. These expectations probably resulted in a greater amount of marital breakdown. Divorces certainly became more numerous and easier to obtain in England, France, the Netherlands, and the United States. As a percentage of all marriages, divorces were still quite low. But what nonetheless seemed to contemporaries to be an alarming and unprecedented wave of divorces did mark a major cultural shift. The modern history of Western divorce had begun. The more traditional grounds of adultery or cruelty on the part of one of the spouses were not, however, abandoned, and certainly they remained in England the only official grounds for separation and divorce. But these traditional grounds were given new meaning in the context of the idea that true marriages were founded on mutual love and the compatibility of the temperaments of wives and husbands. Adultery ceased to be part of the history of cuckoldry and became a domestic tragedy, less a matter for public scorn (though that was still there) and more a part of private pain. A man after 1750 was less likely to divorce his wife because she had become a prostitute; instead it was usually the case that she had eloped with their mutual best friend. The female aristocratic libertine had been tolerable under a system of arranged marriages and separate social lives after marriage: romantic love and companionship in marriage made her intolerable. But after 1760 most adulterous wives were not libertine. They were instead women who had either found true love for the first time or a more compatible friend. It is therefore likely that what the law required a couple to present as a divorce for her adultery was in fact often a divorce on the grounds of incompatibility. But the parliamentary divorce was a device employed largely by the landed classes. The middle-class man was less likely to seek one (table 10.2) from a lack of social self-confidence. But both classes were committed to the new ideals of love that had produced a renewed commitment to the traditional norm that a husband and wife who proved incompatible should be able to end their marriage.[34]

CHAPTER TWELVE

Romance and Adultery

A t the beginning of the eighteenth century cases brought by married women who had been accused of adultery by their neighbors dominated the consistory court. These women sought to protect their marriages by defending their reputations and proving that their husbands were not cuckolds. At the end of the century the adulterous wife still dominated the court, but it was her husband who charged her, and he was seeking a divorce to end the marriage. The plaintiffs at the beginning of the century came mainly from among the less well off; those at the end represented the solid middle class, the gentry, and the aristocracy. At the beginning of the century the adulterous woman's husband had been cuckolded. But in the divorce cases after 1750 that are the subject of this chapter, adultery became a domestic tragedy that very often had had its origin in the heart of a family's intimacy. A similar change from cuckoldry to tragedy has been noticed in the presentation of adultery in the novel. It was perhaps the case that art had copied the actualities of life.[1]

Before 1750 the husbands who sued for divorce complained of wives who had become prostitutes or had deserted them for lovers who were strangers to their husbands. After 1750 the women in the divorce cases had usually fallen in love with one of their servants or with their husband's best friend, or his near relation, or his business partner. The wife who ran off with her husband's best friend can be found in the majority of cases whether in the 1750s (nine of twenty) or the 1790s (twenty-three of fifty-four) as the two parts of this chapter show. The number of divorces initiated by men after 1750 steadily increased, and husbands eventually brought twice as many suits as women, reversing the pattern that had prevailed before 1750 when wives had been the majority of divorce plaintiffs (fig. 10.1). The increase in the number of cases brought by men can

be accounted for by the gentlemen who followed their consistory divorces
with an act of Parliament that allowed them to remarry. This is especially
clear from the temporary decline in the total number of consistory divorces
in the 1780s, when a conservative lord chancellor made it difficult for
divorce acts to pass in Parliament and therefore pointless to go to the
consistory. But in the divorces of the middle-class men who did not seek
acts of Parliament, a very similar kind of adultery was also present. It is
very likely that both groups of men, as well as their adulterous wives and
their lovers, were inspired by the new ideals of romantic love that gave
individuals higher expectations for their marriages and inclined them to
try to make new alliances when their first marriages had not brought them
the kind of love they desired. But it was probably the interplay of the
differences between male and female sexuality that made the husband's
best friend or close associate into his wife's most likely lover. These differences in sexuality were produced by the domestic context in which women
usually enacted their sexual desire and by the new male expectation that
men should be exclusively heterosexual.

   The new male heterosexuality made a radical separation between homosexual and homosocial relations among men. Heterosexuality required a
constant male dominance in which there was no room for the seventeenth-
century practice in which adult men had sexual relations with both women
and boys. From the onset of adolescence all males now could allow themselves to desire only women. Any male who desired another male was
assigned to a despised third gender between the majority of men and
women. To demonstrate that they did not belong to this third gender,
the majority of men fervently pursued women, seducing other men's wives
and going to prostitutes, even though prostitution destroyed marital intimacy and assigned a minority of women to a life that violated the ideals
of the domesticated woman.

   Heterosexuality, however, produced a second dynamic that resulted in
close friendships between men that were not sexual. They were now free
to bring a friend home to share in the warmth of their domestic intimacy
precisely because the bond between the two men was homosocial and not
homosexual. But after husband, wife, and best friend were thrown together, romantic love that was ideally supposed to support marriage disrupted it when a man's wife and his best friend fell in love with each
other. In this erotic triangle husbands suffered not only the loss of their
wives. They experienced as well a sexual subordination to their closest
male friend. A homosocial bond from which homosexual desire had been

carefully excluded thereby became the means of subordinating one male to another. This was an adultery that brought with it the sting of homosexual rape.[2]

The adulterous wives in these divorce cases demonstrate that women in the eighteenth century could take sexual initiative. But the absence for most of the century of third-gender sapphists, who could play the part in women's sexual lives that adult effeminate sodomites played in men's, meant that women's initiatives with men were never organized into an exclusive heterosexuality. Instead the sexual lives of women were usually constrained by their domestic lives as mothers and housekeepers, by their economic dependence on men, and by their subjection to male violence. Women who managed to escape one of these constraints were soon reined in by one or both of the others. Prostitutes did not have to keep house or care for children, but they were dependent on men's financial support and subject to their violence. Young unmarried women lost their livelihoods when they became pregnant. They were likely to be courted in coercive ways, and some men found rape an acceptable prelude to marriage. But sexual experience and the adult status that it conveyed came for most women only in marriage since the majority of women would probably not have masturbated before their first intercourse with their husbands. Sexually active married women were, of course, constrained by motherhood and housekeeping, economic dependence, and the violence of their husbands. In that world before 1750 the widow who remarried came closest to achieving sexual independence. If careful, she could maintain control of her income and choose a younger husband whom she found sexually appealing. But it was harder (as the consistory divorces show) to escape male violence. After 1750 a woman could escape violence if she were lucky enough to marry a man affected by the new romantic and domestic ideals. It is striking, for instance, that almost none of the divorced women in this chapter countercharged that an angry husband had beaten them after their adultery was discovered. The wives of such men were instead much more likely to have a chance to marry their lovers. It was now the divorced wife who remarried rather than the widow. Romance created sexual initiative for women even if the domestic constraints within which they passed their lives meant that they were most likely to take as lovers men who had visited them at home. But there was still punishment for taking initiative, and it came through their roles as mothers when their aggrieved husbands took from their tender care the children who were still legally his alone.

Romantic Love and Divorce, 1750–90

In cases from the middle of the century the new adultery that accompanied the new fashion of making romantic marriages was best displayed when a woman fell in love with her husband's close relative or best friend and the adulterous relationship began in the midst of domestic intimacy. This was true for both the gentry and the middle classes, though the romance might be more self-conscious among the gentry, and they were certainly more likely to try to marry their lovers after a divorce by Parliament. Among the middle classes adulterous intimacy might develop after two married couples had known each other for a long time; or a woman might fall in love with a man whom her husband had recently introduced into their circle; or a young wife after her sexual awakening in marriage might turn not only to her husband's good friend but to other men as well. Among the gentry a wife much younger than her husband could fall in love with a man her own age with whom she might hope to have a more romantic marriage after her divorce; or a woman might become a "slave to passion," despite her best intentions, after a new friend made his way into her household's neighborhood; or two lovers could justify their adultery by believing that it released them both into a marriage of true souls that was more than mere sensuality.

In the case of two middle-class couples who had known each other for some time, the adultery made a strong new bond between the lovers, but they were unable to marry, since although the woman's husband could divorce her by act of Parliament, the man's wife could not divorce him. Richard Glover and Hannah Nunn had married in 1737 when he was twenty-five and she was seventeen. She had a portion of seven thousand pounds, and he became a successful insurance broker. They had a number of children, two of whom survived. In 1753 after sixteen years of marriage the couple took "country lodgings" from April to September at Mr. Smith's, a dancing master at Newington Green. There they were joined by William and Margaret Hollier. The two men were intimate friends, and Glover had helped Hollier out of financial difficulties. During the summer months Glover went once a week to London to his house in Exchange Alley; Hollier made the most of his absences and began an affair with Hannah Glover, who was a more attractive woman than his wife. He threw his arms around Hannah's neck and kissed her as they sat in each other's laps. This his wife must have seen, and they quarreled about it when they were together in bed at night. He did not deny what had happened but damned her blood for mentioning Mrs. Glover's name, since he had often forbidden her to do so. Following this quarrel with his wife, a servant saw Hollier go down into Hannah Glover's bedroom early in the morning and heard the door bolted. This was followed by the sounds of kissing and the bed's creaking with the lovers' exertions. They even went to bed together when Glover came back from London and took his Sunday afternoon walk in the fields for three or four hours. Hollier and Hannah laughed at Margaret Hollier, and Hannah called her a "nasty, ill-conditioned toad." Hollier, with a touch of loyalty, replied, "let her alone, she is an ill-contrived beast, let her go." Margaret Hollier at this point passes out of the story, as do the wives of other adulterous husbands in these cases. She became aware of the affair between her husband and Hannah Glover long before the busy Glover did, and she seems to have tried to check it. But her husband was able to use his authority to silence her. Hollier does seem to have had some affection for her, but it was not strong enough to balance Hannah's charms.

When the two couples returned to London in the fall, Hollier visited Hannah almost daily in the morning, when she would order the servants not to make her bed as they usually did but to wait until the afternoon. In May 1754 Glover discovered the affair, and he and his wife agreed to separate. By the terms of the agreement she was to live in France, where she asked her widowed sister-in-law to go with her. But Hollier evidently told Glover that he would never leave Hannah and would act as her husband. Together they lived in Paris and St. Cloud under the name of Halifax. Glover sued Hollier for criminal conversation, and Hollier was outlawed for not responding. The consistory court then granted a separation, and this was followed by a parliamentary divorce. Hollier and Hannah continued to live abroad, moving from Paris to Antwerp. By the act of Parliament Hannah was now free to remarry, but he could not since Parliament did not grant divorces to women with adulterous husbands.[3]

In the second middle-class case a wife fell in love with a man whom her husband had recently introduced into their family. When Edward Wilford was thirty he courted Rachel Norsa, who was twenty-one. They married in 1746 and had several children, two of whom survived. Wilford had a place in the Exchequer worth three to four hundred pounds a year and lived in a house in New Palace Yard. In 1756, after ten years of marriage and when she was thirty-one, Rachel Wilford began an affair with John Berkley, a new friend of the family's. On a visit a few days before Christmas in 1756, Rachel and Berkley kissed each other, and he put his hands under her petticoat and into her bosom. Her eldest child, who was three, was present in the room and began to cry. When Rachel called the maidservant, and the servant asked the child why he cried, he replied that it was because of the kissing. So the child was taken away, and the love-making continued. To make matters easier Berkley moved and took a lodging next door to the Wilfords' house. On Christmas Eve at eight in the morning he came visiting when Wilford was sleeping. At first the servants would not let Berkley in, but he insisted. Without her stays and with her clothes loosely thrown on, Rachel came to see him in the parlor. When she asked what he wanted, he answered that she knew and began to kiss her. Rachel first made certain that her husband was asleep and that her child was quiet and then bolted the parlor door.

In March when the lovers used the back parlor, the servants heard the easy chair squeaking. One of them listened at the door and heard Rachel "in great ecstasy and rapture call out . . . 'Oh dear Mr. Berkley—Oh Christ, Mr. Berkley.'" This continued for two or three hours. After this the lovers grew bolder. Rachel would signal from her window to Berkley next door that her husband was not at home. If Wilford returned unex-pectedly, Berkley would go out the bedroom window and walk along the gutter and into the back garret of the house where he lodged. Once he had to move from the back kitchen into a closet in the fore kitchen and then into the coal hole until Wilford left again. When Wilford was at home, Rachel would say that she was going to visit a neighbor. But instead she would go to Berkley's, who was seen putting his hands up under her petticoats as she climbed up the stairs ahead of him.

In October Wilford came home and met Berkley in his house, to their mutual consternation. For the first time he became suspicious and decided to sleep in a separate room. But the lovers did not grow more cautious. A candle was placed in Rachel's window either to call her home again when Wilford returned or to tell Berkley that Wilford was gone. The affair became the talk of the neighborhood, and on March 10 Wilford "put her away." Rachel wrote him a letter of confession stressing that she had never slept with Berkley in any bed in Wilford's house or in any other bed. The marriage bed remained inviolate: sex in a chair was less incriminating. But she must have forgotten the night her servants remem-bered when she and Berkley had spent from eleven until three in the morning in bed in Wilford's absence. She had rolled up her shift and petticoat the next morning instead of scattering her foul linen around her room as she usually did. But her servants unrolled them and found the incriminating stains. Wilford was not prepared to forgive her. He filed in the consistory court a month to the day after he received her written confession, but he did not seek a parliamentary divorce. One wonders whether poor Rachel found any lasting support from the lover who had moved her so passionately but whom she could never marry.[4]

In a third middle-class case it may have been less disruptive when Susannah Cooke slept with her husband's good friend, if only because he was only one among the many men whom she saw. Indeed Susannah bears a striking resemblance to the young wives in the previous chapter whose sexual awakening in marriage left them open to all the possibilities of desire. John Cooke and Susannah Cooper had married at the Fleet in 1746 in the presence of her aunt, Thomazin Underwood, when he was nineteen and she was eighteen. After they had they lived together for four years in different sets of lodgings in London, Susannah when she was twenty-two went to visit some relations in Berkshire and stayed three months in Joseph Sayer's house. While she was there, she began an affair with Sayer's son Peter. Peter was found in bed with her by James Grant, who pulled Sayer out of bed and got in himself. When Susannah returned to London, she began an affair with her husband's good friend Jeremiah Morrill.

Morrill venereally infected her, and in January 1752 she passed the disease to her husband. When Cooke accused her of adultery, she confessed in the presence of her mother, Mary Cooper. But Mrs. Cooper later said that she did not believe her daughter had ever had the disease and that Susannah had simply contracted a cold during her lying-in and had suffered a weakness that women often had in that situation. She did admit that Susannah was treated by a surgeon. Cooke himself said that his wife was not treated for the disease until March, after her delivery, since the medicine might have caused an abortion. For her cure Susannah went to Islington and then to Buckinghamshire. But while she was away she began to see other men again and became infected a second time. Cooke, after being entreated by her parents, and after Susannah's contrite assurances, forgave her a second time. Once more she was sent to Islington for her cure. While there she met two friends, Peter Counsil and John Demy, and began to have sex with them. Counsil moved into the house where Susannah lodged and took the room above hers. Mrs. Goodall, another lodger, became suspicious, and after watching Susannah all night, peeped through the keyhole of Counsil's room and saw Susannah undress and get into his bed.

When Susannah came back to London she visited Counsil, who was a journeyman jeweler, in his lodgings in Little Britain. She pretended that she was a maidservant and that her daughter whom she brought along was her master's child. One of Counsil's neighbors heard them together in bed since the head was up against the wall of her closet. Together Susannah and Counsil once went back from a tavern to his lodgings with his friend James Demy and another young married woman, Elizabeth Clarke. Clarke said that as she and Demy lay together on the bed with their clothes on, she watched Counsil and Susannah have sex. Irritated at her lover's lack of forcefulness, Susannah said to Counsil, "Don't lay niggling on me so. I desire that you would mount and let me have as it should be"—so Counsil mounted her.

Susannah's husband now left her, giving her at first seven shillings a week and later agreeing to pay her five pounds a quarter. For her part Susannah wrote Cooke a series of letters in which she begged to be taken back, and she also asked for money and clothes. Several times she pleaded that her daughter be allowed to visit her. Her mother continued to take her side, but her father refused to support her any longer. After her father's death in March 1756, Cooke himself stopped sending her money. Nine months later in January he filed for a separation in the consistory that was granted in June. He also brought a case for criminal conversation against Peter Sayer and was awarded twenty pounds in damages. He finished by receiving from Parliament a divorce that allowed him and his wife to re-marry. But there is no record which if any of her lovers poor Susannah married.[5]

In the first aristocratic case from the 1750s, the marriage may not have been romantic, but the divorce was, when the young second wife of an older man fell in love with a handsome man her own age. In 1746 Charles Hope Weir, a younger son of the earl of Hopetown, married Lady Ann Vane, the daughter of the earl of Darlington. After eight years of marriage and two sons, Hope Weir, who liked to travel, left his wife in England, went abroad, and was gone for twenty months. Five months after his return, Lady Ann gave birth to a child who was obviously not his. In his absence she had fallen in love with George Monson, a younger son of Lord Monson, whom the duke of Newcastle described as "a very pretty young man." (Some would read a degree of sexual ambiguity into Newcastle's statement, but with what accuracy it would be difficult to say.) Monson was twenty-six years old, Hope Weir forty-six. Hope Weir received his consistory divorce in February 1757 and one from Parliament in May. The young couple then married and seem to have lived happily ever after. Gilly Williams, at any rate, wrote in 1765 that Monson's friends saw little of him because "he lives shut up with Lady Anne and is going to settle for life in some remote country." Hope Weir's divorce was not, however, quite the new way. His wife had fallen in love with a man who was not his intimate friend, and the affair began while he was abroad.[6]

But among the aristocracy and the gentry in the 1750s there were women who fell in love with friends of their husband's, and in their divorces the new ideals of romantic love and domesticity played very significant roles. One couple who were desperately in love against the advice of all their friends married as soon as a parliamentary divorce made it possible. And with another pair of lovers even their sexual fantasies were built on the ideals of true marriage and the tender care of children. In the first case Charles Wymondesold had married Henrietta Knight in 1748 when she was eighteen and he was twenty-seven. She was Lord Luxborough's daughter; his father had estates in Essex and Buckinghamshire. She brought five thousand pounds as her portion, and he received five thousand pounds from his father and one thousand pounds a year in land. They had a child who died. In London they had a house of their own, but in the countryside they lived with his father, who had a house at Wanstead. Lord Tylney also had a house in the neighborhood that his brother Josiah Child frequently visited in 1751. Child became friendly with the Wymondesold household and began an affair with Henrietta Wymondesold three years after her marriage. They corresponded, and she kept copies of her letters that were eventually seized and used against her. She told Child that she "never would have yielded myself a slave to passion but you found my heart an easy conquest because it was fraught with esteem and every good opinion of you."

After Wymondesold discovered the affair, the couple agreed to live separately, and she was given four hundred pounds a year. He also asked her to stop seeing Child. But instead the lovers met in Paris and took lodgings in London, where they saw each other. As a result a new deed of separation was drawn up in June 1752. Child's relations disapproved of the affair and (according to Horace Mann, who knew Child's brother in Italy) "dreaded his ruin by that woman and have often given him warning of it." They hoped he would visit his brother, Lord Tylney, who had gone to live in Florence so that he could better pursue his taste for young men. Mann thought that Child would only have "to live abroad till the affair can be made up." He added that in Italy only the woman would have been thought to be at fault and that she "would be punished by the confinement to a villa or be put into a convent at the worst." But the English were different. Wymondesold sued Child for twenty thousand pounds damages (which was part of the ruin Child's family had anticipated) and

was awarded twenty-five hundred pounds in February 1753. In May he
sued for separation in the consistory and received it the following February. That same month he brought a divorce bill into Parliament, and by
April the matter was concluded. Henrietta kept the annuity that had been
agreed to earlier, and in May she married Child.[7]

In the final case from the 1750s the lovers seem to have experienced
their sexual desire for each other only in the context of the true marriage
of souls. In 1750 Admiral Charles Knowles, whose first wife had died,
courted and married the eighteen-year-old Maria Bonget, whose parents
kept a hotel for the nobility and gentry in Aix-la-Chapelle. Since she was
a Roman Catholic, they were married twice, first in a Catholic church and
then in a Protestant ceremony. Two years later Knowles was appointed
governor of Jamaica and went there with his family. In 1756 they returned
to England, but Maria sailed with their three children three months ahead
of him. The captain of the ship was James Gambier, thirty-four years old,
married, and a great friend of Knowles. Before they sailed for England,
Maria and Gambier fell passionately in love. Gambier concealed the affair
from Knowles by appearing to court Maria's unmarried companion, Florence Bletchington, whom Knowles sent home to her family. But Maria's
housekeeper, Elizabeth Bentley, was aware of what was happening.

The lovers first met in March and consummated their affair on April
23 after making vows and exchanging a ring. Gambier later referred to it
as "that awful solemn day, our mutual, happy sacred wedding day that
forever gave the loveliest, tenderest and sweetest, truest of women to the
fondest and faithfullest of men." He called it "the proof of your love [that]
you gave me that day in giving me possession of thy soul and body." He
kept the day sacred and dated his life from it rather than from his birthday.
God had joined them and witnessed their vows. In his prayers at night,
he named Maria as wife and asked God's protection on her. When they
were apart in England, he dreamed of her and her children in a vision of
domestic bliss. He even fought her husband for her in his dreams. In one
dream, finding her alone in a room with another man sitting close to her,
he indignantly asked who the man was. The man replied that he was the
master of a merchant ship and told him, after putting his hand on his
sword, that if Maria belonged to Gambier, Gambier could take her, for
he the master did not care a farthing for her except "for the sake of dying
away in you" (that is reaching sexual climax) and then she might be discarded. Gambier now drew his sword and rushed the man. He intended
to rescue Maria from a husband who only loved her for her body, whereas
his was a more spiritual love. But the dream broke, and he awakened as

his wife in the real world called out to him, "Good God, what is the matter?" Gambier told her that it was nothing: he had been dreaming. She replied, "Yes you have, and quarreling, for you screamed out these words, 'accursed villain, take that.'" Gambier had broken out in a sweat and was as wet as if he had been dipped overboard. This is the only appearance that Gambier's wife makes in the evidence, and as with Margaret Hollier in the first of these six stories, it is not possible to say how she dealt with her husband's obsession with another woman.

Gambier was clearly disturbed by the thought of sex without romantic attachment. He may even have been anxious that his own love for Maria was more sensual than he cared to admit. In another letter to Maria he asked her if she were happy that her sister had married, but he worried that her sister's husband had "only married her for her beauty and to enjoy her, and when the honeymoon is over, she will be wretched." He seems to have dreamed of Maria's children as often as he did of her. Domesticity justified sensual attachment. He saw Maria and himself walking by the riverside, carrying her youngest girl with her two other children following, as he gathered peaches for her from a tree. They agreed that in their letters he would be Torrismond and she Leonora, and he ended by asking "when, oh when shall I sleep in tranquillity and blest in my Leonora's arms."

On the journey home to England, Gambier and Maria supped together every evening and then locked themselves in her bedchamber. Her housekeeper Elizabeth Bentley looked through the keyhole and saw them in bed together. During the voyage, Maria became concerned that she was pregnant. She told Bentley that she would give any sum of money to make it not so. She frequently took "forcing physick" and asked Bentley if she knew of a recipe for making an abortion. Bentley denied understanding such things but said that she had heard that Penny Royal water, saffron, and frequent bleeding would work. Maria tried them but to no effect.

Once they were in England, the lovers agreed to correspond. Maria told Bentley to give her Gambier's letters unopened. They were already aware that her maid and his man, and one or two others, knew of their affair. Gambier visited Maria at her husband's house in London. They arranged and tested a closet in which he could lock himself away if Knowles returned unexpectedly. Maria told Bentley that she wished her husband were dead. The lovers had miniatures of each other made and exchanged a special bracelet. This went on for five months in England.

Bentley, however, had decided to leave Maria's service. When she did, she took two of Gambier's letters, which Maria tried to buy back through the secretary of the imperial ambassador. But Gambier's letters came to light by a different means. As Maria played with her children one day, her handkerchief became disarranged and the letters fell out of her bosom. She was then called away, leaving the letters behind. A young visitor noticed her own name in one of the letters, read them all, and told her mother their contents. This lady was a good friend of Knowles. She went to another of Knowles's friends, a clergyman, who consulted three more of his intimate friends. They all agreed that Knowles should be told and the letters seized. Knowles quickly applied to the consistory and was granted his divorce. He also sued Gambier for damages and was awarded one thousand pounds. He did not, however, seek a divorce in Parliament. But the lovers in any case could not have married since Gambier's wife could not divorce him in Parliament.[8]

The cases of adulterous wives made up two-thirds of the business of the consistory court after 1760, but it would be tedious to describe all four decades' worth of these cases. Some of those from the 1760s and 1770s were printed in the seven volumes of *Trials for Adultery* published in 1779 and 1780. But whoever made the selection of cases for that collection wished to present most divorces as the consequence of adultery in gentle-women. This was achieved by not printing the divorce cases brought by middle-class men and by women. From the 1760s the *Trials* printed ten of the twenty-three cases brought by men in the consistory but only two of the thirteen cases brought by women. In the 1770s the proportion in the *Trials* was the same: twenty-five of the sixty-one cases brought by men were printed but only three of the twenty-one cases by women. The *Trials* also favored the cases in which the aggrieved husband went on to get a divorce from Parliament that allowed remarriage. It printed from the 1770s nineteen of thirty such cases from the consistory but only five of the thirty-one that did not go on to Parliament. This meant that the cases brought by the gentry were emphasized, since they were more likely to go on to Parliament than were middle-class men. This selection was made presumably with an eye to what would interest the reading public. Female adultery and aristocratic vice must have sold better than male cruelty and the failed marriages of the middle classes. But what may have made the greatest sensation was parliamentary divorce and the right to remarry. Remarriage and the divorce for incompatibility went hand in hand. The *Trials* documented the underside of the new romantic marriage, but they failed to note the continuous, unchanged reality of male cruelty that chapter 10 has displayed.[9]

Men brought the majority of consistory cases between 1760 and 1790, and the total number exceeded the previous high between 1700 and 1720.

Both the increase in the total number of cases and the increase in cases brought by men were accounted for by men who after they had received their separations from the consistory went on to seek a divorce by act of Parliament that allowed them to remarry, as a consistory divorce did not. All this is neatly confirmed by the temporary decline in the number of cases in the consistory in the 1780s when Lord Thurlow used his authority as the lord chancellor to discourage divorce acts. Only eight men in that decade managed to have such acts passed after a consistory separation, as opposed to the thirty or thirty-five in the 1770s and 1790s. But the number of men who did not seek parliamentary divorces after a consistory separation remained at thirty or so in each of the last three decades of the century (table 10.2).[10] It is therefore apparent that it was the man who wished to divorce his wife so that they both could remarry who changed the nature of the suits in the consistory court. Such men first appeared in force in the 1750s, when half of the consistory suits by men were followed by divorce acts. But they really took over the court in the last third of the century. As they did so it is apparent that matrimonial suits of all kinds brought by women were excluded. By the 1790s men initiated fifty-seven divorces, but women only twenty-nine. The restitution cases by women had also declined from a midcentury high of twenty-six to seven, to make a total number of thirty-six marital cases brought by women as opposed to fifty-eight (there was one restitution) brought by men.

ADULTERY AND DOMESTICITY IN THE 1790S

The domestic lives of women shaped their sexual experience, and consequently the history of female adultery in the 1790s can be divided in two according to the way in which women met their lovers. In twenty-two cases a woman's lover was a man her husband did not know. This was usually because she was living separately from her husband while he served in the navy during the wars against revolutionary France or had gone to India, or because they had separated privately. In twenty-nine cases a woman took as her lover a man known to her husband. Seven of these were servants in their households. In the remaining cases the man had visited the married couple's house. He might be a relative, the curate, her husband's business partner or associate, or an old or new friend of either one of them. Since there was no streetwalking population of male prostitutes for them, women were most likely to take as lovers men who either regularly visited or lived in their households. In those cases when they did not, they had either separated from their husbands or their husbands were absent because of the demands of their professions.[11]

Women who separated from their husbands, whether by a formal agreement or not, had ample opportunity to meet a lover whom their husbands did not know. In such a case Harriet Harris threw over her much younger husband when he could not sexually satisfy her and settled for a lover of her own age. Harriet had married Thomas Bannister Ball in 1780. Neither of them had married before, but she was twice his age, thirty-four to his seventeen. Her father, James Harris, had died three months before the marriage and left her five thousand pounds in bank stock. This presumably made her an attractive bride, and before the marriage, the interest on the stocks was settled on her husband for life. Ball was his father's heir and had therefore not been trained for any profession. His father was a clergyman, the Reverend Peregrine Ball, who held livings in Gloucester worth over six hundred pounds a year and had an estate at Trellase in Monmouthshire worth over five hundred pounds a year. Ball himself married the couple in London, where her family lived. The new couple then went to live with Ball at Gloucester for three years before moving out on their own to Trellase. But it is apparent that Harriet found her young husband unsatisfactory as a lover. She later said that the marriage was unhappy, that the younger Ball was cruel, morose, and vicious, and that he frequently beat her. She therefore left him in March 1788 and returned to London. There she made a more serious charge that questioned whether the marriage had ever existed. Her young husband, she said, was impotent: Ball's scrotum was diseased. She therefore began an action for nullity in the Court of Arches. Her case failed there, and she appealed to the Court of Delegates, where once again the report of two physicians and two surgeons went against her. (Arches and Delegates were the courts to which one appealed from the consistory.) There was to be no easy escape for her from this mistaken marriage.

In the meanwhile Harriet had found a man more to her taste. In London she lived first with her brother James Harris at Finchley and then with her mother Sarah, who after the death of Harriet's father had married George Ainsworth. At both places Harriet met Robert Allen, a brewer from Wapping. Three months after Harriet's arrival in town, her mother's new marriage fell apart. Mother and daughter now took lodgings together at Islington. There Allen visited Harriet more frequently. By Christmastime their relationship had become a sexual one. The two women then moved to Mile End in Stepney. Six months later Harriet's mother left the lodgings. Allen now started to spend the night with Harriet, and in

September 1789 she bore his son. Allen, who was single, acknowledged the child and arranged its baptism. In January Harriet went to live with him in his house in King Henry's Yard in Nightingale Lane in East Smithfield and started to use his name. By the end of 1790 Harriet's attempt to have Ball declared impotent had failed. At the beginning of the next year Ball sued Allen for criminal conversation and was awarded twenty pounds in damages. At the same time he began divorce proceedings and had his suit granted a year later.[12]

The wives of men who served in the navy or the East India Service were often without their husbands for long periods, and this sometimes opened the way for a lover. Lonely wives at home found that the war against France in the 1790s created opportunities. Two such women found lovers through the military or naval networks in which they and their husbands lived. In the first case William Henry Ricketts had married Lady Jane Lambert in November 1793. She was the daughter of the Dowager Lady Cavan. They lived together in his house at Candover in Hampshire until 1796, when Ricketts was on duty with his ship in the Mediterranean and in the West Indies. At the end of 1796 Lady Jane met John Hargreaves, a captain in the army, who visited her frequently and stayed late at night. They went out together in public, and the signs of the affair were noticed by Lady Jane's friends, who spoke to her with no result. The lovers corresponded, and they met at various inns. The servant at one inn reported their stained sheets to her mistress, who confronted Lady Jane. She confessed the affair and gave the landlady some money for the servant to make certain that she would say nothing. The landlady, however, asked Lady Jane to promise never to see Hargreaves again. This Lady Jane said she could not do, and the affair continued. In April 1798, when he was in the West Indies, Ricketts received a letter informing him of his wife's affair. He obtained leave and arrived back in England in June. He sued Hargreaves for damages and was awarded one thousand pounds. He started his divorce in November and received it in February. His divorce act passed Parliament in April.[13]

Elizabeth Bligh found her lover through what was a clearly very thick naval network. She had married Shuldham Peard in 1791 when he was thirty and ten years her senior. Peard was a surgeon with the rank of lieutenant in the Royal Navy. Elizabeth was the daughter of Rear Admiral Richard Rodney Bligh. The couple lived together for eighteen months and had a child. In May 1793 Peard sailed with the fleet to the Mediterranean and remained there until he returned as a commander in October 1797. In his absence Elizabeth lived in a house in Gosport near her father's. In the town there was an old friend of Admiral Bligh's, Captain James Lys. His son, William Henry Lys, was an army surgeon who also lived in Gosport. The younger Lys visited Elizabeth in her husband's absence. He dined, drank tea, and stayed late at night. In the daytime Lys and Elizabeth shut themselves up alone in the drawing room. He also visited her on Sundays when her guests had gone to church. After Peard's return in October 1797, Elizabeth's mother became sick, and whenever Peard visited as her surgeon, Elizabeth and Lys made the most of his absence. Five months after Peard's return, Elizabeth became ill while they were visiting London and was delivered of a full-term daughter. This made Peard suspicious since he had only started to have sex with Elizabeth five months and fourteen days before. It is unclear why Peard, a surgeon, had not noticed before either that Elizabeth was pregnant or, if he had noticed, how far advanced the pregnancy was. But now he confronted her; she confessed and they separated. Peard sued Lys in April and was awarded four hundred pounds and costs. In November he began his divorce in the consistory. This came through in February and his divorce act passed in June.[14]

Service in India could be as disruptive to a marriage as service in the Navy. In these cases a woman often acquired a lover while she lived in England with the children and her husband was in India. But in some cases, young women who had recently met and married their husbands in India and whose husbands had decided that it was best for them to return to England met their lovers when their ships reached the Cape of Good Hope after five months at sea of the long journey home. John Buller, one of the commissioners of the Board of Revenue at Bengal, was such an unfortunate husband. In May 1795, Buller, who had never married, began to court Elizabeth Catherine Wiggins, who was single and living at Benares. In September they were married. They lived together for ten months until July 1796, when Elizabeth was advised to return to England for her health. She left India in the company of Hetty Treves, the elderly woman in whose house the couple had lived. By October Elizabeth's ship had reached the Cape of Good Hope. There she met William Durban, the captain of a frigate in the Royal Navy, and fell in love with him. When her ship sailed, Elizabeth remained behind with Durban. She sailed with him to St. Helena's when his ship was ordered there five months later in March 1797. Because of the affair, Durban was suspended from his command. He and Elizabeth found lodgings on St. Helena's. There Elizabeth's servant, Frances Blackall, noticed some stains on Durban's shirt, showed them to her husband, and concluded that Durban had had sex with Elizabeth during her period ("connexion with a woman during her menses"). When Durban and Elizabeth sailed for England in August, it became apparent early in the voyage that Elizabeth was pregnant. In May 1798 she bore his child. In the month before that Buller sued Durban and was awarded one thousand pounds in damages. In July he filed for his divorce against Elizabeth. He succeeded in May 1799, and his divorce act went through Parliament in July.[15]

There were, however, women who, while living with a busy husband, met a lover who was not part of her husband's social circle. Two examples from two different social levels make the point. In March 1793 James Fozard, who owned a riding school in Park Lane, married sixteen-year-old Sarah Sophia Leckie. At the end of 1794 Sarah met a young man, William Tubbs, who was serving a clerkship to an attorney in Charles Street. They saw each other at balls and assemblies in the neighborhood. Tubbs was a total stranger to Fozard. The lovers met in his absence and corresponded secretly through one of Sarah's servants. In March 1795 Tubbs hired a back room on the third floor of a turner's house in Jermyne Street so that he and Sarah could meet. He later took other rooms at a sadler's for the same purpose. When Sarah visited Tubbs, she pretended to go to her mother's. At first she went alone, even though Fozard had asked her to go out only if a servant accompanied her. When she did begin to take the footman with her, he told Fozard what was happening. Fozard and a friend then went to the lovers' rendezvous and found them hiding in a closet. This was in March. In April Fozard sued Tubbs for damages and was awarded four hundred pounds. Sarah, who must have been at her mother's, wrote Fozard a penitent letter in July, but he refused to be reconciled, and a year later sued for divorce. After the proceedings were begun, Sarah, who was now nineteen, had a second affair with another man with whom she began to live as husband and wife. Fozard succeeded in the consistory in July 1797. He then applied to Parliament, and a year later his divorce act was passed.[16]

In the second case Edward Jervis Ricketts was a busy lawyer whose wife Cassandra had an affair with a man he did not know. He and his wife were part of an extraordinary cluster of three divorces in their two families that all occurred within a year of each other. The divorce of Ricketts's brother, William Henry, has already been described. He was the naval officer whose wife met a captain in the army while William's ship was on duty in the Mediterranean. The third divorce was that of Cassandra Ricketts's brother, Thomas Twistleton. He was a clergyman whose wife left him after six years of marriage and who after the separation met a

man by whom she had a child. In the case of Edward Ricketts, he had
married the Hon. Cassandra Twistleton in 1790 after more than a year's
courtship. They were both single. He was a barrister by profession and
later became the second viscount St. Vincent. She was the daughter of
the Dowager Lady Saye and Sele. The couple lived at his house at Sutton
in Hampshire and had several children over the first seven years of their
marriage. In March 1797 Cassandra met Charles William Taylor, the
member of parliament for Wells, at her mother's house in Marylebone.
When Ricketts was on circuit as a barrister, Cassandra and Taylor saw
each other in Kensington Gardens and at the opera. When she visited
him, his neighbors noticed because she seemed so cautious when she arrived and left. The lovers corresponded, and Major Ramsey, a relation
by marriage of Cassandra's mother, acted as their courier. But Ramsey
eventually became anxious that Ricketts would discover his role. He therefore told Cassandra that he had burned one of her letters, but instead he
gave it to Ricketts, pretending that he had intercepted it. Ricketts did not
believe Ramsey's story and had Ramsey's desk opened, where he found a
letter of Cassandra's in it that made the matter clearer. The affair between
Cassandra and Taylor had already ended, but Ricketts left Cassandra
nonetheless. In February 1798 he was awarded five thousand pounds in
damages from Taylor. He began his consistory divorce in May, and had it
granted in June. Eight months later his divorce act passed in Parliament.[17]

In the majority of cases a woman met her lover in her husband's house.
In some instances a male servant caught his mistress's eye. This occurred
at all levels of society, whether in a gentleman's townhouse, a professional
man's lodgings, or the house and shop of a master craftsman. It was usually
the case that a woman, after years of marriage and a number of children,
discovered a kind of sexual passion with one of the younger men in her
household that she had never experienced with her husband. Sometimes
the sexual relationship with her husband had ended. A woman in this
situation knew that she took a great risk since she might lose the financial
security of her marriage, not to mention her children. But initially the
financial dependence of her servant on her seems to have been part of the
excitement, not to mention the bodily charms of a man much younger
than her husband. Indeed these relationships would have brought together
two individuals at their sexual peaks—a mature woman in her thirties and
a young male in late adolescence.

The first case of love between a mistress and her servant comes from
the aristocracy. John Wilmot had courted and married sixteen-year-old
Fanny Sainthill in 1776 when he was twenty-six, a lawyer, and a member

of Parliament. Fanny brought six thousand pounds in bank annuities as well as land in Surrey and Hereford that she had inherited from her father. Wilmot, whose father had been the lord chief justice of the Court of Common Pleas, had nearly five thousand pounds a year from his estate as well as his profits as a Chancery master. In the first ten years of their marriage Fanny had six children, but in the last five years of their marriage, there were none. This strongly suggests that (probably as a means of birth control) Wilmot had stopped having sexual relations with his wife in 1786 when Fanny was twenty-six and he was thirty-six. Four years later when she was thirty, Fanny began a love affair with their footman, Edward Washborn, who was twenty-one. By then Fanny had known Washborn for seven years since he had joined her staff of servants as the under-footman when he was fourteen. Fanny had therefore seen Washborn grow into a young man during the years that she bore her last two children and ended sexual relations with her husband. The house in Bedford Row had a full staff of nine. There were four men, a butler, a coachman, a footman (Washborn), and an underfootman, and five women, the lady's maid, the housekeeper, and three maids for the nursery, the house, and the kitchen. After Washborn's fellow servants began to notice the signs of his attachment to his mistress in 1790, he must have quarreled with them. Because of these disputes Wilmot, who did not suspect the affair between his footman and Fanny, gave Washborn warning at the end of January and discharged him on February 7.

Fanny unsuccessfully tried to stop this. Washborn took lodgings nearby and pretended to be a gentleman. With money from Fanny he bought a great amount of linen and elegant clothes so that he could play the role. Fanny began to go out without the liveried servant who had usually accompanied her, and was seen walking arm in arm with Washborn in the public gardens. She also visited him in his lodgings. Fanny got her housekeeper on her side, and with her help, Washborn began to visit the Wilmot house. On the first occasion he supposedly returned to get a reference; on other occasions, Fanny persuaded his former fellow servants to let Washborn dine with them because he was poor and out of work. Soon Washborn began to appear in the street in front of the house. Fanny (who was seen by the neighbors) would signal to him and either let him into the house or go out herself and follow and talk to him. Inside the house their lovemaking was observed. In a mirror's reflection they were seen kissing and embracing; Washborn would kneel down before Fanny and, in the legal phrase, commit then and there the foul crime of adultery together. The couple probably were using cunnilingus as means of avoiding pregnancy since Fanny was no longer sleeping with her husband. On another occasion they were seen as Fanny lay in bed with her petticoats above her knees and Washborn kissed her thighs with his breeches unbuttoned. Perrot Fenton said that he saw Fanny sit on the edge of the bed and Washborn kneel before her and "commit adultery together." They may also have used more conventional means, however, since the servants in the room beneath them could hear the creaking of the sofa above.

Wilmot learned of the affair sometime in April. Through a lawyer he arranged for a friend to take lodgings in Washborn's house. On April 25 when Fanny and Washborn were together in his lodgings, Wilmot was alerted and came and confronted them. He told Fanny that she could not come home again. He also had gotten a court order to have Washborn's boxes and trunks searched. They found money and new clothes but none of the letters that Fanny had sent him. But her love tokens were there, including a pin set with her hair. Wilmot sued Washborn for damages and was awarded five hundred pounds. He also brought his divorce suit in the London consistory. It was appealed to the Court of Arches, where he won. Wilmot then applied to Parliament, and his divorce act was passed in April 1792.[18]

The case of the aristocratic Wilmots can be matched with an example from the ranks of the master craftsmen. William Lovering, who came to London from Tiverton in Devon, had married Elizabeth Bond in April 1774. In the course of fifteen years of marriage they had four children, and Lovering became a master carpenter with a house full of children, apprentices, and servants. In September Elizabeth fell in love with one of her husband's two adolescent apprentices, Gideon Guichenet. Gideon's sister later said that Elizabeth had told her that she loved Gideon and doted on the ground he walked on: she could live happier with him on a crust of bread than with her husband on thousands. Gideon's sister also claimed (but she may have been protecting her brother) that in her presence Gideon always rejected his mistress's advances. Others saw something else. Frances Pomsfird, who took care of Elizabeth's four children, saw Gideon take Elizabeth's hand and kiss it and call her a pretty woman. Gideon would also put his hand into Elizabeth's pocket and try to take out her money. Sometimes when he did not get his way, he called Elizabeth a shabby woman to her face. When Lovering was absent, Elizabeth would call Gideon out of the shop in the morning and give him hot wine to drink. She gave Gideon whatever she thought he would like to eat or drink. When Gideon dined with her in the middle of the day, Elizabeth often kept him with her for the rest of the day even though this disrupted the work schedule. When they had supper together, they sat up after everyone else had gone to bed. When Gideon did go to bed, Elizabeth would carry up brandy and watered wine to him. During the day Elizabeth rang the bell to call Gideon out of the shop so often that the other workmen began to laugh and jeer about it. Whenever the bell that ran from the dining room to the shop rang, the men would call out, "Come, Gideon, your mistress wants you; she can't do without you."

On one night when Lovering was out of town and Elizabeth had gone to bed, Jane Hill needed to take the ironing into her mistress's room. When she entered, Elizabeth told her not to come near the bed, which must have been curtained. Jane then left the room, listened outside the door, and heard Gideon's voice. Whenever Lovering came home late at night, Gideon would suddenly be seen scurrying up to bed wearing nothing more than his shirt. Gideon shared a bed with the other sixteen-year-old apprentice, John Healy, who had to eat in the kitchen while Gideon dined with their mistress. Healy noticed when Gideon was absent from their bed, and once, while he pretended to be asleep, he saw Elizabeth try unsuccessfully to tempt Gideon out of bed. After ten months of this Lovering finally became aware of what everyone else in the house knew or suspected. He stopped sleeping with Elizabeth in May but evidently intended to do no more. Elizabeth, however, must have discovered the delights of adultery. In November she began to have sex with Charles Sadler, a man who kept wine vaults. In January Lovering discovered this affair and took it more seriously. He ordered Elizabeth to leave the house. In July he sued Sadler for criminal conversation and was awarded thirty pounds in damages. About the same time Elizabeth bore a child who (in a letter to Gideon that came into Lovering's hands) she said was Gideon's. In November Lovering sued for his divorce from Elizabeth.[19]

The majority of women took as their lovers a man of their own class and age. He might be a relative of their own or of their husband's, or an old friend of either one of theirs, or an intimate friend of the family they had both known for sometime, or a newly made friend of the couple's, or one of her husband's business associates. But when a woman fell in love with a man from any one of these categories, she was likely to do so in her own house and under the eyes of her husband and her servants. Male relatives from a previous marriage, especially in the form of a brother-in-law, could have a great effect on a woman's heart. Brothers-in-law and sisters-in-law in the English kinship system were the closest of relatives. Two cases show the different ways in which this kind of attraction worked. In the first case Lord Abercorn after the death of his first wife courted and married Lady Cecil Hamilton in 1792. Abercorn's first wife had been Catherine Copley, and Abercorn remained on intimate terms with her family after his second marriage. His first wife's brother, Joseph Copley, who was a lieutenant in the Third Regiment of Guards, continued to be a frequent visitor at Abercorn's after his marriage to Lady Cecil. Ann Copley, the sister of Abercorn's late wife, even continued to live in his house. Four years after the marriage, Abercorn became uneasy about the attentions that Joseph Copley was paying to his young wife. Abercorn told Lady Abercorn of his concern and insisted that she stop meeting Copley in public, and Copley himself was forbidden to visit Abercorn's house. Lady Abercorn agreed to abide by her husband's wishes. Two years later Abercorn, most of whose estates were in Ireland (and worth at least twenty thousand pounds a year), was ordered there in May 1798 as colonel of the Tyrone militia to deal with unrest. Abercorn returned to London for a while in July, but for the six months between May and October, he was mainly in Ireland. In his absence Lady Abercorn and Copley became physical lovers. After Abercorn's return, Lady Abercorn told him on November 6 that she thought she was pregnant with Copley's child and confessed the entire affair to him. Abercorn sent his wife to her mother's in Wimpole Street. From there Copley took her to the Stephens Hotel in Clifford Street, where they passed as a newly married couple, Mr. and Mrs. Copley. In December Abercorn filed for divorce. He also sued Copley for damages. Copley did not plead, and Abercorn was awarded ten thousand pounds by default. The consistory divorce was granted in March 1799, and the divorce act passed Parliament in May.[20]

In the second case Elizabeth Bewicke fell in love with the younger brother of her first husband. As a young widow she married her second husband, the Reverend Calverley John Bewicke, in 1788 when he was twenty-one. In 1791 they lived at Hallaton in Leicestershire where Bewicke had his cure. In July of that year William Welby Vaughan, the younger brother of Elizabeth's late husband, came to visit. It is possible that there had long been an attraction between Vaughan and Elizabeth, but it would have been legally impossible for Vaughan to marry his deceased brother's wife. While Vaughan was visiting, Bewicke learned that he had quarreled with his father, a physician at Leicester. Bewicke therefore invited Vaughan to extend his visit. Vaughan accepted and came frequently thereafter. An affair eventually developed between Vaughan and Elizabeth. The servants saw her frequently go into the bedchamber over the kitchen that Vaughan used and come out with her clothes disordered. Elizabeth took the suspicious precaution of stuffing the keyhole of the room's door with her handkerchief so that the servants could not say what occurred while she was with Vaughan. But elsewhere in the house they did see her sit on Vaughan's knee and put her hand around his neck and kiss him. He in turn put his hand into her bosom and kissed her. Eventually they were seen lying together in bed kissing. Vaughan sometimes went into Elizabeth's room in his dressing gown after Bewicke had left the house. Elizabeth would put her handkerchief around her neck and pin it on in Vaughan's presence, an immodest thing to do in public since it exposed her breasts. The couple met each other several times at a public house and in London. Vaughan also stayed in the house without Bewicke's knowledge when he was away. On one Sunday Vaughan hid himself in a necessary house in the garden until Bewicke left to take the early morning services. Elizabeth then went out and brought Vaughan in. When Bewicke returned from church, Elizabeth hid Vaughan in the linen closet until Bewicke left for the eleven o'clock service. At 12:30, when Bewicke returned, Vaughan went back into the linen closet until it was time for Bewicke to leave at three o'clock for the afternoon service. Vaughan then emerged from the linen closet and left. Vaughan had paid his first visit in July. Bewicke discovered the affair three months later in October. Within two days Elizabeth left her husband's house. A year later Bewicke sued for divorce in the consistory. It was granted in March 1793. He did not sue Vaughan for damages (that was perhaps not appropriate for a clergyman to do), but he did pursue his case in Parliament, where his act was passed in June. It would still, however, have been impossible for Elizabeth and Vaughan to marry legally.[21]

Husbands and wives brought their old friends with them into their marriages, and these friends could eventually become lovers. In 1786 Joseph Seymour Biscoe married Susanna Harriet Hope. For the first four years of their marriage they lived with her father, the Reverend Charles Hope, in Derby, but eventually they set up their own house once they began to have children. In October 1793, because of his business, Biscoe moved to London with his family. There his old schoolfellow and friend, Robert Home Garden, visited him. Biscoe introduced Garden to Susanna, and the three of them became very intimate. In May 1794 Biscoe and his family moved into a house that he rented from Garden. But Garden and Susanna fell in love, and on the evening of Tuesday, October 21, Susanna left her husband and went to live with Garden. Biscoe first sued Garden and was awarded five thousand pounds in damages in December. In March 1795 he filed for a divorce that the consistory granted in December, and in May 1796 his divorce act passed through Parliament.[22]

A woman could also fall in love with an intimate friend whom she and her husband knew as a couple, as Mary Walker did after eight years of marriage. Mary had married Charles Walker in April 1787 after a courtship of many months. She brought one thousand pounds as her portion, but it was not settled on her. Walker was an oil and color manufacturer in Clerkenwell who installed a steam engine at the cost of over five thousand pounds and made two to three thousand pounds a year from his business. Over the eight and a half years of their marriage, they had five children, the last a girl who was not yet christened when Walker filed for divorce. In the summer of 1795 when she was about four months pregnant with her last child by Walker, Mary began a love affair with their intimate friend William Leader, who lived in Wandsworth. Mary made her lady's maid her confidante to carry messages and letters and to keep the rest of the servants out of the way. It was clearly difficult, however, for a married woman with children to conduct a love affair anywhere else than in her own house. But Mary tried too hard to keep the servants in the kitchen when Leader visited her in Walker's absence. This aroused their suspicions. An inquisitive servant girl at first tried standing on a tub and peeking through a hole in the shutters, but she could see nothing. The next day she made three holes in the shutters and had an unobstructed view of Mary and Leader first kissing and playing on the sofa, and then finishing with penetration. Other servants saw them on other occasions. One of them told Walker's brother-in-law, who informed Walker. Mary later claimed that he had actually been warned several times and had ignored the advice of his friends, but one suspects that Walker was reluctant to believe ill of an intimate friend whom he trusted. Mary was about to be delivered of her last child at any moment when Walker finally admitted to himself what had occurred. He therefore did not turn her out of his house immediately but started his divorce suit a week after her lying-in. He won one thousand pounds in damages by default from Leader. His divorce came through a year later.[23]

Sometimes an intimacy developed between a couple and a new friend after the couple or the friend had moved into a new neighborhood. But what began in mutual friendship then became a love affair and ended in the tragedy of divorce and a broken marriage. Henry Cecil, who eventually succeeded his uncle as earl of Exeter and was later created marquess, married Emma Vernon in 1776 when he was twenty-two and already a member of Parliament. Emma was the only surviving child of her father, Thomas Vernon, who had died five years before and left her his estate at Hanbury Hall in Worcestershire, where the young couple lived after their marriage. As patron of the rectory there, Cecil in 1780 presented his friend William Burslem to the living. Three years later when Burslem needed a curate, he engaged William Sneyd, who came and lived in a farmhouse in the parish. At first Cecil occasionally asked Sneyd to dinner. As their acquaintance improved, Sneyd began to come three or four times a week and was soon considered part of the family. Eventually in 1789 Sneyd began an affair with Emma Cecil six years after he had first arrived in the parish. Emma at that point had been married for thirteen years and had had three children. In May 1789 Sneyd became ill at Hanbury House and was taken from there to his father's house at Litchfield. In the meanwhile Cecil and Emma had agreed to go to Birmingham and arrived there on June 12. Emma had told Sneyd of these plans. While Cecil was conducting business, Emma met Sneyd at an inn in Birmingham and eloped from her husband. They passed as man and wife under fictitious names, and Sneyd changed his clergyman's black clothes for colored ones and styled his hair differently. Cecil could not find out where the couple spent their first five days together. But by June 18 they were at Thompson's Hotel in Exeter. Five days later they moved to a house in Devon where they stayed for seven weeks. After this they went to an inn in Somerset for a fortnight. Then the summer ended, and at the beginning of September the couple separated. Sneyd went to Ireland, Emma to London. At Easter Sneyd returned from Ireland and went to London, where he frequently visited Emma at her lodgings. Cecil, who had not lived with his wife since the day she left their hotel in Birmingham, filed for divorce in June 1790. He also sued Sneyd for damages and was awarded one thousand pounds. His consistory divorce came through in March 1791. Cecil applied to Parliament, and by June the couple were completely divorced.[24]

The business associates of a woman's husband who visited her house make up the final category of men from whom a woman might take a lover. There are two cases to consider in both of which the women unsuccessfully attempted a reconciliation with their husbands once it became clear to them that they were otherwise likely to lose all contact with their children. In the first, Benjamin Boddington was Samuel Boddington's cousin as well as his partner. Samuel married Grace Ashburner in 1792 when she was seventeen. For the next five years they lived together in his house in Mark Lane and had children. Two years after they married, Samuel entered into a partnership with his first cousin, Benjamin. They dealt in Exchequer warrants. Benjamin lived with his father at Clapton but frequently dined and slept at Samuel's house in Mark Lane and at his country house at Southgate. Beginning in January 1797 Benjamin seems to have begun to be more attentive to his cousin's wife, who was now twenty-two. His visits grew longer, he took her to plays, he rode with her in her carriage. By June this had become apparent to Samuel, and his friends had mentioned it to him as well. But he did not yet realize that Grace and Benjamin had fallen in love. He decided to take his wife to Bath, hoping that this would break her intimacy with Benjamin. They left London on June 1. On the fourth Samuel received a letter from Benjamin asking him to return to London to deal with a matter affecting the Exchequer warrants. Samuel left Bath that day and arrived in London the next. But the letter was a ruse. Benjamin must already have been in Bath on June 4, and he and Grace eloped once Samuel had left for London.

In London Samuel found a letter from Benjamin. He wrote: "When we parted Wednesday, it was for the last time and this night I go from London *never* more to return. I have deceived you in bringing you up to town—I wished this was the only deceit I have practiced." He asked him to break the news gradually to his father and to take no step until he heard from him again. He ended by saying he had taken seven hundred pounds from the business. When Grace eloped, she wrote to her mother not to "be too much distressed for an unworthy daughter who is many miles off. She did not know it when she last saw you, it would be the last time in her life." Benjamin and Grace knew that their action would cause pain in every direction. They were clearly sorry for that, but they must have felt themselves driven by an inescapable passion. Grace had not fully realized, however, that she had also lost her children. This gave her second thoughts. She wrote to her husband begging him to stop the divorce: "I know after what has happened you must despise me for life; yet I pray you so far forget it, as to stop the divorce. Let me return, take me a house where I may never see a face I have never seen before, but let Mrs. Jelly and my dear children live with me." She also told him that she had hoped that he would have written her if only to say that he forgave her: "Your conduct has been nearly as cruel as mine." But Samuel was implacable. Grace tried writing again about the house and the children; she begged to have at least one child, or if not, to see them all for only an hour so that she could say farewell. It is not likely that Samuel agreed. He won ten thousand pounds in damages from Benjamin by default, sued successfully in the consistory, and saw his act of divorce pass through Parliament all within a year of the day that his young wife and his cousin must have broken his heart.[25]

In the second of these cases James Duberly was clearly the social inferior of the man who became his wife's lover as well as being dependent on his good will for his business. This probably initially contributed to his complaisant acceptance of what the servants found shocking behavior. Duberly had married Rebecca Elizabeth Howard in 1787, and in the next four years they had three children. In 1788 after Gen. John Gunning appointed Duberly as clothier to his regiment, an intimacy grew up between the two families. Duberly sometimes dined with the general and his family at Twickenham. The general and his wife came to Duberly's house in Soho Square, but usually the general came alone. He was sometimes sick and had trouble getting out of his chair. This made it difficult for him to use a hotel, so Duberly offered him the use of his house whenever Gunning came to town on regimental business. Duberly said that he had treated the general with as much attention and respect as if he had been his father. Gunning, Duberly, and Rebecca Duberly became a circle with a fourth person, a Mrs. Gardiner. Rebecca later claimed that the two couples played blindman's buff in the dark, during which Duberly flirted with Mrs. Gardiner while the general flirted with her. She said that the servants in the last two years had declared "that they might as well have lived in a bawdy house," and that some had left as a consequence. But Rebecca could not find any servant to confirm her version. Instead her wet nurse swore that she had heard another servant say that her twenty-five-year-old mistress sat on the general's knee in her husband's presence. In the last year it became a joke that Duberly was a cuckold, and one servant had said of him, "there goes the contented cuckold."

Rebecca and the general began to sleep together in January 1791, two years after their friendship had begun. When Duberly was away for eighteen days, Rebecca pretended to visit her mother but went instead to Gunning. In August when Duberly was absent from his country house at Sheen, Gunning visited Elizabeth. The servants observed the state of the bed afterward. In September the general was arrested for debt and taken to a sponging house in Carey Street. Rebecca visited him several times, and they made love. By September 26 the general was out, and the couple went to the Plough Inn at Clapham. One of the servants immediately told Duberly that his wife had been absent from Sheen. He questioned her when she came to town on the twenty-seventh. Rebecca said she had been at a friend's. Duberly immediately went and inquired and found that she was lying. The general now arrived at the Soho house. He found that Duberly was away, so he wrote a letter to their friend Mrs. Gardiner asking her to save Rebecca, but Mrs. Gardiner instead gave the letter to Duberly. Rebecca therefore left her husband's house that day and put herself under the general's protection. Both he and Rebecca wrote asking Duberly to forgive her. Rebecca said "that our Great Redeemer forgave the woman taken in adultery, oh be my Redeemer and by the love you once bore, by the love you bear our tender babes, soften your heart." But the marriage was over. Within two months Duberly had filed for divorce and sued the general for criminal conversation. In February the jury awarded Duberly five thousand pounds and costs, and his divorce came through in July. He did not apply to Parliament for a divorce act.[26]

Duberly's initial complaisance seems to have had its origins in his financial dependence on his wife's lover. But such complaisance in an aristocratic husband in the 1790s sometimes seems to have been the result of a romantic recklessness in young men and women in their twenties. For them the new ideal of the romantic marriage was interpreted as a freedom to pursue the desires of their hearts wherever they led—which might mean leaving one marriage for another. But when this freedom seemed to threaten the succession to a family's titles and estates, a husband's toleration of his wife's adultery could end. This becomes apparent in the Valentia case. Lord Valentia had married the Hon. Ann Courtenay in 1790 when he was almost twenty and she was almost seventeen. They lived together for a little over three years and had a child. In February 1794 Valentia had to go abroad to avoid his creditors. Lady Valentia was supposed to follow once he had made arrangements. But in March she refused to leave England. Valentia later said that it was because she had begun an affair with his good friend John Bellenden Gawler. In her husband's absence, Lady Valentia went with Gawler to his father's house at Ramridge in Hampshire. Once there they aroused the suspicion of a servant after she saw Lady Valentia leap from Gawler's lap when she entered one of the rooms of the house. The lovers' conversations at night in Lady Valentia's room were also overheard. She took a house near Ramridge, and Gawler visited her. Lady Valentia was soon confessing to her friends that she was pregnant by Gawler. Valentia returned to England in April 1795, but he did not visit his wife until July 21 after he had settled his affairs with his creditors. Lady Valentia at first refused to sleep with him (he was twenty-five, she twenty-two) and told him it was because she was afraid to have more children. But when he complained the next day, she confessed that she had been unfaithful and was pregnant. They separated.

That was Valentia's story. Lady Valentia had a different tale. She insisted that Valentia had known of her affair long before July 22. It had started in 1793 before Valentia went abroad. Nonetheless, Valentia had invited Gawler to visit and had left him alone with his wife. Valentia had frequently said that he wanted a child to prevent any branch of the family of Sir Henry Cavendish from inheriting his property, and that provided his wife bore him children, he "did not care who the devil got them." Valentia had seen Gawler's attentions to his wife, and in November 1793 had asked Gawler if he or his brother had been intimate with her. Valentia had also declared that he knew that the child Lady Valentia had borne was Gawler's. He had even told Gawler not to become venereally infected so that the disease would not be passed along to Lady Valentia. Gawler, Valentia said, did all his business for him with Lady Valentia.

Lady Valentia's story has a plausible ring about it. If it was true that her first child was Gawler's, Valentia must have decided that he could nonetheless plausibly claim paternity and make the child his heir. But then she became pregnant when her husband was out of the country. The legitimacy of any child that she now bore would always be in doubt. And it may be that Valentia was not really prepared to have another man father his children, no matter what he may have said. In any event he left her immediately after he knew that she was pregnant. He successfully sued Gawler and received £2,000 in damages and £366 in costs. He began his divorce in the consistory in November 1796, but it was not concluded until April 1799. He did not apply to Parliament for a divorce, and one wonders why. Did he wish to stop his wife from marrying her lover, or was he afraid that Lady Valentia's story would be believed and that his bill would therefore not pass?[27]

There were clearly limits to a husband's complaisance. Flirtation with a man's wife was one thing—even though in itself it could seem to others to cuckold him. But making her pregnant was beyond the pale for some. A husband who too openly tolerated his wife's adultery might find himself ostracized even among the libertine aristocracy. In 1811 Lady Harriet Granville—whose husband before their marriage had been the lover of her aunt by whom he had discreetly had two children—Lady Harriet supposed that Charles Bagot "will be quite cut out by men when he mixes more in society in town" because he had accepted his wife's affair with Arthur Upton too openly. Society was more inclined to recommend a private separation in such a case. This is what Lady Harriet's aunt, Lady Bessborough, had written to her lover fifteen years before, in 1796, when Lady Webster fell in love with Lord Holland and became pregnant by him. Lady Webster had married her husband Sir Godfrey in 1786 when he was thirty-eight years old and she was Elizabeth Vassall, the sixteen-year-old heiress of a Jamaica fortune. Theirs was not a romantic marriage. Webster (or Vassall as he became) was a notorious rake and a reckless gambler with a violent and ill-controlled temper who sometimes seemed on the edge of insanity. The couple lived together for seven years in England and had three children who survived. It was a difficult marriage, and they frequently quarreled in public. At the end of 1793 they sailed for Italy and arrived in Florence in January. There Lord Granville Leveson Gower (Lady Bessborough's lover and Lady Harriet's husband) introduced them to Lord Holland. In March 1795 Webster returned to England when his father-in-law, Richard Vassall, died. Lady Webster remained in Italy for her health. She and Lord Holland fell in love, and in February 1796 they took rooms and then traveled together in Italy. Holland was twenty-two, and Lady Webster was twenty-five; her husband was forty-eight. Lady Webster arrived back in England on June 18, 1796, and refused to sleep with Webster on the ground that she was ill. On June 28 she eloped with Lord Holland at eleven in the night, and in December she gave birth to his son. Her elopement was blamed for being part of a plan to force her husband to divorce her so that she could marry her lover. "This flight," Lady Stafford told her son Lord Granville, "can be for no purpose but to produce a divorce that he may marry her, as the prelude which they have been performing abroad might have continued in this kingdom without molestation or disturbance."

Some aristocratic women clearly preferred a discreetly tolerated adultery to a public divorce. But for others sexual passion and marriage went together, and where it was possible (as it was not for Rebecca Duberly in a previous case, since she had fallen in love with a married man), it was presumed that individuals should leave a marriage where the partners were not compatible for one in which they were. So the Webster case ground on. Sir Godfrey sued Lord Holland and was awarded six thousand pounds in damages. The consistory gave him his divorce in February 1797, and his divorce act passed later in the year. Lady Webster married her lover and more or less lived happily ever after. Lady Bessborough visited them on their wedding day and wrote to Lord Granville that she "never saw creatures so happy. He flew down to meet me, kissed me several times . . . and can do nothing but repeat her name. Such perfect happiness as theirs scarcely ever was instanced before: Un tel hymen c'est le Ciel sur la terre."[28]

All of the women in this chapter—whether from the middle classes or the gentry—give evidence of having experienced deep and sometimes overwhelming sexual passion. Most if not all of them went as virgins to their wedding beds, and in those beds they had probably first discovered open sexual desire in themselves since it is likely that few of them had masturbated before marriage. But these first sexual experiences usually left them pregnant, and sexual desire became swallowed up in childbearing and motherhood. It is true that occasionally the experience of sex in marriage seems to have released in a woman a voracious sexual appetite that sought fulfillment in every attractive man she met; and it made her demanding in her expectations of her lovers; but such a path must have been exceptional. Instead these divorce cases show that women could experience a second, deeper sexual awakening than their first—one in which desire was freed from its connection to motherhood and childrearing. For younger women who had married older men, this occurred when they fell in love with an attractive man of their own age. But the dynamics of age could also work quite differently. The occasional older woman who married a young husband could throw him aside for a more experienced lover. More frequently a woman after ten years of marriage and childbearing fell in love with a younger dependent man who was her servant or her apprentice. In these cases differences in social class probably reinforced the excitement of the difference in age. But class like age worked in both directions, and some middle-class women could be driven from the safety of their marriages by the attentions of a gentleman.

The sexual desire that we have seen in these women could be direct and bold enough. Hannah Glover, confident in her own attractiveness, scorned her rival as a nasty, ill-conditioned toad. But even a more timid woman like Rachel Wilford still had sex with her lover as her husband slept upstairs and cried out in ecstasy as climax approached, "Oh dear Mr. Berkley—Oh Christ, Mr. Berkley." Susannah Cooke more directly told her lover not to niggle with her but to mount her and let her have it as it should be. Elizabeth Buller and Ann Townshend each had sex with their lovers while they menstruated because, as Ann said of hers, he was so charming and bewitching that no one could resist him. Gideon Guichenet was teased by the other workmen that "your mistress wants you; she can't do without you." Elizabeth Davis scorned her husband to his face because he was not a gentleman like her lover who kept a carriage, and in her frustration she threatened to kill him when he least expected it. Clara Middleton more simply declared that she never knew what love was until she met her groom.

Most of the women in these stories made their marriages and raised

their children under the influence of the ideals of romantic love and domesticity that came to be dominant among the middle and landed classes
after 1750. With these ideas came a new gender role for most women
that stressed their maternal feelings and contrasted those feelings with
what was thought to be the exceptional sexual desire of the women who
became prostitutes. But it is apparent from this chapter that after 1750
romance and domesticity did not eliminate sexual passion from women's
lives, as the historians of the nineteenth century have increasingly recognized.[29] Indeed James Gambier and Maria Knowles used these ideals to
justify their adultery to themselves by claiming that their love for each
other and their devotion to her children was a truer marriage than the
legal ones in which they each found themselves. But a woman's devotion
to her children in many cases made her pay a high price for passionate
adultery. Some women tried to soften a husband's heart by confessing
their fault, and one supposes that this worked in those cases that did not
come to court. But these confessions often only gave a husband the final
piece of evidence for his divorce. It was too late for Grace Boddington
to reclaim her children, even one of them, and perhaps even too late for
her to be given an hour in which to say farewell to them. And Rebecca
Duberly's appeal to our Great Redeemer's forgiveness of the woman taken
in adultery did not persuade her husband to be her redeemer and to take
her back for the sake of their tender babes. Indeed it is likely that the
demands of the new heterosexual role made it harder than ever for a man
to forgive an erring wife since by such forgiveness he might seem to accept
the sexual domination of the close associate who had seduced his wife.
Those women therefore were luckiest who fell in love with an unmarried
man and whose husbands divorced them by act of Parliament. For then
though they lost their children from their first marriage, they could marry
their lovers and make a new family. But for those women whose lovers
were themselves married, this could never be. The middle-class among
them might perhaps move elsewhere and quietly claim to be legally married. But otherwise they could only hope for the continued devotion of
their lovers.

Conclusion

The arguments of the preceding chapters have been constructed through the presentation of statistical series and the explication of particular cases. In conclusion it is useful to review the nature of those series, since they are the spine of the book's structure, and then to ask how they can be brought together to describe the ordinary patterns of male and female sexual development over the course of the century.

The defamation cases establish that by the traditional standard of female chastity a good woman confined her sexual life to her marriage, but the casualness with which a woman could be slandered as a whore or a bitch demonstrates the suspicion generated by women's sexual desires. This was especially true once a woman became sexually active after marriage. Husbands seem to have lived in constant fear of betrayal and the loss of standing they would suffer if they were cuckolded. But it was married women themselves who did the most to maintain these standards through the force of neighborhood gossip. Poor men and women remained committed to this harsh view of female sexuality throughout the century. But men from the elite and the middle class changed their view of female sexuality. As judges and magistrates they discouraged defamation suits. They also ceased to punish adultery as a crime by the middle of the century. Instead they allowed men to sue their wives' lovers for damages and to divorce their wives and remarry.

The magistrates continued to arrest prostitutes, but they dismissed the younger and inexperienced women in the hope that they might return to their families or be redeemed in a hospital for penitent women. This was always a halfhearted effort. Magistrates did almost nothing to find the families of these young women, and the houses of reform could shelter very few. But it is likely that their actions indicate that they no longer viewed all women as potentially whores and that instead they divided women into a majority who were mothers before all else and a minority who from the misfortune of their circumstances fell into the life of prostitution. The world or prostitution probably became more insulated from the families of the poor, since fewer family members bailed women after their arrests. The number of women managing houses of prostitution increased. This may reflect the sentimentalization of prostitution, but it may also have been that strings of houses came to be operated by some men. The location of the houses certainly changes to reflect the new spatial arrangements that came into being as London grew into a single town that incorporated the City, urban Middlesex, and Westminster.

The series of arrests from the first generation of the century establish the kind of men who went to whores. But the magistrates after 1730 ceased to arrest men for doing so. The few men who at the beginning of the century had complained in the consistory that they had been called whoremongers disappeared entirely from the court by midcentury. Some men may have begun to sentimentalize the prostitute, but they all agreed that prostitution was needed as a sexual outlet by many men. The employers of adolescent males therefore no longer brought them to the magistrate for going to whores. Boys instead complained that adult sodomites had attempted to corrupt them, and adult men became so fearful of being charged with sodomy that they could be exploited by blackmailers. The statistical series therefore establish that the pursuit of prostitutes and the avoidance of sodomy became central to the new exclusive male heterosexuality that was subscribed to by men of all social classes. But the widespread resort to prostitutes by men of all ages and social classes brought with it increasing levels of venereal disease. The naval records show this among sailors. The need to find a cure for the disease turns up in the rapes of prepubescent girls and in the numbers admitted to the Lock Hospital. And the married woman infected by her husband can be found at all social levels, among the poor in the Lock Hospital and among the prosperous in the divorce cases.

Many men went to prostitutes, but men of all social classes also seduced the young unmarried woman who was not a prostitute. The women may have started sexual relations in the implicit hope that this was a prelude to marriage, but they admitted that no more than 15 to 20 percent of the men made such promises. The male servants in a parish like Chelsea could not afford to start families with the women they seduced, and the officers and gentlemen in the West End who picked up servants or milliners had no intention of marrying them. In the weaving parishes north of the City wall, men seduced women less literate than the ones they intended to marry. Only in the East End parishes is it likely that sexual relations between unmarried men and women could result in a household if the woman became pregnant since there the distinction between formal marriage and living together was not so important. Poor men and women no doubt fell in love, but for them romance was less of a self-conscious standard than among the middle class and the elite. Courtship and sexual violence were often bound together, and a man who raped a woman could offer to marry her in compensation and expect to be accepted. On the other hand, while richer men may have consciously courted women in romantic ways, once they were married they were as likely to become as violent with their wives as they had ever been when their domination was threatened or they fell in love with another woman. When because of the new romance and domesticity the wives of such men fell in love with another man (which probably occurred more frequently and with a man who was often a part of their domestic circle), they were less likely to tolerate it than they had been in the past and to part immediately once the domestic tragedy was discovered.

These are the minimum conclusions that may be drawn from the various statistical series. They are supported by the foundation of the Foundling Hospital in 1739, the Lock Hospital in 1746, and the Magdalen Hospital in 1758, and the documentation generated by these three institutions. The Foundling Hospital establishes the perception that the number of illegitimate births had grown. The Lock Hospital shows that knowledgeable medical men were certain that venereal disease had increased among the poor. And the Magdalen Hospital demonstrates the anxiety created by high levels of streetwalking prostitution. These three institutions can be seen as brought into existence by the effects of the new exclusive male heterosexuality. By the middle third of the century, when they were all founded, the new gender role for the majority of men would have been in its second generation. In this generation the magistrates ceased to punish adultery and no longer arrested either adult men or apprentices who went to prostitutes. And by midcentury the complementary effects of romantic love were also apparent in the divorce cases in the consistory. By 1750 the entire system that this book has described was fully established.

The patterns of behavior that are apparent in the statistical series can be arranged to demonstrate the normal course of individual sexual development as this varied by gender, class, and generation across the course of the century. They show that for men sex was always tied to the assertion of their power over women (and to some degree over other men) whether in prostitution, seduction, or rape. For women sex was more likely to be controlled by chastity, faithfulness, and relationship. But power was not absent from the sexual lives of the prostitute, the remarrying widow, and the young wife set free after her first experience of sex in marriage; and it is apparent that many women were quite interested in sex and enjoyed it, however reluctant they may have been to say so.

Generational change is clearest in the lives of men. By 1730 men were divided into those who were sodomites and those who were not. For this majority there was no general term since it is always easier to categorize the deviance of the minority than to perceive that the practices of the normal cohere into a system. In the nineteenth century the concept of the homosexual preceded that of the heterosexual, and it remains the case in contemporary society that almost no one ever seeks the etiology of heterosexuality in the way that they endlessly look for the causes of homosexuality. Nonetheless it is reasonable to claim that by 1730 the majority of men of all social classes had a heterosexual identity that in the first generation and throughout the remainder of the century found its most obvious expression in the relentless pursuit of the streetwalking prostitute. The socialization of adolescent males of all social classes into this heterosexual role in the first generation is apparent in the strictures against masturbation and sodomy, even though it is likely that in practice the incidence of masturbation was as high as that of sodomy was low.

In the next generation there were two developments among poorer men. Adolescents were allowed to pursue prostitutes more freely. And men of all ages became more likely to seduce and make pregnant an unmarried woman with whom they did not intend to begin a family. Illegitimacy for men became part of their sexual revolution, whereas for women it continued to be a social disaster. Men from the higher classes also seduced unmarried women, but in this second generation they began to be powerfully affected by sentiment, romance, and domesticity, and as a result their sexual interaction with women of all social classes was transformed. They were now likely to presume that women by their natures were domesticated rather than sexual beings and that the minority who became prostitutes could be redeemed if their circumstances were changed. Some men were even prepared to give up libertinism for domesticity. But they would probably all have thought that some level of prostitution had to be tolerated as a hedge against the threat of sodomy. Some of them resolved this inherent contradiction between heterosexuality and romance by domesticating the brothel. But disease and violence reinforced the contradiction. Men of all classes took home to their wives and children the venereal infections they contracted from streetwalking prostitutes. The sexual violence of poor men in seduction, courtship, and marriage was probably heightened by their new heterosexual identity, especially since for them it was not leavened by romance. Romance, however, seems to have modified the violence of well-off men only to a limited degree. What romance did do for the marriages of such men was to make it more likely in the third generation of the century that their wives would fall in love with a man who gave greater satisfaction to their hearts.

For most of the century there was no exclusive sapphist role against which the majority of women could define themselves as heterosexual. And after 1770 when it becomes possible to document a sapphist role among some aristocratic and middle-class women, it is hard to see that it had on women's behavior anything like the effect that the sodomite role had had on men since the beginning of the century. Throughout the century most women did not have an exclusive heterosexual identity (which is not to say that they were not attracted to men), and they experienced the new male heterosexuality mainly as its victims. The sexual behavior of women was therefore defined by their relationship to men and not in opposition to a sapphist minority. Throughout the century poor women viewed themselves as wives, widows, or maids, any of whom might fall from grace and become a whore even if they did not literally walk the streets to pick up men. In the absence of effective means of birth control, most women ran the risk that their sexual lives might result in the birth of a child. Young women who bore an illegitimate child were certainly not given the kind of license that adolescent males increasingly received. There was no female heterosexual identity with which to justify their libertinism: they experienced only shame and disgrace. Women of all social classes, including the prostitute, found support in religion for their necessary self-restraint. This also meant, however, that they usually depended on men to make all sexual initiatives, and as these initiatives were sometimes violent, they were obliged to accept that rape was part of the continuum of courtship.

Some women did take initiative. The prostitute in some cases chose her life (sometimes as a supplement to her income), rather than being thrust into it by force, inexperience, or poverty, and once she was in the life she learned to be bold enough with men. Sometimes a newly married woman after her discovery of sex in marriage pursued men with the passion that some men pursued whores, but she eventually paid a price in social ostracism that men did not. Some widows used their economic independence to choose a husband whom they found sexually appealing, but other widows were too dependent to do this, and any widow might find that a second husband who did not get his way might beat her into submission. Finally, some of the poor women who became pregnant outside of marriage had been swept away by passion with no thought of a provident marriage. These were the possibilities open to poorer women throughout the century. Middle-class and aristocratic women, however, had a new world of passion opened to them in the last two generations of the century. Adultery could now be justified as the marriage of true souls that was more than mere sensuality. A woman was still more likely than not to find her lover among the men who visited her house, and when she was caught she might lose her children. But some women after years of childbearing and motherhood, experienced a second and perhaps deeper sexual awakening in which romance justified their pursuit of passion wherever it led.

The first generation of the century saw the emergence of a sodomitical minority and a heterosexual majority among men of all social classes. In the second generation landed society and the middle classes experienced the effects of romantic love and the domesticated family. It is reasonable to presume that the changes in these two different generations were related. It is likely that a heterosexual male majority used their new sexual identity to guarantee that the closer association with women brought on by romance and domesticity did not undermine male domination. This can be seen simply as a strategy for reconstructing patriarchy. But it is also true that women usually are more highly regarded in societies where sexual relations between males are organized through an effeminate male minority rather than by differences in age. It is, however, of some interest that while the change in the first generation affected all social classes, the domesticity of midcentury was limited to the prosperous and did not become part of the lives of the poor for another two or three generations. Similarly the sapphist role that emerged in the third generation can at present be documented only among the middle classes and gentlewomen, and it certainly did not have the effect on the lives of women of any class that the sodomite's role had on men of every class. These are the uncertainties that remain in constructing the history of sexual behavior and its relation to gender in the first century of the modern Western world's existence. I hope that others will take them up, and I mean to pursue them myself in a succeeding volume on the history of sodomites and sapphists and the origins of modern Western homosexuality.

NOTES

CLRO   Corporation of London Record Office
DL/C   Diocese of London Consistory Court
FH   Foundling Hospital
GL   Guildhall Library
GLRO   Greater London Record Office (or the London Metropolitan
        Archive)
GRS   Marriage, Sex, and the Family in England, 1660–1800. Ed.
        Randolph Trumbach. 44 vols. Garland Reprint Series. New
        York, 1984–86.
MJ/SR   Middlesex or Westminster Quarter Sessions Roll
R   Recognizances
RCS   Royal College of Surgeons
SP   Sessions Paper, or *Proceedings . . . at the Old Bailey*
SR   Quarter Sessions Roll
WPL   Westminster Public Library

CHAPTER ONE: EXTRAMARITAL RELATIONS AND GENDER HISTORY

1. This distinction was introduced into historical scholarship in Randolph Trumbach, "London's Sodomites: Homosexual Behavior and Western Culture in the Eighteenth Century," *Journal of Social History* 11 (1977): 1–33. David Greenberg, *The Construction of Homosexuality* (Chicago: University of Chicago Press, 1988) has tried to
add two other types of homosexual behavior (between equals in age and across class
lines), but these are actually aspects of the fundamental dual system. Gilbert Herdt,
"Representations of Homosexuality: An Essay on Cultural Ontology and Historical
Comparison, Parts I and II," *Journal of the History of Sexuality* 1 (1991): 481–504,
603–32, confirms the correctness of my original analysis.
2. K. J. Dover, *Greek Homosexuality* (Cambridge, Mass.: Harvard University Press,
1978); Eva Cantarella, *Bisexuality in the Ancient World* (New Haven, Conn.: Yale University Press, 1992); Craig Williams, *Roman Homosexuality* (New York: Oxford University Press, 1998); John Boswell, *Christianity, Social Tolerance, and Homosexuality*

(Chicago: University of Chicago Press, 1980), and *Same-Sex Unions in Premodern Europe* (New York: Villard Press, 1994) (on which see my review in the *Journal of Homosexuality* 30 [1995]: 111–17); Michael Rocke, *Forbidden Friendships: Homosexuality and Male Culture in Renaissance Florence* (New York: Oxford University Press, 1996), and "Male Homosexuality and Its Regulation in Late Medieval Florence," Ph.D. diss., State University of New York at Binghamton, 1989. For an account of the literature on European sodomy before 1700, see the appendix to Randolph Trumbach, "Erotic Fantasy and Male Libertinism in Enlightenment England," in *The Invention of Pornography*, ed. Lynn Hunt (New York: Zone Books, 1993), pp. 388–90.

3. Alan Bray, *Homosexuality in Renaissance England*, 2d ed. (New York: Columbia University Press, 1995); Randolph Trumbach, "The Birth of the Queen: Sodomy and the Emergence of Gender Equality in Modern Culture, 1660–1750," in *Hidden from History: Reclaiming the Gay and Lesbian Past*, ed. Martin Duberman, Martha Vicinus, and George Chauncey (New York: New American Library, 1989), pp. 129–40, and "Sodomy Transformed: Aristocratic Libertinage, Public Reputation, and the Gender Revolution of the 18th Century," *Journal of Homosexuality* 19 (1990): 105–24.

4. A full discussion is forthcoming in the second volume of this work, *The Origins of Modern Homosexuality*. For my earlier discussions, see Trumbach, "Gender and the Homosexual Role in Modern Western Culture: The 18th and 19th Centuries Compared," in Dennis Altman et al., *Which Homosexuality* (London: GMP Press, 1989), pp. 149–69, and "Sex, Gender, and Sexual Identity in Modern Culture: Male Sodomy and Female Prostitution in Enlightenment England," in *Forbidden History: The State, Society, and the Regulation of Sexuality in Modern Europe*, ed. John C. Fout (Chicago: University of Chicago Press, 1992), pp. 89–106. There is a popular account by Rictor Norton, *Mother Clap's Molly House: The Gay Subculture in England, 1700–1830* (London: GMP Press, 1992), which is full of factual error and doubtful interpretation: see my review in the *Journal of the History of Sexuality* 5 (1995): 637–40. For the sodomitical subculture in the Netherlands, see Theo van der Meer, *De Wesentlijke Sonde van Sodomie en Andere Vuyligheeden: Sodomieten vervolgingen in Amsterdam, 1730–1811* (Amsterdam: Tabula, 1984) (of which there is an English summary in van der Meer, "The Persecutions of Sodomites in Eighteenth-Century Amsterdam: Changing Perceptions of Sodomy," in *The Pursuit of Sodomy: Male Homosexuality in Renaissance and Enlightenment Europe*, ed. Kent Gerard and Gert Hekma [New York: Haworth, 1989], pp. 263–301), "Sodomy and the Pursuit of a Third Sex in the Early Modern Period," in *Third Sex, Third Gender*, ed. Gilbert Herdt (New York: Zone Books, 1994), pp. 137–212, and *Sodoms Zaad in Nederland* (Nijmegen: Sun, 1995). For the French subculture, see Michel Rey, "Parisian Homosexuals Create a Lifestyle, 1700–1750: The Police Archives," *Eighteenth-Century Life* 9 (1985): 179–91, and "Police and Sodomy in Eighteenth-Century Paris: From Sin to Disorder," in Gerard and Hekma, *The Pursuit of Sodomy*, pp. 128–46; and Jeffrey Merrick and Bryant T. Ragan Jr., eds., *Homosexuality in Modern France* (New York: Oxford University Press, 1996).

5. Randolph Trumbach, "London's Sapphists: From Three Sexes to Four Genders in the Making of Modern Culture," in Herdt, *Third Sex, Third Gender*, pp. 111–36, and "The Origins and Development of the Modern Lesbian Role in the Western Gender System: Northwestern Europe and the United States, 1750–1990," *Historical Reflections/Réflexions Historiques* 20 (1994): 287–320. Emma Donoghue, in *Passions*

between Women: British Lesbian Culture, 1668–1801 (London: Scarlet Press, 1993), writes from a declared lesbian feminist view that puts all forms of affection between women into the lesbian category and rejects any comparison with the history of male sodomites. She also refuses to see any chronological change even though she admits that women with exclusive desires for women were classified as hermaphrodites early in the century but described as sapphists after midcentury.

6. For discussion of societies that presume that there can be more than two kinds of bodies, and more than two genders, see Herdt, *Third Sex, Third Gender.* Thomas Laquer analyzes the plasticity of Western bodily types in *Making Sex* (Cambridge, Mass.: Harvard University Press, 1990).

7. For aristocratic families, see Lawrence Stone, *The Family, Sex, and Marriage in England, 1500–1800* (New York: Harper and Row, 1977); Randolph Trumbach, *The Rise of the Egalitarian Family* (New York: Academic Press, 1977); and Judith Schneid Lewis, *In the Family Way* (New Brunswick, N.J.: Rutgers University Press, 1986). For the middle classes, see Peter Earle, *The Making of the English Middle Class* (Berkeley and Los Angeles: University of California Press, 1989); John Smail, *The Origins of Middle-Class Culture* (Ithaca, N.Y.: Cornell University Press, 1994); Margaret R. Hunt, *The Middling Sort* (Berkeley and Los Angeles: University of California Press, 1996); and Leonore Davidoff and Catherine Hall, *Family Fortunes* (Chicago: University of Chicago Press, 1987). For the poor, see David Levine, *Family Formation in an Age of Nascent Capitalism* (New York: Academic Press, 1977), and Levine, ed., *Proletarianization and Family History* (New York: Academic Press, 1984); John R. Gillis, *For Better, for Worse* (New York: Oxford University Press, 1985); K. D. M. Snell, *Annals of the Labouring Poor* (New York: Cambridge University Press, 1985); and Anna Clark, *The Struggle for the Breeches* (Berkeley and Los Angeles: University of California Press, 1995). These patterns in family development have been doubted by some: Alan Macfarlane, *Marriage and Love in England, 1300–1840* (Oxford: Blackwell, 1986) (on which see my review in the *Journal of the History of Sexuality* 1 [1991]: 296–309); Linda A. Pollock, *Forgotten Children* (New York: Cambridge University Press, 1983); and Anthony Fletcher, *Gender, Sex, and Subordination in England, 1500–1800* (New Haven, Conn.: Yale University Press, 1995). But most of the recent work on the middle classes, and Anna Clark's on the poor, take for granted the pattern that Stone, Trumbach, and Lewis describe for the aristocracy.

8. The still standard history of London social life is M. Dorothy George, *London Life in the Eighteenth Century* (London, 1925; reprint New York: Harper and Row, 1965). Two more recent general histories: A. L. Beier and Roger Finlay, eds., *London 1500–1700: The Making of the Metropolis* (New York: Longman, 1986); George Rudé, *Hanoverian London, 1714–1808* (London: Secker and Warburg, 1971). I have found my way around London by using H. B. Wheatley and Peter Cunningham, *London Past and Present,* 3 vols. (London, 1891; reprint Detroit: Singing Tree Press, 1968); and Ralph Hyde, *The A to Z of Georgian London* (London: Guildhall Library, 1981). The effect of migration to London and its demographic regime are studied in E. A. Wrigley, "A Simple Model of London's Importance in Changing English Society and Economy, 1650–1750," *Past and Present* 37 (1967): 44–70; John Landers, *Death and the Metropolis: Studies in the Demographic History of London, 1670–1830* (Cambridge: Cambridge University Press, 1993); Peter Clark and David Souden, eds., *Migration and Society in Early Modern England* (Totowa, N.J.: Barnes and Noble, 1988). London's

place in the rest of English urban society: P. J. Corfield, *The Impact of English Towns, 1700–1800* (New York: Oxford University Press, 1982); and Peter Borsay, *The English Urban Renaissance* (Oxford: Oxford University Press, 1989). The London economy appears in L. D. Schwarz, *London in the Age of Industrialization: Enterpreneurs, Labour Force and Living Conditions, 1700–1850* (Cambridge: Cambridge University Press, 1992). For the East and West Ends: M. J. Power, "The East and the West in Early Modern London," in *Wealth and Power in Tudor England,* ed. E. W. Ives, R. J. Knecht, and J. J. Scarisbrick (London: Athlone Press, 1978); Lawrence Stone, "The Residential Development of the West End of London in the Seventeenth Century," in *After the Reformation,* ed. Barbara C. Malament (Philadelphia: University of Pennsylvania Press, 1980); H. Clout, "London in Transition," in *London: Problems of Change,* ed. Clout and P. Wood (London: Longman, 1986); O. H. K. Spate, "The Growth of London, A.D. 1600–1800," *An Historical Geography of England,* ed. H. C. Darby (Cambridge: Cambridge University Press, 1936); John Summerson, *Georgian London,* rev. ed. (London: Barrie and Jenkins, 1970).

9. GRS.

10. Michel Foucault, *The History of Sexuality,* vol. 1, An Introduction, trans. Robert Hurley (New York: Pantheon, 1978); Didier Eribon, *Michel Foucault* (Cambridge, Mass.: Harvard University Press, 1991), p. 316.

11. Jeffrey Weeks, *Coming Out* (London: Quartet Books, 1977), and *Sex, Politics, and Society* (New York: Longman, 1981); Jonathan Ned Katz, *The Invention of Heterosexuality* (New York: Dutton, 1995); Kevin White, *The First Sexual Revolution: The Emergence of Male Heterosexuality in Modern America* (New York: New York University Press, 1993).

12. Stone, *Family, Sex, and Marriage;* Roy Porter, "Mixed Feelings: The Enlightenment and Sexuality in Eighteenth-Century Britain," in *Sexuality in Eighteenth-Century Britain,* ed. Paul-Gabriel Bouc (Manchester: Manchester University Press, 1982), and "Libertinism and Promiscuity," in *Don Giovanni: Myths of Seduction and Betrayal,* ed. Jonathan Miller (New York: Schocken, 1990); Roy Porter and Lesley Hall, *The Facts of Life* (New Haven, Conn.: Yale University Press, 1995); G. J. Barker-Benfield, *The Culture of Sensibility* (Chicago: University of Chicago Press, 1992) (see my review in *Eighteenth-Century Studies* 28 [1994–95] 275–76); A. D. Harvey, *Sex in Georgian England* (London: Duckworth, 1994). For my essays on libertinism: "Modern Prostitution and Gender in *Fanny Hill:* Libertine and Domesticated Fantasy," in *Sexual Underworlds of the Enlightenment,* ed. G. S. Rousseau and Roy Porter (Manchester: Manchester University Press, 1987), and "Erotic Fantasy"; Tim Hitchcock, *English Sexualities, 1700–1800* (New York: St. Martin's Press, 1997), and also his "Redefining Sex in Eighteenth-Century England," *History Workshop Journal* 41 (1996): 75–90.

13. Fletcher, *Gender, Sex, and Subordination,* chaps. 14–20; Clark, *Struggle for the Breeches,* pp. 183–84. For skepticism about the concept of separate spheres, see Amanda Vickery, "Golden Age to Separate Spheres? A Review of the Categories and Chronology of English Women's History," *Historical Journal* 36 (1993): 383–414; Hunt, *The Middling Sort;* Linda Colley, *Britons* (New Haven, Conn.: Yale University Press, 1992); Kathleen Wilson, *The Sense of the People* (New York: Cambridge University Press, 1995). Michael McKeon, "Historicizing Patriarchy: The Emergence of Gender Difference in England, 1660–1760," *Eighteenth-Century Studies* 28 (1995): 295–322, unlike Fletcher, does use the history of modern homosexuality to clarify the differences be-

tween the majority of men and women, but like Fletcher, he sees the early-eighteenth-century changes as a reconstruction of patriarchy.

CHAPTER TWO: REPUTATION AND IDENTITY

1. There is no study of the ecclesiastical courts in the eighteenth century, but some recent works on these courts in the sixteenth and seventeenth centuries are useful: Martin Ingram, *Church Courts, Marriage, and Sex in England, 1570–1640* (New York: Cambridge University Press, 1987); John Addy, *Sin and Society in the Seventeenth Century* (New York: Routledge, 1989); and Laura Gowing, *Domestic Dangers: Women, Words, and Sex in Early Modern London* (Oxford: Oxford University Press, 1996). For an earlier period: Richard M. Wunderli, *London Church Courts and Society on the Eve of the Reformation* (Cambridge, Mass.: Harvard University Press, 1981). G. V. Bennett in *Britain after the Glorious Revolution, 1689–1714*, ed. Geoffrey Holmes (London: Macmillan, 1969), pp. 159–63 makes the point about the effect of religious toleration on the church courts. Lawrence Stone, *Road to Divorce* (New York: Oxford University Press, 1990), p. 41 is mistaken to attribute the decline in moral supervision to anticlericalism and secularization. The actions of the voluntary societies in London show that traditional moral supervision still flourished.

2. There is now a literature on the history of defamation in England, but most of it deals with the sixteenth and seventeenth centuries: W. S. Holdsworth, "Defamation in the Sixteenth and Seventeenth Centuries," *Law Quarterly Review* 40 (1924): 302–15, 397–412; R. M. Helmholz, "Canonical Defamation in Medieval England," *American Journal of Legal History* 15 (1971): 255–68; Rosemary C. Dunhill, "Seventeenth-Century Invective: Defamation Cases as a Source for Word Study," *Devon and Cornwall Notes and Queries* 33 (1976): 49–51; C. A. Haigh, "Slander in the Church Courts in the Sixteenth Century," *Transactions of the Lancashire and Cheshire Antiquarian Society* 78 (1975): 1–13; G. R. Quaife, *Wanton Wenches and Wayward Wives* (New Brunswick, N.J.: Rutgers University Press, 1979); J. A. Sharpe, *Defamation and Slander in Early Modern England: The Church Courts at York*, Borthwick Papers, no. 58 (York, 1980), and "'Such Disagreement Betwyx Neighbours': Litigation and Human Relations in Early Modern England," in *Disputes and Settlements*, ed. John Bossy (Cambridge: Cambridge University Press, 1983); Peter Rushton, "Women, Witchcraft, and Slander in Early Modern England: Cases from the Church Courts of Durham," *Northern History* 18 (1982): 116–32; Polly Morris, "Defamation and Sexual Slander in Somerset, 1733–1850," Ph.D. diss., University of Warwick, 1985; Ingram, *Church Courts;* Susan Dwyer Amussen, *An Ordered Society* (New York: Blackwell, 1988); Addy, *Sin and Society;* Anna Clark, "Whores and Gossips: Sexual Reputation in London, 1770–1825," in *Current Issues in Women's History*, ed. Arina Angerman et al. (New York: Routledge, 1989); Janet A. Thompson, *Wives, Widows, Witches, and Bitches: Women in Seventeenth-Century Devon* (New York: Peter Lang, 1993); Laura Gowing, "Gender and the Language of Insult in Early Modern London," *History Workshop Journal* 35 (1993): 1–21, and *Domestic Dangers;* Steve Hindle, "The Shaming of Margaret Knowsley: Gossip, Gender, and the Experience of Authority in Early Modern England," *Continuity and Change* 9 (1994): 391–419; Karl E. Westhauser, "The Power of Conversation: The Evolution of Modern Social Relations in Augustan London," Ph.D. diss., Brown University, 1994; Tim Meldum, "A Women's Court in London: Defamation

at the Bishop of London's Consistory Court, 1700–1745," *London Journal* 19 (1994): 1–20. This last essay analyzes the defamation cases for 1700–1710 and 1735–45. I have earlier reported on the London cases for 1700–1709, 1750–59, and 1790–99 in "Whores and Bastards: Women and Illicit Sex in Eighteenth-Century London," paper presented at the Northeast American Society for Eighteenth-Century Studies, Toronto, 10 October 1979, "Modern Prostitution and Gender in *Fanny Hill:* Libertine and Domesticated Fantasy," in *Sexual Underworlds of the Enlightenment,* ed. G. S. Rousseau and Roy Porter (Manchester: Manchester University Press, 1987), pp. 73, 83 n. 11, and "Sex, Gender, and Sexual Identity in Modern Culture: Male Sodomy and Female Prostitution in Enlightenment England," in *Forbidden History: The State, Society, and the Regulation of Sexuality in Modern Europe,* ed. John C. Fout (Chicago: University of Chicago Press, 1992), p. 194.

3. Sharpe, *Defamation and Slander,* pp. 27–28 (York); Amussen, *An Ordered Society,* pp. 101–4 (Norfolk); Ingram, *Church Courts,* pp. 292–319 (Wiltshire); Addy, *Sin and Society,* pp. 114, 128–29, 210–12 (Cheshire); Rushton, "Women, Witchcraft, and Slander," p. 131 (Durham). For London, see Gowing, "Gender and Insult." Robert Shoemaker suggests that many defamation cases were also brought in the secular courts (*Prosecution and Punishment: Petty Crime and the Law in London and Rural Middlesex, c. 1660–1725* [Cambridge: Cambridge University Press, 1991]).

4. GLRO: MJ/SR/2384, New Prison Clerkenwell List, 1721–22; MJ/SR/2438, R 86; MJ/SR/2364, New Prison List: March 1720; MJ/SR/2369, New Prison List: May 1721; CLRO: SR, April 1725, R of Matthew Hartley, and of Robert Vero.

5. Husbands charged by wives: GLRO: MJ/SR/2369, R of John Wilder, MJ/SR/2430, R of John Rowse, MJ/SR/2470, R of William Randall, MJ/SR/2485, R of John Barnett, MJ/SR/2492, Gatehouse List: John Barnett, MJ/SR/2436, House of Correction List: Richard Absalom, MJ/SR/2523, R 226; CLRO: SR, January 1722, R of David Jones, SR, July 1722, R of Joseph Melbourn.

6. GLRO: MJ/SR/2340, Bridewell List; MJ/SR/2376, Clerkenwell List: Mary Leech; MJ/SR/2443, Clerkenwell List: Mary Talbot als Veal; MJ/SR/2339, Gatehouse List; MJ/SR/2381, Clerkenwell List; MJ/SR/2422, Clerkenwell List; MJ/SR/2436, Clerkenwell List; MJ/SR/2480, R 68; MJ/SR/2448, Clerkenwell List; CLRO: SR, July 1721, R 33.

7. CLRO: Mansion House Justice Room Charge Book, 1728–33: 16 September, 22 and 23 December 1730.

8. Susan Staves, "Money for Honor: Damages for Criminal Conversation," in *Studies in Eighteenth-Century Culture,* ed. Harry C. Payne (Madison, Wis., 1982), vol. 11, pp. 279–97; Stone, *Road to Divorce,* pp. 231–300.

9. Susan Staves, *Married Women's Separate Property in England, 1660–1833* (Cambridge, Mass.: Harvard University Press, 1990). Staves, pp. 162–95, and Stone, *Road to Divorce,* pp. 149–82, discuss private separations. The evidence for women as the majority of plaintiffs in divorces can be found in Roderick Phillips, *Putting Asunder* (New York: Cambridge University Press, 1988).

10. GLRO: DL/C/152, fols. 17–20, DL/C/249, fols. 306–9.

11. Staffordshire Record Office, D.1778.V.1790. A footman tried to force himself on Mrs. Griselda Murray in the night. The resulting scandal made her try to run away to a convent even though the man was tried and found guilty. See Robert Halsband, "Virtue in Danger: The Case of Griselda Murray," *History Today* 17 (1967): 692–700.

12. GLRO: DL/C/182, 287: Sarah Dantan v. Thomas Clarke Jervoise; Sir Lewis Namier and John Brooke, *The House of Commons, 1754–1790* (London: History of Parliament Trust, 1964), 3 vols., 2:216–17; GLRO: DL/C/151, fols. 52–54.

13. GLRO: DL/C/185: Rose v. Graham.

14. GLRO: DL/C/151, fol. 12, DL/C/248, fol. 411.

15. GLRO: DL/C/151, fol. 377; DL/C/151, fol. 358, DL/C/249, fol. 142; DL/C/150, fol. 378; DL/C/152, fols. 83–85; DL/C/151, fol. 272, DL/C/149, fols. 22–25.

16. GLRO: DL/C/151, fols. 422–27.

17. GLRO: DL/C/151, fols. 387–92, DL/C/249, fols. 144–45; DL/C/150, fol. 237, DL/C/248, fol. 90; DL/C/150, fols. 239–41.

18. GLRO: DL/C/152, fol. 381; DL/C/150, fol. 185; DL/C/151, fol. 441, DL/C/249, fol. 135; DL/C/150, fol. 108.

19. GLRO: DL/C/150, fols. 15–18, DL/C/247, fol. 393; DW/OP/1787/5.

20. GLRO: DL/C/151, fols. 22–23, 26, 263–69, DL/C/248, fol. 417.

21. GLRO: DL/C/153, fols. 429–30; DL/C/152, fol. 344; DW/OP/1783/10.

22. GLRO: DL/C/150, fols. 186–89; fols. 259–61, DL/C/248, fol. 151.

23. GLRO: DL/C/149, fols. 261–62, DL/C/247, fol. 212; DL/C/152, fols. 359–60; DL/C/149, fols. 295–99, DL/C/247, fol. 314.

24. GLRO: DL/C/149, fols. 58–62; other disputes over debt: DL/C/150, fols. 87–88, 148–49, DL/C/247, fols. 336, DL/C/248, fols. 33–34; DL/C/196–99, DL/C/248, fol. 85; DL/C/149, fols. 170–73, DL/C/248, fols. 99, 101; DL/C/172, fols. 45–53, DL/C/638: Burkinster v. Ward.

25. GLRO: DL/C/152, fols. 325–26; DL/C/150, fols. 340–44.

26. GLRO: DL/C/149, fol. 154; DL/C/152, fols. 349–57; DL/C/153, fols. 483–86.

27. GLRO: DL/C/149, fols. 357, 425, DL/C/247, fols. 146–48v; DL/C/150, fol. 302, DL/C/248, fol. 157; DL/C/152, fols. 9–11.

28. GLRO: DL/C/149, fols. 87–88.

29. GLRO: DL/C/150, fols. 303–4, DL/C/248, fol. 314; DL/C/152, fols. 163–64. For widows who ran lodging houses or public houses, see DL/C/172, fol. 248, DL/C/173, fols. 137–39, 199, DL/C/275: Newman v. Smith, Bateman v. Smith.

30. GLRO: DL/C/150, fols. 170–73, DL/C/248, fols. 99, 101; DL/C/150, fols. 178–79, 223–24, DL/C/248, fol. 71; three other cases of economic conflict: DL/C/153, fols. 442–49; DL/C/150, fols. 196–99; DL/C/173, fols. 114–19, DL/C/274: Jones v. James.

31. GLRO: DL/C/149, fol. 353, DL/C/247, fol. 333; DL/C/152, fol. 214; DL/C/151, fols. 355–57.

32. GLRO; DL/C/152, fols. 274–75; DL/C/173, fol. 250; DL/C/174: Spencer v. Leeds; DL/C/150, fols. 151–53, DL/C/247, fol. 450; DL/C/151, fols. 232–33.

33. GLRO: DL/C/173, fols. 357–64.

34. GLRO: DL/C/150, fols. 62–67, DL/C/247, fols. 351–61, 395–402.

35. Impudent servants: GLRO: DL/C/149, fols. 198–200, 399–401; DL/C/152, fols. 89–91, 94–95; DL/C/152, fols. 200–201; DL/C/150, fols. 243–45, 320–22, 370–74, DL/C/151, fols. 213–16.

36. GLRO: DL/C/150, fols. 318–19, 367–68.

37. GLRO: DL/C/149, fol. 177; DL/C/152, fols. 14–15, DL/C/249, fol. 284;

DL/C/151, fols. 271, 397; DL/C/151, fol. 363; DL/C/151, fols. 58–61, DL/C/248, fols. 424–26.

38. GLRO: DL/C/149, fols. 266, 374–75; DL/C/153, fols. 310–19.

39. GLRO: DL/C/151, fols. 207–10.

40. GLRO: DL/C/151, fols. 68–73, 76–90, DL/C/248, fols. 237, 240, 320, 367.

41. GLRO: DL/C/149, fols. 413–14, 402–12.

42. GLRO: DL/C/151, fols. 320–28, DL/C/249, fols. 60, 63; DL/C/149, fols. 20–21; DL/C/152, fol. 402.

43. Public Record Office, KB 1/20, pt. 1 (Affidavits 16 George III), no. 40.

44. SP, no. 5, pt. 2 (1778), pp. 246–50.

45. CLRO: Guildhall Justice Room Minute Books, notebook 50, 20 May 1794.

46. SP (July 1797), pp. 450–54, #464.

47. Randolph Trumbach, *The Rise of the Egalitarian Family* (New York: Academic Press, 1977), pp. 259–62, 280: I was not fully aware that what was being described in this material was the onset of puberty; E. H. East, *A Treatise of the Pleas of the crown* (London, 1803), 2 vols., 1:480.

48. *The Trial of Richard Branson for an Attempt to Commit Sodomy on the Body of James Fassett* (London, 1760), reprint in GRS: Sodomy Trials: Seven Documents, pp. 5–10. I studied these cases in an earlier essay, "Sodomitical Assaults, Gender Role, and Sexual Development in Eighteenth-Century London," in *The Pursuit of Sodomy: Male Homosexuality in Renaissance and Enlightenment Europe*, ed. Kent Gerard and Gert Hekma (New York: Haworth, 1989), pp. 407–29.

49. SP, no. 7, pt. 3 (1755), pp. 317–23. This case takes on a different look if one uses the pamphlet literature: Charles Bradbury, *Mr Bradbury's Case Truly Stated* (London, 1755); John Taylor, *Remarks on Mr Bradbury's State of His Case* (London, 1755); Bradbury, *The Cobbler Undone* (London, 1755). A fuller discussion will appear in the second volume of this study.

50. SP, no. 6 (5–10 July 1749), pp. 127–28.

51. SP, no. 5 (1735), p. 82.

52. GRS: *Select Trials at the Sessions-House in the Old Bailey* (London, 1742), 4 vols., 1:158–60.

53. Frederick A. Pottle, ed., *Boswell on the Grand Tour: Germany and Switzerland, 1764* (London: Heinemann, 1953), p. 278; GRS: *Onania; or the Heinous Sin of Self-Pollution* (London, 1723), p. 64; GRS: *A Supplement to the Onania* (London, 1723), pp. 113, 127; *Onania*, pp. 149–73; James Hudson, *Nature's Assistant* (London, 1794), pp. 158–78. For modern discussions of this literature, see E. H. Hare, "Masturbatory Insanity: The History of an Idea," *Journal of Mental Science* 108 (1962): 1–25; Robert H. MacDonald, "The Frightful Consequences of Onanism: Notes on the History of a Delusion," *Journal of the History of Ideas* 28 (1967): 423–31; and Jean Stengers and Anne van Neck, *Histoire d'une grande peur: La masturbation* (Brussels: Editions de l'Université de Bruxelles, 1984).

54. John Hunter, *A Treatise on the Venereal Disease* (London, 1786), pp. 200–201; GRS: William Buchan, *Observations Concerning the Prevention and Cure of the Venereal Disease* (London, 1796), p. 221; Vicesimus Knox, *Liberal Education* (London, 1783), 5th ed., pp. 329–30.

55. GRS: M. D. T. Bienville, *Nymphomania, or a Dissertation concerning the Furor Uterinus* (London, 1775); Randolph Trumbach, "London's Sapphists: From Three

Sexes to Four Genders in the Making of Modern Culture," in *Third Sex, Third Gender,* ed. Gilbert Herdt (New York: Zone Books, 1994), pp. 111–36; J. H. Gagnon and William Simon, *Sexual Conduct* (Chicago: Aldine, 1973); Harold Leitenberg, Mark J. Detzer, and Debra Srebnik, "Gender Differences in Masturbation and the Relation of Masturbation Experience in Preadolescence and/or Early Adolescence to Sexual Behavior and Sexual Adjustment in Young Adulthood," *Archives of Sexual Behavior* 22 (1993): 87–98; Edward O. Lauman et al., *The Social Organization of Sexuality: Sexual Practices in the United States* (Chicago: University of Chicago Press, 1994), pp. 80–86, 134–45. The recent study of sexual practices in Great Britain unfortunately decided to omit questions about masturbation on the ground that they were too upsetting: Anne M. Johnson et al., *Sexual Attitudes and Lifestyles* (Boston: Blackwell, 1994), p. 146. But see Lesley Hall, "Forbidden by God, Despised by Men: Masturbation, Medical Warnings, Moral Panic, and Manhood in Great Britain, 1850–1950," *Journal of the History of Sexuality* 2 (1992): 365–87. On nymphomania, see Carol Groneman, "Nymphomania: The Historical Construction of Female Sexuality," *Signs* 19 (1994): 336–67.

CHAPTER THREE: MALE LIBERTINISM

1. The history of English prostitution (mainly in London) may now be traced from the later Middle Ages: Ruth Mazo Karras, *Common Women: Prostitution and Sexuality in Medieval England* (New York: Oxford University Press, 1996); Ian W. Archer, *The Pursuit of Stability* (Cambridge: Cambridge University Press, 1991); Paul Griffiths, "The Structure of Prostitution in Elizabethan London," *Continuity and Change* 8 (1993): 39-63; Stanley Nash, "Social Attitudes toward Prostitution in London from 1752–1829," Ph.D. diss., New York University, 1980; A. Henderson, "Female Prostitution in London, 1730–1830," Ph.D. diss., London University, 1992; Frances Finnegan, *Poverty and Prostitution* (New York: Cambridge University Press, 1979); and Judy R. Walkowitz, *Prostitution and Victorian Society* (New York: Cambridge University Press, 1980). I have published some of my argument in three essays: "Modern Prostitution and Gender in *Fanny Hill:* Libertine and Domesticated Fantasy," in *Sexual Underworlds of the Enlightenment,* ed. G. S. Rousseau and Roy Porter (Manchester: Manchester University Press, 1987); "Sex, Gender and Sexual Identity in Modern Culture: Male Sodomy and Female Prostitution in Enlightenment London," *Journal of the History of Sexuality* 2 (1991): 186–203; and "Erotic Fantasy and Male Libertinism in Enlightenment England," in *The Invention of Pornography,* ed. Lynn Hunt (New York: Zone Books, 1993).

2. R. J. Evans, "Prostitution, State, and Society in Imperial Germany," *Past and Present* 70 (1976): 106–29; R. D. Storch, "Police Control of Street Prostitution in Victorian London," in *Police and Society,* ed. D. H. Bailey (Beverly Hills, Calif.: Sage, 1977), pp. 49–72; GL, Broadside, 6.32 (19 November 1689); Malcolm Falkus, "Lighting in the Dark Ages of English Economic History: Town Streets before the Industrial Revolution," in *Trade, Government, and Economy in Pre-Industrial England,* ed. D. C. Coleman and A. H. John (London: Weidenfeld and Nicolson, 1976), pp. 248–73.

3. Dale Underwood, *Etherege and the Seventeenth Century Comedy of Manners* (New Haven, Conn.: Yale University Press, 1957), pp. 10–40; for Italy, see Guido Ruggiero, *The Boundaries of Eros* (New York: Oxford University Press, 1985). James Turner dis-

cusses the varieties of meaning that historians have attached to libertinism in "The Properties of Libertinism," in *'Tis Nature's Fault*, ed. R. P. Maccubbin (New York: Cambridge University Press, 1987), pp. 75–87; for Restoration England, see Warren Chernaik, *Sexual Freedom in Restoration Literature* (Cambridge: Cambridge University Press, 1995); and Harold Weber, *The Restoration Rake Hero* (Madison: University of Wisconsin Press, 1986).

4. Gilbert Burnet, *Some Passages of the Life and Death of Rochester* (London, 1680), in *Rochester*, ed. David Farley-Hills (New York: Barnes and Noble, 1972), p. 56; John Cleland, *Memoirs of a Woman of Pleasure* (London, 1748–49), ed. Peter Sabor (New York: Oxford University Press, 1985), p. 144.

5. Reba Wilcoxon, "Rochester's Philosophical Premises: A Case for Consistency," *Eighteenth-Century Studies* 8 (1974–75): 183–201; J. W. Johnson, "Lord Rochester and the Tradition of Cyrenaic Hedonism, 1670–1790," *Studies on Voltaire and the Eighteenth Century* 153 (1976): 1151–67; Rochester, *Complete Poems*, ed. D. M. Veith (New Haven, Conn.: Yale University Press, 1968), p. 95. See also D. H. Griffin, *Satires against Man* (Berkeley and Los Angeles: University of California Press, 1973).

6. Hume and Walpole, quoted in Farley-Hills, *Rochester*, pp. 200–201; George Etherege, *The Man of Mode* (London, 1676), ed. W. B. Carnochan (Lincoln: University of Nebraska Press, 1966), p. 100; Richard Steele, *The Spectator*, no. 65 (London, 1711), ed. D. F. Bond (Oxford: Oxford University Press, 1965), 5 vols., 1:278–80; John Dennis, *Critical Works*, ed. E. N. Hooker (Baltimore: Johns Hopkins University Press, 1943), 2 vols., 2:495–97; R. D. Hume, *The Rakish Stage* (Carbondale: Southern Illinois University Press, 1983), p. 78; J. W. Johnson, "Did Lord Rochester Write *Sodom?*" *Papers of the Bibliographical Society of America* 81 (1987): 119–53; David Foxon, *Libertine Literature in England, 1660–1745* (New Hyde Park, N.Y.: University Books, 1965), pp. 11, 13.

7. Hertfordshire Record Office, Lady Cowper's diary, D/EP/F29:10, 30 August 1701, 12 October 1702; V. De Sola Pinto, *Sir Charles Sedley, 1639–1701* (New York: Boni and Liveright, 1927), p. 234.

8. M. E. Novak, *William Congreve* (New York: Twayne Publishers, 1971), pp. 41–51; Jeremy Collier, *A Short view of the immorality and profaneness of the English stage* (London, 1699), p. 142; William Congreve, *Complete Plays*, ed. Herbert Davis (Chicago: University of Chicago Press, 1967), pp. 216–17; Thomas Shadwell, *Complete Works*, ed. Montague Summers (London, 1927; reprint New York: Benjamin Blom, 1968), 5 vols., 3:105.

9. Underwood, *Etherege*, p. 16; *Works of Mr. de St. Evremonde* (London, 1700), 2 vols., 1:187, 396–97, 2:211.

10. *Works of St. Evremonde*, 1:221–22, 234; William Burnaby, trans., *The Satyr of Titus Petronius Arbiter* (London, 1694), cited in Donald Thomas, *A Long Time Burning* (London: Praeger, 1969), pp. 76–77; Hertfordshire Record Office, Lady Cowper's diary, D/EP/F29, 1 July 1701.

11. *Works of St. Evremonde*, 1:187; J. C. Hodges, ed., *William Congreve* (New York: Harcourt, Brace and World, 1964), pp. 13, 53, 58–59, 242–43; Samuel Johnson, *Lives of the English Poets* (London, 1779–81) (London, 1967, World's Classics ed.), 2 vols., 2:29, 27; *The Spectator*, no. 189, 2:242, no. 422, 3:585–86; T. F. Mayo, *Epicurus in England (1650–1725)* (Dallas: Southwest Press, 1934), pp. 159–62, 186–223; M. E. Novak, "Congreve as the Eighteenth Century's Archetypal Libertine," *Restoration and*

Eighteenth Century Theatre Research 15 (1976): 35-39, 60; Hume, *The Rakish Stage,* pp. 74-81; E. L. Avery, *Congreve's Plays on the Eighteenth-Century Stage* (New York: Modern Language Association, 1951).

12. A. O. Aldridge, *Shaftesbury and the Deist Manifesto,* Transactions of the American Philosophical Society, 41 (1951), pt. 2, pp. 371-82.

13. R. S. Crane, "Suggestions toward a Genealogy of the 'Man of Feeling,'" *ELH* 1 (1934): 205-30; Ernest Tuveson, "The Importance of Shaftesbury," *ELH* 20 (1953): 267-99; G. S. Rousseau, "Nerves, Spirits, and Fibres: Towards Defining the Origins of Sensibility," in *Studies in the Eighteenth Century,* ed. R. F. Brissenden and J. Earle (Toronto, 1976), pp. 137-57.

14. Lord Shaftesbury, *Characteristics of Men, Manners, Opinions, Times,* ed. J. M. Robertson and Stanley Grean (New York: Bobbs-Merrill, 1964), 2 vols. in 1, 1:310-11. For a recent discussion that is skeptical about Shaftesbury and sex, see Lawrence Klein, *Shaftesbury and the Culture of Politeness* (Cambridge: Cambridge University Press, 1994). Shaftesbury's ambiguous relationship to sodomy did not discredit him as it did Rochester, possibly because it was not widely known: Randolph Trumbach, "Sodomy Transformed: Aristocratic Libertinage, Public Reputation, and the Gender Revolution of the 18th Century," *Journal of Homosexuality* 19 (1990): 105-24.

15. Shaftesbury, *An Inquiry concerning virtue* (London, 1699), p. 177; Robert Voitle, *The Third Earl of Shaftesbury, 1671-1713* (London: Louisiana State University Press, 1984), pp. 198-200; Hertfordshire Record Office, Lady Cowper's diary, D/EP/F29, 16 November 1701. *The Adept Ladies* is discussed by A. O. Aldridge, "Shaftesbury's Rosicrucian Ladies," *Anglia* 103 (1985): 297-319.

16. Voitle, *Third Earl of Shaftesbury,* pp. 135-63, 92-93, 96-97, 256, 78.

17. Ibid., pp. 241-42; Shaftesbury, Characteristics, 2:4, 269, 1:217-18, 2:255, 252-53; Samuel Richardson, *Clarissa* (London, 1747-48) (New York, 1962, Everyman ed.), 4 vols., 2:59; Aldridge, *Shaftesbury and Deist Manifesto,* pp. 380, 297.

18. Shaftesbury, *Characteristics,* 2:261-62; Isaac Kramnick, *Bolingbroke and His Circle* (Cambridge, Mass.: Harvard University Press, 1968), pp. 89-91; Jonathan Swift, *Journal to Stella,* ed. Harold Williams (Oxford: Oxford University Press, 1948), 2 vols., 2:401; Swift, *Works,* ed. Herbert Davis and Irvin Ehrenpreis (Oxford: Blackwell, 1973), 14 vols., 8:134-35.

19. Sheila Biddle, *Bolingbroke and Harley* (New York: Knopf, 1974), pp. 87-96; GRS: *Satan's Harvest Home* (London, 1749), p. 30.

20. Oliver Goldsmith, *Works,* ed. Arthur Friedman (Oxford: Oxford University Press, 1966), 5 vols., 3:439; Swift, *Journal to Stella,* 2:420-21; Hertfordshire Record Office, Lady Cowper's diary, D/EP/F30, 10 January 1702/3.

21. R. J. Allen, *The Clubs of Augustan London* (Cambridge, Mass.: Harvard University Press, 1933), pp. 105-18; Daniel Statt, "The Case of the Mohocks: Rake Violence in Augustan London," *Social History* 20 (1995): 179-99.

22. Hertfordshire Record Office, Lady Cowper's diary, D/EP/F32, 11 November 1707; Allen, *Clubs of Augustan London,* pp. 119-24; Mark Blackett-Ord, *Hell-Fire Duke* (Windsor Forest: Kensal Press, 1982), pp. 42-46, 70-72; GLRO: *Middlesex County Records, 1719-1722,* typescript, pp. 116-18.

23. Mary Davys, *The Accomplished Rake* (London, 1727), in *Four before Richardson,* ed. W. H. McBurney (Lincoln: University of Nebraska Press, 1963), pp. 300-301; Lady Mary Wortley Montagu, *Complete Letters,* ed. Robert Halsband (Oxford: Oxford

University Press, 1965–67), 3 vols., 2:38–40; Blackett-Ord, *Hell-Fire Duke,* p. 83. For the masons, see M. C. Jacob, *The Radical Enlightenment* (London: George Allen and Unwin, 1981).

24. Hertfordshire Record Office, Lady Cowper's diary, D/EP/F29, 10 February 1700/1701, 17 November 1702, F32, 7 February 1706/7, F33, 19–23 July 1709, F29, 30 October 1700; Delariviere Manley, *Secret Memoirs . . . from the New Atalantis* (London, 1709), 2 vols., 1:213–14. See also Ann Kugler, "Prescription, Culture, and Shaping Identity: Lady Sarah Cowper (1644–1720)," Ph.D. diss., University of Michigan, 1994.

25. For the Dilettanti: Cecil Harcourt-Smith, *The Society of Dilettanti, Its Regalia and Pictures* (London: Macmillan, 1932); Lionel Cust, *History of the Society of Dilettanti* (London: Macmillan, 1914); Shearer West, "Libertinism and the Ideology of Male Friendship in the Portraits of the Society of Dilettanti," *Eighteenth-Century Life* 16 (1992): 76–104; for the Hell-Fire Club there are books of various value: L. C. Clark, *The Clubs of the Georgian Rakes* (New York: Columbia University Press, 1942); Donald McCormick, *The Hell-Fire Club* (London: Jarrolds, 1958); D. P. Mannix, *The Hell-Fire Club* (New York: Ballantine, 1959).

26. Betty Kemp, *Sir Francis Dashwood* (London: Macmillan, 1967), pp. 101–4, 116, 137–57; Benjamin Franklin, *Autobiography,* ed. L. W. Labaree (New Haven, Conn.: Yale University Press, 1964), p. 150; Horace Walpole, *Memoirs of the Reign of George III,* ed. G. F. Russell Barker (London, 1894), 3 vols., 1:136–38, 248.

27. Kemp, *Sir Francis Dashwood,* pp. 131–36, Walpole, *Memoirs,* 1:138; Raymond Postgate, *"That Devil Wilkes"* (London: Dobson, 1956), pp. 22–23; Charles Churchill, *Poetical Works,* ed. Douglas Grant (Oxford: Oxford University Press, 1956). Statues of Venus appear in some eighteenth-century gardens as erotic symbols: the Venus at Stowe was accompanied by obscene paintings and verses and soft couches for lovemaking: J. G. Turner, "The Sexual Politics of Landscape: Images of Venus in Eighteenth-Century English Poetry and Landscape Gardening," *Studies in Eighteenth-Century Culture,* ed. H. C. Payne (Madison, Wis., 1982), vol. 11, 343–66.

28. Hamilton's letter was printed in Richard Payne Knight, *Discourse on the Worship of Priapus* (London, 1786), which is reprinted in *Sexual Symbolism,* ed. Ashley Montagu (New York: Julian Press, 1957), pp. 13–23; Brian Fothergill, *Sir William Hamilton* (New York: Harcourt, Brace and World, 1969), pp. 173–74; Lord Herbert, ed., *Pembroke Papers (1780–1794)* (London: Jonathan Cape, 1950), pp. 117–18; Giancarlo Carabelli, *In the Image of Priapus* (London: Duckworth, 1996).

29. Peter Funnell, in *The Arrogant Connoisseur: Richard Payne Knight, 1751–1824,* ed. Michael Clarke and Nicholas Penny (Manchester: Manchester University Press, 1982), chap. 4; G. S. Rousseau, "The Sorrows of Priapus," in *Sexual Underworlds of the Enlightenment,* ed. G. S. Rousseau and Roy Porter (Manchester: Manchester University Press, 1987), pp. 101–53.

30. Payne Knight, *Discourse on Worship of Priapus,* in *Sexual Symbolism,* pp. 26–27, 30, 53–54, 61–62, 67, 72–73, 75, 81, 84, 86–89, 123, 134–35, 200–207, 216.

31. Rousseau, "The Sorrows of Priapus": I reinterpret some of this evidence: I think Rousseau is probably wrong to interpret Walpole's hostility in terms of his sexual fears. He also suggests that Payne Knight was a sodomite, but the evidence for this is problematical.

32. G. V. Bennett in *Britain after the Glorious Revolution, 1689–1714*, ed. Geoffrey Holmes (London: Macmillan, 1969), pp. 159–65.

33. For the societies see G. V. Porteus, *Caritas Anglicana* (London: A. R. Mowbray, 1912); D. W. R. Bahlman, *The Moral Revolution of 1688* (New Haven, Conn.: Yale University Press, 1957); T. C. Curtis and W. A. Speck, "The Societies for the Reformation of Manners: A Case Study in the Theory and Practice of Moral Reform," *Literature and History* 3 (1976): 45–64; Eamon Duffy, "Primitive Christianity Revived: Religious Renewal in Augustan England," *Studies in Church History* 14 (1977): 287–300; T. B. Isaacs, "Moral Crime, Moral Reform, and the State in Early Eighteenth-Century England," Ph.D. diss., University of Rochester, 1979; A. G. Craig, "The Movement for the Reformation of Manners, 1688–1715," Ph.D. diss., University of Edinburgh, 1980; Robert Shoemaker, *Prosecution and Punishment: Petty Crime and the Law in London and Rural Middlesex, c. 1660–1725* (Cambridge: Cambridge University Press, 1991), and "Reforming the City: The Reformation of Manners Campaign in London, 1690–1738," in *Stilling the Grumbling Hive*, ed. Lee Davison et al. (New York: St. Martin's Press, 1992), pp. 99–120; John Spurr, "The Church, the Societies, and the Moral Revolution of 1688," in *The Church of England c. 1689–1833*, ed. John Walsh, Colin Haydon, and Stephen Taylor (Cambridge: Cambridge University Press, 1993), pp. 127–42. These religious societies of the first generation of the eighteenth century had more in common with the societies for urban reform that had been part of the Protestant reformation in England, and like those societies they arrested both men and women for prostitution. After 1730 only the women were arrested: the moral drive behind the later voluntary societies had therefore changed significantly. For the societies before 1660 see Patrick Collinson, *The Birthpangs of Protestant England* (New York: St. Martin's Press, 1988), chap. 2; and Archer, *The Pursuit of Stability*. The history of religious societies after 1730 can be followed in John Walsh, "Religious Societies: Methodist and Evangelical 1738–1800," *Studies in Church History* 23 (1986): 279–302; Henry D. Rack, "Religious Societies and the Origins of Methodism," *Journal of Ecclesiastical History* 38 (1987): 582–95; and Joanna Innes, "Politics and Morals: The Reformation of Manners Movement in Later Eighteenth-Century England," in *The Transformation of Political Culture*, ed. Eckhart Hellmuth (New York: Oxford University Press, 1990), pp. 58–118.

34. The sessions rolls provide the figures for Westminster and Middlesex and the Mansion House Justice Room Minute Books in CLRO those for the City.

35. GLRO: MJ/SR/2364, House of Correction List; MJ/SR/2366, House of Correction List; MJ/SR/2369, House of Correction List.

36. GLRO: MJ/SR/2422, House of Correction List; MJ/SR/2455, House of Correction List; MJ/SR/2431, R of Booth, MJ/SR/2524, R 70, MJ/SR/2468, R 287, 286; MJ/SR/2394, R of Large; *The Fifteenth Account of the Progress made towards suppressing profaneness and debauchery* (London, 1710).

37. GLRO: MJ/SR/2406, Gatehouse List, R of Browne; MJ/SR/2409, R of Vincent; MJ/SR/2416, R of Hainky; MJ/SR/2438, New Prison List.

38. GLRO: MJ/SR/2471, R 81, 80, 79, 78; MJ/SR/2405, R 126; MJ/SR/2451, R 149; MJ/SR/2389, R of Hardy; Isaacs, "Moral Crime," pp. 225–26.

39. CLRO: SR, July 1727, R 29; December 1727, R 1; April 1728, R 7; January 1729, R 14; GLRO: MJ/SR/2373, Gatehouse List.

40. CLRO: Guildhall Justice Room Minute Books, 19 August 1782; *London Eve-*

ning Post, 10 April 1776; *London Chronicle,* 17–20 April 1762, p. 374, 26–29 March 1763, p. 298, 15–17 July 1760, p. 63. See also Parliamentary Papers, *Third Report from the Committee on the State of the Police of the Metropolis* (London, 1818), pp. 114–16.

41. WPL: E. 2574–78.

42. GRS: *The London-Bawd* (London, 1711), p. 163; William Byrd, *The London Diary (1717–1721) and Other Writings,* ed. L. B. Wright and Marion Tinling (New York: Oxford University Press, 1958), p. 136; GLRO: MJ/SR/2440, R of Pendergass, MJ/SR/2358, R of Thacker, Hartwell; MJ/SR/2369, Clerkenwell List: Gill, Lovell, and Bealing for being in Needham's house, R of Hodgson and Lewis to give evidence against her, MJ/SR/2401, R of Tolly, MJ/SR/2425, R of Tolly; *British Journal,* 16 March, 23 March 1723; MJ/SR/2363, House of Correction List; MJ/SR/2520, R 142, MJ/SR/2521, R 123. There is a romanticized account of Needham in E. J. Burford, *Royal St. James's* (London: Hale, 1988), pp. 158–73, which has her running a house continuously in Park Place from 1709 to 1730.

43. R. Campbell, *The London Tradesman* (London, 1747; reprint Newton Abbot, Devon: David and Charles Reprints, 1969), pp. 190–94; GRS: Edward Ward, *The London Spy* (London, 1709), pp. 2, 7, 52, 109, 146, 201–5, 213, 281, 27; Richard King, *The Complete Modern London Spy for the present year 1781* (London, 1781), p. 79.

44. Campbell, *The London Tradesman,* pp. 320, 296–97; CLRO: SR, January 1723, R 20; May 1724, R 55.

45. GLRO: MJ/SR/2456, R 98 (also MJ/SR/2478, Alexander Maplebank in New Prison List); MJ/SR/2448, R 195; *London Chronicle,* 12–15 April 1760, p. 367, 19–22 April 1760, p. 391, 8–10 March 1763, p. 239, 26–28 April 1764, p. 401.

46. *London Chronicle,* 28–30 June 1759, p. 615, 6–8 September 1763, p. 233; *Annual Register* 6 (1763): 62–63. There are vivid descriptions of the houses in Shadwell in the early nineteenth century: Parliamentary Papers, *First Report from the Committee on the State of the Police of the Metropolis* (London, 1817), pp. 51, 128–33, 148, 195, 461.

47. Francis Grose, *A Classical Dictionary of the Vulgar Tongue* (London, 1796), s.v. "dock"; Peter Linebaugh, "The Tyburn Riot against the Surgeons," in *Albion's Fatal Tree,* by Douglas Hay et al. (New York: Pantheon, 1975), pp. 89–102; *London Chronicle,* 28–30 April 1761, pp. 409–10.

48. Tim Harris, "The Bawdy House Riots of 1688," *Historical Journal* 29 (1986): 537–56, and *London Crowds in the Reign of Charles II* (London: Cambridge University Press, 1987), pp. 22–25, 82–91, 166–68, 217, 220–21.

49. Parliamentary Papers, *Report for the Committee on the State of the Metropolis* (London, 1816), p. 222, cf. 232.

50. The traditional relationship in the seventeenth century is described in Steven R. Smith, "The Ideal and Reality: Apprentice-Master Relationships in Seventeenth-Century London," *History of Education Quarterly* 31 (1981): 449–59.

51. GLRO: MJ/SR/2361, House of Correction List; MJ/SR/2361, R of Dennis and Debarr v. Parker; MJ/SR/2386, house of correction: Jones; MJ/SR/2389: house of correction: Hall; MJ/SR/2435, R 128, 129, 130, 127. MJ/SR/2445, Gatehouse List, R 94. There would be evidence of a few more complaints by masters in the 1720s if more of the house of correction lists had survived. There are no complaints, however, in the lists I have seen for 1731, 1733, 1734, 1735, 1737–39, 1744–48, 1752, 1755–56, 1763–65, 1770–72, 1775, which are to be found in GLRO: WJ/CC/B/

135-46, WJ/CC/R/6-12, MJ/CC/R/5-14, 35B, 37-40, 51-57, WJ/CC/R/2-5, 16-20, WJ/CC/R/25-28, WJ/CC/B/234-50.

52. GL, MS 12017, p. 16; H. A. Beecham, "Samuel Wesley Senior: New Biographical Evidence," *Renaissance and Modern Studies* 7 (1963): 93.

53. GLRO: MJ/SR/2458, R 1; GRS: *Select Trials at the Sessions-House in the Old Bailey* (London, 1742), 4 vols., 3:18, 20-22.

54. William Matthews, ed., *The Diary of Dudley Ryder, 1715-1716* (London: Methuen, 1939), pp. 46-47, 49, 66-67, 71-72, 85, 88, 105.

55. *The Autobiography of Francis Place*, ed. Mary Thale (Cambridge: Cambridge University Press, 1972), pp. 34-45, 92-93, 106, 121.

56. Ibid., pp. 71-82, 95-96, 104, 122, 11.

57. *Antimoxeia: or the honest and joint design of the Tower Hamlets for the general suppression of bawdy houses* (London, 1691; Guildhall, B'side 1.43); Craig, "Movement for Reformation," for the best account of this local association; *London Chronicle*, 1-4 September 1764, p. 222; GLRO: MJ/SR/2381, House of Correction List; MJ/SR/2349, R of Ellis; MJ/SR/2027, bond of Sherwood, R 72; MJ/SR/2030, R 130; MJ/SR/2236, R 13.

58. Public Record Office, KB1/11, pt. 1: K. v. Hester wife of John Mills.

59. GRS: Nicholas Venette, *Conjugal Love; or the pleasures of the marriage bed considered* (London, c. 1780), pp. 174-82; for an analysis of this edition, see Roy Porter, "Spreading Carnal Knowledge or Selling Dirt Cheap? Nicholas Venette's 'Table de l'amour conjugal' in Eighteenth-Century England," *Journal of European Studies* 14 (1984): 233-55; Roy Porter and Lesley Hall, *The Facts of Life* (New Haven, Conn.: Yale University Press, 1995), pp. 64-90; *Select Trials*, 1:73; Randolph Trumbach, *The Rise of the Egalitarian Family* (New York: Academic Press, 1977), p. 178; Cleland, *Woman of Pleasure*, pp. 28-33.

60. GRS: *Aristotle's Masterpiece;* the editions of 1694, 1749, and part of 1776 are reprinted in this volume: these represent the three main eighteenth-century editions, *Aristotle's Last Legacy* (London, 1776) being a version of the 1710 edition, though changed again; for a good start at the analysis of the various editions, see Roy Porter, "'The Secrets of Generation Display'd': Aristotle's Masterpiece in Eighteenth-Century England," in Maccubbin, *'Tis Nature's Fault*, pp. 1-21; Porter and Hall, *The Facts of Life*, pp. 33-64; *Autobiography of Francis Place*, p. 45; Foxon, *Libertine Literature*, p. 13, and Thomas, *A Long Time Burning*, pp. 21-22, 78, for Marten's prosecution.

61. GRS: John Dunton, *The Night-Walker; or Evening Rambles in Search of Lewd Women* (London, 1696-97), 2 vols., September 1696, 1:6-7, 11; October 1696, 1:20; January 1697, 2:4; February 1697, 2:14, 10-12; October 1696, 1:10.

62. Daniel Defoe, *Conjugal Lewdness; or Matrimonial Whoredom* (London, 1727), reprint with introduction by Maximillian E. Novak (Gainesville, Fla.: Scholars' Facsimiles and Reprints, 1967).

CHAPTER FOUR: PROSTITUTION: NUMBERS AND TOPOGRAPHY

1. Saunders Welch, *A Proposal . . . to remove the nuisance of common prostitutes from the streets of this metropolis* (London, 1758), in GRS: Prostitution Reform, p. 13n; Jonas Hanway, *A Reply to C—— A——* (London, 1760), p. 20; E. A. Wrigley, in *Towns*

in Societies, ed. Philip Abrams and Wrigley (London: Cambridge University Press, 1978), p. 215.

2. The lists are available in the British Library and the Guildhall Library. The figures of A. G. Craig, "The Movement for the Reformation of Manners, 1688–1715," Ph.D. diss., University of Edinburgh, 1980, p. 117, are more accurate than a slightly different computation in T. B. Isaacs, "Moral Crime, Moral Reform, and the State in Early Eighteenth-Century England," Ph.D. diss., University of Rochester, 1979, p. 256. The lists for 1715–38 are summarized in a table in G. V. Porteus, *Caritas Anglicana* (London: A. R. Mowbray, 1912), following p. 254. They are all combined by Robert Shoemaker, "Reforming the City: The Reformation of Manners Campaign in London, 1690–1738," in *Stilling the Grumbling Hive,* ed. Lee Davison et al. (New York: St. Martin's Press, 1992), pp. 99–120.

3. *London Chronicle,* 8–10 December 1761, p. 554, 13–15 April 1762, p. 354, 29–31 March 1763, p. 305.

4. GLRO: MJ/SR/2230, R 147.

5. GLRO: MJ/SR/2518, House of Correction List.

6. *A Congratulatory Epistle from a reformed rake to John F——g Esq. upon the new scheme of reclaiming prostitutes (London, 1758),* pp. 13–16.

7. John Fielding, *An Account of the origin and effects of a police set on foot by his grace the duke of Newcastle in the Year 1753* (London, 1758), reprint in GRS: Prostitution Reform, p. 45; *London Chronicle,* 4–6 January 1759, p. 17; GRS: *Satan's Harvest Home* (London, 1749), p. 2; GLRO: MJ/SR/3267, Bond 51; GRS: John Marten, *A Treatise of . . . the Venereal Disease* (London, 1708) with an appendix *Gonosologium Novum,* pp. 81, 88, 91; William Brodum, *A Guide to Old Age* (London, 1795), 2 vols., 2:69–70; Randolph Trumbach, *The Rise of the Egalitarian Family* (New York: Academic Press, 1977), pp. 97–113; Jane Austen, *Persuasion* (London, 1818), ed. R. W. Chapman (London: Oxford University Press, 1969), p. 243.

8. WPL: E. 2574, 2575.

9. GRS: John Dunton, *The Night-Walker; or Evening Rambles in Search of Lewd Women* (London, 1696–97), 2 vols., January 1697, 2:3; Daniel Defoe, *Everybody's Business is Nobody's Business* (London, 1725), p. 7; *Satan's Harvest Home,* pp. 4–5; *London Chronicle,* 4–6 January 1763, p. 23.

10. RCS, Lock Hospital Board Minutes, 1771– 73, pp. 218–19; John Butler, *A Sermon preached in the chapel of the Magdalen Hospital,* with an appendix, *General State of the Magdalen Hospital, 10 August 1758–25 December 1784* (London, 1786), p. 4.

11. Dunton, *The Night-Walker,* January 1697, 2:28. Some disorderly houses in the 1720s were prosecuted in King's Bench, so this list of houses is not comprehensive; see Robert Shoemaker, *Prosecution and Punishment: Petty Crime and the Law in London and Rural Middlesex, c. 1660–1725* (Cambridge: Cambridge University Press, 1991), pp. 22, 144 n. 65, 244.

12. WPL: E. 2574–75. The houses in St. Margaret's were possibly prosecuted in the court of burgesses for Westminster: Shoemaker, *Prosecution and Punishment,* p. 22.

13. GLRO: MJ/SR/3158–70.

14. Welch, *Proposal to Remove Prostitutes,* pp. 17–18, GLRO: MJ/SR/2510, R 244, 232.

15. *Satan's Harvest Home,* p. 27.

16. GLRO: MJ/SR/3286, R 279; MJ/SR/3289, R 752, 743.

17. GLRO: MJ/SR/3379, R 344, 318 (Ann Harris); MJ/SR/3225, R 12 (Green); MJ/SR/3340, R 367, 366 (Madden); MJ/SR/3260, R 279, 278; MJ/SR/3300, R 554 (Stewart); MJ/SR/3286, R 283; MJ/SR/3303, R 40; MJ/SR/3289, R 565; MJ/SR/ 3359, R 190 (Farmer and Williams); MJ/SR/3221, R 382, 101 (Egan).

18. GLRO: MJ/SR/3164, R 59; MJ/SR/3169, R 94, 78, 77, 461; MJ/SR/3167, R 449; MJ/SR/3161, R 253; MJ/SR/3158, R 232.

19. GLRO: MJ/SR/3274, R 356, 355; MJ/SR/3278, R 69; *London Chronicle,* 23–25 December 1760, p. 609, 13–15 January 1761, p. 55, 9–11 April 1761, p. 345; *The Life and Character of Moll King* (London, 1747), pp. 19–20; E. J. Burford, *Wits, Wenchers, and Wantons* (London: Hale, 1986), pp. 72–75; *London Chronicle,* 3–5 May 1763, p. 426, 31 May–2 June 1763, p. 522.

20. GLRO: MJ/SR/3264, R 322, 321, MJ/SR/3353, R 38, 37, MJ/SR/3360, R 316, 315 (Grimes); MJ/SR/3221, R 396, MJ/SR/3252, R. 149, MJ/SR/3252, R 141, 109, MJ/SR/3260, R 357, 356, MJ/SR/3264, R 212, 211 (Dyas); MJ/SR/3248, R 360, MJ/SR/3255, bond, MJ/SR/3262, R 99, MJ/SR/3319, R 431, MJ/SR/3343, R 70 (Cassidy); MJ/SR/3237, R 261, MJ/SR/3243, R 199, MJ/SR/3255, R 239, MJ/SR/3260, R 340, MJ/SR/3275, R 187 (Sarsfield); MJ/SR/3237, R 9, 8, MJ/SR/ 3240, R 136, MJ/SR/3271, R 204, 202 (Burne) R 222, 200 (cf. MJ/SR/3275, R 1), 199 (Phenix Alley houses); MJ/SR/3248, R 101, MJ/SR/3250, R 50, MJ/SR/3262, R 98, MJ/SR/3267, R 46, MJ/SR/3271, bond, R 131, MJ/SR/3278, R 85, MJ/SR/ 3303, R 212, 211 (Buckley); MJ/SR/3303, bond, R 141, MJ/SR/3307, R 66, MJ/ SR/3312, R 170, MJ/SR/3353, R 215 (Cowan); MJ/SR/3303, bond, R 71, MJ/SR/ 3307, R 71, MJ/SR/3312, R 185, MJ/SR/5360, 8 September 1778 (Ashley); MJ/ SR/3221, R 442, 441, 421, 418, 348, MJ/SR/3230, R 18, 17, MJ/SR/3252, R 129, MJ/SR/3340, R of Margaret Walker (Foran); MJ/SR/3240, bond, R 43, 44, 45, 30, 326, 335, 334, 333 (Princes Court houses).

21. Sir John Hawkins, *The Life of Dr. Johnson* (London, 1787), pp. 75–76; H. B. Wheatley and Peter Cunningham, *London Past and Present* (London, 1891; reprint Detroit: Singing Tree Press, 1968), 3 vols., 2:126–29.

22. *The Autobiography of Francis Place,* ed. Mary Thale (Cambridge: Cambridge University Press, 1972), pp. 227–28; *London Chronicle,* 17–19 May 1759, p. 477, 2–4 February 1764, p. 118, 16–18 August 1764, p. 166; John Fielding, *Extracts from . . . the Penal Laws* (London, 1768), pp. 66–67.

23. GLRO: DL/C/172, DL/C/274: Hall v. Remnant; MJ/SR/3282, bond, MJ/ SR/3283, R 38, 37, MJ/SR/3284, R 286, MJ/SR/3286, R 65, 64, MJ/SR/3343, R 378, MJ/SR/3360, R 355 (Lemon, Hant).

24. GLRO: DL/C/173, DL/C/274: Reeve v. Hance.

25. GRS: *The London-Bawd* (London, 1711), pp. 9–11; GLRO: MJ/SR/2424, R of John Wiseman, 1724; MJ/SR/2510, R 186; Dunton, *The Night-Walker,* January 1697, 2:18; GRS: Edward Ward, *The London Spy* (London, 1709), pp. 385–86; *Journals of the House of Commons,* 10 April 1770.

CHAPTER FIVE: THE PROSTITUTE'S LIFE

1. CLRO: Guildhall Justice Room Minute Books, notebook 48, 19 August 1791.

2. CLRO: Mansion House Justice Room Minute Books, 27, 28 July 1790.

3. Ibid., 28, 29 May 1790.

4. E. J. Burford, *Royal St. James's* (London: Hale, 1988), pp. 144–45.

5. GLRO: WSP, July 1729, Examinations 1, 2, 3; MJ/SR/2523, Gatehouse List, October 1729, Bond of James and Mary Garrett [sic], R 23, 24; SP, no. 8, pt. 3 (1780), pp. 778–86.

6. John Fielding, *An Account of the origin and effects of a police set on foot by his grace the duke of Newcastle in the Year 1753* (London, 1758), reprint in GRS: Prostitution Reform, p. 46; *London Chronicle,* 24–26 April 1759, p. 391.

7. CLRO: SR, July 1720, R 27, 29; *The Autobiography of Francis Place,* ed. Mary Thale (Cambridge: Cambridge University Press, 1972), pp. 71–72; *London Chronicle,* 10–13 November 1764, p. 459.

8. CLRO: SR, August 1721, R 31; September 1722, R 32; December 1722, R 41, 43.

9. CLRO: SR, July 1721, R 89; July 1722, R 2; January 1722–23, R 14; October 1723, R 23.

10. CLRO: SR, December 1721, R 2; July 1724, R 34; April 1724, R 31; October 1721, R 4, 1; July 1723, R 25; August 1723, R 37; December 1725, R 28.

11. GRS: John Dunton, *The Night-Walker; or Evening Rambles in Search of Lewd Women* (London, 1696–97), 2 vols., January 1697, 2:11–16; GLRO: DL/C/185: July 2, 1795, Shaw v. Shaw; SP, no. 6, pt. 6 (1785), #694, pp. 905–6.

12. GLRO: DL/C/152, fols. 22–25; DL/C/173, fols. 53–60, DL/C/274, Edwardes v. Edwardes; DL/C/181, Carter v. Carter, 284, Carter v. Carter.

13. CLRO: Mansion House Justice Room Charge Book, 1728–33: 16 July 1731, 19 March 1731/2; Guildhall Justice Room Minute Books, 1761–96: 21 January 1778, 25 July 1780, 15 June 1781, 16 August 1782, 3 September 1782, 5 September 1782, 10 July 1786, also 6, 7, July 1786, 24 April 1794.

14. CLRO: Mansion House Justice Room Minute Books, 1 April 1786; *General State of the Magdalen Hospital 1758–1784* (London, 1784), p. 4; *London Chronicle,* 12–14 July 1763, p. 48.

15. Fielding, *Account of a Police,* p. 44; Saunders Welch, *A Proposal . . . to remove the nuisance of common prostitutes from the streets of this metropolis* (London, 1758), in GRS: Prostitution Reform, pp. 3–5, 11–12.

16. R. Campbell, *The London Tradesman* (London, 1747; reprint Newton Abbot, Devon: David and Charles Reprints, 1969), pp. 208–9 (milliners), 227–28 (mantua makers); Adam Smith, *The Wealth of Nations* (London, 1776), Everyman ed., 2 vols., 1:147; M. Dorothy George, *London Life in the Eighteenth Century* (London, 1925; reprint New York: Harper and Row, 1965), p. 124.

17. CLRO: Guildhall Justice Room Minute Books, 21 and 26 January 1778, 29 March 1779; *London Chronicle,* 11–13 February 1762, p. 150.

18. GLRO: FH, Petitioners Admitted, vol. 22 (1798).

19. RCS, Board Minutes, 1763–65 (26 April 1764), pp. 140–42.

20. *London Chronicle,* 10–12 September 1761, p. 255; GLRO: DL/C/275: Leeds v. Leeds.

21. CLRO: Guildhall Justice Room Minute Books, 14 January 1780, 15 January 1791; [John Cleland], *The Case of the Unfortunate Bosavern Penlez* (London, 1749), pp. 9–15; *London Chronicle,* 31 August–2 September 1762, p. 222.

22. CLRO: Mansion House Justice Room Minute Books, 11 October 1690; Guild-

hall Justice Room Minute Books, 22 January 1778; GLRO: MJ/SR/2588, R of Hester Mason; MJ/SR/2488, New Prison List, 1727; MJ/SR/2525, R 23.

23. The materials are extensive. The two trials: SP, no. 3 (February 1753), #158, 159, pp. 109–16; no. 4, pts. 2, 3 (April–May 1754), pp. 157–73. The pamphlets: J. S. Dodd, *A Physical Account of the Case of Elizabeth Canning* (London, 1753); Daniel Cox, *An Appeal to the public in behalf of Elizabeth Canning* (London, 1753); Henry Fielding, *A Clear State of the case of Elizabeth Canning* (London, 1753); John Hill, *The Story of Elizabeth Canning* (London, 1753); *Genuine and Impartial Memoirs of Elizabeth Canning* (London, 1754); *A Full and Authentic Account of . . . Mary Squires . . . and Elizabeth Canning* (London, 1753); *A full relation of everything that has happened to Elizabeth Canning since sentence has been passed on her about the gypsy* (London, 1754). These are a selection of those I have found most useful.

24. Lillian de la Torre (pseud. L. B. McCue), *"Elizabeth Is Missing"* (London: Joseph, 1947); see also B. R. Wellington, *The Mystery of Elizabeth Canning* (New York: Peck, 1940); John Treherne, *The Canning Enigma* (London: Jonathan Cape, 1989); Judith Moore, *The Appearance of Truth: The Story of Elizabeth Canning and Eighteenth-Century Narrative* (Newark: University of Delaware Press, 1994).

25. SP, no. 6 (1762), pp. 153–58.

26. *The Life . . . of Col. George Hanger* (London, 1801), 2 vols., 2:271.

27. WPL: E. 2574–77.

28. GRS: *Satan's Harvest Home* (London, 1749), p. 3; *The History of Colonel Francis Ch——rtr——s* (London, [1730]), pp. 35–48; WPL: E. 2576 #103; GLRO: MJ/SR/2401, R (6 April 1723), MJ/SR/2426, Newgate List, July 8, 1724; *Scotch Gallantry display'd* (London, 1730), pp. 19–21; *Proceedings . . . against Francis Charteris for . . . rape on . . . Anne Bond* (London, 1730).

29. John Cleland, *Memoirs of a Woman of Pleasure* (London, 1748–49), ed. Peter Sabor (New York: Oxford University Press, 1985); Campbell, *The London Tradesman*, p. 209; Edward Ward, *The London Spy* (London, 1709), pp. 73–74, 212–13; Francis Grose, *A Classical Dictionary of the Vulgar Tongue* (London, 1796), s.v. "commodity"; *The Spectator* (London, 1711), ed. D. F. Bond (Oxford: Oxford University Press, 1965), 5 vols., no. 155, 2:108–10; *London Chronicle*, 7–10 November 1761, p. 451.

30. CLRO: Mansion House Justice Room Minute Books, 11 August 1790; GLRO: FH, Petitioners Admitted, vol. 19 (1794); RCS, Lock Asylum Minutes, 1787–90: 7 May 1789.

31. Daniel Defoe, *Some considerations upon street-walkers* (London, 1726), p. 2.

32. SP, no. 1, pt. 1 (1760): Amelia or Millicent Darlow; no. 1 (1761), #7, p. 5.

33. CLRO: Mansion House Justice Room Minute Books, 25 January 1790, 31 December 1789.

34. SP, no. 3, pt. 3 (1768), #240, pp. 126–27; no. 1, pt. 2 (1783), #9, pp. 30–32.

35. GLRO: DL/C/248, fol. 159; SP, no. 1, pt. 5 (1782), #66, p. 91; CLRO: Mansion House Justice Room Minute Books, 30 April 1785; SP, no. 5, pt. 2 (1789), #421, p. 506; *London Chronicle*, 26–28 April 1763, p. 406.

36. CLRO: SR, January 1720, R 70, 57, 56, 38; August 1721, R 19; Guildhall Justice Room Minute Books, 25 September 1784; Mansion House Justice Room Minute Books, 22 March 1790; SR, April 1720, R 83, 82; Mansion House Justice Room Charge Book, 1728–33, 17 and 18 August 1729; *Autobiography of Francis Place*, pp. 57–59.

37. James Boswell, *Journal of a Tour to the Hebrides*, ed. Alan Wendt (Boston: Houghton Mifflin, 1965), p. 255; Welch, *Proposal to Remove Prostitutes*, p. 52.

38. GLRO: MJ/SR/2414, New Prison List and their recognizances; CLRO: SR, January 1727–28, R 29.

39. *A New Description of Merryland* (London, 1741), p. 7; the five cases: CLRO: SR, May 1704, R 3, GLRO: MJ/SR/2679, R 72 (John Williams), MJ/CC/R/7, #119, MJ/SR/3168, bond of Barbara Martin, MJ/SR/3251, R 186; MJ/SR/2488, R 113 (John Spives); MJ/SR/2839, R 124 (Lucy Earle).

40. John Marten, *A Treatise of . . . the Venereal Disease*, with an appendix *Gonosologium Novum* (London, 1708), p. 149; GRS: *Harris's List of Covent Garden Ladies . . . for 1788* (London, 1788), p. 31; Owen Rutter, ed., *The Log of the Bounty* (London, 1937), 2 vols., 2:17.

41. H. Deacon, *A Compendious treatise on the venereal disease* (London, n.d.), p. 24; Alexander Smith, *The School of Venus* (London, 1716), 2 vols., 1:192; Hertfordshire Record Office, Lady Cowper's diary, D/EP/F30, 12 October 1704; *Autobiography of Francis Place*, p. 51; GRS: *Trials for Adultery* (London, 1780), 7 vols., 6:114 (Grosvenor).

42. CLRO: SR, April 1724, R 29; Bond of Bailey, 30 May 1707; GRS: *Select Trials at the Sessions-House in the Old Bailey* (London, 1742), 4 vols., 2:304; *The History of the Human Heart* (London, 1749; reprint New York: Garland, 1974), pp. 123–29; *The Midnight Spy* (London, 1766), quoted in Iwan Bloch, *Sexual Life in England* (London, 1958 ed.), p. 327: Bloch is wrong to say that posture girls appear about 1750; Ward, *The London Spy*, p. 140; CLRO: SR, December 1704, R 49; Mansion House Justice Room Minute Books, 31 December 1789. Christopher Johnson, *The History of the life and intrigues of that celebrated courtezan and posture-mistress, Eliz. Mann* (London, 1724), is a book that does not deliver on the promise of its title.

43. GLRO: MJ/SR/2366, New Prison List, and R 137; CLRO: SR, December 1723, R 35; GLRO: MJ/SR/2424, R of Simon Jones; MJ/SR/2488, R 331; MJ/SR/2236, R 42; MJ/SR/3036, R 38 and MJ/SR/3046, R 30.

44. GLRO: MJ/SR/2836, Gatehouse List, R 228; MJ/SR/2389, R of Peter Dufree; *Life of Col. Hanger*, 1:65; GRS: *The Covent Garden Jester* (London, 1785), p. 68, cf. p. 63.

45. *London Chronicle*, 22–24 July 1762, p. 88; GLRO: MJ/SR/2394, House of Correction List; MJ/SR/2407, Clerkenwell List (Smith); MJ/SR/2841, Gatehouse List (Shipman); *Select Trials*, 1:55; GLRO: MJ/SR/2384, New Prison List (Newell, Tansey, Saunders, Mason).

46. GRS: *Aristotle's Masterpiece*; Marten, *Treatise of Venereal Disease*, pp. 353–84, and *Gonosologium Novum*, pp. 1–63; Richard Payne Knight, *Discourse on the Worship of Priapus* (London, 1786), reprinted in *Sexual Symbolism*, ed. Ashley Montagu (New York: Julian Press, 1957).

47. Cleland, *Woman of Pleasure*, pp. 76–77, 144; John Henry Meibomius, *A Treatise on the use of flogging in venereal affairs* (London, 1718); Thomas Shadwell, "The Virtuoso" (London, 1676), in *Complete Works*, ed. Montague Summers (London, 1927; reprint New York: Benjamin Blom, 1968), 5 vols., 3:139–40, 154, 159, 174, 116 (boy actors); Ward, *The London Spy*, pp. 32–33; *Select Trials*, 2:113–14; Cleland, *Woman of Pleasure*, p. 143; CLRO: SR, January 1723–24, R 11; *Satan's Harvest Home*, p. 9,

quoting Butler's Hudibras; *Gentleman's Magazine* (London, 1780), pp. 462–63: discussed in Ian Gibson, *The English Vice* (London: Duckworth, 1978), pp.10–11, which is mainly on the nineteenth century. See also E. J. Burford, *Wits, Wenchers, and Wantons* (London: Hale, 1986), pp. 227–30. Lawrence Stone, "Libertine Sexuality in Post-Restoration England: Group Sex and Flagellation among the Middling Sort in Norwich in 1706–07," *Journal of the History of Sexuality* 2 (1994): 511–26, suggests that flagellation was inspired by reading pornography. But his evidence does not show this, and one of the men in his group had almost certainly had contact with London prostitutes.

48. *Select Trials*, 1:109, 2:173–74; Cleland, *Woman of Pleasure*, p. 153; CLRO: SR, May 1729, R 2.

49. Hertfordshire Record Office, Lady Cowper's diary, D/EP/F29, 30 October 1700.

50. Dunton, *The Night-Walker*, October 1696, 1:16, 18; Anodyne Tanner, *The Life of . . . Mrs. Elizabeth Wisebourn* (London, [1721]), pp. 2–3; Smith, *The School of Venus;* Charles Walker, *Authentic Memoirs of . . . Sally Salisbury* (London, 1723), pp. 59–60; *Authentic Memoirs of the celebrated Miss Nancy D[a]ws[o]n* (London, c. 1765), p. 11; Burford, *Wits, Wenchers, and Wantons*, p. 134.

51. Matthew Henry, *A Sermon . . . [at] the funeral of the Reverend Mr. Daniel Burgess* (London, 1713), pp. 32, 34; *The Life, death and character of Mr. Daniel Burgess* (London, [1713]), p. 8; Daniel Burgess, *The Golden Snuffers* (London, 1697), p. 77; Johnson, *Life of Eliz. Mann*, pp. vi–viii.

52. GLRO: MJ/SR/2471, R 34; MJ/SR/2389, Clerkenwell List; SP, no. 8 (1762), #287, pp. 198–99; *Autobiography of Francis Place*, p. 229; *Harris's List.*

53. *Annual Register* 13 (1770): 120; *London Chronicle*, 14–16 April 1763, p. 362; CLRO: Mansion House Justice Room Charge Book, 1695–1705, January 1704–5; Guildhall Justice Room Minute Books, 5 February 1791.

54. *London Chronicle*, 23–25 August 1763, p. 186.

55. CLRO: Mansion House Justice Room Charge Book, 1728–33, 15 February 1731/2.

56. *London Chronicle*, 14–17 April 1759, p. 365, 24–26 February 1763, p. 199.

57. SP, no. 3, pt. 1 (1761), pp. 108–43; *London Chronicle*, 9–11 October 1760, p. 353, 11–14 October 1760, p. 362, 18–21 October 1760, p. 386, 21–23 October 1760, p. 397, 23–25 October 1760, p. 407, 1–3 January 1761, p. 15, 10–13 January 1761, p. 43, 7–10 February 1761, p. 139, 24–26 February 1761, p. 194, 28 February–3 March 1761, p. 209.

58. *London Chronicle*, 21–23 October 1760, p. 397.

59. CLRO: Guildhall Justice Room Minute Books, 24 November 1761, 27 January 1778, 20 February 1795; *The Life and Character of Moll King* (London, 1747), p. 5.

60. CLRO: Guildhall Justice Room Minute Books, 13 February 1792; *Select Trials*, 1:109; GLRO: MJ/SR/2023, R 90; WPL: E. 2574, #195, 17, 253, 258, E. 2575, #92; GLRO: MJ/SR/2480, R 149; MJ/SR/2508, R 31.

61. Frances Finnegan, *Poverty and Prostitution* (New York: Cambridge University Press, 1979); Judy R. Walkowitz, *Prostitution and Victorian Society* (New York: Cambridge University Press, 1980).

62. W. B. Ober, *Boswell's Clap and Other Essays* (Carbondale: Southern Illinois University Press, 1979), chap. 1.

63. *Autobiography of Francis Place*, pp. 202–3, 74, 77–78, 57; *General State of the Magdalen hospital*, p. 4.

CHAPTER SIX: PROSTITUTION SENTIMENTALIZED

1. Brian Fitzgerald, ed., *Correspondence of Emily, Duchess of Leinster* (Dublin: Irish Manuscripts Commission, 1949–57), 3 vols., 2:93–94, 3:16–17; Countess of Ilchester and Lord Stavordale, *The Life and Letters of Lady Sarah Lennox* (London: John Murray, 1902), p. 183. G. J. Barker-Benfield, *The Culture of Sensibility* (Chicago: University of Chicago Press, 1992), argues that through sensibility women modified the sexual behavior of men. But he takes his evidence from novels; he does not tie the change to the development of the family; he improbably makes consumerism the principal agent.

2. Samuel Richardson, *Clarissa* (London, 1747–48), 4 vols. (New York, 1962, Everyman ed.); GRS: *Satan's Harvest Home* (London, 1749), pp. 41–43; GRS: Francis Douglas, *Reflections on Celibacy and Marriage* (London, 1771), p. 25.

3. Samuel Shellabarger, *Lord Chesterfield and His World* (Boston: Little, Brown, 1951), pp. 35, 65, 75, 111, 167, 281; Bonamy Dobree, ed., *The Letters of . . . Chesterfield* (London: Eyre and Spottiswoode, 1932), 6 vols., pp. 537, 1931, 278, 893, 2437–39, 2646.

4. Dobree, *Letters of Chesterfield*, pp. 525, 755, 777–78, 1065, 1396, 1491, 1209.

5. Lord Herbert, ed., *Henry, Elizabeth and George (1734–80)*, (London: Jonathan Cape, 1939), pp. 10–41, 387, 394–95; Lord Herbert, ed., *Pembroke Papers (1780–1794)* (London: Jonathan Cape, 1950), pp. 22–25, 34–50, 73, 377–85; Giacomo Casanova, *History of My Life*, trans. W. R. Trask (New York: Harcourt Brace Jovanovich, 1970), 12 vols., vols. 9, 10.

6. Herbert, *Henry, Elizabeth and George*, pp. 46, 53–54, 59, 60, 62, 69, 72, 89, 91, 119.

7. Ibid., pp. 71, 171, 201, 282, 288; Herbert, *Pembroke Papers*, pp. 273–74, 315, 284, 96, 347; for Dartmouth, see Randolph Trumbach, *The Rise of the Egalitarian Family* (New York: Academic Press, 1977), p. 253.

8. For fathers and schools, see Trumbach, *Rise of Egalitarian Family*, pp. 252–80.

9. *Nocturnal Revels; or the history of King's Place, and other modern nunneries . . . by a monk of the order of St. Francis* (London, 1779), 2 vols., 1:25–30.

10. [Richard Morley], *The life of . . . Elizabeth Wisebourn* (London, [1721], pp. 12–17; *Nocturnal Revels*, pp. 12–17; William Byrd, *The London Diary (1717–1721) and Other Writings*, ed. L. B. Wright and Marion Tinling (New York: Oxford University Press, 1958), index s.v. "Mrs. Smith," and p. 339.

11. Byrd, *London Diary*. Lawrence Stone, *The Family, Sex, and Marriage in England, 1500–1800* (New York: Harper and Row, 1977), pp. 563–68, 572–99, has discussed both Byrd and Boswell; Michael Zuckerman, "William Byrd's Family," *Perspectives in American History* 12 (1979): 253–311, gives a different reading on Byrd; see also K. A. Lockridge, *The Diary, and Life, of William Byrd II of Virginia, 1674–1744* (Chapel Hill: University of North Carolina Press, 1987).

12. *Boswell's London Journal, 1762–1763*, ed. F. A. Pottle (New York: McGraw-

Hill, 1950), pp. 83–85, 88–89, 94–98, 100–101, 104, 107, 112–13, 117–20, 126, 135, 137–40, 145, 149, 153–61, 175, 187.

13. Ibid., pp. 143, 164, 227, 231, 237, 255, 260, 264, 272–73, 280, 327, 332–33. For Samuel Johnson, see D. C. G. Allan and John L. Abbott, "'Compassion and Horror in Every Humane Mind': Samuel Johnson, the Society of Arts, and Eighteenth-Century Prostitution," in *The Virtuoso Tribe of Arts and Sciences*, ed. Allan and Abbott (Athens: University of Georgia Press, 1992), pp. 18–37.

14. *Nocturnal Revels*, 2:16–26, 77, 97, 224 and passim; E. J. Burford, *Royal St. James's* (London: Hale, 1988), pp. 194–229; *London Chronicle*, 2–4 February 1764, p. 113; James Graham, *Lectures on the generation increase and improvement of the human species* (London, [1780]), pp. 28–30, 55–58; J. W. von Archenholz, *A Picture of England* (London, 1789), 2 vols., 2:96–97; John Cleland, *Memoirs of a Woman of Pleasure* (London, 1748–49), ed. Peter Sabor (New York: Oxford University Press, 1985), p. 94; Randolph Trumbach, "Modern Prostitution and Gender in *Fanny Hill*: Libertine and Domesticated Fantasy," in *Sexual Underworlds of the Enlightenment*, ed. G. S. Rousseau and Roy Porter (Manchester: Manchester University Press, 1987). Burford, *Royal St. James's*, and *Wits, Wenchers, and Wantons* (London: Hale, 1986), analyzes the change in fashionable prostitution around 1750. His first book deals with the Covent Garden area mainly before 1750, the later book with Soho and St. James's after 1750. He does not indicate how dependent this schema is on *Nocturnal Revels;* and it is sometimes difficult to accept or understand his documentation; but they are useful books.

15. *Authentic and interesting memoirs of Mrs. Ann Sheldon (now Mrs. Archer)* . . . *written by herself* (London, 1787), 4 vols., 1:121–22 and passim, 2:46–57, 153–54.

16. Ibid., 2:244–46, 3:20, 27, 216, 1:227, 4:88–89–107.

17. Ibid., 4:119–68, 185 ff., 202–17.

18. T. H. Hollingsworth, "The Demography of the British Peerage," supplement to *Population Studies* 18 (1964): 16–22; Stone, *Family, Sex, and Marriage*, pp. 541–42, argues for the connection between homosexuality and the incidence of marriage.

19. Hertfordshire Record Office, Lady Cowper's diary, D/EP/F31, 1 March 1704–5; Lincolnshire Record Ofice, 5 Anc 2/A/36; WPL: E. 2574: 163, 165.

20. Casanova, *History of My Life*, 9:320–24; W. S. Lewis et al., eds., *Yale Edition of Horace Walpole's Correspondence* (New Haven, Conn.: Yale University Press, 1937–83), 48 vols., 24:234–35.

21. Archenholz, *A Picture of England*, 2:97–98, 101–2; John Cleland, *The Surprises of Love* (London, 1766), pp. 104–10; Casanova, *History of My Life*, 9:189–90, 194.

22. *Memoirs of the celebrated Miss Fanny M[urray]* (London, 1759), pp. 100–109; Burford, *Wits, Wenchers, and Wantons*, pp. 102–7; GRS: *Harris's List of Covent Garden Ladies . . . for 1788* (London, 1788).

23. *Harris's List.*

24. Ibid.; Tobias Smollett, *Peregrine Pickle* (1751), ed. J. L. Clifford and P. G. Bouc (New York: Oxford University Press, 1983), pp. 432–538; Ilchester and Stavordale, *Lady Sarah Lennox.*

25. Thomas Bray, *A General Plan of a penitential hospital for employing and reforming lewd women* (London, 1698); Christopher Johnson, *The History of the life and intrigues of that celebrated courtezan and posture-mistress, Eliz. Mann* (London, 1724), pp. v–vi; *Satan's Harvest Home*, pp. 33–34. Modern histories of the institution: H. F. B. Compston, *The Magdalen Hospital* (London: SPCK, 1917); S. B. B. Pearce, *An Ideal*

in the Working. The Story of the Magdalen Hospital, 1758 to 1958 (London: H. B. Skinner, 1958); Stanley Nash, "Prostitution and Charity: The Magdalen Hospital, a Case Study," *Journal of Social History* 17 (1984): 617–28, and "Social Attitudes toward Prostitution in London from 1752–1829," Ph.D. diss., New York University, 1980; V. L. Bullough, "Prostitution and Reform in 18th Century England," in *'Tis Nature's Fault,* ed. R. P. Maccubbin (New York: Cambridge University Press, 1987), pp. 61–74; Donna T. Andrew, *Philanthropy and Police: London Charity in the Eighteenth Century* (Princeton: Princeton University Press, 1989); Sherrill Cohen, *The Evolution of Women's Asylums since 1500* (New York: Oxford University Press, 1992); Sarah Lloyd, "'Pleasure's Golden Bait': Prostitution, Poverty, and the Magdalen Hospital in Eighteenth-Century London," *History Workshop Journal* 41 (1996): 48–70.

26. Robert Dingley, *Proposals for establishing a public place of reception for penitent prostitutes* (London, 1758), reprint in GRS: Prostitution Reform, pp. 3, 6; Compston, *The Magdalen Hospital,* pp. 23–36; Saunders Welch, *A Proposal . . . to remove the nuisance of common prostitutes from the streets of this metropolis* (London, 1758), reprint in Prostitution Reform; John Fielding, *An Account of the origin and effects of a police set on foot by his grace the duke of Newcastle in the Year 1753* (London, 1758), reprint in Prostitution Reform.

27. Welch, *Proposal to Remove Prostitutes,* pp. 16–19, 25–30; *An Account of the . . . Magdalen Hospital . . . together with Dr. Dodd's Sermons* (London, 1776), reprint in Prostitution Reform, p. 51. Some account of the changing position on women's nature at midcentury can be found in F. A. Nussbaum, *The Brink of All We Hate* (Lexington: University Press of Kentucky, 1984), pp. 93, 136; M. L. Gates, "The Cult of Womanhood in Eighteenth-Century Thought," *Eighteenth-Century Studies* 10 (1976): 21–39; K. M. Rogers, *Feminism in Eighteenth-Century England* (Brighton: Harvester, 1982), pp. 119–47; C. J. Rawson, "Some Remarks on Eighteenth-Century 'Delicacy,' with a Note on Hugh Kelly's *False Delicacy* (1768)," *JEGP* 61 (1962): 1–13.

28. *An Account of the . . . present state of the Magdalen Charity* (London, 1761), pp. vi–xiii; John Butler, *A Sermon preached in the chapel of the Magdalen Hospital, 10 August 1758–25 December 1784* (London, 1786), pp. 4–5.

29. Nash, "Prostitution and Charity," made the comparison; the rules that describe the daily life may be found in most of the *Accounts* of the charity: I use the 1776 edition, pp. 231–52, 307–27; Lewis et al., *Walpole's Correspondence,* 21:368. It is possible that in the early nineteenth century, institutions like the Magdalen came to be organized more like a penitentiary than a convent; but the convent seems the more likely model in the late eighteenth century.

30. *An Account of the Institution of the Lock Asylum* (London, 1792); RCS, General Court Book, 1773–89, p. 313; Lock Asylum Minutes, 1787–90; Board Minutes, 1768–70, pp. 23, 29, 54, 81, 153, 168, 172, 195, 214, 232, 241, 288, 299, etc.

31. Richard Hill, *The Blessings of Polygamy* (London, 1781), pp. 157 ff.; Thomas Willis, *Remarks on Polygamy* (London, 1781), p. vi; E. B. Greene, *Whispers for the ear of the author of Thelypthora* (London, 1781), p. xxiii.

32. Martin Madan, *Thelypthora, or a Treatise on Female Ruin,* 2d ed. (London, 1781), 3 vols., 1:47, 74–299, 2:76–86. Volume 3 is a history of the way in which polygamy was discredited in Christian tradition, and with it any positive evaluation of sexuality.

33. Willis, *Remarks on Polygamy,* p. vi; John Smith, *Polygamy Indefensible* (London,

1780), pp. 7, 30–33; *A Letter to Dr. P[riestley]* (London, 1781), p. 32, Hill, *The Blessings of Polygamy*, pp. 10–15, 149; Greene, *Whispers for the Ear;* Thomas Haweis, *A Scriptural Refutation of the Arguments for Polygamy* (London, [1781]); [Henry Moore], *A Word to Mr. Madan* (Bristol, 1781), pp. 28–29, 35. The nastiest expression of the Evangelical sense of betrayal that Madan's book brought on was made by Greene (p. xxvii) when he compared Madan to Dr. James Graham, the sexual quack, who had invented a "celestial bed" as a form of sexual therapy. For Graham, see Roy Porter, "The Sexual Politics of James Graham," *British Journal for Eighteenth Century Studies* 5 (1982): 201–6, and "Sex and the Singular Man: The Seminal Ideas of James Graham," *Studies on Voltaire and the Eighteenth Century* 228 (1984): 1–24.

34. Hill, *The Blessings of Polygamy*, p. 71; Haweis, *Scriptural Refutation*, p. viii.

35. RCS, Lock Asylum Minutes, 1787–90; Account of Lock Asylum, pp. 12–13.

36. Welch, *Proposal to Remove Prostitutes*, pp. 8–11, GLRO: MJ/SBP/16.

37. *London Chronicle*, 1–4 November 1760, p. 433, 3–5 May 1763, p. 431, 10–13 September 1763, pp. 254–55, 17–20 September 1763, p. 274, 16–18 August 1764, p. 166, 1–4 September 1764, p. 222.

38. E. G. Rupp, *Religion in England, 1688–1791* (Oxford: Oxford University Press, 1986), pp. 327–30; *A Sermon preached before the former Societies for Reformation of Manners* (London, 1760), p. 36; *London Chronicle*, 11–13 May 1762, p. 454, 9–11 August 1764, p. 141, 13–16 June 1761, p. 574, 22–24 February 1763, p. 191, 28–30 April 1763, p. 413, 21–23 February 1765, p. 191; E. J. Bristow, *Vice and Vigilance* (London: Gill and Macmillan, 1977), pp. 37–50; *Sermon before the Former Societies*, p. 36. The organizers of the society in 1762 were "Messrs. William and Bellamy next to the Mansionhouse, London, Mr. Edward Webber near the East-India-house, Leadenhall street, Mr. William Park, Mercer, behind St. Clement's Church, Strand" (*London Chronicle*, 3–5 June 1762, p. 535).

39. *London Chronicle*, 7–9 January 1762, p. 31; *Hints . . . on the prevalence of vice and the dangerous effects of seduction* (London, 1811), p. 52. For the societies after 1787, see Joanna Innes, "Politics and Morals: The Reformation of Manners Movement in Later Eighteenth-Century England," in *The Transformation of Political Culture*, ed. Eckhart Hellmuth (New York: Oxford University Press, 1990), pp. 58–118.

40. CLRO: Mansion House Justice Room Minute Books, 1785–90; Welch, *Proposal to Remove Prostitutes*, p. 28. On the theory that many of the young girls walking the streets were orphans, an asylum was set up in 1758 for girls whose parents could not be found and whose settlement was unknown, but like the Magdalen and the Loch, it can have made very little practical difference: *An Account of the institution . . . for the reception of orphan girls . . . whose settlement cannot be found* (London, 1763).

CHAPTER SEVEN: THE FOUL DISEASE

1. GRS: John Astruc, *A Treatise of the Venereal Disease*, trans. William Barrowby (London, 1737), 2 vols., 1:1–135; on prostitution's role, 1:86, 52–62; names of the disease, 1:74, 88, 90; decline of the disease, 1:114–20. Modern historians tend to support Astruc's history of the disease in the sixteenth century. See William H. McNeill, *Plagues and Peoples* (Garden City, N.Y.: Anchor Press, 1976), and the literature cited there. For recent general histories of venereal disease, see Claude Quétel, *History of Syphilis* (Baltimore: Johns Hopkins University Press, 1990); John Arrizabalaga, John

Henderson, and Roger French, *The Great Pox: The French Disease in Renaissance Europe* (New Haven, Conn.: Yale University Press, 1997); and Linda E. Merians, ed., *The Secret Malady: Venereal Disease in Eighteenth-Century Britain and France* (Lexington: University Press of Kentucky, 1996).

2. GRS: William Buchan, *Observations Concerning the Prevention and Cure of the Venereal Disease* (London, 1796), p. 13.

3. Edward Shorter, *A History of Women's Bodies* (New York: Basic Books, 1982), pp. 263–67.

4. Allan M. Brandt, *No Magic Bullet* (New York: Oxford University Press, 1985), pp. 12, 13, 31, 54, 77, 97–98, 169. Judy R. Walkowitz, *Prostitution and Victorian Society* (New York: Cambridge University Press, 1980), pp. 49–50; Frances Finnegan, *Poverty and Prostitution* (New York: Cambridge University Press, 1979), pp. 157–58.

5. GLRO: DL/C/155, fol. 253: Jordan (1713), DL/C/156, fol. 486: James (1716), DL/C/157, fol. 59: Belson (1717), fol. 512: Rempell (1718), DL/C/158, fol. 27: Buckland (1719), DL/C/161, fol. 137: Blake (1725), fol. 522: Simson (1725), fol. 595: Wellings (1725), DL/C/162, fol. 109: Ganeron (1727), DL/C/165, fol. 75: Leveridge (1732), DL/C/167, fol. 144: Silvester (1736), DL/C/169, fol. 7: Cibber (1738), fol. 51: Lister (1739), fol. 323: Powell (1741), DL/C/170, fol. 20: Crosby (1743), fol. 38: Koess (1743), fol. 355: Colli (1743). For the nineteenth century, see Gail Savage, "'The Wilful Communication of a Loathsome Disease': Marital Conflict and Venereal Disease in Victorian England," *Victorian Studies* 34 (1990): 35–54.

6. Martin Lister (1694), quoted in John Marten, *A Treatise of . . . the Venereal Disease*, with an appendix *Gonosologium Novum* (London, 1708), pp. 80–85; Buchan, *Observations*, p. 14; *Antimoxeia: or the honest and joint design of the Tower Hamlets for the general suppression of bawdy houses* (London, 1691; Guildhall, B'side 1.43).

7. *London Evening-Post*, 25–28 September 1779, cited by A. E. Simpson, "Vulnerability and the Age of Female Consent: Legal Innovation and Its Effect on Prosecutions for Rape in Eighteenth Century London," in *Sexual Underworlds of the Enlightenment*, ed. G. S. Rousseau and Roy Porter (Manchester: Manchester University Press, 1987), p. 204 n. 57; N. A. M. Rodger, *The Wooden World* (Annapolis, Md.: Naval Institute Press, 1986), pp. 367–68; Greg Dening, *Mr Bligh's Bad Language* (Cambridge: Cambridge University Press, 1992), p. 384; for sex on board ship: Arthur Gilbert, "The *Africaine* Courts Martial: A Study of Buggery and the Royal Navy," *Journal of Homosexuality* 1 (1974): 111–22, and "Buggery and the British Navy 1700–1861," *Journal of Social History* 10 (1976): 72–98; *Fund of Mercy: or an Institution for the Relief and Employment of Destitute and Forlorn Females* (London, 1813), cited in A. D. Harvey, *Sex in Georgian England* (London: Duckworth, 1994), pp. 93, 184 n. 4. I owe the references to the navy to Nicholas Rogers.

8. Marten, *Treatise of Venereal Disease*, pp. 228–29; Daniel Turner, *Syphilis* (London, 1717), p. 11.

9. Marten, *Treatise of Venereal Disease*, pp. 23–24, 39; I. F. Nicholson, *The Modern Syphilis* (London, 1718), p. 7; Astruc, *Treatise of Venereal Disease*, 1:20–21. At this point Astruc rejects the mixture of seeds in one woman as an explanation of how the disease could have existed in the ancient world. But he accepts it as an explanation for its origin in America (103–4). The difference seems to be that the Indians were unusually incontinent and the climate unusually warm. In Europe's temperate climate, men's

seed was not so acrimonious. All torrid zones were infectious: only Christian Europe was cool and clean (95).

10. Marten, *Treatise of Venereal Disease*, pp. 33–34, 149–50; SP (11–14 October 1699) (British Library, 1480, d. 21); John Lord Fortescue, *Reports of Select Cases* (London, 1748), pp. 91–97; Turner, *Syphilis*, p. 19. For sodomy with boys as a means of avoiding disease, see Trumbach, *Sex and the Gender Revolution*, vol. 2, forthcoming.

11. Peter Fryer, *The Birth Controllers* (New York: Secker and Warburg, 1966), pp. 23–30, 273–79; Turner, *Syphilis*, p. 74; William Byrd, *The London Diary (1717–1721) and Other Writings*, ed. L. B. Wright and Marion Tinling (New York: Oxford University Press, 1958), p. 136; Astruc, *Treatise of Venereal Disease*, 1:299–300; James Boswell, *Boswell's London Journal, 1762–1763*, ed. F. A. Pottle (New York: McGraw-Hill, 1950), pp. 231, 237, 255, 272, 227, 262.

12. Fryer, *The Birth Controllers*, pp. 25–26, 276 n. 21.

13. Marten, *Treatise of Venereal Disease*, pp. 61, 63, 65, 67; Astruc, *Treatise of Venereal Disease*, pp. 119, 297, 299; Buchan, *Observations*, pp. 19–36, 42, 229, 247–48.

14. Buchan, *Observations*, pp. 183–86, 24, ii–v, xii–xiv.

15. John Cleland, *Memoirs of a Woman of Pleasure* (London, 1748–49), ed. Peter Sabor (New York: Oxford University Press, 1985), pp. 141–42; GRS: John Dunton, *The Night-Walker; or Evening Rambles in Search of Lewd Women* (London, 1696–97), 2 vols., October 1696, 1:22–23; GRS: *Trials for Adultery* (London, 1780), 7 vols., 6: 109–13 (Grosvenor divorce); W. B. Ober, *Boswell's Clap and Other Essays* (Carbondale: Southern Illinois University Press, 1979), pp. 1–42.

16. Dunton, *The Night-Walker*, October 1696, 1:28; GLRO: DL/C/173, fol. 185; DL/C/274 (Andrew Bell's evidence); DL/C/287, Cheetham v. Cheetham (1798), and DL/C/287 (Harriet Brown's evidence); Marten, *Treatise of Venereal Disease*, pp. 237–39, 284–86.

17. Dunton, *The Night-Walker*, February 1697, 2:2; Marten, *Treatise of Venereal Disease*, pp. 253–54; Buchan, *Observations*, pp. iv–v; R. Campbell, *The London Tradesman* (London, 1747; reprint Newton Abbot, Devon: David and Charles Reprints, 1969), pp. 52–53; W. F. Bynum, "Treating the Wages of Sin: Venereal Disease and Specialism in Eighteenth-Century Britain," in *Medical Fringe and Medical Orthodoxy, 1750–1850*, ed. Bynum and Roy Porter (London: Croom Helm, 1987), pp. 5–28. For the quack's quick cures, see Roy Porter, *Health for Sale: Quackery in England, 1660–1850* (New York: St. Martin's Press, 1989), pp. 149–56, also 50, 52, 99, 100, 108, 112, 114, 118, 197–98.

18. Astruc, *Treatise of Venereal Disease*, 1:170–246; John Hunter, *A Treatise on the Venereal Disease* (London, 1786), pp. 31, 74–87, 12, 93–94, 38; Buchan, *Observations*, p. 293.

19. Buchan, *Observations*, pp. xiii, 7–8, 12; Turner, *Syphilis*, pp. 159–61.

20. GLRO: DL/C/149, fol. 88; fol. 187, DL/C/150, fol. 238; DL/C/149, fol. 258, DL/C/247, fol. 278; Francis Grose, *A Classical Dictionary of the Vulgar Tongue* (London, 1796), s.v. "dock"; GLRO: DL/C/151, fol. 456, DL/C/249, fol. 138; DL/C/173, fols. 159–62, DL/C/284: Pod v. Hardgrove.

21. GLRO: DL/C/150, fol. 32, DL/C/247, fol. 444; Bynum, "Treating Wages of Sin," p. 11; Marten, *Treatise of Venereal Disease*, pp. 221, 127–28.

22. GLRO: MJ/SR/2374, House of Correction List; MJ/SR/2381, House of Cor-

rection List; *London Chronicle*, 10–12 January 1760, p. 42; WPL: E. 3225 (27 June 1727).

23. SP, no. 5, pt. 2 (1774), pp. 237–39, #449.

24. Dunton, *The Night-Walker*, February 1697, 2:3–4, October 1696, 1:28; *The Tryal and Condemnation of . . . Lord . . . Castlehaven* (London, 1699), reprint in GRS: Sodomy Trials, preface: for rape trials, see SP (11–14 October 1699) (British Library, 1480, d. 21.); Marten, *Treatise of Venereal Disease*, pp. 23–25; Walter Harris, *Observationis . . . de Lues Venerae Origina . . .* (Amsterdam, 1715), cited in Astruc, *Treatise of Venereal Disease*, 2:431–32: it was a belief previously current in Italy; Buchan, *Observations*, pp. xvi–xvii.

25. Marten, *Gonosologium Novum*, pp. 81, 88, 91; Peter Laslett, "Age of Menarche in Europe since the Eighteenth Century," *Journal of Interdisciplinary History* 16 (1985): 221–36; Richard T. Vann and David Eversley, *Friends in Life and Death* (New York: Cambridge University Press, 1992), pp. 180–82. Simpson, "Vulnerability," pp. 191–200, bases his analysis of these cases on the trials of girls under ten. But this takes too seriously a legal distinction as to the age of consent and the ability to understand the nature of an oath.

26. *The Battle of Venus* (The Hague, 1760), p. 125, quoted in [H. S. Ashbee], *Index Librorum Prohibitorum* (London, 1877), p. 125; GRS: *Satan's Harvest Home* (London, 1749), p. 2.

27. RCS, Lock Hospital, General Court book, 1746–62 (24 March 1753), p. 95. This was reported in the *Gentleman's Magazine*, March 1752, in a slightly different way. But the phrasing used implied that some of the children would have been boys infected by women. The manuscript minutes do not discuss the point. Cases involving boys did not, presumably, come to trial because females could not be conceived to rape males. For similar reasons women who had sex with women could not be tried for sodomy. Men, of course, who approached boys were tried for sodomy, and in at least one case the boy did become venereally infected (SP, no. 8, pt. 1 (1779), #447, pp. 502–14). But a cure does not seem to have been a significant part of this case, and in the other cases between men and prepubescent boys, there is no mention of disease.

28. SP, no. 7, pt. 1 (1778), pp. 340–43, #641.

29. SP, no. 1, pt. 2 (1770), pp. 23–25, #40.

30. SP, no. 6, pt. 6 (1778), pp. 630–34, #496.

31. GRS: *Select Trials at the Sessions-House in the Old Bailey* (London, 1742), 4 vols., 1:198–208 (1722).

32. SP (September 1796), pp. 787–95, #469.

33. SP, no. 7, pt. 2 (1766), pp. 281–85.

34. SP, no. 4, pt. 2 (1769), p. 169, #303; SP, no. 1, pt. 2 (1770), pp. 23–25, #40; SP (17 February 1796), pp. 304–7, #191.

35. SP, no. 7, pt. 2 (1768), pp. 319–20, #538; SP, no. 7, pt. 2 (1748), pp. 262–64; *Select Trials*, 1:368–69 (1723).

36. SP, no. 7 (1733), pp. 197–98; SP, no. 6, pt. 2 (1771), p. 328, #460.

37. SP, no. 5, pt. 2 (1749), pp. 91–94.

38. SP, no. 7, pt. 2 (1779), pp. 427–29, #394.

39. RCS, Lock Hospital Board Minutes, April 1765–November 1766, p. 272; January 1761–July 1763, p. 133.

40. RCS, General Court Book, 1746–62, 1762–73. The account of the Lock Hos-

pital by Donna T. Andrew, *Philanthropy and Police: London Charity in the Eighteenth Century* (Princeton: Princeton University Press, 1989), pp. 69–72, 133, 161–62, is unsatisfactory. It overplays Martin Madan's role and seems unaware that Bromfeild was its founder (his name is even misspelled). See instead James Bettley, "Post Voluptatem Misericordia: The Rise and Fall of the London Lock Hospitals," *London Journal* 10 (1984): 167–75; David Innes Williams, *The London Lock: A Charitable Hospital for Venereal Disease, 1746–1952* (London: Royal Society of Medicine Press, 1995); and Linda E. Merians, "The London Lock Hospital and the Lock Asylum for Women," in *The Secret Malady,* pp. 128–45.

41. RCS, Board Minutes, 1771–73, pp. 218–19; 1755–57; General Court Book, 1746–62, pp. 203, 243; General Court Book, 1773–89, p. 165 (29 April 1782).

42. RCS, Board Minutes, 1763–65, pp. 119–20, 1766–68, pp. 28, 71, 93; 1768–70, pp. 302, 241; 1766–68, p. 84; 1766–68, p. 181, 1768–70, p. 264; 1765–66, p. 148; 1768–70, p. 270; 1766–68, p. 193.

43. RCS, Board Minutes, 1780–83, pp. 107, 109, 118, 121, 129.

44. RCS, Board Minutes, 1766–68, p. 187; 1768–70, p. 314.

45. RCS, Board Minutes, 1766–68, pp. 149, 165, 170.

46. RCS, Board Minutes, 1761–63, p. 90; 1766–68, p. 197; 1768–70, pp. 1, 57, 69, 191.

47. RCS, Board Minutes, 1765–66, p. 216; 1766–68, pp. 265, 271; 1768–70, p. 47; 1780–83, p. 188; General Court, 1762–73, p. 59; Board Minutes, 1768–70, p. 56; 1766–68, p. 225.

48. RCS, Board Minutes, 1766–68, p. 81; 1777–80, pp. 62, 64; 1786–89 (11 June 1789).

49. RCS, General Court, 1762–73, p. 137; 1773–89, pp. 71–73.

50. RCS, Board Minutes, 1766–68, p. 197; 1765–66, p. 198; 1768–70, pp. 19, 8; 1783–86 (10, 17 February, 3 March, 11 August); General Court, 1773–89, p. 182.

51. RCS, Board Minutes, 1793–97 (20 April 1795); 1768–70, p. 342; 1766–68, p. 184; 1766–68, pp. 115, 142; 1765–66, p. 134; 1766–68, p. 127; 1786–89 (1 February 1787).

52. RCS, Board Minutes, 1766–68, pp. 90, 161, 193; 1768–70, p. 181.

53. RCS, General Court, 1773–89, pp. 76, 79, 88–92, 112–15, 145, 177–78, 184–85, 312; F. K. Brown, *Fathers of the Victorians* (Cambridge: Cambridge University Press, 1961), pp. 73–74, 501.

54. RCS, General Court, 1773–89, pp. 197–98, 204–5, 313; Board Minutes, 1786–89 (17 May 1787).

55. RCS, General Court, 1762–73, pp. 77, 169; 1773–89, pp. 68, 166.

56. Saunders Welch, *A Proposal . . . to remove the nuisance of common prostitutes from the streets of this metropolis* (London, 1758), in GRS: Prostitution Reform, p. 13.

57. GLRO: DL/C/149, fols. 1–2. For two studies of venereal disease in marriage, see Mary Margaret Stewart, "'And Blights with Plagues the Marriage Hearse': Syphilis and Wives," pp. 103–13, and Betty Rizzo, "Decorums," pp. 149–67, in Merians, *The Secret Malady.*

58. GLRO: DL/C/185: Rea v. Rea.

59. GLRO: DL/C/182: Beeby v. Beeby; DL/C/183: Holland v. Holland, Knibbs v. Knibbs.

60. Mary Hyde, *The Thrales of Streatham Park* (Cambridge, Mass.: Harvard University Press, 1977), p. 166; GLRO: DL/C/150, fols. 294–97; DL/C/172: Fitzgerald v. Fitzgerald; DL/C/181: Timmings v. Timmings.

61. GLRO: DL/C/173: Cooke v. Cooke; DL/C/181: Carter v. Carter.

CHAPTER EIGHT: COURTSHIP OR LIBERTINAGE

1. Peter Laslett in "Introduction: Comparing Illegitimacy over Time and between Cultures," in *Bastardy and Its Comparative History*, ed. Laslett, Karla Oosterveen, and Richard M. Smith (Cambridge, Mass.: Harvard University Press, 1980), pp. 29–31; John R. Gillis, *For Better, for Worse* (New York: Oxford University Press, 1985), p. 186; Roger Finlay, *Population and Metropolis* (New York: Cambridge University Press, 1981), pp. 149–50.

2. Edward Shorter, *The Making of the Modern Family* (New York: Basic Books, 1975); Nicholas Rogers, "Carnal Knowledge: Illegitimacy in Eighteenth-Century Westminster," *Journal of Social History* 23 (1989): 355–75.

3. Adrian Wilson, "Illegitimacy and Its Implications in Mid-Eighteenth-Century London: The Evidence of the Foundling Hospital," *Continuity and Change* 4 (1989): 103–64; Ruth K. McClure, *Coram's Children: The London Foundling Hospital in the Eighteenth Century* (New Haven, Conn.: Yale University Press, 1981). For doubts on Wilson's findings, see Richard Adair, *Courtship, Illegitimacy, and Marriage in Early Modern England* (New York: St. Martin's Press, 1996), chap. 7.

4. For the nineteenth-century working-class family, see Gillis, *For Better, for Worse;* Anna Clark, *The Struggle for the Breeches* (Berkeley and Los Angeles: University of California Press, 1995); and Ellen Ross, *Love and Toil* (New York: Oxford University Press, 1993).

5. D. A. Kent, "Ubiquitous but Invisible: Female Domestic Servants in Mid-Eighteenth Century London," *History Workshop Journal* 28 (1989): 111–28; and more generally on servants, J. Jean Hecht, *The Domestic Servant Class in Eighteenth-Century England* (London: Routledge and Kegan Paul, 1956); Randolph Trumbach, *The Rise of the Egalitarian Family* (New York: Academic Press, 1977), chap. 3; Bridget Hill, *Servants: English Domestics in the Eighteenth Century* (New York: Oxford University Press, 1996); and Tim Meldrum, "London Domestic Servants from Depositional Evidence, 1660–1750: Servant-Employer Sexuality in the Patriarchal Household," in *Chronicling Poverty*, ed. Tim Hitchcock, Peter King, and Pamela Sharpe (New York: St. Martin's Press, 1997), pp. 46–69.

6. Daniel Defoe, *A Tour through the Whole Island of Great Britain* (London, 1724–26), ed. G. D. H. Cole and D. C. Browning (New York: Dutton, 1962), 2 vols., 1: 315, 2:11; H. B. Wheatley and Peter Cunningham, *London Past and Present* (London, 1891; reprint Detroit: Singing Tree Press, 1968), 3 vols., 1:376. See also Tim Hitchcock, "'Unlawfully Begotten on Her Body': Illegitimacy and the Parish Poor in St Luke's Chelsea," in Hitchcock, King, and Sharpe, *Chronicling Poverty*, pp. 70–86.

7. GLRO: P74/LUK/121–26.

8. GLRO: P74/LUK/121, Honour Harris, Martha Cleason.

9. GLRO: P74/LUK/122, Amy Nixon, Elizabeth White; P74/LUK/121, Priscilla Howard.

10. GLRO: P74/LUK/121, Catherine Price, Mary Neal; P74/LUK/122, Jane Tapsell.

11. GLRO: P74/LUK/121, Mary Handbrooke; P74/LUK/122, Ann Hunt, Lucy Robinson.

12. GLRO: P74/LUK/122, Sarah Powell; P74/LUK/121, Mary Drew; P74/LUK/122, Mary Morris, Elizabeth Edwards.

13. GLRO: P/74/LUK/121, Ann Mackenny, Sarah Randall, P74/LUK/122, Ann Crockford, Sarah Baldwin.

14. GLRO: P74/LUK/121, Elizabeth Bucknall, Elizabeth Inwood, Martha Howard.

15. GLRO: P74/LUK/121, Mary Hughes, Mary Snoggs; P74/LUK/122, Jane Rumbell; P74/LUK/121, Rebecca Clements, Jane Phillips.

16. GLRO: P74/LUK/122, Hannah Bradby; P74/LUK/121, Barbara Frampton.

17. GLRO: P74/LUK/122, Martha Elmes, Elizabeth Davis, Dorcas Edmonds.

18. GLRO: P74/LUK/121, Catherine Watson, Susan Street; P74/LUK/122, Elizabeth Powell.

19. GLRO: P74/LUK/121, Margaret Lumbey; P74/LUK/122, Elizabeth Carpenter.

20. GLRO: P74/LUK/123, Ann Lentler; P74/LUK/124, Elizabeth Coleman. For two examples from midcentury, see P74/LUK/121, Mary Morris; P74/LUK/122, Jane Temple.

21. GLRO: P74/LUK/124, Esther Philpot; P74/LUK/125, Elizabeth Hunt; P74/LUK/124, Susannah Broom, Elizabeth Foley. In the case of the second Irishwoman from the 1790s, Eleanor Murphy said after she had a child that she used to live with Joseph Gough, an Irishman without a settlement, but that he had deserted her (P/74/LUK/125).

22. GLRO: P74/LUK/124, Ann Spond; P74/LUK/123, 20 August 1783, 1 December 1784, 6 December 1786, Catherine Wingate; P74/LUK/124, 16 October 1790, Catherine Wingate.

23. GLRO: P74/LUK/125, Elizabeth Wheeler.

24. Nicholas Rogers in "Carnal Knowledge" has discussed some aspects of bastardy in St. Margaret's, but he has also included material from the parishes of St. Martin in the Fields and St. Clement Danes.

25. J. P. Malcolm, *Anecdotes of the Manners and Customs of London during the Eighteenth Century* (London, 1808), p. 116.

26. GLRO: P91/LEN/1216, Mary Pellett.

27. WPL: E. 2574, Sarah Leek, Lydia Page, Martha Hurrell, Frances Mills; E. 2575, Mary Fulford; E. 2574, Mary Banbridge, Arabella Fowke, Jane Jones, Ann Squire, Ann Wigham, Ann Fairfax, Margaret Stewart; E. 2575, Rebecca Bottomley, Mary King, Margaret Newport, Elizabeth Coots.

28. Ibid., E. 2574, Alice Greenwood, Elizabeth Ovelever, Mary Roberts, Elinor Jones, Frances Buckley.

29. Ibid., E. 2574, Mary Young, Mary Deacon, Elizabeth Turner.

30. Ibid., E. 2574, Elizabeth Howey, Jane Minen, Rachel Wood, Johanna Pereya,

Barbara Katherine Clay, Mary Batchell, Eleanor O'Bryan, Bridget Tudor, Susan Smith.

31. Ibid., E. 2574, Elizabeth Woodyar; E. 2575, Jane Jones; E. 2574, Ann Jarvis, Margaret Baines.

32. WPL: E. 3232, 3233 contain the examinations of these vagrant soldier's wives.

33. M. Dorothy George, *London Life in the Eighteenth Century* (London, 1925; reprint New York: Harper and Row, 1965), pp. 176–95; Peter Linebaugh, *The London Hanged* (New York: Cambridge University Press, 1992), pp. 257–87; George Rudé, *Hanoverian London, 1714–1808* (London: Secker and Warburg, 1971), pp. 185–89, 197–203.

34. George, *London Life*, pp. 191–92.

35. GLRO: P91/LEN/1200–1217.

36. George, *London Life*, pp. 191–92; David Cressy, *Literacy and the Social Order* (New York: Cambridge University Press, 1980), pp. 144–54. The literacy rate for unmarried women in both St. Margaret's and Aldgate becomes two or three points higher and closer still to that for poor married women if one excludes from the total figure those instances in which a declaration had neither a signature nor a mark. It is apparent from comparing individual years with each other at St. Margaret's that most of those who neither signed nor marked probably were illiterate, since in those years when these ambiguous declarations are fewer, the illiteracy rate is higher.

37. GLRO: P91/LEN/1200–1201.

38. GLRO: P91/LEN/1205: Alice Broderick; George, *London Life*, p. 199: on which see Gillis, *For Better, for Worse*, chap. 6, who argues that irregular unions became widespread in early-nineteenth-century London. There are seventeen long-term liaisons in the Shoreditch declarations, lasting from four to thirty-three years, with a median of nine years. Ten couples had two children, five had three, and two had four. The occupations of a dozen men were given: two weavers, two bakers, a waiter, an embosser, a silver engraver, a shoemaker, a dealer in fish, a laborer, a stonemason. Three women signed, seven put their mark, and for seven there was no indication given. Seven women gave Shoreditch as their parish; there was one each from Spitalfields, Piccadilly, and Hanover Square; there was no indication for seven. The seventeen cases are spread out over the four decades from the 1760s to 1790s more or less in proportion to the overall number of declarations in each decade, except that there is only one in the 1770s, but three in the 1760s, six in the 1780s, and seven in the 1790s. There are perhaps more gaps in this information than in the other cases, and this may indicate a high level of uncertainty about the parish of settlement of these women. These relations did not fit neatly into the legal grid.

39. GL, MS 2676, vol. 1, Rachel Peters; vol. 2, Elizabeth Ripshaw, Sarah Smithson, Mary Walker, Mary Norman.

40. Ibid., vol. 1, Elizabeth Haines; vol. 2, Mary Huggins, Sarah Leggatt; vol. 1, Mary Ludgate.

41. Ibid., vol. 1, Elizabeth Lockwood; vol. 3, Elizabeth Barber; vol. 1, Elizabeth Phillips; vol. 3, Isabel Morgan.

42. Ibid., vol. 4, Eleanor Miller.

43. Ibid., vol. 2, Martha Snell, Mary Stevens (who is probably also Elizabeth Ste-

venson, since they both slept with a Thomas Arnold, a shoemaker or a cordwainer, at the Falcon, Old Fish Street; but it is possible that Arnold slept there with two different women); vol. 1, Diana Bully, Ann Jones, Elizabeth Freebody; vol. 3, Sarah Primer; vol. 2, Catherine Taylor, Ann Bond, Frances Sparks.

44. Karla Oosterveen, Richard M. Smith, and Susan Stewart, "Family Reconstitution and the Study of Bastardy," and Anthea Newman, "An Evaluation of Bastardy Recordings in an East Kent Parish," in Laslett, Oosterveen, and Smith, *Bastardy*, pp. 94–157; Finlay, *Population and Metropolis*, pp. 149–50.

45. Finlay, *Population and Metropolis*, pp. 149–50.

46. Gillis, *For Better, for Worse*, pp. 190–228.

47. WPL: E. 3222, E. 3224. For Fleet marriages, see Roger Lee Brown, "The Rise and Fall of the Fleet Marriages," in *Marriage and Society*, ed. R. B. Outhwaite (New York: Europa, 1981), pp. 117–36; R. B. Outhwaite, *Clandestine Marriage in England, 1500–1850* (London: Hambledon Press, 1995).

48. WPL: E. 2574, Elizabeth Yarnel, Esther Morris (late Esther Rice), Elinor Typto, Mary Wheetly, Margaret Baines; E. 2575, Ann Higgons.

49. See chap. 11 for the case, which is to be found in GLRO: DL/C/181: Nash v. Nash.

50. GL, MS 2676, vol. 18, Hannah Puffey; vol. 19, Jane Stoneham.

51. GL, MS 2676, vol. 22, Mary Playford, Eleanor Connor. This situation persisted until Roman Catholic marriages were made legal in 1837: see Lynn Hollen Lees, *Exiles of Erin: Irish Migrants in Victorian London* (Ithaca, N.Y.: Cornell University Press, 1979), p. 152; see also John Bossy, "Challoner and the Marriage Act," in *Challoner and His Church*, ed. Eamon Duffy (London: Danton, Longman and Todd, 1981), pp. 126–36.

52. GL, MS 2676, vol. 19, Jane Fairbrother; vol. 20, Peggy Smith. Irish Roman Catholic weddings also turned up in seven cases in which a woman was pregnant or had had a child. Mary Redmond was married in the Catholic chapel in Virginia Street, St. George, Middlesex (vol. 11), as were Martha Cropper (vol. 18) and Mary Lewis (vol. 21). Owen Rairdon's sister was married by a priest in a house (probably a chapel) in Moorfields, and her child, who was legally a bastard, was baptized in the Virginia Street chapel (vol. 19). Eleanor Roach was also married in the Moorfields chapel (vol. 20). Helen Sullivan married her husband in a parish church, but he told her that twenty years before he had been married by a Roman Catholic priest to another woman by whom he had had two children, for whom Helen seems to have been responsible (vol. 22).

53. GL, MS 2676, vol. 4, vol. 9, Sarah Wickham.

54. GL, MS 2676, vol. 17, Hannah Gotschin; vol. 21, Ann Howard.

55. Ibid., vol. 4, Rachel Clark, Ann Rubee; vol. 6, Renee Tring; vol. 22, Sarah Hollindrake. There are cases of women not from Aldgate who also said that they had not been apprenticed or served as servants: vol. 4, Sarah Bonham; vol. 6, Jane Louzey.

56. Ibid., vol. 14, Sarah Hemming; vol. 10, Carolina Bell; vol. 11, Elizabeth Profitt; vol. 14, Grace Dalton.

57. Ibid., vol. 14, William Tatum; vol. 17, Catherine Bleasdale; vol. 20, Joseph Bull; vol. 22, Elizabeth Tipton.

58. Ibid., vol. 15, Alice Thomas, Elizabeth Gready; vol. 21, Ann Hannah; vol. 17,

Helen Gibbs; vol. 21, Amelia Ross; vol. 17, Frances Smith; vol. 16, Elizabeth Gloster; vol. 19, Jemima Joyce, Jane Drummond.

CHAPTER NINE: SHAME AND RAPE

1. GLRO: FH, Petitioners Admitted, vol. 6 (1775), Martha Freeman, Ann Stafford, vol. 1 (1768–69), Mary Jewitt, Elizabeth Hall, vol. 1 (1768–69), Mary Teat; Adrian Wilson, "Illegitimacy and Its Implications in Mid-Eighteenth-Century London: The Evidence of the Foundling Hospital," *Continuity and Change* 4 (1989): 103–64. For the history of the Foundling Hospital, see Ruth K. McClure, *Coram's Children: The London Foundling Hospital in the Eighteenth Century* (New Haven, Conn.: Yale University Press, 1981). The nineteenth-century declarations are studied by John Gillis, "Servants, Sexual Relations, and the Risks of Illegitimacy in London, 1801–1900," *Feminist Studies* 5 (1979): 142–73; and Franoise Barret-Ducrocq, *Love in the Time of Victoria* (New York: Verso, 1991).

2. GLRO: FH, Petitioners Rejected (1799), Sarah Duke, Petitioners Admitted, vol. 7 (1776), Mary Mose, vol. 17 (1787–91), Isabel Anderson, vol. 18 (1792–93), Elizabeth Jennings.

3. GLRO: FH, Petitioners Admitted, vol. 1 (1768–69), Ann James, vol. 8 (1777), Mary Moorson, vol. 22 (1799), Winnifred Richard.

4. Ibid., vol. 1 (1768–69), Sarah Harbour, vol. 6 (1775), Elizabeth Jardine Reynolds, vol. 21 (1797), Mary Whitcomb, vol. 6 (1775), Ann Fleming, vol. 22 (1798), Ann Tuckey.

5. Ibid., vol. 5 (1774), Maria Hershaw, vol. 1 (1768–69), Elizabeth Hall, F[rances] Story.

6. GLRO: FH, Bundle 1763, Sarah Salt, Petitioners Admitted, vol. 8 (1777), Susannah Samworth, vol. 9 (17788), Sarah Picke, vol. 10 (1779), Elizabeth Eaton, vol. 17 (1787–91), Ann Barnes; see also vol. 22 (1797), Elizabeth Hardy.

7. GLRO: FH, Petitioners Admitted, vol. 6 (1775), Mary Abbotts, vol. 17 (1787–91), Catherine Jones, Petitioners Rejected (1799), Ann Robinson.

8. GLRO: FH, Petitioners Admitted, vol. 1 (1768–69), Mary West, Leticia Smith, Jane Slater, vol. 2 (1770–71), Mary Hewitt, vol. 7 (1776), Hannah Frankling, vol. 22 (1797), Mary Taylor.

9. Ibid., vol. 2 (1770–71), Mary Griffis, Mary Smith, vol. 4 (1773), Elizabeth Hill.

10. Ibid., vol. 1 (1768–69), Christian Bear, Elizabeth Lumley.

11. Ibid., vol. 2 (1770–71), Sarah Aviary, vol. 3 (1772), Susannah Scorfield, vol. 5 (1774), Jane Whitaker, vol. 3 (1772), Ann Stephens.

12. Ibid., vol. 3 (1772), Mary Brown, vol. 4 (1773), Ann Brown.

13. Ibid., vol. 5 (1774), Frances Moore, vol. 19 (1794), Mary McGowen, vol. 22 (1797), Kitty Plume, Hannah Millington.

14. Ibid., vol. 1 (1768–69), Mary Jewitt, Thomasine Whely, vol. 19 (1794), Mary Harpur, vol. 1 (1768–69), Elizabeth Hunt.

15. Ibid., vol. 1 (1768–69), Mary Hendrie, vol. 19 (1794), Amy Girling.

16. Ibid., vol. 2 (1769–70), Mary Edwards, vol. 4 (1773), Mary Taylor, vol. 19 (1794), Frances Layton, Elizabeth Pernick, vol. 20 (1795), Ann Pedder, vol. 21 (1796), Elizabeth Morris, Catherine Pearce.

17. Ibid., vol. 1 (1768–69), Sarah Page, vol. 4 (1773), Elizabeth Williamson, vol.

2 (1770–71), Grace Scott, vol. 6 (1775), Sarah Brown, vol. 7 (1776), Sarah Williams, vol. 7 (1776).

18. Ibid., vol. 7 (1776), Elizabeth Owen, vol. 1 (1768–69), Mary Smith, Elizabeth Beety, Elizabeth Jones.

19. Ibid., vol. 20 (1795), Elizabeth Barrow, Mary Livesy, vol. 22 (1797), Elizabeth Barrett, vol. 20 (1795), Charlotte Sophia Roberts, vol. 22 (1797), Ann Peter, Rebecca Lambert.

20. Ibid., vol. 19 (1794), Sarah Guerry, vol. 20 (1795), Susan Smith, vol. 19 (1794), Ann Hayward, vol. 17 (1787–91), Mary Allen, vol. 22 (1797), Elizabeth White, Sarah Mason, vol. 19 (1794), Ann Macarty, vol. 20 (1795), Sophia Wilson, vol. 17 (1787–91), vol. 20 (1795), Elizabeth Finck.

21. Ibid., vol. 21 (1796), Sarah Moore, Elizabeth Vinall, vol. 18 (1792–93), Hester Broad, vol. 22 (1797), Charlotte Williams, vol. 21 (1796), Sarah Clark, vol. 18 (1792–93), Jan Totty, vol. 22 (1797), Ann Sugg.

22. Ibid., vol. 19 (1794), Mary McGovern, vol. 17 (1787–91), Sarah Benton, vol. 22 (1797), Elizabeth Gibson.

23. WPL: E2575, #10 (25 February 1718–19); SP, no. 1 (1733), pp. 10–11; GRS: *Select Trials at the Sessions-House in the Old Bailey* (London, 1742), 4 vols., 3:40–41; *London Chronicle,* 30 March–2 April, 13–16 April, 16–18 April 1765. In 1762 Philip Defour, a tailor from Bethnal Green, was sentenced to six months and the pillory for seducing his eleven-year-old niece and sixteen-year-old stepdaughter (*London Chronicle,* 16–18 December 1762). A tradesman from St. Sepulchre ran away after he made his daughter pregnant (ibid., 26–28 December 1765).

24. GLRO: FH, Petitioners Admitted, vol. 19 (1794), Ann Windell, Sarah Hamerton, Mary Harpur, Amelia Freind.

25. Ibid., vol. 19 (1794), Ann Mockett, vol. 17 (1787–91), Ann Grainger, vol. 19 (1794), Elizabeth Powell, vol. 21 (1796), Elizabeth Pearson, vol. 22 (1797), Mary Barrett, vol. 19 (1794), Amy Webb.

26. Ibid., vol. 2 (1770–71), Mary Browne, Mary Smith, Eleanor Richardson, vol. 3 (1772), AB, vol. 5 (1774), Elizabeth Atwood, vol. 19 (1794), Elizabeth Archer.

27. Ibid., vol. 1 (1768–69), Susannah Herbert, Elizabeth Bloxam, Mary Nelson.

28. Ibid., vol. 21 (1796), Ann Bartleet, vol. 19 (1794), Mary Pamplin, vol. 21 (1796), Mary Partridge.

29. SP, no. 8, pt. 10 (1784), pp. 1221–23, no. #925.

30. For the changing nature of infanticide prosecutions, see Peter C. Hoffer and N. E. H. Hall, *Murdering Mothers: Infanticide in England and New England* (New York: New York University Press, 1981); R. W. Malcolmson, "Infanticide in the Eighteenth Century," in *Crime in England, 1550–1800,* ed. J. S. Cockburn (Princeton: Princeton University Press, 1977), pp. 186–209; Mark Jackson, *New-Born Child Murder: Women, Illegitimacy, and the Courts in Eighteenth-Century England* (Manchester: Manchester University Press, 1996); Ann R. Higginbotham, "'Sin of the Age': Infanticide and Illegitimacy in Victorian London," *Victorian Studies* 32 (1989): 319–37; Philippe Chassaigne, "L'infanticide à Londres à l'epoque victorienne: Essai d'approche quantitative," in *Annales de Démographie Historique 1990* (Paris, 1990), pp. 227–37. For maternal feeling, childbirth, and medical opinion, see Randolph Trumbach, *The Rise of the Egalitarian Family* (New York: Academic Press, 1977), chaps. 4, 5; and Judith Schneid Lewis, *In the Family Way* (New Brunswick, N.J.: Rutgers University Press, 1986).

31. SP, no. 6 (1755), pp. 237–40.

32. Ibid., no. 3, pt. 2 (1793), pp. 370–76, #232.

33. Ibid., no. 1, pt. 3 (1778), pp. 56–60, #59.

34. Ibid., no. 4, (1762), pp. 99–100, #41.

35. Ibid., no. 4 (1735), p. 79; no. 8 (1737), pp. 202–4; no. 5 (1744), pp. 115–16; no. 4 (1737), pp. 89–91; no. 3 (1746), pp. 82–83; no. 3, pt. 2 (1760), pp. 111–14.

36. Ibid., no. 2 (1735), pp. 24–25; *Ordinary of Newgate's Account* (1735), pp. 10–11.

37. SP, no. 1 (1762), pp. 24–26, #28, pp. 26–28, #29.

38. Ibid., no. 7, pt. 1 (1765), pp. 258–59, #459; no. 1, pt. 3 (1775), pp. 91–94, #105, 106; no. 8, pt. 2 (1761), pp. 408–10, #31; see also no. 3 (1760), pp. 88–90; no. 8, pt. 10 (1784), pp. 1221–23, #925.

39. Ibid., no. 8, pt. 2 (1770), pp. 383–86, #687; no. 6, pt. 2 (1766), pp. 243–44, #372; no. 1, pt. 3 (1793), pp. 74–79, #31; no. 6, pt. 2 (1769), pp. 310–14, #366; no. 8, pt. 2 (1773), pp. 471–72, #720.

40. The eighteenth-century cases from the Old Bailey have previously been studied by A. E. Simpson and Anna Clark. Simpson, in "Vulnerability and the Age of Female Consent: Legal Innovation and Its Effect on Prosecutions for Rape in Eighteenth Century London," in *Sexual Underworlds of the Enlightenment*, ed. G. S. Rousseau and Roy Porter (Manchester: Manchester University Press, 1987), looked at the entire century and argued that the court became increasingly unsympathetic to rape charges. He discussed the connection between venereal disease and the rape of children, but he was conservative in his estimate of the number of these cases. Simpson was also skeptical about the possibility of blackmail in rape cases: "The 'Blackmail Myth' and the Prosecution of Rape and Its Attempt in Eighteenth-Century London: The Creation of a Legal Tradition," *Journal of Criminal Law and Criminology* 77 (1986): 101–50. See also Susan Staves, "Fielding and the Comedy of Attempted Rape," in *History, Gender, and Eighteenth-Century Literature*, ed. Beth Foukes Tobin (Athens: University of Georgia Press, 1994), pp. 86–112. Anna Clark in *Women's Silence, Men's Violence: Sexual Assault in England, 1770–1845* (New York: Pandora, 1987), mentioned venereal disease only once in passing. She analyzed the cases from the last thirty years of the century, but her interest was in using them to make a contrast with the early nineteenth century, when (she argued) women were terrorized with rape as a means of keeping them out of public spaces. If Simpson was right, however, in contrasting the early and the late eighteenth century, it is likely that domesticity and the doctrine of the separate spheres had begun to have an effect on rape cases before the nineteenth century. The decreased public sympathy for rape victims that was probably a result of domesticity needs to be balanced, however, by the increased sympathy for women who killed their children, inspired by the same belief that women were by their natures maternal and domestic. The similarities between rape and seduction were noted for Renaissance Venice by Guido Ruggiero in *The Boundaries of Eros* (New York: Oxford University Press, 1985). Nazife Bashar, "Rape in England between 1550 and 1700," in *The Sexual Dynamics of History*, ed. London Feminist History Group (London: Pluto Press, 1983), pp. 28–42, argued that it was only in the last half of the seventeenth century that significant numbers of poor adult women brought rape cases against men of their own social class. Before that rape had been prosecuted as a crime that gentlemen committed against propertied girls. But the courts almost never convicted in the cases involving adult

women. Nonetheless, it would seem that by 1700 rape had been reconceptualized as a crime against a woman's person rather than against her property. For a notorious eighteenth-century rape, see Wallace Shugg, "The Baron and the Milliner: Lord Baltimore's Rape Trial as a Mirror of Class Tensions in Mid-Georgian London," *Maryland Historical Magazine* 83 (1988): 310–30.

41. SP, no. 6 (1734), pp. 161–64.

42. Ibid., no. 4 (1752), pp. 84–86, #119.

43. Ibid., no. 8, pt. 1 (1775); see also no. 8, pt. 2 (1775), pp. 551–56.

44. Ibid., no. 4, pt. 3 (1781), pp. 222–27, #242; no. 7, pt. 2 (1771), pp. 425–26, #578, 579, 580.

45. Ibid., no. 7, pt. 2 (1771), pp. 425–26; no. 6 (1730), pp. 18–20.

46. Ibid., no. 7, pt. 1 (1768), pp. 306–7, #519.

47. Ibid., no. 1, pt. 4 (1778), pp. 75–82, #75.

48. Ibid., no. 7, pt. 2 (1777), pp. 321–32, #522; see also no. 8 (1743), pp. 270–74.

49. Ibid., no. 8, pt. 6 (1786), pp. 1271–74, #813.

50. Ibid., no. 4, pt. 2 (1745), pp. 136–38.

51. Ibid., no. 6, pt. 1 (1769), pp. 290–99, #347, pp. 299–301, #348.

52. Ibid., no. 3, pt. 1 (1771), pp. 95–102, #135.

53. Ibid., no. 6, pt. 3 (1779), pp. 388–402, #361

54. Ibid. (1797), pp. 484–95, #495.

55. Ibid., no. 7, pt. 2 (1737), pp. 194–95.

56. Ibid., no. 4, pt. 1 (1772), pp. 147–50, #317.

57. Ibid., no. 8, pt. 2 (1777), pp. 386–91, #628; see also no. 7, pt. 4 (1787), pp. 954–61, #702.

58. Ibid., no. 7, pt. 2 (1735), pp. 130–32.

59. Ibid., no. 6, pt. 2 (1772), pp. 340–42, #571; no. 1, pt. 3 (1772), p. 65, #147.

60. Ibid., no. 6, pt. 2 (1772), pp. 340–42, #571; no. 8, pt. 2 (1776), pp. 460–66, #747.

61. Ibid., no. 3, pt. 3 (1793), pp. 406–11, #242.

62. Ibid., no. 2, pt. 3 (1758), pp. 100–101; no. 4, pt. 2 (1771), pp. 191–98.

63. Ibid., no. 8, pt. 3 (1780), pp. 778–86, #603, 604, 605. In another case a woman who met a gentleman in St. James's Park later tried to charge him with rape. But he pointed out that he had met her in a standard pickup spot, the Birdcage Walk, and that she had not been wearing gloves, as a respectable woman would have been (no. 4, pt. 3 (1757), pp. 158–75).

64. Ibid. (13–18 January 1727).

65. Ibid., no. 7, pt. 3 (1787), pp. 699–703, #544.

66. Ibid., no. 4, pt. 1 (1768), pp. 153–57, #284.

Chapter Ten: Violence in Marriage

1. Margaret Hunt, "Wife Beating, Domesticity, and Women's Independence in Eighteenth-Century London," *Gender and History* 4 (1992): 10–33, has studied the consistory cases from 1711 to 1713. She finds that there was a new level of disapproval of wife beating early in the century, but she discounts its significance on the ground

that it drew the "veil of silence" over wife beating. This is unduly pessimistic, but she may be right to some extent, and the reluctance to discuss the issue in public may explain the decline in the number of cases brought by women after 1750. Roderick Phillips, *Putting Asunder* (New York: Cambridge University Press, 1988), also discusses the growing disapproval of wife beating over the course of the eighteenth century and places it in the context of the development of romantic love throughout western Europe (pp. 323–44). Most of the rest of the literature on wife beating deals with the nineteenth and twentieth centuries. For London, see Nancy Tomes, "A 'Torrent of Abuse': Crimes of Violence between Working-Class Men and Women in London, 1840–1875," *Journal of Social History* 11 (1978): 328–45; Ellen Ross, "'Fierce Questions and Taunts': Married Life in Working-Class London, 1870–1914," *Feminist Studies* 8 (1982): 575–602; and Anna Clark, "Humanity or Justice? Wifebeating and the Law in the Eighteenth and Nineteenth Centuries," in *Regulating Womanhood*, ed. Carol Smart (New York: Routledge, 1992), pp. 187–206.

2. GLRO: DL/C/149, fols. 439–42, DL/C/247, fols. 251–67.

3. GLRO: DL/C/174: Briggs v. Briggs.

4. GLRO: DL/C/150, fols. 163–68, DL/C/248, fol. 73.

5. GLRO: DL/C/151, fols. 9–10, DL/C/248, fol. 197.

6. GLRO: DL/C/173, fols. 319–28, DL/C/275: Ferrers v. Ferrers; W. S. Lewis et al., eds., *Yale Edition of Horace Walpole's Correspondence* (New Haven, Conn.: Yale University Press, 1937–83), 48 vols., 21:183–84, 367, 394–403; *The Trial of Lawrence Earl Ferrers* (London, 1760).

7. GLRO: DL/C/182, DL/C/287: Cheetham v. Cheetham.

8. GLRO: DL/C/185: Swinton v. Swinton; Irvine Loudon, "'The Vile Race of Quacks with Which This Country Is Infested,'" *Medical Fringe and Medical Orthodoxy, 1750–1850*, ed. W. F. Bynum and Roy Porter (London: Croom Helm, 1987) pp. 106–28.

9. Public Record Office, KB 1/11, pt. 1: King v. Nesbitt; for the new childbearing regime see Randolph Trumbach, *The Rise of the Egalitarian Family* (New York: Academic Press, 1977), pp. 165–85; Judith Schneid Lewis, *In the Family Way* (New Brunswick, N.J.: Rutgers University Press, 1986); and Adrian Wilson, *The Making of Man-midwifery* (Cambridge, Mass.: Harvard University Press, 1996).

10. GLRO: DL/C/173, fols. 295–306, DL/C/275: Brogden v. Brogden.

11. GLRO: DL/C/182: Adams v. Adams.

12. GLRO: DL/C/172, fols. 1–28, DL/C/638: Adams v. Adams.

13. GLRO: DL/C/149, fols. 149–253; DL/C/150, fols. 354–55; DL/C/153, fol. 5; John Quick, *A Serious Inquiry into that weighty case of conscience whether a man may lawfully marry his diseased wife's sister* (London, 1703), reprint in GRS: The Marriage Prohibitions Controversy: Five Tracts; GLRO: MJ/SR/2340: Bridewell Calendar, #31. The discussion of siblings is taken from Trumbach, *Rise of Egalitarian Family*, pp. 26–33; see also Polly Morris, "Incest or Survival Strategy? Plebeian Marriage within the Prohibited Degrees in Somerset, 1730–1835," in *Forbidden History: The State, Society, and the Regulation of Sexuality in Modern Europe*, ed. John C. Fout (Chicago: University of Chicago Press, 1992), pp. 139–69. There was a deceased wife's sister case in the London consistory in the 1780s, but unfortunately I neither read it nor took down the reference.

14. GLRO: DL/C/182, DL/C/287: Dance v. Dance. An aristocratic woman took

a similar case to Parliament; see DL/C/287, DL/C/182: Addison v. Addison; *Journals of the House of Lords*, vol. 43. In GRS: *Trials for Adultery* (London, 1780), 7 vols., vol. 3: Oliver v. Oliver, there is a case from 1774 of a man who made his wife's adolescent sister pregnant. He tried unsuccessfully to procure an abortion for the girl. The manuscript record can be found GLRO: DL/C/177.

15. GLRO: DL/C/152, fols. 364–72.

16. GLRO: DL/C/150, fols. 294–300.

17. GLRO: DL/C/150, fols. 141–47, DL/C/247, fol. 442.

18. Lawrence Stone, *Road to Divorce* (New York: Oxford University Press, 1990), pp. 167–69; William Ll. Perry-Jones, *The Trade in Lunacy* (London: Routledge and Kegan Paul, 1972), pp. 8–10, 17, 75, 244; GLRO: DL/C/182: Eagleton v. Eagleton. For Eagleton as an entrepreneur, see Hoh-Cheung Mui and Lorning H. Mui, *Shops and Shopkeeping in Eighteenth-Century England* (London: Routledge, 1989), pp. 257, 268–75, 279, 281. For another woman confined in Newton's madhouse see GLRO: DL/C/154, fol. 509.

19. GLRO: DL/C/150, fols. 325–35.

20. GLRO: DL/C/172, fols. 123, DL/C/274: Ryves v. Ryves.

21. GLRO: DL/C/173, fols. 147–53, DL/C/454–577: Peirse v. Peirse.

22. GLRO: DL/C/150, fol. 221, DL/C/248, fols. 50–62.

23. GLRO: DL/C/151, fols. 240–45.

24. GLRO: DL/C/153, fols. 8–11. For a widow who misled her second husband as to the health of her finances, see DL/C/149, fols. 365–72, DL/C/247, fols. 224, 241.

25. GLRO: DL/C/184: Oliver v. Oliver. Lawrence Stone and Jeanne C. Fawtier Stone, *An Open Elite? England, 1540–1880* (Oxford: Oxford University Press, 1984), pp. 122–25, noted that the marriages of elite males (or men of higher status than those who appear in the widow cases in the consistory) to widows declined from 20 percent of all marriages in the sixteenth century to 3 percent by 1800. They account for this on the grounds of romantic love as a motive for marriage and the greater protection given to widows by prenuptial settlements, which made them less financially attractive. Susan Staves, *Married Women's Separate Property in England, 1660–1833* (Cambridge, Mass.: Harvard University Press, 1990), pp. 215–16, captiously disputes this but offers no viable alternative. Irene Q. Brown argues that what she calls an early Enlightenment form of domesticity allowed widows in the first half of the eighteenth century to decline offers of remarriage; "Domesticity, Feminism, and Friendship: Female Aristocratic Culture and Marriage in England, 1660–1760," *Journal of Family History* 7 (1982): 406–24. For a general discussion of remarriage among the elite, see Trumbach, *Rise of Egalitarian Family*, pp. 50–61. Barbara J. Todd has shown that in Abingdon in a social range rather like the consistory cases the percentage of widows who remarried declined from a half to a quarter between the mid-sixteenth and the early eighteenth centuries for two reasons: marriages lasted longer and produced fewer young widows, and even more strikingly, women widowed after long marriages became much less likely to remarry. Women were discouraged from remarrying because their first husbands attached economic penalties to doing so as a means of protecting their children and because of their loyalty to their dead husbands ("The Remarrying Widow: A Stereotype Reconsidered," in *Women in English Society, 1500–1800*, ed. Mary Prior [New York: Methuen, 1985], pp. 54–92). For the demography of remarriage, see Roger Schofield

and E. A. Wrigley, "Remarriage Intervals and the Effect of Marriage Order on Fertility," in *Marriage and Remarriage in Populations of the Past,* ed. J. Dupquier et al. (New York: Academic Press, 1981), pp. 211–27. The history of the London widow can be traced in Barbara A. Hanawalt, "The Widow's Mite: Provisions for Medieval London Widows," in *Upon My Husband's Death: Widows in the Literature and Histories of Medieval Europe,* ed. Louise Mirer (Ann Arbor: University of Michigan Press, 1992), pp. 21–45; Caroline M. Marron and Anne F. Sutton, eds., *Medieval London Widows, 1300–1500* (London: Hambledon Press, 1994); Vivien Brodsky, "Widows in Late Elizabethan London: Remarriage, Economic Opportunity, and Family Orientations," in *The World We Have Gained,* ed. Lloyd Bonfield, Richard M. Smith, and Keith Wrightson (New York: Blackwell, 1986), pp. 122–54; Jeremy Boulton, "London Widowhood Revisited: The Decline of Female Remarriage in the Seventeenth and Early Eighteenth Centuries," *Continuity and Change* 5 (1990): 323–55; and Barbara J. Todd, "Demographic Determinism and Female Agency: The Remarrying Widow Reconsidered . . . Again," *Continuity and Change* 9 (1994): 421–50.

26. GLRO: MJ/SR/2035, R 167; MJ/SR/2037, R 78; MJ/SR/2225, R 72; MJ/SR/2230, R 124; MJ/SR/2236, R 13; MJ/SR/2223, R 1 and New Prison Kalendar; MJ/SR/2668–87 for 1737.

27. CLRO, Guildhall Justice Room Minute Book of Proceedings, 17 November 1761, 5 December 1775, 7 August 1782, 13 August 1782, 23 March 1790, 18 September 1791, 28 March 1793.

28. Ibid., 23 April 1793, 16 February 1796. This series of notebooks is too incomplete to make it worthwhile to calculate the total number of separations that came before these justices. The notebooks of Henry Norris, a magistrate in Hackney, survive for a decade (1730–40: GLRO). It has cases of wife beating, adultery, fornication, and indecent acts like putting a man's hands up a woman's coats. But Hackney was clearly still out of the orbit of truly urban London: there were no prostitutes, sodomites, or disorderly houses in the notebook. See Ruth Paley, ed., *Justice in Eighteenth-Century Hackney: The Justicing Notebook of Henry Norris and the Hackney Petty Sessions Book* (London: London Record Society, 1991). For further discussion of popular divorce and separation, see D. Kent, "'Gone for a Soldier': Family Breakdown and the Demography of Desertion in a London Parish, 1750–91," *Local Population Studies* 45 (autumn 1990): 27–43; Pamela Sharpe, "Marital Separation in the Eighteenth and Early Nineteenth Centuries," *Local Population Studies* 45 (autumn 1990): 66–70; and K. D. M. Snell, *Annals of the Labouring Poor* (New York: Cambridge University Press, 1985), pp. 359–64.

CHAPTER ELEVEN: DESERTION AND INCOMPATIBILITY

1. GLRO: DL/C/173, fols. 95–110.

2. GLRO: DL/C/149, fols. 16–17.

3. GLRO: DL/C/185: Williams v. Williams, Webster v. Webster.

4. GLRO: DL/C/185: Ward v. Ward.

5. GLRO: DL/C/150, fols. 381–84, DL/C/248, fol. 180.

6. GLRO: DL/C/153, fols. 304–9; DL/C/150, fol. 42, DL/C/247, fol. 380; DL/C/151, fols. 431–35.

7. GLRO: DL/C/151, fol. 352, DL/C/249, fol. 211.

8. GLRO: DL/C/152, fols. 403–5.

9. GLRO: DL/C/153, fols. 1–3; for a similar case from the 1750s, see DL/C/ 173, fols. 217–24, DL/C/275: Goodflesh v. Goodflesh; Private Act: 33 Geo. II. c. 14.

10. GLRO: DL/C/172, fols. 270–82; DL/C/274: Henley v. Henley. For a young man deceived into marrying a prostitute, see DL/C/151, fols. 114–30; DL/C/248, fols. 346–66, 431–34.

11. GLRO: DL/C/173, fols. 53–60; DL/C/264: Edwardes v. Edwardes. For a similar case, see DL/C/152, fols. 22–25.

12. GLRO: DL/C/172, fols. 340–47. For similar cases, see DL/C/152, fol. 408; and DL/C/185: Shaw v. Shaw.

13. GLRO: DL/C/151, fols. 197–205; DL/C/248, fols. 338–410. For the sapphist role, see Randolph Trumbach, "London's Sapphists: From Three Sexes to Four Genders in the Making of Modern Culture," in *Third Sex, Third Gender*, ed. Gilbert Herdt (New York: Zone Books, 1994), pp. 111–36, and "The Origins and Development of the Modern Lesbian Role in the Western Gender System: Northwestern Europe and the United States, 1750–1990," *Historical Reflections/Réflexions Historiques* 20 (1994): 287–320. See also Emma Donoghue, on *Passions between Women: British Lesbian Culture, 1668–1801* (London: Scarlet Press, 1993), which, however, fails to see change over the course of the century.

14. GLRO: DL/C/181, DL/C/284: Carter v. Carter.

15. GLRO: DL/C/150, 351–53; DL/C/149, fols. 222–32; DL/C/149, fols. 245– 47; DL/C/151, fols. 445–47; DL/C/151, fols. 295–98. The best introduction to the law on these promises of marriage is GRS: Henry Swinburne, *A Treatise of Spousals or Matrimonial Contracts* (London, 1686); and see also Lawrence Stone, *Uncertain Unions: Marriage in England, 1660–1753* (New York: Oxford University Press, 1992); R. B. Outhwaite, *Clandestine Marriage in England, 1500–1850* (London: Hambledon Press, 1995); Peter Rushton, "The Testament of Gifts: Marriage Tokens and Disputed Contracts in North-East England, 1566–1630," *Folk Life* 24 (1985–86): 25–31; and Diana O'Hara, "The Language of Tokens and the Making of Marriage," *Rural History* 3 (1992): 1–40.

16. In 1700–1709 in the consistory there were six cases over private contracts and three over Fleet marriages. In 1750–59 there were five cases of Fleet and Mayfair marriages and no private-contract cases. In 1790–99 there were twenty-two cases over the age of a spouse involving fifteen female minors and seven male. In 1700–1709 there were also five disputes over private marriages by Roman Catholic priests, which were valid but illicit until 1753. In the 1790s there were two cases involving Jewish marriages, which were legal under the act of 1753. For Fleet marriages in St. Margaret's, see chap. 9, and also see Roger Lee Brown, "The Rise and Fall of the Fleet Marriages," in *Marriage and Society*, ed. R. B. Outhwaite (New York: Europa, 1981), pp. 117–36; for Roman Catholics, see Bossy, "Challoner and Marriage Act," pp. 126–36; and for London in the late seventeenth century, see Jeremy Boulton, "Itching after Private Marryings? Marriage Customs in Seventeenth-Century London," *London Journal* 16 (1991): 15–34, and "Clandestine Marriages in London: An Examination of a Neglected Urban Variable," *Urban History* 20 (1993): 191–210; Tony Benton, *Irregular Marriage in London before 1754* (London: Society of Genealogists, 1993).

17. GLRO: DL/C/174, 275: Meigham v. Meigham. For the legality of marriages

between cousins, see Randolph Trumbach, *The Rise of the Egalitarian Family* (New York: Academic Press, 1977), pp. 19–21. The marriage in September 1700 between Michael Gentill, the French steward of Lord Brudenall, and Elizabeth Cross, the daughter of a Roman Catholic Lancashire gentleman, raised similar questions. They were married by a Roman Catholic priest and had two children. But Gentill later pretended that there had been no marriage and married another woman in the Church of England. He was indicted for bigamy at the Old Bailey, and the consistory accepted the validity of the first marriage (GLRO: DL/C/151, fols. 299–301, DL/C/249, fol. 1).

18. GLRO: DL/C/173, fols. 183–89.

19. George Farquhar, *Complete Works,* ed. George Stonehill (1930; reprint New York: Gordion Press, 1967), 2 vols., 2:134, 159, 191; Martin A. Larson, "The Influence of Milton's Divorce Tracts on Farquhar's *Beaux' Strategem,*" *PMLA* 39 (1924): 174–78.

20. GRS: [George Booth, Earl of Warrington], *Considerations upon the institution of marriage . . . wherein is considered how far divorces may or ought to be allowed* (London, 1739); J. V. Beckett and Clyve Jones, "Financial Improvidence and Political Independence in the Early Eighteenth Century: George Booth, 2nd Earl of Warrington (1675–1758)," *Bulletin of the John Rylands Library* 65 (1982): 8–35, esp. 21–22.

21. *The Ordinary of Newgate, his Account of James Hall* (London, 1741), p. 4; GLRO: DL/C/152, fols. 130–39; Daniel Defoe, *Moll Flanders* (1722), ed. Juliet Mitchell (New York, 1978), pp. 142–45, 171–73.

22. GLRO: DL/C/185: Webb v. Webb. It was legal to marry the daughter of your sister-in-law; see Trumbach, *Rise of Egalitarian Family,* pp. 22–23.

23. GLRO: DL/C/181: Nash v. Nash.

24. Samuel Pyeatt Menafee, *Wives for Sale: An Ethnographic Study of British Popular Divorce* (Oxford: Blackwell, 1981); Stone, *Road to Divorce,* pp. 143–48; E. P. Thompson, *Customs in Common* (New York: New Press, 1991), pp. 404–66; for other popular forms of marriage and divorce, see John R. Gillis, *For Better, for Worse* (New York: Oxford University Press, 1985).

25. GL, MS 1075, vol. 20.

26. *General Evening Post,* 15–18 March 1735, *Grub Street Journal,* 27 March 1735; *Lloyd's Evening Post,* 14–17 March 1766; *Annual Register* 9 (1766): 75; *London Chronicle,* 2–4 June 1767.

27. *Public Advertiser,* 25 June 1791; *Morning Chronicle,* 13 June 1791; *London Chronicle,* 13–15, 25–27 June 1797; *Morning Chronicle,* 29 July 1797; *Morning Chronicle,* 22 December 1797; *London Chronicle,* 28–30 November 1797.

28. Kent Record Office: U908: L10/1, 2, 6, 8, 26, 28; L19/6, 24, 25, 26; G. D. Squibb, *Doctors' Commons* (Oxford: Oxford University Press, 1977), p. 188.

29. GLRO: DL/C/183: Kemp v. Kemp; Defoe, *Moll Flanders,* p. 145.

30. Susan Staves, *Married Women's Separate Property in England, 1660–1833* (Cambridge, Mass.: Harvard University Press, 1990), pp. 163–95: Staves would not necessarily agree with my reading of the information on these contracts that she presents; they are also discussed by Stone, *Road to Divorce,* pp. 149–82 in a way that ties them to the history of the family more than does Stave's feminist critique of judicial thinking.

31. GLRO: DL/C/181: Goldsmith v. Goldsmith.

32. GLRO: DL/C/185: Woodmason v. Woodmason, *Journals of the House of Lords*, vol. 41.

33. GLRO: FH, Petitioners Admitted, vol. 19, Elizabeth Lishman. For divorce in Sweden and France, see Roderick Phillips, *Putting Asunder* (New York: Cambridge University Press, 1988), pp. 197–200, 256–76.

34. The eighteenth-century transformations in family life are the subject of a growing literature. For England: Lawrence Stone, *The Family, Sex, and Marriage in England, 1500–1800* (New York: Harper and Row, 1977); Trumbach, *Rise of Egalitarian Family;* and Judith Schneid Lewis, *In the Family Way* (New Brunswick, N.J.: Rutgers University Press, 1986). For France: Cissie Fairchilds, *Domestic Enemies* (Baltimore: Johns Hopkins University Press, 1984); and Margaret H. Darrow, *Revolution in the House* (Princeton: Princeton University Press, 1990). For the United States: Philip Greven, *The Protestant Temperament* (New York: Knopf, 1978); Daniel Blake Smith, *Inside the Great House* (Ithaca, N.Y.: Cornell University Press, 1980); and Jan Lewis, *The Pursuit of Happiness* (New York: Cambridge University Press, 1983). There is now also a very full general history of divorce since 1500 in all of Western society, Phillips, *Putting Asunder,* as well as a legal study for essentially eighteenth-century England by Stone, *Road to Divorce* (New York: Oxford University Press, 1990). I have discussed Phillips's book and his earlier *Family Breakdown in Late Eighteenth-Century France* (Oxford: Oxford University Press, 1980) in two essays: "Kinship and Marriage in Early Modern France and England: Four Books," *Annals of Scholarship* 2 (1981): 113–28, and "Is There a Modern Sexual Culture in the West; or, Did England Never Change between 1500 and 1900," *Journal of the History of Sexuality* 1 (1990): 296–309. The six central chapters of Phillips, *Putting Asunder,* place the emergence of divorce for incompatibility in the context of the changes that were occurring in the family in England and in all the rest of Western society. Some westerners in the generation after 1770 first began to practice what was rapidly enacted as the law of divorce in all Western societies in the generation after 1960. The replacement of divorce for the fault of one spouse by the standard of incompatibility and marital breakdown has come to be accepted even by the marriage courts of the Roman Catholic Church, despite the official doctrine that divorce violates God's law: see John T. Noonan Jr., *Power to Dissolve* (Cambridge, Mass.: Harvard University Press, 1972).

CHAPTER TWELVE: ROMANCE AND ADULTERY

1. Tony Tanner, *Adultery in the Novel* (Baltimore: Johns Hopkins University Press, 1979).

2. The discussion of these two triangles has in part been inspired by Eve Kosofsky Sedgwick, *Between Men: English Literature and Male Homosocial Desire* (New York: Columbia University Press, 1985). Paul Taylor pointed out to me the similarities between the triangles I had found and those in Sedgwick.

3. GLRO: DL/C/173, fols. 72–86; DL/C/274: Glover v. Glover; Private Act: 29 Geo. II. c. 344.

4. GLRO: DL/C/173, fols. 375–89; DL/C/275: Wilford v. Wilford; DL/C/545–77: Wilford v. Wilford. For a similar case, see DL/C/172, fols. 292–97.

5. GLRO: DL/C/173, fols. 210–14; DL/C/275: Cooke v. Cooke; Private Act: 32 Geo. II.

6. GLRO: DL/C/173, fols. 279–84, DL/C/275: Weir v. Weir; Sir Lewis Namier and John Brooke, *The House of Commons, 1754–1790* (London: History of Parliament Trust, 1964), 3 vols., 2:639, 3:151. For an argument that Tobias Smollett meant to make sodomitical suggestions about Newcastle, see Peter Miles, "Smollett, Rowlandson, and a Problem of Identity: Decoding Names, Bodies, and Gender in *Humphry Clinker*," *Eighteenth-Century Life* 20 (1996): 1–23.

7. GLRO: DL/C/172, fols. 356–75; DL/C/545–77, 1753: Wymondesold v. Wymondesold; *Correspondence of Horace Walpole*, 20:355–56; Private Act: 27 Geo. II c. 35.

8. GLRO: DL/C/173, fols. 225–49; DL/C/275: Knowles v. Knowles; *Admiral Knowles against Captain Gambier*, in GRS: *Trials for Adultery* (London, 1780), 7 vols., vol. 6. For the case of a husband very much in love with his wife who did his best to endure her infatuation with another man in the hope that the affair would end, see DL/C/172, fols. 304–24.

9. *Trials for Adultery.*

10. Stuart Anderson, "Legislative Divorce—Law for the Aristocracy?" in *Law, Economy, and Society, 1750–1914*, ed. G. R. Rubin (Abingdon: Professional Books, 1984), pp. 412–44.

11. Katherine Binhammer suggests that the adultery cases from the 1790s under the pressure of fears generated by the French Revolution produced "The Sex Panic of the 1790s," *Journal of the History of Sexuality* 6 (1996): 409–34. But the material in this chapter shows that concern had mounted over the issue for thirty years before that decade.

12. GLRO: DL/C/181, DL/C/284: Ball v. Ball. For a similar case, see DL/C/182: Belmore v. Belmore.

13. GLRO: DL/C/185: Ricketts v. Ricketts; *Journals of the House of Lords*, vol. 42.

14. GLRO: DL/C/184: Peard v. Peard; *Journals of the House of Lords*, vol. 42. In one naval case, the wife's lover was a relative of her husband's and had been the couple's friend; see DL/C/182, DL/C/287: Donnelly v. Donnelly. In another case, the wife was an actress who in her husband's absence became the duke of Hamilton's mistress; see DL/C/182: Esten v. Esten. In a third case, the long periods alone over most of her married life eventually led Mary Williamson to drink and to involvement with an abusive lover; see DL/C/185: Williamson v. Williamson. For two other naval cases, see DL/C/181, DL/C/284: Columbine v. Columbine; *Journals of the House of Lords*, vol. 42; and DL/C/184: Parker v. Parker; *Journal of the House of Lords*, vol. 42. Esten and Williamson did not seek parliamentary divorces, probably because of their social class. Esten was only a purser and Williamson, a half-pay officer who served in the merchant navy.

15. GLRO: DL/C/182, DL/C/287: Buller v. Buller; *Journals of the House of Lords*, vol. 42. Sex during menstruation turns up in another case. After the Honorable Ann Townshend fell in love with a man who lived in a cottage on her husband's estate, her lady's maid noticed from her mistress's clothes that she must have had sex even though she was menstruating. The maid was shocked and told her that this was indelicate and improper. Ann replied, "What could I do, Jenny? He is so charming and bewitching a man that no one can resist him" (GLRO: DL/C/185: Wilson v. Wilson). For other Indian divorces, see DL/C/182, DL/C/287: Bonham v. Bonham, DL/C/185: Ramus v. Ramus, DL/C/181: Liege v. Liege, and DL/C/181: Eastabrooke v. Eastabrooke.

16. GLRO: DL/C/183: Fozard v. Fozard; *Journals of the House of Lords*, vol. 41. In another case Sarah Elwes said that the two lawyers she was accused of having sex with were not strangers to her husband, as he claimed: he had invited them home, and she had gone to see them on business. She also said that in the case for criminal conversation against one of the lawyers who had supposedly been her lover, the lawyer had agreed not to call any witnesses of his own, and that her husband's solicitor had undertaken to repay whatever costs and damages were awarded. The court must not have believed this, since it granted her husband his divorce (GLRO: DL/C/182: Elwes v. Elwes). Sidenham Teast, a Bristol merchant, after he was awarded five hundred pounds in damages and sixty-eight pounds in costs at the Gloucester assizes, declared that the damages did not have to be paid because he did not wish to profit from his wife's adultery (GLRO: DL/C/185: Teast v. Teast).

17. GLRO: DL/C/185: Ricketts v. Ricketts. For the divorce of the Honorable and Reverend Thomas James Twistleton, see DL/C/185: Twistleton v. Twistleton; *Journals of the House of Lords*, vol. 41.

18. GLRO: DL/C/181, DL/C/284: Wilmot v. Wilmot. For abstinence as a means of birth control, see Randolph Trumbach, *The Rise of the Egalitarian Family* (New York: Academic Press, 1977), pp. 171−76. For a middle-class case of mistress and servant, see DL/C/185: Sabine v. Sabine.

19. GLRO: DL/C/181, DL/C/284: Lovering v. Lovering. For the case of another master craftsman, see DL/C/185: Thompson v. Thompson. In the *Trials for Adultery* there are cases from the 1760s and 1770s of mistresses and servants; see, vol. 1, Draper v. Draper; vol. 2, Worgan v. Worgan; vol. 5, Lockwood v. Lockwood. There were two such cases in the consistory records from the 1750s and the 1790s that came from outside London. The most detailed for the entire century was from the 1790s: Middleton v. Middleton (DL/C/184, DL/C/286), which has been recounted by Lawrence Stone in *Broken Lives* (New York: Oxford University Press, 1993), pp. 162−247. The Middletons were a Roman Catholic gentry family from Yorkshire. Although the couple seemed to have had a romantic marriage and a domesticated family of the new kind, which made it impossible for a long time for William Middleton to believe in his wife's adultery, it is clear that Clara Middleton had never really experienced sexual passion in her marriage. After nine years of marriage, when she was twenty-eight Clara fell in love with one of their grooms and declared that until she met John Rose, she never knew what love was. The second case (this one from 1753) involved a tenant farmer from Essex and his wife. Mary Ennever complained of her husband's cruelty. John Ennever replied that after thirteen years of marriage, Mary had had an affair with his cowman, Jonathan Harvey. Mary countercharged that John had an affair with her best friend, Mary Nicholas. Mary bore Harvey's child and probably ended as a prostitute in London (GLRO: DL/C/172, fols. 70−75, DL/C/638).

20. GLRO: DL/C/182, DL/C/287: Abercorn v. Abercorn. For the role of siblings-in-law in the English family system, see Trumbach, *Rise of Egalitarian Family*, pp. 26−33.

21. GLRO: DL/C/182: Bewicke v. Bewicke. The Reverend Thomas Twistleton also did not bring an action for criminal conversation against his wife's lover: see n. 17 above; but the Reverend William Brook Jones did: see DL/C/183: Jones v. Jones; *Journals of the House of Lords*, vol. 40. Hanna Bright fell in love with a distant relation of her husband's who lived with them, see DL/C/182: Bright v. Bright.

476 NOTES TO PAGES 416–424

22. GLRO: DL/C/182: Biscoe v. Biscoe; *Journals of the House of Lords*, vol. 39.

23. GLRO: DL/C/185: Walker v. Walker. For a similar case, see DL/C/183: Houlditch v. Houlditch.

24. GLRO: DL/C/181, DL/C/284: Cecil v. Cecil; *Journals of the House of Lords*, vol. 39. For a similar case, see DL/C/182, DL/C/287: Crewe v. Crewe.

25. GLRO: DL/C/182, DL/C/287: Boddington v. Boddington. For a business associate lower in the social scale, see DL/C/183: Kibblewhite v. Kibblewhite.

26. GLRO: DL/C/181, DL/C/284: Duberly v. Duberly. In a case from Yorkshire, Richard Moorson, a timber merchant, seems to have deliberately shut his eyes to Henry Clarke's very flirtatious behavior with his wife Elizabeth. As in the Duberly case, Clarke was a gentleman, a magistrate, and local landowner, the master of ceremonies at the assembly house in Whitby, and he was also Moorson's best customer. For this reason, Elizabeth and her family later charged, Moorson had been complaisant. It became the gossip in Whitby that Moorson was "laying by" for a divorce. The boys in the street held up their fingers on their foreheads in the sign of the horns when he went by and said that he carried his horns in his pocket (GLRO: DL/C/184: Moorson v. Moorson; *Journals of the House of Lords*, vol. 40).

27. GLRO: DL/C/185: Annesley v. Annesley.

28. Virginia Surtees, ed., *A Second Self: The Letters of Harriet Granville, 1810–1845* (London: Michael Russell, 1990), pp. 20, 46; GLRO: DL/C/185: Vassall v. Vassall; *Journals of the House of Lords*, vol. 41; Namier and Brooke, *House of Commons*, 3:617; Castalia Countess Granville, ed., *Lord Granville Leveson Gower (First Earl Granville) Private Correspondence, 1781–1821* (New York: E. P. Dutton, 1916), 2 vols., 1:50, 52, 123, 162.

29. Nancy F. Cott, "Passionlessness: An Interpretation of Victorian Sexual Ideology, 1790–1850," *Signs* 4 (1978): 219–36; Lucy Bland, "Marriage Laid Bare: Middle-Class Women and Marital Sex, 1880s–1914," in *Labour and Love: Women's Experience of Home and Family*, ed. Jane Lewis (Oxford: Blackwell, 1986), pp. 123–38; Carl Degler, "What Ought to Be and What Was: Women's Sexuality in the Nineteenth Century," *American Historical Review* 79 (1974): 1467–90; Peter Gay, *The Education of the Senses* (New York: Oxford University Press, 1984); M. Jeanne Peterson, *Family, Love, and Work in the Lives of Victorian Gentlewomen* (Bloomington: Indiana University Press, 1989); Judith R. Walkowitz, *City of Dreadful Delight* (Chicago: University of Chicago Press, 1992).

A. Manuscript Sources

1. Corporation of London Record Office

Quarter Session Rolls, 1704, 1720–29, 1737, 1770, 1777
Mansion House Justice Room Charge Book, 1695–1705, 1728–33
Mansion House Justice Room Minute Books, 1784–90
Guildhall Justice Room Minute Books, 1752–86, 1786–95

2. Greater London Record Office
(or the London Metropolitan Archive)

Diocese of London Consistory Court
Allegations, Libels, Sentences: DL/C/148–54 (1700–1709), 170–74 (1750–59), 181–85 (1790–99) all read; 153–72 (1710–49), 174–80 (1760–79), divorce cases counted
DL/C/246–52, 274–75, 282–87, 638, Deposition Books for 1700–1709, 1750–59, 1790–99
DL/C/545–77, Divorce Exhibita
DL/C/627, Index to Causes, 1818–57

Diocese of Winchester Consistory Court
DW/OP, Defamations, 1730–99

Foundling Hospital
Petitioners Admitted, 1768–1800, 25 volumes
Petitioners Rejected, 1799

Middlesex and Westminster Quarter Sessions
MJ/SR/2023–41 (1704), 2221–39 (1714), 2340–2525 (1720–29), 2607–26 (1734), 2668–87 (1737), 2831–51 (1745), 3028–46 (1755), 3158–70 (1765), 3221–3381 (1769–79), 3452–66 (1785)

Middlesex Process Register of Indictments
MJ/SBP/11–13, 16 (1720–29, 1752–59)

Examinations
WJ/SP, 1700–1730

House of Correction Rolls
Middlesex CC/R/5–14, 35B–40, 51–57
Westminster CC/R/2–12, 16–20, 25–28
Westminster CC/B/54–63, 134–252 (calendars of commitment)

Clerkenwell Magistrates
Henry Norris, Magistrate's Book, 1730–41

Poor Law Examinations
P/91/LEN/1200–1217, St. Leonard Shoreditch
P/74/LUK/121–26, St. Luke Chelsea

3. Guildhall Library
MS 1075, St. Ann Blackfriars Poor Law Examinations, 1778–84
MS 2676, St. Botolph Aldgate Poor Law Examinations, 1745–99
MS 8913, St. Giles Cripplegate Poor Law Examinations, 1780–99
MS 9096, St. Sepulchre Poor Law Examinations, 1793–99
MS 12017, Autobiography of Sir John Fryer

4. Hertfordshire Record Office
Panshanger (Cowper) Manuscripts
Diary of Dame Sarah Cowper

5. Kent Record Office
Streathfield (Earls of Leicester) Manuscripts
U.908/L10,19.

6. Lincolnshire Record Office
Ancaster Manuscripts

7. Public Record Office
King's Bench Affidavits
KB/1/11/parts 1, 2 (1753)
KB/1/20/part (1776)

8. Royal College of Surgeons
Lock Hospital Manuscripts
General Court Book, 1746–89
Board Minutes, 1755–1800
Lock Asylum Minutes, 1787–90

9. Staffordshire Record Office
Dartmouth Manuscripts
D. 1778 V. 1790

10. Westminster Public Library
E. 2574–78, St. Margaret's, Westminster (Bastardy Book)
E. 3221–36, St. Margaret's, Westminster (Poor Law and Vagrant Examinations)

11. British Library
Additional Manuscripts, 27825-6, 36625, 47028

B. PRINTED SOURCES

An Account of the institution . . . for the reception of orphan girls . . . whose settlement cannot be found. London, 1763.
An Account of the Institution of the Lock Asylum. London, 1792.
An Account of the . . . Magdalen Hospital . . . together with Dr. Dodd's Sermons. London, 1776. Reprint GRS. New York, 1985.
An Account of the . . . present state of the Magdalen Charity. London, 1761.
Annual Register. London, 1770.
Antimoxiea: or the honest and joint design of the Tower Hamlets for the general suppression of bawdy houses. London, 1691: Guildhall, B'side 1.43.
Archenholz, J. W. von. *A Picture of England.* 2 vols. London, 1789.
Aristotle's Last Legacy. London, 1776. Reprint GRS. New York, 1986.
Aristotle's Masterpiece. London, 1694, 1749, 1776. Reprint GRS. New York, 1986.
Astruc, John. *A Treatise of the Venereal Disease.* Trans. William Barrowby. 2 vols. London, 1737. Reprint GRS. New York, 1985.
Austen, Jane. *Persuasion.* London, 1818. Ed. R. W. Chapman. London: Oxford University Press, 1969.
Bienville, M. D. T. *Nymphomania, or a Dissertation concerning the Furor Uterinus.* London, 1775. Reprint GRS. New York, 1985.
Boswell, James. *Journal of a Tour to the Hebrides.* Ed. Alan Wendt. Boston: Houghton Mifflin, 1965.
———. *Boswell's London Journal, 1762–1763.* Ed. F. A. Pottle. New York: McGraw-Hill, 1950.
Bradbury, Charles. *The Cobbler Undone.* London, 1755.
———. *Mr Bradbury's Case Truly Stated.* London, 1755.
Bray, Thomas. *A General Plan of a penitential hospital for employing and reforming lewd women.* London, 1698.
The British Journal. London, 1723.
Buchan, William. *Observations Concerning the Prevention and Cure of the Venereal Disease.* London, 1796. Reprint GRS. New York, 1985.
Burgess, Daniel. *The Golden Snuffers.* London, 1697.
Butler, John. *A Sermon preached in the chapel of the Magdalen Hospital.* London, 1786.
Byrd, William. *The London Diary (1717–1721) and Other Writings.* Ed. L. B. Wright and Marion Tinling. New York: Oxford University Press, 1958.
Campbell, R. *The London Tradesman.* London, 1747. Reprint Newton Abbot, Devon: David and Charles Reprints, 1969.
Casanova, Giacomo. *History of My Life.* Trans. W. R. Trask. 12 vols. New York: Harcourt Brace Jovanovich, 1970.

Chesterfield, Philip Dormer Stanhope, Earl of. *The Letters.* Ed. Bonamy Dobrée. 6 vols. London: Eyre and Spottiswoode, 1932.

Churchill, Charles. *Poetical Works.* Ed. Douglas Grant. Oxford: Oxford University Press, 1956.

[Cleland, John]. *The Case of the Unfortunate Bosavern Penlez.* London, 1749.

Cleland, John. *Memoirs of a Woman of Pleasure.* London, 1748–49. Ed. Peter Sabor. New York: Oxford University Press, 1985.

———. *The Surprises of Love.* London, 1766.

Collier, Jeremy. *A Short view of the immorality and profaneness of the English stage.* London, 1699.

A Congratulatory Epistle from a reformed rake to John F——g Esq. upon the new scheme of reclaiming prostitutes. London, 1758.

Congreve, William. *Complete Plays.* Ed. Herbert Davis. Chicago: University of Chicago Press, 1967.

The Covent Garden Jester. London, 1775. Reprint GRS. New York, 1986.

Cox, Daniel. *An Appeal to the public in behalf of Elizabeth Canning.* London, 1753.

Davys, Mary. *The Accomplished Rake.* London, 1727. In *Four before Richardson,* ed. W. H. McBurney. Lincoln: University of Nebraska Press, 1963.

D[a]ws[o]n, Nancy. *Authentic Memoirs of the celebrated Miss Nancy D[a]ws[o]n.* London, [c. 1765].

Deacon, H. *A Compendious treatise on the venereal disease.* London, n.d.

Defoe, Daniel. *Conjugal Lewdness; or Matrimonial Whoredom.* London, 1727. Reprint with an introduction by Maximillian E. Novak. Gainesville, Fla.: Scholars' Facsimiles and Reprints, 1967.

———. *Everybody's Business is Nobody's Business.* London, 1725.

———. *Moll Flanders.* 1722. Ed. Juliet Mitchell. New York, 1978.

———. *Some considerations upon street-walkers.* London, 1726.

———. *A Tour through the Whole Island of Great Britain.* London, 1724–26. Ed. G. D. H. Cole and D. C. Browning. 2 vols. New York: Dutton, 1962.

Dennis, John. *Critical Works.* Ed. E. N. Hooker. 2 vols. Baltimore: Johns Hopkins University Press, 1943.

Dingley, Robert. *Proposals for establishing a public place of reception for penitent prostitutes.* London, 1758. Reprint in Prostitution Reform, GRS. New York, 1985.

Dodd, J. S. *A Physical Account of the Case of Elizabeth Canning.* London, 1753.

Douglas, Francis. *Reflections on Celibacy and Marriage.* London, 1771. Reprint GRS. New York, 1984.

Dunton, John. *The Night-Walker; or Evening Rambles in Search of Lewd Women.* 2 vols. London, 1696. Reprint GRS. New York, 1985.

East, E. H. *A treatise of the Pleas of the crown.* London, 1803.

Etherege, George. *The Man of Mode.* London, 1676. Ed. W. B. Carnochan. Lincoln: University of Nebraska Press, 1966.

Farquhar, George. *Complete Works.* Ed. George Stonehill. 2 vols. 1930. Reprint New York: Gordion Press, 1967.

Fielding, Henry. *A Clear State of the case of Elizabeth Canning.* London, 1753.

Fielding, John. *An Account of the origins and effects of a police set on foot by his grace the duke of Newcastle in the Year 1753.* London, 1758. Reprint in Prostitution Reform, GRS. New York, 1985.

———. *Extracts from . . . the Penal Laws.* London, 1768.

The Fifteenth Account of the Progress made towards suppressing profaneness and debauchery. London, 1710.

Fortescue, John Lord. *Reports of Select Cases.* London, 1748.

Franklin, Benjamin. *Autobiography.* Ed. L. W. Labaree. New Haven, Conn.: Yale University Press, 1964.

A Full and Authentic Account of . . . Mary Squires . . . and Elizabeth Canning. London, 1753.

A full relation of everything that has happened to Elizabeth Canning since sentence has been passed on her about the gypsy. London, 1754.

General Evening Post. London, 1735.

General State of the Magdalen Hospital 1758–1784. London, 1784.

Gentleman's Magazine. London, 1780.

Genuine and Impartial Memoirs of Elizabeth Canning. London, 1754.

Goldsmith, Oliver. *Works.* Ed. Arthur Friedman. 5 vols. Oxford: Oxford University Press, 1966.

Graham, James. *Lectures on the generation, increase and improvement of the human species.* [1780].

Granville, Leveson Gower, First Earl. *Lord Granville Leveson Gower (First Earl Granville), Private Correspondence, 1781–1821.* Ed. Castalia, Countess Granville. 2 vols. New York: E. P. Dutton, 1916.

Greene, E. B. *Whispers for the ear of the author of Thelypthora.* London, 1781.

Grose, Francis. *A Classical Dictionary of the Vulgar Tongue.* London, 1796.

Hanger, George. *The Life . . . of Col. George Hanger.* 2 vols. London, 1801.

Hanway, Jonas. *A Reply to C—— A——.* London, 1760.

Harris, Walter. *Observations . . . de Lues Venerae Origina. . . .* Amsterdam, 1715.

Harris's List of Covent Garden Ladies . . . for . . . 1788. London, 1788. Reprint GRS. New York, 1986.

Haweis, Thomas. *A Scriptural Refutation of the Arguments for Polygamy.* London, [1781].

Hawkins, Sir John. *The Life of Dr. Johnson.* London, 1787.

Henry, Matthew. *A Sermon . . . [at] the Funeral of the Reverend Mr. Daniel Burgess.* London, 1713.

Herbert, Lord, ed. *Henry, Elizabeth and George (1734–80).* London: Jonathan Cape, 1939.

———. *Pembroke Papers (1780–1794).* London: Jonathan Cape, 1950.

Hill, John. *The Story of Elizabeth Canning.* London, 1753.

Hill, Richard. *The Blessings of Polygamy.* London, 1781.

Hints . . . on the prevalence of vice and the dangerous effects of seduction. London, 1811.

The History of Colonel Francis Ch——rtr——s. London, [1730].

The History of the Human Heart. London, 1749. Reprint New York: Garland, 1974.

Hunter, William. *A Treatise of the Venereal Disease.* London, 1786.

Johnson, Christopher. *The History of the life and intrigues of that celebrated courtezan and posture-mistress, Eliz. Mann.* London, 1724.

Johnson, Samuel. *Lives of the English Poets.* London, 1779–81. 2 vols. World's Classics ed., 1967.

Journals of the House of Commons. 1770.

Journals of the House of Lords. Vols. 39–43. London.

King, Richard. *The Complete Modern London Spy for the present year 1781.* London, 1781.

Leinster, Emily, Duchess of. *Correspondence.* Ed. Brian Fitzgerald. 3 vols. Dublin: Irish Manuscripts Commission, 1949–57.

A Letter to Dr. P[riestley]. London, 1781.

The Life and Character of Moll King. London, 1747.

The Life, Death, and Character of Mr. Daniel Burgess. London, [1713].

Lloyd's Evening Post. London, 1766.

The London-Bawd with her Character and Life. London, 1711. Reprint GRS. New York, 1985.

London Chronicle. London, 1759–65, 1767, 1790–92, 1797.

London Evening Post. London, 1776.

Madan, Martin. *Thelypthora; or a Treatise on Female Ruin.* 3d ed. 3 vols. London, 1781.

Malcolm, J. P. *Anecdotes of the Manners and Customs of London during the Eighteenth Century.* London, 1808.

Manley, [Mary] Delariviere. *Secret Memoirs . . . from the New Atalantis.* London, 1709. In *The Novels,* ed. Patricia Koster. 2 vols. Gainesville, Fla., 1971.

Marten, John. *Gonosologium Novum.* London, 1709. Reprint GRS. New York, 1985.

———. *A Treatise of . . . the Venereal Disease.* London, 1708. Reprint GRS. New York, 1985.

Meibomius, John Henry. *A Treatise on the use of flogging in venereal affairs.* London, 1718.

[Morley, Richard]. *The Life of . . . Elizabeth Wisebourn.* [1721].

Morning Chronicle. London, 1791, 1797.

[Moore, Henry]. *A Word to Mr. Madan.* Bristol, 1781.

M[urray], Fanny. *Memoirs of the Celebrated Miss Fanny M[urray].* London, 1759.

A New Description of Merryland. London, 1741.

Nicholson, I. F. *The Modern Syphilis.* London, 1718.

Nocturnal Revels; or the history of King's Place, and other modern nunneries . . . by a monk of the order of St. Francis. 2 vols. London, 1779.

Onania; or the Heinous Sin of Self-Pollution and *A Supplement to the Onania.* London, 1723. Reprint GRS. New York, 1986.

The Ordinary of Newgate, his Account of James Hall. London, 1741.

Parliamentary Papers. *First Report from the Committee on the State of the Police of the Metropolis.* London, 1817.

Parliamentary Papers. *Report for the Committee on the State of the Metropolis.* London, 1816.

Parliamentary Papers. *Third Report from the Committee on the State of the Police of the Metropolis.* London, 1818.

Payne Knight, Richard. *A Discourse on the Worship of Priapus.* London, 1786. Reprint in *Sexual Symbolism,* ed. Ashley Montagu. New York: Julian Press, 1957.

Place, Francis. *Autobiography.* Ed. Mary Thale. Cambridge: Cambridge University Press, 1972.

Proceedings . . . against Francis Charteris for . . . Rape on . . . Anne Bond. London, 1730.

Proceedings . . . at the Old Bailey. London, 1700–1799.

Public Advertiser. London, 1791.

Quick, John. *A Serious Inquiry into that weighty case of conscience whether a man may lawfully marry his deceased wife's sister.* London, 1703. Reprint in The Marriage Prohibitions Controversy: Five Tracts, GRS. New York, 1985.

Richardson, Samuel. *Clarissa.* London, 1747–48. 4 vols. New York: Everyman ed., 1965.

Rochester. *Complete Poems.* Ed. D. M. Veith. New Haven, Conn.: Yale University Press, 1968.

Rutter, Owen, ed. *The Log of the Bounty.* 2 vols. London, 1937.

Ryder, Dudley. *The Diary of Dudley Ryder, 1715–1716.* Ed. William Matthews. London: Methuen, 1939.

St. Evremonde, Charles de Saint-Denis. *Works of Mr. de St. Evremonde.* 2 vols. London, 1700.

Satan's Harvest Home. London, 1749. Reprint GRS. New York, 1985.

Scotch Gallantry Displayed. London, 1730.

Select Trials at the Sessions-House in the Old Bailey. 4 vols. London, 1742. Reprint GRS. 2 vols. New York, 1985.

A Sermon preached before the former Societies for Reformation of Manners. London, 1760.

Shadwell, Thomas. *Complete Works.* Ed. Montague Summers. 5 vols. London, 1927. Reprint New York: Benjamin Blom, 1968.

Shaftesbury, Anthony, Earl of. *Characteristics of Men, Manners, Opinions, Times.* 1710. Ed. John M. Robertson and Stanley Grean. New York: Bobbs-Merrill, 1964.

———. *An Inquiry concerning virtue.* London, 1699.

Sheldon, Mrs. Ann. *Authentic and interesting memoirs of Mrs. Ann Sheldon (now Mrs. Archer) . . . written by herself.* 4 vols. London, 1787.

Smith, Adam. *The Wealth of Nations.* 2 vols. London, 1776. Everyman ed.

Smith, Alexander. *The School of Venus.* 2 vols. London, 1716.

Smith, John. *Polygamy Indefensible.* London, 1780.

Smollett, Tobias. *Peregrine Pickle.* 1751. Ed. J. L. Clifford and P. G. Boucé. New York: Oxford University Press, 1983.

Steele, Richard, and Joseph Addison. *The Spectator.* 1711–14. Ed. D. F. Bond. 5 vols. Oxford: Oxford University Press, 1965.

Swift, Jonathan. *Journal to Stella.* Ed. Harold Williams. 2 vols. Oxford: Oxford University Press, 1948.

Swinburne, Henry. *A Treatise of Spousals or Matrimonial Contracts.* London, 1686. Reprint GRS. New York, 1985.

Tanner, Anodyne. *The Life of . . . Mrs. Elizabeth Wisebourn.* London, [1721].

Taylor, John. *Remarks on Mr Bradbury's State of His Case.* London, 1755.

The Trial of Lawrence Earl Ferrers. London, 1760.

The Trial of Richard Branson for an Attempt to Commit Sodomy o the Body of James Fassett. London, 1760. Reprint in Sodomy Trials: Seven Documents, GRS. New York, 1986.

Trials for Adultery. London, 1779–80. 7 vols. Reprint GRS. New York, 1985.

The Tryal and Condemnation of . . . Lord . . . Castlehaven. London, 1699. Reprint in Sodomy Trials, GRS. New York, 1986.

Turner, Daniel. *Syphilis.* London, 1717.

Venette, Nicholas. *Conjugal Love; or the pleasures of the marriage bed considered.* [1780]. Reprint GRS. New York, 1984.

Walker, Charles. *Authentic Memoirs of . . . Sally Salisbury.* London, 1723.
Walpole, Horace. *Memoirs of the Reign of George III.* Ed. G. F. Russell Barker. 3 vols. London, 1894.
———. *Yale Edition of Walpole's Correspondence.* Ed. W. S. Lewis et al. 48 vols. New Haven, Conn.: Yale University Press, 1937–83.
Ward, Edward. *The London Spy.* London, 1709. Reprint GRS. New York, 1985.
[Warrington, George Booth, Earl of]. *Considerations upon the Institution of Marriage.* London, 1739. Reprint in Prostitution Reform, GRS. New York, 1985.
Welch, Saunders. *A Proposal . . . to remove the nuisance of common prostitutes from the streets of this metropolis.* London, 1758. Reprint GRS. New York, 1985.
Willis, Thomas. *Remarks on Polygamy.* London, 1781.
Wortley Montagu, Lady Mary. *Complete Letters.* Ed. Robert Halsband. 3 vols. Oxford: Oxford University Press, 1965–67.

INDEX

Roe, Elizabeth, 208
Rogers, K. M., 454n.27
Rogers, Nicholas, 230, 456n.7, 460n.2, 461n.24
Roman Catholics, and irregular marriage, 269–71, 379–80. *See also* Irish women
Romantic love: and sexual desire, 110–11; and prostitution, 169–75; and domestication of the brothel, 175–84; and illegitimacy, 259–60, 282–83; and rape, 320–22. *See also* Adultery, female
Rosamund, Ann, 159
Rose, Elizabeth, 143
Rose, Katherine, 36
Ross, Amelia, 274
Ross, Ellen, 460n.4, 468n.1
Rottam, Thomas, 360
Round, Elizabeth and John, 361
Rousseau, G. S., 441n.13, 442nn. 29, 31
Routledge, Mrs., 288
Row, Mary, 151
Rowden, Esther, 300
Ross, Mrs., 38
Rowse, Ann and John, 28
Royston, William, 368
Rubee, Ann, 272
Rudé, George, 433n.8, 462n.33
Rudge, Judith, 50
Ruell, Hester, 50
Ruff, William, 93
Ruggiero, Guido, 439n.3, 466n.40
Rumbell, Jane, 240
Rupp, E. G., 455n.38
Rushton, Peter, 435n.2, 436n.3, 471n.15
Russ, Elizabeth, 316–17
Russell, Elizabeth, 315
Russell, John, 273
Russell, Lucy, 41
Ryder, Dudley, 103–4, 109, 189
Ryves, John, 350–54

Sabine, Thomas, 54–55
Sackville, George, Lord, 180

Sailors, 270–71; and prostitutes, 99–100; and venereal disease, 199–200, 261–62
Sainthill, Fanny, 410–12
Saints Cosmos and Damian, 87–88
St. Evremonde, Charles de, 76–77, 81
St. John, Oliver, 48
St. Margaret's, Westminster, 118, 121, 129, 138, 151; illegitimacy, 248–56; and Societies for the Reformation of Manners, 248–51; gentlemen and military officers as seducers, 250–55; servants and seducers, 255–56; wives and widows with bastards, 249; time of declaration, 249–50, 266–67; servants pregnant by masters, 251–52; sexual and experience and frequency of intercourse, 253–54; sexual locales, 254–55; intention to marry, 255–56; literacy levels of seduced women, 258–59; long-term liaisons and Fleet marriages, 255–56, 268–69
St Martin in the Fields, and illegitimacy, 242–45
St. Sepulchre, and illegitimacy, 242–43
Sais, Elizabeth, 43
Salisbury, Sally, 162
Salt, Sarah, 284
Samuel, Mary, 299
Samworth, Susannah, 284
Sands, Betty, 157
Sarsfield, Ann, 129
Sarson, Thomas, 28
Satan's Harvest Home, 185
Saunders, Margaret, 160
Savage, Edward, 252
Savage, Gail, 456n.5
Sayer, Joseph, 399
Sayer, Peter, 399–400
Scarborough, Lord, 35
Schofield, Roger, 470n.25
Schulman, Maria Christina, 365–66
Schwarz, L. D., 434n.8
Scofield, Sussanah, 286
Scott, Grace, 290
Scott, David, 214
Scott, Sarah, 311–12